WEIMAR CINEMA AND AFTER

German cinema of the 1920s is still regarded as one of the 'golden ages' of world cinema. Films such as *The Cabinet of Dr Caligari*, *Dr Mabuse the Gambler*, *Nosferatu*, *Metropolis*, *Pandora's Box* and *The Blue Angel* have long been canonised as classics, but they are also among the key films defining Germany as a nation uneasy with itself. The work of directors like Fritz Lang, F.W. Murnau and G.W. Pabst – having apparently announced the horrors of fascism, while testifying to the traumas of a defeated nation – still casts a long shadow over cinema in Germany, leaving film history and political history curiously intertwined.

Weimar Cinema and After: Germany's Historical Imaginary offers a fresh perspective on this most 'national' of national cinemas, re-evaluating such labels as 'Expressionist film' and 'The New Sobriety' and even putting 'fascinating fascism' and film noir in a different, international context. Thomas Elsaesser questions the conventional readings which link these genres and movements solely to the legacy of German romanticism and nationalism, and offers new approaches to analysing the function of national cinema in an advanced 'culture industry'.

Elsaesser reads the major films as well as popular entertainment cinema against the contradictory background of avant-garde modernity and consumerist modernisation from the 1920s to the late 1930s. He argues that Weimar cinema's significance lay less in its ability either to promote Socialism or predict fascism than in its contribution to the creation of a community sharing a 'historical imaginary' rather than a 'national identity'. In this respect, German cinema in the Weimar period anticipated some of the problems facing contemporary nations in reconstituting their identities by means of media images, memory and invented traditions.

Thomas Elsaesser is Professor of Film and Television Studies at the University of Amsterdam.

WEIMAR CINEMA AND AFTER

Germany's Historical Imaginary

Thomas Elsaesser

LONDON AND NEW YORK

First published 2000
by Routledge
2 Park Square, Milton Park, Abingdon, Oxon OX14 4RN

Simultaneously published in the USA and Canada
by Routledge
270 Madison Avenue, New York, NY 10016

Reprinted 2004, 2008

Routledge is an imprint of the Taylor & Francis Group, an informa business

Typeset in Baskerville by Taylor & Francis Books Ltd

British Library Cataloguing in Publication Data
A cataloguing record for this book is available from the British Library

Library of Congress Cataloging in Publication Data
Elsaesser, Thomas.
Weimar cinema and after: Germany's historical imaginary / Thomas Elsaesser
p.m.
Includes bibliographical references and index.
1. Motion pictures–Germany–History. I. Title

PN1993.5.G3 E58 2000
791.43′0943′09042–dc21 00–021661

ISBN 978-0-415-01234-8 (hbk)
ISBN 978-0-415-01235-5 (pbk)

CONTENTS

ILLUSTRATIONS

Part I

HAUNTED SCREENS

Caligari's cabinets and a German studio system

1

INTRODUCTION

Weimar cinema's impersonations

The Möbius strip: German cinema and its double

The German cinema of the Weimar Republic is often, but wrongly identified with Expressionism. If one locates Fritz Lang, Ernst Lubitsch and F.W. Murnau on the mental map of Berlin in the twenties, home of some of Modernism's most vital avant-garde directors, then Expressionist cinema connotes a rebellious artistic intervention. If one sees their films grow from the studio floors of the Universum Film Aktiengesellschaft (UFA), the only film company ever to think it could compete with Hollywood, this golden age of silent cinema takes its cue more from commerce and industry than art. Either way, coming so soon after a catastrophic military defeat and a failed socialist revolution, the emergence of a national cinema of international fame in Germany was as unexpected as it proved to be exceptional. No single stylistic label could hope to cover the many innovative ideas about film decor, the distinctive *mise-en-scène* of light and shadow, or the technical advances in cinematography usually attributed to Weimar film makers. And yet, in retrospect, a unity imposed itself on the films, their subjects and stories. Unique among film movements, Weimar cinema came to epitomise a country: twentieth-century Germany, uneasy with itself and troubled by a modernity that was to bring yet more appalling disasters to Europe. This legacy, embodying the best and worst not only of a national cinema, but of a nation and its people is largely the consequence of two books: Siegfried Kracauer's *From Caligari to Hitler* and Lotte Eisner's *The Haunted Screen*. Their works, more than any other, have encouraged a potent analogy between film culture and political history, where experience (of key films) so uncannily matches expectation (of what German cinema should 'reflect') that the convergence of image with its object has for nearly fifty years seemed all but self-evident.

The present study wants to take a new look at Weimar cinema. Since the films refuse to be divorced from the history of their reception as masterpieces of film art and their reputation as social sensors – identifications that now belong inseparably to Weimar cinema – the new look cannot be with fresh eyes, and this book cannot but begin with a re-reading of Kracauer and Eisner. If, as their different arguments imply, the German nation is haunted by its cinema screen, and the films are haunted by German history, then their books are themselves haunted by the history that came after the films. The *Zeitgeist* said to be speaking from their images and stories is thus a doubly mediated one, refracted across two defeats, in 1918 and 1945, and their books 'successfully' write the second disaster into the aftermath of the first. This casts over the whole enterprise a Freudian *Nachträglichkeit*, or deferred action, as if an event was looking for its cause, of which it could claim to be the consequence. And vice versa: their interpretations make such a perfect fit that the films appear as the books' illustrative evidence, retrospectively becoming the effects of a narrative of which they started out being the cause. A Möbius strip is forming before one's eyes, which catches a nation's history in a special kind of embrace. Whether there is an appropriate term for such a screen history (here, of Weimar cinema) onto which other histories and screen memories (here, persecution, exile, trauma) project themselves or are being overwritten, I am not sure. Weimar cinema is not just (like) any other period of German cinema, it is this cinema's *historical imaginary*, which suggests that it is 'the German cinema and its double': in fact, it became a *Doppelgänger* of its own pre-history: foreshadowed in the 'kino-debate' of the 1910s, it shadowed the Nazi cinema that selectively tried to (dis)inherit it in the 1930s. On the other side of the Atlantic, in the 1940s, it legitimated – almost equally selectively, as film noir – the work of German émigré film makers, before it was dug up again in the 1970s, to lend a historical pedigree to the New German Cinema of Syberberg, Herzog and Wenders.

Why historians, soon after the end of the monstrous realities of Hitler's rule, should have seized on the cinema, even more than on literature, philosophy or politics for explanation of the inexplicable is perfectly understandable. Kracauer, for one, gives an elaborate justification for his methodology. What my opening chapters try to address, however, is a slightly different question: was there something about this cinema that allowed such a 'fit' between film and history to remain convincing for so long? Can one pinpoint particular features in the films usually cited, such as *The Cabinet of Dr Caligari*, *Dr Mabuse the Gambler*, *Nosferatu*, *Warning Shadows*, *Metropolis*, *Faust*, *Pandora's Box*, *M* or *The Blue Angel*, that warrant or encourage the kind of slippage between cinematic representation and a nation's history, and consequently produce a historical imaginary? It seems that, starting with *The Cabinet of Dr Caligari*, the films usually indexed as Weimar cinema have one thing in common: they are invariably constructed as picture puzzles. Consistently if not systematically, they refuse to be 'tied down' to a single meaning. One could say that thanks to a film language that resists reference, Weimar cinema has allowed all kinds of 'realities' (including an all too real history) to shape a special semblance of sense: 'from Caligari to Hitler'.[1] Kracauer's Möbius-strip effect, it will be argued, is due to a set of formal and stylistic devices, whose equivalences, inversions and reversals facilitate but also necessitate the spectator constructing 'allegories of meaning': the political meaning offers itself first, perhaps because of the energy still absorbed into the 'black hole' that Nazism has been for the twentieth century.

The second part of my argument follows from the first in the form of a question: why should it be Weimar cinema that encourages such special hermeneutic activity? The tentative answers given are not always as interesting as the question. Apart from the ambiguity after which all art strives, Weimar cinema's rebus images – readable, like Wittgenstein's duck–rabbit picture as either one or the other, but not both at the same time – have to do with mundane matters of film economics and marketing, with the film industry and its objectives and constraints. These function as the 'historical symbolic', the limits and horizons that outline and yet vanish in the historical imaginary. Historians of Weimar cinema are, in a sense, fated to already 'know' what these films are about and how one is to experience them, making it difficult to cast off the notion that film history is necessarily the metaphoric double of another history, rather than driven by its own determinants, or merely the story of its films and its makers. On the other hand, it cautions against treating them as 'mere entertainment'.[2]

A study of Weimar cinema easily becomes a meta-critical discourse, and this book is no exception. Although I offer close readings of individual films and of individual directors, these interpretations have themselves a symptomatic character, taking as their starting point the observation that many of Weimar cinema's classics are films about film making itself, that is, self-referential. Such 'reflexivity' is, however, in this case due less to the directors belonging to a specific aesthetic avant-garde and pursuing a modernist agenda. Instead, I see it as evidence of a historical conjuncture in which a prominent segment of the Weimar film community (counting next to producers, directors and screenwriters also set designers and cameramen) found itself in an intense dialogue or even struggle on at least two fronts: domestically, they had to compete with the other, more established arts and their social institutions, and internationally, with the permanent threat of Hollywood hegemony, both on the German market and in the rest of Europe. This twofold contest over cultural recognition at home and commercial sucess abroad forms a background to all the chapters. The first two chapters also trace a shift among the films' target audiences, as early Expressionist cinema modulates into late Weimar cinema, and the battle between popular culture and high culture tilts notably in favour of the popular. One could say that from the mid-1920s, the films address not only a different social class (the so-called *Angestellten*, i.e. the white-collar workers of the emerging service industries), but also a different gender mix, reversed by Kracauer when he shifts attention from the 'little shopgirls at the movies' (in his writings from the late 1920s) to the anxious males of the immediate post-1918 years, 'tossed between rebellion and submission' (in *From Caligari to Hitler* in 1947). But this is itself a highly metaphoric argument, which the first chapter tries to nuance, by also re-reading Lotte Eisner's essentially stylistic history. Her argument about Romanticism, Expressionism and the 'will to style' is reviewed across another paradigm altogether: that of style as design, and of design as at once a form of disguise and enhancement, suggesting that so-called 'Expressionism' in Weimar cinema has determinate modernising or constructivist functions, creating for the cinema a space not only among the arts but making it a vehicle also of the emergent lifestyle technologies and leisure industries, such as fashion, decor and display. That Expressionism also served internationally as a brand-name recognition for the 'better' Germany – initially a pariah nation after the First World War – merely underscores its strategic use in designating Weimar cinema as a whole. The high-culture associations, however, also help to explain why at mid-decade, with the growing success of UFA productions in Europe and its ambitions about breaking into the US market, Expressionism as a label was abandoned in favour of other, more Americanised marketing strategies, associated with big-budget special-effects productions on national themes, such as *The Nibelungen* or *Faust*, and futurist visions such as *Metropolis* and *The Woman in the Moon*.

One of the most persistent imaginaries of the German cinema as a national–nationalist cinema thus focuses on the leading company, UFA, the giant studio machinery and media empire, whose military origins are taken as proof of its right-wing influence on German picture-making *and* politics. The chapter entitled 'Erich Pommer: "Die UFA" and Germany's bid for a studio system' (Part I, Chapter 4, this volume) challenges this causality and tries to reconstruct another possible logic, one that first of all suggests that UFA was a modern multi-national company and media conglomerate and second, that it was a company so aware of Hollywood that it constantly tried to emulate it, rival with it or differentiate itself from it – contradictory objectives that had paradoxical results. When one examines UFA's production strategy and corporate policy, one notes that it was organised according to principles of product differentiation and niche marketing, with the so-called stylised film a deliberate attempt to create an art cinema for export, while a domestic genre- and star-based commercial cinema was to be the economic bedrock, and a palette of super-productions (*Großfilme*), designed and budgeted also with export in mind, aimed to break into the American market (rarely achieved after 1923). For especially these last objectives, it was essential that nationalist or propaganda aims should be kept well in the background, at least as far as the production of feature films was concerned. UFA's market dominance was in any case due to its hold on distribution, its export network and its early diversification into many merely film-related services, rather than based on the number of films it made. This also revises the orthodox account, according to which the company's nemesis was a consequence of its success: that in its bid to enter the world market and rival the Americans, UFA overreached itself with super-productions like *Metropolis*. By considering its management practices and policy objectives, other explanations can be put forward for the financial difficulties it encountered around 1925–7, when it came so perilously close to bankruptcy.

Economically and institutionally, the most appropriate criteria for an international perspective on the Weimar film business are thus industrial indicators: division of labour and management practices, markets and exports, diversification of services and product differentiation, advertising and distribution, infrastructural investment in plant and new technologies. How different really was the German cinema from Hollywood by such a comparison? The similarities outweigh the differences, and the relative ease with which, once they were given the chance to work, German émigré directors, cameramen, set designers, composers and even screenwriters were able to adapt to Hollywood studio practice confirms the parallels between the respective film industries.

The story of UFA as a diversified media company also brings to the fore another dialogue or contest which, all through the 1920s, the cinema conducted with other popular entertainment forms, such as operetta, folk theatre and cabaret, from which even some of the classics borrowed plots and often the best ideas for their sets. How compelling, in this light, is the logic that links the disparate visual styles of German films of the early 1920s to the legacy of Romanticism, to Biedermeier cosiness, the Gothic-uncanny and Expressionist pathos, rather than to *Jugendstil*, orientalist fashion and *Kaiser Wilhelm* medievalism? In an advanced 'culture industry', are premonition, or dark foreboding at all appropriate terms for the ways a national cinema engages its audiences? Why not assume that the films were 'looking back in banter' rather than forward in *angst*, that they made a bonfire of Wilhelmine Germany's eclectic tastes and historicist pastiches with their ham-theatrical acting, their camera wizardry and spectacular special effects?

Innocence restored

That such heretical thoughts can come to mind at all perhaps indicates the gap that separates the 'present' from which I speak, from the post-1945 present of Kracauer and Eisner. One could point to several (disparate) factors that since the mid-1980s have made Weimar cinema once more topical: the revival of expressionist stylisation over realist modes in mainstream Hollywood in the form of neo-noir, sci-fi and horror genres; the turn in film studies from apparatus theory to gender studies; or the sustained interest in Walter Benjamin and Siegfried Kracauer as theorists of a modernity based on the metropolitan cityscape, the popular mass media, the ephemeral stimuli of anonymous spaces and the surface effects of neon lights or shop windows. In addition, the trigger was also something more simple and immediate: the re-experience of many of the so-called 'German Expressionist' classics in the 1980s and 1990s, when freshly minted copies became visible again, thanks to restoration efforts by archives and cinematheques, and festival screenings in places such as Pordenone, Paris and Bologna. I first saw a tinted version of *The Cabinet of Dr Caligari* at the Royal Academy London in 1983, then Enno Patalas's archive version of *Metropolis* in 1984. Since then, I have watched *Nosferatu*, *Madame Dubarry*, *Die Nibelungen*, *Faust*, *Waxworks*, *The Hands of Orlac*, *Pandora's Box* and *Warning Shadows* – mostly performed with live music, projected on big screens and occasionally even at outdoor venues, as open-air shows under star-studded night skies. Such evenings turned out to be an overwhelming visual and audio experience, attracting large enthusiastic audiences. Experience of what? Less of doom and gloom as of youthful zest, an ironic self-confidence, sustained by a rather dry humour and mischievous make-believe. I was confronted with hyper-real images saturated with sensuous–tactile surfaces, and the sets vibrated with inventive exuberance, flourish and verve. Strangely familiar worlds opened up, peopled by even stranger and yet even more familiar bodies: androgynous, parodically patriarchal, erotically ambivalent, openly bisexual; sleek or bulky; flowing or solid, languid or melodramatic. For the space of an evening's performance, Emil Jannings, Conrad Veidt, Pola Negri and Lya di Putti, Fritz Kortner and Louise Brooks, Werner Krauss and Lil Dagover, Paul Wegener, Peter Lorre were suddenly contemporaries.

From these turbulent rather than tormented sensations, a somewhat presumptuous desire came to the fore: could these Weimar films also be 'revived' for film history? Just as a generation of archivists had assured their physical survival by restoring them, I thought it ought to be conceivable to restore something else. What would it mean, for instance, to 'give back' to them some of their other possible futures, rather than keep them the ones that history (the historical imaginary) seems to have locked them into?[3] I first tested this idea with *The Cabinet of*

Figure 1 Conradt Veidt as Cesare in Robert Wien's *The Cabinet of Dr Caligari* (1920)

Source: BFI films: stills, posters and designs

Dr Caligari,[4] and then applied it to Fritz Lang's *Metropolis*, about which I wrote when Giorgio Moroder's version came out in the mid-1980s. With deliberate provocation, the essay was called 'Innocence Restored'.[5]

The naivety of the provocation and the somewhat brutal revisionism it implied were brought home to me in 1985 when I came across Peter Sloterdijk's *Kritik der zynischen Vernunft*, a book that sets itself the task of diagnosing Weimar culture in a radically different way from the studies I was previously familiar with, such as Peter Gay's *Weimar Culture* (1968), Walter Laqueur's *Weimar – A Cultural History* (1974), or even John Willett's *The New Sobriety* (1978). Detecting what he calls an enlightened false consciousness at all levels of political and cultural life, Sloterdijk remarks that Weimar was the

> most wide-awake epoch of (German) history, a highly reflexive, thoughtful period, full of imagination and extremely articulate, ploughed through with self-irony and self-analysis. To talk 'about' Weimar as if it was behind us is to remain seriously beneath it.[6]

What made Weimar especially vital and confusing were three 'fronts of complexity, [...] deforming the body politic': the impossibility of recognising among the profusion of political parties a clear polarity of pro- and anti-democratic power formations; the stresses and strains of a 'pluralist' public sphere in which a bewildering diversity of interest groups fought each other both inside and outside the law; and finally, the conflict between a traditional ethics of scarcity, production and work, and the emerging culture of consumption, mobility and mediatisation. Sloterdijk also noted two aspects that all of Weimar cultural life seemed to share: the radical *Abbau* (deconstruction) of metaphysics and bourgeois idealism, where Martin Heidegger turned out to be a more poker-faced Dadaist than Raoul Hausmann, Walter Serner and Johannes Baader put together, and the pervasive performativity of the arts and political action:

> Theatricality appeared to be the common denominator of all manifestations of life – from Expressionism to Marlene Dietrich's spectacular legs in *The Blue Angel*, from the bloody comedy of Hitler's 1923 Putsch to Brecht's *Threepenny Opera*, from the impressive funeral of [the assassinated Walter] Rathenau to the calculated banditry of the Reichstag fire of 1933. The permanent crisis that everyone talked about proved to be an excellent *metteur-en-scène*, one who knew how to direct quite a few memorable effects.
>
> (Sloterdijk 1985, vol. II: 705)

Needless to say, Sloterdijk constantly underlines how much the 1980s resembled his 1920s, arguing that only with the disillusionment that followed the 'defeat' of 1968 had the 'cynical' and 'melancholy' consciousness of Weimar finally come home to roost (ibid.: 707) Strangely enough, however, apart from the obligatory nod in the direction of Marlene Dietrich's legs, he makes no mention of the cinema, and yet, it is there that one finds ample source material for several of his 'fronts of complexity'. For instance, the cinema is directly in the firing line of the 'modernisation' front, where the 'Americanisation' of leisure and consumption raises its flag. Weimar cinema also knows one of the most flagrantly intelligent as well as self-reflexive representatives of the enlightened false consciousness, Fritz Lang, as I argue in the chapter on *Dr Mabuse* (Part II, Chapter 1, this volume), which revises my own revisionist 'Innocence Restored' (Elsaesser 1984b) and gives this study its motto: 'Duplicity Restored' could be said to be the thread that runs through all the subsequent chapters.

In the realm of the look

Lang is also the director whose entire work has traditionally been read as an extended metaphor on the vicissitudes of vision, making the theories of the cinematic apparatus as elaborated by film studies in the 1970s seem particularly apt. His films are veritable anthologies of the proto- or para-cinematic devices, elaborating the most sophisticated architecture of the gaze by his deployment of off-screen space, the insert shot and point-of-view editing, in the many stories that revolve around voyeurism and detection, hypnosis and auto-suggestion, spying and surveillance. Lang could have been on Sloterdijk's mind when he says that we need 'a logical and historical "cubism", a simultaneous thinking and seeing in several dimensions' if we are to understand 'the Weimar symptom' (Sloterdijk 1985: 710).

Yet my argument is that Lang is not the only one to whom this applies, and that the discourses of power across the *dispositifs* of vision as theorised by Michel Foucault can also be found in the work of a director as unlikely in this context as Ernst Lubitsch. His *Madame Dubarry* both enacts and deconstructs Weimar cinema's peculiar (over-) valuation of the gaze, just as earlier Lubitsch films, such as *Die Puppe*, had made fun of male obsessions with female automatons, homunculi and other test-tube creatures so well known from the genre of the 'Expressionist' film. The gender issue in *Madame Dubarry* subtly undercuts the class discourse of social mobility in the fantastic genre, ironizing it via its operetta subtext, where power appears a charade of costumes and a matter of imposture and disguise. As Weimar cinema's first export success into the United States, *Madame Dubarry* secured Lubitsch a ticket to Hollywood, making him the vanguard of a long line of émigrés and proving that politics was not the only motivation for film makers leaving Germany.

F.W. Murnau, another top UFA director and also one who left for Hollywood at the height of his fame in Germany, is usually identified with a very individual kind of lyricism, but in his work, too, the Weimar duplicity is sustained with almost clairvoyant precision. The chapter on the director stresses not so much his 'personal' themes as his creation of a 'persona'. His predilection for magic transformations and the hesitations between display and disguise are placed within a broader framework, that of producer Erich Pommer's international ambitions, backed by UFA's gamble with high production values and technological innovation. There, Murnau emerges as the ideal catalyst for the hard-nosed experiments of cameramen like Karl Freund and Carl Hoffmann and the idiosyncracies of a brilliant designer team like Robert Herlth and Walter Röhrig. Catalyst also, in that he understands like no other Weimar director how to infuse the barrage of special effects in a super-production like *Faust* with an intimate atmosphere and heart-breakingly melancholy moments. Extending the blend of romantic motifs and ironic understatement from the small-scale experimental film into the era of the exportable prestige blockbuster, Murnau's work, with its 'secret affinities' between Romanticism and a high-tech studio style both confirm and deconstruct a key element of Eisner's thesis on the persistence of Romanticism in the constitution of the German soul, giving it a wry twist in the direction of *Grand Guignol* and dandy *désinvolture.*

Pommer's ambitions and Murnau's career moves illustrate that a national cinema does not exist in splendid isolation. Weimar cinema was engaged in complex manoeuvres, at once competing with and imitating its rivals. It made 'national cinema' mean little more than a differential relation of domestic producers to foreign ones, usually those of Hollywood.[7] For the movie-going public, however, the nationality of a film was only a secondary matter, exposed as audiences were to foreign films and especially to foreign stars, some of whom – when one thinks of the reputation of Douglas Fairbanks, Mary Pickford and Charles Chaplin in Europe during the 1920s – spectators often idolised even more than their own domestic talent. Chapter 1 in Part III ('*Hallo Caesar!* Reinhold Schünzel – a German Chaplin?') is an attempt to demonstrate around a once highly popular director, who was also his own star performer, the logic of such national–international cross-referencing in Weimar cinema. The image of Schünzel, as reflected in the trade journals, was doubly relational, playing off Schünzel the director against Schünzel the star, and Schünzel the (German) comedian against Chaplin, Harold Lloyd or Buster Keaton. It suggests that the German film market, even for mainstream films, was international rather than national, with Schünzel trying to provide the indigenous equivalent of what audiences had already learnt to like from American films. That Schünzel was able to engage in a kind of masquerade of masculinity that leaves considerable room for ambiguities of gender perhaps distinguished his comedy from that of his American models.

The complex of masculinity is also taken up in Part II, Chapter 4, on G.W. Pabst's *Pandora's Box*, the film that may well in retrospect have become the most defining, but in its time the most puzzling, document of late Weimar cinema. The persona of Louise Brooks in this, her most famous film, has given rise to a lively debate in recent years, not least sparked off by Brooks's own – Sloterdijk might call them cynical–sensual – memoirs, as well as the wider interest in female empowerment through masquerade and self-conscious play with (sexist) stereotypes, like the *femme fatale*.[8] The chapter also gives a functionalist analysis of the representations of masculinity, which echoes other, more recent debates about masculinity in Weimar Germany, sparked off by studies such as Klaus Theweleit's *Male Fantasies*.[9] The American actress in *Pandora's Box* continues the oblique but none the less abundant references in Weimar cinema to America, the American dream and above all American image making in the latter half of the 1920s.

Transparent duplicities

On the other hand, G.W. Pabst's other classic film, *The Threepenny Opera*, reworks similar issues of gender and stereotype – the *homme fatale* – in a quintessentially 'Weimar' context. While Brecht's play is as much an icon of the period as Marlene Dietrich's legs, Pabst's film is also the culmination, summary and (self-) critique of Weimar cinema's filmic iconography. Like Lubitsch's *Madame Dubarry* that, together with *The Cabinet of Dr Caligari* opens the period, *The Threepenny Opera* at its close represents at once a deconstruction in the mode of parody and the rearticulation of this Weimar aesthetic as a transnational, if not 'international' style. Its elaborate play with theatrical props and tailors' dummies, seemingly interchangeable with human beings and their feelings, gives a specially ironic turn to Brecht's own brand of aggressively displayed cynicism, so that, despite the author's famous lawsuit against Nero, the production company, *The Threepenny Opera* remains symptomatic of Weimar's 'transparent duplicities'.

A similar game of hide and seek, of disavowal and double negation characterises another late Weimar film, *Das Lied ist aus* (*It's the End of the Song*), written by the Jewish screenwriter Walter Reisch and directed by one of his best friends, the Nazi sympathizer Geza von Bolvary, for whom Reisch also wrote *Das Flötenkonzert von Sanssouci* (*The Flute Concert of Sanssouci*). The 'transparent duplicities' here take on a dangerously political dimension, a kind of 'moral cubism' which makes it appear that any work that cannot or will not sustain the 'complexity fronts' ends up working for the propaganda front – in this case, abandoning the typical Weimar resistance to reference in the course of the film itself, for the sake of a simpler political metaphor.

The chapter devoted to the cinema of the early 1930s tries to understand this apparent reduction of complexity across the dynamics and competing forms of modernity and modernisation, once more returning to the issue of high-culture and popular culture, of the avant-garde and the invention of tradition, processes which in the 1930s took place under the sign of the technologies of make-believe, the *schöne Schein*, but feeding off the energies which in the 1920s were still associated with 'Americanism'. With the coming of sound, the late and post-Weimar film industry undertook the kinds of modernisation entirely in line with previous UFA developments, but also – more contentiously perhaps – in keeping with developments in the international and Hollywood film industry. Hence the Nazi cinema's emphasis on genres and stars, hence its successes at home and – for much of the 1930s – even abroad.

If, from the vantage point of 1945, one can detect proto-fascist tendencies in Weimar cinema, they reside less in the supposed allegories of leader figures and demonic seducers distilled by Kracauer and Eisner. Rather, the Nazi entertainment industry, in crucial respects, took over the carnival of styles, the 'imperso-Nation' of roles and poses, tailoring them to the new rulers' chief ideological requirement on the home front: to appropriate national history by inventing for its own *idées fixes* a 'tradition', a historicist legitimation and a pedigree. The principle of disguise and make believe became Joseph Goebbels' political principle *par excellence*, the Möbius strip was arrested, cut in half, and life took a cynical lesson from art, as Kracauer had woefully noted. Thus, Nazism as a regime of both theatricality and camouflage had an uncanny capacity for 'inheriting' its different political predecessors and indeed even its ideological enemies, such as the socialists and communists. In this respect, Nazi culture was a kind of mimicry of modernity *and* of tradition, but also a sort of dress rehearsal for some of the attitudes and values of consumer culture. As a society of the spectacle, it energetically forged ahead with the uses of cinema and the visual media for propaganda purposes: uses which, before, during and after the Hitler regime, continue to be practised as 'advertising' and 'marketing'.

Some of the émigrés who had to flee Germany in 1933 did in fact think, upon arrival in California, that out of the frying pan, they had landed right in the fire. With a certain shock of recognition they realised that the commercial culture they encountered in the United States recalled nothing more vividly than the 'administered culture' they had fled, especially in the way the arts under both capitalism and Nazism had been – as it seemed to them, cynically – appropriated and pillaged in the form of a masquerade, with the entertainment industry busy producing cunningly seductive simulacra of every style, every ideology, every pleasure or value, and treating these styles – but also the pleasures and values they connoted – as commodities. This shock of recognition may well have armed the Weimar exiles, and reminded them of the need not to drop their guard too much, and instead, maintain their camouflage and mimicry. The result was one of Weimar cinema's most enduring legacies which is also one of its most powerful imaginaries. The German exile community in Hollywood, these 'strangers in paradise' are credited with having found their most existential self-representation in a quintessentially American film genre, held to be quintessentially 'German' and 'Expressionist'. I am referring, of course, to film noir, a genre that is not one, and a style that perhaps refuses and resists reference as cunningly as the great Weimar classics. Chapter 3 in Part 4 is devoted to the historical imaginary of film noir and picks up the discussion of the movements between Berlin, Paris and Hollywood briefly introduced in the chapter on Walter Reisch and *Das Lied ist aus* (Part III, Chapter 3), before presenting a more sceptical but also multi-layered genealogy of the German 'influence' on film noir, arguing that these émigrés have had, in the 1930s at least, an equally strong contribution to make to (musical) comedy, and in the 1940s and 1950s, to melodrama, thus somewhat complicating the (imaginary) 'fit' between personal fate, political persecution and a cinematic genre. And yet, nothing seems to speak more vividly to movie audiences today than 'noir' – in all its shades.

It returns me to an earlier point, namely my own experiences with the Weimar classics, and more generally, the reception of 'Expressionist' cinema in the 1990s, as (projective) objects of an energy and of youthful vitality that now (or once more?) seems to be emanating from the films themselves. Are we witnessing the 'pop-appropriation' of a rather heavy legacy, 'Weimar light', so to speak? With 'pop-appropriation' I am alluding to the camp mimicking of Weimar classics by rock artists and pop-singers: apart from Giorgio Moroder, super-stars such as Madonna, Freddy Mercury, David Bowie and Mick Jagger have all borrowed from *Metropolis*, *Pandora's Box* and *Dr Caligari* for their music videos. These high-culture films have been given legitimacy, or rather 'street-credibility' by the very epitome of commercialised popular culture – the music business. Suitably 'sampled', Weimar cinema has become a collection of 'film clips with attitude'. What exactly is the appeal? Where is the moment of recognition? Is there another 'historical imaginary' in the making? My initial inference was that it is the energy and the body language, the androgyny, gender ambiguity and bisexuality of Weimar cinema that is instantly familiar. But maybe it is also a certain knowingness – Sloterdijk's enlightened false consciousness, which I have called 'transparent duplicity' – at the heart of so many of the films, with which we have no difficulty of entering into a dialogue: the 'devil' for whom, Jagger *dixit*, we have a great deal of 'sympathy'. Weimar cinema has a serious sense of self-parody: even its tragic moments are not without tongue-in-cheek, sign of a culture finally unable to take itself altogether too seriously. However, the contemporary recognition effect may also be fuelled by a new media culture of 'transgression' and 'excess', especially where these moments beyond the limits are associated with technology, automatons, the borderline between body and machine, the cyborgs of today recalling the somnabulists and hypnotists of Weimar. In other words: the secret affinities are with a drug culture and psychic prosthetics, with techno-energy and the body electric. In this respect, the Nazi shadow over Weimar cinema may simply have become its new neon sheen.

Although pop culture's act of re-appropriation thus has undoubtedly its darker side, it oddly corroborated my sense of an oxymoronic 'innocence restored', endorsing a desire to restore to the past its other futures. Madonna and co. confirmed an intuition that a different look at Weimar cinema was indeed possible, even if, as it happened, it was not only initiated by film historians and archivists. It was as though the films had to be 'loved' differently – differently even from the way they were by Eisner, Kracauer and their followers (among whom I count myself). Has the pendulum begun to swing once more the other way? My hope is that the Weimar films, now that they have been embraced by today's popular culture, can once more become objects of 'serious' study, and besides being appropriated, can also be appreciated: maybe even giving rise to a new 'kino-debate'?

The present book has been in the making for about a decade. Its starting

Figure 2 The 'false' Maria (Brigitte Helm) seducing the pleasure-seeking young men of Fritz Lang's *Metropolis* (1927)

Source: BFI films: stills, posters and designs

point were three essays on aspects of Weimar cinema, two of which are incorporated, one in substantially revised form.[10] For other chapters reprinted I want to thank the editors of *European Popular Cinema*, *G.W. Pabst An Extra-Territorial Cinema*, *Home, Exile, Homeland* and the journal *Iris* for their kind permission.[11] The chapters in this volume on Murnau (Part II, Chapter 3), on 'Modernity and modernisation' (Part IV, Chapter 2) and on the UFA studio (Part I, Chapter 4) have drawn on, respectively, material first published in *Sight and Sound*,[12] and *The Oxford History of World Cinema*,[13] whose editor, Geoffrey Nowell-Smith has been a most invaluably incisive commentator in the final phases. Among the many other colleagues and friends from whose invitations, conversations and comments I have drawn encouragement and help for this project are Dudley Andrew, Janet Bergstrom, Ansje van Beusekom, Hans-Michael Bock, Warren Buckland, Michael Budd, Barton Byg, Richard DeCordova, Mary Ann Doane, Pamela Falkenberg, Malte Hagener, Miriam Hansen, Anton Kaes, Peter Krämer, Tarja Laine, Patricia Mellencamp, Leonardo Quaresima, Don Ranvaud, Rick Rentschler, Phil Rosen, Tom Saunders, Jennaro Talens, Cynthia Walk, Michael Wedel and John Willett. Finally, my editors at Routledge, Rebecca Barden and

Alistair Daniel are to be warmly thanked, first for their persistence and then for their patience.

Notes

1 Klaus Kreimeier (Kreimeier 1998) pointed out a further turn of this Möbius strip: in a post-script to his essay on Pabst, he mentions that the director had intended to cast Werner Krauss, the actor who played Dr Caligari in 1919, as Hitler in his 1955 *Es geschah am 20. Juli* (*The Jackboot Mutiny*).

2 It took the so-called 'New Film History' to convince scholars that film production and motion picture exhibition already in the early years were highly international affairs, suggesting that the idea of a national cinema must be set alongside international developments. For the German Cinema of the pre-1918 period, see my 'Early German Cinema: A Case for Case Studies or Recasting it All?', in J. Fullerton (ed.) *Celebrating 1895* (London: John Libbey, 1998): 264–77 and Elsaesser (1996).

3 Paul Ricoeur once called for 'returning to the past its own future'. This evokes the whole complex of '*Nachträglichkeit*' or deferred action which, while not the same as counterfactual history ('what-if ... ' or 'it could have been otherwise, but wasn't'), gives a historical period the sense of 'a transferential function, whereby the past dissolves in the present, so that the future becomes (once again) an *open question*, instead of being specified by the fixity of the past' (Homi K. Bhaba *The Location of Culture* (London: Routledge, 1994): 219, quoting from John Forester, *Dead on Time*: 206).

4 'Social Mobility and the Fantastic', *Wide Angle* vol. 5, no. 2 (1982): 14–25.

5 'Fritz Lang's *Metropolis*: innocence restored', *Monthly Film Bulletin* (December 1984): 363–6.

6 Peter Sloterdijk (1985): 708.

7 For this reason, film historians have generally ceased to find 'national cinema' a useful category. If one focuses on the mode of production, one has to choose between commercial cinema and an art or avant-garde fringe as typically 'national'. In the first case, what is considered nationally significant are the genres and stars that make a cinema popular with domestic audiences. In the cases where the art cinema stands for the 'national', it requires not domestic audiences but the existence of an international circuit of film festivals, film journals and art houses for its critical validation. In the 1920s, the situation was almost the reverse: the commercial cinema was written about as if it had no cultural significance, being merely a money machine for producers, equally reprehensible whether these were indigenous or foreign. It was the 'artistic film' (and its ability to appeal to a national audience) that carried the hopes and fears for a 'national cinema'.

8 See Mary Ann Doane, *Femmes Fatales* (London: Routledge, 1992).

9 Klaus Theweleit, *Male Fantasies* (Minneapolis: University of Minnesota Press, 1989).

10 Apart from 'Social Mobility and the Fantastic' (see note 4, above), of which parts are taken up in 'Caligari's Family' (Part I, Chapter 3, this volume), and 'Lulu and the meter man: Louise Brooks, G.W. Pabst and *Pandora's Box*' (Part II, Chapter 4, this volume), first published in *Screen* vol. 24, nos 4–5 (June–July 1983): 4–36 (reprinted here and revised and expanded), published 'Film History and Visual Pleasure: Weimar Cinema' in P. Mellencamp and P. Rosen (eds.) *Cinema Histories / Cinema Practices* (Frederick, MD: University Publications of America, 1984): 47–85.

11 'Author, actor, showman: Reinhold Schünzel's *Hallo Caesar!*' in R. Dyer and G. Vincendeau (eds) *Popular European Cinema* (London: Routledge, 1992): 72–86;

'Transparent duplicities: *The Threepenny Opera*' in Rick Rentschler (ed.) *The Films of G.W. Pabst An Extra-Territorial Cinema* (New Brunswick, NJ: Rutgers University Press, 1990): 103–15; 'Ethnicity, authenticity and exile: A counterfeit trade?' in H. Naficy (ed.) *Home, Exile, Homeland* (London: Routledge, 1998): 97–124; 'A German ancestry to film noir? – Film history and its imaginary', in *Iris* (Paris/Iowa City), no. 21 (Spring 1996): 129–44.

12 'Secret Affinities – F.W. Murnau: A Centenary Tribute', *Sight and Sound* (Winter 1988/89), and 'Hollywood–Berlin', *Sight and Sound* (November, 1997).

13 'Germany – the Weimar years', in G. Nowell-Smith (ed.) *The Oxford History of World Cinema* (Oxford: Oxford University Press, 1997).

2

EXPRESSIONIST FILM OR WEIMAR CINEMA?

With Siegfried Kracauer and Lotte Eisner (once more) to the movies

Expressionist film – everyone's favourite nightmare?[1]

The German cinema of the early 1920s, sandwiched by film historians between the pioneering effort of American directors Griffith, de Mille and Chaplin in the 1910–19 era and the Soviet cinema of the late 1920s (Eisenstein, Pudovkin and Vertov), is invariably associated with 'Expressionism'.[2] Not least to advertise the turn from plebeian amusement to high modernism, this label, borrowed from the German pre-First World War avant-garde movement in literature and the fine arts became the generic term for the cinema of the period as a whole.

From the perspective of the 1990s, this is a contentious, but passably benign view. It somewhat too readily assumes the 'baton relay' or 'roving spotlight' narrative of 1920s cinema history,[3] and it takes as representative a rather small sample of films, favouring often carefully crafted export productions at the expense of a wide array of domestically targeted films: detective films and comedies, (male and female) star 'vehicles', operetta subjects, social and erotic melodramas, epics and costume films enjoyed by popular audiences. Expressionist cinema, on the other hand, was an *auteur* cinema: self-conscious, sophisticated, state-of-the-art film making that was initially calculated to promote a company – Decla – its producer Erich Pommer, and his team of directors, screenwriters, cameramen, set designers and male acting stars.[4] Nowhere near as well known today are other leading figures not associated with Expressionist films, such as Joe May, Richard Oswald, Max Mack, Ludwig Berger, Reinhold Schünzel, Richard Eichberg. They were prolific directors, often more successful and sometimes no less accomplished than the famous names.[5] Given this preference of high-art films over popular mainstream cinema as an index of Germany's national cinema, it is the more surprising how many films that subsequently became part of the canon carry titillatingly sensationalist titles: besides *The Cabinet of Dr Caligari*, there is *Dr Mabuse The Gambler*, *Destiny/Der Müde Tod*, *The Golem*, *The Street*, *Backstairs*, *Waxworks*, *Warning Shadows*, *Metropolis*, *Nosferatu The Vampire*, *The Hands of Orlac*, *Pandora's Box*, *Joyless Street* and *Secrets of a Soul*.

Either popular taste was taking its toll after all, or another story was being told as well. One of these stories is the canonical one: establishing film as art and signifying the unexpected flowering of creative talent in a defeated nation, Expressionist film came to connote that sudden, brief *frisson* of a never-to-be-forgotten glimpse into the abyss – of unconscious urges, of the German soul, of Germany's fatal destiny. The nightmare visions and psycho-horrors have not only led to conjectures about the society giving birth to these monsters on the screen. Testifying to the troubled political reality of post-First-World-War German society or already foreshadowing the ideological turmoil to come, both rang true, depending on whether one thought of the lost war of 1918 or of the rise of Nazism at the end of the decade.

Trying to decide why these films seem so morbid, traumatised and full of foreboding has kept a lively but also often murky debate smouldering, thanks largely to two well-known books, Siegfried Kracauer's *From Caligari to Hitler* (1947) and Lotte Eisner's *The Haunted Screen* (1969) (the latter published originally in French: *L'Écran démoniaque*, Paris: Le Terrain Vague, 1952). Rarely before or since has a body of films exerted such a pull towards verbal paraphrase, in which epithets like 'dark' and 'demonic', 'twisted', 'haunted' and 'tormented' leap onto the page. A narrative of fear and trembling, instinct and drive, Eros and Thanatos have fed the notion that the German cinema is 'psychological' and 'inward', prompting other historians, in the wake of Kracauer and Eisner, to speculate about the national character responsible for these aberrant fantasies or eccentric fictions. As a case study of a 'movement', a period, a national cinema or the relation between cinema and society, German Expressionist film is still a favourite in textbooks,[6] film style surveys,[7] in books about the sociology of cinema,[8] and in general film histories.[9]

The general cultural memory, on the other hand, has retained neither the directors nor the convoluted story lines of the films. It is the often eponymous heroes, or rather villains, that have caught the imagination: the mad doctor and magician Dr Caligari; the underworld mastermind Dr Mabuse; the cruel tyrant Ivan the Terrible or the serial killer Jack the Ripper from *Waxworks*; lean weary Death from *Destiny/Der Müde Tod*; the legendary Golem; Attila and Hagen from *The Nibelungen*; the student of Prague and his murderous double; the vengeful scientist Rotwang and the robot Maria from *Metropolis*; Orlac of the severed hands; the vampire Nosferatu, the German Dracula; Haghi the super-spy; the leering Mephisto of *Faust*; the insinuatingly smooth Tartuff and the creepily pitiable child murderer in *M*. These figures are often indissociable from the (male) actors who incarnated them: Conrad Veidt, Emil Jannings, Rudolf Klein-Rogge, Max Schreck, Werner Krauss and Peter Lorre. Their roles and the films' titles come, however, from *Grand Guignol* or the fairground (a frequent setting, as Kracauer noted) and the villains resemble the bogeymen of children's fairy tales and folk legend, precisely the regions of the popular imagination and entertainment that Expressionist films are said to have helped the cinema leave behind.

The irony almost suggests that the film makers and writers involved may have had their tongues firmly in their cheeks. This would be the other story: the present chapter equally firmly keeps in mind the possibility that these art films may have functioned on a double register – straight-faced and put-ons, performative 'expression', not only of Expressionism, but of neo-romantic decadence and *Jugendstil* as well as of Bauhaus modernism and constructivist futurism. If some of the films do look back to the traumas of trench warfare in the muddy fields of Flanders, others (or the same in another register) also look forward to the time of style warfare in the high streets of Berlin.[10] Technological bonfires of eclectic tastes and daring fashions, they certainly ignited and delighted an international public that was otherwise deeply suspicious of everything German.

What in the films is identified with 'Expressionism' is the unusual lighting,[11] the stylisation of the sets and the acting,[12] the 'Gothic'-story material and fairy-tale motifs, angular exteriors, claustrophobic interiors,[13] and above all, that excess of soul ascribed to things 'typically German'.[14] The political–ideological readings challenge the inherent formalism of such a label and prefer the term 'Weimar cinema', in order to distinguish the period style 'Expressionism' from the broader analysis of a mentality and political conjuncture, identified with the still fascinating phenomenon 'Weimar culture', lasting from 1918 to 1933.[15] Such a distinction invites one to re-read the canonical version, perhaps deconstruct it a little, without dismissing it, and instead, try and locate the ground on which both terms find a new place in (film-)history.

Our two standard works reflect these divisions, if they did not actually create them. Kracauer's *From Caligari to Hitler* and Eisner's *The Haunted Screen* appeared almost simultaneously, but largely independently from each other, after the Second World War and in response to it. It is telling that the books were published, respectively, in the United States and in France, rather than in Germany, where their publishing history is a chapter all by itself.[16] Each is the work of a Jewish exile, who in the 1920s wrote as a professional film critic or journalist, and each in its distinct way is a profoundly personal attempt to grasp through the cinema, something of the tragedy that had befallen the country and the culture they had loved and even over-identified with. Hence also the vehemence of their ambiguity about this cinema, reflected in the appropriately lurid and brilliantly suggestive titles they chose for their books. As with the films they so prominently featured, the sensationalist slant has paid off in recognition value, but it has also given their interpretations a certain mirror illusion of intuitive truth, making one at times forget that this perspective alignment is one that imposes itself only with hindsight: in this instance, the view of insiders looking back and of outsiders looking in, as much in sorrow and pain as in anger. While *The Haunted Screen* is the work of an art historian trying to account for the prevalence of the fantastic in the themes of the German cinema, as well as explain the pervasive elements of stylisation, by demonstrating the persisting legacy of Romanticism and the Gothic revival in German art and culture, Kracauer's title is itself an interpretation. *From Caligari to Hitler* boldly suggests that the madmen, machine men, tyrants, supermen and charlatans populating the German screens from the end of the First World War onwards are the prototypes of those madmen, charlatans and tyrants who took Germany, Europe and finally most of the rest of the world, into another disastrous war.[17] There have been many objections to *From Caligari to Hitler* and *The Haunted Screen*, ever since they were published,[18] with Kracauer's methodology and Eisner's assumptions continuing to arouse criticism.[19] None the less, the central idea of these books has imposed itself with singular self-evidence: in Kracauer, the claim for a demonstrable relation between Weimar films, social upheavals and Nazism; in Eisner, the demonstrable relation between German Romanticism, Expressionist films and Nazism.

Thus, 'Expressionist film' and 'Weimar cinema' continue to signal ready-made, self-evident identities, the former slanted towards the artists that produced the films, and the latter focusing on the society that consumed them – two halves of a whole that to this day spells Germany's national cinema. Yet, it is this very self-evidence that must make one pause. Are the two books not based on an imaginary, an ideological fiction? Each names an entity that is retrospectively given coherence, because seen from a particular vantage point that compellingly serves a deep-seated need. As suggested, the two books' interpretative sweep of Germany's national trauma, seen across its cinema, bears itself the marks of personal trauma for their authors. One only has to remind oneself of the fact that Eisner worked in Paris and Kracauer in New York, to realise that they addressed themselves (or had reason to believe they addressed themselves) to a doubting, hostile and suspicious audience (of non-German readers), with whom they were trying to make (em)phatic contact, by accommodating distinct sensibilities. Eisner, for instance, quotes a Frenchman:

> In 1817, in a letter to the archetypal Romantic Rahel Varnhagen, Astolphe de Coustine wrote: 'Behind the lives and writings of the Germans there is always a mysterious world whose light alone seems to pierce the veil of our atmosphere; and the minds disposed to ascend towards that world [...] will always be alien to France'. It was in this mysterious world, attractive and repugnant at the same time, that the German cinema found its true nature.[20]

As exiles, both Kracauer and Eisner served their host countries well, mediating between the respective national predilections or prejudices, and a West Germany trying to face up to its responsibilities as the legal successor of the 'Third Reich'. At the same time, on an even more personal level, both exiles also enjoyed patronage, and their books can be understood as addressing their benefactors – Eisner was working for Henri Langlois, and Kracauer wanted to express his gratitude to Iris Barry at MOMA and the Institute of Social Research, as well as offering his services to the US government. In other words, and once more with considerable hindsight, one can discern in these influential texts certain kinds of mirror relations at work, providing an occasion for recognition/miscognition effects, which in turn favoured discourses and perspectives on their subject that necessarily occluded other, equally well-founded film-historical approaches and film-aesthetic evaluations, or at any rate, they made these others more difficult to articulate. For instance, there is a third publication, also by an émigré journalist and also published immediately after the Second World War in 1947, but virtually forgotten: H.H. Wollenberg's *Fifty Years of German Film* (1947). Wollenberg, who from 1920–33 was an editor of the influential trade paper *Die Lichtbildbühne*, writes primarily an economic, production-oriented history that gives *Dr Caligari* barely seven lines and concludes:

> There is a general contention abroad that German studios of the 'classic' period between 1920–30 preferred to use macabre themes and that this obviously had its psychological basis in the mentality of the Germans. I have tried to show here that this view is entirely wrong. The probable reason for it is that only a very few films out of the great mass of German productions are still being shown to students of the cinema today. To generalise about all German films, using these outstanding works as proof, is certainly a mistake. The vast majority of films never survived the one season for which they were intended.[21]

The first extended study of 'Expressionist film' by Rudolf Kurtz had already appeared in 1926.[22] Kurtz refers himself to the art historian Wilhelm Worringer and his notions of abstraction and empathy, and he favours musical and architectural analogies, rather than discussing somnambulist anticipation. Where Kurtz draws political parallels, they point in the opposite direction to Kracauer:

> Expressionist film in Germany did not appear out of nowhere. It required a certain contemporary disposition, in order for the impulses to fall on fertile soil. The period around 1919 was propitious for its popularisation. […] Due to the voluntarist stance of Expressionism and its constructivist character, it proved attractive to all those whose goal it was to seize, reshape and newly-create [the world]. Additionally, there is its decorative–revolutionary appearance, opposed to all conventionality and adapting itself easily to every revolutionary intent. […] It is this disposition, which gave Expressionism, during the first storm years in Russia, the stamp of official art. It would be easy to write a treatise about Bolshevism and Expressionism, but even if one wants to avoid all [political] references, the world-feeling of radical change would have to seek its spiritual source in Expressionism.[23]

Any of the now almost inevitable associations with terrifying doubles, mysterious strangers, Faustian pacts and deadly wagers, idyllic towns visited by stern figures dressed in black, gingerbread houses dwarfed by giant skyscrapers, and cities peopled by petty despots wearing white gloves or hiding mad scientists with piercing eyes would not have occurred to Kurtz, who, by 1926, was himself already writing retrospectively. In the guise of a programmatic manifesto, his extended obituary is a form of damage limitation, arguing that filmic expressionism has to be rescued from its externally applied repetitions, because only in the 'absolute film' (of the German avant-garde around Richter, Ruttmann, Egeling) does its spirit find its 'new radical form'.

Kracauer's and Eisner's seminal interventions dating from the end of the Second World War, thus mark a decisive break in film criticism and film historiography. Especially Kracauer's book recasts and effectively contradicts the reputation that the German cinema enjoyed from about 1920/1 to the early 1930s all over Western Europe, Russia and the United States as a model of aesthetically and often enough also politically progressive film making. It began with French enthusiasm for the 'Caligarisme' (Delluc),[24] which was shared in the Soviet Union (Caligari was imitated on stage and screen, Eisenstein published admiring articles on German cinema).[25] German cinema had a unique reputation in the US after the success of *Dr Caligari* and Lubitsch's *Passion.* It was a model cinema for the Dutch Filmliga;[26] in Britain, it inspired the London Film Society movement and the journal *Close-up* whose writers championed especially G.W. Pabst as a political progressive.[27] By way of 'influence', the German cinema had a formative role for Luis Bunuel, discovering his calling after seeing films by Lang (*Destiny/Der Müde Tod*).[28] Alfred Hitchcock, also impressed by Lang (*Destiny*, *Dr Mabuse*), Leni (*Waxworks*) and Dupont (*Variety*), worked at Ufa in Berlin, where he watched Murnau on the set of *The Last Laugh* while co-directing *The Blackguard* on the adjacent stage; he directed his first features *The Pleasure Garden* and *The Mountain Eagle* for Emelka in Munich in 1925/26.[29] The articles written about the German cinema in the 1920s are legion, yet none of them discovers 'demonic' traits, 'haunted' characters or proto-fascist tendencies in the films or the film makers.[30] Some typical examples, such as *The Cabinet of Dr Caligari*,[31] *Nosferatu*,[32] or *Destiny*,[33] were considered key works of avant-garde cinema, while others, equally typical, such as *Madame Dubarry*, *The Last Laugh*, or *The Joyless Street*, had an appreciable influence on fixing norms of mainstream narrative cinema, and not only in Europe.[34]

That this estimation changed after the Second World War is all too understandable, in the wake of international demands for accountability and explanations: how could it have come to Nazism, the brutal exiling and extermination of Jews, tolerated or supported by a majority of the population? The cinema fell under suspicion not least because of the role films had had in the Nazi propaganda machine. For the subsequent two decades, almost all major studies of both Weimar and Nazi cinema were written by exiled Germans or non-Germans, a fact that honours their authors, yet these ideological accounts of the take-over of the film industry after 1933 tended to generate rigid explanatory models, almost all of them binary. The style and genre paradigm fell into the two categories – fantasy and realist; the art historical periodisation knew two phases – Expressionism and *Neue Sachlichkeit*; the aesthetic judgements divided between avant-garde or commerce; and the political tendencies were assessed under either 'nationalist' (i.e. reactionary) or 'international' (progressive). German film history became a series of oppositional discourses, mirroring structures of embattled or ideological terms, even when the labels were subsequently taken apart.[35]

Hence the difficulty of writing about the films without falling into such categories: their symmetry seems to repress something, and therefore, the choice of either Expressionist *film* or Weimar *cinema* is never an arbitrary one. The terms cannot be simply 'deconstructed', nor can the labels lay claim to any obvious historical truth, other than that they, too, represent different kinds of 'imaginaries' which, fetish-like, hide as much as they reveal. In order to understand why Expressionist or Weimar films still – once more? – fascinate, one has to recognise that the labels and their imaginaries now belong to the films, and are part of their identity for cinema history. Even though the assumption that films 'reflect' their society directly is surely untenable, the historical imaginary attached to a national cinema show the films working at (different) constructions of (different) identities. But this 'working-at' is also a 'trying-out', alerting one to the mirror-relations, to the processes of cultural self-fashioning through the eyes of 'significant others', and the ritualised masks across which communities speak to each other – or fail to do so. In their oppositions and successions, the historical imaginaries around Germany's national cinema from the 1920s onwards make up a fabric that holds the individual films in place and lends a semblance of consistency if not to the term 'national cinema' itself, then to the possibility of a period paradigm.[36] Despite the retrospective construction of Weimar cinema, then, to take another look at the German films of the 1920s, means necessarily to take Eisner and Kracauer once more to the movies.

The Haunted Screen: image and influence

Lotte Eisner concentrates on the stylistic continuities of a number of motifs, both literary and from the fine arts, as they persist, transform themselves and permutate through more than a hundred years of German aesthetic sensibility. She is persuasive on the intertextualities existing between film, theatre and painting, as she traces the extraordinarily resilient legacy of German Romanticism from the 1820s to the 1920s, with its predilection for extreme states of feeling, the sublime in nature, torn and divided personalities and a ready penchant for grotesque or morbid fantasies. The cinema of the 1920s seems to her the culmination of a long development of the 'demonic', exacerbated by the lost war, and testifying to a national character inclined at times of crisis or disgrace to turn irrational, choleric and manic–depressive:

> Mysticism and magic, the dark forces to which Germans have always been more than willing to commit themselves, has flourished in the face of death on the battlefields. […] A new stimulus was thus given to the eternal attraction towards all that is obscure and undetermined,

> towards the kind of brooding speculative reflection called *Grübelei* which culminated in the apocalyptic doctrine of Expressionism.
>
> (Eisner 1969: 9)

Apart from 'the national character', Eisner also has another protagonist determining this cinema's aesthetic identity. Much of her book focuses on the charismatic personality of Max Reinhardt, whose stage-craft dominated design and *mise-en-scène*, but who was also the Godfather–Caligari in another sense, since almost the entire personnel of the German screen trained with him or owed him their artistic breakthrough.[37] But Eisner's central historical category is 'influence': her study details how specific individuals or artists influenced film style, documenting the many links from nineteenth-century paintings to 1920s set design, decor, and the use of (chiaroscuro, or Rembrandt-type) lighting in the key films of the 'Expressionist' mode. That paintings by Caspar David Friedrich are quite evidently the inspiration for certain compositions in Fritz Lang's *Destiny*, or that the importance of lesser painters like August Böcklin and Hans Thoma for film iconography has not been fully appreciated are among her major insights. Her sensitivity towards the mutations that the Romantic heritage underwent as it entered the cinema makes *The Haunted Screen* still an important source book.[38] As more films have become viewable again, this aspect of Eisner's work could well be extended to include the popular image culture of Germany at the turn of the century, indicating the migration of motifs and the permeability of the arts in relation to each other.[39] Her eye for the vibrant multi-media space which the German cinema shared with the theatre, architecture and the visual arts give a range to Eisner's argument that makes one almost forget its central weaknesses: in order to describe the dynamics of this 'new romanticism', the term 'influence' fails as an explanatory concept. The appeal to the idea of the 'Gesamtkunstwerk' does not convince either, nor does 'Expressionism' seem finally the appropriate name for the pressures of stylisation at work.

First, there are quite other ways of analysing the stylistic elements and peculiarities of Expressionist films. Barry Salt, for instance, has challenged both Kracauer and Eisner. In his essay 'From Caligari to who?' he points out, among other things, that the particular lighting that Eisner traces in German cinema and attributes to the influence of Max Reinhardt can be found much earlier in American films; he demonstrates that of the films generally listed as 'Expressionist', only very few show actual features of expressionist style, and he also avers that any ideological reading of the films is so selective as to remain unconvincing.[40] In another important essay, Salt goes on the counter-offensive and persuasively shows to what extent German set design and film architecture was adapting or copying theatre design, tracing the various productions – and not exclusively by Reinhardt – which might have stood as models for style features of specific films.[41] Summing up his research, Salt mentions seven films at most that seem to him to qualify, having either elements of Expressionist visual design, Expressionist acting, or are based on Expressionist plays with theatrical mass-stagings.[42]

Along similar lines, Kristin Thompson has inscribed Expressionist style in a more materially and historically grounded film poetics, in so far as she has demonstrated how complexly determined the choice of style actually was, or how premeditated so-called 'Expressionism' was when first launched in *The Cabinet of Dr Caligari*, in order then to be deployed equally calculatedly but ultimately without lasting success.[43] She also offers a set of formal criteria which, while having little to do with Expressionist painting or literature, none the less make sense within the constructivist framework sketched by Rudolf Kurtz and cited above:

> Expressionism will here serve as a stylistic term applying to a general attempt to minimise the differences among the four aspects of mise-en-scène: lighting, costume, figure disposition and behaviour, and setting. The expressionist film makes, as much as possible, a single visual material of these aspects; the result is an emphasis on overall composition. Expressionism lends the expressivity of the human body to the entire visual field, while simultaneously trying to make of the body a purely compositional element.[44]

Thompson corroborates implicitly that here, too, the attempt to create for this cinema a level of consistency, or to account for a perceived coherence by an appeal to either psychology or mentality risks becoming trapped in an imaginary – that of style as self-expression of an epoch, as it had famously been proposed by Alois Riegl or Heinrich Wölfflin.[45] Both Salt and Thompson confirm, by different routes, that not only Expressionism but the very conception of a 'will-to-style' (lending art-historical credibility to expediency) is not applicable to this cinema. Most banally, it does not apply for pragmatic reasons, if one accepts Erich Pommer's claims of the material constraints he was confronted with immediately after the war, which apparently necessitated the 'Expressionist' stylisation in *Dr Caligari* as a consequence of power-rationing and the lack of technical infrastructure.[46] Lotte Eisner has a similar explanation for Max Reinhardt's innovative styles of symbolic and dramatic lighting, arguing that war-shortages obliged him to use *ersatz* materials for his sets which had to be disguised with light.[47] But even if these stories are apocryphal, and invented after the fact, as a diversionary or mythologising manoeuvre, there remain other more decisive considerations. For instance, Pommer's awareness, after the success of *Dr Caligari* in Paris, of the potential for the name 'Expressionism' to be used as a 'brand-name' for connoting things German, rather than adopt the French coinage 'Caligarisme':

> The German film industry made 'stylised films' to make money. […] Germany was defeated: how could she make films that would compete with the others? It would have been impossible to try and so we tried something new; the Expressionist or stylised films.[48]

Expressionism in the technical sense, as Salt has argued, is applied consistently in very few of the films commonly traded under this name. When viewing them with an art-historical eye, one notes many self-conscious references to several recognisable styles, as well as other more or less subtle forms of stylisation: German cinema across the genres presents an eclectic mixture of *Heimatkunst*, orientalism and ornamentalism à la mode, from Chinoiserie, 'Madame Butterfly' exoticism and Egyptian art, to African or Aztec colonial spoils, *Jugendstil* furnishings and Expressionist paintings, art deco interiors and even Bauhaus easy chairs, as in the later films of Pabst. These stylistic idioms are borrowed from the stage (in Leni's *Waxworks*, for instance), taken from children's book illustrations (in the case of Lang's *Die Nibelungen*), or they look as though they are out of home-furnishing catalogues and advertisements from ladies' journals (as in Pabst's *Pandora's Box*). In less-well-known films, like military comedies or costume dramas, the styles allude to postcards (*Feldpostkarten*),[49] newspaper comics, illustrations in popular magazines and other kinds of commercial art.

So why this persistence of the term 'Expressionism' not just as a stylistic term for some of the films from the early 1920s, but as a generic term for most of the art cinema of Weimar, and beyond Germany, echoing down film history across the periods and the genres, turning up in the description of Universal horror films of the 1930s and film noir of the 1940s, until it became, according to the *Monthly Film Bulletin* 'such a general description for any stylistic departure from strict naturalism as to be virtually meaningless'?[50] The anonymous writer adds, however: 'perhaps Expressionism was the first movement which allowed the cinema broadly to formulate certain ideas about itself'. These ideas can be read in several ways: as indicative of the self-reflexive turn of Germany's film avant-garde, as a sign of the cinema's growing self-confidence, and as a decisive rejection of the assumption that the cinema's task is to reflect phenomenal reality. Whatever the answer, such 'ideas' as Expressionism formulated about the cinema are certain to lead directly to Weimar versions of Modernism and modernity. But they also point beyond Weimar: in the first instance, to the expulsion and exile of so many film producers, directors, writers, actors, musicians after 1933. For some of them, Expressionism represented just about the only cultural capital they could take with them. It advertised their creativity and their professionalism, but also their adaptability and survival skills, which the Hollywood dream factory made good use of. The fact that a potent imaginary clustered around the German émigrés once they found themselves in California is nowhere more in evidence than in the existence of that famous 'Expressionist' genre, the film noir, somewhat erroneously but irresistibly combining the haunted screen of the early 1920s with the lure of the sinful metropolis Berlin of the late 1920s (the *femmes fatales* Louise Brooks and Marlene Dietrich), mixed and stirred with the presumed *angst* of the German émigrés during the 1930s and 1940s, as they contemplated personal tragedies and national disaster: as if modernist self-reflexivity had given way to morbid introspection.

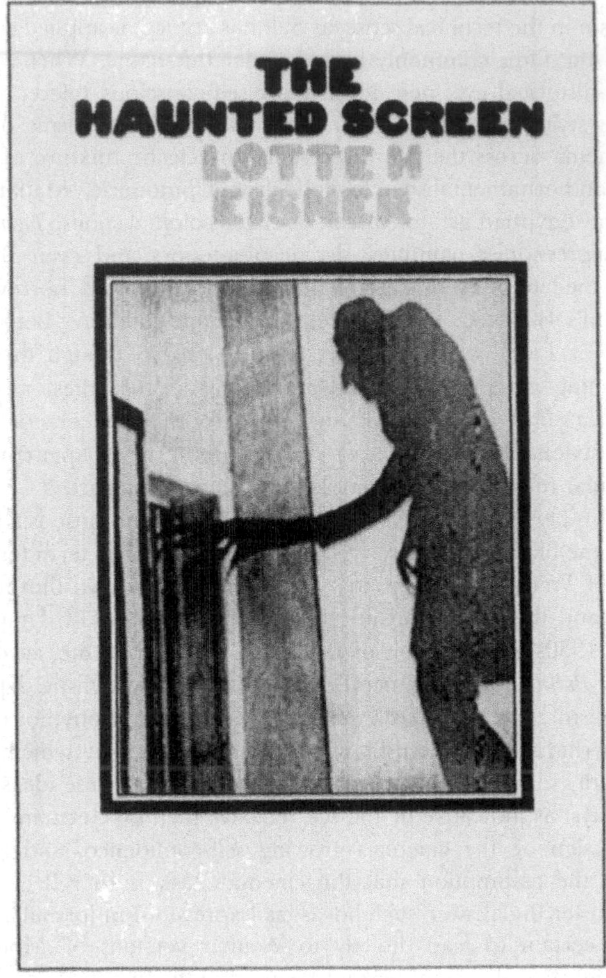

Figure 3 Lotte Eisner's *The Haunted Screen* (cover of the 1973 paperback edition, with still from *Nosferatu*)

Source: University of California Press

From Caligari to Hitler: 'working over' in order to 'work through'?

Expressionism in this sense has little or nothing in common with Eisner's concept of an art-historical period style. Rather, film noir's nightmare visions and paranoia states from the late 1940s and early 1950s curiously parallel the historical mindset of Kracauer's work, and may even illuminate why he assumes that films like *Dr Caligari*, *Nosferatu*, *Hands of Orlac*, *Warning Shadows*, *Secrets of A Soul* give clues to the 'psychic dispositions' of the public for whom the films were intended. Yet to read his book as a film noir tale, would personalise his project too much and simplify it:

Figure 4 Siegfried Kracauer's *From Caligari to Hitler* (cover of the 1971 paperback edition: 'cover deisgn based on scenes from *The Cabinet of Dr Caligari* and *Triumph of the Will*')

Source: Princeton University Press

where he detects a 'German soul' which is 'tossed between rebellion and submission', the inner states of the characters function precisely not as subjective expressions: they are the screens filtering out or disguising non-individual, social symptoms. Traumatised as well as revolutionised by the nation's defeat on the battlefield and – even more dangerously devastating to national identity – defeated in the peace 'dictated' at Versailles in 1920, the German lower middle class found itself deadlocked politically by the Weimar democracy. Recognising in the social-democratic public discourse neither their regret nor their resentment, they were attracted to extreme politics, and extremely contradictory fantasies, often mixed with aggression and violent anger. Yet these fantasies were none the less, so Kracauer's argument runs, like a concave mirror in which their class-conditioned moral and material misery could be read.[51]

However, Kracauer is famous less for tracking the after-shocks of the First World War in Weimar cinema than for arguing that the films show foreboding of a dictatorship to come, indeed, that they had wittingly/unwittingly helped prepare the climate for such tyranny. In this respect, *From Caligari to Hitler* is still the most thorough attempt at outlining a coherent framework for a relatively large body of films, whose common denominator is neither author nor genre, neither film style nor taste and popularity, but the mentality of the historical period itself, manifest in a kind of super-text, held together by family resemblance and the migration of motifs.[52] Unlike Eisner, whose focus is often the single image, Kracauer treats Weimar cinema as predominantly a narrative cinema: one that through its choice of stories – whether by accident or by design – *works over* a political–cultural heritage situated in the past, which combines literary allusions with folk-art illustrations, mass-culture stereotypes and shared thematic and visual tropes, even taking in *fait divers* gleaned from the newspapers, all in order to *work through* a present sociopolitical trauma, in view of a scenario of future *action*. One additional strength of this 'history of mentalities' approach to the films, from which he extracts political references and ideological subtexts, is that it does not rest on an *a-priori* distinction between high culture and popular culture, mainstream and experimental cinema, self-consciously aesthetic value and calculating commercialism. This contrasts with Eisner, who makes high-culture claims for her favoured directors, such as F.W. Murnau and Fritz Lang, and summarily dismisses the non-*auteurs*.[53]

Kracauer supports his analyses mostly with plot synopses and the interpretation of certain iconographic or thematic configurations. He is quite selective in his choice of examples, leaving out many films which could be said to belong with equal right to the period he scrutinises. While the ideological effects are thus attributed to the mass-audience, the films discussed are in the main *auteurs*' films for specialised audiences.[54] None the less, the persuasive force of his argument derives from the strikingly consistent and repeated use of the motifs he identifies and their narrative emplotments, across seemingly distinct generic codes, tracked over a relatively long period, during which styles changed as the German film industry underwent major technical and managerial transformations.[55]

Implicitly, Kracauer posits a structural convergence between story and history, dramatic conflict and social conflict. He deduces a level of determination that lies above or outside the individual films, whose coherence only emerges in the light of these extra-cinematic factors, although Kracauer nowhere assumes a directly determining instance.[56] For him, society has to be seized at the phenomenal level, where historical agency and the individual subject remain suitably anonymous, immersed in ephemeral perceptions and 'distracted' by surface effects. Intentionality and purpose remain latent almost by default, while on the manifest level the human agents (whether characters in the film, or the director) ostensibly pursue other objectives while being blind to their true motives. Such psychoanalytic or symptomatic readings make his argument almost unassailable, since any counter-evidence adduced (such as statements by the film makers themselves, reviews from the trade press, or audience opinion polls) can be relegated to the overt level, which by definition disavows, denies or represses latent motives and unconscious content. Kracauer never quite opts for such a stark contrast. Instead, the Weimar cinema appears in his study a field of fluid contours and of seemingly indeterminate epiphenomena,[57] where history writes itself in traces, often so lightly as to need a very acute investigator indeed. The film critic or historian has to turn detective, alert to every index or clue: one occasionally senses Kracauer's euphoria alongside his melancholy, at having discovered so many hitherto unsuspected skeletons in Weimar cinema's cupboard. In fact, the desire to see the films as elaborate social hieroglyphs or riddling metaphors of political dilemmas and national traumas means that Kracauer has to fill gaps, smooth out the narrative logic, mitigate intensities, and often brush over or put aside the very resistance that makes these films different from realist–illusionist (that is to say, classical Hollywood) narratives. In other words, the forces of stylisation and excess, of indirection and ambiguity that so evidently mark many of the films and are the very features that thrill Lotte Eisner into fervent art-historical exegesis, barely rate a mention in Kracauer's interpretation, let alone lead to a sustained analysis, beyond occasionally commenting on the painted back-drop flimsiness of the worlds present on the screen.[58]

On closer inspection, of course, Kracauer's argument is more sophisticated and nuanced. When he speaks of unconscious dispositions pervading public life and official culture, it is the despised and neglected forms in which they manifest themselves that attract his attention: pulp novels and serial literature, cheap illustrations and the mass-production of genre-art. He recognises that the cinema, more than the other emergent mass media, touches on the transitoriness of everyday life, filling it with a new kind of energy and vitality, aside from the poetry of the fleeting moment. As entertainment made for profit, Weimar cinema was responsive to the point of clairvoyance to the desires and pleasures, as well as anxieties and secret fears of its primary audience: this premise, fundamental to the study of mass culture and to the analysis of commodity consumption is implicit in almost every line Kracauer writes, indeed it is one of his key contributions to our understanding of film as a socially significant phenomenon. After several decades of popular culture studies, he may appear more conservative today than he did to his contemporaries: T.W. Adorno, for one, thought Kracauer a 'splenetic realist', dangerously soft on mass culture and too easily seduced by the charms of the inauthentic and the ephemeral.[59]

Yet Kracauer, too, has to be read for certain omissions. Not the least disconcerting gap is his dismissal of German cinema before 1919, and his oversight to inform his (American) readers of the long literary and pictorial tradition standing behind the narrative and figural motifs he so assiduously interprets, in the blinding light of hindsight, as topical, symptomatic or typical of Weimar

Germany. In the same vein, one could take issue with his selectivity about the films he chooses: those which do not particularly advance his thesis, such as comedies, popular parodies of serious drama and operetta films, for instance, are scarcely mentioned or get short shrift. For instance – a most notable absence – he pays almost no attention to comedy directors such as Lubitsch or Reinhold Schünzel. This bias in favour of certain genres is aggravated (for the plausibility of his argument) when one realises that Kracauer deals with roughly 8 per cent of the films made during the years 1919–33, and with no more than 25 per cent of the films that have survived.[60] Finally, Kracauer does not always convince as a close textual scholar. His account of the history and meaning of the framing device in *The Cabinet of Dr Caligari* is a case in point – one that, among others, earned him the undying anger of Fritz Lang.[61]

Passing over other contexts which might offer competing explanations for the prevalence of the themes Kracauer dwells on, has often been judged damning for the thesis put forward in *From Caligari to Hitler*.[62] Given that he relies for his readings on a taxonomy of plot lines, story motifs, character constellations and recurring dramatic situations, instantiating a number of symptomatic master narratives, it is not surprising that his selectivity of films has come under scrutiny, since the credibility of his central thesis must stand and fall with the representivity of his sample. His critics, often taking their cue from Kracauer when reading the narratives as reflection of a given national identity or ideological formation, have therefore tried to correct what they saw as his methodological flaws by putting forward more empirically verifiable criteria. They have compiled lists of the most popular films for the years in question, noting that the titles Kracauer discusses rarely figure among the top twenty even of German productions, not counting the vast number of very successful American films seen by the German public.[63]

Paul Monaco, for instance, bases himself on a content analysis of the statistically most popular films.[64] He classifies them according to certain themes, e.g. betrayal, foreigners, exoticism. Adding to his statistics copious evidence from the machinery of studio publicity, advertising, press reviews and criticism,[65] Monaco concludes that German films of the 1920s are obsessed by guilt (responsibility for the war), by the conflict of generations (fathers and sons), and by suicides. Although he talks about the 'psychology of movies',[66] Monaco takes Kracauer to task on virtually every point of method and detail. Yet his objections to Kracauer are well founded only if one grants him the unspoken premise that Kracauer's 'sociology of cinema' is methodologically similar to his, based on statistical evidence and content analysis. Monaco implicitly assumes an even more unmediated relation between films and society or film and psychological dispositions than one could ever attribute to Kracauer, whose 'weaknesses' as an empirical sociologist turn out to be his strength as a cultural historian, given the complexity of his model of social interaction and symbolic forms. For if he posits a structural convergence between story and history, dramatic conflict and social conflict, he always points to a level of determination above or outside the individual texts, whose coherence can only be understood in the light of these extra-cinematic factors, that is, the cultural master narratives that hide in the cinematic texts more like rebus pictures in children's books than 'content' to be peeled from 'form' and classified according to social or political relevance.

Kracauer's imagination was sociological, but of a particular kind. An avid reader of Kant, he kept aloof from his friend T.W. Adorno's preoccupation with dialectical thought and Hegelian system building, though he shared with both Adorno and Benjamin an abiding admiration for Kierkegaard and his psychological paradoxes.[67] The medium of his thinking was lived experience, and he tried to render the 'thick' description of the everyday in a richly poetic and metaphoric language, which is why it would be inaccurate to describe him as a normative realist. Neither was Kracauer a Marxist, however much his innate bent towards phenomenology made him worry about the place of the sensuously perceived material data within critical thought and the world of concepts, caught as he felt himself to be between fundamental epistemological reflections and the empiricist methods of analysis prevalent in the social sciences.

It is against this philosophical background that one can see the double process of abstraction by which he tried to validate his form of analogical reasoning. Both German society and the films appear to him as tropes, picture puzzles or even dreams, as the characters' movements through the filmic fiction become symbolic of the movements of classes, groups or historical subjects: constructions which he names (with more self-irony than is often realised) by such terms as 'the German soul', 'the collective mentality'. In many ways, *From Caligari to Hitler* is itself built like a 'classical narrative' (with a 'noirish' voice-over 'Out of the Past'), made up of two parallel strands, the argument cross-cutting between the condensed master narrative of a hundred-odd feature films (many of which Kracauer had first reviewed as a critic for the *Frankfurter Zeitung* before viewing them again at the Museum of Modern Art in New York), and the political fate of the German people during the same period.[68] Treating the films almost as if it was one single mega text ensures the coherence and cumulatively persuasive power of this narrative, but it also gives it that 'paranoid' 1950s post-war–Cold-War feel. What anchors the various moments of both the social and the fictional text is the psycho-critical description of a recognisable disposition, occasionally condensed into the character typology of 'the adolescent', 'the father', 'the prostitute', pastiching the Expressionist drama's penchant for abstract types rather than proper-name protagonists.[69] Kracauer, similar to the Freudo-Marxist émigrés Erich Fromm or Wilhelm Reich, regarded the emphasis on psychological and emotional conflict in mass cultural products as itself a bourgeois displacement, a 'personalisation' of problems and contradictions whose roots were in the last instance political and social. One must assume that he was aware of the irony of his personifications, echoed in his suspicion about 'the national character' and, instead, confirming him in the need to conduct a class analysis of audiences and the Weimar social formation.[70]

Kracauer, while sensitive to the essentially metaphoric role of his character typology, thus tends to read the fictional protagonists of his films as emblematic representations of conflicts that have their reality elsewhere, or rather, conflicts that are fought by proxy in oedipal form because they cannot find their outlet in politics, organised labour or the street. At the same time, this makes Weimar cinema more radical than it would otherwise appear: it becomes the stage where in coded language, society can speak of things which it ruthlessly represses or censors in its public discourse. Yet 'if class conflict is repressed by Weimar cinema, we cannot expect it to be explicitly linked with character typology.'[71] But Kracauer is difficult to fault on this. Not only did he recognise the structure of reverse identification and disavowal in his spectators, he also understood the ideological benefit and hegemonic power that such a structure of miscognition brings to the ruling classes. What Kracauer consistently argued was that identification in the mass media under capitalism may be a form of self-alienation, but none the less, spectators, unconsciously and yet lucidly, recognise their own subjectivity in the alienated, doubly mirrored representations: they may be dreaming, but they are 'not duped'. Perhaps it is these kinds of insights that have ensured that the book and its author, despite being so often chided as a conspiracy theorist or even as politically opportunist, has retained a towering presence, seemingly unassailable and indestructible.[72]

The two imaginaries

The labels 'Expressionist film' and 'Weimar cinema' and by extension, the two books, name two imaginary identities, dialogically positioned across an anxious self-interrogation, which tries to bridge an abyss. From such an imaginary face-to-face, Eisner's and Kracauer's views are not contradictory, but neither do they altogether complement each other. As already hinted at, their methods pose different problems to the scholar, and their insights lead in different directions. This particularly powerful and persistent view of the classical German cinema could best be described as the invention of a tradition (in the case of Eisner) and the invention of an anti-tradition (in the case of Kracauer), or as I have chosen to call it, different constructions of one of the German cinema's 'historical imaginaries'. Kracauer and Eisner, in their distinct ways, have helped to popularise and at the same time demonise this cinema, making it, under a double conjuncture, in one case representative of broader tendencies within society (Kracauer's collective soul of the recipients),[73] and in another, more art-historical turn, of the German 'genius' (Eisner's individual soul of the creators) in art, reflected, expressed and embodied in German cinema. If their underlying assumptions have become questionable to film historians, they did grasp what for several generations of viewers has rendered this cinema distinctive: its Janus-faced ambivalences, its journeys into the interior of cultural Modernism, some of whose intellectual *tours de force* the films enthusiastically perform at the same time as they eclectically transform them. The blend of sophistication and sensationalism, of art and kitsch, the exploration of pathological perception and psychic borderline states make many of the films produced between 1919 and 1929 into historical documents precisely where they appear most fictional, fantastic and ahistorical.[74]

Both Kracauer and Eisner knew first hand why there might be readers willing to listen to their *après coup* Cassandra calls. It is as if the enormity of the suffering inflicted by Germans on millions all over Europe in the six years of warfare, genocide and destruction was so unimaginable that it demanded – even more than argument or narratives – 'images', 'symbols', 'metaphors', which Eisner and Kracauer seemed to find in the films made twenty years earlier. Since history itself in this case required the in(ter)vention of an imaginary, in order to become once more conceivable, though scarcely less incomprehensible, the films became somehow the shadows that allowed the unspeakable to enter into an order of temporality and discourse, however inadequate or banal. In a sense, the cinema became that history's double: the tangible, visible, inspectable mirror of something which, Medusa-like, could not, or so it seemed, be looked at or examined otherwise. An unrepresentable history found less its 'objective correlative' than its negative image and thus the illusion of a hidden truth, experienced the more strongly, since unsuspected by all concerned: the conscious motives of film makers, the reception by historical audiences, the expressed opinions of contemporary critics counted for little in the face of a symptomatology, so perfectly readable – with hindsight.

In this respect, Eisner's and Kracauer's two kinds of imaginary constructs, Expressionist film and Weimar cinema are antithetical, in that Eisner values in the films and film makers she admires that they were able to produce 'art', while Kracauer, committed to a constructivist–materialist aesthetics, denounces this very 'artistic' aspiration as historically false, a simulation, a disguise and manipulation, and thus a travesty of what cinema could be in a technologically developed industrial society like the Weimar Republic.[75] At another level, however, these two critics–historians respond to each other, having provided for this cinema a psychologically coherent incoherence and a bafflingly contradictory self-evidence. Whether intended or not, they have contributed significantly to an ominous sort of radiance emanating from the films to this day. In what are undoubtedly also subjective, as I suggested, even autobiographical allegories, they have succeeded in identifying a set of images, of icons and clichés, plausibly circumscribing a totality, in which isolated artefacts or individual images metonymically stand for a whole, sum it up, imbue it with the instant force of an explanation. One might say that the two imaginaries are distinct but belong together, by virtue of their author's own historical subjectification via the trauma of 'loving' Germany and having to learn to hate what became of it, of being exiles and no longer having a place from which to speak.

From another perspective, faced with the (extravagant) expectations from the readers, the books respond in their (extravagant) arguments, so that the desire for explanations, where there may be none, creates itself a powerful form of subjectification, precisely an imaginary relation between the reader, the authors, the films and German history. The question this raises is the one already alluded to in my introduction: how far do we need this imaginary today? Are we still looking to films for explanations of Nazism, and if not, what is the imaginary to which the films' revival in pop culture respond today? If they now serve another/new imaginary, does it have to do with Germany at all, or does it appeal to current fantasies of the designed and stylised 'body', of the performative self and the perpetual parade of 'authentic fakes'?

To this extent, the Expressionist film/Weimar cinema doublet, and the persistence of the two books' appeal is but one sign of contemporary culture's historicist masquerade, with its delight in drastically foreshortened, but iconically suggestive period identities.[76] That one turns increasingly to the cinema to supply such short-hand history may be part of the 'Expressionist' films' good fortune, in this respect not so different from other retrospective, nostalgic constructions, which, in the age of television make up the 'heritage industry' and for which Jean Baudrillard, in his explanation of the 'retro-fashion' for Second World War stories has introduced the term 'fetish-history'.[77] Whatever knowledge one can therefore bring to these films, from cinema history or art history, from economics, from textual analysis, from film theory or audience research, it is unlikely that it will dislodge that now quasi-existential bond between a group of films and the subsequent fate of the society that produced and consumed them. In short, Kracauer and Eisner have become part of this film history, have become themselves Caligari-like and Cassandra-like figures, at least as long as the history of Nazism 'haunts' the history of modern Germany. Having in their books given voice to this powerful imaginary, they are themselves caught in the mirror mazes of its self-fulfilling prophecies.

The Constructivist turn: from style to design

How, then, to preserve the insights of Kracauer and Eisner, while at the same time avoiding the implied tautologies? How to understand the cinema's function in a modern society, without metaphorising its political history, and how to valorise style as historically significant, while not being trapped into art-historical thinking about 'influence' and the 'will-to-style', indexed as the self-expression of an artist or an epoch? Kracauer's argument wants to provide categories for a reception study of Weimar cinema. But to paraphrase him in another context, he finally does not go far enough, at least not in *From Caligari to Hitler*, because in the guise of analysing it, the book in fact has set the terms for the Weimar cinema's posthumous reception. As indicated above and argued further in the following chapter, his unique ability was to grasp Weimar films in their multitude as a single 'super-text', and Weimar Germany as a 'social-text', writing and rewriting itself at its most transient surface. It permits one to compare Kracauer to his own past, and thereby confront him with other aspects of the period itself, where, paradoxically perhaps, his concerns look once more very pertinent for the present, grappling with the fact that these films still speak to us, even though the historical moment to which Kracauer ties them so tightly, has apparently receded further and further.

This is not a problem for Eisner, for whom the films remain documents of an artistic avant-garde whose 'genius' she tries to demonstrate and thereby also celebrate. Focusing on production in its widest sense, rather than reception, she goes, as we saw, into technical aspects like sets and decor, as well as cultural thematics. But her approach, too, does not go far enough, because she attaches these stylistic features to a number of particular individuals, be they Max Reinhardt, F.W. Murnau, Karl Freund, Hermann Warm or Robert Herlth, without reflecting at all the institutional, semi-industrial, profit-driven context in which these individuals were constrained or encouraged to work. What would be needed, it seems, is to extend her art-historical notion of a movement or group style, to include a concept of style immanent to a given productive context, understood as the material as well as discursive conditions of production *and* reception, where style intervenes in – i.e. actively translating and transforming – the relations between an industry, its products and the meanings given to these products in the act of reception or consumption. The name for this idea of style is 'styling' or 'design', and it would seem to fit several features of the distinctiveness of Weimar cinema implied by both authors, but not specifically analysed by either. For instance, Eisner and Kracauer both discuss the Weimar cinema's technical excellence and craftsmanlike proficiency: features that after all, were the first to be admired among film-industry professionals internationally, and were regularly commented on by critics well into the 1930s. Virtuosity and ingenuity were shown off in the camera work of Guido Seeber, Eugen Schüfftan's special effects and Karl Freund's 'unchained camera'.[78] The lighting of Fritz Arno Wagner, Theodor Sparkuhl, Günther Krampf and others practically defines the German look, and no contemporary review of any major film misses praising set construction, decor and costumes, the areas where Hermann Warm, Erich Kettelhut or Robert Herlth and Walter Röhrig made their – and UFA's – reputation.[79] Directors, too, were often known for their detailed technical know-how. Fritz Lang, for instance, was feared for his exactions, perfectionism and sadistic patience when it came to trying out new special effects.[80] Pabst was an equally hands-on director, insisting at Nero on state-of-the art equipment. In fact, even the most 'spiritual' of Weimar directors, namely F.W. Murnau was something of a film-technology freak, as were E.A. Dupont, who began as a screenwriter, and Paul Leni, who throughout his directing career also doubled as a set designer.

By studying, for instance, Leni's career, as one of the outstanding set-designers-turned-director, one arrives at a good sense of the professional exchanges that took place in Berlin between the various crafts and trades concerned with the graphic arts, including newspaper cartoons, the stage, cabaret design and poster art.[81] It allowed not only Leni to move with relative ease, and substantial financial rewards, between different kinds of professions and tasks, including directing.[82] Leni's career also shows just how eclectic and 'opportunist', how tongue-in-cheek and playful, iconoclast and sarcastic the visual arts scene and film world were in the early 1920s, as the German cinema tried to build up a domestic market share and an internationally competitive industry. Many of the film architects, costume makers and set designers were just as likely to frequent Dadaist circles and cabarets in their spare time as to attend Herwarth Walden's Expressionist *Sturm* gallery evenings. This did not prevent them, during the day at the studio, from dressing the most sumptuous set of orientalist follies or *Jugendstil* elegance, which indicates that the concept of 'influence' becomes too loose to have any purchase on the underlying dynamics of style as 'special effect'. As a means to a mood, an atmosphere, the rapidly sketched and foreshortened invention of a period triggered historical or exotic connotations, and above all, served as a repertoire of visual icons and quick-reference clichés that could tie together disparate elements of story, character and setting. Walter Reimann, for instance, pleaded for more mobile sets and smaller units that could be flexibly combined:

> I am often astonished at the truly grotesque senselessness with which sets are built and then torn down again. With just a little foresight and planning it could be so easy to combine a number of similar set pieces in such a way that, with few modifications, they can serve for different scenes. Such a system of combinations saves time and money, but should only be undertaken by gifted designer–architects. […] Today's set building is still rigid and cumbersome, the totally antiquated notions of 'dimensional' or 'authentic' sets have to make way for a mentality of adaptable improvisation. [… We need] simplification, rationalisation in our trade; prejudices and preconceptions no longer belong to our age.[83]

Reimann, known for his work on *Dr Caligari*, had just finished (in a minor capacity) a year on Lang's *Metropolis*.[84] His reflections on the potential for proficiency in film technique and film design suggest that the look of a film and the definition of its style were indeed a matter of creative teams, working in close collaboration towards unifying different elements and 'coordinating' details of decor as well as large-scale sets. Film makers and art directors were as much alert to the fashion and clothing business as they were engaged with expressing individual talent (though they clearly were keen to promote their careers). Reimann put it very bluntly:

> good set design belongs to a film like fur to a dog and a suit to a gentleman. We all know that clothes make the man! On questions of decor and the effects of furnishings one had best consult with a lady, only then does one begin to understand the mystery of cause and effect, and the relation between wrapping and core.[85]

In so far as particular styles were 'made to measure', by functionally re-tooling and adapting recognisable idioms to answer purposes defined by other agendas, 'Expressionism' in film, too, falls under this verdict of a 'borrowed' or 'poached' style, though one where, for the reasons discussed above, the sense of a 'national' style, the adequate formal language for the promotion of luxury products aimed at an international market, was among the most sought-after 'effects'.

As discussed in the next chapter, there is a precedent for this apparent reversal, with content following form, in the *Autorenfilm* of the 1910s: the background to Paul Wegener's/Guido Seeber's/Hanns Heinz Ewers'/Urban Gad's *The Student of Prague* from 1913. Once the underlying dynamics of technological change in the film industry and the productive force of the *Autorenfilm* offensive from the 1910s are factored in, 'Expressionist cinema' may perhaps be better understood as the German variant of Constructivism, concerned with giving technologically produced art and artefacts a wholly different space – literally and discursively – from that traditionally occupied by paintings, literature and even the theatre. The major difference would be that this cinema challenges the bourgeois arts on their own grounds, and in their own idiom of cultural consumption, such as high fashion and interior design, rather than joining a self-consciously political, aesthetic avant-garde, as in the Soviet Union. Expressionism would then be the period name for a 'toolbox' of style features,[86] whose functions do not coincide with art-historical connotations at all. On the other hand, if the attribute 'Expressionist' refers to an effect, it is one that disguises itself as 'cause', impersonating the aesthetic revolt and subjective expression of a 'will to style', for the purpose of authenticating a technological prototype, and of culturally validating a new form of prestige in the hotly debated arena of the *Kino-Debatte* around the cinema's drive to respectability. It is in this sense, that through Expressionism, the cinema did indeed formulate something about itself, namely its technical capacity to simulate stylistic authenticity, organic coherence and formal adequacy.[87] The more appropriate name for this process, then, is again, not 'style', but 'styling', not 'self-reflexivity' but 'design': in the sense of the look, surface or shape given to objects of consumption and daily use once they enter into a circuit of commodities, becoming part of the market. In design, the appearance of the object stands in a certain relation to its function, to the materials it is made of, and to the processes of production to which it owes its existence. As a design manual puts it:

> styling is the application of surface effects to a product after the internal mechanism has been designed. The intention can be either to disguise or to enhance the relationship between form and function. It is invariably a device for stimulating consumer expectations.[88]

To think about style in the cinema under the aspect of design would seem at first glance to be the very antithesis of Expressionism. In this sense, Herbert Jhering, in his review of *Dr Caligari*, saw this discrepancy, criticising the makers for 'not being Expressionist enough', that is to say, calling its bluff:

> It is telling that Carl Mayer and Hans Janowitz rendered their photoplay *The Cabinet of Dr Caligari* expressionistically only because it is set in an insane asylum. It opposed the notion of a sick unreality to the notion of a healthy reality. In other words, impressionism concerns the arena in which one remains accountable, expressionism the arena in which one is unaccountable. Insanity becomes the excuse for an artistic idea. But we want to assume that in his next film the risk of expressionism will appear less frightful to Robert Wiene, leaving him able to laugh at the motivation underlying his initial attempt.[89]

Such contemporary views of Expressionism in the cinema as Impressionism gone mad shows how aware critics were of the pressures on 'style' to simulate subjectivity or authenticity, but how ambivalent they none the less remained. Commercial art in this sense dates back to the arts and craft movement of the late nineteenth century and is associated with styles such as Neo-Gothic, with *Jugendstil* or Art Nouveau, i.e. styles crucially dependent on modern materials and production techniques. Since *Jugendstil*, however, was the very style that Expressionist artists like Oskar Kokoschka, the 'Blaue Reiter' and 'Die Brücke' groups originally had fought to overcome, the emergence of cinematic Expressionism could be regarded as the return of *Jugendstil*, dressing itself up in the plumage of its opponent to extract a belated revenge. The same would apply, *mutatis mutandis*, to the other major style identified as belonging to German cinema in the 1920s: the cinema of the *Neue Sachlichkeit*. Along with the different idioms of 'realism' with which the later Weimar cinema is associated (ranging from the 'new photography', the Bauhaus aesthetic, different versions of functionalist and constructivist aesthetics to the 'gritty naturalism' of its social melodramas), the new matter-of-factness, too, would be symptomatic of the reversal of roles between style and design. By assimilating as design these styles and their programmatic connotations, films engaged in a game of hide-and-seek with their high-art rivals, displaying and showing off a range of effects simulated in order to please, to seduce or advertise. But since especially the Bauhaus and the New Photography were themselves not averse to creating (or entering into) a marketplace, the question would be: who in this trade of design elements and style features benefited more from the other's self-advertising? This line of thought intimates that the reasons for the peculiarities of the post-First World War German cinema in its stylistic eclecticism and successive transformations up until the late 1920s, may have to be sought in the alliance – by no means unique in capitalist countries moving towards a consumer culture – of a technicist–functionalist imagination with certain lifestyles and changing demographics, breaking up older community habits by teaching people urban tastes and introducing the behaviour of consumers.

Design as disguise: the 'honesty' of kitsch

The design style that most conveniently served this double purpose of convincingly exhibiting the signifiers of artistic value, while manufacturing them industrially was evidently not 'Expressionism' with its emphasis on artistic subjectivity, 'primitive' technique and tactile immediacy, but the eclectic range of pictorial or decorative idioms often summarised under the name of neo-romanticism, a generic term familiar since the German arts-and-crafts movement of the 1880s. The preferred aesthetic techniques, sites and forms of Neo-Romanticism (just as of *Jugendstil*) were the ornamentation of utility objects or the exteriors of houses, of interior murals or advertising posters, the predilection for mythological figures and historical subjects. They served the function of making the object or event thus ornamented known in the marketplace as something of value, while masking its (industrial) mode of production. Perhaps the impact of this style on Weimar cinema of the early 1920s can best be compared to that of *Jugendstil* at the turn of the century on architecture and domestic furnishings, except that in the cinema, mechanical reproduction and its industrial base throw into even sharper relief the social complicity of Neo-Romantic art. Thus, the accusation of 'kitsch' levelled against Weimar films is more profoundly apt and more necessarily 'honest' than their detractors probably intended, because kitsch characterises not the artefacts thus described, but the standards and social vantage points of those judging them thus.

Neo-Romanticism and *Jugendstil* are kitsch in the very precise sense that they are support styles externally applied: they rely on a material support whose appearance they can transform, and thus they function as arts of disguise. They hide a facade of plain brick behind scroll-work and stucco, they transform into luxuriant foliage and natural growth such products of industry as cast-iron gates or Metro-entrances, and they supply the fantasy forms and erotic accretions around objects of daily use: lamps and hat-stands, candlesticks and sugar bowls, vases and even radiograms. As such, the purpose of kitsch and its idiom is to attenuate or anthropomorphise the stark functionalism of amorphously formless materials such as Bakelite, iron or plaster, and of mass-production methods such as moulding and casting. Its ideological character is thus one of softening, mediating, insinuating and pleasing: important attributes for objects of utility that need to become commodities. In this respect, even *Jugendstil* promotes the naturalisation of consumption through the borrowed graces of organic growth. Hence the hostility of a Walter Benjamin, viewing its idealism as a consciously dishonest but unconsciously revealing form of kitsch:

> [*Jugendstil* is] the style in which the old bourgeoisie camouflages the intimations of its own weakness; cosmically reaching for the spheres and drunk with future possibilities, it misuses the word 'youth' as its mantra. Here, for the first time, the retreat from the social into the biological and natural world manifests itself. […] It has been said that the

> tortured ornaments which once covered domestic furniture and facades of buildings were an attempt to take back the breakthrough of technology by a simulation of arts-and-crafts. *Jugendstil* is indeed the great unconscious attempt at retreat. Its language of forms expresses the will to evade, by a premonition that vehemently rears up against the inevitable.
>
> (Benjamin 1933: 56)

Benjamin, steeped as he was in battles on behalf of Modernism and a constructivist aesthetic, was none the less suitably intrigued by the historical processes he was describing to allow for a measure of ambiguity around the significance of kitsch, whether analysing its self-conscious variant in the surrealist *objet trouvé*, or the 'dream-kitsch' of popular culture, including garish neon-lighting and the flamboyant bad taste of cinema.[90] But *Jugendstil* is kitsch also because it evokes emotions of nostalgia that promise the owner participation in a realm already given up as lost. Yet, instead of acknowledging this loss, it fills the loss with presence. But this is precisely the dialectical moment for the cinema to make its entry, and engage its dialogue with art and high culture: it places itself on the side of the amorphous 'material' and its functional starkness, and it need not mourn the loss of aura, since it embodies the energies of modernity. If it then puts itself forward in forms which a bourgeois taste elite denounces as kitsch, its camouflage is both strategic and tactical. Tactical, in that the cinema can play the Trojan horse inside the fortress of culture, and strategic in that its 'disguise artists' are both cynical and honest, answering the 'primary' imposture needed to enter this fortress with another layer of disguise: the second one showing up not only the first, but also the general bad faith that makes the first one necessary. If kitsch is the defensive attribute given to films by those who rightly fear the cinema for destroying the 'authentic' in art, the cinema can wear it as a badge – if not of honour then perhaps of its energetically cynical courage. Its energy, as well as its identity, is precisely the ability to simulate and impersonate, to mimic styles and wear them as helmets of invisibility, rather like the young Siegfried wears Alberich's *Tarnhelm* to help Gunter in the conquest of Brunhild in Fritz Lang's *Die Nibelungen*.

The fact, for instance, that directors such as Lang so easily made the transition from *Jugendstil* to so-called 'Expressionism' to so-called 'New Objectivity' is not a contradiction, but merely underlines the point, namely that the shifts in style in Weimar films throughout the 1920s are the signs of the ongoing (and in view of Berlin's cultural climate, possibly unresolvable) conflicts of a film industry (especially in the person of Lang as UFA's flagship director) that always had at its disposal modern state-of-the-art studio technology, aware of the resistance to cinema among a conservative-taste elite, whose opinion it none the less needed for publicity purposes. Weimar cinema's underlying constructivist modernity is thus paradoxically most in evidence where it mimics a gamut of styles, including the more notoriously conservative ones, thereby providing in its moments of 'inauthenticity' (measured by either the ideal of *Stilwillen*, or by the standards of a realist agenda) the surest sign of its modernist technological–commercial identity, ultimately cocking a snook at a critical establishment that was looking for authenticity from an inauthentic medium, by looking over its shoulder towards the mass audience.

That the German author's cinema of the early 1920s, starting with *The Cabinet of Dr Caligari*, via *Waxworks*, *Nosferatu*, *Warning Shadows* to *Faust* and *Tartuff* should adopt such strategies of insinuation and pastiche indicates the degree to which the pressure towards cultural assimilation went a similar route of domestication as *Jugendstil*, disavowing the cinema's industrial conditions of production by promoting it as art, while at the same time ensuring that this art did not alienate those whose habit of 'going to the cinema' was to become part of an economically desirable modernity of consumption, with the cinema, like the department store, gradually becoming accepted as a place to choose one's home decor, to confirm one's lifestyle and to identify one's fashion preferences. Thus, if kitsch applies to a mass-produced object that disguises its technological-industrial origin by reproducing meticulously the forms, textures and attributes of value associated with a unique, hand-crafted or cult object, then Weimar cinema was by definition kitsch,[91] for these were precisely its conditions of possibility, making for itself a place within traditional culture, but also for a mass public. Its legitimacy was that of an alloy, so to speak: an alloy that had become the new gold-standard not only of the cinema, but – as Benjamin and Adorno were to argue – of all art.[92] The kind of 'truth' that kitsch and cinema both speak about would reside not so much in the fact that commercial considerations penetrate them equally (and with it, the whole of modern art), but that they herald a changed relationship between ideology and subjectivity, endowing those participating in social life mainly via culture and consumption with peculiar survival skills: cynical *sang-froid*, schizophrenic self-reflexivity, and an 'enlightened' false consciousness.[93]

Design as enhancement: the utopian aspirations of style

The contradiction between the Romantic or post-Romantic cultural codes – Lotte Eisner's 'romantic fancies' – and the advanced technologies of their presentation, performance and stylised re-embodiments only resolves itself by a fundamentally different evaluation of the perceptual proximity that surface textures, fleeting encounters and humble everyday objects began to connote for the modern sensibility and for metropolitan life.[94] Cheered by Charles Baudelaire, ambiguously relished by Oscar Wilde, this modernity of the moment, of the transitory and the tactile was comprehensively theorised by Walter Benjamin, who gratefully drew on Kracauer for some of his key concepts and insights.[95] Before returning to Kracauer for a final comment on the relation of cinema, design and society, though, an alternative route taken by style into design should be briefly examined: that of design as enhancement.

The aspect which one takes from Eisner as cinematic expressionism's single most distinctive feature is undoubtedly lighting, the famous *clair-obscure* of *Stimmung*. It did impress cameramen from abroad, some of whom came to Berlin, like Charles Rosher, and by a not altogether convincing sequence, lighting is often said to be the most demonstrable 'influence' of German cinema on Hollywood style in the 1940s, thanks to film noir and its profuse use of key-lighting.[96] More specifically, German cameramen from the mid-1920s on preferred lighting that was assumed to come from hidden, irregularly diffused or invisible sources,[97] a practice which in many of the classic films, notably in Murnau's, but also those on which Paul Leni, Henrik Galeen or Arthur Robison were involved, has very particular narrational functions, when one thinks of the implications of indirect lighting for character motivation and story causality. But apart from adding mystery and indeterminacy to a scene, such a conception, as argued in the next chapter (Chapter III), fitted in with Weimar narratives and the desire for a reversibility or 'suspension' of the direction of action, glances and motion. One wonders whether this feature of Weimar cinema so often pinpointed, namely the UFA lighting styles, fit into a larger conception, for it seems that the cameramen were not only famous for their techniques using shadows, but they also tried to create with their black-and-white cinematography the tactile values of oil painting (before the invention of colour photography), evoking through its representations both a desire of wanting to touch the images, and the frustration of not being able to.[98] Lighting turns the image into an object endowed with a special luminosity (being lit and at the same time radiating light) which is to say, light appears as both cause and effect, active and passive. In short it suggests 'authenticity' and 'presence', while remaining 'hidden' and 'ineffable'. The object, and the human actor as object become irreducibly immanent, more-than-real in their 'there-ness' and 'now-ness', but by a process that confers this presence on them from off-frame, off-scene – especially in the films of F.W. Murnau – the luminous becomes ominous becomes numinous.

Equally remarkable is the surplus value this lighting style contributed to international cinema (including Hollywood). Given the different story construction of American films, it may have been less a new psychological language, or the soulful inwardness and radiant loveliness celebrated by Lotte Eisner, but a way of displaying objects, part objects, details – surrounding them with a luminous halo, caressing them with light, making both the animate and the inanimate world available for what is best described as a pervasive, but also perhaps perverse eroticisation, or more tersely, making them 'glamorous'.[99] This erotic sheen given to the detail when seen by the cinema may itself be taken in several directions, perhaps symptomatic of Weimar Germany's dual project of Modernity and Modernisation. On one side would be the argument that there is, after all, an emancipatory dimension inherent in the eroticisation of the everyday, an essential aspect of the transformation of matter on the way to de-realisation in the new cult of the beautiful, not unconnected with the different 'visibility' extolled, for instance, by Bela Balasz, in *Der sichtbare Mensch.*[100] Cinematic Expressionism and the *Neue Sachlichkeit* would in this perspective be merely complementary idioms of a 'liberation' that is also a separation, a new way of disposing the world before the eye, in view of mastering it – in short, they would partake in the confidence of a constructivist ethos, whose utopian dimension should not be underestimated, especially if one sees the *Neue Sachlichkeit*, the new sobriety, not as the opposite of Expressionism (which in my version is the style of an embattled duplicity having to disguise itself), but as its more serene, because finally, more self-confident variant. The Weimar cinema, having achieved its measure of cultural recognition, can by the mid-decade present itself in the public realm with a progressive ideology, defending the principles of a pleasingly attenuated functionalism, which no longer has to confront the contradictions between the traditional art work, commercial art and industrial design. An example of just such a synthesis, in which the cinema finds its place between high culture and mass-entertainment, between constructivist art and the commercial display can be found in *Das Neue Berlin*, a collection of urbanist essays from 1929:

> The best art exhibition of Berlin is also its cheapest. There is no entrance fee and it stays open day and night: the shop windows along the boulevards. [...] Here constructivism, so often pronounced dead, is alive and well, without profaning its principles, for its will and desire has always been to dissolve into daily use and daily need. True, the constructivism of the lighting engineers, designers and window-dressers looks different from that of the painters. The latter was severe and serious, this one is frivolous to the point of flirtatiousness. But it is thanks to its witty nonchalance, its serene amiability that it wins over the masses who shunned the artist and his seriousness. Sociologically speaking, the modern shop-window fulfils an important function: it brings the masses to a new level of art, bridges the gap that yawned like an abyss and slowly paves the way for new pioneers. [...] How does art reach the people today? Not through galleries, lectures, books, but with the gramophone, fashion, film and the illustrated weekly.
>
> (Behne 1929: 22)

If a similar nonchalance is indeed at the core of Weimar cinema's self-confidence, then, both the apparently reactionary aspect of design as disguise, and the modernist aspect of design as enhancement are driven by the same aspects of 'modernity', notably the move towards a consumer culture that takes over the urban environment, not necessarily only for profit, but in order also to 'improve' the face of the city and the lives of ordinary people.[101] Conspicuous consumption is here already seen not as profligacy (the nineteenth-century attitude), but as embellishing the quality of life, in its ability to fashion the everyday like a work of art.[102]

The contribution made to this self-fashioning by the cinema, and by lighting techniques in particular would be the increased possibilities of stylising decor, the 'coordination' of designed environments.[103] It would highlight the work of the set designer as 'ensemblier', as someone who can take the phenomenal realm, separate it into discrete visual components, and from these re-assemble a 'world', able to make each element count at the same time as he imbues it with sign value, adding attraction to the film-as-artefact, while giving the film-as-experience, i.e. going to the movies, a quality of objecthood, with its own fascination and appeal, its own tactility and spatial presence. In this sense, what in the 1930s became Hollywood's 'modelling for glamour' might be one route by which 1920s German lighting styles of psychological mystery found their way into mainstream practice,[104] allowing themselves to be translated into a more straightforward commercial idiom. In the chapter on Murnau (Part II, Chapter 3), I shall discuss in more detail how this adaptation of a technique – first elaborated with the aim of creating the illusion of 'art' (for a doubting taste elite) – transformed itself into the exigencies of erotic display. Yet, if the differing context of Hollywood brought out lighting's other side, namely its ability to enhance market value and create a new kind of objecthood, then such an instrumentalisation may reveal a truth that the German practice kept conveniently hidden, namely the possibility that the intensification of the erotic aspect of filmed reality was already a heightening of the commodity aspect, with the luminosity and the glamour seizing not only the characters but also the objects. This is certainly one way of reading Walter Benjamin's comments on the new photography,[105] which he saw as creating the technological equivalent of the aura of the artwork, whose reverse, as he noted elsewhere, was 'the phoney spell of the commodity'.[106] It would point in the second direction of eroticisation and modernity, adding another dimension to the quotation about Expressionism formulating ideas about the cinema itself: here it could refer, in addition to modernist self-reflexivity and anti-realism, to the medium's participation in those aspects of modernity that exude confidence in the skill to impersonate 'authentically' any style or 'reality', and therefore, asserting the cinema's growing self-confidence before it became hubris: if it is able to 'sell' itself, it is capable of 'selling' anything![107]

Thus, the question of how the cinema fits into twentieth-century history and society, what its place is within the dialectic of Modernism and mass-culture can be seen to have shifted the terms of the argument as presented by Kracauer, who – like Benjamin, but more pessimistically than Benjamin – saw clearly that the history of modern art had to be re-written as the history of the technologies that artists were able and willing to make use of. However, when Kracauer spoke about the increasing abstraction of the 'contents' (human or political) which gave aesthetic forms their sociological importance, he might have been referring to the technology of the cinema – as discussed above around special effects, lighting and camerawork – which appears in the films themselves only as a further stage of abstraction (in the first instance, eroticised and commodified).

This abstraction is 'design', and it is the design that constitutes the film's mode of address, and thus its sociological moment, rather than its characters, actions or situations, and the way these might 'reflect' social or political realities.

Between design and mass ornament: the cult(ure) of distraction

With this the argument has come full circle, back to Kracauer, or rather, that thanks to Kracauer, Benjamin was able to formulate a theory of modernity that overcame the deadlock between *Kunst* (art) and kitsch (its simulation) that so bedevilled the discussion of mass culture in Weimar Germany immediately after the war. Yet for thinking productively about Weimar cinema in these terms, one cannot rely on *From Caligari to Hitler* and must instead turn to Kracauer's earlier writings. There, Kracauer had, in fact, recognised a problem that is still with us, even though he perhaps foreshortened its inherent dialectic, namely the question of what sort of historicity or historical agency can be attributed to the cinema in general, of which individual films would be both the embodiments and the products. In a number of essays dating from the late 1920s,[108] Kracauer had argued that as a mass medium that owes its existence entirely to capitalism, the cinema was indeed a historically ambivalent phenomenon, where 'progressive' elements could not be that easily disentangled from 'reactionary' uses.[109] Following a lead by Georg Lukacs, Kracauer was especially struck by how ambivalently the cinema represented causality and agency, convinced that the medium would affect traditional Enlightenment notions of history, since films showed a world where human action is suspended between effect and cause, indeed, in its dominant genres – melodrama and comedy – testifies to its experience as effect without cause.[110]

Kracauer's early work, centrally concerned with this suspension of history through modern forms of mythology, helps to situate the ideological and conceptual climate in which the cinema became an issue for a left-liberal intelligentsia: against the prevailing tendency of trying to decide if cinema could be art, Kracauer even more than Lukacs or Benjamin, took a pragmatic view and looked at the sociological–materialist base, elaborating a theory of mass entertainment that places the cinema in a wider social field, the rise of a new (non-)class, the service industry workers, in competition with both professional white-collar and traditional working classes. He also sketches a new demographic–architectural context, in which the cinema is an urban entertainment space among others, but with vanguard function. In the uneven development of the technological recording media, dividing into still photography as a private art and into film as a public event, the cinema is given a quasi-anthropological role, that of translating the experience of time into spatial categories.[111] It shares this task with other, more directly participatory and performative events, such as parades, public spectacles, revues, sporting festivals. The typical entertainment forms of urban life for Kracauer are collective, but none the less generate powerful effects of subjectivity and subjection. The theoretical concept to capture this spatialising tendency is that of the mass ornament, a notion first introduced in an essay in 1927. It is Kracauer's most sophisticated attempt to explain why surface effects, such as geometrical design, serial repetition or abstract patterning, increasingly informs not only the arrangement of objects, the representation of industrial processes, but also of people and the masses, generating a peculiar bodily fascination and aesthetic absorption. By mass ornament Kracauer initially meant the then hugely popular female revue numbers, like the Tiller Girls.[112] But he also had in mind the growing popularity of gymnasts in formation at athletic events or in a stadium. More generally, Kracauer anticipated the importance which highly ornamentalised and decorative patterns at parades or in the visual representation crowds and armies would assume when displayed to a detached or distant observer, from an Olympian perspective, or when staged in order to be perceived by a camera (Kracauer 1995: 26).

Representing the relation of self to body in terms of vision and self-display, the mass ornament creates a powerfully social space for the articulation of subjectivity (as 'bound' violence, or 'ritualised' masquerade). In the mass ornament, visual display is not representational but a configuration of easily identifiable cultural icons and emblems in a space devoid of any signified other than confirming the spectators' own presence: in Kracauer's terms, spectacle becomes 'the rational and empty form of the cult.'[113] Social space, the external environment, is transformed into the site of figural 'play', at once repeating and inverting conditions of 'work'. For in an affirmative, quasi-utopian reversal of values, the revues and sporting contests parody the reality of the Taylorised assembly-line factory system, by celebrating a happily reified consciousness:

> The legs of the Tiller Girls correspond to the hands on the machines in the factory. But beyond the manual aspect, emotional dispositions are also tested for their psycho-technical aptitude. The mass-ornament is the aesthetic reflex of the rationality to which our economic system aspires.
> (Kracauer 1995: 79)

What makes the mass ornament pleasurable is the degree to which an oppressive working routine appears in it transfigured and transcended in the very act of being repeated, mimicked and reproduced. What is particularly useful in Kracauer's early analysis is the connection he makes between the mass ornament, understood as a form of 'institutionalised spectacle' whose sign/image character is the mirror of capitalist production, and the mass ornament as a mode of collectively experiencing subjectivity. For one of the central features of Kracauer's theory of distraction is the analysis of certain processes that the cinema shares with other industrial modes of production: the combination of discrete components and parts in such a way as to create the impression of a unified commodity, the 'two-dimensionality' of the industrial object (ibid.: 328). '

'The Cult of Distraction' offers a new departure point for the high culture–mass culture debate, because:

> [a]udiences act more in their own deeper interest, if they increasingly avoid high-culture events and instead prefer the superficial glamour of stars, films, revues and expensive production numbers. Here, in pure externality, they encounter themselves: in the rapid succession of disconnected sensory stimuli they see revealed their own reality.
>
> (ibid.: 326)

Kracauer argues that distraction, for a modern urban population, is a legitimate mode of aesthetic experience, more truthful to their historical situation than the experiences put in circulation as high culture. The question was essentially whether the mass ornament as 'authentic' forms of urban experience would find an articulation and practice that preserved their historical truth value, or whether its power for generating surface effect, immediacy and pure presence would, on the contrary, be instrumentalised: harnessed for an illusion of coherence, taken in charge by 'art' – or politics. It was the re-injected cultural cachet, the new psychologism and inwardness, but also the new activism that Kracauer objected to. Why should the 'motley sequence of externalities' be glued back together and offered up 'as organic creations' (ibid.: 327–8)? The cinema, this technologically based mass medium, was in danger of merely mimicking traditionally crafted, bourgeois art:

> Externality has honesty on its side. Truth is not in jeopardy because of it, rather, it is threatened by the naive affirmation of cultural values that have become illusory, by the unscrupulous abuse of terms such as personality, feeling, tragedy, etc.: words designating no doubt noble ideas, but social change has stripped them of a good deal of their credibility and basis in reality, so that in most cases, they now have acquired a bad taste, because they unduly divert attention from the objective ills of society and personalise the issues.
>
> (ibid.: 326)

Kracauer's ambivalence about Weimar cinema was due at least as much to the 'naive affirmation of cultural values', as to his missing in the films a 'basis in reality'. He objected, for instance, to Fritz Lang's productions, because of their supposed pomposity:

> Things that breathe in pamphlet form suffocate in polished leather bindings. This is literally true: on [Lang's] *Spione* opening night, critics were handed a volume that was a marvel of the art of bookbinding and that contained nothing more than Thea von Harbou's novel.
>
> (ibid.: 317)

Yet he seems to have underestimated the extent to which Lang and Harbou were in on the joke, so to speak, knowingly mimicking high-culture forms, impersonating them, but also deploying this mimicry as a tactical manoeuvre. Half-acknowledging this fact, Kracauer admitted to preferring what he called 'colportage' to some avant-garde positions (for instance, Brecht's). In a fallen world, a swashbuckler like Harry Piel does at least not strut about with too many pretensions:

> Colportage is the projection of major issues onto the level of triviality. The clash of good and evil, the marvellous, reconciliation – many important themes are represented in however distorted a manner by colportage. This is what justifies Harry Piel's sensational films, which do have some excellent crafted moments; indeed, there is certainly nothing objectionable about nice confidence-men pieces like *Casanova's Erbe.*
>
> (ibid.: 316)

Kracauer not only looked at the films. He noticed the sites where they were shown and the people who flocked to them other than on opening nights. He described the dance halls and amusement palaces that movie-goers went to afterwards, or young men took their dates, wondering at the fashion-driven exotic decor, the sentimental but also cynical reproduction of regional and national stereotypes, the themed musical evenings and tinsel glamour. One of the largest, the 'Haus Vaterland' by the Potsdamer Platz, was owned by UFA and had several live bands with different kinds of music, the 'Spanish Room', the 'Vienna Salon' and simulacra of other popular tourist spots. What Kracauer found among the new class of office workers and service-industry employees whom he interviewed for his book *Die Angestellten*, was a cool acceptance of themselves as part of a façade art and carnivalesque masquerades, and a clear-sighted preference for these special effects, style hypes and show-biz razzamataz over more stolidly bourgeois aspirations of cultural self-improvement.[114] He documents forms of entertainment and a lifestyle that has weathered the destruction of popular Berlin haunts like the Residenzkasino, the demise of the Adlon Hotel five o-clock *thé dansant* because the conditions that made them profitable have survived.[115] Glamour as a value enjoyed for its own sake, and self-estrangement as a mode of disguise or identity-costume, so Kracauer, allow the new shop girl's or office worker's fantasy self to experience itself as the true self: a split subjectivity under the sign of pleasurable self-alienation was the social basis for Kracauer's cinematic imaginary, against which he then proceeded to read individual films in *From Caligari to Hitler*, some twenty years later.

In his writings of the 1920s, Kracauer, in other words, was willing to face up to both sides of the (classical) argument about reified subjects as the inescapable consequences of modernity. If he followed early Lukacs or Adorno, he had to concede that the cinema stood merely in the vanguard of those forces that turn social exchange and interpersonal intercourse into relations of things among things, a 'stripped' world for which the moving image provides the anthropomorphised skin. If he endorsed popular taste uncritically, he deprived himself of the sociopolitical perspective on modernity as a dialectical process. Hence he conceived of the 'cult of distraction' as double-edged: the Weimar cinema may anticipate the mass ornament of Nazi parades and the society of the spectacle when viewed 'from above', but it also had room for a subjectivity 'from below', responding to the restless search for sensory and tactile stimulation that agitated the mass of spectators and made them seek distraction and fast-moving thrills. The contract between the entertainment industry and its public did have a measure of 'honesty'. In this respect, Kracauer and Eisner complement each other only across a significant ideological divide: what to Eisner is the re-subjectification of cinema thanks to the art of great *auteurs* was for Kracauer a sign that abstraction or reification had penetrated all aspects of creativity-as-style, and not only of a particular style, whether Expressionism or *Neue Sachlichkeit*. 'Colportage' and kitsch being thus notions about which his writings show a commendably open and even indulgent ambiguity, Kracauer saw them as a possible refuge for a collective subject, even though objectively they, too, served an industry geared for profit.[116] Pushing a point, one might say that whereas Eisner sometimes gives kitsch the benefit of the doubt by calling it art, Kracauer, knowing that cinema needed to be kitsch and 'colportage', became highly suspicious when it masqueraded as art.

As this chapter has moved back and forth between Expressionist film and Weimar cinema, from stylisation and the will-to-style to kitsch and the will-to-design, it would seem that despite his general hostility to Weimar cinema, it is Kracauer who after all comes closest to seizing a moment of its historical truth, when arguing that the competing claims of both high modernism and popular culture are better served by a cult(ure) of distraction than by a mass medium promoting its exceptions as art. On the other hand, Eisner was also right. Expressionism has triumphed in the cinema, though not as a style nor the signature of singular sensibilities, but as the historical imaginary of all filmic representation, now perhaps rather too complacently distrusting the truth claims of photographic realism, making stylisation and fantasy the default value of motion picture reality. Yet the challenge of Weimar cinema was precisely this: in its very first 'masterpiece' – *The Cabinet of Dr Caligari* – Expressionism chose to enlist the cinema not in issues of realism at all, not even in the quest for 'truth', but in a search for enduringly equivocal, fundamentally sceptical, and duplicitously ironic forms. This might be its legacy, worth once more to be navigated, past the Scylla and Charybdis of Kracauer and Eisner, into the uncharted waters of the post-photographic future.

Notes

1 I am playing on the title of David Bordwell, 'Our dream cinema: Western historiography, and the Japanese film', *Film Reader* no. 4 (1979): 45–62.

2 The best-known example is still Robert Wiene's *The Cabinet of Dr Caligari* (1920), now the epitome of Germanness (see also the next chapter (Part I, Chapter 3), but in its day also celebrated in Europe for having transformed the cinema from a fairground attraction into 'the seventh art' in, for instance, Paul Rotha 1930 and Eric Rhode 1976.

3 It corresponds to what David Bordwell has called 'The Standard Version' of film history, which assigns to this period the task of 'unfolding the cinema's essence'. See Bordwell, *On the History of Film Style* (Cambridge Mass: Harvard University Press, 1997): 32.

4

> Just as we intend to enter the export markets, so Britain, France, Italy and the United States want to re-conquer the German film market. These countries remember very well from the time before 1914 that the entire central European market is determined by German taste and German programmes. [...] Without our concentration of capital and the fusion of companies, the international film industry could now rule the German film business just as it pleased, flood us with their products and make any kind of competition impossible. Only because of the foresight of the larger firms are we now in a position to play a regulative role and put pressure on foreign firms and make them treat Germany with respect.
>
> Erich Pommer, 'Die Bedeutung der Konzerne'
> *Das Tage-Buch* no. 35 (11 September, 1920)

5 According to a leading trade journal, the top ten directors of 1927 were (ranked according to popularity): Richard Eichberg, Fritz Lang, Richard Oswald, Friedrich Zelnick, Joe May, Gerhard Lamprecht, Dr Franke, Franz Osten, Georg Jacoby, Holger Madsen. See *Filmbühne* no. 8 (1927): 5.

6 Examples of such textbook accounts would be *Film Art* by David Bordwell and Kristen Thompson (New York: McGraw & Hill, 1993); and *A History of Narrative Film* by David Cook (New York: Norton, 1981).

7 For example, Rhode 1976.

8 See Huaco 1965; Tudor 1974; Monaco 1976; Jarvie 1970.

9 See Gomery and Allen 1985.

10 *Nosferatu*, for instance, premiered with a high-society ball and had as 'prologue' a modern dance performance. After the film 'the guests quickly turned the "symphony of horror" into a delightful symphony of merriment' *Film-Kurier* (6 March, 1922).

11 Lotte Eisner, in 'A contribution to the definition of the Expressionist film', speaks of 'light [...] like a frenzied cry of anguish devoured by the greedy maws of the shadows.' Cited in Jürgen Kasten, *Der expressionistische Film* (Münster: MaKs, 1990): 151.

12 The question of film acting was vividly discussed at the time. See Herbert Jhering, 'Der Schauspieler im Film' (1920), in Herbert Jhering *Von Reinhardt bis Brecht. Vier Jahrzehnte Theater und Film*, vol. I (Berlin (GDR): Aufbau Verlag, 1958): 378–414; Julius Bab, *Schauspieler und Schauspielkunst* (Berlin, 1926). For more recent discussions, see Dennis Calandra, 'The nature of Expressionist performance', *Theatre Quarterly* 21 (Spring 1976): 45–53 and Barry Salt, *Film Style and Technology: History and Analysis* (London: Starword, 1983): 198.

13 In her various definitions, Lotte Eisner took over the metaphors of animism and pervasive anthropomorphism of Rudolf Kurtz:

> Streets twist in pain, fall on top of each other, [...] trees are a phantastically yearning tangle, ghostly bald, tearing the pictorial space into shreds with their cold shivers. Protuberant buildings fill the space like parasites, angular stairs groan underfoot, mysterious powers liven up the doors which are actually hollow, greedy apertures.

Rudolf Kurtz, *Expressionismus und Film* (Berlin: Verlag der Lichtbildbühne, 1926; facsimile reprint, Zurich: Verlag Hans Rohr, 1965): 63.

14 Michael Budd and Kristin Thompson have studied the ambivalent reception of *Dr Caligari* as 'German' in France and the United States. See Budd 1990: 56–102; Thompson 1990: 139–56.

15 The books on Weimar culture fill a library. Among the earliest and still very useful are Peter Gay, *Weimar Culture. The Outsider as Insider* (New York: Harper, 1968), Walter Laqueur, *Weimar – A Cultural History* (New York: Putnam, 1974) and John Willett, *The New Sobriety* (New York: Pantheon, 1978). In all three books, Weimar culture is itself a 'historical imaginary', a cluster of contradictory representations and mirror relations, formed around the names Marlene Dietrich, Martin Heidegger, Bert Brecht, Berlin in the twenties and Christopher Isherwood's Sally Bowles. See also Anton Kaes, Martin Jay and Edward Dimendberg (eds) *The Weimar Republic Sourcebook* (Berkeley: University of California Press, 1994).

16 See Karsten Witte's Preface to *Von Caligari zu Hitler* (Frankfurt: Suhrkamp, 1978): 7–14.

17
> Homunculus walked about in the flesh. Self-appointed Caligaris hypnotized innumerable Cesares into murder. Raving Mabuses committed fantastic crimes with impunity, and mad Ivans devised unheard-of tortures. Along with this unholy procession, many motifs known from the screen turned into actual events.
>
> (Kracauer 1947: 272)

18 For a discussion of the initial critical response to *From Caligari to Hitler*, see Karsten Witte, 'Nachwort', *Von Caligari zu Hitler* (Frankfurt: Suhrkamp, 1979): 605–15. Sophisticated methodological critiques from sociological and Marxist points of view can be found in George A. Huaco, *The Sociology of Film Art* (New York: Basic Books, 1965): 27–91; Andrew Tudor, *Image and Influence* (London: Allen and Unwin, 1974): 155–77; and John Tulloch, 'Genetic structuralism and the cinema', *The Australian Journal of Screen Theory* 1 (1976): 3–50.

19 See, from very different vantage points Salt 1979 and Carroll 1978. Most recently, in Martin Sopocy, 'Re-examining Kracauer's *From Caligari to Hitler*', *Griffithiana* (October 1991): 40–2.

20 Eisner 1969: 17.

21 H.H. Wollenberg, *Fifty Years of German Film* (London: Falcon Press, 1947): 19.

22 Rudolf Kurtz, *Expressionismus und Film* (Berlin: Verlag der Lichtbildbühne, 1926; facsimile reprint: Verlag Hans Rohr. Zurich, 1965).

23 Kurtz 1926 [1965]: 61.

24 Louis Delluc, 'Le Cabinet du Docteur Caligari', *Cinéma* 44 (10 March 1922). For an extended discussion of *Dr Caligari* in France, see Thompson 1990: 149–56.

25 Yuri Tsivian, 'Caligari in Russland', in O. Bulgakowa (ed.) *Die ungewöhnlichen Abenteuer des Dr Mabuse im Land der Boschewiki* (Berlin: Freunde der deutschen Kinemathek, 1992): 169–217.

26 German cinema's supporters were – apart from Joris Ivens – L.J. Jordaan, Mannus Franken and Menno ter Braak. See Ansje van Beusekom, *Film als Kunst: Reacties op een nieuw medium in Nederland 1895–1940* (Amsterdam: Vrije Universiteit, 1998): 134–230.

27 One of the first film historians to canonise Expressionist cinema as a distinctly 'national', i.e. German film style was Paul Rotha. His *The Film Till Now* (London: Johnathan Cape, 1930) served as a model for several generations of historical surveys.

28 Luis Bunuel, *My Last Breath* (London: Jonathan Cape, 1984): 88.

29 Hitchcock was much impressed by the tricks of the trade employed at UFA, especially the foreshortening of perspective, to give scenes 'American' depth. See Russell-Taylor 1972: 39–42 and Spoto 1984: 72–8, 85–91. Michael Balcon, Hitchcock's producer, had a special agreement with UFA, as a consequence of which, Oscar Werndorff

and Alfred Junge, two young German art directors, came to London and began very successful careers. See Tim Bergfelder, 'Rooms with a view' in Jörg Schöning, *London Calling* (Munich: text + kritik 1993) 55–68.

30 This was also the argument made by Nick Browne, in a paper presented at the Society for Cinema Studies, University of Iowa, 1989.

31 Standish D. Lawder, *The Cubist Cinema* (New York: New York University Press, 1975): 96–7.

32 Michel Bouvier and J.L. Leutrat, *Nosferatu* (Paris: Gallimard, 1981).

33 Noel Burch and Jorge Dana, 'Propositions', *Afterimage* 5 (Spring 1974): 44–66.

34 Ernst Lubitsch was called 'the European Griffith'. See W. Lacqueur: German edition (Frankfurt/M and Berlin: Ullstein, 1977: 291) of *Weimar – A Cultural History* (1974).

35 For a superior, but standard account, see Eric Rhode, *A History of the Cinema* (London: Allen Lane, 1976) 157–206.

36 A useful summary of the debate on national cinema can be found in Steve Crofts, 'National cinemas' in J. Hill and P. Church Gibson (eds) *The Oxford Guide to Film Studies* (Oxford: Oxford University Press, 1998): 385–94.

37 On Max Reinhardt and Weimar cinema, see Jo Leslie Collier, *From Wagner to Murnau* (Ann Arbor: UMI Research Press, 1988): 77–104.

38 In the introduction to her *Fritz Lang, Filmbilder, Vorbilder* (1992) which details the echoes from art, painting and architecture in the films of Lang, Heide Schönemann cites a number of authors in this iconographic tradition. Besides Eisner, she mentions Rune Waldekranz, Jurek Mikuz and Frieda Grafe, who have all worked on Lang's imagery. On Lang's *Siegfried*, see also Sabine Hake, 'The architectural style of *The Nibelungen*', *Wide Angle* 12/13 (July 1990); and Angelika Breitmoser-Bock, *Bild, Filmbild, Schlüsselbild* (Munich: diskurs film, 1993).

39 For recent work along these lines, see Jacques Aumont, *L'Oeuil Interminable* (Paris: Seguier, 1989); Brigitte Peucker, *Incorporating Images* (Princeton: Princeton University Press, 1995) and Angela Dalle Vacche's *Cinema and Painting* (Austin: University of Texas Press, 1996), which has a chapter on Murnau's *Nosferatu* (pp. 161–96).

40 See Salt 1979: 119–23.

41 See Salt 1990: 402–22.

42 These films are *Dr Caligari* (1920), *Genuine* (1920) – both Robert Wiene; *Von Morgen bis Mitternacht* (1920, Karl Heinz Martin), *Torgus* (1921, Hans Kobe), *Raskolnikov* (1923, Robert Wiene), *Das Wachsfigurenkabinett* (1924, Paul Leni) and (because of its acting and indebtedness to an Expressionist play) *Metropolis* (1926, Fritz Lang). See Salt 1991: 198.

43 See Thompson 1992: 127–39.

44 Kristin Thompson, 'Expressionistic mise-en-scène', in her *Eisenstein's Ivan the Terrible* (Princeton: Princeton University Press: 1981): 173.

45 The idea of stylistic coherence as the expression of a nation's or culture's 'will-to-style' was introduced by Alois Riegl, *Spätrömische Kunstindustrie* ([1901] Vienna, 1927) and Heinrich Wölfflin, *Grundprinzipien der Stilgeschichte*' (Leipzig, 1915).

46 Herbert G. Luft, 'Erich Pommer', *Films in Review* 10/8 (1959): 461. An account of the various claims and counterclaims can be found in Wolfgang Jacobsen (ed.) *Erich Pommer* (Berlin: Argon, 1989): 38–42 as well as in Thompson 1990: 127–39 and Hardt 1996: 45–51.

47 Eisner 1969: 19.

48 Erich Pommer, quoted in Huaco 1965: 35.

49 Both Fritz Lang and Carl Mayer for a time earned their living as young men in the postcard trade (Kracauer 1947: 62).

50 Anon., 'Aspects of Expressionism (3) it lives again', *Monthly Film Bulletin* (August 1979): back page.

51 For an argument extending Kracauer's point see my 'Social mobility and the fantastic', in Budd 1990.

52 The term 'super-text' I borrow from Nick Browne 'The political economy of the television (super) text', in Nick Browne (ed.) *American Television* (Langhorne, PA: Harwood, 1994): 69–80.

53 The leaning towards violent contrast [...] and the inborn German liking for chiaroscuro and shadow, obviously found an ideal artistic outlet in the cinema. [...] This explains why the first films of second-rate directors such as Robert Wiene or Richard Oswald misled people into thinking them remarkably gifted. These works blithely married a morbid Freudianism and an expressionist exaltation to the romantic fantasies of ETA Hoffmann and Eichendorff, and to the tortured soul of contemporary Germany seemed, with their overtones of death, horror and nightmare, the reflection of its own grimacing mirage, offering a kind of release.

(Eisner 1969: 17)

54 One of the most perceptive critics was Kracauer's friend, Richard Krautheimer, commenting on the 'Caligari' chapter as early as July 1944:

You use the movie itself and interpret it directly as reflecting a political situation. This interpretation is correct, no doubt. I wonder whether this direct method should not be buttressed by indirect, 'archeological' evidence: what did the Kreuzzeitung say? what the Rheinisch-Westfälische? what the Rote Fahne? How was the box office success in Catholic Dortmund? in [Berlin] Wedding? the Kurfürstendamm theatres? Probably you can't find out – I am merely thinking out loud.'

(cited in Volker Breidecker (ed.) *Siegfried Kracauer/Erwin Panofsky: Briefwechsel 1941–1966* (Berlin: Akademie Verlag, 1996): 96

55 Kracauer's strength is not as an economic historian. Classic studies of the German film industry are Karl Zimmerschied, *Die deutsche Filmindustrie* (Stuttgart, 1922), which Kracauer does not list in his bibliography. More recent studies include Peter Bächlin, *Der Film als Ware* (Königstein/Ts: Athenäum, 1972, originally 1948) and Jürgen Spiker, *Film und Kapital* (Berlin: Volker Spiess, 1975). The definitive studies on UFA are Klaus Kreimeier, *Die UFA Story* (Munich: Carl Hanser, 1992) and H.M. Bock and M. Töteberg (eds) *Das UFA-Buch* (Frankfurt: Zweitausendeins, 1992).

56 Marc Silberman has pointed out that: 'Kracauer's one-sided emphasis on the decline of democratic content [in the films] produces a momentum of inevitability which parallels the very ideology of fatalism in the films that he criticizes' (Silberman 1982: 375). This is particularly evident in the book's final paragraph, but there one senses Kracauer as much exhausted from his own labours as he was grieving for his country: 'Irretrievably sunk into retrogression, the bulk of the German people could not help submitting to Hitler. Since Germany thus carried out what had been anticipated by her cinema from its very beginning, conspicuous screen characters now came true in life' (Kracauer 1947: 272).

57 For a valuable introduction to Kracauer's intellectual formation, see Tom Levin's Preface and Bibliography in Siegfried Kracauer, *The Mass Ornament* (Boston: Harvard University Press, 1995 [1969]): 1–30.

58 Of Lang's *Die Frau im Mond*, he writes: 'The lunar landscape smelled distinctly of Ufa's Neubabelsberg studios' (Kracauer 1947: 151), which makes one wonder what else he had expected Lang to do.

59 T.W. Adorno, 'The curious realist: on Siegfried Kracauer', *New German Critique* 54 (Fall 1991): 77–94.

60 Kracauer mentions about 230 film titles, of which he discusses in detail no more than 40. It is estimated that Germany produced something in the region of 3,000 feature films in the fourteen years of the Weimar republic, of which perhaps 500 have survived, though these would not have been accessible to Kracauer in the post-war years, even if his research funding had been more generous.

61 See the letter by Lang, reprinted in the pamphlet *Caligari und der Caligarismus*, (Berlin: Stifting Deutsche Kinemathek, 1970): 23–5.

62 The motif tyranny vs chaos is not *specifically* characteristic for the period after the last war [i.e. The First World War]. It characterizes likewise the period from 1810 to 1830 (E.T.A. Hoffmann). I do not deny that it has political implications also at that earlier time, but I wonder whether I should not bring out the *specific* characteristics of the 1920 situation as contrasted with the 1820s. In either period [...] it is perhaps not so much a polar but a triangular conflict which dominates the scene; not tyranny vs chaos in other words, but tyranny vs chaos vs reason.

(Richard Krautheimer to Kracauer, July 1944, in Volker Breidecker (ed.) *Siegfried Kracauer/Erwin Panofsky: Briefwechesel 1941–1966* (Berlin: Akademie Verlag, 1996): 96)

63 The most extensive work-in-progress along these lines has been undertaken by Joseph Garncarz, 'Hollywood in Germany. Die Rolle des amerikanischen Films in Deutschland 1925–1990', in Uli Jung (ed.) *Der Deutsche Film* (Trier: Wissenschaftlicher Verlag, 1993): 167–214.

64 Monaco 1976: 115 ff. See also Salt 1990.

65 Monaco 1976: 77.

66 Monaco 1976: 75–8.

67 See Preface by Karsten Witte to *Von Caligari zu Hitler* (Frankfurt: Suhrkamp, 1978): 7–14.

68 For his version of German history, Kracauer seems to have relied mostly on Arthur Rosenberg's *Geschichte der deutschen Republik* (Karlsbad, 1935, repr. Frankfurt: Fischer, 1961).

69 Kracauer's chapter headings have a distinctly novelettish tone that mimics the sensationalist titles of the films: 'The Shock of Freedom', 'Caligari', 'Procession of Tyrants', 'Destiny', 'Mute Chaos', 'Crucial Dilemma', 'From Rebellion to Submission', 'Decline', 'Frozen Ground', The Prostitute and the Adolescent', etc. Weimar's mocking irony veils the exile's helpless melancholy.

70 Kracauer, for instance, takes to task those who read the figure of the double in *The Student of Prague* from a depth-psychological perspective without seeing the class motifs (Kracauer 1947: 30–1).

71 See Doane 1978.

72 See especially Meyer Shapiro's comments on Kracauer's earlier 'Propaganda and the Nazi War Film' (1942), where the art historian and close friend of Kracauer severely takes the author to task for setting up an opposition between propaganda and information that is itself a form of propaganda. He then goes on:

the second big point of disagreement is your characterization of the German people. [...] I am shocked to read of the 'natural inclination of Germans for thinking in anti-rational mythological terms'. This is what the Nazis want people to believe; as for me, habits of thought are cultural and historical, not 'natural' [...]. The 'secret' of the Nazis is to be found in the Weimar Republic, but in its full internal and international contexts.

(Cited in full in Ingrid Belke, 'Der Kunsthistoriker Meyer Shapiro über Siegfried Kracauer's erstes Filmbuch', *Film-Exil* 4 (1994): 35–49)

73 Here, Kracauer's theory of the cinema needs to be elucidated before even analysing his views of German cinema before 1933. See the two issues of *New German Critique* devoted to Weimar Film Theory (40, Winter 1987) and Siegfried Kracauer (54, Fall 1991).

74 As I have argued in the Introduction and elsewhere, the periodisation of German cinema is one of the most vexed questions in film history: the period of 'Expressionist cinema' can be moved forward to 1913 or confined to the years 1917 to 1924/25, but it is increasingly doubtful if the kind of convergence between film history and political history can be sustained, which would like to locate this cinema between the years 1919 and 1933.

75 'Art in the cinema is reactionary, because it symbolizes totality and thereby pretends to a continuity of beliefs, which appeal to physical reality while at the same time they cover it up. The result are films which support the dominant abstractions' (Kracauer 1960: 364). In this respect, he may have heeded Meyer Shapiro's points mentioned earlier.

76 If the case of Germany is at once extreme and extremely untypical, it has none the less become a more general tendency of the contemporary media worlds to think of nations and their national identities, but also of social processes and political change in terms of handy turns of phrase, image icons, catchwords and sound bites.

77 See Baudrillard 1978.

78 For a study of the cameramen of Weimar, see Esser 1994.

79 A number of useful interviews, statements and biographies of leading set designers are collected in Walter Kaul, *Schöpferische Filmarchitektur* (Berlin: Deutsche Kinemathek, 1971). See also the collection published as Robert Herlth, *Filmarchitektur* (Munich: Hochschule für Film und Fernsehen, n. d.).

80 'Dictator that he was, he was also "hands on", whether completing the make up of an actor, setting up a complicated special effect, or himself aiming the arrow that had to hit bulls eye' Robert Herlth, *Filmarchitektur* (Munich: Hochschule für Film und Fernsehen, n. d.: 49). For a report on a day's shoot on *Metropolis*, see also Curt Siodmak, *Unter Wolfsmenschen* vol. 1 (Bonn: Weidle Verlag, 1995): 107–10.

81 On Leni, see Bock 1982. For an earlier period, see Bottomore 1995.

82 See Bock 1982.

83 Walter Reimann, 'Filmbauten und Raumkunst' (1926), reprinted in Kaul 1970: 14–15.

84 Hans-Peter Reichmann, *Walter Reimann. Maler und Filmarchitekt* (Frankfurt: Deutsches Filmmuseum, 1997).

85 Kaul 1970: 13.

86 Robert Herlth, 'Zur Technik der Filmarchitektur', in Robert Herlth *Filmarchitektur* (Munich: Hochschule für Film und Fernsehen, n. d.): 60.

87 Almost all testimony about film making in the Pommer era stresses the intensity of the work atmosphere, and the sense that on the set, the world outside no longer mattered. Robert Herlth has vividly described the 'spirit of a medieval Cathedral building site which animated everyone: director and actors, cameraman and art-director not only felt a common bond with the key grips, the carpenters and painters, they were also dependent on each other' (Robert Herlth, *Filmarchitektur*, 48–52). As to the often also tense dynamics between director, cameraman and art director in the heyday of the UFA *Großfilme*, see Robert Herlth, 'Tournage avec Murnau', in Eisner 1964: 63–78.

88 See 'Styling' – *Study Notes of The Design Museum*, 1990: 1.

89 Herbert Jhering, 'Ein expressionistischer Film', *Berliner Börsen-Kurier*, February 20, 1920, reprinted in A. Kaes, M. Jay and E. Dimendberg (eds) *The Weimar Source Book* (Berkeley: University of California Press, 1994): 620–1.

90 See also Miriam Hansen, 'Benjamin and cinema: Not a one-way street', *Critical Inquiry* 25/2 (Winter 1999): 306–43.

91 By a reverse irony, *Jugendstil* objects now tend to come across as strangely uncanny, probably because, after Modernism, Functionalism, and the backlash to both, the gesture of hiding their industrial provenance seems so excessive, and so excessively obvious.

92 T.W. Adorno, *Aesthetische Theorie* (Frankfurt: Suhrkamp, 1970): 89–97.

93 See references to Peter Sloterdijk in the 'Introduction', Part I, Chapter 1, this volume. Further reflections on the idea of the enlightened false consciousness and Weimar cinema are in the chapter on Fritz Lang (Part II, Chapter 1, this volume).

94 The majority of German critics at the time well recognised the strategy, but – falling into the hole they had dug for themselves – they had to denounce it as kitsch, unable to specify what they considered art, except forever pointing to Charles Chaplin. See Saunders 1992 and also Hake 1994, 'Chaplin's reception in Berlin'. The Weimar left, on the other hand, used, in the late 1920s, the 'Russenfilme', i.e. the work of Eisenstein, Pudovkin and Vertov as their yardstick, though they clearly did not promote this cinema as a traditional art form, but as in the quotation from Rudolph Kurtz, in order to keep alive the avant-garde element in Expressionist film, with an eye to the general public.

95 See Walter Benjamin, 'The work of art in the age of mechanical reproduction', in Walter Benjamin, *Illuminations* (New York: Schocken, 1969): 217–52.

96 See Marc Vernet, 'Film noir on the edge of doom', in Joan Copjec (ed.) *Shades of Noir* (London: Verso, 1993).

97 Joseph von Sternberg, in order to get his particular effects used a special, irregularly perforated diffuser which he called a 'cookalourus', an Americanisation of the German word 'Kokolores', meaning 'thingamajig'. See Kevin Brownlow, *The Parade's Gone By* (London: Abacus, 1968): 237.

98
> In recent years, the art of lighting pictures has made marvellous strides. Hardly a week passes that some new discovery is not announced, and experimentation is going on all the time by directors and lighting experts. The day is coming – and coming soon – when the light expert will be as a skilful painter, using light rays as the artist does pigments.
>
> (*Photoplay* (November 1923): 44, cited in Brownlow 1968: 251)

99 For a discussion of lighting styles in US cinema, see Lea Jacobs, 'Belasco, De Mille and the development of Lasky lighting', *Film History* 5/4 (1993): 405–18.

100 Balasz 1924 [1982]: 43–143.

101 High modernism's claim to design the new man (and woman) through technology and (social) engineering pervades the post-First World War period from Le Corbusier's houses as 'machines for living' to Lenin's advocacy of Fordist assembly lines and bio-mechanics. For the fault-lines and possible mediations between high modernism, the avant-garde and mass culture, see among others, Huyssen 1986.

102 In this light, the implacable hostility of the political left in the 1920s to UFA productions, speaking from the expectations of a socially committed, agitational cinema, appears doubly tragic: disappointed by virtually all Weimar films, the hope was also disappointed by subsequent history. The working class was to welcome consumption and commodity culture, and the *promesse de bonheur* it entailed. A Soviet journalist had to report back to Moscow his deep disappointment that the *Russenfilme* did much better on the Kurfürstendamm than in the working-class districts of Berlin. See catalogue *Berlin-Moskau 1900–1950* (Munich: Prestel, 1995): 195.

103 A more detailed consideration of the ideal of total design and the modernist 'ensemblier' in Weimar Germany would have to start with Johannes Itten, Walter Gropius and the Bauhaus aesthetic, as well as the architect–designers Hans Poelzig and Bruno Taut. See, for instance, H.M. Wingler, *The Bauhaus: Weimar, Dessau, Berlin, Chicago* (Cambridge, Mass: MIT Press, 1977) and Gillian Naylor, *The Bauhaus Reassessed: Sources and Design History* (London: Herbert Press, 1985). For Poelzig, see Hans Peter Reichmann (ed.) *Hans Poelzig. Bauten für den Film* (Frankfurt: Deutsches Filmmuseum, 1997), for Taut, Ian Boyd-White, *Bruno Taut and the Architecture of Activism* (Cambridge: Cambridge University Press,1982).
104 See Charles Rosher's account of his stay in Berlin and visiting UFA, in order to watch Murnau at work, in Kevin Brownlow, *The Parade's Gone By* (London: Abacus).
105 See Benjamin 1973a, 'The author as producer'; and Benjamin 1979 'A short history of photography': 240–57. See also Mellor 1978: 69–76.
106 Walter Benjamin, 'On some motifs in Baudelaire', in *Charles Baudelaire: A Lyric Poet in the Era of High Capitalism* (London: New Left Books, 1973b): 171–6.
107 It is surprising to find how many films, especially in the early 1920s, were produced to coincide with the opening of new picture palaces in Berlin. It points not only to the relation between real estate and film production, but also to how carefully a specifically bourgeois audience was solicited in metropolitan Berlin. The champion of eye-catching facades for first run houses at UFA was Rudi Feld. Renowned critics would be invited to speak before the film, and the ambience was that of an important theatrical opening. By the late 1920s, advertising campaigns had been perfected, especially for a 'Grossfilm', as had the press book. For *Die Nibelungen* (1924), *Faust* (1925) or *Metropolis* (1926) it gave explicit advice about local and regional marketing strategies and envisaged audience appeal, supplying sample reviews, suggestions for foyer decoration and a choice of posters. Indeed, Fritz Lang's interviews and (often ghosted) essays in the quality monthlies and weekly press throughout his German career were always conscious of what cultural prejudices he had to flatter in order to subvert. The detailed planning and the studio-orchestrated publicity around the pre-production of a film like *Metropolis* suggests that its expensive special effects and other apparently profligate production values were undertaken also to allow UFA to invest massively in new film-making technology, not only with the purposes of making the film suitable for US export but of bringing the infrastructure in line with that of UFA's potential or actual domestic and European competitors.
108 The most important pieces are collected in Kracauer 1963. In English: Kracauer 1995.
109 On Kracauer's position, see also my 'Cinema, the irresponsible signifier' (Elsaesser 1987a): 65–90.
110 See also Lukacs 1913 [1978]: 112–17. Lukacs' views are discussed at greater length in the Chapter on Lubitsch (Part II, Chapter 2, this volume).
111 The spatialisation of time was a topic which – around the theme of 'ends' of history – preoccupied Kracauer throughout his life. See, for instance, his book *History – The Last Things before the Last* (Princeton: Wiener, 1994).
112 The Tiller Girls were first imported to Berlin by Eric Charell, directors of revues and operettas at the Große Schauspielhaus and responsible for *Der Kongress Tanzt* (1931), one of the most famous of early German musicals. For a contemporary account, see Giese 1925.
113 'The mass ornament', Kracauer 1995: 84.
114 Siegfried Kracauer, *Die Angestellten. Berichte aus dem Neuesten Deutschland* (1930), in *Schriften* I (Frankfurt: Suhrkamp, 1972).

115 The Berlin Adlon has in the meantime been rebuilt in the old style. It re-opened in 1997 to national and international attention, a full-fledged kitsch pastiche of its former self, which was already a pastiche of a Paris luxury hotel from the times of the Empire. See Jane Kramer, 'Berlin Building Site' in *The New Yorker*, June 1999.

116 For examples of his 'dialectical' argumentation, see especially 'Calico World', 'The Little Shopgirls go to the Movies' and 'Film 1928' (Kracauer 1995: 281–322).

3

CALIGARI'S FAMILY

Expressionism, frame tales and master-narratives

The cabinet of Dr Caligari: which end of the telescope for Weimar history?

Historians of Weimar culture have often viewed the cinema part of what makes Weimar 'Weimar', but they rarely give it the privileged status it has for Kracauer and Eisner, unlocking the *Zeitgeist*, the ever-elusive essence of an epoch, and mockingly summarised by John Willett:

> 'When we think of Weimar' writes Peter Gay in the preface to his *Weimar Culture*, 'we think of *The Threepenny Opera*, *The Cabinet of Dr Caligari*, *The Magic Mountain*, the Bauhaus, Marlene Dietrich'. More recently that other eminent historian Walter Lacqueur has defined its Zeitgeist in very similar terms as 'the Bauhaus, *The Magic Mountain*, Professor Heidegger and *Dr Caligari*'.[1]

Willett none the less confirms what one has always suspected, namely that among the classics of Weimar cinema, Robert Wiene's *The Cabinet of Dr Caligari* (1919) is not only the best-known enduring icon, it is the part that denotes the whole. Because of Kracauer's brilliantly telescoping title, *From Caligari to Hitler* 'Caligari' even stands for German history this century, the epitome of Germanness in its fatal conflation of art and politics. Credited at the time for having transformed the cinema from a fairground attraction into 'the seventh art', this rather short film about two friends and a woman, whose lives are tragically affected by an itinerant hypnotist and his medium, has launched a thousand explanations and interpretations: Not only did it become the benchmark of Expressionism in the cinema, with its world of distorted perspectives, dreamscapes, murder, mayhem and menacing shadows; it made the avant-garde movement itself seem like the emanation of a sick brain. Not only did the frenzied body language and angst-ridden faces of its protagonists symbolise a new subjectivity and inwardness; one of its screenwriters later claimed that it was a polemical–parodic joke directed against the upcoming fashion for psychoanalysis. Not only did Kracauer allegorise anticipations of the spell that Hitler was to cast on the German people; just as convincingly *Dr Caligari* was read as the definitive allegory of the cinema itself, in its power over mind, perception and the imagination. And as to the distorted sets, it was all due to mishearing the name of (Alfred) Kubin as 'Cubism'. ...

This chapter only reluctantly adds yet another such interpretation. The question is rather why *The Cabinet of Dr Caligari* should have exerted such a hypnotic as well as hermeneutic fascination on the critics of its day and continue to do so for every generation since. As the crystallisation point of different historical and imaginary constructions of Weimar cinema, the film retains its central, 'originary' function. In fact, *Dr Caligari* can be regarded as a kind of probe, lowered into turbulent waters of its time. These the film seems to have channelled, because they now barely ripple the surface of the film itself, so powerfully are they held in check by its narrative strategies and cinematic devices. First, all but imperceptible have become the film politics to which Expressionism in the cinema once owed its existence. Second, the narrative construction and the character-constellation continue to be enigmatic. Third, the discussions around the significance of the framing story and the undecidable truth status it creates, as well as the implied suspension of narrative authority are unabated. Finally, imitating the manner of a 'frame tale', this chapter re-frames *Dr Caligari*'s family relation to the (German) genre of the fantastic within the struggle for legitimation between high culture and popular culture known as the *Kino Debatte*. There, *Dr Caligari* appears like the rebus picture of much of Weimar cinema, pointing to a double 'social reality' – that of its public, changing its tastes and demographic make-up over the period of the 1920s, and the reality of the film makers, at once Caligaris and Cesares, at once sorcerers and sorcerers' apprentices, increasingly aware of the precarious control that 'creative artists' have over a mass medium that was to follow its own logic and was gathering political momentum at alarming speed.

From Dr Caligari to the Student of Prague: expressionism as rearguard action?

To begin with the film–political context, from which *Dr Caligari* stands out thanks to certain moments of retrospective rewriting. Kristin Thompson, among others, has vigorously challenged what she considers the myths put about notably by Erich Pommer, then head of Decla, the film's production company, regarding his role in the project and the 'origins' of the stylised sets.[2] But the claims and counterclaims about who was the producer (Pommer or Rudolf Meinert), who suggested the 'frame tale' story line (Fritz Lang, Robert Wiene or Carl Mayer himself), who had the idea of Expressionist sets (Mayer and Hans Janowitz, or Walter Reimann), who was responsible for approving the sets (Wiene or Pommer), who had famously said 'the film image must become graphic' (Hermann Warm, as is often claimed, or Walter Röhrig):[3] all this mystification and jostling for positions actually fits this film rather well, seemingly repeating at the level of production history the shifting frames of authority in the story itself.[4] Before one has really 'entered' the *Cabinet of Dr Caligari*, one is already in a *Spiegelkabinett*, a hall of mirrors.

This, too, has its historical logic with a domestic and an international dimension. Although Decla weathered the uncertainties of the war rather well, its director Erich Pommer, like any German film producer after 1918, saw himself confronted by significant obstacles, if he wanted to export films abroad, which in view of foreign competitors once more having access to the German market, became a vital necessity for survival. In addition, most countries in Europe operated a boycott of German goods, creating the need to either find a protected niche, or to market such products under a label that an international audience was likely to associate positively with a provenance from Germany. 'Expressionism', already in circulation before the war, connoting revolt against the established order, and yet elevated enough as high culture, helped supplant the then current (and wholly negative) association of 'German' with militarism, brutal aggression and the Kaiser, the 'Beast of Berlin'.

Here the function of 'Expressionism' was to establish a historical imaginary: a mirror style in which the negative image one thinks or knows that the Other has of oneself could be reversed-out. Acting or re-acting accordingly, *Dr Caligari* mobilises Germany's cultural patrimony (i.e. romanticism) and avant-garde credibility in the medium of high art (Expressionism) as 'propaganda' or 'camouflage' in another medium (the cinema), for the purposes of (national or commercial) self-promotion. But inside this cross-cultural mirror construction that was *Dr Caligari*, foreign audiences could, if they so wished, 'recognise' the evil, mad doctor, thus confirming the negative image of the German 'beast' of Allied war propaganda,[5] which the positive associations of the high-art style did not disavow or displace, but merely placed in an infinitely reversible frame, by allegorising it in the nested narrative of the flashback prologue, which forever vacillates between two interpretations: the story of a mild-mannered doctor and his mad (or simulating) patient, or that of a sane patient, criminally imprisoned by a malevolent hypnotist.

In Germany, the situation was reversed once more: the reviews of *Dr Caligari* published by such critical figureheads as Kurt Tucholsky or Herbert Jhering after the film's Berlin opening spoke of imposture and phoney effects and an attempt to hoodwink the public by speculating with two different kinds of audiences.[6] But after its unexpectedly triumphant success abroad, opinion began to change, with audiences and critics basking in the nation's damaged pride in the sunshine of the film's foreign acclaim.[7] As a quality label, 'Expressionism' was in this case not altogether far from the epithet that Dr Mabuse in Fritz Lang's 1921 film of that title applies to it, when he says: 'Expressionism – it's just a game'.[8] The lack of conviction, after the first surprise had worn off, that critics detected in the self-consciously stylised films following *Dr Caligari*, notably *Genuine*, *Das Haus zum Mond*, *Raskolnikov*, *Torgus* and *From Morning to Midnight* seem to bear out the suspicion that the film industry was passing off as gold what was merely gilded: a calculated, but perhaps too transparent put-on, pastiching itself, even before Ernst Lubitsch sardonically parodied such stylisations in *The Mountain Cat* (1921) and Paul Leni was able to invest the fashion with a new parodic zest in *Waxworks* (1924), by which time 'Expressionism' had more in common with Shéhèrezade and other *Ballet russe* fantasies than with either shell-shocked war veterans like Hans Janowitz or futurist artists from *Der Sturm* like Walter Reimann.[9]

How to understand such apparently cynical reactions? As some historians have argued, 'Expressionist cinema' was a self-conscious attempt at wooing a bourgeois public, meant to persuade the middle class to accept the cinema as authentic art.[10] In this, it replayed earlier attempts at legitimation from 1913, the so-called *Autorenfilm-Debatte.*[11] At that time, several different formulae were tested, from the Asta Nielsen films of Urban Gad, via popular novels and plays turned into films by Augustus Blom and Max Mack, to the fairy tale, folk legend, or gothic films with Paul Wegener, inaugurated by the justly famous *The Student of Prague* (1913). There, one can follow rather well how cinema technology, cultural battles, and the self-understanding of the film makers found their textual condensation and expression. When Wegener approached Guido Seeber early in 1913 because he had seen some astounding trick photography in a French film, the two decided that they needed suitable story material. They contacted Hanns Heinz Ewers, who wrote a romantic tale for them, a collage of standard Gothic motifs involving lost shadows, Faustian pacts and *doppelgängers*, just what Seeber needed for best displaying the special effects he was planning, and for Wegener to astonish the world by playing opposite himself! In 1919, for instance, Seeber published an essay entitled 'Doppelgängerbilder im Film' in the trade journal *Die Kinotechnik*, in which, after detailed descriptions of how to overcome the difficulties of creating flawlessly illusionist doubles for the moving image as opposed to still photography, he concludes:

> The first large-scale application [of my new technique] in a feature film was demonstrated in *Der Student von Prague*, shot by me in 1913 with Paul Wegener in the lead and as his own double. The result caused a major sensation at the time. The illusion was so perfect that many experts simply would not believe me when I told them that I had exposed the relevant scenes twice in succession.[12]

The Student of Prague is symptomatic for the importance of Wegener's work from the 1910s when trying to place the cinema in the emergent public sphere of urban entertainment culture. For Wegener was not only attracted to fantastic motifs because they gave him the chance to explore different techniques, such as trick photography, superimposition, special effects in the manner of Méliès' féeries and French detectives series like *Zigomar*, but because he wanted to develop these 'numbers' further in the direction of a stronger narrative motivation, that is to say, longer narratives – a decisive move for the economic consolidation of the film industry.[13] Wegener's fairy-tale films also promoted the ingenious compromise which the *Autorenfilm* wanted to strike between countering the hostility shown towards the cinema by the intelligentsia and the educated middle class, and at the same time exploiting what was unique about the cinema, its immense popularity across all classes and ages.

The reason, therefore, for the prevalence of the fantastic in the German cinema may be simpler than that given by either Lotte Eisner or Siegfried Kracauer, who enlist it as proof of the German soul baring itself on the screen. By reviving gothic motifs, Biedermeier settings and imitating the romantic *Kunstmärchen*, the fantastic film achieved a double aim: it militated for the cinema's legitimacy (the *Kino Debatte* being one of the first rounds in this century's battle between high culture and popular culture) by borrowing from middlebrow Wilhelmine 'culture'. Yet it also countered the 'international' tendency of early cinema, offering instead nationally identifiable German films. Up until the *Autorenfilm*, film subjects and genres were remarkably standard and international: film makers were either inspired by other forms of popular entertainment, or they copied the successful film subjects of their foreign rivals and commercial competitors – old wine in new bottles. With the *Autorenfilm*, national literature became an integral part of the notion of national cinema, and a certain definition of the popular also came to the fore, in which the agrarian-*völkisch* and the national–romantic were central. At the same time, the two pioneers reached the new urban masses by providing sensationalist show values, such as the 'special effects' described by Seeber.

The Wegener tradition thus set a pattern that was to repeat itself from the 'teens into the twenties and even extended to sound films: romantic, nostalgic and national themes contrast sharply with the experimental and avant-garde outlook that almost all film makers shared about advancing the medium's technical possibilities. Blending a middle-class concept of national literature with a pseudo-folk culture as the well-spring of the popular, the Wegener combination of romanticism and technology successfully took the wind out of the establishment's critical sails, making the fantastic film a mainstay of the German cinema for at least a decade (from 1913 until about 1923), before bifurcating into two versions of Rococo: Ruritanian musical comedies and Prussian male melodrama. It suggests that the celebrated 'Expressionist film' is the tail-end of this first truce between highbrow culture and a lowbrow medium, rather than a new departure. What breathed new life into the vogue was, of course, *The Cabinet of Dr Caligari*, mainly because of its extraordinary reception in France (and subsequently in the United States), which in turn made producers and directors self-consciously look for motifs the export market would recognise as German. Both the character of Scapinelli in *Der Student von Prag*, and the mysterious doctor in *Caligari* are, however, traditional figures, referring back to the magicians, shadow-players (*montreurs d'ombres*) and magic lanternists with their phantasmagorias at fairgrounds and other popular entertainment shows all over Europe: their manipulation of illusionism might be seen as typical of a German obsession where the films self-consciously elaborate parallels with the cinema itself, suggesting the increasing social (and political) power accruing to those who have control over the image (as in the films from the early 1920s, such as *Waxworks, Warning Shadows, Tartuffe*). In this guise, the fantastic films presented Mephisto figures tempting young, petit-bourgeois Fausts: as in Murnau's 1925 *Faust*, a vehicle for some hitherto unseen technical feats and special effects and harking back to *The Student of Prague* also with its motif of temptation. *The Student of Prague*, then, is indeed the first Expressionist film, even though its style bears little resemblance to the angular sets and starkly stylised interiors of *Dr Caligari*, which it predates by seven years. Nor is it because *The Student of Prague* has the literary motif of the double that it deserves its vanguard role. Rather, it embodies a key principle behind 'Expressionist film' in general, not stylistic at all, but part of the period's cultural politics: story and style are driven by the exigencies of developing and testing state-of-the-art film technology, not the other way round, while the films 'intervene' in a debate about the re-alignment of cultural capital, rather then 'reflecting' inner states of mind or collective mentalities.

Romantic fancies in modern dress

This context also casts a different light on a well-known passage by Lotte Eisner: 'It is reasonable,' she writes, 'to argue that the German [Expressionist] cinema is a development of German Romanticism, and that modern technique [i.e. cinematography] merely lends a visible form to Romantic fancies.'[14] Eisner does not address the question whether one can assume that 'modern technique' leaves the meaning of these romantic themes unaffected. As the medium of the moving image appropriates them, do they not turn into pastiche, imposture or ironic quotation? In other words, if 'Romantic fancies' were 'made visible', they were none the less a response to contemporary pressures that found in them at once their expression and their disguise, which is to say, an acceptably ambiguous resolution. The revival of the Gothic novel in the nineteenth century, as indeed much else in the romantic arsenal, was a Europe-wide phenomenon, usually attributed to a reaction against Enlightenment rationality. But it was also a more explicitly political response to the French Revolution (in Britain) and the Napoleonic Wars (in Germany). However, if the rapid industrialisation following the Vienna Congress provoked another major site of dislocation, where the contrast between city and country was central and the relation to nature became profoundly re-figured,[15] often with the result of making nature itself seem uncanny, haunting, then the re-staging of social conflicts solved half a century earlier in a new medium signals its own kind of politics. One of Siegfried Kracauer's earliest correspondents already suggested that much:

> The motif tyranny vs chaos is not *specifically* characteristic for the period after the last war [i.e. the First World War]. It characterizes likewise the 1810–1830 (E.T.A. Hoffmann). I do not deny that it has political implications also at that earlier time, but I wonder whether [if I were you] I

> should not bring out the *specific* characteristics of the 1920 situation as contrasted with the 1820s.[16]

Especially popular in the 1830s, for instance, were fantastic tales where the natural world was poised to avenge itself on those despoiling the earth in search of mineral wealth, or taking over rivers, lakes and waterfalls as sources of mechanical energy. In the wake of the Brothers Grimm, figures such as Undine, Rumpelstilzkin, or the gingerbread house of Hansel and Gretel allude to this split, featuring characters hovering between earth-bound space and encroaching civilisation, on whom are projected the fears and fascination of the protagonists. Their bad conscience treats all manner of natural habitats as picturesque sites or idyllic spaces, while at the same time, the tales make dangerous monsters out of those that guard them. One thinks of the Giant Rübezahl (celebrated in one of Wegener's film, *Rübezahls Hochzeit*, 1916) haunting the woods and villages of the Erzgebirge (a mining region in Thuringia). Even the figures of Mime, Alberich and Etzel in Lang's *The Nibelungen* have both a mysterious communion with nature and pose a powerful threat to the more 'civilised' protagonists.

Additionally, in mystery stories of the Romantic agony, what is often at stake are contested forms of political authority or social control, with the elements of horror or the supernatural both disguising the historical conditions of socio-economic struggles *and* foregrounding their destructive effects, by insistently imagining different, i.e. fantastic forms of agency and legitimacy. Revived in the 1920s, these conflicts become the historical garb for other kinds of violence, whose topical urgencies and sources of irruption are often set in another, more distant age. Surprisingly many films of the early Weimar cinema thus take up these shifts of period and social structure. Medieval courts (*The Golem*, 1914), Renaissance principalities (*Die Pest in Florenz*, 1917), *Lucrezia Borgia* (1922), episodes in *Destiny* (1921) and *Faust* (1925), or the struggles of the Reformation and counter-Reformation provide the scenery for depicting class relations and for characters giving vent to hostile feelings towards clergy and other father/authority figures. The vaguely Italianate name Caligari, and the mysterious medieval manuscript that the doctor is trying to test thanks to the new inmate conform to this paradigm of temporal–topographical displacement.

Yet even without assuming the 'out of phase' political development of modern Germany, it would be possible to find parallels between the 1820s/1850s in Europe, and the Germany of the 1890s/1920s, such as rapid economic expansion putting special pressures on political institutions and social life. For while the unification of the German Reich under Bismarck in 1871 had finally done away with the small feudal courts and petty aristocratic principalities that had blocked Germany's industry-driven transformation from a wholly rural patchwork of communities into a modern, bourgeois nation-state, Wilhelmine Germany remained none the less a predominantly agrarian society. Its peasant morals and closed community values equipped it badly for the transition to urban living, factory work and office employment without the strains showing in the body politic. The recurrence of Romantic and fantastic motifs might therefore be explained as a 'working through' of this uneven development and the time lag that separated Germany from its European neighbours, especially Britain (with its strong colonial and industrial base) and France (with its democratic institutions and centralised administration). The Bismarck 'revolution from above' had left intact a powerful caste system, and a culture as well as an educational system deeply saturated with an elitist, feudal heritage. The survival of an Imperial Court and a bureaucratic–military administration, even after the defeat in 1918, along with the emergence of a heavily politicised working class, gave the struggle of the various sections of the bourgeoisie for power and hegemony quite distinctive features in Germany.[17]

But the struggle in the 1920s was also on a different front: if one compares Germany with the United States, where the forces of capitalist modernisation were such that the economic imperative for the cinema was to help spearhead a modern culture of consumption, it is true that Germany in 1919 was not quite ready yet. Such an economic–ideological objective in post-First World War Germany was still at odds with an innate conservatism and the persistence of agrarian ways of life as they structured the family and determined authority and identity, even in such cities as Berlin with its wholly rural *Hinterland*. Hence, the significance of the efforts to win for the cinema respectability and cultural capital which, again starting with *The Student of Prague*, found in stylised films a unique compromise solution, seemingly addressing two very distinct constituencies. In order to carve out a space that was acknowledged as part of high culture, the film industry needed to produce works whose value advertised itself in the terms familiar from the traditional arts, be they visual, dramatic or literary: originality, individual authorship, stylistic uniqueness and formal coherence were the criteria, with films implicitly compared to canonical literary texts or cultural events like the theatre, whether based on the masterpieces of the past or featuring the avant-garde art of the present. Although usually described as gloomy, dark and full of anxiety, this cinema (and the emergent film culture to which it belonged) was also brash and aggressive, youthfully experimental and status-seeking, sensing itself on a winning streak as well as beleaguered, caught in the dilemma of having to legitimise itself to a national, but internationally oriented taste élite of intellectuals, while for economic reasons, it also had to make itself acceptable to middle-class patrons at home, whose tastes were not at all intellectual, avant-garde or experimental – the latter expectations fostered abroad after the success of *The Cabinet of Dr Caligari*, but disappointing avant-garde critics like Kracauer or Rudolf Arnheim, who felt Caligari's successors as phoney and opportunist.[18]

The ideological contours of this transformation of a culture of scarcity and toil into one of display and consumption provide thus a further reason why just these 'stylised' films were produced in Germany, at this particular point in time. Apart from the permanent tensions in German cinema that pitted film makers against intellectuals and the cultured establishment, who acted as the opinion makers, supplying the critics working for the daily press, the weekly journals and reviews with brilliantly formulated verdicts, there was a mass audience to be seduced into changing its spending habits and leisure pursuits. While many intellectuals remained guardedly sceptical or openly hostile to the cinema, especially in the years 1910–14 and 1919–23, the very periods that saw the emergence and consolidation of the German film industry and the flowering of the *Autorenfilm*, the mass audience had no problem adopting the cinema as its entertainment of choice. The central thrust of the German author's cinema was thus to find a compromise between attaining cultural status and the means of doing so, persuading both a class-divided domestic audience and a foreign, generally anti-German public to accept German films as 'art', even if it was an art invariably found wanting by its critics: at least the cinema was now fighting for its corner on the plateau of high culture, where even 'failure' was a form of victory.

But *Dr Caligari* was no failure. Despite legends to the contrary, it proved an instant success domestically as well as internationally.[19] Just how sensational it must have been at the time is difficult to recapture, now that the film has become the 'must-see' chore of dutiful film students and an all-weather stand-by of educational matinee shows. But in 1920 it clearly danced to a different drum, or rather, it glowed in different hues, as one can again see for oneself, thanks to the tinted print restored in 1985, with its luminous, almost stereoscopic effects, its tactile surface feel of velvet or polished metal, of cool blues and rosy-fingered dawns. Even ten years after its premiere, Paul Rotha called it 'a drop of wine in an ocean of salt water.'[20] In the early 1960s, Parker Tyler opened his review with an equally vivid metaphor: 'Like a steel spring responding to violent compression, *The Cabinet of Dr Caligari* sprang onto the post-war scene of film-making.' He went on to justify its historical relevance, arguing that 'people had suffered from the universal calamity of war, and some artists among us visualised its social blight as a product of the morbid imagination secreted in the lust for power, the drive towards the destruction of man by man', before conceding that 'it has remained, in any case, an illustrious museum piece, reproached by the fast set of film aesthetes and simon-pure documentarists for its militant artificiality, static manner of progressing and general archaic flavour.'[21] Yet, in the film-industry context outlined above, *Dr Caligari* was important precisely because it could not be repeated. Such *haute couture* one-offs or (engineering) prototypes have a special strategic importance in their respective domains, even if they do not lead to serial production.[22] They energise, by their event character, an unusually wide field, and like a magnet, they gather up and bind very different kinds of filaments, which underscores, but also situates the tactical significance of films like *The Student of Prague* or *The Cabinet of Dr Caligari*, and later, *Variety*, *The Last Laugh* and *Metropolis*. Their common denominator is that they were hybrids as well as one-off films, impossible to fit into a linear film history of 'influence' or cause-and-effect, however much they came to 'stand for' Weimar cinema as a whole.

Additionally, with *Dr Caligari*, the Weimar cinema's marketing practices followed those in use for perishable consumer goods, sports events or fashion-driven novelties, rather than those appropriate for the arts with an eye to 'immortality' – and yet, this is effectively what *Dr Caligari* achieved.[23] But measured by literature's standards, the film's claim to being 'art' must have seemed an imposure, fraudulently foisted on a gullible public, which was in fact just what critics thought about the sensationalist advertising campaign devised for the launch of *Dr Caligari*. 'Du musst Caligari werden' ('You, too, have to become Caligari') was one of the mysterious slogans plastered on posters on street corners and in newspaper headlines. Other commercial interests were quick to latch on:

> In the shop-windows, one is greeted by [expressionist] book-covers, all beating the same resounding gong. On fairgrounds and in bars, zigzag flames. In arts-and-craft displays, convulsive tremors. Shop-window signs, weekly journals and printed matter mail-drops are jiggling and cannot keep steady. In a big department store, not so long ago, they had an exhibition called 'futurist handicrafts'.[24]

Wherever the mimicry of stylistic authenticity was felt to be successful, Expressionist films passed as 'art', wherever the mimicking gimmick effect was too transparent, critics shouted 'Kitsch!' – to which one might simply add that in the cases where it was understood to be tongue-in-cheek, it was indeed appreciated as 'design' and marketing, as Rudolf Arnheim noticed:

> The success of this film at the time was less due to its gripping story or the acting, but because of the 'expressionist' sets, here seen for the first time. But ever since the gag of drawing all right-angles askew, showing houses collapse on top of each other, and of squeezing every round shape into a pointed edge has become *de rigeur* for interiors of cabarets, theatres and cinemas, and ever since the walls of even the shabbiest café speak the fiery tongue of this extravagant fashion language [. . . it has become] obvious that none of this has anything to do with Expressionism, the representation of the essence of things. It only means that the exterior surface of objects has been reworked according to the principles of ornament. [The result is] a delightful design for wallpaper.[25]

Thus, within a year or two of *Dr Caligari*'s release, and possibly because of the image impact of this celluloid bastard, Expressionism as an art movement had itself adapted to the 'market' and become just that, a commercial art idiom in interior design and a fashion accessory. As can be seen from the quotations, notorious spaces of this new popular culture decking itself out with the signifiers of high-culture were, besides the cinemas with their modernist architecture and plush interiors,[26] deemed to be the cafés and bars of Berlin. One extraordinary fact about *Dr Caligari* was therefore its radiance and ripples beyond the film text, and even beyond the film theatre, into the culture at large, making cinema history, and – as indicated in the opening quotation – becoming a (portable, visible) emblem of the age.

The oedipal scenario as master-narrative

The crisis of the pre-First World War *Autorenfilm* and the attempts to re-align the economic and cultural stakes of the German cinema after the war are thus among the historical foils against which to hold *The Cabinet of Dr Caligari*, created as a quality product for an international public. But like *The Student of Prague*, the symptomatic value of *Dr Caligari* should not be reduced to its production circumstances, nor merely explained by its reception history, however controversial both continue to be.[27] The logic of the film itself encompasses the film–political situation just sketched, 'translated' into textual relations of unequal exchange, which manifest themselves as a peculiar narrative economy. For instance, Rudolf Kurtz in 1926 (mis)remembers the film:

> like a fever dream, having its premiere in wild days, surrounded by dark streets, across which echo commands shouted by republican paramilitary units; elsewhere, the piercing voices of streetcorner orators, and in the background, the centre of town plunged into total darkness, occupied by radical insurgents, machine-gun rattle, soldiers forming human chains, [falling] roof-supports and hand-grenades.[28]

It is as if Kurtz had added to *Dr Caligari* yet another frame tale, locating the film's opening in the street battles of the November Days of 1918, but forgetting that it was only shot a year later, in November–December 1919. But with his recollection of war and revolutionary unrest he anticipates the *post festum* controversies claimed by Hans Janowitz between him, Mayer and Robert Wiene about the political 'message' of the film.[29] While Janowitz was able to pass his version of the story to Kracauer, and Warm gave his recollections to Lotte Eisner, Pommer, in the guise of a tribute to Carl Mayer, made sure that he, too, was on the record.[30] In the cinema (as in advertising), 'telling is selling' and *Dr Caligari* is a particularly vivid example for what Roland Barthes called a 'contract-narrative', by which he meant stories, character constellations and modes of narration, especially frame tales, flashback structures or nested narratives, which are 'determined not by a desire to narrate, but by a desire to exchange: (narrative as a medium of exchange, an agent, a currency, a gold standard).'[31] The longer one looks at *Dr Caligari*, the more its historical protagonists and purported authors seem to become part of the plot, engaged in a complicated series of exchanges and reversals.[32]

Such a *mise-en-abyme* effect is, of course, a perspective illusion induced by hindsight, and yet it is one which the film itself promotes, by the way it deploys some basic techniques of story-telling: narration, focalisation, tense and point of view generate a tissue of relations and the gradients of knowledge which secure a kind of deep-structure coherence that spectators experience not only as the narrative's own intelligibility, but also as a form of interpellation, turning the viewer into a participating subject, identifying with the film, at once inside the fiction and outside, poised between puzzling over and instantly recognising its 'master-narrative'. History, cinema history, biography and film text here fit or fuse together so startlingly that one can understand why Kracauer, already in October 1942, exiled in New York, the city of *Dr Caligari*'s international triumph some twenty years earlier, conceived of *Dr Caligari* as the key text for his idea of 'A History of the German Film':

> From the beginnings the German film contained dynamite. […] Chaos spread in Germany from 1918 to about 1923, and as its consequence the panic-stricken German mind was released from all the conventions that usually limit life. Under such conditions, the unhappy, homeless soul not only drove straightaway toward the fantastic region of horrors, but also moved like a stranger through the world of normal reality. […] That free-wandering soul imagined the madmen, somnambulists, vampires and murderers who were haunting the expressionistic settings of the *Caligari*-film and its like.[33]

That this master-narrative, here sketched by Kracauer, should have come to be so widely accepted is largely explicable by the very events happening in Europe as Kracauer was writing his outline, seemingly repeating the political madness remembered by Kurtz. But looked at from the other end of the telescope, as it were, the story of *Dr Caligari* opens out towards other master-narratives, not exclusively German, such as pulp-fiction murder mysteries and romance stories of sexual jealousy. In *Dr Caligari* they do, however, combine to create, at the very least, a 'family resemblance' with surprisingly many other Weimar films. Among these *Dr Caligari* was unusual in that it proved popular with urban sophisticates as well as attracting large audiences also in the provinces. Abroad it blazed the trail for what came to be known as 'art cinema' and the '*art-et-essai*' or 'little cinema' secondary exhibition circuits.[34] In Germany, part of the excitement stemmed from the fact that it promised a cinema of broad appeal achieved by a new technology and not by the kind of universality associated with Shakespeare. However, as argued above, its promise was based on a number of compromises, emblematically preserved in the conflicting stories of how the film had come into being, and in the hybridity of the narrative itself: the clash of expressionistic sets, realist objects and naturalistic acting; the use of an Edgar Allen Poe-like detective story, given a *Grand Guignol* theatrical treatment, with a *Ballet russe*-like musical brio; the transformation of the Golem/machine-man/homunculus theme of folklore and science fiction into the register of hypnosis, psychiatry and psychoanalysis. But whereas Kracauer saw 'symptomatic value' in the film for an analysis of political dispositions (notably the failure of Weimar social democracy), others regarded such heterogeneity as the modern form of mythological 'bricolage', where binary structures (of cultural attributes and antagonistic character conflicts) serve what Claude Lèvi-Strauss had called 'the imaginary resolution of real contradiction'.[35] For mainstream Hollywood narrative, the formula yielded a sort of template. Centred on a male protagonist and leading to the formation of a heterosexual couple, the narratives symbolically re-staged Sigmund Freud's 'resolution of the oedipal complex' at the heart of all male identity. As to crises in masculinity generally, there is indeed a good deal of similarity between classical Hollywood and classical Weimar narrative, if one accepts *Dr Caligari* as both symptomatic and representative.[36] But there are also differences that can be explained by pointing out that *Dr Caligari* belongs to a European 'art' cinema, whose 'Modernism' has since the 1920s always involved a distinct mode of narration.[37] At issue are the nature of the central enigma and the treatment of character causality, as well as the terms of closure, i.e. the general absence of a happy ending in European cinema, compared to Hollywood. If this disparity between Hollywood practice and Weimar cinema does exist, then the challenge of Kracauer's symptomatic reading is to ask if it can explain what purposes these differences serve.

Before taking up this challenge, though, it may help to recapitulate just what the oedipal master-narrative entails in the case of *Dr Caligari*, and how the film seems to fit into the 'family' of Weimar films. For instance, what initiates the story and drives the narrative in German cinema has often to do with sibling rivalries, overpowering father figures, absent mothers, problematic 'princesses' or impossible object choices. Typical conflicts arise from struggles with established authority in which the place of the father and the place of the son are particularly heavily marked, but that of the woman (as a sexual being and object of desire) is far less clearly defined than in comparable Hollywood films. *Dr Caligari* is a story of two friends, of a monstrous father figure, and of an ethereal fair lady, whose sexuality is only acknowledged by a murderous night creature. Many of the German stories centre on doubles, representations of a split in the central character, attributable to an unsuccessful challenge to authority. In *Dr Caligari*, one of the two friends is murdered, the other wants to avenge him. Suspecting the sinister doctor, he ends up in the doctor's power instead. Narrative closure does not follow the double path of adventure and heterosexual romance as it does in classical Hollywood, but seems the result of desire exhausting itself and regressing into narcissistic over-identification with the objects of aggression. In *Dr Caligari*, Francis is strapped into a straight-jacket and lives out his days in an insane asylum, as if doing the doctor's bidding were the ultimate form of resistance.

The second point to retain is that many Weimar narratives do indeed involve the kind of triangulation of conflicts familiar from plots often referred to as oedipal:[38] violent confrontations between an older and a younger man over the same woman (e.g. *The Student of Prague*, *Phantom*, *Dr Mabuse The Gambler*, *Variety*,

Pandora's Box), where the rival might be different in class (*The Student of Prague*, *Phantom*); he could be the young man's father (*Pandora's Box*, *Metropolis*) or the young woman's father jealous of a suitor (*Shattered*). The 'father' might fantasmatically appear as Death (*Destiny*) or as a vampire (*Nosferatu*), as the Tsar, Harun-al-Rashid (*Waxworks*), or Jack the Ripper (*Waxworks*, *Pandora's Box*). The 'other' might be a brother disguised as a monk (*Schloss Vogeld*, *Das Geheimnis des Abbé X*), an enemy brother (*Chronicle of Grieshuus*, *The Brothers Schellenberg*), a cousin (*Secrets of A Soul*), the hero's double (*The Student of Prague*, *Der Andere*), his moral opponent (the contest between von Wenk and Mabuse in *Dr Mabuse The Gambler*) or, as in *Dr Caligari*, his 'best friend'.[39]

Further prominent features of the Weimar oedipal narrative are the protagonist's suicidal states of mind (*The Student of Prague*, *The Street*, *Sylvester*), the frequent representation of 'the other' as monstrous (a double, an undead, a robot, a homunculus, a test-tube human or a medical abnormality), the repeated incest motif as explicit motivation (*Backstairs*, *Sylvester*, *Shattered*) and the horrifying but also petrifyingly fascinating spectacle of abuses of power and manipulation in the exercise of legal or paternal authority (*Waxworks*, *Dr Mabuse*, *Nosferatu*, *The Golem*). The underlying dynamic typifying these patterns is the instability of the paternal instance and a blank or absence around the place of the mother, regardless of whether the films take place in a bourgeois milieu or a working-class setting. Although only some of the titles belong to the genre of the expressionist or 'stylised' film, and irrespective of their literary or non-literary source, one frequently finds the same configuration of characters, the same kinds of conflicts. A fantastic film like *Dr Caligari* (whose heroine has a father, but apparently no mother) is thus remarkably similar in its narrative conflicts centred on the family, authority, oedipal struggles, to a popular melodrama with a contemporary Berlin setting, such as *Das Mädchen aus der Ackerstrasse* (Reinhold Schünzel, 1919, the story of an orphan whose step-parents collude in blackmailing the young woman's fatherly protector). It is this recurrence of motifs across the genres and across the class nature of the characters that prompted Kracauer to think of them as somehow representing aspects of the national character, and therefore as trans-individual manifestations of deep-seated mentalities.

One merit of Kracauer's study was to have pointed to this systematic overcoding of oedipal situations across a wide variety of fictional plots and narrative situations. His range, as argued in the previous chapter, not only challenges the generic division between 'fantastic' and 'realistic' films, but also the stylistic period distinction between Expressionism and *Neue Sachlichkeit*. On the other hand, the father–son conflicts and their resolutions in favour of the father have long been recognised as part of the standard tropes of Expressionist literature and drama, to the extent of constituting in the minds of some cultural historians Weimar culture's most explicitly overall identity. Peter Gay, for instance, calls his book on Weimar a study of 'The Outsider as Insider' and regards as crucial for the Weimar period, besides the blood sacrifices made by young men in a war started by the father generation, the trauma of a rebellion that failed, after which the 'fathers' Ludendorff, Ebert, Hindenburg exacted terrible revenge.[40] For Gay, just as for Kracauer, the oedipal conflict or generational revolt does double duty as a metaphor for the aborted class struggle and the absence of political renewal. Correlating plot structure, family conflict and class division, Kracauer, however, was the first to argue that it was Weimar cinema that most insidiously (because so cunningly disguised) stages the submission of the son to the father, interpreting it as evidence of an authoritarian or sadomasochistic personality structure, unable to resolve the affective ambiguity between rebellion and submission.[41] At the same time, Weimar cinema, no different from other mainstream national cinemas, relied heavily on the family as the setting for narrative intrigue and dramatic confrontation. Films tend to depict social conflicts indirectly, via primary affective relations in the family, or between friends, in locations drawn from a variety of historical, mythological, literary or popular sources. In contrast to the way civil war, for instance, was dramatised across families breaking apart, with the son of one family falling in love with the daughter of the other (as in D.W. Griffith's *Birth of the Nation*), Weimar cinema screens out the war setting, turning it instead into an urban nightmare scenario, as in *Dr Caligari* or *Waxworks*. While there were many German films from the 'teens that depict especially the Franco-Prussian war of 1871 (and the dilemma of Alsace-Lorraine) in such a split-family constellation. The exception is the anti-Russian (disguised as pro-Polish) propaganda film *Das Tagebuch des Dr Hart* (Paul Leni, 1916) using almost newsreel-like footage of battle-scenes to put across its message via the brother of the hero's fiancé fighting on the enemy side. The Great War, as source of the Weimar trauma, only starts to become an explicit screen subject after 1927.[42]

From Weimar cinema's oedipal master-narrative, film historians have drawn different conclusions: Kracauer, as we saw, argued that the films obsessively and compulsively turn on and return to the father–son axis.[43] Paul Monaco, in his study of French and German films, classified his corpus according to the themes of betrayal, foreigners, exoticism, the 'Dolchstoss Legende' (which explained defeat by claiming that Germany had been 'stabbed in the back', as in *Siegfrieds Tod*). For Germany, he concluded that films of the 1920s were obsessed by guilt (responsibility for war), by the conflict of generations (fathers and sons, again), and by suicides. John Tulloch has argued that in Expressionist cinema one can follow the working out of a conflict between two kinds of conservative ethics *vis à vis* capitalism, one neo-feudal, the other technicist–functional.[44] Pam Falkenberg has seen in the same narratives that Kracauer cites a re-transcription – in terms of sexuality and the family – of the feudal and bourgeois relations between classes and social groups.[45] In this way, Weimar narratives become socially symbolic acts, with the cinema re-appropriating history, by figuring it in the self-image of the dominant classes, themselves highly split and unstable after the lost war. Michael Henry, finally, has analysed the films in terms of the relation between narrative authority and political authority, seeing Expressionist cinema as an 'excessively' metaphoric textual system, where the institution itself, i.e. the film maker, the audience, the screen appear as a *mise-en-abyme* and mirror images of each other, in infinite regress.[46]

Single space, multiple perspectives: motivation, melodrama and the tableau scene

Such broadly 'structural' approaches highlight the family resemblance of the films to which *Dr Caligari* undoubtedly belongs, with its rivalry between two men over a woman, its patriarchal *Übervater*, and its 'rationalisation' of defeat both by disavowing agency via the fantasy of remote-controlled somnambulism, and by a 'retreat' into madness and thus denial of accountability. In fact, *Dr Caligari* belongs rather too well to all these constellations: the 'evidence' suggests that many of the themes just identified as typical of Weimar cinema appear indeed indicative of larger cultural patterns. Yet my argument will be that the formal means by which these patterns are articulated frustrate the very possibility of locating them unambiguously in the texts or in the society to which they are supposed to refer. Rather, so much does displacement, disavowal, denegation and reverse causality at the level of narrative join the pastiching, hybridising, camouflaging impulse at the level of stylisation, that one can only speak of the film as a conjurer's 'now you see it, now you don't' disappearance act, a Möbius strip put together by a Cheshire Cat. Thus, when one interprets, as both Kracauer and his critics have done, *Dr Caligari*'s supposedly social, political or gender themes – say, the oedipal rivalry between fathers and sons, the place of the woman,[47] or the difficult transfer of authority and responsibility from one generation of males to the next; the taboos on social rise and class mobility;[48] or the tensions between pre-modern agrarian values and modernist urban ones – references that seem to fit neatly into what one knows from other sources about Weimar society and the sexual politics of the post-war years – one is merely adding to the Weimar cinema's 'historical imaginary', that is, providing mutually confirming metaphors between the film text and the context: in this instance, a number of political discourses, social 'facts' and gender-and-culture subtexts, long settled into historical clichés.

There is nothing wrong with this interpretative principle or practice. But what is peculiar about *Dr Caligari* (and other Weimar films) is that its textual form allows so many, potentially contradictory narrative strands and social themes to manifest themselves within the space of one fiction, making this space a multi-layered one, in which visual stylisation and narrational strategies support each other, even though, as critics have noted, the clash between style and story seems to violate the film's aesthetic 'unity'. To test the effectiveness of this violation, and maybe discover a *raison d'être* for these strategies, one could start by assuming the film to be a standard Hollywood murder mystery, and then ask the sort of questions of basic character motivation appropriate to such a narrative. For instance, why does Francis, the narrator in the frame tale, and Caligari's chief antagonist in the story itself, go mad? Or, what is the relation between the murder of the town clerk and the murder of Allan, Francis's friend? And what goes on between Francis and Cesare? The film seems to treat these matters – obvious queries if the film had been a detective story in a realist genre – as somehow irrelevant, as it strives for one bizarre visual effect after another. But this impression is misleading: *Dr Caligari* very much cares about what motivates the chain of events, but it expends even more narrational and figural energy into displacing these motivations away from the characters' conscious designs and goals. In the process of transforming the script from a conventionally written tale into the 'stylised' film that it became, made up of a series of self-contained, mainly static tableaux scenes,[49] questions of motivation have become almost illegible, at least if one expects classical, character-centred causality. But as in other examples from early Weimar cinema, the static quality of much of *Dr Caligari* need not be taken for inexperience or identified as avant-garde neo-primitivism.[50] Rather, true to its melodramatic mode, stasis is a function of too much agitation which, unable to articulate itself in the linear form of goal-oriented action, creates the kind of compression alluded to by Parker Tyler's image of a coiled spring. Ever so often, these moments of stillness are punctuated with bursts of frenzied commotion, like a chase, or a violent struggle to subdue one of the protagonists. In these scenes, *Dr Caligari* cites a popular and well-established film form, which it displaces by making it strange: the genre of the detective serial, extremely popular in Europe from the mid-1910s onwards, depicting not only suave detectives like Joe Deebs and Stuart Webbs,[51] but also master-criminals like Fantomas or Dr Gar-El-Hama, of which Dr Caligari is a medically and metaphysically supercharged specimen.

This particular narrative economy of *Dr Caligari* obliges one to think of the characters' motivation in different terms, namely not expressed in a contest of action, of move and counter-move, as in the traditional detective story (of which there are still plenty in *Dr Caligari*), but also as a contest of action at one remove, conducted as struggles over narrational authority: Whose story is it? Who tells it, and to whom? If one follows accounts like Kracauer's, it is the story of Caligari, a mysterious, manipulative and most likely mad doctor of psychiatry, the premonitory materialisation of a long line of tyrants, an image of German military dictatorship and its demonic, mesmerising hold over an unsuspecting, somnambulist population. Yet one can construct for Caligari's behaviour a motivational logic that derives from the terms of story itself and remains within its textual boundaries. The doctor, one recalls, while researching in his archives finds a manuscript containing the secret of successful hypnosis and he manages to bring a somnambulist patient under his control. Disguising himself as a fairground operator, he uses this power for both scientific purposes and financial gain – a common conjunction for the time, not only in medicine, but also in cinematography, when one thinks of the first generation of inventor-showmen, from Edison and the Lumière brothers to W.R. Paul and Oskar Messer. Caligari, however, smarting from lack of status recognition, first avenges himself on the town clerk and subsequently lures a young woman into his tent, after having the night before eliminated one of her suitors. He beckons Jane inside, showing her the upright box, flings it open with a leer to reveal the rigid figure of Cesare, who, as she gets closer, opens his eyes, whereupon she stands transfixed in fascination, until she breaks away with a terrified, distraught expression on her face.

The sexual connotations of the scene are hard to avoid, and here Caligari's powers of hypnosis are like a childish attempt to compensate for an attraction and youthful prowess clearly lacking in his person. His behaviour towards Jane is that of the 'dirty old man' exposing himself: showing Cesare is literally an 'exhibition'. Cesare's abduction of the young woman strengthens this strand of the narrative: the medium becomes, as it were, the detachable part of Caligari, not so much his double as his tool. Told from Caligari's point of view, the story is centred on a pathological relationship to sexuality and political power, in which (social) impotence (his humiliation by the town clerk) is overcompensated by (sexualised) exhibition ('I'll show you!'), but where 'showing' involves an alternation of hiding and revealing, here pictured as the flamboyant opening of the coffin and Cesare's blinking single eye. Cesare, the medium, unlike the Golem and other 'creatures' does not turn against his master, although his attitude to

Figure 5 Werner Krauss as the psychiatrist turned fairground exhibitor, showing Jane (Lil Dagover) into his tent in *The Cabinet of Dr Caligari* (1920)

Source: Stiftung Deutsche Kinemathek, Berlin

Jane displays the same Victorian ambiguity between rape and rescue as other male monsters of the fantastic. When pursued by Francis, Cesare drops Jane, visibly losing strength until he withers and fades away. In this respect, he is a cousin to Dracula (or Nosferatu), fading with daylight – both of them not only creatures of the night, but hyper-sensitive to light (easily 'over-exposed', one might say, like film stock). When Cesare does return to his creator, the very sight of him, signalling the necessity to recognise in the creature part of himself, and thus to acknowledge his own responsibility for the crimes, seems to make Caligari lose his senses.[52]

But is the spectator in fact asked to read the film as centred on Caligari? The story is initiated by Francis, and in this sense it is his story, too, about how he came to be at the place from which he tells it, as the recollection of a series of events whose memory is activated by the sight of a figure in white passing by, who turns out to be Jane. What, then, is Francis's story and why does he go mad? From his point of view it is, essentially, the tale of a suitor who is ignored or turned down: the narrative comes full circle when Francis pleads with Jane to marry him, and she replies that 'we queens may never choose where our hearts dictate'. In the story itself, the choice was between Francis and Allan. After the visit to the fairground, where Allan is told by Cesare that he has only until dawn to live, the friends part with the remark, 'we must let her choose. But whatever her choice, we shall always remain friends'. This seems like protesting too much. In such a situation of rivalry, the main beneficiary of Allan's death is Francis, a benefit which his reaction to the news both expresses and suppresses, manifest in his largely futile efforts to track down the perpetrator. For Francis's moment of recognition (in the script it appears as 'a look of comprehension') is itself turned into an enigma and disavowed: 'I shall not rest until I get to the bottom of these events,' he says, which opens up the detection narrative, with its false trail and its false suspect, inaugurating a typical chain of substitution. In this respect, Cesare is Francis's double: he kills the rival and abducts the bride, acting out Francis's secret desires. The fact that throughout the rape/abduction scene both Francis and Caligari sit stupidly in front of a box containing Cesare's life-size rag doll dummy, not only accentuates the gesture of disavowal, it also establishes a parallelism of desire between Francis and Caligari, underlined later by the repetition of an identical composition and shot: first, Caligari is put in a strait-jacket and locked into a cell, and then Francis, too, has to be identically restrained. The investigation of the series of crimes thus culminates in the visual statement that the criminal is the alter ego of the detective, the story of Oedipus, in other words: sufficient reason to make Francis, too, lose his senses. But this version is itself held in suspense by the reversibility which the framing of the tale imposes on any attempt at a final decipherment.

For it is equally plausible to read *Dr Caligari* as Jane's story, in which case, her doctor–father and Dr Caligari feature as doubles of each other, and Cesare as the disavowed phallus-fetish of a curiosity, which the scene in Caligari's tent marks as explicitly sexual. One recalls that she is motivated to visit Caligari by 'her father's long absence' (there being no mother, she is scared of living alone), and that in the face of Francis's protestations that it could not have been Cesare who abducted her, Jane insists vehemently on being right, as if to defend her version of events against the rival claims of Francis.[53] What implications is one to draw? It appears that the makers of *Dr Caligari* found a visual form and a mode of narration, where several different 'versions' or narrative perspectives converge and superimpose themselves on the same fictional space: its economy is that of condensation, itself the outcome of a series of displacements that de-centre the narrative, while also creating entry points for a number of distinct spectator-fantasies, figuring male and female oedipal scenarios – as well as their disavowal.[54] The multiple readings are facilitated by the film's subtle manipulation of temporality, cross-cutting and suggested simultaneity of actions on the one hand, and a muting of action time in favour of narrated time on the other, so that one never quite knows whose narrative one actually inhabits at any given moment. Additionally, this multi-perspectivism gives a fairly precise function to the decor, which is striking not only for its borrowings from Expressionism as such, but for the uses it puts this stylisation to: the sets' angularity at once creates an indeterminacy of space and metaphorically comments on the many different 'angles' one can attribute to its central story line.[55] The balancing of narrative agents brings to the fore the many parallels and instances of repetition, but by eliding the links and attenuating their relationship, the story becomes lacunary and elliptical, so that the figures of the fantastic are as much what 'explains' the story as they are the (formal) consequences of the film choosing this particular textual economy of narrative perspectivism and spectator positioning.

Paradoxically, such an economy works towards opening up the film to its many interpretations, while condensing its elements into an even tighter oedipal logic. For *Dr Caligari* knits together its various characters, letting them function as substitutes for each other, either as doubles or (fetishised) part objects. The 'overdetermined' nature of the psychic repression is named, shown, hinted at, only to become in turn the object of further repression. It is as if the social motif (the doctor's humiliation) is substituted by a sexual motif, but both are themselves distorted by the force of narration itself, so that the film offers 'solutions' that leave everything open, or rather, produce radically equivocal textual moves. At first sight, it illustrates the tendency observed by Kracauer that in the Weimar cinema, social conflicts become internalised, psychologised, but it also shows that this process happens not without exacting a price: the interiorisation is of so virulent a kind that it threatens to disturb the very attempt at psychological containment and ultimately 'prevents' a resolution. Typical are the scenes that seem to break off and fade out in mid-gesture, on a note of suspension, so to speak: they connote a force of resistance, of disavowal, without which there would be no nested narrative, and even more so, no need for so many narrators and narrator perspectives. For it seems that the act of narration establishes itself in *Dr Caligari*, and in other films of the German cinema of the twenties, as a veritable struggle for control over the right to narrate, and thus over the intensities of the filmic discourse itself, so that the apparent indecisiveness hovering over both the temporal and causal order of the film, as well as the opaqueness and blur in the emotional texture of the relationships between the three initial figures Francis, Jane and Allan, is evidence not of an absence of tension and suspense, but of contradictory desires unable to attach themselves to their proper objects, thereby giving rise to the emergence of Caligari and Cesare in the first instance, as excessive signifiers of the 'normal' characters' too muted ambivalences.

Frame tales and nested narratives

Another way of defining some of the strategies of narration in Weimar cinema would be to borrow the term of 'narrative braiding' that Roland Barthes invented for *S/Z*, his study of a novella by Balzac, with its taxonomy of narrative codes, including the semes (thematic groupings of a text), the hermeneutic code (the voice of truth) and the proairatic code (referring to actions in a narrative) the symbolic and the referential codes. Significantly, the tightly woven interdependence of these codes which Barthes saw as typical for the classical realist text is much looser and disjointed in the German cinema where the hermeneutic and the proairetic codes seem weak, that is, the semantic material that gives information about the enigma and its resolution is often missing, as are indications about the temporality of the actions and their causal nexus. As a consequence, the narration gives few clues and circumstantial detail about the characters' motives. What Barthes calls the voice of truth is curiously muted and frequently very oblique. Using the vocabulary of Barthes helps to explain why these films lack suspense, why the characters have no motives for their actions, and the viewer is not told why one event follows another. The hermaneutic and proairatic codes assume less importance than do the symbolic code and the semes attached to it, i.e. what Barthes calls 'the place for multi-valence and reversibility', where the text allows for 'the instability, the dispersion characteristic of motes of dust, flickers of meaning'.[56] It explains why (especially American) critics have often complained about German films being 'slow' and lacking suspense: judgements that confirm the comparative indifference to the action codes, neglected in favour of the code(s) that organise structural relations of symmetry, of antithesis, but which also form the basis for systems of substitution, both functional and referential. It is the 'semes of dispersion' that spawn the 'over-interpretation' mentioned earlier, since they encourage viewers to try to disambiguate and make sense of certain scenes by bringing in extra-cinematic referents. The symbolic code blocks discursive mastery on the part of the spectator, in contrast to the illusion of narrative control the audience enjoys in the classical Hollywood cinema, for example, by often knowing more than the characters. Compared to this classical story telling, whose compliance with the spectator's desire 'to see and to know' makes it appear invisible, Weimar films often foreground the question of who authorises or controls the act of narration.[57] The profusion of nested narratives, framed tales, flashbacks, *mise-en-abyme* constructions and interlacing of narrative voices is an index of the differences that established German silent cinema as historically specific.[58]

Why the films should show these formal–narrational peculiarities has rarely been discussed. But it is one of the secrets of their fascination for critics that they play hide-and-seek (or, like *Dr Caligari*, peek-a-boo) with the spectator: the very obliqueness of the narratives both encourages all kinds of speculation and frustrates definitive interpretation, making them resistant to the very temptations they invite, namely to pin down their referentiality. One argument would be that German art cinema represents a kind of 'meta-cinema', in the sense that all the prominent films of this tradition are also, and maybe even mostly 'about' the cinema itself: about the act of seeing, about vision and visuality. The films seem to convert the violence and aggression inherent in the viewing situation of cinematic spectacle not into chase, adventure, spectacle, nor into comedy, slapstick or grotesque fantasy (as is the case in the cinema of the period 1910–1919 in France or the USA), but into uncanny moments, hesitation and horror, into the drama of (violent) fantasy and (surreal) dream reality, as it plays between the spectator and the screen. The audiences' artificial restriction of motility typical of the cinematic experience translates itself into the narrative material across the 'oedipal' conflicts, as if a 'primary' violence had to undergo 'secondary' elaboration in terms of the story, without fully disappearing into this secondary revision, creating the typical effects of excess, 'expressionist' body language and seemingly 'unmotivated' over-emphasis.

This repeated self-reference might in turn explain the unusual prominence given to the figure of the narrator, or more abstractly, the instance of narration. Among Weimar cinema's master-narrators one finds the mysterious figure of Scapinelli, in *The Student of Prague*, the itinerant showman of *Dr Caligari* or the equally itinerant *montreur d'ombres* in *Warning Shadows* who entertains the aristocratic company at the mansion with his truth-telling phantasmagoria. If one adds all the other eponymous string-pullers of human puppets like Dr Mabuse, Nosferatu, Tartuffe and the figure of 'Death' in *Destiny*, then the line of master-narrators is very long indeed, coinciding with, but by no means collapsable into Kracauer's 'procession of tyrants'.[59] Some, for instance, are external to the fiction, others are internally generated, as in *Dr Caligari* and *The Golem*, but also in *Nosferatu* and *The Nibelungen*. In *Nosferatu* in particular, there are so many sources of narrative authority that the meaning of the tale is crucially altered by each one competing for narrative authority. But instead of feeling threatened by its tyrannical power (as Kracauer maintains), the spectator is more likely to be threatened by his lack of control, acutely aware as he is of the absence of the voice of truth. Despite the many narrators or because of them, these figures are not to be trusted, since they cannot but add yet another layer of uncertainty.

The device that most readily introduces these further uncertainties is probably also the most distinctive feature of narration in Weimar films: the framed tale.

The very name 'frame' could suggest a stabilising function, a way of containing textual excess, but instead, its deployment seems more often designed to merely complicate matters. The best-known example of such complication is, of course, the framing device of *Dr Caligari* itself, whose origin and function, as already indicated, has given rise to so much discussion and surmise that it has become a 'crux' of film history all by itself.[60] What *Dr Caligari* exemplifies is a mode where the narrative is 'framed' by another tale, which acts as a motivation, a commentary and thus an interpretation of events immanent to the text. But, as this narration is itself overturned at the end, the *mise-en-abyme* denies in a more radical fashion the truth value of what one has just seen, not only because of doubts about the reliability of the narrators, but of their very sanity: even the final frontal shot of the good doctor hardly reassures about his state of mind, never mind his intentions. In such an extreme form, unreliable narration is relatively rare even in the German cinema.[61] But *Dr Caligari* is by no means the first German film to employ this device, which has been familiar in popular literature since the Middle Ages, for example, *1001 Arabian Nights*, Boccaccio and Chaucer. A social melodrama from 1910, *Grausame Ehe/Brutal Marriage*, for instance, features the story of a woman who murdered her husband. It is framed by her telling a court of law about how she was driven to the deed, with the courtroom setting providing the frame.[62] This is similar to the frame in *Variety*, which opens when the imprisoned protagonist, Boss Huller, is led to the appeal tribunal's hearing and tells the judge how he came to murder his rival. *Variety* closes with the prisoner being paroled and released, an unusually symmetrical and circular ending, possibly explaining why it was one of the most successful German films ever seen in the United States. Generally, the framing device in German films acts as a lure or trap for one or more of the characters either to give themselves away or to give away a secret, as in *Schloß Vogelöd* and *Tartuffe*. In *Warning Shadows* it is the cinema in a complicated form of doubling, as a Balinese shadow play that becomes the film we are actually watching, which serves as a screen for projection. Used by the magician for ultimately benevolent ends, it ostensibly allows the characters to confront themselves, attain a degree of self-knowledge about their fears and obsessions, jealousies and murderous rages.

A similar situation obtains in *Hands of Orlac* (Robert Wiene, 1924). Without the framing device, the film is a story, typical of a number of films from the period, modelled on the fairy tale of the sorcerer's apprentice, or the Hegelian master–slave dialectic. An aristocratic concert pianist gradually realises the hands that had been grafted on to his arms after losing his own hands in a rail crash have a life of their own. It is a particular shock when he learns that they once belonged to an executed murderer! He no longer has any control over his hands and is forced to recognise the 'other' in himself, and to decide whether to accept or reject this other, or to mutilate himself again. This conflict is similar to that of F.W. Murnau's *Der Gang in die Nacht* (1921), where the hero, also played by Conrad Veidt, would prefer to go blind again, rather than benefit from a sacrifice based on crime. With the stark conflict of either internalization or exterior projection, the hero's predicament in *Hands of Orlac* stands for an evident if excessive moral about repressed desires, the beast within and the process of alienated labour in which the product of one's own work confronts one in monstrous form. However, because of the frame tale, this aspect of the narrative is, as it were, taken back, given another twist, and the narrative of a nemesis one cannot get rid of when bidding dark forces for assistance, becomes a story about fascination itself, about hypnosis and manipulation, making the 'gothic' tale into yet another meta-narrative about the cinema itself. But the relation of frame to tale in *Hands of Orlac* also gives some especially clear insight into another function of complex narratives in German cinema. For the reversibility between tale and frame either yields a cognitive dissonance or contradiction that, once posited, is irresolvable unless it causes a shift in the terms in which it is posed (the shift being signalled or accomplished by the different levels of the tale following their own logic), or it shows that a dialectic of cognition and miscognition operates between tale and frame, in which case the moment of 'truth' is deferred indefinitely, as in *Dr Caligari*.

Frame tales, besides foregrounding the act of telling itself, thus draw attention to the personality, the state of mind or motives of the one who is narrating the tale. This is the case when a character is telling 'his' story to another character (like Francis, in *Dr Caligari* talking to a fellow inmate, after he has seen his former fiancée, Jane, pass by in the garden). Or he may be tormented by a memory, reliving it or being reminded of it by something or someone, as with the hero of *Phantom* (F.W. Murnau, 1922), finally plucking up the courage to relate his terrible tale to his wife. The split story world may be in the form of a dream, as in *Hands of Orlac*, or the hero's own fictional stories may come alive and appear to him, as he falls asleep, exhausted (*Waxworks*, Paul Leni, 1923). The latter is similar to *Destiny* (Fritz Lang, 1921), which *Waxworks* both imitates and parodies. As in many fairy tales, both films establish through the frame a narrative situation, in which one of the characters allows another three chances, three wishes, three adventures, with the protagonist appearing both inside the stories and in the framing tale. These cases are in turn related to films where a visitor, arriving unannounced or under slightly mysterious circumstances, sets in train a chain of events that necessitates the putting on of a play or a charade (*Schloß Vogelöd*, *Tartuffe*, both F.W. Murnau), or where the visitor is a strangely melancholy magician (*Warning Shadows*, Arthur Robison, 1923; *Der Verlorene Schatten*, a Paul Wegener film, 1921). Flashback structures without a double plot line acting as a frame can also be found in *Zur Chronik von Grieshuus* (Arthur von Gerlach, 1925) and several other films adapted from well-known nineteenth-century short stories by Theodor Storm or Hermann Sudermann.

Two of the most interesting films of this type are the already mentioned *Destiny* and *Waxworks*. In both films, there is not only a framing device, but in addition, a narrative in which three episodes are linked: episodes which in time, setting and mood seem very different from each other, but have elements in common that function at one and the same time iteratively as repetition, and cumulatively as intensification. Are the different episodes meant to illustrate the framing tale, or is the frame merely there to motivate the episodes? If the latter, does the frame tale, by creating a full-length, multi-reel feature film out of essentially single-reel story material, refer back to the conditions of production and exhibition of an earlier period of the institution of cinema, or rather, is the film 'citing' this earlier moment of film history, and thus creating a transtemporal, transnational *mise-en-abyme*? For with a film like *Destiny* one immediately thinks of D.W. Griffith's *Intolerance* (1916), which might be said to have brought the form of longer narratives to perfection, assembled from episodes different in setting and characters, but united by a common theme. But the parallel with *Intolerance* makes the differences the more noticeable. In the German film, the iterative structure serves not a moral point or a historical argument, and instead, responds to a problem that the frame itself posits. In *Destiny*, it is the relation between the heroine, her lover, the community and the stranger who comes to town that the frame at first hierarchises and then reverses. In fact, one senses that the story of the three candles is mostly there to articulate a particular sense of transgression felt by the young woman, though the reason for her trespass is not clear, except that it expresses itself in two initial gestures: covering the (all too phallic) head and neck of a goose in the carriage, and picking up an innocent kitten (as in *Nosferatu*), as if she were aware of Death as the alien presence, yet secretly in league with him – also rather like Nina in *Nosferatu*, who is (unconsciously) in league with the vampire. In both films, then, female desire – as in *Dr Caligari* and Jane's demon-lover Cesare – would seem to be the hidden narrative trigger as well as a source of spectatorial attraction.

In *Waxworks* the relation between framing story and the episodes at first seems simpler than in *Destiny*. Each story not only doubles the basic situation of the young writer in love with the daughter of the fairground owner, but each episode also provides both a punishing father figure and a benevolent one, until, in the final episode in which frame and tale come together, Jack the Ripper acts as the murderous father, allowing the girl's 'real' father to come to the writer's rescue, in a scene in which initially, the penniless writer could not hope to be accepted as suitor by the gruff fairground showman. Thus, quite craftily, the different episodes 'resolve' the problem, work out the contradiction of how the man who gives the hero a job, apparently so lowly in status that by that same token, he would not give him his daughter, can become his employer as well as his father-in-law. The two episodes therefore depict a young man, stand-in for the hero-dreamer, engaged in a gesture or act of defiance against a potentate, with disastrous results, were it not, in each case, for a young woman, prepared to commit an act of perfidy or treason in order to help her lover. Two limbs – a severed arm in one episode and the disembodied dummy in the other, underscore the 'castration' motif that *Waxworks* shares with *Hands of Orlac*, while exchanging more than a knowing wink with both *Dr Caligari* and *Destiny*. That the writer, as he falls asleep, seems to 'stab' himself with his pen, only adds (a) further (l)ink to the chain of castration anxieties, but with a sarcastic–sadistic comment on the central conflict of the *Kino-Debatte*, namely the rearguard battle of the literary establishment – the writers – to retain their cultural capital, while some of their less high-minded colleagues are prepared to 'sell out' to the cinema, here once more, as in *Dr Caligari*, depicted as a fairground.

Ambiguous narratives or narratives of ambiguity?

Destiny and *Waxworks* both employ repetition, as a way of making – in this comparable to myths and folk tales – a deep structure apparent that might otherwise be missed. However, while this imitates the 'three wishes' division of folk tales and fairy tales, the actual effect of the nesting of the narratives in the films is to create an ambivalence of affect or mood, to suspend and retain as indeterminate the primary relations between the characters, and in particular, the feelings between father and son (and enfolded into it, between father and daughter, as in *Waxworks*). In other words, unlike some of the examples quoted above, where the frame appears to be 'inverting' the tale by undermining the referentiality of the narrative, the frame may also act as something that signals a disavowal, while at the same time sustaining a central emotional tension or cultural (gender) contradiction.

An intriguing case is Murnau's *Phantom*, the story of the solitary bookworm who is accidentally run over by the chariot of a woman dressed in white, and who after recovering, develops a passion for the phantom lady. This unhappy love leads him to theft, embezzlement and finally to becoming an accessory to murder. After his release from prison, he is met by the young woman he had spurned in favour of the mystery lady, but who had, of course, remained faithful to him all the while. Accompanied by her father, they return to a house in the country where, once married, they can live happily ever after. However, the film is framed by the new bride entreating her husband to write down the story of his obsession, in order to rid himself of the troubling vision. This idea, to confess and thus to liberate himself from the phantom, motivates the story that is then told. The plot of the film is almost too complicated and there are also gaps in the story, possibly due to an incomplete print, so that it is the frame tale and several other moments that enable the viewer to condense a complex sequence of actions into a relatively simple narrative scheme. A contradiction between the story and its narration is evident right from the start (with a man, deeply troubled for no apparent reason, being led back into the house by his wife), which seems to be the main reason for the narrative convolutions. It is as if the film needed not only the frame tale and its displacements, but in addition, all the twists and turns of the plot in order to simultaneously reveal and conceal the complexity or contradictions at issue. Assuming the frame story's function as a signifier of disavowal, one realises that the knowledge *Phantom* cannot admit to is the hero's incestuous fixation on his sister, which – necessarily repressed – produces the phantom lady, in the end no more than a pretext for him to be able to follow his sister, get involved with her underworld lover, and prove himself as his equal, if necessary, in crime: in a bungled robbery, they brutally murder an old lady. However, while on one level the framing story acts as a therapeutic device, meant to rid the hero of his phantom, when at the end of the film the action returns to the frame, one notices that the contradiction has only deepened, for while telling his story may have therapeutically cured the hero of his phantom lady, the incestuous desire it was supposed to 'screen' and disguise, has – quite logically, in a sense – been rekindled in its full ambiguity. On the very path from which the wife has, at the beginning of the film, recalled her husband to sit at his desk, the sister suddenly arrives, as if conjured up by the writing of the story and the intensity of her presence is evoked in the hero. In this respect, *Phantom* can usefully be compared to *Dr Caligari* and even more so to *Variety*, where the framing device also exacerbates the original obsessions of the Emil Jannings character, and his sadomasochistic penchant, even though, here, too, the frame tale is motivated by a confession and the desire for atonement. Another, especially convoluted example of multiply nested narratives via a flashback structure is *Der Turm des Schweigens* (1924, Johannes Guter) in which two stories of betrayal – that of an aviator by his friend, and that of a husband by his wife are narrated not only as mirrors in relation to each other and shifted in time across two successive generations, but also joined through a flashback structure and a letter left by the older man, into a kind of endlessly reversible Möbius strip. Announcing the family melodrama of Rotwang and Frederson over the lost Hel from *Metropolis* and adapting the central plot conjunction of Murnau's *Schloß Vogelöd*, the film combines a contemporary setting of motor cars and aeroplanes with medieval bell towers, terrible family secrets and oedipal rivalry.[63]

Similarly related to the frame tale in this respect is the extremely elliptical story telling in films like *The Last Laugh*, *Schloß Vogelöd*, and *Shattered*, the repetition of near-identical incidents, or the proliferation of plot situations in *Phantom*, *Waxworks* and *Variety*. A frame tale, gaps in the story and complex plots produce convolutions in the narration, by withholding and yet underlining information: mechanisms necessitated by the contradictory emotions of remorse, anxiety and desire attached to the dramatic predicaments. The story, rather than becoming difficult to follow because of ellipses and inversions, can only be told by using such devices. They allow simultaneously both affirmation *and* denial, camouflaging what needs to be there but cannot be said out loud or openly endorsed. The framing device acts as a barrier or bar, an instance of narrational self-censorship, becoming the sign of a contradiction that the layered narration is called upon to repair, but where the (oedipal) configuration might itself be no more than a ruse, smoothing over other conflicts. One wonders if the oedipal triangles are themselves already an elaboration and at the same time, a containment of something else? Their very excessiveness hints at them being not the structure of the structure, but its rationalisation. What is at stake is that the films posit insoluble problems, which are either put in repetition, *ad infinitum* and *en-abyme*, or they are given an inadequate solution by a closure through reversal and narrative framing. Since this feature is again constant in both the so-called 'expressionist' films of the early decade and the 'realist' ones of the second, it suggests that the strategy is itself a secondary effect of another structure. Once again, the narrative of *Dr Caligari* can stand as an exemplar, for reasons that are distinct from the so-called Expressionist sets.

For besides alerting the spectator to the different levels of credibility of the tale being told, framing can also suspend reference across a dual circuit of mediation, but also miscommunication. In *The Nibelungen*, for instance, not only are there competing narrators, e.g. Mime and Rüdiger, but the effect of their intervention is to kindle in their respective addressees a desire for one another. Because neither realises that they thus become both subject and object for each other, an almost imperceptible nesting of the two narratives sustains a self-deceiving idealising dialogue between these two lovers-to-be, but one that only the spectator can recognise as such. Siegfried, after forging his sword in Mime's hovel chances to overhear the men outside speak of Kriemhild, which promptly makes him fall in love with her as a result of the stories they tell about her. Also, while Kriemhild listens to Rüdiger singing of Siegfried's heroic deeds, she, too, is determined to fall in love with him. Each is thus 'destined' for the other, before either has met. Desire here becomes the desire for the narrative image the self has of the other, in a double narcissism that creates a powerful 'absence' of agency and drive, in which the spectators can invest their own imaginary: the often noted 'static effect' of Lang's film has here its rationale because the apparent lack of movement is the result, as in the tableaux of *Dr Caligari*, of too many contesting forces finding themselves compressed in one shot or scene. The drama is not only initiated this way but subsequently continues to turn on the presence of mutually sustaining or confirming narrators, to which different positions of knowledge and secrecy correspond, such as Kriemhild knowing about Siegfried having defeated Brunhild in Gunther's stead: registers of information and trust are brought into play, as the drama unfolds, with eventually tragic consequences, as when Kriemhild fatally entrusts Hagen with the secret of Siegfried's vulnerability.

More generally, in *The Nibelungen*, none of the relations that the characters have with one another are ever directly dialogical.[64] This is also true of other couples in Weimar cinema, who rarely if ever simply interact with each other, face to face, as it were. In clear contrast to classical Hollywood, where the formation of the couple is so central to the narrative economy, such forms of closure in Weimar cinema are rare. Not only is there rarely a 'happy ending', but the couples involved seem too self-engrossed, too reluctant or charged with too much negative energy to even touch each other. On the few occasions when they do, as Emil Jannings and Lya de Putti in *Variety*, Gustav von Wangenheim and Grete Schröter in *Nosferatu*, Carl Fröhlich and Brigitte Helm in *Metropolis*, Fritz Kortner and Ruth Weyher in *Warning Shadows*, or for that matter, Rudolf Forster and Carola Neheri in the *The Threepenny Opera*, it is either a prelude to disaster or there is the implied presence of an 'Other' in relation to whom the encounter is structured, the scene staged, and to whom it is therefore ultimately addressed. The audience is thus not automatically drawn into the image, via the character's movement or his and her look. Spectator identification has to be mobilised more cognitively through inference or intellect, rather than direct perception: the many instances of frontal staging prevent the so-called 'diegetic effect' as does the position occupied by the camera, which generally prevents views that can be identified with the field of vision or point of view of a character in the fiction. Although the example of *Die Nibelungen* is an extreme case, even for Weimar cinema (though not for Fritz Lang, as his other films prove), quite generally it is rarely a question of knowledge or the unravelling of a secret that is revealed at the end of a Weimar narrative. Instead, at issue is the position of knowledge put in crisis, and thereby affecting the spectator's relationship with the symbolic (the voice of truth). At the same time, as the films also consistently question perception as a register of truth, this troubles the spectator's own relationship to the image. The predilection for stylisation, the priority of the act of narration over narrative action, and the emphasis in the films on both the power of vision and its fallibility are some of the more noticeable textual consequences.

A strategy that is complementary to the frame tale are 'over-plotted' plots and parallel narrative strands, as they can be found in virtually all the films of Fritz Lang (e.g. *Dr Mabuse*, *Metropolis* or *Spione*) as well as in some of the films of G.W. Pabst, notably *Secrets of A Soul* (which, famously, thematises the psychoanalytic process),[65] and *Die Freudlose Gasse*, where, in place of a frame tale, Pabst manages an intricate interweaving of four separate plot lines, much the preferred strategy for the latter half of the 'twenties, when frame tales appear far less frequently. Other films in this group, with double or triple plot lines, include: *Tragödie einer Liebe* (Joe May, 1922) *Die Verrufenen* (Gerhard Lamprecht, 1925) and *Mensch ohne Namen* (1932), the latter one of the many films from the early 1930s centring on an amnesiac protagonist,[66] a staple of the films noir of Robert Siodmak and Curtis Bernhardt in France in the 1930s and Hollywood in the 1940s. For more than key lighting or Expressionist stylisation, it is the technique of narrated time determining action time and the split or doubled story world that seems to be the 'legacy' that *Dr Caligari* and Weimar cinema took into exile. Film noir voice-over and flash-back narration, while preserving the Weimar predilection for indirect narration, rarely confuses the logic of the actions. Instead of ambiguity arising from the ellipses and gaps that oblige the viewer to infer the causal links between segments or even between shots, film noir generally adheres to the rules of continuity editing, while none the less making use of off-screen space and, as in Weimar cinema, presenting weak, drifting male protagonists.[67]

Narrational features such as unattributable points of view or multiple story tellers, rather than character psychology (often melodramatic) confer on Weimar cinema the reputation of interiority, since the protagonists' motives have to be guessed or otherwise presumed, which is another consequence of the priority given in Weimar films to the coherence of space: time in Weimar cinema is neither the medium of duration nor of change. There is little sign, for instance, of such typical Hollywood devices as the deadline structure or of 'timing' as a source of suspense. Instead, the progress of the narrative depends on making sense of the image as a motivated view, as an image for somebody, by somebody: attributing something to a subject. Power relations are articulated via the gaze, that is, who is controlling the field of vision, who is looking at whom without being seen, who can immobilise whom by looking at whom. The most extreme example of this structure is *Dr Mabuse the Gambler*, but it is equally in evidence in films like *Shattered*, *Variety* and *The Last Laugh*. Yet the gaze and its power also encompass another pole, the pleasure of constituting oneself as the object of someone's look: it, too, is a form of subjectivation. A film like *The Last Laugh* (1924) is entirely structured around the ambivalences of catching the other's look, the hero oscillating between the anxieties of being detected (as a lavatory attendant) and the corresponding pleasures of being admired (as a doorman). A similar obsession can be found in Karl Grune's *Die Straße/The Street* (1923), which plays on the dialectic of guilty voyeurism and repressed exhibitionism. The protagonist, a middle-aged hen-pecked husband is lured to the outside world by the bright lights of the city reflected on the ceiling of his stuffy room. He breaks out, in search of 'life', falling prey to a prostitute whose pimp manages to frame him for a murder he did not commit. Eventually freed, he returns ruefully to his wife. Again, much of the drama of his sudden temptation, moral fall and therapeutic restitution is played out across the metaphors of sight. For instance, a shot of the prostitute blinking with her eyes (rather like Cesare in *Dr Caligari*) is followed by a huge pair of eyes, the sign outside an optician's shop, suddenly lighting up, as if to mock the hero's curiosity. At the street corner, a blind old man is led by his granddaughter, who twice makes a spectacle of herself in order to attract the attention of the police, once to alert the officers to the scene of the murder, the second time to bring the traffic to a halt. The murder victim, a man from the country, shows off his fat wallet, and in one of the most phantasmagoric scenes, the prostitute next to him turns into a death's head, though only the spectator is aware of this transformation, since the hero looks straight into the camera, dividing the plane of the picture into two, rather like the famous anamorphic projection in Hans Holbein's *The Ambassadors* in which the skull falls like a blur across the frontal composition. In *Die Strasse*, too, the spectator is obliged to adopt two viewpoints at once – one alluring, one horrific – as if the film were less concerned with 'punishing' the hero's rebellion, than with gleefully tabooing the spectator's visual pleasure, demonising it, before giving it an 'oedipal' twist with its imagery of castration anxiety and violent murder. Interiorisation and subjectivisation seem to converge with the weak male, to configure a particularly potent form of powerlessness.

The uncanny, or the powerless power of the gaze

The Street here follows the practice of several Weimar films that revolve around the motivated view (often not identical with the classic point-of-view shot) and the power of off-screen space, as a double structure that regulates, but also suspends the characters' positions within the film. In particular, off-screen space becomes the signifier of a source of power that forever escapes the protagonists' control. It creates the structure of excess already mentioned and which the point-of-view shots can never quite recover or contain. As in *The Street* and *The Last Laugh*, there always seem to be more pairs of eyes in a Weimar film than there are characters on the screen. While motivated views are very frequent, the reverse-field shot is in fact rather rare, and off-screen space retains its powers of suggestion, menace, dread.[68] One might generalize and say that what typifies this cinema is that power is equated with vision, and vision with knowledge, and knowledge with control, and control with anxiety in a power/anxiety/knowledge nexus almost entirely mapped on the axis seeing/unseen/being seen. The dynamic is thus circular, or rather, it functions according to interlocking gradients, rather like the children's game where scissors, stone and paper each has the power to defeat or neutralise the other. This very dialectic of motivated look, on-screen and off-screen space in the German cinema also determines the viewing positions of the spectator, and is responsible for the problematic status of the image, where one often has the impression that the image is both hyper-real (because invested with emotional significance) and unreal (because insufficiently articulated within a time–space continuum or a chain of cause and effect). Attention is directed towards off-screen space, emphasising what is not seen but must be there, and thus invoking a (symbolic) absent cause, invested by the spectator with imaginary power, encouraging him to give shape and substance to the invisible. Conversely, the sheer weight of this invisibility makes the space and action that the audience does see an always-already-seen-space, readable either as a visual configuration that 'belongs' to some other presence, or as an iconographic allegory that requires interpretation.[69] As Janet Bergstrom has suggested, especially in relation to Murnau and Lang, narrative progress in Weimar cinema is achieved by discontinuity and gaps, binding but also 'trapping' the spectator in elliptical constructions, so that one of the filmic codes most relevant for narrative development is not seeing/seen, but seen/unseen, or seen/inferred, that is, the action advances across the imaginary space generated by the off-screen gaze.[70] Perception being so often the most fallible and deceptive of indices to truth, it can be questioned by and subordinated to off-screen space. Following Mary Ann Doane, one might say that in the German cinema, there is also a problem about object relationships: seeing/seen is differently valorised because the gaze so often does not have an object, or does not 'fetishise' its object. Instead of the reverse-field, point-of-view structure so central to classical narrative, one finds that no clear subject–object relations are allowed to develop, on which the narrative referents might be mapped. Rather, the field of vision tends to lead to phobic or paranoid states, often connoted by the 'double', which is to say, giving rise to a narcissistic structure, where the subject appears in the place of an 'Other' along either a temporal or spatial axis of division and discontinuity.[71]

Spectator positions are thus marked by the same lack of knowledge, the same anxiety that characterises the protagonists: torn between on-screen space, which seems insufficient and off-screen, which is ('dread-fully') unknowable, the spectator is locked into the fiction as a split subject. It is this uncomfortable, anxious subject position that makes Weimar films often seem to be a taxingly concentrated experience. American cinema of the 'teens, and especially the early films of Griffith were not without their own forms of non-continuity and tableau shots, but they avoided narrational ambiguity (Griffith, for instance, was not comfortable with off-screen space), even where the settings were stylised (as in the 'expressionistically' lit interiors of Ralph Ince and Cecil B. de Mille).[72] Yet by the 1920s the German cinema had developed a narrative system that classical Hollywood had begun to marginalise,[73] and this divergence between American and German practice may be why the German films have elicited so many divergent psychological, sociological and ideological–political readings, appearing incomprehensible unless made coherent thanks to an imagined referent (in the case of Kracauer, nascent Nazism; for others, the trauma of the First World War). Retrospectively identified, such historical referents must be secondary effects, in the eye of the beholder, because the films withhold such certainty. Kracauer's political thesis, for instance, requires that he interprets the films' special visuality and non-linear temporality as 'premonition'. He treats Weimar narratives as if the default value was the Hollywood norm, with a clear articulation of space and time, whose lack in Weimar films he interprets as a sort of future perfect of 'anticipation'. But the films put in crisis the very notion of a textual norm, along with a stable authority, a reliable narrator and a voice of truth. It would seem that the underlying indecidability of many of the key Weimar narratives are a further indication that what is at issue is a particular kind of engagement with the spectator, rather than a 'representation' of external reality, social or psychological, present, past or future. What one retains from the films is thus not the political tendencies one can extrapolate, but their *resistances* to such extrapolations, their constitutive hesitation or doubleness – in short, their investment in something other than, or apart from, narrative as the depiction of character-centred action.

Weimar directors, in other words, had a very precise notion of the relation between narrative structure, genre and narration, but paradoxically, they were in the service of sustaining indeterminacy at all costs, at all levels, as it were: narrational ambiguity, created by non-continuous editing, off-screen space and the deferred optical point-of-view, as in films like *Nosferatu*, *The Last Laugh*, *The Nibelungen*, but found also in lesser-known films such as *Shattered* or *Phantom*; indecidability of the shot, as in *Faust* or *Warning Shadows*; and finally, hybridity and anachronism of genre, as in the gothic–fantastic detective films that range from

Dr Caligari, *Dr Mabuse the Gambler* (Fritz Lang, 1921) and *The Street*, to *Secrets of a Soul* (G.W. Pabst, 1926), *Spione* (Fritz Lang, 1928) and *Asphalt* (Joe May, 1929). One concept that has seemed useful in accounting for such plot ambiguity and inversion of agency is that of 'The Uncanny', as proposed by Freud in his analysis of *The Sandman*, a novella by E.T.A. Hoffmann, an author often cited as precursor for the screenwriters of *The Student of Prague* or *Dr Caligari* because of his tales of lost shadows, sudden doubles and the 'return of the repressed'. Samuel Weber has drawn some very pertinent implications from Freud's concept:

> Uncanny is a certain indecidability which affects and infects representations, motifs, themes, and situations. […] But the uncanny is not merely identical with this in-decidability: it involves and implies a second moment or movement, namely the defence against this crisis of perception and phenomenality, a defence, which is ambivalent and expresses itself in the compulsive curiosity, […] the craving to penetrate, discover and ultimately to conserve the integrity of perception: perceiver and perceived, the wholeness of the body, the power of vision, all this implies a denial of that almost-nothing which can hardly be seen, a denial that in turn involves a certain structure of narration, in which this denial repeats and articulates itself.[74]

Weber explicitly links perception and the gaze with both indecidability and its disavowal. Although he is discussing literature of the fantastic, from Hoffmann via Poe to Dostoevsky and Henry James, the borrowings of romantic and gothic motifs in early Weimar films not only fit his description, his analysis might point to an important function which uncanny moments and their 'un'location in time fulfil in Weimar cinema: they are part of a strategy of defence. Rather like the remnants of the detective plots in *Dr Caligari*, the uncanny preserves an ambivalence of wanting to know and not wanting to know, in an attempt to keep intact the body of the perceiver in the act of perception, hoping to give himself control over his own lack of control.[75]

Such a notion of 'defence' and protection from knowledge opens up a new perspective on Kracauer's analysis of the contemporary target audience: the anxious male of the Weimar petit-bourgeoisie, whom he claimed the lost war and inflation had robbed not only of savings and a job, but of pride, dignity and manliness. Driven by fear and resentment, unsure of his social status and class identity, so the theory goes, the visions, dreams and nightmares on the screen spoke on his inner behalf. And indeed, the initial situation of *Dr Caligari* contains a social aspect involving class/status differences. One sees Caligari, shortly after he has arrived in Holstenwall, deferentially asking for a permit to put up his tent-show, only to be treated to insult and humiliation by the town clerk and his subordinates. The scene deftly conveys the psychologically fraught experience of feeling at once outraged and powerless in the face of an arrogant, petty

Figure 6 Humiliated by the town-clerk, Dr Caligari (Werner Krauss, left) contemplates revenge
Source: BFI films: stills, posters and designs

bureaucracy: but while the spectators in Caligari's situation could only murmur exasperated imprecations, he is in a position to act on his impulses, taking revenge on the hated town clerk via his medium, Cesare, setting off the chain of events that make up the narrative. But if Kracauer found these fears reflected in the films, he did not go far enough in analysing the processes of their representation. For such feelings (if they existed) underwent on the screen a double inversion: fear of humiliation, first of all, disguised itself as its opposite, the ambition of social mobility and economic success, but by another inversion, it returned as horror and uncanny, because experienced as transgression. The ambition is heavily punished, the revolt is defeated. In order for this whole complex to become representable, it furthermore undergoes a generic transformation: from being 'in reality' a very modern, metropolitan anxiety about how to survive in an upwardly mobile meritocratic–democratic society, social status in *Dr Caligari* is represented as a 'fantastic–gothic' motif, with wizards, somnambulists and sorcerers' apprentices. Even in this disguised form, it is curiously disavowed. The narrative may start with hinting at a problem of class or status, but then veers off in a quite different direction, never coming back to the issue of status or class. Instead of Caligari's humiliation expressing itself in open revolt, a commensurate omnipotence becomes associated with his powers of hypnotism, which seem to overcompensate for his social impotence, relating the story structurally also to the fairy tale of the sorcerer's apprentice. With Caligari's medium Cesare, as in the Golem, Frankenstein and other machine-men, a force is set free that escapes its creator's control and may even turn against him. One is never quite sure whether the medium's nightly sorties are all planned and ordered by his master or if they take on a momentum of their own. But Cesare is also Caligari's double: the medium is the embodiment of his master's rebellious, anti-authoritarian streak, itself standing in apparent contradiction to Caligari's own authoritarianism.

From these examples, one can conclude that the frame tale and its related devices neither serve a merely formal function nor do they symbolise extra-cinematic referents. Their purpose is to retain for the narrative a fundamental ambiguity and indecipherability, mainly, as suggested, to 'protect' the male hero from self-knowledge, and to displace into issues of memory and trauma (and thus present as a crisis of perception, recollection and cognition) what are typically ambivalent feelings of hostility – resentment or rebellion – in these instances, towards a father, a friend or incestuous desires for a sister. Yet such psychological-narrative motives are themselves more like metaphors, allowing the films to maintain duality, reversibility and ambivalence, whose correlative is not irrationality, but irony, scepticism and an affirmation of radical doubt. In promoting these kinds of enlightened ambiguity, the films are indeed formally extremely inventive, in so far as the device of the frame, inherited from the short story, and in *Dr Caligari* radically transformed for the cinema, is only one of the strategies deployed by Weimar films to this end. Hence the purpose of this chapter, to argue that one needs to be cautious about both formalist readings of 'Caligari's family' and about attributing direct socio-historical referentiality to their symbolic actions. Even the modernist move, where Weimar films partake of a 'meta-cinema' that speaks only 'about' itself, runs the risk of reducing the films' effects of instability to a static allegory. It abstracts from a dynamic cultural listing, ignoring the vivid sensations of synaesthesia as well as the cognitive dissonances that such a form of textuality leaves as its film-historical legacy.

Portrait of the artist as Caligari

At the beginning of the chapter, I put forward the argument that some of the anxieties, but also some of the aggression that cluster around the genre of the Expressionist film in general, and *Dr Caligari* in particular, have to do with a double 'legitimation crisis' affecting the cinema in relation to high culture, and the German film industry in relation to Hollywood. Subtending both, I also suggested, is the social status of the film maker, compared to that of the 'artist' in other fields of cultural practice. As to the latter, film makers such as Wegener, Wiene, Lang and Leni, Murnau and Robison (with their screenwriters Mayer, Galeen and Harbou, art directors Warm, Reimann, Herlth, cameramen Seeber,

Freund and Hoffmann) may well have allegorised their own cultural politics – half-seriously, half-ironically – through their protagonists: their showmen–demiurgues are the wizards of a new magic, not sure whether it was black or white. Sorcerers of a fabulous technology, they seem both reckless and wary of the forces they have summoned. Exercising control as 'artists', afraid of losing control in the corporate bureaucracies of the giant UFA, they may have vampirised traditional culture and the more established arts, but they also learnt how to seduce the public, half exultant, half genuinely concerned about the social consequences. Fritz Lang's interviews and essays in the illustrated magazines and the weekly press throughout his German career were always conscious of what cultural prejudices he had to flatter in order to 'play game', but he also defended film makers on the cinema's own terms: 'Kitsch, Sensation, Kultur und Film.'[76]

Such self-reflexivity and textual mythification can in turn be further contextualised and historicised. For another dimension of this legitimation crisis between high culture and low medium, is the astonishing quality of the films *and their critical reception*: Weimar cinema provoked an unparalleled sophistication among German-speaking intellectuals theorising, commenting and analysing films in the 1920s. 'Today's Film Enemies, Tomorrow's Film Friends' was the title of one of Hans Richter's polemical mid-decade treatises, and it came after Georg Lukacs, Emilie Altenloh, Malwine Rennert, Bela Balasz, Siegfried Kracauer, Rudolf Arnheim, Kurt Tucholsky, Egon Fridell, Rudolf Kurtz and Guido Bagier (to mention only the best-known names) had already published widely on the cinema, while Berlin film critics such as Herbert Jhering, Willy Haas, Hans Siemsen, Alfred Kerr, and of course, Lotte Eisner had, besides day-to-day reviewing, also theorised about the cinema as a new cultural phenomenon.[77] Partly caught in similar contests of legitimation, post-Second World War (German) film historians have, in their perspectives on both Wilhelmine and Weimar cinema, largely followed in the shadow of these authorities, and they have tended to privilege the literary and intellectual 'response' to the emergence of cinema.[78] Given such a preference in favour of the artistic film, the author's film, in short, of a cinema that had to make its own peace with high culture, assessments of Weimar cinema seem often caught more anxiously in the double reflection of high modernism and mass culture than the films themselves, quite self-confidently displaying their ironic militancy.[79]

Thus, the fascination and horror with which subsequent generations would look at the 'Germanness' of this cinema, is in part a mirror effect produced by a strategic over-emphasis on the Expressionist films that, as Wollenberg reminded his readers in 1942, were in the context of overall film production the exceptions, elevated (by cultural, often also commercial, but at any rate historically quite comprehensible factors) to the status of a cinema revelatory of hidden truths, possessing clairvoyant powers or concluding Faustian pacts. It is as if in the films of the fantastic subsequent generations of *cinéphiles* had recognised themselves with a particular kind of *frisson*, the very *frisson* that gave the films the air of divining the future and thus being part of shaping it. Such a meta-historical observation, however, must not be taken too far. It would be foolish to claim that the films now canonised as the 'classics' of the period have nothing more to offer than to be cited as evidence for the intellectual debate of cultural legitimacy or as coded allegories of the film maker's self-understanding, however ironic or complicit the films are about their own ambiguous position between art and the mass-market.[80] Seeing the formal features of Weimar cinema discussed above within the double frame of reference national/international, as well as high culture/popular culture, for example, gives the strategies of hiding and revealing around the narrator and his authority a historical place as instances of mediation in the skirmishes of cultural intervention that have accompanied the cinema ever since. The changing critical fortunes of the German 'classics', often hated by the critics at the time, and in some cases also spurned at the box office,[81] indicate that in the cinema, film text and reception context, aesthetics and film industry interpenetrate each other. The tighter the mesh, the more 'classical' or canonised the work in question, and 'Caligari's family' documents an encounter with the social reality of the Weimar Republic not in direct references to street battles, inflation or unemployment. It testifies to something else, in the end no less historical.[82]

What opens the films of the fantastic towards society are, as argued above, the artist-intellectuals, whose changing relations to cultural capital and cultural production are condensed in the neo-romantic motifs of the sorcerer's apprentice and that of the producer confronting the product of his labour/desire as an alienated self-image. To return to Lotte Eisner's 'romantic fancies': one side of the equation is that the Romantic project of arming the subject against historical experience through inwardness, and transforming inwardness into the sensuous perception of immediacy has found its 'realization' in the cinema, but with a vengeance. Nature returns in the form of the uncanny and the fantastic, because Romanticism wedded to technology produces a reified and thoroughly mediated form of immediacy. Yet the films encounter social reality, besides in the artist as producer, also on the side of the spectators and reception, where self-alienation may take on a different meaning: the new immediacy, this second nature of the technological apparatus, has its own logic. The cinema entered the public sphere of the early 1920s not, as its implacable avant-garde critics had hoped, by 'realistically' documenting the class conflicts and social injustices, but by a bricolage appropriation of a shared stock of fictions, narrative and pictorial, drawn from popular and high culture alike. None the less, as this chapter has argued, even the most 'fantastic' films intervened politically – perversely perhaps – by refusing to take sides, by resisting referentiality, which is to say, refusing to be used either on behalf of rhetoric or reality. By practising stylisation, abstraction and the skills of simulation, they did engage themselves on the other side of the Romantic divide, where technologically mediated immediacy 'realises' the mirror reverse of the uncanny and the fantastic, namely the sensuous presence of the commodity, a realm of images and their 'surface-effects', which solicit aesthetic perception but also social action mainly in the mode of consumption.

It is this emergent other social reality of Weimar culture, with its emphasis on the metropolis and modernity, on the new woman, on life styles and the 'designs for living', which the fantastic cinema on one level attempted to resist, with its oedipal master-narratives acting like fetish-objects of fascination, as if wanting to taboo the changing gender relationships which increasingly shaped Weimar society as it consolidated itself economically. Yet when read from the late 1920s, one can see how the traumatised masculinity of the stylised films abundantly indicates an awareness of its 'other' by the many strategies of disavowal and 'protection from knowledge'. Also, the insistence on ambiguity does not exempt sexual identity from appearing 'reversible' or suspended, and male protagonists in Weimar films are allowed to be effete, to behave childishly and to occupy symbolic positions traditionally coded as 'female':

> In Weimar cinema [...], class identity is usually as strongly marked in both iconographic and narrative terms as sexual identity, and the two are almost always won or lost in the same moment. Typing by social class was so important to Weimar narratives that it often obscured the significance of sexual definition. In Murnau's films, however, [...] femininity, insofar as it can be associated with eroticism or sexuality, has been displaced from the woman's body to several kinds of substitutes. [It] is at a loss literally in that it has a reduced physical presence, lacking a sexual dimension; metaphorically, the symbolic function of the woman's body in establishing sexual difference is greatly diminished.[83]

A reorientation of an 'erotics of looking' was taking place in the direction of contemplation, and thus a redistribution of the relation between sexual object (coded in terms of male or female) and sexual aim (identified around active and passive), with the consequence that identification was supported not by the markers of gender or sexual difference, but by the structure of the fetish and disavowal ('I know, but all the same'). In one of his 1928 essays Kracauer gives a trenchant description of such identification and its subject-effects:

> Films do not cease to reflect society. On the contrary: the more incorrectly they present the surface of things, the more correct they become and the more clearly they mirror the secret mechanisms of society. In reality, it may not often happen that a scullery maid marries the owner of a Rolls Royce. But doesn't every Rolls Royce owner dream that scullery maids dream of rising to his stature?[84]

The twice reversed structure here posited between fairy-tale fantasy, narrative motifs, social structure, class relations and gender gives a good indication of the kind of *mise-en-abyme* of social observation, political formation and popular entertainment that the films in the Caligari tradition were engaged in, distilling those uncanny moments of recognition that may indicate the oblique ways in which film spectators organise and experience their (psychic and social) reality in the cinema. One notes that Kracauer speaks of 'scullery maids,' and the essay is entitled 'Little shopgirls at the movies': his anxious males of the de-mobbed early 1920s had, in the meantime, either found an office job and joined the *Angestellten*, or had joined the street thugs of the Nazi party storm troopers. But Caligari's family had also taken note of the *Zeitgeist*. The actor who so memorably incarnated Cesare in *Dr Caligari* was spotted by the American screenwriter Anita Loos, on a visit to Berlin in 1927:

> Any Berlin lady of the evening might turn out to be a man; the prettiest girl on the street was Conrad Veidt, who later [sic] became an international film star.[85]

If some of the most anxious males could coolly cross-dress as 'one of the girls', maybe all was not lost. Caligari, Anita Loos might have added, was probably using his dummy-double Cesare to model clothes rather than commit nocturnal crimes, though it was the Weimar dandies of the *Neue Sachlichkeit*, writers like Bert Brecht and Alfred Döblin, painters like Otto Dix and George Grosz who were developing *Lustmord* into an art form.[86] Social rise continued to be a film subject – in fact, more than ever – but as Kracauer suggests, in comedies, musicals and revue-films. Class mobility, he once sarcastically remarked, now took the 'up' escalator in a department store.[87] The young men at Decla-Bioskop had consolidated their reputations inside UFA, and the studio executives, including Erich Pommer, knew all about mobility: from the vantage point of gaining respectability and cultural status, Germany's premier film production company had, not least thanks to *Dr Caligari* and its world-wide success, arguably made the steepest rise of all.

Notes

1 John Willet, *The New Sobriety* (London: Thames & Hudson, 1978): 10.

2 Kristin Thompson also punctures Pommer's story of the power shortages, by scrutinising the model that Hermann Warm built in 1970 of the Lixi Studio in Weissensee near Berlin where *Dr Caligari* was filmed (Thompson 1990: 127–36).

3 Kracauer writes: '"Films must be drawings brought to life": this was Hermann Warm's formula at the time', adding that it was a quotation from Rudolf Kurtz 1926: 66. But it is now generally agreed that the phrase is Röhrig's.

4 Hermann Warm later claimed that the film was made in spite of Wiene rather than because of him, and that Pommer refused to authorise the stylised designs. Herman Warm, 'Gegen die Caligari Legenden', in W. Kaul (ed.) *Caligari und der Caligarismus* (Berlin: Stifting Deutsche Kinemathek, 1970): 11–16.

5 One of the odder responses in France seems to confirm the effectiveness of the strategy: 'The Folies-Bergère staged an elaborate review titled "En Pleine Folie", in which Dr. Caligari figured. Interestingly, Caligari appeared as a German arch criminal threatening France – a sort of Dr. Mabuse-like villain.' (Thompson 1990: 154). The Alice-in-Wonderland effect, here, of course, is that Dr Mabuse was Fritz Lang's version of Louis Feuillade's *Fantomas*, his caped and hooded figure famously looming over Paris.

6 Kurt Tucholsky asks sarcastically where, in these rickety houses, would one find such smart clothes and stiff starched collars like those the male characters are wearing? *Die Weltbühne* 16/1 (11 March 1920): 347; Herbert Jhering also notices the female lead's sturdy iron bedstead, arguing that the film lacks the courage of its convictions, dithering too much between popular appeal and highbrow affectation, 'Ein expressionistischer Film', *Berliner Börsen Courier* (29 February 1920).

7 Rudolf Kurtz' *Expressionismus und Film* (1926) (discussed in Part I, Chapter 2, this volume) is a reassessment in response to the international acclaim of *Dr Caligari*.

8 In Lang's case, the sarcasm is understandable, given the intially hostile domestic reaction to his 'expressionist' *Der Müde Tod/Destiny* which turned into grudging praise when critics realised just how unanimously and positively the film was being received in France and elsewhere (see Kracauer 1947: 88–9).

9 Louis Delluc, in his seminal review of *Dr Caligari*, mentions the *Ballet russe* productions of *L'Après-midi d'un faune, Shéhèrazade, Parade* and *Le Sacré du Printemps* in *Cinéa* 44 (10 March 1922): 5.

10 See Leonardo Quaresima, 'Der Expressionismus als Filmgattung', in Jung and Schatzberg 1992: 174–94; and Jürgen Kasten, *Der expressionistische Film* (Münster: MAkS, 1990): 25–38, 175–80. Mike Budd takes a similar view in 'The moments of *Caligari*' (Budd 1990: 19–25).

11 For an overview in English, see Anton Kaes, 'Literary intellectuals and the cinema: The *Kino-Debatte*', *New German Critique* 40 (Winter 1987): 7–34.

12 Guido Seeber, 'Doppelgängerbilder im Film', *Die Kinotechnik* (1919/21): 12–17. See also Guido Seeber, *Der Trickfilm* (Berlin: 1929), reviewed by Sergei Eisenstein in *Close-Up*, May 1929.

13 Corinna Müller, *Frühe deutsche Kinematographie* (Stuttgart: Metzler, 1994).

14 Lotte Eisner, *The Haunted Screen*, 1969: 113.

15 For a scholarly survey, see Raymond Williams, *The Country and the City* (London: Paladin, 1975).

16 Richard Krautheimer to Kracauer, July 1944, in Volker Breidecker (ed.) *Siegfried Kracauer/Erwin Panofsky: Briefwechesel 1941–1966* (Berlin: Akademie Verlag, 1996): 96.

17 A suggestive comparative study of such uneven developments and their effects on family structure, political institutions and culture is J. Barrington-Moore, *The Social Origins of Democracy and Dictatorship* (Harmondsworth: Penguin, 1968).

18 Rudolf Arnheim, 'Expressionistischer Film' (1934), in *Kritiken und Aufsätze zum Film* (Frankfurt: Fischer 1979): 148–50. In France, it was Blaise Cendras who most famously denounced *Dr Caligari* (originally in *Cinéa* (2 June 1922): 11)).

19 The legend of it initially being a flop comes from Erich Pommer: 'At first *Caligari* was a big box-office flop […] so I forced *Caligari* through a poster and publicity campaign. We had posters all over Berlin, with Conrad Veidt and the words "You must see *Caligari*", "Have you seen *Caligari*", etc.' Cited in George A. Huaco, *The Sociology of Film Art* (New York: Basic Books, 1965): 34. This, in fact, repeats an advertising campaign from 1913, around the Max Mack film *Wo ist Coletti.* See Michael Wedel, *Max Mack, Showman im Glashaus* (Berlin: Freunde der Deutschen Kinemathek, 1996).

20 Paul Rotha, *The Film Till Now* (London: Jonathan Cape, 1930): 94.

21 Parker Tyler, *Classics of the Foreign Film* (New York: Bonanza, 1962): 13–14.

22 Rudolf Kurtz argued that '*Caligari* sounded a chord whose volume and resonance has not been augmented by its successors', adding:

> from the point of view of the commodity-form film, Expressionism disappears like a thin shadow. […] Schematically speaking, the product must be able to earn as much as it cost to make, plus profits. A situation must exist, where this relation can

be guaranteed. In Germany, the lower limit of consumers for the film industry stands at around ten million. Any film that cannot win the approval of this number is bad for the film industry, because it damages its capital base.

(*Expressionismus und Film* (Berlin: Lichtbildbühne, 1926): 69, repr. Zurich: Rohr, 1965)

23 Kristin Thompson has pointed out that exhibition practice at the time of *Dr Caligari* was still that of the 'Monopolfilm' introduced in Germany around 1911/12, i.e. with a limited run at an exclusively booked venue. Only with the mid-1920 *Grossfilme* did UFA adopt the 'open run' practice of the blockbuster. It was the 1925 revival of *Dr Caligari* that, with its international fame securely surrounding it like a halo, that established its canonical status.

24 Max Osborn, 'Die Lage des Expressionismus', *Vossische Zeitung* 8 November 1920, cited in Quaresima 1990: 175.

25 Rudolf Arnheim, 'Dr Caligari redivivus', *Das Stachelschwein* 19 (October 1925): 47.

26 The trade journal *Die Lichtbildbühne*, in its issue of 11 September 1920 reports on a newly opened Decla-Bioskop cinema in the Berlin suburbs, 'entirely decorated in the Expressionist manner'. Evidently, *Caligari*'s production firm quickly realised the film's value as a brand-name promoter.

27 For implicit and explicit rejoinders to Thompson, see Hardt 1996: 45–51 and David Pratt, 'Fit food for madhouse inmates.' The Box Office Reception of the German Invasion of 1921. *Griffithiana* 48/9 (October 1993): 97–157. For a recent discussion of the history of the screenplay, as well as the French novelisation, see Leonardo Quaresima, 'Die Geburtsurkunde des *Caligari*', *film-dienst* 5 (1992): 16–18.

28 Kurtz 1926: 46.

29 Janowitz's story and Kracauer's endorsement of it have been largely discredited by Gero Gandert's acquisition, on behalf of the Stiftung Deutsche Kinemathek Berlin, of an early version of the screenplay from the estate of Werner Krauss, the actor playing Dr Caligari. There, it transpires that the script had always opened with a prologue leading into a flashback. This prologue 'neutralised' the supposedly revolutionary message more effectively than the framing tale of the film as it was eventually made. For a summary, see Budd 1990: 28–9.

30 Erich Pommer, 'Carl Mayer's debut', in *The Cabinet of Dr Caligari* (Classic Film Scripts, New York: Simon & Schuster, 1972): 27–9. For a discussion of the contract between Mayer, Janowitz and Decla, see Jürgen Kasten, 'Die Vetrăge des *Dr Caligari*' in M. Schaudig (ed.) *Positionen deutscher Filmgeschichte* (Munich: diskurs film, 1996): 75–90, which also discusses the subsequent history of the screenplay, the rights, litigations and the attempted and actual remakes of *Dr Caligari*.

31 Roland Barthes, *S/Z* (New York: Hill and Wang, 1975): 90.

32 On Robert Wiene, see Uli Jung and Walter Schatzberg, *Robert Wiene, der Caligari Regisseur* (Berlin: Henschel, 1996): 60–81 and also Mike Budd, 'The Moments of *Caligari*' for another account of the question of rights and remakes (Budd 1990: 32–6).

33 Siegfried Kracauer, 'Notes on the planned history of the German film', appended to a letter to Erwin Panofsky, dated 16 October 1942 (see Breidecker 1996: 17 in note 16 above).

34 Thompson 1990: 156–61 gives a concise summary of the role played by *Dr Caligari* in the origins of the 'art-house' circuits in France, the United States and Britain from 1921 to 1931.

35 Claude Lévi-Strauss, 'The structural study of myth', in *Structural Anthropology* (Harmondsworth: Penguin, 1963): 216–17.

36 For more rigorous structuralist analyses of Weimar films, see Alan Williams, 'A structure of narrativity in Fritz Lang's *Metropolis*', *Film Quarterly* 27/4, (Spring 1974); and John Tulloch, 'Genetic structuralism and the cinema: a look at Fritz Lang's *Metropolis*', *Australian Journal of Screen Theory* 1 (1976): 3–50.

37 'Art cinema narration', in David Bordwell, *Narration in the Fiction Film* (Madison: University of Wisconsin Press, 1985): 234–73.

38 For a concise presentation of 'oedipal' narratives in classical Hollywood, see 'Alternation, segmentation, hypnosis: interview with Raymond Bellour', *Camera Obscura* 3–4 (1979): 71–103.

39 This is a summary of the analysis of some 25 films in a seminar on 'Weimar Cinema', which I taught during the Winter Semester 1977–8 at the University of Iowa. Among the main contributors were Mary Ann Doane, Richard de Cordova, Pamela Falkenberg, Elizabeth Cleere, Tom Powers, Karen Nulf and Van Mensing. See also my 'Film History and Visual Pleasure – Weimar Cinema' (1984).

40 Peter Gay, 'The revolt of the son', 'The revenge of the father', *Weimar Culture* (1968): 102–45.

41 There is a certain tradition to reading this motif in German history and the arts. T.W. Adorno, for instance, in his book on Wagner called him ' a rebel who had changed sides'. T.W. Adorno, *Versuch über Wagner* (Frankfurt: Suhrkamp 1974): 132.

42 Films with First World War settings began to apear around 1927. The first major production to deal with the question of responsibility for starting the war was *1914. Die letzten Tage vor dem Weltbrand* (Richard Oswald, 1931), by which time war films had become a source of controversy (cf. the reception of Lewis Milestone's *All Quiet on the Western Front* (1930) and of G.W. Pabst's *Westfront 1918* (1930)) as well as a mainstream genre of late Weimar sound cinema. See Bernadette Kester, *Filmfront Weimar* (Hilversum: Verloren, 1998).

43 For a discussion of the formation of the family and its oedipal scenarios as the key to a country's social formations, see Barrington-Moore 1968, arguing that kinship serves as the structure through which class conflicts and question of loyalty, authority, betrayal, alliance and rivalry are encoded in literature and the arts. With respect to the cinema, Martha Wolfenstein and Nathan Leites have similarly identified recurring patterns in father–daughter and father–son narratives whose resolution significantly differ in French, American and British cinema of the 1940s and 1950s. Martha Wolfenstein and Nathan Leites, 'The good–bad girl', in *Movies: A Psychological Study* (New York: Atheneum, 1970): 153–69.

44 See John Tulloch, 'Genetic structuralism and the cinema', *Australian Journal of Screen Theory* no. 1 (1976): 16–29.

45 One of the things we have noted about oedipal structures in the German films of the 20s and 30s is their peculiar instability, particularly in the instability of the place of the father. Fathers are displaced and replaced, and those that are displaced reappear to reclaim their place (e.g. *The Testament of Dr Mabuse*). Even when more 'positive' father figures appear to take the place of the ones which have been cast by the narrative as dangerous or destructive, these 'positive' figures, either overtly or covertly, tend to take on the characteristics of the original figure, e.g. the supposedly kindly psychiatrist at the end of *Dr Caligari* [cannot be distinguished from the evil Caligari. …] The position of the mother in these oedipal configurations is also peculiar. Father and son figures compete for her, but they are also ambivalent about her, and in some cases desire to eliminate her altogether. (*The Last Laugh*, *Pandora's Box*, *The Blue Light*).

(Pamela Falkenberg, 'Oedipal structures in French and German Cinema' (unpublished paper, University of Iowa, 1978)

46 Michel Henry, *Le cinéma expressioniste allemand* (Fribourg: Edition du Signe, 1971).

47 Cathérine Clément, 'Charlatans and hysterics', in Budd 1990: 191–204.
48 Thomas Elsaesser, 'Social mobility and the fantastic', in Budd 1990: 171–90.
49 The theatrical or pictorial tableaux scene as a form of 'negative' dramaturgy has been important since Diderot and was taken up by Brecht. In film studies it is associated with melodrama, as part of a particular rhetoric of muteness and self-repression, which also provides a convenient link between social drama, melodrama and early German cinema. See Peter Brooks, *The Melodramatic Imagination* (New Haven: Yale University Press, 1976) and also Patrice Petro, *Joyless Street* (Princeton: Princeton University Press, 1989): 25–36.
50 Noel Burch and Jorge Dana, in 'Propositions', *Afterimage* 5 (Spring 1974): 40–66, discuss *Dr Caligari* as an example of avant-garde neo-primitivism.
51 Tilo Knops, 'Cinema from the writing desk: detective films in Imperial Germany' and Sebastian Hesse, 'Ernst Reicher alias Stuart Webbs; both in T. Elsaesser (ed.) *A Second Life* (Amsterdam: Amsterdam University Press, 1996b): 132–50.
52 Similar to *The Student of Prague*'s thwarted ambitions to status, the violence provoked by the doctor's humiliation is displaced in *Dr Caligari* to another level. For a reading of *The Student of Prague* as an example of the genre of the fantastic overcompensating for the hero's self-perceived lack of social status, see my 'Social mobility and the fantastic', in Budd 1990: 174–8.
53 For an elaboration of how to read the film from Jane's point of view, see Patrice Petro, 'The woman, the monster and *The Cabinet of Dr Caligari*' in Budd 1990: 205–20.
54 One might call *Dr Caligari*, anachronistically, displaying the *Rashomon* effect, after the film by Akiro Kurosawa that famously, after the war, voiced its radical scepticism as to evidentiary truth in the cinema. My contention is that this scepticism is at the heart of much 'Expressionist' cinema.
55 *Dr Caligari* contains a number of (German) visual puns. For instance, Cesare in his box immediately evokes the notion of 'Kadavergehorsam' ('corpse- or coffin-obedience'), the term used in the Prussian army and during the First World War to indicate absolute military submission.
56 Roland Barthes, *S/Z* (trans. Richard Howard; London: Jonathan Cape, 1975): 19.
57 An example of a (late) 'Weimar' film which has given rise to a debate about narration, disambiguation and impossible narrators is Carl Dreyer's *Vampyr* (Germany/Netherlands/France, 1932). See Mark Nash, '*Vampyr* and the fantastic', *Screen* 17/3 (Autumn 1976): 29–67; and D. Bordwell, *The Films of Carl-Theodor Dreyer* (Berkeley: University of California Press, 1981): 107–16.
58 German cinema of the 1920s may have taken over its indirect modes of narration, such as frame tales and flashbacks from Swedish and Danish cinema of the period 1910–1920. But, depending how one defines framing devices and flashbacks, there are many American and European precedents (see Salt 1989: 100–102). Tom Gunning discusses flashback films, e.g. *After Many Years* (1908) in *D.W. Griffith and the Origins of American Narrative Film* (Chicago: University of Illinois Press, 1991): 117–18 (a reference kindly supplied by Karel Dibbets). Charles Musser, in *The Emergence of Cinema* (New York: Scribner, 1990): 478 mentions *When we were Boys* (1907), in which two old men reminisce about their childhood while the film cuts back and forth between the old men and scenes from their childhood. To my knowledge, there exists no systematic discussion of frame tales and other such narrational features in silent cinema. However, a very stimulating theory and history of flashbacks is Maureen Turim, *Flashbacks in Film: Memory and History* (London: Routledge, 1989).
59 'Procession of tyrants' is a chapter heading in Kracauer 1947: 77.
60 Apart from the references above to the accounts of Hans Janowitz, Hermann Warm and Erich Pommer, see Kracauer 1947: 61–72, Walter Kaul (ed.) *Caligari und der*

Caligarismus (Berlin: Stiftung Deutsche Kinemathek, 1970); and David Robinson *The Cabinet of Dr Caligari* (London: BFI Classics, 1996). More recent accounts are in Helga Belach, H.M. Bock (eds) *Das Cabinet des Dr Caligari* (Munich: edition text + kritik, 1997) and Leonardo Quaresima, 'Wer war Alland? Die Texte des *Caligari*', in Bernhard Frankfurter (ed.) *Carl Mayer. Im Spiegelkabinett des Dr Caligari* (Vienna: Promedia, 1997): 99–118.

61 For unreliable narration in classical narrative, see Kristin Thompson, 'Duplicitous narration in [Alfred Hitchcock's] *Stage Fright*', in Kristin Thompson, *Breaking the Glass Armor* (Princeton: Princeton University Press, 1989): 135–61, and Warren Buckland on Fritz Lang's *Secret Beyond the Door* in 'The pragmatics of unreliable filmic narration', in Jürgen Müller (ed.) *Towards a Pragmatics of the Audiovisual*, vol. II (Münster: Nodus 1995): 55–66.

62 Heide Schlüpmann, who first drew attention to the film, raises the interesting issue of narrative authority, given that this is a woman's narrative, addressed to men who have juridical power over her. According to Schlüpmann, women as narrators are very rare, and never appear without being set in an explict framing device. Heide Schlüpmann, *Unheimlichkeit des Blicks* (Frankfurt: Stroemfeld, 1990): 44–5.

63 Wolfgang Jacobsen calls the complex plot and its improbabilities 'grotesque', but concedes that *Der Turm des Schweigens* is an instructive 'failure' because its bricolage of recognisable Weimar plot elements make it seem like a prototype for other, more integrated films, W. Jacobsen, *Erich Pommer* (Berlin: Argon, 1989): 64.

64 For all of Lang's uniquely idiosyncratic talent as a director of interlaced narratives, it is useful to remember that his style did not spring from nowhere, and instead, can be understood as an elaboration of the narrational complexities shared by much of Weimar cinema from the late 1910s onwards.

65 See two detailed essays by Paul Riess: 'Popularize and/or be damned: Psychoanalysis and film at the crossroads in 1925' (1995), and 'Geheimnisse einer Seele: Wessen Film und wessen Psychoanalyse' (1996).

66 The film is discussed in Kracauer 1947: 212.

67 Besides the films of Siodmak and Bernhardt, one could call Jacques Tourneur's female melodrama *Experiment Perilous* (1944) and his film noir *Out of the Past* (1947) outstanding examples of the 'Weimar' style transposed to Hollywood. Generally, 1940s film noir and 1950s melodrama are considered the genres most likely to extend the limits of classical narrative. In both genres, 'seeing/seen' is frequently enfolded in the drama of imaginary sight, indicating their affinity (or pedigree) with Weimar cinema narration.

68 What a detailed analysis of a classic German film, such as *The Student of Prague* suggests is that the filmic code seeing/seen can play an important part in a textual system, without being necessarily tied to the action codes of narrative. Especially in early cinema one finds other filmic codes, such as on screen/off screen, deep staging/shallow staging and the code near/far, which can determine narrative progress and the terms of conflict resolution. See Leon Hunt, 'The *Student of Prague*', in T. Elsaesser (ed.) *Early Cinema: Space, Frame, Narrative* (London: BFI Publishing, 1990): 389–401.

69 For a more extensive discussion of off-screen space, see Pascal Bonitzer, *Décadrages; cinéma et peinture* (Paris: Edition de l'Etoile, 1985).

70 Janet Bergstrom, discussions with the author, Los Angeles, Paris and Berlin, May–August 1983.

71 Mary Ann Doane, *The Desire to Desire: The Woman's Film of the 1940s* (Bloomington: Indiana University Press, 1987).

72 See Barry Salt 1983: 139–43 on elements of 'expressionist' lighting in the 1910 films of Ralph Ince and Cecil B. de Mille.

73 A brief discussion of Griffith and his European followers can be found in T. Elsaesser (ed.) *Early Cinema: Space, Frame, Narrative* (London: BFI Publishing, 1990): 306–13.

74 Samuel Weber, 'The sideshow: or remarks on a canny moment', *Modern Language Notes* 88/6 (1973): 1133.

75 'The strategy through which the Weimar cinema confronts the gaze – a strategy of simultaneous appropriation as representation and implementation as a formal means of structuration – is also the strategy through which it confronts the notion of the 'double and the concept of doubling or repetition.' Mary Ann Doane, 'Narrative strategies in Weimar cinema' (unpublished paper, University of Iowa, 1978): 2.

76 Fred Gehler and Ullrich Kasten (eds) *Fritz Lang: Die Stimme von Metropolis* (Berlin: Henschel 1990a): 202–6. The volume is a montage of Lang quotations, with a reprint of most of the director's public statements to newspapers and the trade press between 1922–32.

77 For a range of the responses to the cinema, see, besides, Anton Kaes (ed.) *Kino-Debatte* (Tübingen: Niemeyer, 1978); also Jörg Schweinitz (ed.) *Prolog vor dem Film* (Leipzig: Reclam, 1990). An English-language account can be found in Sabine Hake, *The Cinema's Third Machine* (Lincoln: University of Nebraska Press, 1994).

78 Among the monographs and anthologies are Ludwig Greve *et al.* (eds) *Hätte ich das Kino* (Stuttgart: Kösel, 1976); Heinz B. Heller, *Literarische Intelligenz und Film* (Tübingen: Max Niemeyer, 1985); Fritz Güttinger (ed.) *Kein Tag ohne Kino* (Frankfurt: Deutsches Filmmuseum, 1984); Helmut Diederichs, *Anfänge deutscher Filmkritik* (Stuttgart: R. Fischer, 1986).

79 Following Noel Burch, I called this essentially male stance the 'Edisonian imaginary' of Weimar cinema. See my 'Film history and visual pleasure: Weimar cinema' (1984a).

80 A number of films, especially in the early 1920s, were produced as advertising fanfares for new (UFA-owned) picture palaces in Berlin. This points to the relation between real estate and film production, and also shows how carefully a specifically bourgeois audience was solicited in metropolitan Berlin. Known critics would be invited to speak before the film, and the ambience was that of an important theatrical opening, with curtain calls for the cast. A vivid description of such a gala opening is by Joseph Roth, cited in Kreimeier 1992: 136–7. By the mid-1920s, press and advertising campaigns had been perfected, especially for a *Großfilm*. The press books for *Die Nibelungen* (1924), *Faust* (1925) or *Metropolis* (1926), for example, feature extensive instructions about marketing strategies and envisaged audience appeal.

81 One thinks of *Metropolis* or *Faust*, but these were box office failures only to the extent that they did not fulfil what turned out to be unrealisable, because unrealistic expectations, tied to the Parufament Agreement: to break into Hollywood's domestic market, and become block-busters in America itself.

82 See, for instance, Fritz Lang's own account of the first day of shooting on his film *Halbblut*, during the Spartakist uprisings. Its probably apocryphal character merely adds to its allegorising gesture (cited in Gehler and Kasten 1990: 19).

83 Janet Bergstrom, 'Sexuality at a loss: The films of F.W. Murnau', *Poetics Today* 6/1–2 (1985) 186–92.

84 'The little shopgirls go to the movies', Kracauer 1995: 292.

85 Anita Loos, *A Girl Like I* (New York: Viking, 1966): 128.

86 Maria Tatar, *Lustmord: Sexual Murder in Weimar Germany* (Princeton: Princeton University Press, 1995).

87 Siegfried Kracauer, *Die Angestellten*, in *Schriften* in Karsten Witte (ed.), vol. 1 (Frankfurt/M: Suhrkamp, 1971): 286.

4

ERICH POMMER

'Die UFA' and Germany's bid for a studio system

Introduction

The Universal Film Aktien Gesellschaft, better known as UFA, and founded in 1917, was the largest film corporation Germany has ever had. During its heyday in the 1920s and already well before it became a state monopoly under Nazi rule in the course of the late 1930s, it dominated the national film business. Engine and power-house, obliging domestic competitors to do battle on its terms, UFA also held a commanding position in international and transnational trade. Throughout Continental Europe, but also in South America and the Middle East, it had no rival except for the Hollywood Majors.

This much can be stated without courting controversy. But almost every other assertion about UFA remains disputed territory. Why was UFA founded: as the propaganda arm of the German military or as a belated but none the less far-sighted business venture? Who controlled it? Was it the banks, the politicians, the German chemical and electrical industry or film-obsessed entrepreneurs? What were its management principles? Was the main objective to become a media empire in order to wield political influence, or was management geared (not always successfully, as it turned out) to maximise profit for its corporate shareholders? Was UFA a company that proved to be a seedbed of technical innovation, or did it simply plunder and swallow up the best talents from among the independent production sector, before it turned them into desk-bound bureaucrats? Was UFA an important centre for production or did its power come from controlling film distribution? Did it sacrifice financial prudence and gamble away its assets with *Großfilme*, the super-productions from the mid-1920s, self-consciously advertised as filmic masterpieces in order to win American audiences, or was it bread-and-butter productions, the home-grown genre films, with which it periodically regenerated itself, but also often miscalculated?

Fortunately, the literature on UFA is now so copious and accessible that most interested readers may form their own judgement.[1] But in so far as UFA has become virtually synonymous with the 'grandeur and decadence' of the German cinema in its (first) classical period, the 'historical imaginary' surrounding UFA has given rise to a number of 'master-narratives', which need to be briefly sketched before putting a slightly different perspective on the vexed question of whether there ever existed an UFA style of cinema, and what might be its characteristics.

Dream factory of the people or ideological arms factory of the nation?

Accounts of UFA generally follow a path, where chronology and periodisation shadow quite closely the sociopolitical development of the Weimar Republic. A less than perfect democracy is struggling to survive between revanchist feudalism and technocratic modernity, leading to failure and collapse, for which UFA is sometimes held responsible. What gives a semblance of credibility to UFA's sinister role is that its history does bring together a number of military, political and high-finance protagonists (Erich Ludendorff, Emil Georg von Stauß, Alfred Hugenberg and Ludwig Klitzsch), whose role in the politics of Weimar has been, at the very least, ambiguous. Paralleling this political narrative, UFA can be presented as the sorry tale of waste and profligacy by its managers, of megalomania and hubris by its directors, before falling into the hands of Joseph Goebbels, Hitler's propaganda minister, with the consequence that the UFA empire was speedily dismantled by the Allied Control Commission in 1945, thereby assuring that Germany would never again have a film industry to challenge the supremacy of Hollywood. This story schema, inherited from writing about the origins of the 'Thousand Year Reich', has long served as the narrative foil for UFA in the more popular literature. In more recent scholarship, prompted to some extent by the 75th anniversary of the company in 1992, a number of versions of UFA's history are vying for accuracy and acceptance. They can be summed up as follows:

- UFA is the child of the *Wehrmacht*, and therefore Government-instigated in order to coordinate German war propaganda. Such inauspicious beginnings account for UFA's militaristic, Prussian, right-wing, ultra-conservative outlook, an ideological mix that remains intact right through to the company's takeover by Alfred Hugenberg in 1927. This contains many of the features of the causal narrative just mentioned: 'from Ludendorff to Hugenberg, from Hugenberg to Goebbels'. It focuses on the 'field-grey' productions during the last year of the war, the *Nibelungen* films of the mid-1920s, the *Fredericus Rex* films from *Die Tänzerin Barberina* to *Der Herrscher*, or films from the early sound period such as *Der Weltkrieg*, *Das Flötenkonzert von Sanssouci*, *Flüchtlinge* and *Morgenrot*.
- UFA's history is 'overdetermined' in its economic, political, industrial structure, allowing for exceptions (artistic masterpieces), ideological ruptures (films with a liberal slant) and seeming blunders (the disastrous Parufament agreement). Nevertheless, these erratic phenomena do not alter the company's right-wing, reactionary tendency, where each level of command,

power structure, or creative input reinforces the company's basic cultural and artistic conservatism. This explains why even a technical *tour-de-force* like *Metropolis* or an artistic masterpiece like *The Last Laugh* display deeply authoritarian traits.

- UFA was the ideological rearmament factory for Hitler and national socialism. Based on the above-mentioned history of UFA's pro-nationalist ownership and management in 1917 and again, in 1927, this case is supported by putting less emphasis on the (often financially barely profitable) prestige productions and author's films that one now remembers as the glories of UFA (the works of Fritz Lang, F.W. Murnau, or E.A. Dupont), and instead, focusing on the countless genre films: comedies, costume dramas, operetta and adventure films popular with German (provincial) audiences, and revelling in the past glories of Prussia, the monarchy and German military and diplomatic history. Such ideologically loaded entertainment prepared the (blood-and-) soil for populist demagogues and fascist propagandists.
- In the founding of UFA, General Ludendorff and the government were merely the pawns for Dr Stauß and the Deutsche Bank, who pursued their own goals (notably in relation to rival business and banking interests). Their aim in involving the government was to minimise the financial risk for a venture into the film business, which in Germany before the war had high failure rates.[2] Second, government backing facilitated favourable legislation, necessary for the envisaged mergers and acquisitions policy, but also in order to gain tax concessions. Once established with government help, UFA was run as a business on strictly commercial lines.

What these four accounts demonstrate is that already at the moment of UFA's inception, a complex field of force is in place, where governmental, economic, ideological and military objectives are difficult to separate. How much harder, then, to derive from these conflicting accounts of UFA's origins direct causal links that might explain its subsequent history, and even more, to draw conclusions from them about what films were being made, and why? While film policy and political history can at certain points determine each other (e.g. when it is a matter of legislation, such as censorship, or company law), it is generally safer to assume that they develop according to quite separate dynamics, if they do not actually show major points of divergence: German post-First World War inflation, for instance, affected the film business quite differently from the way it hit artisans or the middle class, and as studies in the United States have shown, a period of economic depression such as that of the early 1930s need not necessarily affect adversely the number of cinema-goers and thus the profitability of the cinema industry.

A more reliable starting point, then, for trying to reconstruct the logic of UFA in the 1920s is to compare its structures and *modi operandi* with those other film industries. Given what was said in the opening paragraph, it suggests UFA should be judged within a national and an international context, where the company's fortunes are less a reflection of purely or even typically German obsessions, ideologies and aspirations, but result from (re)acting in a climate of competing and (most likely,) contradictory demands. What follows is thus not a potted history, but more a series of snapshots, focused mainly on the role of Eric Pommer, and intended to highlight the configuration most crucial to him – that between Germany and Hollywood.[3] Since the points of comparison have to do mainly with managerial style and business strategies, it will lead away from the films as texts. They will be present, as in the previous chapters, more in the form of material manifestations of compromise formations, where the traditional divisions between 'art' vs 'commerce', 'expressionism' vs 'new objectivity', realism vs 'kitsch' are so many labels seemingly kept in circulation for the benefit of the contemporary debate between high art and popular culture, but also in this opposition's national/international variant, the competition between Europe and America.

Models for a film industry

To begin with a flash-forward from 1917: 1921 is one of the most crucial years for UFA. By March 1921 the company had paid off the Reich through the Deutsche Bank. Later the same year, it acquired with Decla-Bioskop the fourth pillar of its corporate structure (the other three being Nordisk, Messter and PAGU). Also in 1921, UFA had its first major export successes in the United States with *Madame Dubarry* (*Passion* opens in New York in December 1920) and *Anna Boleyn*.[4] In France, *The Cabinet of Dr Caligari* (a Decla production) is enjoying a huge critical success, giving rise to 'le Caligarisme' and inaugurating a new cultural *rapprochement* after the disastrous war between the 'arch-enemies' France and Germany. Both successes highlight the nature of UFA. It is a business that is in the business of mass entertainment, but also of 'art'.

As such, it is best understood on a comparative basis. Two kinds of comparisons are conceivable: UFA's financing, management structure and economic performance can be judged against other large industrial conglomerates emerging in Germany from the First World War (say, the press and publishing-industries).[5] Second, and more crucially, UFA stands in comparison with national, and especially international film industry competitors and predecessors. If one could run UFA through a kind of diagnostic test programme, in order to assess the company's competitive strengths and weaknesses *vis á vis* its rivals, one might get closer to answering the question why UFA was an impressive achievement during the 1920s, but also why its success was so short-lived.[6] It might also give one an insight into the apparent paradox of UFA films enjoying their highest critical acclaim when the conglomerate's finances were most precarious, while economic prospects recovered sharply towards the end of the decade, reputedly a time when the firm's artistic reputation plummeted. The conventional answer is that political interference and crass commercialism stifled creativity and talent. As more research is being done on company records, the trade press and studio memos, a somewhat revised picture emerges, which complements or even modifies the much better-known and better-researched political and ideological story of UFA.[7]

Two successful models were available to the founders for reference in 1917: the French and the American film industry. In Paris, Pathé Frères dominated the national film business over its rival, Gaumont, while in New York, Edison's MPPC (Motion Picture Patent Company) represented a number of fully fledged, vertically integrated firms. By the end of the war, Pathé, which in 1914 was probably the strongest film producing and distribution company in the world, with sister-companies or subsidiaries in Germany, Russia, Italy, the United States,[8] was on the verge of bankruptcy. However, it had been the first to identify the chief features of a successful film industry: division of labour in the production process, centralised distribution (introducing the shift from buying to renting, and creating the crucial marketing differential of monopoly exhibition known as 'first-run' or 'exclusivité'), and a strong export drive. It had also worked out some of the most popular genres: physical comedy, melodramas and historical reconstructions, including Passion plays.

The United States had also developed an industrialised model for making films, based on the pooling of patents, on cross-licensing and on controlling distribution: in other words, they had formed an industrial Trust. The Americans had also, by 1917, already reorganised and revolutionised their film industry twice over. Once, when independent producers defied and finally defeating through the courts the MPPC's restrictive practices in 1916, relocating the centre of film making from New York and New Jersey to the outskirts of Los Angeles, better known as Hollywood. The second reorganisation was inaugurated when the major producers, all of whom pursued an aggressive acquisitions policy, in order to become vertically integrated companies, formed among each other a cartel, the so-called 'studio system'. This meant that they were able to keep competition out (both domestic and especially foreign), but also assume a high degree of self-regulation. In addition, by standardising the chief product (the full-length feature film), the service (the type and amenities of first-run theatres), and distribution (via zoning and clearing agreements), they shifted the terrain of competition to brand-recognition, the star system, 'studio style' and advertising rather than to price differential or product difference.

While the French film industry knew it had to gain export markets to keep production costs competitive, the American film industry did not at first have to be international because of its vast internal market, and only expanded internationally towards the end of the war. None the less, competition among the studios was so fierce that its products were internationally of a very high standard, and they therefore found it relatively easy to enter the European market. People all over the world, it soon turned out, wanted to see American films, and by the early 1920s, the United States supplied something like 88 per cent of the world's films.

The German case before 1917

Prior to 1917 and the foundation of UFA, a film industry in this sense, either made up of cartels that pooled patents and controlled their use, or of a centrally organised film distribution, that could define quality of product and enforce pricing, did not exist in Germany. The film business, such as it was, consisted of a number of medium-sized companies, some of which could boast a certain degree of (horizontal) integration at the level of production (notably Messter Film).[9] Others, for instance Nordisk, were aiming at vertical integration, meaning that they owned and controlled, apart from extensive production facilities, a number of theatre outlets. This was also the case of PAGU (Paul Davidson's Union), built as it were 'from the bottom up', because it moved into production from exhibition, when its supply of films from different sources did not keep pace with the demand. Both PAGU and Nordisk were national and international companies. The difference between them was that whereas PAGU *imported* heavily from abroad, especially from Pathé in France, Nordisk was a very successful *exporter* of films. Originally a Danish company, it not only made major inroads on the German market, but also traded in the rest of Europe, and was one of the very few European companies, with major (mainly distribution) interests in the USA.

Therefore, despite the boost to production occasioned by the import embargo, the German film business was dispersed (with regional production centres, such as Munich, Frankfurt, Hamburg, as well as Berlin) and decentralised, in so far as many producers competed with each other for very different trading advantages in an as yet unstructured market: from a business point of view, the industry was at an earlier stage of capitalist development than either the French (a duopoly: Pathé and Gaumont) or the American (an oligopoly). More specifically, one could identify two models of commercial film making that prior to 1917 had not yet been fully integrated: simplifying a little, one could call one the Messter model and the other the PAGU model (with Nordisk showing signs of being a combination of both). The Messter model was organised from the production side, and quite diversified in its business interests, stretching from patents and apparatus manufacture to film production, and in the area of film making, stretching from entertainment uses of cinema (fiction films, *Tonbilder*, newsreels – the *Messterwoche*) also to scientific uses (the introduction of film as a record in science laboratories and medical facilities) and military applications (reconnaissance equipment for Air Force and Navy). Its financing ranged from commercial exploitation to government contracts, from direct sale and rental of films, to 'research and development' in sound and image reproduction technologies. In this sense, the Messter firm could be called a horizontally integrated company, but it was also very much the creation of a single individual.

The PAGU model on the other hand, represents an exclusive concentration on cinema as mass entertainment, and here the key feature was production organised from the exhibition side, as a consequence of marketing and consumer research: it was a demand-driven mode,[10] and not an equipment- or production-driven mode (as were the very beginnings of cinematography in almost all countries). Paradoxically, thanks to his contacts with Pathé, a foreign firm, PAGU became a significant force in the German film business. However, this also left it vulnerable: Paul Davidson suffered tremendous losses, when with the onset of the war, his supply of Pathé films was cut off. This was the moment for Nordisk to come up from behind, using Denmark's neutrality to expand its distribution in Germany, and on the back of that, its production. Davidson began his association with Nordisk, as an alternative supplier of films.[11] What Germany lacked at this point, apart from a normal export market, was a well-organised distribution network. Nordisk, however, helped to pioneer the star system in Germany (with Asta Nielsen), which, as in America, was a prerequisite for a demand-driven production system, which is to say, a business mode where distribution could regulate and coordinate both exhibition and production. The fact that other companies followed suit (Messter with Henny Porten, May Film with Mia May, etc.) indicates that by the mid-'teens, efforts were well under way to create 'vertically integrated' film companies, along the American model, though nothing yet suggests that they were operating as a cartel.

However, the conjunction of a boom in demand and a war-economy had, by the end of the war, led to an unsustainable number of small, undercapitalised production firms competing with each other, some of which had tried to gain an advantage via mergers or takeovers. The first such association of small producers was the Deutsche Lichtbild A.G. (Deulig) in 1916, backed by heavy industry interests in the Ruhr, headed by Alfred Hugenberg, then a director of Krupp, and also owner of a newspaper and publishing empire. One of Hugenberg's chief lieutenants, Ludwig Klitzsch, saw the advantage of diversifying into a potentially profitable medium. He also had a veritable mission to use the cinema as a promotional tool for both commerce and lobby politics. Klitzsch occupied a leading function in the German Colonial League, one of the two nationally organised initiatives – the other being the German Navy League – which had, from about 1907 onwards, relied heavily on the cinematograph in order to promote its aims. Especially the Navy League provoked the anger of cinema exhibitors, since it provided unfair competition by getting free advertising for their shows in the local press, and captive audiences from school officials or local army commandants.[12]

The formation of UFA

It was this initiative by Deulig that led to a counter-offensive, bringing together a consortium of firms from the electrical and chemical industries, headed by the Deutsche Bank. They were able to persuade military circles to use the government-owned film propaganda unit, the Bild und Film Amt (Bufa), to front a large-scale merger operation. Under considerable secrecy, the Universum Film Aktien Gesellschaft (UFA) was founded in December 1917, combining the

Messter GmbH, PAGU, Nordisk, along with a handful of smaller firms. The Reich provided funds to buy out some of the owners, while others were offered shares in the new company, with Paul Davidson becoming the new firm's first Head of Production. By the time UFA was operational, however, Germany had been defeated, and the new conglomerate's goal was to dominate the domestic as well as the European film market. Its chief assets were in real-estate (extensive studio capacity, luxury cinemas all over Germany, laboratories and prime office space in Berlin), while owning Messter brought UFA horizontal diversification into film equipment, processing and other cinema-related service industries, and the Nordisk stake extended both the exhibition basis already present from PAGU, and gave UFA access to a world-wide export network. The establishment of a horizontally and vertically integrated company of this size meant that not only Deulig was dwarfed, but a great many other middle-size companies became increasingly dependent on UFA as Germany's chief domestic exhibitor and export distributor.

Production at first continued under the brand names of the merged firms: PAGU, Messter, Joe May Film, Gloria, BB-Film, some using the new purpose-built studios in Potsdam-Babelsberg, soon to become the heart of UFA and the German film industry. The PAGU team around Davidson and Lubitsch rose to international fame with a series of historical spectaculars and costume dramas, sometimes based on operettas. Specializing in exotic *Großfilme* (*Das Indische Grabmal*), Joe May's multi-episode serials like *Die Herrin der Welt* proved particularly popular to Germany's war-exhausted spectators, not least because each episode featured a different continent, with the heroine travelling from China to Africa, from India to the United States.

Among the firms that initially did not form part of the UFA conglomerate, the most important was Decla, headed by Erich Pommer. Decla's first major films after the war were *Die Spinnen* (1919), an exotic detective serial written and directed by Fritz Lang, and *Die Pest in Florenz* (1919), a historical adventure directed by Rippert and scripted by Lang. Together with *Das Cabinet des Dr Caligari*, directed by Robert Wiene and written by Carl Mayer and Hans Janowitz, these three films made up a production programme that by and large defined the course the German cinema was to take in the early 1920s. Popular serials, with exotic locations and improbable adventures, historical spectaculars, and the 'stylised' (or 'Expressionist') film complemented the strategy, with the economic backbone a genre and star cinema aimed at the domestic audience that broadly continued along the lines first developed in the mid-'teens.

Neither the strategy of the UFA merger, nor the use of a special interest group for the purposes of creating a film propaganda instrument were the invention of UFA's backers. Both obeyed a certain commercial logic, and both belonged to the political culture of Wilhelmine society, making UFA an expression not so much of the war, as of a new way of thinking, on the one hand, about corporate capitalism, and on the other, about public opinion and the (technological) media. The orthodox version, therefore – that it is the Oberste

Heeresleitung that wanted UFA, secretly financed by the Reich and openly by the banks – cannot in itself tell one much about UFA as a business, unless one is expecting an altogether different (non-industrial, non-capitalist) mode of film making.

What is significant, from an economic perspective, is that the German film industry at the end of the First World War was poised towards the formation of a cartel of more or less equally-sized companies (Messter, Nordische, PAGU, Decla, Terra, Bioskop, May Film, Emelka, DLG, etc), some of which would in any case have merged (as did Decla-Bioskop), others may well have gone bankrupt. Erich Pommer, writing in 1920 about 'the importance of industrial conglomerates for the film industry' in the trade journal *Film Kurier* recognised the imperative for amalgamation:

> Only thanks to their far-sighted policy are Germany's large companies now in a position to play a regulatory role in these issues [how to stop foreign film firms from taking over]. If the German film business were still made up of nothing but small, isolated firms, then the trusts in England, America, France and Italy would, with a single gesture, simply sweep away these molecular specks in German economic life, or at best, buy up the profitable ones, in every case the aim being to bring them under their control.[13]

An argument can, however, be made that the forcible merger of PAGU, Messter, Nordische (with Oliver Film, May Film, etc.),[14] under the name of UFA also seriously distorted the balance of forces. Rather than helping to form such a cartel, it created a situation which was neither a monopoly, nor an oligopoly, with the consequence that everyone still had to compete with everyone else, to the detriment of all sectors of the industry.[15] Through no particular doing of UFA, the situation was furthermore distorted during the inflation period, giving an artificial boost to production, and allowing German films to enter the world market at dumping prices as well as making foreign films uneconomical for importers. As Tom Saunders has pointed out:

> In the cinema as in society and the economy as a whole, inflation, though ultimately catastrophic in proportions and impact, massively aided the cause of postwar recovery. By sheltering the domestic market from foreign interference and encouraging industrial concentration, it fostered experimentation and growth.[16]

Inflation, however did not 'solve' the structural problem of the German film industry: too many small companies always at the brink of bankruptcy, contributing to chronic over-production, that in turn led to a chaotic distribution system, with exhibitors eternally at war with producers and distributors (350–400 production companies, 100 distributors, more than 300 films per annum). Price wars, no coordinated export drive, no effective government lobby regarding censorship or the levy of amusement tax made it an ideal opportunity for outsiders (e.g. the Americans) to enter the market, taking up strategic positions in distribution and offering their films below the going rate. A good example of how far US companies were able to penetrate even into the field of production was the EFA (European Film Alliance) initiative.[17] In fact, it was not least because of the worsening inflation that Famous Players pulled out of EFA, leaving much of its German personnel the option to emigrate to Hollywood, which the entire team around Lubitsch (with the exception of Davidson) promptly took up.[18]

As far as the regulation of the industry was concerned, it was almost entirely external, via two mechanisms: taxation (entertainment tax)[19] and censorship. Regarding the re-introduction of censorship for films, so soon after the Weimar Republic had abolished all other forms of curtailing the freedom of expression, an interesting point emerges. While the film law of May 1920 is usually blamed on the post-war wave of 'Aufklärungsfilme' (sex-education films), Saunders has pointed out that the absence of party-political debate shows a surprising consensus across the political spectrum about the cinema being regarded undesirable and a nuisance.[20] For as pointed out in an earlier chapter, the kind and degree of hostility which the medium faced in Germany among the educated classes was an important factor in its overall development. On the other hand, it is equally true that film producers' interests are not necessarily opposed to those of censorship, and in actual fact only rarely did they find themselves in conflict with censorship boards.[21]

UFA's corporate structure

Such was the picture at the end of 1921, after UFA had acquired the debt-ridden, but asset-rich Decla-Bioskop, and in two stages had increased its capital from a modest 25 million to 200 million.[22] With Decla-Bioskop, UFA not only became economically a European player: the addition of Erich Pommer gave the company a far-sighted, European-minded producer who championed an internationally recognised art cinema and brought about the confluence of industrial and creative trends which built UFA's enduring reputation. Historically, therefore, one needs to distinguish quite clearly several periods. The first phase is from 1917 to 1921; the second, from 1921 to 1923 (the end of inflation); the third from 1924 to 1927 (the so-called consolidation period, where the dynamics of UFA are broadly in line with the developments of the German economy at large), and the fourth, which goes from 1928 to 1937 (with 1933 not altogether the incision which it is usually taken to be). UFA's own internal development is marked by its acquisition policy which somewhat slowed down after the stabilisation of the currency; the second phase was ruled by worries over the increased market share of the Americans (by the mid-1920s it had risen to about 50 per cent), while towards the end of the decade, UFA had recovered its domestic profitability, and had achieved a degree of European dominance, thanks to the introduction of sound. The strategic aim, in each phase, was to be able to produce films that could, either domestically, or internationally, compete with Hollywood.[23] While the first few successes in 1921 gave some substance to these ambitions, hopes were soon dashed, and for the rest of the decade, it was an uneven struggle, where UFA had to compete externally as well as internally with the Americans, while internally, it had its domestic rivals, such as Emelka, and later Nero, Tobis as well as many others, and in terms of publicity, against a largely hostile press, not forgetting the most crucial point of all, the pressure from its shareholders, notably the Deutsche Bank, which a few years later, was responsible for pulling the plug on the company in 1927. The only weapon was a quota system and import restrictions, a system which the Germans pioneered, but which has never been successful, and was not always welcome, even among producers. Pommer, for instance, was not at all in favour of import restrictions. Already in 1922 he wrote:

> Away with today's quota-system ['Kontingentierungssystem'], which may give a few producers short-lived financial advantages, but because of the uses and abuses to which it is open, no longer serves its intended purpose. Bring in free trade, if necessary mitigated by a system of compensation and import tax.[24]

There can be no doubt that UFA was conceived as an industrial conglomerate that wanted to be 'state of the art' in the international film business. Less certain is whether it was a conglomerate to which the description 'advanced capitalist' applies. And if so, how much influence did those who held the company's stock exert, as opposed to those who managed its day-to-day decisions.[25] Nominally, in the early phases, the director (Bratz) acted in close consultation with a four-member Executive Board, made up of Stauss (accounts), Pommer (production), Grau (distribution) and Jacob (exhibition). How much discretion this Board had to reinvest profits in the company, as opposed to paying them out as dividend is not clear. For instance, as one industrial analyst (Schildt) remarked, in the key accounting period of 1924–5, the entire profit of 3m Reichsmark went into paying a 6 per cent dividend. Because so much of the UFA stock was in the hands of banks, or institutional investors, this is surprising, since it should have allowed the company to plough back its profits into investments and production.[26] Such a short-term dividend-oriented policy (with hindsight regarded as one of the mistakes that aggravated the debt crisis of 1925–6) was rarely if ever taken by the Hollywood majors, whose own management structure was much more hierarchical, running the business from the accounting side and the exhibition side (located in New York), with the actual production side ('Hollywood') occupying a subordinate role in the company pyramid.[27]

Among economic historians of the American film industry, there are two schools of thought: one considers ownership of stock as the key to business decisions, the other sees management as the crucial factor in performance. The post-Second World War historians of UFA always follow the former,[28] perhaps because it appears to back up the 'political' and ideological argument. However, more recent studies of the American film industry, and of the collapse of Pathé strongly argue for analysing management structure, in order to understand why a company succeeds or fails.[29] What the American example also suggests is that historians may have placed too much emphasis on the production side of UFA, using the available statistics (not very copious or reliable at that) as an index of how 'successful' (at the box office, in export) the films were, when it is clear from these same statistics that UFA's different kinds of assets performed very differently during the period, yielding a profit profile that has yet to be fully analysed. We know, for instance, that throughout the 1920s, the distribution sector in Germany remained highly fragmented (up to 100 companies), and that the industry did not achieve a centralised policy which could steer both production and exhibition into an equitable and profitable relationship.[30] The exhibitors were complaining about blind booking, which however, was crucial from the producers' point of view, if they were to plan the annual output. Fluctuating admission prices on the other hand, as well as regional variation in the amusement tax, made it impossible for the distributor to calculate rentals, which in turn put pressure on the monies that distributors could advance to the producer. Because of this distribution situation, chronic over-production was built into the very structure of film making in Germany.[31] At the same time, given UFA's assets in the field of studio capacity, it had to encourage other firms to rent its studio space for their productions, in order to make these facilities profitable. This, too, was a question of management and especially in the early years proved a problem, which the trade press hoped would be resolved after the fusion with Decla-Bioskop:

> The terrible years of the interregnum, with yawningly empty studio-lots that cost UFA millions upon millions, are now hopefully a thing of the past for the company.[32]

UFA's mode of production: the Pommer model

By contrast, UFA's film production structure compared more directly with United States practice. While the US management model in the early 1910s was the 'director-unit system', where the director has control over a given film and is involved throughout its stages, virtually all studios replaced this with the central producer system towards the mid- to late-1910s.[33] The changeover occurred at a time when the studios' production volume and capacities had expanded significantly, but it was equally in line with new theories of 'scientific management' introduced widely also in other branches of the US manufacturing industry. The 'central producer system' functioned by giving a head of production control and responsibility over all of a studio's annual product output, implying a much greater division of labour for the various tasks and phases of film production, as well as a very strict assignment of shooting schedules, budgets and release dates. Furthermore, the script acquired a different function: from directors using the 'scenario-script', the industry-standard becomes the 'continuity-script', the film making equivalent of a technical blueprint, not just for the action, the players, the number of scenes, the locations and dialogue, but for the entire budget calculations, set constructions, time schedule, and other dispositions. It therefore could not be altered during shooting, nor was there consultation on the set between the writer, the director and the art director. While the director still had complete control over the shooting itself, many of the other elements had become pre-designed and pre-determined. In the 1920s, the most publicised central producer unit was that commanded by Irvin Thalberg at MGM, not least because here the transition from the director-unit system to the central producer system exacted its most illustrious casualty: the film *Greed*, and Erich von Stroheim's subsequent fate as director.[34] It prompted the saying that 'a Thalberg is to a movie what a Hamburger is to a beefsteak'.[35]

What kind of Head of Production, then, was Pommer at UFA in the 1920s? Was he either able or willing to impose the kind of central-producer system practised in Hollywood? As founder of Decla, and production chief of Decla-Bioskop, Pommer's film-making concept had two salient features. With his background in distribution (as agent for Gaumont, and then Eclair, in Germany and Austria) Pommer, like Davidson, conceived of production as driven by exhibition and export.[36] He recognised the importance that export had also for the domestic market itself, as shown in his efforts as deputy director of the 'Exportverband der deutschen Filmindustrie', founded in May 1920, to put pressure on 'the internal organisation of the market, if necessary by sidestepping the people who currently feel themselves to be in charge of the German film business.'[37]

Regarding his production policy, however, Pommer preferred initially to stay with the director-unit system. Decla-Bioskop did not only bring into the UFA conglomerate valuable production facilities, a sizeable theatre park and real-estate, it had some of the youngest and most creative teams in the business: Fritz Lang, Ludwig Berger, E.A. Dupont, Arthur von Gerlach, F.W. Murnau, Robert Wiene, to name only the directors, though the writers (Carl Mayer, Thea von Harbou, Robert Liebmann), cameramen (Fritz Arno Wagner, Karl Freund, Carl Hoffmann, Günther Rittau), set designers and film architects (Otto Hunte, Hermann Warm, Erich Kettelhut, Robert Herlth, Walter Röhrig) were almost equally important.[38] As Pommer proudly announced:

> I hold the view that the value of a film does not lie in the quantity of players, nor in the size of the sums invested in the negative, but in the careful selection of subjects, the tasteful direction, the quality of the cast, and last but not least in the creative collaboration of the director with good designers and camera operators. Only under these conditions can we hope to achieve acceptable product for export.[39]

Because he himself travelled extensively, in order to realise his vision of UFA with a strong export business and a brand-name of international dimension, Pommer let his director units work under conditions of great autonomy and freedom from interference or supervision.[40] This was a high-risk but none the less deliberate strategy, based on what he himself called 'Zweiteilung der Produktion' (i.e. product differentiation). Whereas in the United States production was divided according to the type of market and exhibition venue: A-pictures and B-pictures, in Pommer's case, the differentiation ran more between 'stylised film' and *Großfilm* on one side, and popular genre films and star vehicles on the other.

> A film company that wants to survive, needs, for the foreseeable future, to make sure it knows how to toss to the taste of the large public the kind of strong meat which it craves, regardless of whether it wants to satiate its appetite for sentimentality or belly-laughs. […] The artistic film, on the other hand, has seen, from the point of view of its profitability, quite few changes. […] There is no reason why it should not be possible to implement the highest artistic means and aims, and still stay as much in business as with the loud bangs for the broad mass. […] I am convinced that a canon of classics will emerge from the bulk of movies which in no way lags behind the classics of the theatre. *The Cabinet of Dr Caligari* and *Der Müde Tod/Destiny* will be among them, proof positive that the artistic film need not be a financial liability.[41]

The highest risks (with open-ended budgets and time schedules) were taken with the *Großfilme*, since these were made with a number of objectives in mind. They often coincided with the opening of a new UFA luxury cinema in Berlin or other major cities (e.g. *Tartuffe* and the Gloria Palace); second, their extensive technological investments allowed the company to upgrade its equipment, and thus keep its infrastructure high-tech and competitive (the case with *Der Letzte Mann*, *Faust* and *Metropolis*);[42] third, these films were targeted to compete directly with American super-productions above all in Europe, but if possible also in the United States. The latter remained UFA's Achilles heel, but it, too, was a calculated risk. On the basis that *Madame Dubarry* in the US and *The Cabinet of Dr Caligari* in Europe had broken the international post-First World War boycott of German films, Pommer clung to his concept of trying to service two markets: the mass audience at home, always in danger of deserting to Hollywood imports, and the international art cinema outlets, where the art cinema ('künstlerische Film') generated the prestige which ever since has attached itself to the German cinema. Yet, as indicated, the initial export successes were greatly facilitated by hyper-inflation, since depreciation automatically amortised a film's production cost: in 1921, for instance, the sale of a feature film to a tiny market like Switzerland earned enough hard currency to finance an entire new production. But with the stabilisation of the mark in 1923, this trading advantage disappeared for German production, and Pommer's twin strategy became increasingly precarious.

In response Pommer tried to establish a common European film market dominated by Germany and UFA. He entered into a number of distribution and co-production agreements under the banner 'Film Europe', demonstrating his awareness that despite its size and concentration, UFA on its own was in no position to brave Hollywood even in Europe, not to mention penetrating the US market. Pommer brought C. Th. Dreyer, Holger-Madsen and Robert Dinesen from Denmark, Graham Coutts, Alfred Hitchcock and Herbert Wilcox from Great Britain, and René Clair and Julien Duvivier from France. The UFA–Aubert distribution contract, the ACE initiative, and other schemes[43] showed that he knew very well why UFA could not function as an effective cartel by itself, and needed to undergo modernisation and rationalization.[44] Despite their ultimate failure, the 'Film Europe' initiatives laid the groundwork for the very extensive contacts that were to exist throughout the late 1920s and lasting well into the 1940s, between the German and French film-making communities. For instance, it gave Pommer, after his forced expatriation in 1933, an initial foothold in Paris and allowed him to find work for scores of other UFA exiles, among them Lang, Robert Siodmak, Curt Bernhardt, Billie [Billy] Wilder and Max Ophuls.[45]

Until 1926, when he left for the United States, Pommer's production system at UFA remained the director-unit system, with its teams assembled around a major director. The benefits of this policy are well-recognised: they make up the splendour of the so-called UFA-style, with scope for technical and stylistic experimentation and even improvisation at almost every stage of a project. This led to heavy reliance on studio work, which UFA's admirers thought 'atmospheric', and others merely 'claustrophobic'. There were drawbacks, too: often it seemed that with perfectionism and the craft ethos permeating all departments, time and money were no object. Furthermore, the refusal to divide and control the labour processes of film production as was standard practice in Hollywood often came into conflict with a production policy geared towards exhibition schedules. Given the German film industry's chronic over-production, few of UFA's more expensive films could be fully exploited, making Pommer's production concept deficit-prone, and as illustrated by the loan and distribution agreement concluded with US Majors (the Parufamet Agreement), ultimately fatal to UFA's fortunes as a manufacturing company run on industrial lines with commercial imperatives. The aesthetic and stylistic results of Pommer's concept, on the other hand, were more lasting: revolutionary techniques in special effects (*Destiny*, *Faust*, *Metropolis*), new styles of lighting (*Phantom*, the *Kammerspiel* films), camera movement and camera angles (*Variety* and *The Last Laugh*) and set design fully integrated into style and theme (as in *The Nibelungen*). These achievements gave UFA film technicians and directors their high professional reputation, making the German cinema of the 1920s, paradoxically, both a financial disaster and a film makers' Mecca (Hitchcock's admiration for Murnau, Bunuel's for Lang, not to mention the influences on Joseph von Sternberg, Frank Borzage, Rouben Mamoulian, Orson Welles and on Hollywood film noir of the 1940s).

Stylistic features of the German mode of production

In actual fact, the film making practised at UFA in the mid-1920s showed not only distinct stylistic features as far as lighting, camera work and set design were concerned.[46] It also was distinct in the editing patterns and the kind of narrative continuity which made these films both less obvious in the logic of the action, and gave them a slower tempo. While such an editing style may not appeal to the larger public, it did account for what international critics thought most astonishing: the psychological depth and complexity, the emotional inwardness and dream-like obliqueness of the character's motivation. With this, the German stylised film was much closer to an earlier American film-making practice: that of D.W. Griffith, who, in films like *Intolerance* (1918), developed complex editing patterns and correspondences which impressed Lang and Murnau, with cross-cutting that enthused the young Pudovkin and Eisenstein, but which made

Figure 7 A relay of ambiguous looks: Fritz Kortner (left) surprises his wife bidding farewell to her lover in Arthur Robison's *Warning Shadows* (*Schatten*,1923), produced by the independent Pan-Film company

Source: Stiftung Deutsche Kinemathek, Berlin

Intolerance all but incomprehensible even to an American public that only two years earlier had hailed *Birth of a Nation* as a miracle of movie magic.[47]

Therefore, one of the reasons why German and Russian directors could learn from and refine the Griffithian model of editing (the Germans in the direction of dream and inwardness, as in Murnau's most Griffithian film *Nosferatu*, and the Russians in the direction of cross-cutting and montage, as in *The End of St Petersburg*) was that both film industries – though for very different reasons – were for some time protected from the full force of the market, and the need for mass audiences. While in the classical Hollywood system we see a greater and greater convergence between narrative economy and industrial efficiency, in Germany under Pommer, the kinds of narrative style directors were interested in (or were driven towards in their battle for artistic legitimation and respectability) stood in a tension with the practical ways of producing it. This more 'experimental' mode was possible because, unlike the American system (which already by the mid-1910s was entirely demand-driven and organised in view of release dates), the Pommer model was still director-driven, and did not (yet) have the same sophisticated feedback as the American industry with its public.[48] Instead, Pommer had an all too sensitive feedback with the Berlin cultural intelligentsia, a taste elite that demanded film to be art or would denounce it as 'kitsch'. Although it was a demand he had to take seriously, Pommer showed his exasperation in print, complaining about the critics' 'remoteness from the realities of film.'[49] Two concepts of 'quality' were seen to clash, the European one (quality as artistic excellence and originality) and the Hollywood's criterion of quality (the essentially industrial one of 'quality-control', i.e. standardisation, reliability and uniformity of the product), which was intended to give audiences a secure horizon of expectation, a virtue well recognised by Pommer.[50] At the same time, the industrial basis of the German film industry could not come to terms with what was effectively an avant-garde ideology, where production schedules were uncertain, budgets open-ended and release dates volatile.[51] Pommer appeared to take such risks with his creative personnel, teaching the directors on the job, in order to develop prototypes and stay in the international vanguard.[52]

Vertical integration: strength or weakness of UFA?

In the light of the financial crisis of 1925, the Parufamet agreement,[53] and the collapse of the company in 1927, it was easy to argue that Pommer's product-differentiation strategy failed, and that the battle with the Americans should never have been undertaken.[54] It is indeed ironic that, during Pommer's high-profile strategy, the cost to export earning ratio should have fallen to its lowest (20 per cent).[55] But, given that this is only one pocket of the UFA's production plan, and that production is only one of its profit-generating activities, should the blame for the crisis not also be sought elsewhere?[56]

Current research suggests that on the eve of the banks foreclosing on UFA, and necessitating the Hugenberg rescue package, the American companies via their subsidiaries in Berlin had spread rumours not about the losses on super-productions like *Metropolis*, but about the fact that the UFA theatres were making such huge losses that the company would have to sell off its real-estate (it did, of course, sell Haus Vaterland to the Kempinski hotel in January 1927).[57] Did the banks get cold feet, because they always considered real estate like the cinemas, the Romanische Haus or Haus Vaterland as UFA's key assets?[58] Due to the fact that UFA was a vertically integrated company, it both enjoyed an enormous advantage over its rivals, but at the same time, if the distribution and exhibition sectors were in disarray, it could indeed threaten the financial survival of the company, especially if, as I suggested, the management structure did not allow this part of UFA's activity to determine production policy.[59]

Might it have been that a major weakness of UFA was not in the films but in the distribution, especially domestic? Could it have been that UFA, despite its 10 per cent of the cinemas and 40 per cent of the audiences, was not strong enough to 'standardise' the distribution market? Why, in the end, was the Parufamet Agreement so bad financially?[60] Surely, the US imports and Parufamet productions, if properly exploited in UFA cinemas and elsewhere, could have made a profit for the company as a whole?[61] The argument that UFA collapsed because *Metropolis* and other big budget films, such as *Tartuffe*, failed to win audiences in the US is unconvincing. It seems mostly based on the kind of anti-American propaganda which the cartoons in a 1925 SPIO pamphlet spread in order to lobby for a reduction of amusement tax.[62]

The distribution sector generally was at war with production, and both were at war with exhibition, which did give UFA, as a vertically integrated company, the strategic advantage it had, despite producing only a small percentage of Germany's overall number of films.[63] Yet these conflicts hurt its profitability, as can be gauged from the so-called 'Kampf um die Kinotermine' (the battles for the cinema booking dates), which Jürgen Spiker argues were responsible for distributors becoming, by 1926, the real power in the film business, holding both exhibitors and producers to ransom.[64] But precisely because distribution was the most profitable branch of the business, it became the easiest prey for predators, with foreign firms buying up German distribution firms – a situation not that dissimilar to the post-Second World War period, and definitely decisive in the decline of the European cinema since the 1980s. On the other hand, if out of the 21 core production firms, 15 had their own distribution arm (with the four largest companies also among the six largest distributors), then distribution could have been a cartel (e.g. in imposing prices and conditions, as happened in the US studio system), except that anti-trust laws were enforced, and even UFA's vertical integration did not allow it to weather the fluctuations of admission prices, amusement tax and rental income.

Since most films in Germany at that time were produced via distribution guarantees, this should have mopped up over-capacity, especially since the saturation figure for annual exhibition was known (max: 275 films).[65] But high production volume was necessary to amortise fixed costs of plant and capital investments, in turn leading to dumping practices on the German market, a process where the Americans could hold their own, since they were not dependent on their export earnings, which were pure profit.[66] With over-capacity in Germany, films were pulled from the cinemas too fast to reach their optimum potential, and UFA's *Großfilm* (blockbuster) mentality did indeed contribute to hurting the market. Finally, given that so many independent firms were producing films, and that family-owned cinemas and small distributors existed to show them, one could assume the existence of a wide variety of film forms, film subjects and film styles in Germany. However, it seems that the economic precariousness of the independents actually enforced conformity.[67]

Horizontal integration: the UFA *Medienverbund*

Another specific aspect of UFA's internal structure which compared interestingly with the American system was the degree to which, right from the start, UFA was also a horizontally integrated company, following on from the way that the Messter group had diversified into technological research and non-entertainment applications. Pommer's ethos of craft and experiment, of creative autonomy within a business conglomerate harked back to the values of a Oskar Messter or a Guido Seeber, who saw themselves as inventors and technicians rather than as salespeople and businessmen. In contrast to this kind of diversification of the uses of the cinematographic apparatus, UFA also formed part of another kind of horizontal integration altogether, which saw the cinema in its technical 'Verbund' (photographic, precision engineering, optical, electrical and chemical industries), an example of which would be the acquisition of Afifa, in order to control film processing and the supply of prints. Similarly, knowing itself to be part of the burgeoning entertainment industries, the company diversified by acquiring, for instance, sheet music rights and later, gramophone interests. An important aspect of this diversification was UFA's leading role in educational and cultural films, for schools and for theatrical release (the famous *Kulturfilmabteilung*, the documentary unit, first run by Nicholas Kaufmann, and then Alexander Grau).

Just as significant, however, was the fact that already in the early 1920s, UFA formed a 'Verbund' with other media interests, notably in the print and publishing industry, aware of the financial benefits of exploiting the same material or 'property' in several media simultaneously.[68] The Ullstein deal with Joe May Film (later Decla-Bioskop) on their serialised novels, resulting in the formation of a separate production company, Uco-Film, is a frequently cited example.[69] But one can find cooperation agreements across the whole area of literary and musical property acquisition, and it would pay to study more closely the UFA script departments, the royalty and rights specialists, as well as the connection of UFA to the trade press, journalism and the feuilleton, not to mention to the theatrical and creative talent agencies. For instance, according to A. Jason, up until 1932 only 3 per cent of the scripts used in German film production were original stories. The rest were, in one form or another, adaptations from literature, stage, operetta and newspaper feuilletons. This was confirmed by Walter Reisch, who argued that the influx of Budapest and Vienna writing talent in the early 1930s was as much a consequence of UFA's need for original material for sound films as it was motivated by the political climate.[70]

Certainly, UFA's elaborate multi-media advertising policy – which stretched from gala openings to book-publishing tie-ins (Thea von Harbou proved especially inventive in this respect), to fully UFA-designed front-of-house decorations for cinema foyers (famously for *The Last Laugh*, *Die Frau im Mond*, *Asphalt* by Rudi Feld) illustrated programme notes (by among others, Stefan Lorant), magazine features in fashion journals, and endless publicity material for the regional press – had little to fear or, for that matter, to learn from the Hollywood studios' publicity machinery.[71]

Figure 8 The witching hour: Yvette Guilbert (as Gretchen's mother) falling for the charms of Emil Jannings (as Mephisto) in F.W. Murnau's *Faust* (1926)

Source: BFI films: stills, posters and designs

The trade organisations and industrial self-regulation

There was, however, one area where the organisation of the German film industry in general, and UFA in particular appeared to differ markedly, when compared to the American industry. This was the structure and function of the trade organisations. On the face of it, little separates the MPPDA (the Motion Picture Producers' and Distributors' Association) from its German equivalent, the SPIO. But given the cartel-like nature of the Hollywood Majors, the MPPDA developed into a formidable body, whose importance for the American film industry cannot be overestimated.[72] While to the general public, the MPPDA, founded as early as 1922, with Will Hays as its chairman, was best known for its self-censorship code of practice (the often ridiculed Hays Code), its actual role and function was much wider. The MPPDA was the film industry's lobby and pressure group both nationally and internationally, dealing with all branches of government, on a much wider range of questions than sex and morality, including for instance, tax laws and anti-trust legislation. As to its international role, not only did it immediately form a separate department dealing with foreign matters, with Frederick Herron in charge, where all the Majors had their export interests represented, it also acted as a kind of second diplomatic corps all over the world.[73] Most importantly, however, its purpose domestically was as the industry's self-regulatory body, policing its members in order to minimise or avoid altogether, outside interference: 'it was conceived in fear of regulation of the industry by the public and is dedicated to the proposition that outsiders should never dictate its policies.'[74] For the MPPDA it did not matter whether these outsiders are the state via legislation or taxation, or outside competitors trying to enter the American market.

In Germany, by contrast, the industry never found such a voice that could speak effectively on its behalf. Given UFA's hegemony, and because the individual firms were so unevenly matched, the companies, instead of acting as a cartel, were engaged in outright competition. There was, for instance, throughout the period, no organisation that collected reliable statistics either on rental income from films or did market research on audience preferences, what Peter Bächlin has called 'the testing of public taste prior to releasing the final version', i.e. the practice of 'sneak previews'.[75] Even UFA did not gather reliable statistics on how well or badly its films did, where and when until the early 1930s.[76] Second, the trade organisation SPIO was, for most of the decade, not able to speak on behalf of all its members (the South German companies boycotted SPIO), nor for all the different branches of the film business.[77] For instance, it seemed to do little to mediate successfully in the conflicts of interest between exhibitors and producers, and on the contrary, occasionally appeared to aggravate them.[78] Equally detrimental perhaps was the German industry's inability for concerted action in matters of export and foreign relations, for each company acted on its own account. The smaller firms not distributing via UFA, such as Emelka, Deulig, Südfilm, Terra and Nero maintained their own export network, by also entering into agreements with American and British firms, thus further splitting the German market, to the ultimate advantage of Hollywood.[79] Pommer, who was convinced that more needed to be done by the government to improve Germany's export chances, tried to involve the various branches of the executive in his efforts, as also happened in the US:

> Our contacts with the government was continuous and such that Stresemann would ask me to meet him informally for dinner. This provided the opportunity to air our problems and wishes at the highest level.[80]

What caused the most serious divisions inside the film industry was the local entertainment taxes levied on cinemas and depressing their economic viability. At the same time, legislation adopted to protect national producers from Hollywood competition was, as indicated, ultimately ineffectual: import restrictions and quota regulations helped boost the production of 'quota-quickies', hurting distributors who needed quality American films and aggravating the general glut of cheaply produced films clogging exhibition outlets.[81] In other respects, too, politicians wielded only a blunt instrument: although the government occasionally banned uncomfortable films on the grounds of endangering public order, it could do little to foster a prosperous and united national film business, since import restrictions and the entertainment tax not only put the state and the regions in conflict with each other, but also played one section of the film industry (the producers) off against another (the exhibitors).

The 'war' on several fronts

Given the many other weaknesses of the Weimar political system, the chances of decisive action for the cinema were, thus, minimal. Besides, fending off American competition was not the only front on which UFA did battle in the 1920s, and while it dominated exhibition, it did not make up much more than 18 per cent of the national production. As a capitalist conglomerate, UFA was the target of critics on the left, foremost among them the writers from liberal and social-democratic press, whose cultural distrust of the cinema was hardly less pronounced than that of their conservative colleagues, but for whom UFA was clearly a tool in the hands of the nationalist right. The arts pages of the quality press also showed a somewhat contradictory attitude to the popular: denouncing the 'artistic' films as 'kitsch', they despised popular or genre films as 'Schund', i.e. trash, thus operating a concept of film art where in the mid-1920s only Chaplin and in the late 1920s only the Soviet cinema could pass muster. Another group to interest themselves ideologically in the cinema were professional pedagogues, lawyers, doctors and the clergy of both Protestant and Catholic denominations. As early as 1907 their organisations had promoted debates about the dangers of the cinema for youth, work discipline, morals and public order (the so-called 'anti-dirt-and-smut-campaign'). Lobbying continued in the 1920s, when the aim increasingly became not a ban on the cinema, but one to promote 'cultural' films, that is, educational and documentary cinema, a market for which UFA very quickly – and successfully – catered. There was thus an intellectual climate in Weimar Germany that may have been hostile to German films, but none the less fostered an informed and discriminating film culture heavily politicised, as implied in the term 'Weimar cinema'. The organised radical left was, throughout most of the decade, almost uniformly hostile towards the cinema, lambasting UFA for poisoning the minds of the masses with reactionary celebrations of Prussia's glory,[82] while chiding the masses for preferring such films to party meetings and street demonstrations. Only after the successful screening of the so-called *Russenfilme* in 1925 did Willi Münzenberg, the left's most gifted propagandist, find support for his slogan 'Conquer the Cinemas', the title of a pamphlet in which he argued that films were 'one of the most effective means of political agitation, not to be left solely in the hands of the political enemy'. Münzenberg's International Workers' Aid set up a distribution company, Prometheus, to import Russian films and also to finance its own productions. Apart from documentaries, Prometheus made features such as the comedy *Überflüssige Menschen* by the Soviet director Alexander Razumny, and Piel Jutzi's proletarian melodrama *Mutter Krauses Fahrt Ins Glück* (1929). Not to be outdone by the Communists, the Social Democrats also financed feature films, among them Werner Hochbaum's *Brüder* (1929) and several documentaries dealing with housing problems, anti-abortion legislation and urban crime. Earlier, the trade unions had sponsored *Die Schmiede* by Martin Berger (1924), who also made *Freies Volk* in 1925 and *Kreuzzug des Weibes* in 1926. Prometheus's best-known film was *Kuhle Wampe* (1930), directed by Slatan Dudow and Hanns Eisler, with a script by Bert Brecht, which opens with the suicide of an unemployed adolescent, and follows the fortunes of a young working-class couple as they try to find jobs and a home in order to start a family, finally realising that only when marching with their fellow workers can they change the world, and thus improve their own fate.

Very rarely did films with a party-political affiliation succeed in providing what critics missed in almost all UFA productions: 'realism', and a commitment to themes from everyday life. Such a demand, comprehensible from a critical establishment still under the impact of literary naturalism, was none the less not always compatible with the export objectives pursued by Pommer. Abroad, the reality of Germany was still too much associated with the First World War for subjects with a contemporary setting to appeal to international audiences. While before 1918, the German cinema extensively used various locations, realistic decor and contemporary themes, after the war only productions mainly intended for the domestic market (comedies and social dramas, such as Reinhold Schünzel's *Das Mädchen aus der Ackerstrasse* or Harry Piel adventure films) were filmed in realist settings. Most of the prestigious productions that later became associated with the realism known as '*Neue Sachlichkeit*', whether those by G.W. Pabst (*Die Freudlose Gasse*, *Die Liebe der Jeanne Ney*, *Die Büchse der Pandora*) or Joe May (*Asphalt*, *Heimkehr*) remained, both before and after the coming of sound, wedded to the UFA studio look, regardless of the period in which the action was set.

In the United States, by contrast, German films were unpopular because they had unclear and weak plots, but mostly because there were no major film stars. The star system has always been fundamental for international film making, because a major popular film star transcends national boundaries in a way that the film setting and subject matter often do not. One of the problems UFA had in this respect was that as soon as actors and actresses became famous, they tended to be lured by the attractions of Hollywood, as did Lubitsch's first international discovery, Pola Negri. The only truly international star in the 1920s who also worked in Germany was Emil Jannings, and he was indeed a commanding presence in a disproportionate number of Germany's American successes: *Madame Dubarry*, *Variety*, *The Last Laugh*, *Faust*, *The Blue Angel*. Not only did he have a reputation in the United States – even winning the first-ever 'Oscar' for acting, in Josef von Sternberg's *The Last Command* – he also had a very keen grasp of the dynamics of the international film business, often initiating projects and working very closely with Pommer throughout the 1920s.[83]

Attempts to launch international stars by importing American actresses in the latter part of the 1920s were only intermittently successful.[84] Louise Brooks never became popular in the 1920s. Anna May Wong (directed by E.A. Dupont and Richard Eichberg in films like *Piccadilly* and *Song*) failed to catch the attention of American audiences, and Betty Amann – Pommer's American 'discovery' for May's *Asphalt* never developed her star potential. The cast of Murnau's *Faust* (with Emil Jannings, Yvette Guilbert and Gösta Ekmann) was a deliberate attempt to have an internationally attractive cast: the fact that Camilla Horn was given the role of Gretchen, originally offered to Lilian Gish (to echo her success in Griffith's *Way Down East* and *Broken Blossoms*) did not help these transatlantic ambitions. It was even more remarkable that none of Fritz Lang's leading men or women (including Rudolf Klein-Rogge or Brigitte Helm) ever became international stars. When he and Pommer visited Hollywood, Lang apparently was irritated by Douglas Fairbanks, insisting that what mattered in American picture making was the performer, not the set, nor the originality of the subject. Only with the coming of sound – and after using (on Jannings' suggestion), American directors such as Josef von Sternberg – did UFA develop successful stars, such as Marlene Dietrich, Hans Albers, Lilian Harvey, Willy Fritsch and Marika Rökk, all of them closely modelled on American stars of the early 1930s.

Ludwig Klitzsch and the management structure in 1927

By 1927, the fortunes of the German cinema as a national and international cinema had become even more closely allied to the fate of UFA. In January

Figure 9 Eye-catching and double-framed: Lilian Harvey at the bar in Wilhelm Thiele's *Die Drei von der Tankstelle* 1930

Source: BFI films: stills, posters and designs

1926 Pommer had resigned, several months before the completion of both *Metropolis* and *Faust*, to take up an old offer from Paramount, which prompted major soul searching in the press and made 1926–7 the second most crucial season for UFA.[85] Following severe losses in 1926, the company's major creditor and stock holder, Deutsche Bank, was prepared to force UFA into receivership unless new outside capital could be found. Alfred Hugenberg, thwarted in his ambitions when UFA was first set up in 1917, seized his chance and acquired majority holdings. His new director, Ludwig Klitzsch, set about restructuring the company, following the Hollywood studio system. Klitzsch probably developed the concept that finally welded together the different models of running a national–international film conglomerate, but more than that, he also had the vision to add to it another model – that of a media communication business.

Klitzsch' concept of film making, as mentioned, dated back to 1916 at a meeting of the Deutsche Lichtbild Gesellschaft (DLG), when the idea of using the cinema for propaganda ends was first mooted. This appeared to be in the first instance not for political and nationalist ends, but for economic propaganda in certain markets in the Middle East and Far East, to support the principle that trade not only follows the flag but that trade likes even more to follow the movies! At the time, Klitzsch's concept was not adopted by the backers of the DLG, but he caught the attention of its then public relations manager, Alfred Hugenberg. Klitzsch's background in publishing meant that his model was both consumer-driven, and had a public-service (in this case, national–patriotic) remit. However, there was no doubt in Klitzsch's mind that it had to be built on sound commercial principles, with political motives being secondary. He saw what today one would call a 'synergy' between the electronic industry, the energy industry and the transport industry, into which publishing and the cinema fitted as part of an integrated communication strategy.

Reading the re-structuring plan,[86] it becomes clear that Klitzsch reorganised UFA in 1928, not only according to the management principles of the American studios, with a strict separation of the finance department from production, but also with a reorganisation of distribution and hiving off some of the subsidiary companies. Klitzsch thus brought to UFA the central producer system, overseen by Ernst Hugo Correll, who divided production up between different heads of production ('Produktionsleiter' such as Günther Stapenhorst, Bruno Duday and Erich Pommer), thereby achieving both greater central control and greater division of labour.[87] He introduced strict shooting schedules,[88] tight budgets, and accountability. If the Hugenberg takeover sealed the fate of UFA ideologically, as most commentators have argued, it is equally true that from a business perspective, it was thanks to Klitzsch that for the first time, UFA was run along strictly commercial lines.[89] Pommer, having worked in the United States in 1926, was rehired by Klitzsch in 1927.[90] When he returned, he – entirely in keeping with Klitzsch's ideas – appeared happy to implement and then preside over a central-producer system.[91]

The Klitzsch regime allowed UFA to catch up rapidly with major international developments, such as the introduction of sound, which the previous management had been very slow to take an interest in. UFA converted production to sound in just over a year, while the company was also able to avoid costly competition, by agreeing terms with its major domestic rival, Tobis Klangfilm. From 1930–31 onwards, UFA once more began to make a profit, not least because it proved to be successful in aggressively marketing foreign-language versions of its films in France and Great Britain, in addition to exploiting its interest in gramophone and sheet music. It also seems that Klitzsch's and Pommer's ideas about production were compatible, especially because both thought in international terms, and because both understood the business of film making. A new mood of self-confidence (though not without a hint of anti-intellectualism – or worse) had entered the film trade.

> How many principles and theories had to founder, until air and space could finally be created for the new kind of international German films, such as it is here [i.e. with *Heimkehr*] presented! Complete severance from the avantgarde, no concession to the so-called experts, and a willingness to sacrifice the bulky studio superstructure.[92]

However, it was not with its star directors of the 1920s that UFA achieved financial recovery: Murnau had left for Hollywood early in 1927, Lang had formed his own company, Pabst was working for Seymour Nebenzahl's Nero Film, while Dupont had gone to Britain, like Carl Mayer, who after following Murnau to Hollywood had settled in London in 1931. Efficient genre directors such as Karl Hartl, Gustav Ucicky and especially Hanns Schwarz, put UFA back into the black, the latter with six films, among them some of the biggest box office successes until then: *Bomben auf Monte Carlo*, *Einbrecher*, *Ungarische Rhapsodie*, *Die Wunderbare Lüge der Nina Petrowna*):

> The laws of cause and effect are suspended, gravity is no more, only time runs and runs. As if by magic it gives us the most beautiful image of the living rhythm of the world, of history, of being.[93]

Musicals and comedies became the mainstay of the internationally focused German cinema, with super-productions like *Der Kongress tanzt*, star vehicles like *Die Drei von der Tankstelle* and *Ein blonder Traum*, the zany comedy *Viktor und Viktoria* and the domestic melodrama *Abschied*. These films conveyed quite a different image of German cinema than that of the 1920s. Even before the Nazi take-over in 1933, transformation of the German film industry from a twin-track 'artistic film'/prestige production cinema to a mainstream entertainment cinema was well on the way, forced by economic necessity and technological change even more than by political interference. While the migration of personnel to Hollywood, having begun with Ernst Lubitsch in 1921 and followed by Murnau, Dupont and Leni, had also gathered pace by 1927–8, its motives were, at least until 1933, personal and professional as much as political.

Klitzsch also had ideas about how to reshape the industry's trade organisation. He undertook steps to turn SPIO into an industry-wide body, much along the lines of the MPPDA, which, of course he had seen in action on his US visit.[94] The change of direction provoked, as a counter-measure, the formation of Dacho, whose first president was Lupu Pick, followed by G.W. Pabst. SPIO, on the other hand, gradually transformed itself into a body disciplining and policing its members. While this undoubtedly helped pave the way for the Nazi take-over, it also – again paradoxically – brought the German film industry in line with American practice, by creating a more overtly self-regulatory body, which allowed the industry to fend off outside interference. This, too, Klitzsch copied from Will Hays: intransigent at home, while staunchly defending the nation's film industry interests abroad, especially during his visit to the US in order to renegotiate the Parufamet stipulations.

The dilemmas of UFA: directions and directors

By these criteria, the history of the Weimar film industry is not that it was too right wing, nor too much a product of the Prussian military, nor even that it

Figure 10 Renate Müller and Adolf Wohlbrück in Reinhold Schünzel's *Viktor und Viktoria* (1933)

Source: Stiftung Deutsche Kinemathek, Berlin

behaved too much like a tool of the ruling elite. The dilemma may have been that it remained for too long a 'craft and cottage industry', that even in the case of UFA it both centralised too much and did not centralise consistently enough, that it was undercapitalised and that it provided its creative personnel with not enough management discipline. In other words, its problem may have been not too much capitalism, but too little. Its failures were due less to knaves or villains or conspiracies, but to risks and gambles, to winning some battles and losing others, to sometimes shrewd and sometimes bad management decisions.[95] The moral would seem to be the one espoused by Pommer (who embodied some of the very best of UFA, but also shares responsibility for mistakes): if UFA wanted to be successful and powerful enough to compete with the major American film companies, it had better do it the capitalists' way, or not at all. The Weimar film industry hesitated too long, or did not have the organisational structures to carry out this policy. The political master-narrative about UFA, with which this chapter started is, at the very least, incomplete. On the other hand, the fact that UFA 'failed' to do it the Americans' way may also have been its glory, for it gave the world films that by strictly economic criteria should not have been made at all.

What, however, is also symptomatic about UFA is that many of the problems and decisions facing Pommer in the 1920s are still dilemmas today. In fact, they might be said to plague not so much the German film industry, as they define the European cinema: what is its identity? What might a European cinema be, in the face of Hollywood hegemony? The various options tested by Pommer have been tried many times since, with variable success. UFA's afterlife, as it were, is therefore not only the popularity of its classic films, especially from the 1930s and 1940s, with German television audiences or the hundreds of thousands of visitors to UFA anniversary exhibitions. By chance and coincidence, in 1992 the old UFA studio in Babelsberg celebrated its 75th anniversary just in time to see its site sold by the 'Treuhand' to a French conglomerate, the 'Compagnie Général des Eaux' (CGE), whose subsidiary, the aptly-named 'Compagnie Immobilière Phénix S.A.', appointed the French-trained 'New German Cinema' director and only post-war German Oscar-winner, Volker Schloendorff as (caretaker-) director. Whether this is the sign for the German cinema to become its own museum, or whether this phoenix will indeed rise from the ashes, still remains to be seen. But the very moves to revive German cinema through the buildings and movie icons associated with UFA, makes of the studio and its history perhaps the most poignant site of the German cinema's historical imaginary. Apart from Erich Pommer, the most prominent embodiment of UFA, its human face, so to speak, is undoubtedly Fritz Lang, himself both object and source of still potent imaginary identifications.

Notes

1 This chapter contains sections initially published in German as 'Kunst und Krise' in Hans Michael Bock, Michael Töteberg (eds), *Das Ufa Buch* (Frankfurt: Zweitausendeins, 1992) and in English as 'Germany: The Weimar Years' in Geoffrey Nowell-Smith (ed.) *The Oxford History of World Cinema* (Oxford: Oxford University Press, 1997): 136–51. Among the books consulted for the revision, the most important are: Wolfgang Jacobsen, *Erich Pommer, ein Produzent macht Filmgeschichte* (Berlin: Argon, 1989), Thomas J. Saunders, *Hollywood in Berlin* (Los Angeles and Berkeley: California University Press, 1994), Klaus Kreimeier, *The UFA Story* (New York: Harcourt Brace, 1996) and Ursula Hardt, *From Caligari to California: Eric Pommer's Life in the International Film Wars* (Providence/Oxford: Berghahn Book, 1996).

2 For a lucid general overview of the political narrative around UFA, see Julian Petley, *Capital and Culture: German Cinema 1933–1945* (London: British Film Institute, 1979). As to the reluctance of investing in the cinema, Peter Bächlin argues that the Prussian establishment viewed businessmen in general with deep distrust, and considered those with an interest in the cinema as little better than criminals. See Bächlin 1972 [originally 1947]).

3 Erich Pommer was born in 1889 in Hildesheim, and died in 1966 in Los Angeles. The best biographical and career study is that of Ursula Hardt, *From Caligari to California – Eric Pommer's Life in the International Film Wars* (Providence and Oxford: Berghahn Books, 1996). The best collection of documents, writings by and about Pommer is the catalogue for the centenary retrospective at the Berlin Film Festival, edited by Wolfgang Jacobsen, *Erich Pommer, ein Produzent macht Filmgeschichte* (Berlin: Argon, 1989).

4 'German experts noted proudly that an American compilation of the ten best pictures at the box office in 1921 placed *Madame Dubarry* first, ahead of *Way Down East* and *The Kid*, while *Caligari*, *Anna Boleyn*, *The Golem* and *Carmen* were placed fourth, fifth, seventh and eighth, respectively. They concluded that 'German pictures generally surpassed American in appeal as well as quality' (see Saunders 1994: 63–4). For a more detailed study of the reception of *Caligari* in the US, see Budd 1992. On the export performance of Hollywood, see Kristin Thompson, *Exporting Entertainment* (London: BFI Publishing, 1985).

5 G.D. Feldmann (ed.) *Die Nachwirkungen der Inflation auf die deutsche Geschichte, 1924–1933* (Munich: Oldenbourg, 1985), especially the chapter by Heidrun Homburg on the AEG–Siemens merger proposals. Thus, the German heavy industry (coal, steel), the German chemical and electricity industries, as well as the German communication industries would provide comparable cases.

6 A good model for comparison would be David Bordwell, Janet Staiger and Kristin Thompson, *Classical Hollywood Cinema: Film Style and Mode of Production to 1960* (London: Routledge and Kegan Paul, 1985) especially Janet Staiger, 'The Hollywood mode of production to 1930': 85–153. In the following footnotes, I shall refer to this chapter, unless indicated differently in the footnote.

7 Klaus Kreimeier's *The UFA Story* extensively supports itself with archive material. However, given the scope of Kreimeier's task and the ambition to tell a 'story', he necessarily leaves some detailed questions unanswered. For an example of the yields from a more limited perspective, an examination of the trade press in the US and Germany for the years 1920–7, see Jan-Christoph Horak, 'Rin-Tin-Tin erobert Berlin', in Jung and Schatzberg 1992: 255–70.

8 Richard Abel, *The Cine Goes to Town* (Berkeley: University of California Press, updated edition 1994): 19–58 and *The Red Rooster Scare* (Berkeley: University of California Press, 1999) which extensively discusses the Pathé organisation in the US. Pathé's model of both horizontal and vertical integration is also described in Thompson 1985: 59–60.

9 The best introduction to the industrial organisation of German cinema prior to the First World War is Corinna Müller, *Frühe deutsche Kinematographie* (Stuttgart: Metzler, 1994). For an English-language account of early German cinema, see Thomas Elsaesser (ed.) *A Second Life: German Cinema's First Decades* (Amsterdam: Amsterdam University Press, 1996b).

10 Paul Davidson originally came from the clothing trade and ladies' fashion in Frankfurt, moving first into cinema exhibition, and from there into distribution and production. See Peter Lähn, 'Paul Davidson and the Frankfurt Film Scene,' in Elsaesser 1996b: 79–85.

11 On Nordisk and one of its chief trading partner, David Oliver, see Evelyn Hampicke, 'The Danish Influence: David Oliver and Nordisk in Germany' in Elsaesser 1996b: 72–78.

12 Martin Loiperdinger, 'The Kaiser's cinema' in Elsaesser 1996b: 41–50.

13 Erich Pommer, 'Bedeutung der Konzerne in der Filmindustrie', *Film-Kurier* no. 204, 13 September1920, reprinted in Jacobsen 1989: 32–3.

14 Nordisk film sold its subsidiary, Nordische Film GmbH (together with its other foreign interests), as well as Oliver Film GmbH; Oskar Messter sold his Messter Film, with the glasshouse in Tempelhof; Paul Davidson sold PAGU and a second glass house in Tempelhof; other, much smaller firms were also added (see Kreimeier 1992: 39–42).

15 Critics at the time talked about UFA as a cartel (on the basis of the various tax concessions granted by the government). In the United States cartels (with price-fixing and other non-competitive agreements) were officially illegal, though in practice tolerated. Later historians, such as Douglas Gomery use the word 'oligopoly'.

Hermann Wollenberg (*Fifty Years of German Film*, London: Falcon Press, 1947: 15–16) argues that, unlike in the USA, no cartelisation and concentration was in place in Germany to encourage diversity and experimentation.

16 See Saunders 1994: 52.

17 See Saunders 1994: 60–3.

18 Lubitsch's departure coincides with the beginning of the accelerated period of inflation because his company was associated with Famous Players, who wound up their business in Germany in 1921. Janet Staiger notes that Famous Players hired Hans Dreier in 1923 as its chief art director, emulated the German manner. See note 6 above, Bordwell, Staiger and Thompson 1985: 148.

19 The second official expedient by which to control the movies, the entertainment tax or Lustbarkeitssteuer. This, a prewar practice borrowed from regulation of circuses and other public amusements, was a surcharge imposed by the municipality on ticket prices. It fluctuated so widely from one locality to the next that any generalization about its severity is hazardous, but in the early 1920s it ranged in the neighbourhood of 20 to 30 percent. In some cities it rose well above these values, however, and was blamed for bankrupting otherwise profitable cinemas.

(Saunders 1994: 31)

20 The parliamentary discussion late in 1919 which preceded introduction of formal legislation underscored near unanimity on the need for action. That a Nationalist deputy who decried movies as a pestilence unleashed by unscrupulous capitalists won the applause of both the Centre and the SPD gives a fair indication of the prevailing mood.

(Saunders 1994: 28)

21 One often commented feature of the censorship law was that it could be – and was – used to exert political pressure on distributors and exhibitors not to show films that might cause public disorder. This was a strategy used by the Nazis towards the end of the decade, e.g. around *All Quiet on the Western Front* (see W. Petzet, *Verbotene Filme*, Frankfurt 1931).

22 The history of the merger of Decla-Bioskop and UFA is detailed in Jacobsen 1989: 49–50, who gives some idea of the complexity, the machinations and the sheer fragmentation of the German film business, even among the market leaders.

23 In August [1923] Willy Haas looked back on a year of German production and judged it qualitatively incapable of competing abroad. Its export continued only because it underbid all competitors. In October Wolfgang Martini, a leading trade journalist in Munich, asserted that in the public mind American film had already achieved victory in Germany.

(Saunders 1994: 65)

24 *Film-Echo* 31 July 1922, quoted in Jacobsen 1989: 44.

25 The restructuring of 1921, when the government share (and that of Robert Bosch and Graf Donnersmarck) was taken over by the Deutsche Bank, as well as the financing of the Decla-Bioskop acquisition, does not seem to have shifted the balance of power as far as ownership was concerned (see Kreimeier 1992: 85–6). The *Filmkurier* 27 May 1921 carried a very critical article about the methods used to acquire the Decla-Bioskop.

26 In Germany, the large companies are A.G. (i.e. publicly quoted companies) while medium-sized companies are generally GmbH, 'reflecting the risks of film production' (Bächlin 1972: 49).

27 See Douglas Gomery, *The Hollywood Film Industry* (London: Macmillan, 1986).

28 For example, Bächlin (1972 [1947]), Spiker (1975) and W. Becker, *Film und Herrschaft* (Berlin: Volker Spiess, 1973), whose counterparts would be F. F. Klingender and S. Legg, *Money Behind the Screen* (London: Lawrence & Wishart, 1937).

29 See Gomery (note 27 above), and Tom Schatz, *The Genius of the System* for the US, and Richard Abel, *The Cine Goes to Town* (Berkeley: University of California Press, 1990), for France.

30 This put them in a good position in Europe. Because there were so many small 'independent companies', American producers were able to gain an easy foothold, which was helped with the quota quickies for securing an import licence (Kontingentschein). But not only the Americans benefited: Michael Balcon from Britain also invested in Germany. In 1925 he sent Alfred Hitchcock to Munich, where the Emelka studio wanted to attract foreign capital. See Donald Spoto, *The Dark Side of Genius: Alfred Hitchcock* (London: Plexus, 1984: 85–9).

31 Jacobsen 1989: 75 gives details. The percentage of American films in German cinemas were: 1922, 36 per cent; 1924–5, 54 per cent. The fact that fewer films were being made (1921: 600; 1923: 300) has to be seen in the context of the estimates for the ceiling of around 230 films that the German market could make (Bächlin: 1972 [1947]: 49).

32 *Lichtbild-Bühne* 6, 10 February 1923.

33 Staiger, in Bordwell, Staiger and Thompson 1985: 128–41 (see note 6 above).

34

> If the approximation between German practice and von Stroheim's style constituted one recurring theme in commentary on *Greed*, the element of excess or fanaticism was the other. Critics confirmed that UFA had correctly sensed, though falsely understood, the deviation of *Greed* from American motion picture convention.
>
> (Saunders 1994: 137)

35 See Bächlin 1972 [1947]: 43. He also discusses the central producer system.

36

> Art assured export and export meant salvation. An ardent partisan of this doctrine, Pommer had moreover an incomparable flair for cinematic values and popular demands.
>
> (Kracauer 1947: 65)

37 See Jacobsen 1989: 44.

38 For a more detailed list, see Jacobsen 1989: 48. As Klaus Kreimeier points out, with Decla-Bioskop UFA acquired some of the best ideas for marketing and merchandising, and one of the first cross-media sales campaigns (the Decla-Ullstein Uco-Film) (Kreimeier 1992: 88).

39 Erich Pommer, *Film-Kurier* no. 1, 1 January 1922, quoted in Jacobsen 1989: 43–4.

40 Jesse Lasky returned to director units in 1917:

> Each director in our four studios will be absolutely independent to produce to the best of his efficiency and ability. With the discontinuance of a central scenario-bureau, each director will have his own writing staff, and the author will continue active work on every production until its conclusion, staying by the side of the director even when the film is cut and assembled.
>
> ('Jesse L. Lasky announces plans', *New York Daily Mirror*, 77, no. 2003, 12 May 1917: 22 (quoted in Staiger 1985: 137))

Lasky was the studio-head who hired Pommer in 1926 (*Hotel Imperial*).

41 Erich Pommer, 'Geschäftsfilm und künstlerischer Film', *Der Film* no. 50, 10 December 1922, quoted in Jacobsen 1989: 44–5.

42 See review of *Metropolis* by Hans Siemsen (*Berlin Börsen Courier*), but also Jacobsen 1989: 71, where Lang shows himself impressed by the equipment available at the First National Studios. There Pommer bought an American Mitchell camera. The film *Metropolis* used a French Debrie, a Mitchell and a German Stachow.

43 Andrew Higson, 'Film Europe', in Sibylle M. Sturm (ed.) *Hallo? Berlin? Ici Paris!* (Munich: text + kritik, 1996): 63–76.

44 Erich Pommer, 'Die Bedeutung der Konzerne…' cited in Jacobsen 1989: 32–3.

45 See Sibylle M. Sturm (ed.) *Hallo? Berlin? Ici Paris!* (Munich: edition text + kritik, 1996) for essays on the German film emigration in Paris.

46 Pommer, cited in in Jacobsen 1989: 54–5.

47 Well into the early 1920s, Griffith continued to work with the outline script, so that very little division of labour was either possible or desirable. As an independent producer–director, he was not tied into release schedules, nor did he have anyone supervising his budgets. One contemporary writer commented:

> Mr Griffith's method of working has its advantages and, under certain circumstances, it would have its grave disadvantages. Mr Griffith, being his own employer, can take all the time he wishes on the making of his productions. A director working on a schedule that makes some consideration of time would be quite at a loss in working without a script.
>
> (Peter Milne, quoted in Bordwell, Staiger and Thompson 1985: 139, see note 6 above)

48 The screenwriter Walter Reisch commented on the change of attitude to feedback from audiences in an interview with me. See 'Vienna–Berlin–London–Hollywood: Greetings to the Sun', *Pix* no. 3, 2000.

49 For Pommer's complaints about 'Filmfremdheit der Kritik' (i.e. critics arguing from non-cinematic assumptions), see also 'Vorstellungen' (reprinted in Jacobsen 1989: 56–7). Among critics trying to mediate was Roland Schacht, 'Der Film und die Gebildeten', *Der Kunstwart* 2 (November 1925), also quoted in Jacobsen 1989: 56–7.

50

> The Americans taught us the meaning of the term 'entertainment value'. We have learnt to select story material, so that […] Minna Schulze's interest is as much roused as that of the disciple of science and art, of the banker, the engineer.'
>
> (Pommer, quoted in Jacobsen 1989: 57)

51 *Kriemhilds Rache/She Devil*, the second part of the blockbuster *The Nibelungen*, for instance, reportedly premiered without its final act, because Lang was unable to finish editing in time, while the opening date could, of course, not be postponed, after a massive budget had been spent on press promotion and cinema advertising, with the result that the film received very mixed reviews (see Bock and Töteberg 1992: 54).

52 Ludwig Berger, another of UFA's top directors, but also a man of the theatre, praised Pommer for teaching him the 'American style', and a wholly new type of *mise-en-scène* (Ludwig Spitzer, 'Gespräch mit Dr Ludwig Berger', *Reichsfilmblatt* no. 49, 5 December 1925: 37–8).

53 See Saunders 1994: 69–72.

54 This was the view of an article in the *Berliner Tageblatt*, no. 581, 9 December 1926. Pommer resigned on 22 January 1926, and was succeeded by Alexander Grau, by then Head of the Kultur(film)abteilung. Emil Jannings, in his autobiography *Theater – Film. Das Leben und ich* (Berchtesgaden, 1951), blames Pommer for being too lenient with his directors. See also Jacobsen: 1989: 79.

55 The impact of inflation can be seen from the following figures: German films in 1921–3 managed to recoup 60–70 per cent of their cost via export, while between 1924–6 export dropped to 20 per cent. It was to rise again, by the early 1930s, to around 50 per cent.

56 Stefan Grossmann, 'Erich Pommers Sturz', in *Das Tagebuch* no. 5, 30 January 1926, pays a fulsome tribute to the Pommer era.

57 See Jan-Christopher Horak, 'Rin-Tin-Tin erobert Berlin', in Jung and Schatzberg 1992: 264–5. It is quite possible that there were dirty tricks campaigns. The US strategy for entering Europe was flexible and adaptable: the Hollywood majors entered on different levels and by different means; via official government channels as well as through purely economic-industrial ones. US studio executives travelled to Europe (especially Fox, Universal and Paramount) to make films in Germany via subsidiaries (cf. Kontingentschein laws). They also offered contracts to F.W. Murnau, E.A. Dupont and Wilhelm Dieterle, among others.

58 It could be argued that UFA as an investment opportunity was mainly judged by its real-estate assets.

> The conclusion one can draw is that the large-scale acquisition [by production companies] of film theatres, which represent the safest form of capital investment in the high risk film industry, persuaded the banks to somewhat relax their earlier caution vis a vis the film business.
>
> (Bächlin 1972 [1947]: 41–2)

59 Little is known about Siegmund Jacob as the Generaldirektor of the Ufa-Verleihbetriebe, and about Alexander Grau's performance as head of theatres (see Kreimeier 1992: 39).

60 Anti-Hollywood sentiment did not come from either exhibitors or the movie-going public. This is how Dr. R.B. [Rudolf Beissel] argued in 'Die amerikanische Gefahr' (Danger from America), *Reichsfilmblatt* (23 February 1924): 9–10, quoted in Saunders 1994: 105.

61

> In its mid-decade crisis UFA carried out a confidential audit in the distribution sector to compare the company's fortunes with domestic and American feature films. The report, never published, paints a picture of crushing financial loss through pre-Parufamet commitments to handle American film. In the crucial season 1925/26 ten of eleven pictures from Paramount, twelve of fifteen from Goldwyn, ten of fifteen from First National, and seven of twelve from Warner Bros. each entailed losses of 10,000 marks or more for UFA. Fully three-quarters of UFA's American releases fell into this category, for losses totalling 1,283,796 marks! Only 3 American pictures (Rin Tin Tin in *Lighthouse by the Sea*, Buster Keaton's *The Navigator* and Victor Sjöström's *He Who Gets Slapped*) showed significant profits.
>
> (Saunders 1994: 155)

62 As Peter Bächlin points out, the Parufament agreement is only one in a long line of similar agreements that the US companies had with German producers and distributors, making it clear that it was only another variant of the *Kontingent* laws (see Bächlin 1972 [1947]: 46–7).

63 UFA produced 15 films in 1927, out of a total production of 242, 16 in 1928, and 13 in 1929. However, the remaining films were produced by 83 companies, which means that many of them made only one or two films per year, far too few to have leverage in the exhibition sector, or to have a chance in the 'battle for the bookings'.

64 Jürgen Spiker, *Film und Kapital* (Berlin: Volker Spiess, 1975): 39, quoting Annemarie Schweins, 'Die Entwicklung der deutschen Filmwirtschaft', PhD dissertation, Nürnberg, 1958.

65 See table in Bächlin 1972 [1947]: 118, according to which there was 100–150 per cent over-capacity right up to 1927, when supply gradually comes close to demand (1929–30). During the 1930s, production was cut back drastically, so that the German industry could actually cope with producing no more than 150 films per annum to satisfy demand, which meant that each film could be exploited more effectively.

66 Americans had up to 40 per cent of the German market, and this despite German overproduction. Precise figures: 1923: 24.5 per cent; 1924: 33.2 per cent; 1925: 40.7 per cent; 1926: 44.5 per cent (France: 78.5 per cent; Britain: 83.6 per cent in 1926).

67 For an idea of the genres, diversity and tendencies within the annual national production and exhibition, see Gero Gandert, *Der Film der Weimarer Republik. Ein Handbuch 1929* (Berlin: Walter de Gruyter, 1993).

68 In *Pandora's Box* Dr Schoen advises his son to put Lulu in his up-and-coming variety review, saying 'my newspapers will guarantee her success'. Anticipating the launching of Susan Kane in Welles's *Citizen Kane*, Pabst/Schoen also refer to the Berlin newspaper and publishing industries generally, which from the mid-1920s were keen for tie-ins with the film industry. The Hugenberg UFA 'rescue deal' in 1927 can also be understood in the context of his desire as owner of Scherl to diversify into industries with 'synergy', before his rivals do: in Hugenberg's case, these were Ullstein and Mosse. See Irmalotte Guttmann, *Über die Nachfrage auf dem Filmmarkt im Deutschland* (Berlin: Wolffsohn, 1928).

69 See Kreimeier 1992: 104–5; Jacobsen 1989: 47.

70 Interview with Walter Reisch, *Pix* 3 (2000).

71 Lubitsch's *Madame Dubarry*, for instance, was timed to open the new UFA Palast in Berlin-Zoo, 18 Sept 1919. The history of the stage shows and gala openings of Weimar cinema is yet to be written. Although they can be seen as part of the cinema's drive for middle-class respectability, the extent to which they not simply imitated the theatre – Max Reinhardt's theatre – but mimicked and parodied it, suggests that a more colourful form of negotiation was taking place. For a description of some of the sophisticated effects, see Joseph Roth, *Frankfurter Zeitung* 19 November 1925, quoted in Kreimeier 1992: 136–7.

72 See Richard Maltby, 'Censorship and self-regulation', in G. Nowell-Smith (ed.) *The Oxford History of World Cinema* (Oxford: Oxford University Press, 1997): 235–40.

73 See Ruth Vasey, *Diplomatic Representations: The World According to Hollywood* (Madison: University of Wisconsin Press, 1995).

74 Quoted in Bächlin 1972 [1947]: 191.

75 See Bächlin 1972 [1947]: 196.

76 For top ten lists from 1925 onwards (and their rationale), see Joseph Garncarz, 'Hollywood in Germany', in U. Jung (ed.) *Der deutsche Film* (Trier: Wissenschaftlicher Verlag, 1993): 167–214.

77 For a history of SPIO, whose first chief officer was Erich Pommer, see Jacobsen 1989: 49. SPIO was founded in October 1923, bringing together twelve interest groups, including the 'Spezialausschuß der Filmindustriellen' (standing committee of the film industry). See *Film-Kurier* 226 (6 October 1923).

78 Another question would be how strong the trade unions were at UFA: there is frequent mention of crippling strikes during the inflation period. See Michael Töteberg, 'Wir hier oben, ihr da unten' *Das Ufa-Buch* 1992: 240–4.

79 The European efforts were not encouraging, after the UFA-Aubert deal went wrong, the Pathé-Westi fiasco further discouraged such arrangements. See essays by J.P. Goergen and A. Higson in Sibylle M. Sturm (ed.) *Hallo? Berlin? Ici Paris!* (Munich: text + kritik, 1996).

80 Cited in Ursula Hardt 1996: 80.

81 In 1926 Fox-Europa released its first productions, among them *Der Trödler von Amsterdam* and *Die Mühle von Sanssouci*, and later produced Walter Ruttmann's *Berlin, Sinfonie einer Großstadt*. United Artists extended its field of operations first with Phoebus-Film – here cooperation included appointment of Joseph Schenck to the Phoebus board – and then with Rex-Film under the directorship of Lupu Pick. First

National enlisted prominent German personnel, initially Friedrich Zelnik and then Wilhelm Dieterle, for its production company.

(Saunders 1994: 81)

82 As a response to the right sabotaging the public screenings of *All Quiet on the Western Front,* the left caused disturbances around the screenings of *Das Flötenkonzert von Sanssouci.* On Walter Reisch, see Chapter 3 in Part III, this volume.

83 If a book on Pommer can with some justification be called 'From Caligari to California', a book on Weimar cinema, might, instead of being 'From Caligari to Hitler', be entitled 'From *Madame Dubarry* to *The Blue Angel*': to signal the importance of Jannings, an actor whose ambiguously public role during the Nazi years (similar to that of his colleagues Werner Krauss and Heinrich George) has discouraged scholars from comprehensively assessing his career.

84 In 1927 Pommer wrote in the trade journal *Variety*:

When Europe has made a star, Europe cannot long retain that star – for a very simple reason – money. Europe cannot now, nor, I fear, for some time, pay the salaries America can – because Europe cannot get that salary back in box office returns. The possibilities of profit […] are too restricted.

(Quoted in Hardt 1996: 109)

85 On the background to Pommer's departure, see Jacobsen 1989: 76–81; Kreimeier 1992: 146–57; Hardt 1996: 94–106.

86 See Spiker 1975: 45.

87 Other production heads were Alfred Zeisler, Noel Bloch, Gregor Rabinovitch and, from November 1927, Erich Pommer. Major production units in the 1930s were Hans Ritter (who uses Steinhoff for *Hitlerjunge Quex*) and Alfred Zeisler (who uses Karl Hartl for *Gold*), along with Günther Stapenhorst's unit. See also Kreimeier 1992: 202–3, 215. The trade journal *Film-Kurier* 106 (4 May 1928) published an essay 'Was ist ein Produktionsleiter' ('What is a Head of Production'?), written by Joe May and Hanns Schwarz.

88 From Hollywood, Pommer imported to UFA the famous 'Drehplan', his version of the continuity script (see Jacobsen 1989: 88).

89 Whatever his political agenda, Hugenberg and his right-hand man, Ludwig Klitzsch, were committed to contesting Hollywood's home turf. Rapid revision of the Parufamet agreements and repayment of the accompanying loan did not mean that they intended to solve the problems of German film production without reference to Hollywood.

(Saunders 1994: 248)

90 See Jacobsen 1989: 83. Pommer came back to Germany, on loan from the Producers' Service Corporation, to which UFA had to pay royalties.

91 In Pola Negri's *Memoirs of a Star* (New York, 1970), a passage describes Pommer's introduction of the 'composite set' into Hollywood practice, at the time of his production of *Hotel Imperial* and *Barbed Wire.* Pommer's first experience in Hollywood was a chequered one. He was first at Paramount, then moved to MGM, where Thalberg wanted to assign him to a B-production, which Pommer refused. See *Film-Kurier* no. 278 (24 November 1927), also quoted in Jacobsen 1989: 84.

92 See Ernst Jäger, *Film Kurier* no. 207 (30 August 1928).

93 See Oscar Bie, 'Eric Charell's *Der Kongress Tanzt*', *Der Filmkurier*, June 1931.

94 See a passage in Ilya Ehrenburg's *Die Traumfabrik* (Berlin: Malik 1931), about a (fictional?) meeting between Klitzsch and Zukor, where Zukor is reported to have said: 'But this Klitzsch guy! Not a patch on our own Will Hays', quoted in Jacobsen 1989: 76.

95 So Herr Hugenberg, representative of the German-national heavy industry, has bought Ufa, […] lock, stock and barrel. The left-wing press is demoralised, and everyone, yet again, speaks of the catastrophic crisis of German cinema. True, there is a crisis. But it has absolutely nothing to do with the fact that a huge, inert, comatose mass – having been openly offered by the Deutsche Bank for years to anyone willing to pay a halfway acceptable price – has finally found a taker. […] Herr Hugenberg will have to follow market trends [and] presumably do what they all do: make pictures on this or that, depending on what was last successful and promises to be so again. […] Film is a business; a special firmness of character is not one of the requirements.

(Willy Haas, 'Filmkrise und kein Ende', *Die Literarische Welt* nos 15/16 (15 April 1927): 7)

Part II

IN THE REALM OF THE LOOK

Lang, Lubitsch, Murnau and Pabst

1

FRITZ LANG'S TRAPS FOR THE MIND AND EYE

Dr Mabuse the gambler and other disguise artists

our chaotic age, when it will have frozen into a formula long ago[1]

Enigma variations on Weimar cinema identities

Besides *The Cabinet of Dr Caligari*, German Expressionist cinema is often synonymous with Fritz Lang: *Der Müde Tod*, *Dr Mabuse der Spieler*, *Die Nibelungen* and *Metropolis* are the titles one associates with a distinctly German film style in the 1920s.[2] This is paradoxical, considering that Lang always denied having been an Expressionist film maker, even during the heyday of UFA's Expressionist export successes in the early part of the decade.[3] The 'misunderstanding' underscores Lang's emblematic status, but also complicates the question of Weimar cinema's stylistic identity, for Lang's work could equally well stand for eclecticism and diversity: *Der Müde Tod* (1921), a mock-Gothic fairy tale, showed special effects never seen before; *Die Nibelungen* (1924) made a spectacular two-part disaster movie out of the nation's favourite 'boys-own' medievalising epic, and *Metropolis* (1926–7), a sci-fi urbanist dystopia with a happy ending, was the most hyped film ever made in Germany, in the hope of catching American attention. *Spione* (1928) and *Die Frau im Mond* (1929) were block-busters, with advertising campaigns as canny as anything seen today.[4] *M* (1931), capturing Weimar culture's morbid but already 'post-Freudian' fascination with serial killers, became one of the masterpieces of early sound cinema, probing the psychology of the crowd, as well as the darker side of the urban *flaneur*, thanks to Peter Lorre's unforgettable portrayal as the pathologically cunning child murderer, Beckert. Lang's last film in Germany, *The Testament of Dr Mabuse* (1933), was banned by the Nazis and had to have its premiere in Vienna and then Paris.

The case *against* Lang's German films has often been made, but nowhere more damagingly than in Siegfried Kracauer's *From Caligari to Hitler*. The book set the tone for what has in essence remained the same complaint: that Lang's cinema was coherent and entirely consistent. Replete with authoritarian figures projecting conservative–nationalist values, its mystic–mythical iconography of Wilhelmine and Weimar Germany was underpinned by fables that offered proto-fascist solutions to economic and social ills.[5] The name of 'Fritz Lang' stood for films where human relations revolved around power, control and domination, and the individual was a mere puppet of hostile forces, malevolent tyrants or super-spies. When not depicting master minds, Lang's films prefigured a possibly even more insidious tyranny – the 'mass-ornament' of modern urbanised societies, the abstract, calculatedly aesthetic figures whose fascination for the eye Kracauer brilliantly analysed in *Die Nibelungen* and *Metropolis*.[6] Lang's presumed virtues: his irony and distance, the conceptual clarity in his visual compositions and the classical simplicity of his narrative designs turned out to be merely the reverse of his faults: his pessimism, his misanthropy, his convoluted stylistic arabesques and dandy sadism.[7]

Lang's reputation and films have been so well discussed and documented that it is a thankless task to disentangle the author from his works, his works from their various interpretations, the interpretations from their hidden assumptions, and the assumptions from even larger claims about the Weimar *Zeitgeist*. But some attempt is necessary, if only to understand what was eventually to lead to a fundamental reassessment of Lang. Kracauer's animus, for instance, is itself historically locatable: it forms part of a generally cautious sizing up between Lang and his Weimar contemporaries in their Californian exile, notably T.W. Adorno and Bert Brecht. Adorno and Lang met frequently, though mainly through their spouses. At first, his relationship with Brecht was also quite cordial, until they quarrelled when working on *Hangmen also Die*.[8] However, in spite of professional differences, there was mutual admiration. What they had in common – apart from their disgust at Californian-style consumer-capitalism – was their distrust of so-called human nature, which is to say, they all rejected psychological 'realism'. In Lang's films, it is artifice that triumphs even more than 'evil' – a fundamentally ironic strategy that earned him the reputation of being an anti-humanist and probably contributed to the somewhat frosty climate even under a Californian sun! Kracauer, who was living in New York rather than on the West Coast, was, by the end of the Second World War, very much the poor relation, both economically as well as intellectually in this illustrious community. His personal approaches to Lang, such as they were, seem to have been rebuffed, unlike those of Lotte Eisner who courted Lang with flattering perseverance long enough to be eventually permitted to be his first biographer.

Her efforts, fortunately for Lang, paid off, so that he remained not only a German director with an American passport but also, thanks, in part, to a seminal article on his style that appeared in Paris in 1947,[9] his reputation began to undergo a sea change, and he also became a director of French films. This was not in the sense that he 'returned' to France from Hollywood as had Jean Renoir and Max Ophuls (though Lang had made one film in France in 1934 – *Liliom*, and had starred in Godard's 1962 *Le Mepris*). Rather, his films had acquired a reputation in Parisian cinephile circles that made his work – in this respect second only to Alfred Hitchcock's – the very epitome of a certain idea of what was cinema.[10] The film makers Eric Rohmer, Alexandre Astruc, Jacques Rivette, Jean-Luc Godard and François Truffaut were among his admirers, and their respect is echoed in important articles on Lang as the master of *mise-en-scène* and of 'pure cinema' in the otherwise rivalling journals *Cahiers du Cinéma, Positif,* and *Présence du Cinéma* by Jean Douchet, Philippe Demonsablon, Michel Mourlet and Gérard Legrand.[11]

For Raymond Bellour, Noel Burch and Thierry Kuntzel, writing in the late 1960s and 1970s, Lang's work is exemplary not so much because it illustrates certain problems in film theory but because it helped define the agenda of what these problems were: questions of figure and ground, of off-screen space, of the single image and narrative flow, the importance of the point-of-view shot and the close-up or fragment.[12] To Noel Burch, for instance, Lang was an avant-garde director, whose work exhibits strategies of formal permutation in the treatment of space, narrative and editing that, given other circumstances, might have taken the cinema in completely different directions: away from novelistic forms of story telling, or using illusionism to represent action.[13] One of the strongest claims for Lang's pre-eminence came from Bellour:

> For today, with Fritz Lang entering legend in France, far from America which never really fathomed him, and from his native Germany which was unable to reclaim him, the audiences flocking to the Cinématèque are coming more or less consciously to admire the man who, in his work, has envisaged film as the ultimate metaphor.
>
> (Bellour 1981: 29)

Figure 11 'Expressionism: it's all a Game!' Sharpsuits and Divine decadence in *Dr Mabuse, the Gambler* (1921)

Source: BFI films: stills, posters and designs

'The ultimate metaphor' is a suggestive term, one that prompts the question: metaphor of what? Of fate, destiny and tyranny, as in Kracauer's thesis? As a metaphor of the cinema experience or of the workings of the mind itself, as it makes sense of conflicting sense perceptions? Emerging from the subtle and searching formal analyses of 'French Lang' is the director's importance for a history of the cinema as the history of 'seeing–knowing–believing' and their contending claims: a critical, reflexive and vigilant discourse of the visible, in the age of mechanical mimesis and the technological supports of eye, brain and ear. In this perspective Lang's *mise-en-scène* formulates the norms of what has come to be regarded as the classical cinema at the same time as it situates itself at the limits of this mode, so that the very functioning of the system, the preconceptions and premises on which it rests, become demonstrable and evident: 'French Lang' is a theorist's and director's director.

The enigma of Lang, therefore, cannot be pinned merely to the ideological ambiguities that surrounded him for much of his life, when he was retrospectively suspected of having harboured Nazi sympathies in his 1920s films *Die Nibelungen* and *Metropolis*, while he consistently made anti-totalitarian films in the United States during the 1930s and 1940s, pleading against 'mob rule' while being accused of communist sympathies.[14] From *Fury*, his first Hollywood picture, onwards, Lang espoused liberal views, though he still took what could be regarded as a sceptical or fatalistic view of the masses as dupes seduced by demagogues. Crowds might be made up of decent simpletons, but they could turn, as in *Fury* (repeating scenes from *Metropolis*), into a fierce lynch mob. In many of Lang's subsequent films, especially *The Blue Gardenia*, *The Big Heat*, *While the City Sleeps*, *Beyond a Reasonable Doubt*, it is the mass media, the legal profession, local government, organised crime and corporate business that are shown colluding with each other, representing a threat to individual liberty. Could one detect a 'reformed' Lang who had quickly learnt the lessons of Nazi Germany, or was the American Lang the same as the German Lang, belatedly converted to democracy, but with his cynicism and fatalism merely turned inside out? How was one to reconcile a supposedly 'proto-fascist' Lang with a 'democratic' Lang, and what would be gained by playing off the 'formalism' of French cinephilia against the 'political' agenda applied to Lang's films in the US or West Germany?

I think the case *for* Lang can be made on grounds other than by recalling a wizard of film technique and an austere perfectionist with an upper-class conservative social agenda who in the United States trimmed his sails to the prevailing wind. If *Metropolis* – an art director's Aladdin's cave to steal from – has always remained a favourite, somehow transcending its author (along with its social message of the hand needing the heart to reconcile it with the head), the other German films from the late 1920s are nothing less than remarkable. *Spione*, watched today, is striking for its sharp look at conspiracies: criminal ones at the ostensible plot level, but perceiving how much Haghi the master spy is made to resemble Lenin, and his headquarters a prison designed by Piranesi, one wonders what this parallel wanted to point up. *Die Frau im Mond*, despite a leaden-footed intrigue about professional rivalry, jealousy, romance and the quest for gold, incorporates very advanced ideas about jet propulsion and rockets, for which Lang acknowledged receiving advice from space scientists Willy Ley and Hermann Oberth, the latter being Wernher von Braun's teacher and boss prior to the V1 'doodle-bug' experiments in the 1940s. Lang also claimed to have invented the countdown when trying to figure out how to create for the audience a sense of suspense around the launch. However pedestrian the elements of Lang's plot for *Die Frau im Mond*, his story-telling technique is that of an engineer: the pieces, pre-formed by pulp fiction and sensationalist cliché are none the less fitted together with the utmost precision, the narrative gears engaging with flawless logic and according to a quite beautiful abstract design.

Equally striking are Lang's takes on surveillance and the cinema's complicity in the militarisation of perception. Already such mythologising vehicles as *Die Spinnen*, *Der Müde Tod* and even *Die Nibelungen* are complex vision machines. The films are full of proto- and pseudo-cinematic apparatuses, made to appear playfully exotic or part of a folk-legend world, as in the sombre and eery fairy tale *Der Müde Tod*, where death plays magic lanternist to the hapless bride. Such self-reflexivity is there from the start, for already an adventure serial like *Die Spinnen* displays its folding mirrors, peepholes and spyglasses as the ingenious tools of trade of an exotic femme fatale – Lio-Sha – doubling as *metteuse-en-scène*: in both films Lang makes himself the ironic archivist of the pleasures and dangers, profits and terrors of assisted sight. Even in his epic family saga, *Die Nibelungen*, the cinema finds itself – apparently incongruously – refigured. There, it is Alberich, the guardian of the Nibelungen treasure, who plays the projectionist of deferred desire, taunting Siegfried with images of fabulous wealth suddenly cast on the smooth stone wall of Alberich's underworld cave dominion. Siegfried, the proverbial *thumbe Thor*, or hero without guile, succumbs to the spell of this phantasmagoria, stretching out his hands, wanting to grasp at the images that conjure up a golden crown on a mountain of diamonds. The contemporary audience would have recognised and enjoyed how Siegfried unwittingly mimicks the proverbial 'Rube', the country bumpkin of early cinema, too unsophisticated to realise that these are mere representations. Yet the Simple Simon of the Nibelungen legend is a quick learner: in the event, Siegfried wins Kriemhild by deviousness and deception. Fighting Alberich for his *Tarnhelm*, the magic cloak of instant invisibility, he puts it to good use as the device to 'body double' Gunther like a stunt-man, in feats of combat that finally defeat Brunhild. It is as if Lang had decided to let the whole Burgundian tragedy hinge on a trick taken straight out of Georges Méliès' box of movie magic, but played out on a stage that foreshadows the looking-glass worlds of Thomas Pynchon's *Gravity's Rainbow* and John Le Carré's Cold War double-crosses.

To see, to know, to believe: this is the triad whose contending claims on perception and reason the radical sceptic in Lang never ceases to play off against each other. Technologically, in that the trick effects of the early films dazzle with sights that the mind knows are impossible, thrilling us with cognitive dissonances that would have made today's digital images a welcome addition to the UFA imagineers' arsenal. Politically, in that Lang's German films know everything about advertising and how to build a brand-name image, but at the same time, they let us look inside the mechanisms of power and persuasion that make such manufacturing possible. Hagen, the sinister figure behind the Burgundian throne, is a consummate 'spin-doctor', taking in Kriemhild to confide in him the secret of Siegfried's weakness, while managing a political assassination so nimbly as to deflect suspicion from his boss, King Gunther.

In Lang's often quoted conviction that 'cinema is *the* art of our time' – a sentiment by no means unique to him[15] – is contained the belief that film was instrumental in a shift in modern culture, where sight, motion, transport and flight combined to become a formative bodily, but also cognitive experience, thanks to the way technically assisted vision appropriates its objects and assigns meaning to sense perception as well as to sense deception.[16] As argued earlier, the cinema of Weimar is hyperconscious of how social life and individual subjectivity respond to specular embodiments and visual seduction, suspecting that the technological media would affect the way political power came to be exercised and social agency – the aggregate states of the people as mass, crowd or spectators – be shaped and controlled. These are also the overriding concerns of Lang's films: the relation of vision to knowledge, of knowledge to power, of power to falsehood, and of duplicity to the pleasures of complicity, of 'being in the know'. Despite their often exoticising guises, Lang's films place the viewer squarely amidst an industrialised civilisation, where apparatuses such as cinema, radio and other recording technologies are the dominant factors of wealth creation, manufacturing and trade, no less than of artistic production, access to information and political intervention.[17]

The idea that vision – the act of seeing and being seen – was in a productive crisis had been a recurrent cypher among German sociologists of the 1910s, such as Max Weber and Georg Simmel.[18] In their writings, as in those of the French décadence poets since Baudelaire,[19] acute sensory attentiveness and perceptual overstimulation appear as the very indices of life in the metropolis and of the mass in a technological society.[20] In Simmel, the 'disembodied eye' made new demands on 'mental life' and in Weber it called for new kinds of 'mediation'.[21] No longer merely the extension of an individual body in space, vision had emancipated (or reified) itself and acquired the techniques and technologies that were fashioning collective social bodies, of which the cinema was at once the most emblematic and only one among many such apparatuses.[22] Walter Benjamin's work on Paris in the nineteenth century has become the encyclopedia of the motifs associated with this moment of perceptual modernism.[23]

Enlightened false consciousness

Kracauer is thus right in detecting particular historical inscriptions in Weimar cinema as represented by Fritz Lang, but they cannot be deciphered merely across the political alternatives of order/chaos, tyranny/liberty. What has become abundantly clear is that the cinema permeated Weimar society as a very contradictory cultural force, at once part of oppositional Modernist avant-gardes and in the forefront of capitalism's own modernising tendencies (as technology, industry and fashion) and for this very reason, invested with the hopes of revolutionary changes while susceptible to being used as the instrument for their containment (in the form of specular seduction, nostalgia, propaganda).[24] Echoes of the contradictions can be found in the various *Kinodebatten*, the campaigns by both left and right against the cinema discussed in a previous chapter, where the suspicions of the literary establishment (fearing for their livelihood and cultural prestige, as the upstart cinema courted new literary talent), inversely mirrored the hostility of the avant-garde on the radical left, who complained that 'progressive' technical apparatuses, such as the mass media of radio and cinema, were used to merely reproduce 'kitsch' and to pacify the public with sentimental melodrama.[25]

In this sense the cinema does indeed function as a metaphor, representing an 'apparatus' as well as a 'dispositif': an arrangement of technologies and bodies, where material and immaterial conditions intersect, where artistic vanguard and engineering skills, modernist experimenters and modernising marketeers, international prestige thinking and national self-stylisation all combine to create a double reference system, parallel universes and possible worlds, at once radically new and ruthlessly parasitic on the history of the visual and performing arts.[26] If the term had not become too over-extended, one could say that Lang was a 'modernist', in the way he responded to the technical challenges posed to the arts: his stance was both self-reflexive and detached. But he was also a mass-culture 'moderniser', and one must be careful not to claim him too eagerly for an avant-garde from which he dissociated himself, aware of how much aesthetic experiment among the avant-gardes was either reacting to or actively imitative of the techniques and technologies that mass culture owed to capitalism.[27] Lang's own work, in this sense, participates fully in the processes of mimetic appropriation of advance developments in engineering and industry (as in his popularising use of 'cutting edge' space research), a mimesis not of subjective perception or sensory phenomena, but rather one moulded by the bureaucratic habitus of the modern state and industry, 'naturalised' to the point of invisibility. Among the modernist principles thus mimetically isolated in Lang's cinema are divisibility, seriality and exchangeability. Where the commodity form treats the products of consciousness and human labour (technical or cultural artefacts and styles, but also sensory experiences) as material manifestations, discrete and inert, until put in circulation as so many potential discourses of power, profit and pleasure, Lang's cinema mimics such reification in its focus on the fragment, the detail.

The way he deploys repetition and outward resemblance as the prompts or cues of his editing highlights the reactive, automated reflexes in the body language of his characters and their wholly non-psychological motivation. It is from this perspective that I want to look once more at the German Lang, as distinct from the French and the Anglo-American Lang, and to evaluate some of his central preoccupations in the Weimar period, concentrating in the main on this 'portrait of the times', the two-part *Dr Mabuse der Spieler* from 1922.

To historicise these automated reflexes in Lang's cinema, as well as the several dimensions of dissimulation, mimesis and mimicry they entail, one can usefully turn to Peter Sloterdijk's *Critique of Cynical Reason*, which makes the Weimar period its acid test for a more broadly cultural–philosophical essay about 'cynical' and 'kynic' modes of critique, subversion and reflection.[28] Sloterdijk begins by pointing out that the Weimar period has survived in the minds of cultural historians as two apparently incompatible but perhaps discretely symmetrical paradigms. Either the events, ideas, decisions, dominant attitudes are seen as leading inexorably towards fascism and National Socialist ideology, or Weimar represents the unredeemed moment in modern German history, where the fatally wrong turn (possibly going back to the Reformation, and certainly to German Romanticism) might have been put right, and a historical alternative for Germany seemed possible, for which Weimar in retrospect remains the receding but luminous image. Against these rival paradigms, Sloterdijk asserts something he calls the 'enlightened false consciousness', which he finds pervasive at all levels of political, intellectual and artistic life.[29] Its mark on cultural production is either a manipulative, Machiavellian advocacy of means divorced from ends, or a categorical refusal of 'single vision', i.e. a refusal to take anything at face value or for what it says it is.

According to Sloterdijk, the identity of Weimar culture lies in 'di-vision': the dual perspective, when deliberately suppressed, becomes a demagogic or self-deceiving expediency, but when fully and consciously articulated manifests a cynical or ironic intelligence, constantly dividing and divided against itself, whose (philosophical) enemy is nominalism, empiricism, scientific realism, i.e. the thing's identity with itself. Sloterdijk's treatise is an attempt to think the contradictions of the Weimar period without having recourse to the political labels of left and right, bourgeois or radical, socialist or nationalist, since the era in its significant utterances attended school from the same three nineteenth-century thinkers: Nietzsche's genealogy of morals, Marx's notion of ideology, and Freud's concept of the unconscious.[30]

In so far as Lang's films have contributed to this ambiguously scintillating sociopathological space associated with Sloterdijk's diagnosis, it would be well to take into account when re-assessing his work the double vision, the dialectical reflex whereby the Weimar intelligentsia dissociated itself from the age and at the same time implicated itself, regardless of their explicit political affiliation or lack of it – a typically 'modernist', but also 'modernising' stance. As Sloterdijk also points out: the Weimar representative figures knew more about themselves than either their critics or historians are likely to ever know, and they were more sophisticated conceptually than any of the explanatory models later adduced to account for their motivations and practice. It suggests, in the case of Lang, that hindsight histories and symptomatic interpretations risk committing a certain hermeneutic violence on his films, whose own kind of 'violence' – about which, more below – may be part of a refusal to yield to such interpretations, as argued in a previous chapter about Weimar cinema generally. The mesmerising or hallucinatory effects on spectators so often attributed to Lang's films could in this regard be the result of *both* kinds of violence: the film viewer's interpretative violence, and the violence of the film's resistance to interpretation. This chapter examines this mutual collusion and collision, seeing *Dr Mabuse der Spieler* exemplary for the gap that opens up between its self-description as a 'portrait of an epoch', and the film-theoretical idea that Lang's cinema functions as the 'ultimate metaphor'.

Why 'gap', one could ask, since the image of Mabuse as a metaphor (of the many kinds of paranoia and apocalypse that are said to have stalked Weimar society) fits perfectly the assertion of the film as a portrait of the times? But Sloterdijk's 'enlightened false consciousness' warns against such simple analogising. The split or doubled perception he notes does enforce a separation, as it were, in the very idea of Weimar self-representations as metaphorical relay, between the cinema and society, between the film *Dr Mabuse*, its eponymous hero and its historical or sociopathological referent.[31] This bar I want to call 'mimicry' or 'parody', in the first instance merely to indicate the underlying 'doubleness' of gesture, the ironically broken self-awareness and distance. But in the second instance, the distance folds back into the film itself, into the hero's awareness of his own activity, for Mabuse as a metaphor merely reproduces the slippage that allowed Kracauer to go from Dr Caligari via Mabuse to Hitler, putting Lang either in the position of being himself one of the Weimar 'masterminds', or (in Lang's self-defensive version) the one who prophesied the reign of terror that was in store. In both cases the director becomes the full subject 'in the know', standing god-like outside or above not only his work, but the present and the future – the very stance the enlightened false consciousness is designed to subvert.[32]

Mimicry as metaphor, metaphor as mimicry, then: Lang has often been regarded as the director of appearances that prove to be deceptive, which is true, but it presumes to judge these appearances by a standard of 'reality' of which there is little evidence in the films. The difficult delights of his work are that strictly speaking, there never seems to be a 'ground', a solid world from which the realm of appearances might be confidently asserted to be either true or false. So thoroughly do Lang's nested narratives and *mise-en-abyme* compositions suspend unmediated access to the real that each viewer is obliged to either fantasise or metaphorise a 'meaning' into the images, and to decide on the frame of reference. Because so often this frame is missing, viewers feel frustrated, making Lang responsible for the paranoia or vertigo his films induce. One of Lang's keenest critics of the 1980s, Klaus Kreimeier, for instance, describes this vertigo very concisely, even situating it historically. By holding the films against the foil of Weimar, he sees in Lang's German films images that always cite other images, while behind them loom 'Chaos, Abgrund, Hölle, Tod' (chaos, abyss, hell, death): terms that cumulatively spell in their negative connotations a 'positive', namely the Nazi regime, prefigured in its by now metaphorised – and somewhat clichéd – historical significance. Kreimeier then confronts Lang's adventure yarns of hidden treasures or subterranean sources of wealth, such as *Die Spinnen* or *The Nibelungen* with a lucid Marxist analysis of the world economy and its crises in the late 1920s, against which Lang emerges as a political somnambulist, nostalgic for archaic, pre-capitalist notions of money as gold, and capital as the hidden hoard.[33]

Kreimeier's critique tries to lift Lang a little out of the narrow 'proto-fascist' groove. Yet what legitimates the gesture that invokes these political foils, in order then to critique Lang's ideology? Do the films not devote all their textual dexterity to a sustained relativism, without supplying their own reality checks? In Lang, there are always several worlds, set in contrast, supporting each other only in so far as they comment on each other. For instance, what strikes one in *Die Spinnen* is how pointedly the episodes contrast the contemporary world of motor cars with the exotic locations of South American Incas, where an aeroplane suddenly appears to pick the hero in the nick of time from a horse in the pampas, or where a Chinese opium den turns out to be equipped with ultra-modern means of telecommunication. In *Der Müde Tod*, the fairy-tale frame provides the setting for, once again, exotic and faraway locations, with episodes located in China or Renaissance Venice, turning the episodic structure of Griffith's *Intolerance* into a modern form of time travel. Would the backdrop of Weimar chaos that critics after Kracauer never fail to invoke as symptomatic of future catastrophe,[34] be the 'repressed' of which Lang's films cannot speak, but around which they somehow turn, deploying the historicist and exotic trappings merely as a further layer of disguise?[35] Kreimeier points out how Lang's films are like involuntary documentaries – half-ironic, half-ostentatious – of the hideously overstuffed styles and tastes in architectural facades, ornamental design and interior decor with which the Wilhelmine bourgeoisie and Berlin parvenues tried to give themselves historical solidity and cultural cachet. As an instant 'inventor of tradition', however, Lang gives with one hand what he takes away with the other. His contrasting worlds comment on each other mainly in the mode of irony, each pastiching the other by an act of repetition: the same stories, the same conflicts, the same futility, each time merely in another costume, a different fancy dress, the eternal return of the same. One of the most extended commentaries on these Nietzschean deconstructive impulses is *Dr Mabuse der Spieler*, where more than anything, one is introduced, right in the heart of the modern metropolis, to several worlds that already look false even before they become real, or rather, where the clever fake is that which is most real about reality.

Dr Mabuse, I am suggesting, can be seen as a film of the enlightened false consciousness, in the sense that its central character is not so much a person, as the embodiment of a move, a gesture and a stance. Rather than prefiguring political tyranny, he is 'the spirit that says "no"'. In other words, a Mephistophelian principle of negation and corrosion, becoming, in Sloterdijk's terms, a 'kynic' force of revolt. For like Mephisto, Mabuse is endowed with a special energy, that of doubling and repetition, of disguise and mimicry. He embodies a process that breaks up and undermines the status quo, by cutting violently into the surface of things. On the other hand, he also threatens order by his impersonations, because they relieve the senses from keeping up civilised norms, by exposing them as pretences. Both cases confirm Mabuse's function as metaphor, either working as the semiotic principle of rupture and transfer, or by suspending reference, perfectly performing the appearance of things as ironic impostures. In this chapter, then, I want to argue this Mabuse move of Mephistophelian mimicry, across six interrelated aspects that outline a particular cinematic figure in Lang's work, what I am calling the disguise artist. First, narrative 'incoherence': the film offers an exceptionally involuted narrative that appears incoherent, if judged by the criteria of a self-directed central protagonist. Mabuse's erratic behaviour and jerky body language instantiate a continual break-up, coupled with an emphasis on detail that seems non-integrated into its surroundings, at least not in the way viewers are used to, and more like the surrealists' practice of *exquisite corpses*: a fragment or object orphaned from its context, migrates like a vagrant to new locations. Second, an impression of violence is generated, not so much by the actions themselves, and rather by the shocks that the disjunctures, the shifts of attention and the variations in size or scale, force on the spectators' sensory system. Third, a systematic doubling or *mise-en-abyme* of vision occurs, centred on the look and the exchange of glances structuring the film, which acts as a 'trap' but also a lure and bait, calling upon the scene a new distribution of power. Fourth, such a power is 'the power of the false': Lang's 'excessive' symmetry turns out to provoke a therapeutic irony, which is able to resist brute force by a form of camouflage that doubles the real, making actions, characters and things seem like copies of themselves. Fifth, this effect of actions, feelings and objects appearing as their own copies is often known as the 'uncanny return'. This typically Langian uncanny, of a reality appearing as its own copy, has in the sphere of style also another name: it is often called kitsch. Not only the decor and ornaments that in *Dr Mabuse* crowd the fashionable salons are kitsch. The graphic shorthand of the emblems, trade-marks and props (ghostly writing, spectacles, spoken mantras) with which Mabuse, media mogul and self-advertiser, surrounds himself – is kitsch, too: in its preposterous efficiency as a materialisation of the image, it authenticates the inauthentic, by condensing melodramatic gesture and erotic sign into 'action', under the conditions of the market and the circulation of material objects. The importance of kitsch in Lang, finally, will bring me back to the beginning of this chapter, namely in what sense Lang, a self-confessed fake Expressionist, can help us redefine Weimar cinema.

Dr Mabuse, Weimar disguise artist

Dr Mabuse der Spieler (1922) was Lang's break-through film in Germany, as well as an early example of a special marketing ploy with media synergy, in which the serialised novel and film became each others' mutual selling points.[36] Announcing itself in its title as a 'portrait of its time' (pt 1: 'der große Spieler, Bildnis der Zeit') and a portrait of its men and women (pt 2: Das Inferno: Bildnis der Menschen'), *Dr Mabuse* was loosely based on motifs from Norbert Jacques' tabloid opus, peppered up with topical material by Lang and his then wife Thea von Harbou, a well-established mass-circulation novelist in her own right and one of UFA's top screenwriters. The four-hour film starts at a furious pace, with a meticulously timed train robbery leading to a stock-exchange fraud. It then moves to Mabuse hypnotising a young American industrialist into making large debts at gambling, before concentrating on winning the favours of an aristocratic lady, driving her husband to suicide and eventually kidnapping her. Time and again outwitting the public prosecutor, by a mixture of brutality, practical jokes and *agent provocateur* demagoguery, Mabuse is finally cornered in his secret hideout, and either goes mad or feigns insanity when he is finally captured. The film was originally said to have had a pre-credit sequence depicting street battles from the 1919 Spartacist uprisings, the assassination of Walther Rathenau and other scenes of disorder masterminded by Mabuse ('"Who is responsible for all this" – "Me"' was apparently the film's first intertitle).[37] Although this opening is now lost or was never made, the various scams Mabuse is involved in (industrial espionage, stock-exchange fraud, forged banknotes) as well as the felonies he perpetrates (he runs a drugs lab manufacturing cocaine, his gang controls gambling, prostitution and it plots assassinations) all vividly point to the post-war era, especially to Germany's raging hyperinflation between 1921–4, with its black-market economy that pauperised the middle classes, while creating urban subcultures of war profiteers, Mafia-like racketeer organisations and vigilante units, recruited from the growing army of unemployed. The political references were not lost on contemporary reviewers or the censors.[38] Even now, Mabuse's several disguises seem taken out of a catalogue of Weimar types, familiar from the drawings of Otto Dix and George Grosz: stock-broker in top hat, derelict drunk in a housing tenement, Jewish peddler at the street corner, bearded *rentier* in flashy limousine, industrialist with monocle and moustache, pimp, psychiatrist, hypnotist and opium-smoking Tsi-Nan-Fu in a gambling den. A British viewer might see shades of Conan Doyle's Dr Moriarty, the Victorian villain who displayed a similar ubiquity in iniquity and crime. French movie-goers would have recognised Louis Feuillade's *Fantomas*, and especially the caped and hooded figure silhouetted over the city-scape in the poster was reminiscent of the French serial king from the 'teens. In Germany, Mabuse was taken to be modelled on Hugo Stinnes, a steel magnate who from humble beginnings amassed a fortune and occupied a key position in the post-First World War (illegal, according to the Versailles Treaty) rearmament industries. But Mabuse also doubles as a Houdini-like vaudeville artist, he passes himself off as soul-doctor from Vienna, and even has a dash of the Bolshevik agitator in the Karl Radek mould.[39] The final showdown was modelled on the 'Fort Chavrol' bank-robbers and their famous shoot-out with the police from a barricaded house in the *banlieus* of Paris in 1921.[40] In short, Lang's 'portrait of the times' with its atmosphere of ruthless, energetic raffishness corresponds rather well to the image one still has of Berlin during the fabled twenties, though they had hardly begun when the film premiered in 1922.

It was only after the Second World War that *Dr Mabuse* in the eyes of the critics took a less topical and more overtly metaphoric turn. Kracauer ties virtually every significant trend of his diagnostic psychogramme of Weimar veering towards totalitarian madness to one of Lang's films, acknowledging the director as a key figure, but making him very nearly the evil genius of the faltering Republic's film culture:

> Dr Mabuse's family likeness to Dr Caligari cannot be overlooked. He too is an unscrupulous master-mind animated by the lust for unlimited power. […] The film succeeds in making of Mabuse an omnipresent threat that cannot be localized, and thus reflects society under a tyrannical regime – that kind of society in which one fears everybody because anybody may be the tyrant's ear or arm.
>
> (Kracauer 1947: 82–3)

Lang later argued back, pointing out that if he had predicted the rise of Hitler in his films, then Kracauer was pinning the blame for the bad news on the messenger.[41] But Kracauer's version stuck. As Ann Kaplan once remarked: '*From Caligari to Hitler* […] effectively damaged Lang's critical reputation for at least a decade.'[42] Evidently, to the degree that *Dr Mabuse* is more than a sensationalist exploitation film, its immense popularity at the time and subsequent status as a classic testify to a surplus of meaning, best readable perhaps across the curious supplement of Mabuse's epithet '*der Spieler*', meaning the gambler, but also the dissembler, or pretender. In a sense, the epithet literalises one meaning of the word metaphor, as a disguise, a form of indirection and irony, speaking 'as-if'. Highlighting both playfulness and risk, both a refusal of identity and a slippage of reference, it announces the question of what kind of agency Mabuse embodies, as he 'stands behind' events as well as 'fronting' a conspiratorial gang bent on mayhem and mischief. For this reason, Mabuse as disguise artist dissimulates both identity and agency, suggesting that he belongs to the rather large family of such creatures in the Weimar cinema, whose kinship, but also generic diversity (Caligari and Nosferatu, Hagen and Haghi, Tartuffe and Mephisto) allow some conclusions about the self-representation of the cinema during the Weimar period. If Lang's German films are indeed inventories of styles, and if he provided much of the wallpaper for Weimar Germany's national or avant-garde ambitions, he also always showed how flimsy it was. Take 'Expressionism', the style that like no other was intended to create an internationally valid quality brand-name for German cinema in the early 1920s: as Mabuse himself says, asked what he thinks of it: 'Expressionism! – it's a game of make-believe! But why not? Everything today is make-believe.' Mabuse both implicates and distances himself, in a gesture that joins mimicry and parody, a mottled person for a mottled ground, which raises the question of how mottled the ground has to be on which Mabuse moves, in order to make him part of 'picture of the times'.

There are several moments of mottled mimicry or camouflage in *Dr Mabuse.* One would be the scene of Mabuse at the stock exchange, in which he destabilises both stock prices and currencies by selectively planting the information gleaned from the treaty captured during the train robbery. The scene ends with the superimposition of Mabuse's face on the emptied stock exchange, gradually surging from the background, like a water-mark on a banknote when held against the light. Such a double exposure is also like a hologram, as if to say: just tilt the image a few degrees, and look again. Lang, in *Dr Mabuse*, constantly tilts the world he is creating, making something else become visible: not the ground for a hidden 'truth', but *the recto of a verso.* Watching Lang construct such a scene as that of the stock exchange is to watch the act of metaphorisation at work, but as a process, not as established analogy or equivalence. One sees how a reality becomes image becomes sign, and the sign a kind of hieroglyph. What is left is a rebus world, barely readable, apparently incoherent, but consisting of nothing but the most familiar elements.

Narrative 'incoherence'

Lang's cinema has often seemed aberrant when judged under the aspect of story telling. Even sympathetic critics have complained about the incoherence of his plots, based so much on sudden turns, implausibly contrived coincidences and a strategy of shock and surprise. Compared to, say, Hitchcock's close-knit weaving of suspense or the build-up of drama from a character's conflicting choices, Lang's manner of withholding character motivation and evidence seems wilful and irritating. David Bordwell has pointed out how the American Lang 'frequently constructs a "paranoid" spectator through a narration that brutally and abruptly manipulates point-of-view in order to conceal gaps and force the viewer to false conclusions'.[43] Discussing *Dr Mabuse*, Paul Jensen, finds the film 'too long and too diffuse', full of 'logical flaws', and 'confused thematic thinking': 'we see these thing happen, but we are given no plot or character motivation for either the specific events or [Mabuse's] general decline.'[44]

Other critics did not care for the pace, thinking it slow and disjointed, or missed verisimilitude and psychological depth. Some put these supposed defects down to the serial format and the random accumulation of episodes (comparing *Dr Mabuse der Spieler* with *Die Spinnen*) and to the epic ponderousness (Jensen speaks of 'elephantine grandeur') of the subjects (*Der Müde Tod*, *Die Nibelungen*, *Metropolis*). A Lang admirer, Eric Rhode, regrets that the whole of *Dr Mabuse* did not live up to the clockwork precision of the editing in its opening scenes with the train robbery and stock-exchange fraud:

> *Dr Mabuse*, the four-hour epic made in 1922, [thematises] a sense of doom, a society enervated by city pleasures, a mastermind controlling and manipulating just about everybody. [...] *Dr Mabuse* has formally much of the serial about it. The plot appears improvised, and the narrative inconsequential, sometimes to the point of being cryptic. [...] Odd for the serial form, though is its lack of action: after a brilliantly conceived robbery at the start [...] the film settles down comfortably to a series of dialogues and arias, only now and then interspersed by some burst of activity. Still, in spite of its shaky development *Dr Mabuse* rivets the attention. Why so?
>
> (Rhode 1966: 89)

Why indeed? The question is less rhetorical than it may seem. Lang was a reteller of familiar adventure fare and a fervent admirer of Karl May, perhaps Germany's greatest popular story-telling genius since the Brothers Grimm.[45] Where other Weimar directors resorted to literary classics such as Goethe's *Faust*, to Biedermeier tales of the fantastic, or to middle-brow novels like those of Gerhard Hauptmann and Theodor Storm, Lang was not above also picking current pot-boilers.[46] In the form of illustrated comics (as they appear in the boy's knapsack in *Die Frau im Mond*, for instance), this reading matter made up the bulk of mass-market publishing sold at news stands (like the one in *Spione*) or circulating by subscription from door to door (as in the opening scenes of *M*). The German critic Frieda Grafe even thinks that Lang had studied the problem of what makes a successful film story more closely than other directors who rely on more intelligent scripts:

> The frozen, stencilled, and stilted pieces of language and literature make evident the fact that stories in the cinema are always pre-formed and stereotyped, that they belong to a stock of available clichés. [...] The script for *Dr Mabuse* was written by Thea von Harbou after a serialized novel that had appeared in Ullstein's Berlin Illustrated News. The Ullstein Brothers had founded their own production company for turning the serial novels into films. For Lang these were entirely adequate as sources for his scripts. Later, in the United States, he took the facts as true stories from the newspapers and the phrases from the comics. [...] At the beginning of his career he wanted material for the

> new medium that had as little as possible in common with traditional cultural values. Popular inventions, accessible to the masses, cast in a visual idiom that bypassed the domination of language. Von Harbou's ready-made figures of speech and a-personal formulas where the Id speaks louder than it does in situations or stories that want to appear original: it was exactly what Lang needed to build up the things he could communicate via the cinema.
>
> (Grafe 1976: 24–5)

'Where the Id speaks louder' is a telling point with which to answer Rhode's question: not in the sense that Lang appeals to the dark, demonic forces of the national psyche, as Kracauer would have it, but that the narrative engine of Lang's cinema appears stalled only to some viewers, and for a reason. One could say that the films are made up of pre-formed blocks or set-piece tableaux because they eschew what Freud called 'secondary' psychological elaboration, not wishing to achieve smooth transparency as narratives, and they do so in order to direct attention elsewhere. Lang is only the more extreme example among German directors of the 1920s to use narrative continuity differently from American cinema, concentrating on the individual image, the shot and the frame, as opposed to the scene and the sequence (the latter the building blocks of Hollywood cinema). From this it could be argued that Lang's film making rests on a fundamentally antithetical or contrapuntal conception of cinematic form, proof that throughout his life he remained true to silent cinema.[47] Or that he belonged to the avant-garde: Noel Burch places Lang, within the terms of classical film theory, on the side of a formalist 'montage-cinema'.[48] Yet it would be misleading to identify his editing with the Russian school, however much Sergei Eisenstein via Esfir Shub is said to have learnt from Lang.[49] Lang had, from as early as *Die Spinnen* demonstrated an effortless facility with Hollywood continuity editing, and he never dispensed with basic principles of scene dissection. For instance, in the opening segment of *Dr Mabuse*, by exploiting point of view cutting, Lang devised some bold and startling effects of scene transition, such as Mabuse's summoning of his coke-snorting servant, or the glance at his watch, which takes the viewer to another pocket watch and into the train compartment and a close-up of a wrist-watch. By the very shock that these shot transitions and ellipses produce, Lang tends to highlight the artifice and construction principles of 'Hollywood' editing conventions, while reserving himself the right to continue in a different key. Even this 'classically' mounted opening scene, in which the cuts – alternatively following hands, looks and gestures – contribute a rapid forward thrust to the action, the effect is 'excessive' by the way energy is so melodramatically transferred to (and focused on) Mabuse's desk-cum-dressing table, his preferred action space, whose control-and-command position the scenes thus establish, not least by an obsessive frontality, whenever a shot shows Mabuse himself.[50]

What 'rivets attention' subsequently is not so much the drive of events: it is the very lacunary, apparently disjointed advance of action, so often folded back into the mirror shot of Mabuse looking at us looking at himself. This redefines the tasks given to the spectator: to take in the virtuoso performances that are the visual deceptions Mabuse is able to perpetrate on the public space (giving the illusion that he is 'behind' everything of consequence that happens in society, the economy and politics), but at the same time, to beware of being too dazzled by these deceptions. For in practice Mabuse exerts power through disguises and through his look, two quite different modalities, as I shall try to argue. In other words, the film fosters an attitude of fascination and scepticism at the same time. A split awareness, a double vision, an oblique or even anamorphic perspective is generated by this mode of discontinuity, where isolated detail and synoptic tableaux alternate with each other, precisely without being motivated psychologically. Instead, the central character appears in control of the events only in so far as he is himself driven by them. It is this self-mobilising, self-energising aspect that characterises the disguise artist Mabuse: he becomes someone else, it would seem, mostly in order to gain control over himself, that is, to exploit the flows of energy set free by mimicry: where the Id speaks is the place where disguise lies.

'Cynical' and 'kynic' energy

Some of the most perceptive comments on Lang's narrative style have come not from a film critic or theorist, but from a novelist, via one of his fictional characters, a very close reader indeed. Franz Pökler, the Fritz Lang fan in Pynchon's *Gravity's Rainbow* is no *Cahiers du cinéma* cinephile, yet he is clearly drawn to the dynamic of fragment and flow, of deception and the manic look that lies at the heart of Lang's depiction of Weimar modernity and its cynical, split consciousness. A scientist who during the last years of the Nazi Regime worked on Hitler's secret weapon, the V2 Rocket System, Pökler is being de-briefed by his American captors shortly after the collapse in April 1945, when he begins to ruminate, recalling the Weimar years 'through inflation and depression'. The 'Spirit of the Age ...] came to have a human face attached to it, *natürlich* that of the actor Rudolf Klein-Rogge whom Pökler idolised and wanted to be like'.[51] Rudolf Klein-Rogge, it will be remembered, was Lang's Dr Mabuse, his Attila the Hun in *Die Nibelungen*, Rotwang the scientist in *Metropolis*, and Haghi the master spy in *Spione*.[52] *Dr Mabuse* especially makes Pökler want to surrender to the 'enormous bleak eyes' of Klein-Rogge, for him the symbol of Weimar also in a specific sense:

> You were meant to think of Hugo Stinnes, the tireless operator behind the scenes of apparent inflation, apparent history: gambler, financial wizard, arch-gangster, ... a fussy *bürgerlich* mouth, jowls, graceless moves, a first impression of comic technocracy ... and yet when the rages came over him breaking through from beneath the rationalized look, with his glacial eyes becoming windows into the bare Savanna,

> then the real Mabuse surfaced, vital and proud against the gray forces surrounding him, edging him toward the doom he must've known he couldn't escape, the silent inferno of guns, grenades, streets full of troops attacking his headquarters and his own madness at the end of the secret tunnel. ... And who brought him down but matinee idol Bernhard Goetzke as State prosecutor von Wenk! Goetzke who played tender wistful bureaucratic death in *Der Müde Tod*, here too running true to form, too tame, too gentle for the jaded countess he coveted – but Klein-Rogge jumped in, with all claws out, drove her effeminate husband to suicide, seized her, threw her on his bed, the languid bitch and took her! while gentle Goetzke sat in his office among his papers and sybarites – Mabuse trying to hypnotise him, drug him, bomb him to death in his own office, nothing worked, each time the great Weimar inertia, files, hierarchies, routines kept saving him.
>
> (Pynchon 1972: 675)

Compared to Kracauer's analysis, Pynchon changes the sociopolitical accent. Mabuse's crimes take on the character of a battle, a 'one man's war' after the trauma of the Great War, a capitalist entrepreneur's war against a neo-feudal bureaucracy, but also a war against democracy, in the name of macho intelligence, unbridled libido and animal cunning, with the peculiarly modern tools of theatricalised, open deception, supported by technology. Mabuse becomes the 'character-mask' of which Adorno was to speak when he analysed captains of industry and finance in America, seeing the Rockefeller, Ford and Vanderbilt dynasties as the ultimately unacceptably human face of the anarchic forces of capital, especially in the sphere of public opinion.[53] In Lang, the image of the stock-exchange speculator becomes emblem of the struggle between capitalism (monopoly capitalism, multinational capitalism) and civil society, democracy. If this has something to do with instinct, it is the 'instinctual' side of capitalism and the market economy. In this sense, Mabuse is not an anticipation of a self-proclaimed dictator such as Hitler, but someone who works both behind the scenes and in public, on behalf of the anarchic forces of money and its cycles of inflation/deflation, to which he lends his face as a cartoon mask. If anything, he is more a Weimar precursor of Orson Welles's Charles Foster Kane: both are 'larger-than-life' figures of a buccaneer capitalism that responded to the 'revolutionary' energies of industrialisation, warfare and the world-economy with a regime of speculation, manipulation and disguise on the grandest possible scale.[54] If Mabuse '*is*' Hugo Stinnes, he has the same relationship to him as 'Citizen Kane' has to Randolph Hearst or Howard Hughes. In each case, an increasingly abstract logic of production and circulation gives itself a human face, in order to be comprehensible by becoming representable. That this face takes on monstrous and mythological traits marks the dimension of the gap between the socio-economic reality it claims to represent and the popular fantasies of fabulous wealth that the representations are supposed to channel, with fantasy and monstrous figure compensating for the fact that such representations cannnot finally dispel the incomprehension.

What is new about this personality cult is that representation itself seems to have passed into the hands of those interested only in self-representation, and both Mabuse and Citizen Kane forge instruments of manipulation out of their mastery of the emerging mass media, not hesitating to exploit democracy's weaknesses or to control individuals by preying on their passions and vices. The spectator succumbs to fascination, and thus to being duped, because he is encouraged to be pleased with himself for not being deceived.[55] The Nietzschean motifs in Lang might be understood as anthropomorphised revolutionary forces, the unleashed powers of modernity's innovations also in the sphere of image making, but in the 'cynical' mode of a Mabuse, quite open about the game he is playing. At the same time, plugged into this circuit of wrenching social change, where Wilhelmine traditions have become mere impostures, but are still strong enough to clash with the brash impersonations of the new performative imperative of the spectacle and the show, Mabuse also embodies the subversive, 'kynic' energies from below, appropriated by the nonconformist rebel, playing *agent provocateur* to the permanent revolution in the sphere of tradition, truth, stable values and single vision.[56]

The violence of partial vision: the detail as disruption

The most intriguing part of Pökler's testimony, however, is not his attribution of Mabuse as a recognisable Weimar icon, but the way he evokes the extraordinary climate of violence that emanates from Lang's films, when there is in fact surprisingly little violence shown, at any rate in the German films. Some of Mabuse's bloodiest deeds have to be surmised, anticipating the classic example of violence by inference in Lang – the murder of little Elsie in *M*.[57] Such memories of destruction and cruelty that one takes away from Lang's films stand in direct contrast to what one can only call the extraordinary chasteness of the images themselves, when viewed individually, and divorced from the contiguous spaces of their narrative implication. The impression of violence comes from the nakedness with which the framing and editing exposes the act of representation as an interference, an incision almost of a surgical operation, and Lang's cinema reminds us of the violence done to things made visible when representing them. Something seems to slip between the confrontations that can lead to violence and the manner in which they are rendered visually, producing a kind of disjuncture or hiatus experienced by the viewer, who notes the startling care lavished on details, without being at all sure how to 'place' such detail: is it meant to contribute to the credibility of the story or on the contrary, condemn it to a mere melodramatic pretext?[58] In addition, details or close-ups of fragments are usually presented as insert shots (common in silent cinema), rather than as point-of-view shots familiar from classical continuity editing. Inserts interrupt the flow of an action scene, but they also emancipate the camera from its role as bearer of a (diegeticised) human look.[59] Lang's films here recall the early cinema's fascinated love affair with scientific, medical or instructional documentaries, in which German cinema since Oskar Messter was to be so prolific. Reminiscent of the so-called *Neue Sachlichkeit* 'photo-eyes' of Renger-Patsch and Blossfeldt, these optical forays into the phenomenal world seemed the more fantastic by their very claims to scientific truth and precision.[60] Estranged through magnification or an unusual angle, the images are meant to make the viewer temporarily lose the coordinates of size, scale and perspective, locating the eye either too close or too far away, depriving the mind of its cognitive default value, the human body image as reference point. Pynchon has accurately grasped this moment in Lang when he describes Pökler watching *Die Nibelungen*:

> He kept falling asleep, waking to images that for half a minute he could make no sense of at all – a close up of a face? a forest? the scales of a dragon? a battle scene? Often enough it resolved into the features of Rudolf Klein-Rogge. [...] Pökler would nod back into sleep with bursts of destroying beauty there for his dreams to work on.
>
> (Pynchon 1972)

In his semi-conscious state Pökler makes an instructive conjecture. Apart from anthropomorphising a sequence of images by superimposing on them a human intentionality and a face, he also mistakes the violence *of* the screen (the force emanating from the act of representing the world in images) for violence *on* the screen (the force emanating from an object or body represented in the image). Lang widens the gap between the act of representation and the represented: either in order to produce a hesitation, an oscillation, or to send the viewer into a state of stunned fascination. The potential for violence stems from the fact that every cut commits a violation of the viewing position established or implied by the previous shot. It is this violence (which it is the task of 'classical' continuity editing to mask) that makes Pökler fantasise the terrible but reassuringly human face of Klein-Rogge as a unifying presence. The 'burst of destroying beauty' i.e. the impression of violence marks the gap that surfaces between the image and the narrative to which it belongs, an effect all but hypnotic to Pökler/Pynchon, but merely irritating to critics complaining of Lang's incoherences, which now emerge as the verso of his refusal to submit to the appeasement politics of Hollywood narrative.

As Pynchon also noticed, discontinuity in Lang is exacerbated by a kind of unreadability of the image, an indecipherability that provokes both anxiety and pleasure. It is as if Pökler has to repress the narrative, in order to cope with the images. To see in close-up the cross that Kriemhild stitches on Siegfried's hunting jacket (in *Die Nibelungen*) is to see either an abstract object or a textured shape: an insect, a huge spider even, but never simply a sign or mark on a coat, however much the close-up is also part of the sequence that joins two images in a cause-and-effect logic, each stitch sealing Siegfried's fate, because Kriemhild's needlework is intercut with Hagen 'already' selecting the lance he will aim at the stitched cross on Siegfried's back. The close-up doubly connotes attention: Kriemhild's loving solicitousness and Hagen's concentration on the murderous deed, but the look embodied in the close-up cannot be the convergence of the two, since they are diametrically opposed in both intention and consequence. Is this puzzled swelling of contradictory meaning in the image evidence of Lang's 'fatalism'? The look implied is the depersonalised gesture of dramatic irony, while the attention is that of the spectator's split awareness and dread anticipation, so that the violence of the shot derives from the viewer having to hold and contain in one image a fatal and incompatible duality, rather than because this image connotes the violent death of the hero. Similarly, the director's famous inserts of his own hands, of an empty plate or an angled desktop are so disconcerting, because the emphatic gesture that the isolation of an object or detail conveys does not work to the benefit of the narrative, and on the contrary, deflects attention, forcing the eye to scrutinise and decipher an image become strange because taken from a vantage point or distance that once more reveals the shocking (or shockingly comic) 'obtuseness'[61] of the world when seen by a camera, before this very obtuseness works to the benefit of the image becoming a hieroglyph and the world an allegory.

Lang's refusal to subordinate himself to the linearity and psychological motivation demanded by continuity editing is thus a studied provocation. By holding on to the insert shot he resists classical narrative cinema, which quickly harnessed this aggressive potential, translating the assault exerted by the cut into the diegetic energy of a chase, a battle, a tangible goal, or by giving this violence an agent and its agent a subjective point of view, both of which serve to re-motivate the inherent arbitrariness of the image, subjecting it to the force of a logic that propels an intrigue, the pursuit of an objective, the resolution of a conflict. The nervous energy, the frayed jerkiness of that restless busybody and insomniac schemer Mabuse is more like a parodic manifestation of power than power *per se*. His erratic behaviour is like the reflection of an aggregate irritation accumulated in the act of seeing but not comprehending, surfacing when the originary arbitrariness of editing is not fully 'covered' or used up by the narrative. Whenever it becomes impossible to locate the affective charge emanating from the close-ups in *Dr Mabuse* in the story world, their free-floating meaning feeds the violence of the cinematic process itself.[62]

In the complaint about Lang's narrative incoherence lies thus a definition of his style and method. Less a rejection of classical continuity editing or a retention of early film form, and instead the exploitation of both for another end, namely to preserve a fundamental equivocation about cinematic representation as signification, putting the onus on the spectator who has to make sense of even the slightest difference and disjunction, if he is not to be overwhelmed by the violence of enunciation itself.[63] Usually achieved by reframing an image or shot, Lang 'primes' the spectator at the micro-level, just as, at the macro-level, his narratives are invariably 'nested' and internally framed. In an example given by

Bellour from *Die Nibelungen*, Lang does not even depend on reframing to make the image change radically and yet remain unsettled and unsettling:

> In *Siegfried*, for instance: three warriors occupy almost the entire surface of the screen; they are so close that they cannot be seen in their entirety; between them are blank spaces, in the background a bare wall; the image is perfectly flat and the soldiers look like cardboard cut-outs; when Kriemhild's women pass behind them, following her, perspective suddenly returns so vividly that one feels it as being too deep, and it seems like another illusion.
>
> (Bellour 1981: 35–6)

Similarly, the first shot of the rocket in *Die Frau im Mond* shows a white cylindrical shape with two black slanting apertures being slowly wheeled out of a hangar. Its size becomes startling only once one becomes aware of the large crowd of people toiling at its base to keep it moving. The beauty of the composition is sinister not so much because of what the object denotes, but derives from a kind of self-sufficiency, where the image returns to its two-dimensionality and the shape is readable as pure surface, no longer the representation of an object but its graphic abstraction, on whose behalf an army of human beings expend their energy.[64] Is the image 'impersonating' an object, one wonders, or is the object the hallucinated effect of a graphic shape? What remains as a surplus is a 'gestic' principle peculiar to Lang, whose caution against the image as 'proof' competes with his 'irony' as the preferred mode of narrational authority, never missing an opportunity to give the viewer a split vision between the graphic and the photographic, effected by reframing and repetition. The gesture exhibits an aggressiveness that can transfer to the spectator, who not surprisingly, feels threatened by such loss of imaginary coherence and specular mastery, pointing to the act of enuniciation and suture, the very processes that classical narrative disguises and elides. Confronted, as in *Dr Mabuse*, with a character whose existence is nothing but disguise, elision and camouflage, Lang's gestic principle doubles the exposure, but also takes it back: Mabuse's disguises *in* the film denounce (through mimetic enactment) the disguises *of* the (classical narrative) film, but each is a comment on the other. The pleasure, once one submits to this play of elision and exposure, comes from the energies it frees up, the transfer it makes possible from narrative logic and representational space to the more figural space subtending them and which develops its own vertiginous pull.[65]

The shock effects, the moments of narrative incoherence, the violence that leaves no marks on the image (because it overpowers the mind) prepare the senses for the epistemological as well as semiological fact that an image is never identical with what it represents. This non-identity is established in Lang along two distinct but equally important axes. The first confirms that his shots are often motivated from outside the diegetic world, their fastidious framing meant to enact the gesture of showing, and thus re-working the early cinema practice of 'monstration' (with its implied gesture of showing), but within the self-conscious idiom of 'distanciation' and 'estrangement' of the Modernist avant-gardes: every shot indicates that it is there because it is meant to be seen, and before we see it, it has been seen by someone else. Right from the start, *Dr Mabuse*, as do so many of Lang's films, operates in the space of the non-identity of the camera look, the protagonists' looks and the spectatorial look: a 'Modernist' type of reflexivity *par excellence*. The spectator is witness not only to the self-referring *mise-en-scène* of the film's successive episodes, but shares what is put there to be seen with several, often disempowered diegetic characters. An example is the opening sequence, where the punctuation marks of iris-in and iris-out, heavily and perceptibly underline the logic of a gaze whose potency crystallises in the shocked reaction of Spoerri, Mabuse's substance-abusing manservant. The iris and the two circular pocket watches, linked by the speeding train and the repetition of hands holding them like stop-watches in a race, arrange the world so it can be seen, but mark it as a world both arranged and primed by looking: metaphors of the bare elements of cinema – the camera (iris), the watch (the timing and the cut) and the director (the hand that arranges, chooses and selects). The effect is that of a closed circuit of communication, a circulation of desired objects (literally, the commercial treaty; metaphorically, narrative authority, the fame of authoring a film) happening thanks to an agency of the look that is materialised and made mobile via the most advanced technologies of transport: express train, motor car and telephone.

The second axis on which the image is non-identical with itself almost contradicts the first, because it involves not self-reflexivity but the effect of the uncanny. In Lang, the uncanny emerges whenever an image or shot brings with it the sensation that besides having already been seen, the look belongs to someone whom the audience cannot see, or in *Dr Mabuse*, someone whom the viewer suspects of possessing a cold, malevolent eye. The audience, in other words, is not allowed to 'see for itself' (as the phrase goes), being deprived of the illusion of making a discovery, of directly participating in the world becoming image: we only see what we are meant to see – so much and no more. It is the epitome of a paranoid vision, the spectator being caught in someone else's vision or having one's sense perceptions 'prepared for in advance', which necessarily marks them as sense deceptions. And to this extent Lang's cinema does not afford a voyeuristic pleasure or mastery, never quite covering up for this sense of the uncanny or compensating for it through proffered moments of transparency and vicarious participation. What I am trying to describe here is another form of 'disguise', where the film offers resistance to (single) meaning and (determinate) reference not by a lack of specificity, but by suggesting that there is always something 'behind' the image, just as Mabuse insinuates that he is 'behind' the chaos, the crimes and spectacular actions that disrupt public order and 'bureaucratic inertia'. It is as if Lang's film wears its own meaning like a mask, to irritate and to delight, according to temperament, but never endorsing the epistemic drive that seeks out a unitary source and origin, hoping for a 'reality' beneath appearance. Instead, the viewer is offered involuted, self-generated and mutually sustaining fictions whose apparent inconsistence is a benevolent form of imposture, distracting the mind, possibly the better to ensnare the eye. For as one puzzles about the 'ground' of Mabuse's grand design, one finds oneself already 'figuring' inside its design as mere 'ornament'.

The *mise-en-abyme* of vision

That the two-part *Dr Mabuse* is about 'a master-mind controlling just about everybody' as Eric Rhode (and Kracauer) asserts, may be true, but this is not what makes it cast its spell, unless one includes among those 'controlled' by Mabuse the audience itself. It is easy to get caught up in the feverish pace of its opening, a stock-exchange fraud on an international scale, executed with manic precison by an organisation in which the financial genius, virtuoso impersonator and strategic planner Mabuse commands crooks, gamblers, drug addicts and forgers by a scowl or frown, but also politicians, rich industrialists, society ladies and effete aristocrats. The effect at first is of character-types and life styles, seen already as if from a great distance and in retrospect. Gradually, the forces of the law embodied by Chief Prosecutor von Wenk, penetrate the power structures of imposture and intrigue, of erotic fascination and sexual exploitation that Mabuse has built up, but the settings, locations and interiors that come into view are like a display case, a shop window or catalogue of fashionable eclecticism in styles, designs and fads: orientalism in the opium den, *Jugendstil* in Mabuse's private appartments; African masks and South Sea fetishes in Count Told's salon; elaborate mechanical gadgets in the gambling casino, a dance hall with a sunken floor and painted shadows on the wall, as if to reproduce the asylum from *Dr Caligari*. In the scene already quoted, Mabuse himself suggests that Expressionism itself has degenerated into a mere affectation, the style no longer 'expression of self' but its disguise, no longer 'will to style' but skilful 'styling'.

Befitting such a design, the plot is at the same time simple and convoluted.[66] Once Mabuse's powers are established, the action focuses on Mabuse's mistress – Cara Carozza – a cabaret performer and on the assignment Mabuse gives her to seduce the industrialist Edgar Hull, whom Mabuse wants to blackmail, but who is eventually killed. Cara commits suicide after being imprisoned and refuses to testify against her lover, even though he cold-bloodedly abandons her. All the while, the State Prosecutor is on the master-criminal's trail, yet Mabuse manages to evade him, even playing practical and almost lethal jokes on his pursuers. The second part has a slightly different pace and cast. In extended move and countermove the action becomes less breathtaking and more interiorised, as hypnosis and telepathy take their place alongside the motor car, the telephone, hard drugs and theatrical disguises. The central couple whom Mabuse both seduces and destroys are now Count and Countess Told: he a world-weary, effete aristocrat, she a bored, pleasure-hungry society-beauty.[67] In a series of tableaux, the world of salons, night clubs, hotel lobbies and gambling houses is contrasted with

Mabuse's apartment which combines office, consulting room, boudoir, chemical laboratory and weapons stockpile. Von Wenk is also seen in his office, or making raids, mixing incognito with high-society diners, at swanky restaurants or orientalised speakeasies, braving Mabuse's stare at a public performance of the doctor's hypnotising skills and conjuring tricks. In the end, after Count Told has also committed suicide and Mabuse has kidnapped the Countess, von Wenk surrounds Mabuse's lair, but in the pitched battle that ensues the old fox escapes down some secret corridors into his underground bunker, staffed by a gang of blind men engaged in printing banknotes. There, von Wenk finally seizes Mabuse, seemingly having gone mad and throwing fake paper money in the air.

As the title 'portrait of the times' suggests, a rapid snapshot effect is intended.[68] But the film is nevertheless no mere kaleidoscope made up of a series of splinters from the period, even though reviewers at the time were much impressed by the sharply etched vignettes and the break-neck speed with which the plot picks up so many pieces from the shattered post-war world of Weimar Germany.[69] For despite the loose sequence of set pieces, several narrative strands link the scenes and give the film the edgy energy that still makes viewing so compulsive. Generating this intensity are not the actions, incidents or even extravagant decors, as much as the sensation that every scene is also the *mise-en-scène* of the 'seeing' of this scene, either by one, two or even three characters. The sequence early on in the film is typical, where Mabuse, in disguise, goes to the Folies Bergères night club and there engineers an encounter with Edgar Hull, his future victim. The encounter is exclusively dramatised in terms of vision: while the mainly male spectators are riveted to the stage, devouring the star (Cara Carozza) with their eyes, Mabuse himself is scanning the audience.[70] Since she is his mistress, he already possesses Cara and instead can fix Hull with his stare. His awareness of Hull's visual interest in Cara gives Mabuse a double control, structured *en abyme*, putting him at the apex of a triangle that consists of Hull gazing at Cara who is seeking the approving gaze of Mabuse. The question of control and possession is here manifestly linked to the gaze, as if to give a blueprint of how the film intends to structure itself within the terms of a mediated, remote-controlled relay of looks and scenes. Later in the scene at the Incognito Club, Hull loses at cards by succumbing to Mabuse's eyes, and henceforth never escapes his role as a mere instrument and tool. The initiative is no longer Hull's, even when he is most sure of taking it, as in his pursuit of Cara at the Excelsior Hotel: the headlong flight down the stairs to catch her at the bottom of the elevator merely underlines his downfall. We see him setting up a *tête-à-tête* with Cara in his apartment, arranging chocolates and flowers and preening himself, when all the while he is the one being set up by Mabuse who knows about the intimate assignment.

What Mabuse wants of Hull is evidently not money, even though he defeats him at the gaming tables. It is to place Hull as the receptor of a look, in order to bring about a configuration in which he, Mabuse is the voyeur through an intermediary, whose desire or vision he also controls. Thus, at the Excelsior Hotel,

Cara is the eavesdropper, in order that Mabuse can experience Hull's desire for Cara, suggesting that Mabuse's aim is not even the world domination that the plot suggests, except in the sense of wanting to dominate a world of sight and display, playing mediator in acts of deferred and delegated vision. What seems a megalomaniac's craze for power turns out to hide its own vulnerability and anxiety, crucially dis-placing sight, in order to include a third term in its structure. Mabuse plays through the triangulation of desire so typical of the 'romanesque', in René Girard's term, but sited entirely in the field of vision, the intermediary ensuring control over the terms of one's desire, which is depicted over and over again, as Mabuse's desire to possess someone else's desire.[71] It is, of course, tempting to give a Freudian reading to this desire, by interpreting the film as yet another version of Weimar masculinity in crisis, but here less intent to wrest phallic power from the Father, represented by von Wenk, and to possess the mother, embodied by Countess Told, the inexplicably unattainable love object of Mabuse. However, Mabuse's oedipal quest centres on his attempts to occupy a position where he can *be* the phallus, that is, the master signifier from which the other systems of exchange (and those who participate in them) have to take their cue. Such a reading would take the question of disguise into the psychoanalytic register, since the phallus is by definition a 'signifier without signified', the 'veil' that stands for its own lack, making Mabuse's desire ultimately the desire for his own disappearance behind his stand-ins, themselves only recognisable by the effects they produce.[72] This might explain why Mabuse has to fail, or rather why failing is the condition of his success. The instrument of this success-in-failure is his antagonist von Wenk, the Chief Prosecutor, curiously if not comically ineffectual until the end, when he can merely lead away the mad Mabuse. Earlier on, von Wenk has a more positive function, namely that of circuit-breaker and Mabuse's energiser. He literally interrupts the show that Hull is putting on for Cara, thereby breaking up the triangle Hull–Cara–Mabuse and establishing the double circuit (that adds Count and Countess Told) and which is to traverse the film from then on. Von Wenk offers protection in the form of surveillance, laying claim to the position occupied by Mabuse – to watch Hull and Cara. In addition, his is the social climber's and class voyeur's entry into a world of the spectacle of beautiful women, elegant apartments and high living. As Hull says to Cara: '[von Wenk] wants me to introduce him to secret clubs'. With von Wenk's action also identified as the pleasure of seeing, the plot from this point onwards serves to flesh out and articulate the interlocking mechanisms of these asymmetrically placed desires for possession through vision. Von Wenk, in due course, is to replace Hull, in order to challenge Mabuse on his own ground: disguises and the fixed stare. But for this to succeed, a complicated set of symmetries has first to be set up.

For instance, constructed classically as a series of repetitions is the 'Hugo Balling' episode at the Incognito gambling club (where Hull loses so heavily to the disguised Mabuse that he has to issue an IOU). It finds its mirror-equivalent in the stale-mated confrontation in the backroom of the Andalusia Palace between von Wenk and Mabuse, once more over a game of cards. Hull is used by von Wenk to infiltrate Mabuse's world via Cara, in the same way that Mabuse uses Cara as his intermediary, symbolically ceding his position to von Wenk when he gives him the secret passwords, the 'Sesame that opens all doors', as Cara at one point remarks. The particular meshing of these transfers and exchanges generates a number of scenes that have their visual or narrative counterparts elsewhere: Hull, for instance, leaves von Wenk's visiting card for Cara to find (a Freudian slip, in the light of his extreme irritation over von Wenk's intrusion), while Cara leaves Mabuse's instructions for Hull to find, who promptly informs von Wenk, just as Cara had alerted Mabuse, with one important difference however, that Hull's phone call to von Wenk is already part of Mabuse's plan, thereby introducing another *mise-en-abyme* or Chinese box puzzle, which results in a typically complex relay of intersubjective dependencies: Cara has set up Hull, who with the help of von Wenk thinks he is setting up Cara, when in fact it is Mabuse who is setting up von Wenk. The scene in the gambling casino has, consequently, more than the false stage that is so splendidly shown in action, since it is also a narrative trap door designed to put each key player into free fall, or at least reversing the hierarchies of power and control, even if only momentarily. The question is always: who is playing what part in whose script, the theatricality of the *mise-en-scène* being the sign of the incremental hold of power. One is reminded of the children's game 'scissors, stone and paper' where each item presented is both superior and inferior, depending on the other it finds itself confronted with.

The repetitions also work laterally: von Wenk's position at the club in Haydn Street appears to echo that of Mabuse at the Folies Bergères, though von Wenk's control is an illusory one, and he is doubly frustrated; not only does the raid not catch Mabuse and inadvertently makes von Wenk responsible for Hull's death, at another level, Mabuse controls von Wenk by talking to the Countess at the séance, where the Countess is desirable to Mabuse for the oedipal reason that she is also the object of von Wenk's desire. What von Wenk fails to achieve, namely a conversation with the Countess (the butler tells him on the phone that Told and his wife are busy), Mabuse manages by sending von Wenk on a fool's errand to the gambling casino. As in several other instances, von Wenk's reliance on the telephone proves to be less effective than Mabuse's trust in the delegated gesture. Mabuse's conversation with the Countess at the séance establishes not only a key visual parallel: the hands ranged around the dining table recall the circular disc of the sunken gaming table. The scene is also symmetrically placed to a previous one, when after gazing at the Countess in rapt enchantment, von Wenk follows her inside the black marketeer and war-profiteer Schramm's private salon, in order to strike up a conversation which is similarly set apart from the rest of the company as is Mabuse's with the Countess. But while von Wenk's is invariably single vision, or pure specular fascination, Mabuse's attention and gaze are always mediated, at one remove. Von Wenk falls for the Countess, almost like Hull fell for Cara, while with both Cara and the Countess,

Mabuse seems to have one eye on the here-and-now, while his other is already one move ahead: at Schramm's, von Wenk believes himself to be keeping an eye on Hull and Cara, but it is in fact Mabuse who watches von Wenk, alerted by Cara's secret glance in his direction.

At this point, by an intricate interlocking of narrative segments whose apparent parallelism tends to mask the underlying ratchet-action that propels the narrative towards the next stage, the triangle Hull–Cara–Mabuse, which dominated the first part, is progressively substituted by the one that determines the second part: Mabuse–Countess Told–von Wenk. The second part of the film is therefore not so much a continuation of the first, as it is a return to the same themes, now in a different key, with the substitutions effected through a series of relays and eliminations, themselves often triangular. At Schramm's the Countess asks von Wenk to allow her to escape unseen when her husband enters, a complicity he is eager to accept, and which gains him entry into the Countess's apartment. This visit in turn leads to her becoming complicit in von Wenk's desire to observe Cara in prison. The two triangular relationships (von Wenk–Countess–Told, and Cara–Mabuse/von Wenk–Countess: the latter actually a double one, in which Mabuse supersedes von Wenk) are in some sense played in a minor key. Yet they none the less act as narrative transformations that bind the protagonists into their characteristic patterns of interaction, serving mainly to confirm the object status of the two women (the Countess here identifying with Cara) and the instrument status of the two men unable to sustain Mabuse's stare: Hull and Count Told.

The privileged position of the Countess, on the other hand, as object of desire for von Wenk and Mabuse is established in the scene where the woman with the Tiffany necklace succumbs to Mabuse's eyes, and the Countess interrupts von Wenk with an excited look, remarking how fascinating it is to watch a woman lose at cards. She, too, like Mabuse, knows the pleasures of vicarious vision, but in her case, it is a masochistic identification with the woman thus subdued by the male gaze: Mabuse possesses the Countess through the intermediary of the losing woman's anguished eyes. The scene is 'doubled' and 'crossed' by the intervention of Cara, who 'transvestively' identifies with the punishing stare, saying 'nobody looks like a saint when they are gambling' as well as identifying with the Countess, in whose direction she sends a witheringly jealous look, and who seems to acknowledge this look, by suddenly turning away, thereby just in time noticing her husband at the door, before he notices her. The Countess's escape under cover of darkness, pursued by Cara, is thus motivated both by the arrival of her husband and the punishing stare from her rival for Mabuse's favour.

Among the other moments that bind the characters together in this fashion are the first visit of von Wenk to see Cara in her prison cell in which she warns him that his life will be in danger if he does not release her, which corresponds to the scene where the Countess, now Mabuse's prisoner, warns him that her disappearance will not go unnoticed by her friends, meaning von Wenk. These reminders in turn underscore the growing propinquity between von Wenk and Mabuse, most noticeable in the parallel positionings of the camera, the near identity of their respective offices and the scenes showing each in front of a make-up mirror trying out disguises. Finally, the film expends much care on demonstrating actions as processes, in the form of mini-documentaries: there are, for instance, Mabuse's various gadgets, such as the phoney taxi with the rotating license plates and the pressurised anaesthetic bottles famously imitated decades later by the James Bond films; the complicated mechanism of the gambling casino displayed at length and seemingly for its own sake; or the scenes painstakingly informing the viewer how to make cocaine or extract venom from a snake.

Lang's *mise-en-abyme* of Griffith: parallel editing as question and answer

Such precise meshing of gears, repeated at several levels of the action and the *mise-en-scène* suggest that the plot is not as 'improvised' as Rhode and others have claimed, and on the contrary, follows a most classical logic of the repetition-

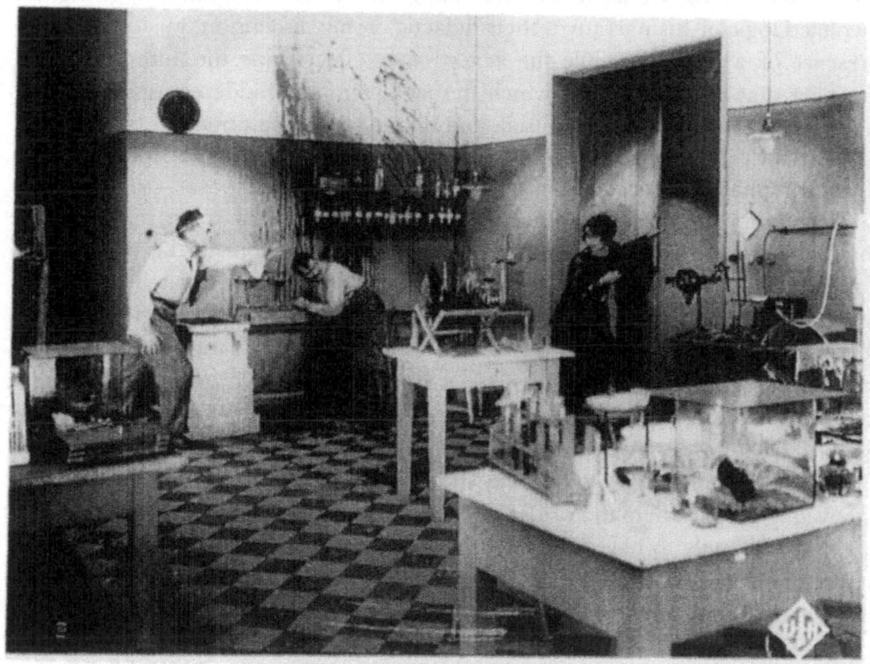

Figure 12 Too many cooks: Dr Mabuse (Rudolf Klein-Rogge, left) surprised by the Countess Told (Gertrude Welcker, right) in his cocaine-lab

Source: Stiftung Deutsche Kinemathek, Berlin

resolution schema, except more extensive and more involuted than any Hollywood film of the time.[73] The nature of the web of interactions and the degree of their complexity, engineered almost solely around the exchange of looks, makes it understandable that the story should have been perceived as 'inconsequential' and its progression as non-existent. Down to almost the last detail (including the deadly snake that reappears as a fabric motif on the dress Cara is wearing on the night she goes to prison, when poison is presumably administered to her there by the same hand that in close-up held the live snake when Mabuse extracted the venom), the narrative is made up of internal rhymes, repetitions, echoes, and counterpoints, drawn from a strictly limited repertoire of elements: typically, generated from the two couples Cara/Hull, Countess Told/Count Told, flanked by two men: von Wenk and Mabuse, and their multiple disguises and aids. These couples are, as can be seen from the preceding examples, invariably mirrors, doubles and split halves of each other.

The ultimate sense of closure of *Dr Mabuse* is thus partly achieved by anchoring the narrative in a series of '*en-abyme*' effects that contrast strongly with the first impression of a story made up of nothing but loosely woven set-pieces. Such continuity, at once open-ended and tightly stacked as a series of Chinese boxes, is supported by the impression of watching Mabuse always trying to re-establish control, by capping, topping or inverting the counter-strategies undertaken by von Wenk. It is one of Lang's most typical signatures, giving the involuted logic of his narratives their didactic, ironic dimension, for it signals the presence of a narrator, while the *mise-en-abyme* effects hide the authorial voice, ensuring that the place from which it speaks remains hidden, suspended, but ready at any moment to show itself and then again to be obscured by doubling back on the facts that the spectator had been encouraged to infer – in short, by assuming 'phallic' power.

This doubling or double-backing may take the form of overt references or may even parody symbolic references. To return once more to the show at the Folies Bergères, where the number in which Cara stars is being watched by Hull, who in turn is being observed by Mabuse, stages a graphically explicit version of the drama unfolding in the auditorium. Cara plays a dancer provocatively teasing and then being threatened by at first one, then two grotesquely phallic faces, laboriously negotiating the stage, and thus providing an image of the double structure of feuding masculinity in which she, and later the Countess Told are held in thrall. Another way in which narration makes itself felt by not motivating its paradigmatic use of repetition is the scene when Cara drops her handkerchief, only to have it brought back to her by Hull. It has the same effect as the inadvertently or deliberately dropped messages mentioned earlier in the chapter, and resumes the didactic function of the Hugo Balling episode. Mabuse 'drops' Cara at the Excelsior, so that Hull can find her, as if she was quite literally the *fort* tossed at Hull for his *da* game: a scheme reproduced, Russian doll-like, in the displacement from Cara as person to her handkerchief as signifier of this person. This is reminiscent of another famous example of displacement in Lang: that of Elsie to her ball rolling onto waste ground in the film *M*. Lang thus builds on a series of embedded moments, in which particular scenes become metaphors of the film as a whole, or rather, of its narrative-specular mechanisms.

What is true for the way certain scenes are structured, namely the tromp l'oeil effects, also applies to the editing. It seems deceptively classical in that it seems to follow D.W. Griffiths' model of parallel montage, with the various strands of the action running concurrently. Thus, the seance is inter-cut into the sequence of the gambling casino being opened and then raided. This at first suggests mere temporal simultaneity, but on reflection implies a particular hierarchy, once one realises that the inter-cut scene actually dominates and determines the one it interrupts: Mabuse controls what goes on at the gambling casino, which is established by showing that the underlying purpose of the scene at the gambling casino is to show Mabuse talking to the Countess. The film establishes a causal chain that is driven less by character psychology than by editing patterns, a peculiarity not only of Lang's *mise-en-scène*, but typical of Weimar cinema's distinct approach to the legacy of Griffith, whose film *Intolerance* was first shown in Germany in 1920, and whose impact (on film makers) cannot be overestimated.[74]

Apart from Lang, F.W. Murnau must also be considered to be an heir to Griffith (to which of course, one must add within the European cinema, Sergei Eisenstein, Abel Gance and Alfred Hitchcock – each one interpreting the master's example differently). Murnau's development of sight lines and a contrasting use of action spaces indicates a creative and highly self-conscious reworking of the lessons of the director of *Enoch Arden*, for example in *Nosferatu*, where two locations distant from each other are linked by a complex use of off-screen space.[75] Lang also creatively reworks Griffith: whichever film one chooses, cross-cutting and alternation never bring two spaces together. On the contrary, repetition tends to highlight their differences, however slight, and even more important, the scenes will either form a hierarchy or they will give the impression of a system of 'Chinese-boxes', since Langian cinematic space always contains a 'trap-door', though its exit is usually, so to speak, blocked *and* bolted. In the case of a hierarchy of spaces, as in the seance–casino example from *Dr Mabuse*, a sort of 'serial' alternation hints at an absent cause or hidden agency, locking the scenes into a rhythm that finally gives an impression of 'wheels within wheels'.[76] One can find an outstanding example of a 'two-step' causality in Lang's *Metropolis*: the figure of the steps is 'literalised' in the descent of the workers into the catacombs, intercut with master of the city – Fredersen – looking at his watch and deciding to visit the sinister inventor Rotwang, a scene 'boxed into' the other narrative centred on Freder, the son, standing at the controls as if he were Christ at the cross. The sequence interlaces four strands: Fredersen visiting Rotwang in order to obtain information about the mysterious plans of the workers; Freder receiving a similar plan from a worker; Fredersen looking at his watch/the wall clock in the machine room ticking towards the shift change; the workers walking down the steps into the catacombs/Freder becoming ever more frantic at the controls.

By inter-cutting scenes that are separate in space, or editing together images that do not at first seem to fit, Lang builds sequentiality into a very complex labyrinth, or a mysterious architecture of point and counterpoint, action and consequence, all of which results in the kinds of effects that critics, rather misleadingly, have referred to as the director's determinism, his penchant for everywhere seeing the workings of an inexorable necessity. It is true that in some respects, Lang's editing functions like a clockwork mechanism; over and over again, scenes are fitted into each other like cogs in a complicated piece of machinery. But in a gesture more ironic than fatalistic, Lang both literally and figuratively, lays his cards on the table in the opening scene of *Dr Mabuse*: the five or six different photos of theatrical disguises, the pocket watch, the forged banknotes and the telephone are Mabuse's repertoire of props that thus become another metaphor for the film's textual construction, in the way a series of simple elements are brought into play, their permutation and combination providing the toolbox of the subsequent narrative. Yet, the actual effects are stranger, and the consequences more complex than is suggested by the analogy of a clock or a toolbox, though only frustration at the puzzle they pose would make one conflate them with fate or destiny. Instead, these effects of absolute power or inevitable necessity are only the reverse side, the illusionist effect, so to speak, of an arbitrariness that refuses to smooth out the signifying work of editing and montage, and instead, underlines it. With these discontinuities, these sudden breaks, the film literally disappears, its heartbeat coming to a stop, so that when starting up again, it can take the viewer in any direction whatsoever, except that this, too, is a trick the director plays on his viewers. What greater way of being in control than making the audience lose *their* control, but then to catch them, just as they think they are falling?[77]

There are a few more examples of the Langian labyrinth of forked causality and doubled-up consequence working laterally in space, but also within a temporality of deferral. A scene of Cara Carozza in her dressing room is inserted into the game between Hull and Hugo Balling at the Incognito Club. The instructions she finds in the bouquet of flowers sent to her by Mabuse already anticipate the outcome and the sequence to the game, and thus opens up a new space even as it ends the Folies Bergères episode. As with the example of the seance, inter-cut with the casino about to be raided, the dressing room scene thus resumes an action and passes it on like a baton. The alternating montage establishes a contiguity, forging a link in the syntagmatic chain, but it also creates a hierarchy of values, so precarious it could just as easily be overturned. We might even describe a triad of scenes – a triangular relationship of shot/insert shot/countershot – which develops dialectically (thesis/synthesis/antithesis) and where the synthesis becomes once more the thesis of another chain. By contrast, when the scene with the snake whose venom is about to be extracted is intercut into a conversation between von Wenk and Hull, it opens up a chain whose other links (and thus ultimate meaning) appear only much later, after we learn that Cara has committed suicide in her prison cell.

However, one of the most dramatic examples of a triad of scenes occurs at Schramm's private club. After the Countess Told has made her hurried exit, Cara confronts von Wenk by the curtain and asks him 'What does this mean'? Before von Wenk has time to answer, the shot/countershot set-up with Cara and von Wenk on either side of the curtain is crossed by a page-boy announcing a message for Hull, his announcement visually and metaphorically cutting into the opposition between von Wenk and Cara, introducing a third strand. We then see Hull reading the message (i.e. the return of his IOU which concludes the Hugo Balling gambling episode), whereupon von Wenk joins him (saying: 'Keep the police out of it!') before the scene fades out with the triumphant stare of Cara, still in an elevated position on the threshold. The triangles are here explosively dynamic, charged with redefining the sudden shifts in the power relations, with von Wenk's apparent superiority when he turns off the lights to stop people leaving once more inverted, as Cara occupies von Wenk's position and Mabuse has regained dominance in absentia, by literally crossing von Wenk, because he manages to have his message successfully delivered to Hull via an intermediary. The intercutting is here done within one single sequence, with the page-boy entering functioning like an edited-in insert, dividing the shot in half.

Gambling, gamesmanship and paranoia plotting

In this manner, the narrative develops an intricate logic in which temporal flow and spatial contiguity are subsumed or doubled by a game of argument and counter-argument, question and answer, cause and consequence, anticipation and implication. Any number of further instances could illustrate the point: there is a scene where Countess Told talks to her husband, saying she would rather not see Mabuse on Thursday. At this point von Wenk is announced and enters (thus the mention of 'not-seeing Mabuse' is made to entail 'seeing von Wenk'). He persuades her to spy for him and says 'I'm going to arrest you!' Lang cuts to Mabuse's house, with Spoerri being told by Mabuse: 'Get the room ready, I'm expecting somebody!' (meaning that he will kidnap the Countess and lock her up), whereupon we cut back to the Countess's house to von Wenk saying 'I expect you at 7 p.m. at the police headquarters!' The double ironies are evident, as the two men both 'expect' her, and intend to imprison her, each engaged in a piece of dissembling and disguise, at her expense. It is a typical example of how Lang works with intertitles in *Dr Mabuse*, anticipating Bert Brecht's epic or gestic principles of counterpoint and commentary. The 'erotetic' or question/answer type of editing is the one most frequently employed, as in the following rather special case, which involves the sort of 'framing' of a message that was to become one of Lang's preferred devices for marking reversals through recontextualisation in his American films (e.g. a reverse tracking shot in the prison in *Fury*, or in and out of the newspaper headlines in *You Only Live Once*). When Mabuse's sidekick Poesch is killed by a sniper to stop him being questioned by the police, von Wenk furiously berates his men and one of them says, 'God only knows who stirred up all these people.' At this point, Lang cuts to an iris shot of the agitator first seen at the bar at Schramm's, as if to answer that it is not only God who knows. As the iris opens up, one realises that the shot is in fact not a flashback to the scene in the bar, but shows Mabuse at his desk with the make-up mirrors. By the time the image is full frame, Mabuse has pulled off his wig, revealing the agitator's true identity, as if providing a mocking answer to von Wenk's men looking in vain for the agent provocateur. The death of Poesch is furthermore a typical staging of a deception that 'dis-covers' its own efficacy only through repetition: the bomb attack on von Wenk's office having failed and Mabuse's man being captured, the task is now to either free the prisoner or to eliminate him before he can be taken in for questioning. The agitator stirs up a mob as the police van with the captured Poesch is sighted, demanding to free another prisoner, Gutter. The police, cornered, show Poesch, to reassure them that he is not the man they want, whereupon a sniper's bullet can comfortably target the unfortunate Poesch. The 'wrong' man was of course the right man.

Such plotting in 'paranoid' series, inverting cause and effect by backtracking along the same chain of events, serves to create not so much an optical *mise-en-abyme*, as one of agency and action. It establishes an ambiguity about who in a given situation exploits whom, or is led by the nose by whom, two power structures mutually either reinforcing or cancelling each other through their *Nachträglichkeit*, their after-the-event causality. Nothing is what it appears to be, each 'reality' being necessarily the disguise that another gives itself, but the causal inversion also presupposes a universe of radical objectification of human beings, their sense perceptions, emotions, motives or actions. In *Die Spinnen, Dr Mabuse,* and *Spione* as in virtually all his other films, Lang depicts power as the ability to create and maintain networks of dependencies. For instance, in *Die Frau im Mond*, the villain (played by Fritz Rasp) uses for his own ends the scientist's ambition to be first *man* on the moon, who himself exploits the unhappiness of Helius, the hero, who in turn relies on the loyalty and sense of duty of Friede, who banks on the jealousy of her financé. The rationale of the trip to the moon thus becomes a *mise-en-abyme* of the protagonists' different motivations, each reified to the point where it materialises as a calculable variable in the technical/technological operation of the moon landing. The human agents become mere extensions of the apparatus. They are the added 'risk factors', which creates suspense for the viewer, but which the villain controls and 'contains' in the manner of a logistical or engineering challenge.

'Cynical' or ironic narration of this kind relies on the same receding vistas of belief worlds and causal schemata existing in the spectator, whose positions of knowledge and embedded assumptions have to be trained to believe conflicting hypotheses simultaneously. Lang's films multiply these hypothetical realities, undercutting one level of reference by another, either through ellipsis/discontinuity or repetition/reversal. The causal nexus thus shaped is neither one of linear sequence and temporal succession, nor of parallel action and simultaneity, but works by implication and inference, by an interrogative interpellation of the spectating subject, whose active engagement is needed to fill the gap in 'motivation'. That one thereby enters oneself into the power networks and specular apparatuses set up by the film is one of the ironies once more confirming how Lang securely springs his traps for the mind *and* eye.

Given the title, *Dr Mabuse der Spieler*, i.e. Mabuse the gambler, it is not surprising that, there are frequent references to gambling. Mabuse, for instance, several times remarks how life is a game, how sex and love are merely a game, and the Countess berates him for treating people as if they deserve no better than to be played with. The grandly Nietzschean gesture of the 'as-if', licensing those in the know to dissimulate and deceive, doubles the game metaphor, which applies first and foremost to the 'portrait of the times', in the sense that the film shows a society at once ravaged *and* buoyed by inflation, suffering *and* profiting from free-floating value systems, speculating on *and* condemning the high-risk gambles of its leaders. As in any game, the film keeps repeating, there are winners and losers.

Within the fiction itself, the game that is being played is the cat-and-mouse one between Mabuse and von Wenk. In the interplay of move and countermove, Mabuse stays on top just as long as he can either up the stakes, or implicate von Wenk in contests that invert or upend themselves, symbolised in the capsized rowing boat that nearly cost von Wenk his life. Mabuse, though masterminding just about everybody, is evidently unable to establish ascendancy over the ongoing sequence of events or fix his position, so that, even when winning, he is already caught in his own devices and is as much a cog in the machinery he sets in motion as those on whom he seeks to impose his game plan. In the end, his restless and nervous energy merely feeds the see-saw motion of his own strategems, none of which look like becoming the more balanced for it.[78] This may have generic reasons as much as existential and psychoanalytic ones. In common with its literary origins, *Dr Mabuse* belongs to the genre of serial fiction, which is one reason why the film needs to take as long as it does for the plot to unravel and why it is divided into two parts (comparable to other Lang/Harbou projects from the early 1920s, such as *The Indian Tomb* and *Die Nibelungen*).[79] Its serial form may also legitimate that the driving force is not character psychology or goal orientation, but an episodic and cumulative principle predicated on anecdotal variation within a structure of repetition.

On the other hand, the game metaphor functions as a description of the film's own formal operation and signals Lang's transformation of this popular genre. The plot may still bear traces of the serial and the *Fantomas* or *Zigomar* prototypes that most probably inspired Lang, but now a more abstract, quasi-mathematical conception governs it, formulated according to the set of rules laid out in the opening scene.[80] Thereafter, Lang proceeds by a kind of aleatory logic, putting in place a number of paradigmatic situations, then letting the possible permutations develop their own momentum. The film *Dr Mabuse*, just as much as the character of Mabuse himself, plays through the constellation, and the film comes to a stop when all the combinations into which it can place its triangulated characters have been whittled away. After having, by attrition, eliminated most of its secondary players, *Dr Mabuse* not so much ends as it dies of exhaustion: just as the Countess is emotionally spent at the end, so the film is structurally spent. This, less abstractly, is also what impels the agonistic structure of the game Mabuse plays with von Wenk: in order to 'stay on the winning side' (Mabuse's phrase), he has to cap von Wenk's moves, and while von Wenk never looks like a winner, Mabuse has to play all his trumps, and despite winning on one level, he depletes himself of his aces. But since Mabuse seems to make up the rules as he goes along, the game is in a manner rigged, and this being a game of dissimulation and deception, winning is also cheating, a paradox that aptly describes the somewhat absurd dimension of Mabuse's final fate.

This ending seems the more anticlimactic as it does not tie up loose ends, but merely abandons the scheming maze it has sustained for so long, leaving the viewer contemplating a ruined architecture of cause and effect as elegantly involuted and deceptively self-evident as an Escher drawing.[81] Mabuse may be mad, but has he really been defeated? Why spend so much time out-staring von Wenk, instead of out-manoeuvring him? What was Mabuse's stake – money, sex, power – or was he 'in it' for no more than the game itself? The lack of a narrative centred on a clearly goal-oriented hero, and a story seemingly fanning out in all directions, only then to double up on itself prevents the film from straightening out its Byzantine design, and in this respect it is less a popular serial than second cousin to the paranoia fiction and labyrinthine narratives familiar from the novels of Franz Kafka, J.L. Borges, Thomas Pynchon and Kurt Vonnegut. In view of its serial origin and Lang's own transformation of it, however, *Dr Mabuse* may also be compared to another kind of 'game', where bifurcating story lines and optionally permutable characters are the rule: the modernist novel. To think that James Joyce's *Ulysses* was published in 1922 and that Leopold Bloom is thus an exact contemporary of Dr Mabuse allows a glimpse of the kind of allegory and hieroglyphic writing that appears inside 'the ultimate metaphor'.

For given the meta-levels of meaning generally attributed to Lang's cinema, *Dr Mabuse* might be regarded as allegorical, in the sense of becoming the metaphor of its own metaphor. For instance, the different kinds of *mises-en-abymes* discussed seem to establish metaphoric links between Mabuse as *metteur-en-scène*, and the *metteur-en-scène* of *Dr Mabuse*, enfolding the director himself in the schemes of his arch-villain and power-broker. It has led critics to argue against any anticipatory or cautionary parallels between Mabuse and Hitler, and to read *Dr Mabuse* instead as a cautioning finally addressed to Lang himself, about the ambiguous role the film maker has as master of the machinery of public power fantasies.[82] But as already suggested, Mabuse's reliance on vision and disguise is contradictory, not only because he seems caught in his own devices but he is finally hoist by his own petard.

Emerging in the gap between representation and what is being represented is what I have called the Langian uncanny, the feeling that this has already been seen by someone else or is being seen by someone not himself seen. A relay of roles joins the spectator, the film, the main protagonist, his disguises and other characters as his dupes. Over this relay, it is true, presides the director, invisible *metteur-en-scène* of all these roles. Yet, by the disjunction in the relay of roles as well as their proliferation he also disperses his presence, or rather, by the elaborate staging of different layers of camouflage and their uncovery, he manifests his presence as absence, putting himself under 'erasure'. The 'ultimate metaphor' would here be Mabuse as *metteur-en-scène* of a world he intends to control, 'capped' by the film maker Lang as ironic – rather than manic – Mabuse, ensnaring his audience the more firmly, by first 'arming' and then 'disarming' his hero: demonstrating how it is done, while letting complicity trouble the irony. Disguise artist, *Übermensch* and phallic *Übervater* here implicate and complement each other, with the director wearing Mabuse as his own mask, or rather, as the stand-in for an all-seeing eye.

The look as the locus of power?

So, have we finally tracked 'him' down, and secured a position from which to divide 'figure' from 'ground' and perhaps resolve the enigma posed at the beginning, about Lang's symptomatic complicity or prescient anticipation? Is his cinema at once 'sign of the times' and 'the ultimate metaphor' because it can speak about the cinema as a locus of power and thus, *through* the cinema, warn *about* the cinema? It is an idea that, as Bellour has also observed, links the three *Mabuse* films:

> The Mabuse series are, within classical cinema, the most important reflection on the cinema ever produced by a director (to the point that, with their forty year span, they could be said to mark the beginning and end of the classical period). The three films […] deal with the central power of vision and diffusion, defined by the three major phases of the development of cinema: the cinema as such (silent cinema), sound cinema, and cinema confronting video and television.[83]

In this respect, the three Mabuse films that mark such crucial turning points in his career are indeed veritable essays on the social symbolic represented by the new technologies of surveillance as dissembling machines at once fascinating and terrifying. The first *Dr Mabuse* makes the homology between Mabuse as *metteur-en-scène* of vision and the cinematic spectacle most explicit in Mabuse's role as Dr Weltmann, professional hypnotist and showman extraordinaire: the audience witnesses a film-within-the-film, which is capped by the desert caravan riding right through the auditorium. The social dimension emerges in *The Testament of Dr Mabuse*: at the very beginning of the sound film period, Lang singles out the human voice, via loudspeaker and gramophone, to demonstrate how readily it lends itself to the manipulation of 'presence'. A dummy Dr Mabuse, wired up to perform sinister deeds of simulated authority, issues commands and bellows instructions, intimidating his gang into believing him to be the more powerful for being heard but not seen. Finally, in *The 1000 Eyes of Dr Mabuse* it is the array of television screens, video monitors and other, more diabolical surveillance devices installed at the Hotel Luxor, a site which the Cold War inherited from Nazi terror, that serve Lang to press home the notion of a looking-glass world in which sight is not only the sense most easily deceived, but also the one most easily seduced.

How might such a conclusion affect my reading of the first *Dr Mabuse*? In one crucial respect, it obliges me to retrace it in order to apply another turn of the screw, because it would seem that right from the start the director veiled his own power by giving the audience comic, spectacular or even derisory simulacra of the cinema itself, as if to deflect attention from his own invisibility. For while Lang's German films are indeed built around perception and power, the deployment of what I have named as his vision machines do not offer the spectator any direct means of accessing the kind of illusory mastery on which the pleasure of classical cinema is normally predicated. Rather, the vision machines become additional occasions to reflect on the motives Lang's heroes might have for wanting to access this mastery, especially in *Dr Mabuse*, where neither the master-criminal's ambitions are straightforward, nor the forces that thwart him. For what is it that ultimately brings Mabuse down? Not von Wenk and his men laying siege to his house, nor the Countess and her refusal to submit to his passion. Such setbacks are already the consequences of another failure, that of Mabuse's own look. It fails because it harbours a secret: it is at its most powerful when exercised via intermediaries. Mabuse's gang is not only made up of valets, drivers, fixers, forgers, fences and errand boys. They are in each case also intermediaries, his helpers of the delegated look. Situations that oblige him to abandon this delegated look and instead, make him rely on the direct gaze, such as the scenes of hypnosis are the high point of danger, as much for himself as for his victims. Delegation is also one reason he needs to change appearance, making himself his own messenger and intermediary, usually thanks to an alert use of new 'media' technologies such as the telephone, the motor car and other gadgets of remote control: the stock-exchange, the gambling casino, the variety theatre offer him the public spaces where different kinds of mediations and exchanges take place that keep his power 'in place'.[84] It suggests that the desire animating Mabuse and engendering the film is not the desire to possess or even to manipulate someone for ulterior gain, be it money, power or sex, but the need to maintain a very particular state: control through the gaze and the means of vision, but ideally via the vision and gaze of someone else, most evident in the relation between Cara, himself and Hull. Lang makes 'possession' ultimately a question of how to hold in balance a triangular dynamic that involves seeing oneself mirrored in another through the mediation of a third. Once he allows this dynamic to be disturbed by the intrusion of another exigency – the urge to 'face down' the other directly, Mabuse enters a contest he seems bound to lose. The film operates a double strategy of empowerment: it gives Mabuse a repertoire of dissimulation and disguise, and it endows him with a piercingly direct look, a petrifying stare. These two tactics at first seem to complement each other, in that Mabuse the 'mastermind' uses both indiscriminately to further his ends. But what the ferocious contest of looks has shown is that the narrative actually tilts like a see-saw: the more direct the look of Mabuse, the less power he seems to wield. The *mise-en-abyme* of vision, with its hypnotic stares, glowering scowls, conspiratorial looks and furtive acts of surveillance, weaves together a network of power that allocates the protagonists their places, but only just. It is an unstable system, eventually winding down and thinning out, like a power-grid, fed by a battery going flat.

Mabuse's downfall can thus be traced to his having to confront ever more directly, i.e. without narrative mediation, the two key antagonists that make up his basic constellation: von Wenk and the Countess. By turning up in von Wenk's office, for instance, Mabuse takes back the elaborate structures of human intermediaries he had previously built up, putting himself in jeopardy. The same is true of his relationship with the Countess, especially from the moment he announces: 'The game between us must end!' When Mabuse threatens her, saying 'I will destroy anyone who comes between us', the irony is that by destroying all that comes between him and the object of his desire, he destroys his own power (-base). The narrative therefore progresses by proxy moves, rather than by Mabuse defeating his antagonists. Successively, he is stripped of all his available helpers, whose mediating look he needed to ensure himself of this relay of reliable power. This is the function of his 'victims': Cara, Hull, Count Told. On the other hand, it equally applies to his domestic 'assistants': Poesch, George, Spoerri and Frank. These protagonists and their actions seem to function like fetishes – figures of disavowal – of the mediated look to which Mabuse has no access. In *Dr Mabuse*, then, despite its obsession with vision, to look is the opposite of 'seeing'. The world of the film, broken down into discrete 'moves' or exploits, is reassembled around Mabuse's look whose involuted hierarchies appeared to control the logic of the actions and the sequence of events, but which finally turns out itself to be beholden to another system, for which it acts as the cover-up and decoy. Plugged into the distributive networks of sight without seeing, both protagonists and spectators seem to follow a more or less hidden economy of interpellation and injunction, which is to say, of subjectification.

At another level, the film tries to figure out what this implies for the political function of the cinema as an instrument of social control. And here it also seems as if the direct look is not a look at all, at least not in the sense that it gives access to power. For instance, the opening scene, with Mabuse facing the audience facing himself in the imaginary dressing-table mirror is the 'zero degree' of the film's fix on the look as power, but this 'zero degree' is built as an infinite regress: Mabuse faces the spectator across a mirror which is also the screen. Like all the other looks that circulate, Mabuse's own does not finally seem to belong to him, but is, as it were, a look 'on loan'. Yet since Mabuse initially accedes to power via the look and eventually loses power via the look, these must be two kinds of look, the unmediated, imaginary one and the mediated, symbolic one.[85] His downfall is, classically, the consequence of his rise, in that he makes a tragic mistake: the further he rises, the more the look he has access to and relies on reveals its underside, namely of being a look borrowed from the technologies of vision.

As a consequence, Mabuse's hard stare resembles a totemic mask, designed to terrify those who look at it. As a look, the stare is not an expression of power, but yet another form of the disguise of power. On the one hand, Mabuse dons disguises whose purpose it is to make him blend with the urban fabric, becoming a Jewish peddler or a drunk working-class husband berating his wife, both deployed as diversionary gestures of metropolitan mimicry. On the other hand, there are forms of disguise that draw attention to themselves, for instance, when Mabuse plays the boo-man and buffoon, by putting on the airs and manners of the clownish jester and the manic laughter of the fool – terrifyingly disconcerting, but also meant to fascinate and distract the onlookers, paradoxically to focus and disperse their attention. In these cases, one is faced with a kind of Mabuse–Medusa, explicitly in the scenes where he faces down von Wenk at the gambling table and hypnotises him as Dr Weltmann. But as a kind of ritual mask, the rigid face with the piercing eyes can also be a form of disguise that hides the bearer from himself. In its anthropological sense, a mask is designed to ward off evil spirits, it is the bearer's gesture of defence, in the language of the 'enemy', whereas a disguise that operates as camouflage is the currency the bearer tries to acquire in order to enter into circulation and exchange. Disguise in general would thus be a look that does not see, because it functions in a double system: it assimilates or 'absorbs' the look of the other in the form of mimicry and camouflage, and it 'wards off' the look of the other in the form of the mask.[86] One inference of this interpretation of the hard stare would be that the scenes of Mabuse as Dr Weltmann, conjuring up the 'living pictures' of the camels in the desert, and his subsequent hypnosis of von Wenk are less proof of his power, but as suggested, merely more derisory effigies of the cinematic apparatus, of the kind described above in *Der Müde Tod* and *Die Nibelungen*, because the apparatus is not to be metaphorised in terms of vision at all: its signifiers are material, and its effects are semiotic rather than optical.[87] Instead of foregrounding the act of looking, as is so often claimed, Lang's cinema captures looking in a relay of devices or machines that mock human sight at the same time as they lend it the illusion of new forms of mastery.

Technologies of vision are, however, blind. The empty look, the frozen stare, the Medusa's gaze: Lang progressively descends into some very cold regions of visuality, in which apparently no-one is in control, and yet everyone struggles for control over others, which suggests that the question of the cinema's vision machines poses itself differently: no longer is the look to be thought of as a metaphoric extension of power, but in fact, power is that which interrupts the exchange of looks, by which human beings signal each other's recognition. The cinema, taken to its (techno)logical conclusion, for Lang, is the ultimate metaphor not of social control through the power of the look, but – more in line with Paul Virilio's thinking about cinema and warfare – proof of the end of this metaphor: the all-seeing eye of surveillance finally sees nothing at all.

Kitsch, sensation, kultur: the revenge of *Jugendstil*

One comes back to the apparent contradiction between *Dr Mabuse* as a 'portrait of the times' and of Lang's cinema as 'the ultimate metaphor'. It resolves itself if we see Mabuse as a metaphor not of political power, Nazi or otherwise, but of a rebellion against power, in the idiom of imposture, the mask and the disguise, with Lang rescuing his cinema from its all-seeing blindness by aligning it with the different modes of the cynic–ironic *Uneigentlichkeit* (the 'as-if' stance) of the 'enlightened false consciousness' of Weimar's 'Spieler' or gamblers. *Dr Mabuse* can be read as a 'pastiche' of (Expressionist) revolt, mimicking already at the start of the decade the make-believe dandyism of Weimar intellectuals, politicians and artists with their postures of open duplicity and disloyalty towards what came to be known as the *Vorbehaltsdemokratie* (the 'yes-but' democracy). Yet, by wanting to stay ahead of the game, the master-mind is also liable to overreach himself: Mephistophelian spirit of the metropolis, he descends into the fast-moving traffic in souls and goods, eventually lost in a new kind of social agency: performative yet impersonal, it moulds a space out of sight lines and architectural prospects, stencilling command-and-control figures out of its technologically assisted theatricality. No wonder post-modern pop 'recognises itself' in Lang, always poised to 'strike the pose'.

Such dandyism, however, makes the desire to deceive by disguise appear in yet another light: its purpose would be to ward off the look, in the sense of stopping the circuit of imaginary looks that has no purchase on the symbolic economy of desire. It implies that the opposite of disguise is not truth, immediacy or 'authenticity', but rather, whatever it takes to instantiate this symbolic, that is, the condition of possibility of discontinuity, disjuncture, non-identity. Specifically, it would mean to introduce into the kinds of imaginary relations that, in the case of *Dr Mabuse*, seem to play themselves out on both sides – on the side of the looks and on the side of the disguises – the force or trace of a break: in other words, to be able to 'place a rupture'.

Biographically, this rupture came in 1933, when Lang decided to leave Germany. Although right from the start in his American films, most conspicuously in *Fury*, his very first Hollywood production, the question of how cinematic representation can appeal to a reality outside representation was central, it is perhaps fitting that it was ten years later, in 1943, in a film about 'Germany', that he can be seen to 'place his rupture'. When working with Bert Brecht on the anti-Nazi propaganda film *Hangmen also Die*,[88] the fictional treatment of the assassination of Heydrich, the hated SS-commander of occupied Prague, Lang had to stand his ground about the cinema's particular suspension of the opposition between truth and falsehood under especially difficult circumstances, both personally and politically. While for Brecht, the script was an occasion to show the heroic struggle of the Czech people against Nazi terror, for Lang, the film became an occasion for constructing a scenario around different kinds of lies and falsehoods; the fight for moral truth in the film – as it is in Lubitsch's anti-Nazi black comedy *To Be or Not to Be* – is entirely conceived within the deceptive realm of images, which is to say that the moment of truth of an image is always another image. Hence the film's narrative development proceeds by nothing but a series of false doors, false bottoms, traps for the mind and for the eye.[89]

Yet this is precisely the point: in the cinema, the desire to deceive, or at any rate, the desire to make deception the 'zero-degree' of all representation, turns out to be more 'honest' than any asserted claims made in the name of truth. Since the cinematic apparatus in all three Mabuse films merely figures as a metaphoric extension of the manipulations of power, it cannot in this respect be 'turned against itself': in other words, there is no voice of truth that within the cinematic apparatus can speak about truth. The question that the disguise artists of Lang's (and Weimar's) cinema put to the historian is finally, what might be the truth of which the disguise wanted to be the open simulacrum? Under certain conditions, they seem to be saying, one has to disguise oneself in order to be true to oneself, one has to counter the many strategies of unacknowledged dissimulation – the 'cynicism' in its public form – by mimicking the very form of untruth one encounters.[90] Dissimulation as mimicry would here be a survival strategy, and in the artistic and intellectual milieux of the Weimar Republic it could be seen as part of how to find one's bearings in this looking-glass world, this inside-out reality, so often described.[91] Mabuse's ferocious need for disguises, as well as his ferocious masks are in this sense nothing but 'performances' of the many forms of imposture encountered in the 'image of his times'.

Such a dissembling redeemed by its own double, as repetition and 'excessive' symmetry brings us back to the question of 'style', and to the function of Expressionism within the imaginary of Weimar cinema. If the 'enlightened false consciousness' turns out to both provoke and sanction an open duplicity, which installs the simulacrum, where the self performs itself as a 'copy without an original', then this effect, when applied to objects rather than subjects, can be compared to kitsch, the naive, naively knowing or derisive dissembling of authenticity. As discussed in a previous chapter, kitsch in the film debate of the 1920s figured as an unquestioningly negative category: Lang himself entered the fray several times, with essays like 'Der künstlerische Aufbau des Filmdramas' and 'Kitsch – Sensation – Kultur und Film' (both 1924).[92] But one can also recognise in kitsch a number of important tension and realignments in the relation between art and its public, technology and the commodity, style and subjectivity. In this sense, the question of kitsch joins the problematics of the disguise artist as 'self-cancelling' resistance fighter, and can be seen to apply very specifically to the situation of the cinema in Weimar, in the way it situates itself within a society that could plausibly be described as perhaps the first modern society not so much of the spectacle, but of the simulated spectacle.

It is now easier to understand Lang's own discomfort with the label 'Expressionist' when applied to his work. For if as argued earlier, 'Expressionism' is one of the stylistic effects which Weimar cinema was successful in mimicking – and marketing – then to call Lang an Expressionist is a backhanded compliment, since it takes the first level of imposture as a truth, when Lang's pride as a true stylist of the cinema must lie in the second layer of imposture, capable of producing the first, flawlessly and convincingly. Some of the director's abiding formal obsessions – ornament and abstraction, technology and sentiment, violence and petrification, arabesque and stasis – can be traced back to the aesthetics but also the historical problematics of *Jugendstil*. As early as *Der Müde Tod*, culminating in *Die Nibelungen* and finding its most functionalist form in *Metropolis* and *Die Frau im Mond*, human affect and expression are not only frozen in gesture but 'absorbed' in the decor, tending towards an immobility that transmits desire to the figural and ornament, where it 'dies' in the beauty of an abstract composition, almost in the manner of Henry van Velde or Egon Schiele, or takes on a terrifying aspect of serene indifference.[93] What in the films just named is often experienced as a pictorialist effect, the reversal of figure and ground typical of art nouveau ornament,[94] emerges in *Dr Mabuse* as what I have called the mottled figure on a mottled ground, the mimicry of mobile energy in the ornamental labyrinth of the modern metropolis.[95]

Lang's Viennese background, as well as his early talent as a precociously gifted pasticheur of, for instance, Gustav Klimt, suggest that from early on he knew first-hand the sensibility as well as sociocultural side of *Jugendstil* as kitsch, and there is evidence in his German films, besides *Die Nibelungen* where it is most explicitly apparent,[96] that *Jugendstil* is the style he remained most faithful to, as if its legacy of playful feigning licensed him to mimic other styles, among them the style of Expressionism, itself the declared enemy of *Jugendstil*.[97] If the so-called 'Expressionist cinema' of which Lang is said to be one of the chief representatives, was – as I suggested in an earlier chapter, only half in jest – the revenge of *Jugendstil* on the style that claimed to replace it, then one might with equal aptness say that this part of Weimar cinema was the revenge of Vienna, as the cultural centre of the pre-war period, on Berlin, the city that replaced it as the city of the post-war decade. The director's enigmatic as well as emblematic place within Weimar cinema can thus be seen as an ongoing self-reflection about the cultural politics of a *Jugendstil* aesthetic carried into the Berlin of the 1920s, indicative of the cinema's modernity as both camouflaged and confident, both self-deprecating and self-assertive. Kracauer's argument about Lang as the director of the new mass ornament of the fascist public sphere is no more 'false' than *Cahiers du cinéma*'s praise of Lang as the most consummate representative of 'pure cinema'. Both, however, leave out the dimension of disguise that concerned me here: the double *mise-en-abyme* in which both ornament and abstraction in Lang hold each other suspended. It makes not only Lang's many-sided villain Mabuse but also the director a 'disguise-artist' of cynical/kynic reason, perhaps more truthful in his mimicry and masks than those who, thinking to be in possession of the truth, enjoy the wisdom of hindsight. For how did Sloterdijk critique the critiques of Weimar? 'They risk remaining more naive than the consciousness they set out to unmask'.[98] '"All Cretans are liars" – says a Cretan' goes the famous paradox of Zeno. It is a conundrum that Fritz Lang, the 'Cretan' from Vienna, finding himself in the Spree-Athens of the Weimar Republic, might well have carried as his secret motto.

Notes

1 'unser chaotisches Zeitalter, wenn es längst zu seiner Formel erstarrt sein wird', Fritz Lang, 'Kitsch – Sensation – Kultur und Film', cited in Gehler and Kasten (eds) 1990a: 203.

2 'Lang's rise in the German cinema, which reflects most of its tendencies, is in itself something like an allegory' (Gavin Lambert, quoted in Gehler and Kasten 1990a: 8).

3 Lang is emphatic about this in his interview with Michel Ciment, Goffredo Fofi, Louis Seguin and Roger Tailleur 'Fritz Lang à Venise'. *Positif*, no. 94 (April 1968): 9–10. See also Michael Töteberg: 'All his life, Lang vehemently denied that *Dr Mabuse* belonged to expressionist cinema [...]: "it's the theme that dictates the style" he would say, adding "I don't know what I took from Expressionism. I may have used it, maybe to get it out of my system" (Töteberg 1985: 38).

4 'For anyone abroad, German film equals Fritz Lang, whose childish giant's toys happily fit the hoary idea foreigners have of German fairytale romanticism and philosophical brooding' (Rudolf Arnheim, 'Die Frau im Mond [1929]', *Kritiken und Aufsätze* (Frankfurt/M: Fischer, 1979): 222)

5 See Huaco 1965; Tudor 1974; Monaco 1976.

6 See Kracauer 1947: 149–50. See also Kracauer 1995.

7 'Was Lang a sensitive and compassionate artist, as well as a lover of famous women? Or was he a sado-masochistic beast whose tortuous on-set behaviour was mirrored, off the job, in a sordid love life crowded with prostitutes and mistresses?' (McGilligan 1997).

8 For the Brecht–Adorno contacts, see my essay on 'Fritz Lang and Lily Latté', in B. Eisenschitz and P. Bertetto, *Fritz Lang* (Paris/Turin, 1993): 177–8. For the Lang–Brecht relationship, see Lyon 1980: Chapter 2, esp. pp. 58–72. Kracauer, who lived in New York and did not visit California, remained in contact with Adorno throughout his life. See Martin Jay, 'The extraterritorial life of Siegfried Kracauer', and 'Adorno and Kracauer: Notes on a troubled friendship', both in Jay 1986.

9 See Eisner 1947: 22–4.

10 Here is Eric Rohmer:

> Mise en scene was for us a critical concept, not a battle cry. We rejected the word 'realisiteur' because we were convinced that the work of cinematic mise en scene was not a question of realising a scenario or directing players, but a matter of conception. Mise en scene is an unsuitable term insofar as it is derived from the theatre, but correct if we understand by it an organization of space and time. Fritz Lang's films embody the precise example and the most demanding conception of the mise en scene.
>
> (Jenkins 1981)

11 Michel Mourlet wrote in 1959:

(In Lang) 'Expressionism was cast into a Euclidian mould which transformed its meaning....So a liturgy was created, based on a purely formal hieratism. Already the principal feature of Lang's later attitude to actors is prefigured in this liturgy, where they are its servants: in other words, turning them into a completely neutralised vehicle for mise-en-scene considered as pure movement, whereas the reverse is generally true of other filmmakers, for whom mise-en-scene is a means to glorify the actors. Hence Lang's predilection for actors who are more negative than positive, and whose reticence, diffidence or passivity more readily suffers the annihilation imposed on them.'

Quoted in S. Jenkins (ed.) Fritz Lang, *The Image and the Look*, (London: BFI, 1984): 13.

12 See Thiery Kuntzel, 'Le Travail du film', *Communications* 19 (1972): 25–39.

13 See Noel Burch, 'From Mabuse to M', in Richard Roud (ed.) *Cinema. A Critical Dictionary*, vol. II (London: Secker & Warburg, 1980): 583–99.

14 Fritz Lang 1947: 52–5. For Lang's brush with the McCarthy hearings, see McGilligan 1997: 365–7.

15 For testimony from contemporaries, see among others, Kaes 1978; Schweinitz 1992; Hake 1994.

16 As to the importance of (space-)flight in the archaeology of modernity, see Asendorf 1997.

17 The ideas and practices of Bert Brecht, Erwin Piscator, and Sergeij Tretjakov are among the best known, not least because of Walter Benjamin's 'The artist as producer' in *Understanding Brecht* (Benjamin 1973a).

18 See, for instance, Georg Simmel, 'The metropolis and modern life', [1903], translated in Kurt H. Wolff, *The Sociology of Georg Simmel* (Glencoe, Ill: The Free Press, 1950).

19 See Jameson 1974.

20 See Simmel 1997: 24–40.

21 See Jameson (1973) 'Vanishing mediator: Narrative structure in Max Weber', *New German Critique* no. 1 (Winter 1973): 52–89.

22 In the 1920s, philosophers from Georg Lukacs to Martin Heidegger were to recast the relation of the senses to self-presence, and writers otherwise as diametrically opposed as Walter Benjamin and Ernst Jünger made the category of 'perceptual shock' central to their analysis of modernity: both saw in the cinema and photography the media that registered most accurately this shock experience. On Benjamin and Jünger, see Bohrer 1978.

23 See Benjamin 1983.

24 Among the most ideologically critical assessments of Weimar cinema from a Marxist perspective are W. Becker *Film und Herrschaft* (Berlin: Volker Spiess, 1973) 1977 and Spiker 1975. A more nuanced assessment can be found in Saunders 1994 and in Kreimeier 1992, as well as in his essay on Fritz Lang, 'Der Schlafwandler' in Berg-Ganschow and Jacobsen 1987.

25 The Brecht–Lukacs debate over 'realism', or the so-called *Expressionismusdebatte* would be places to go for a context and further arguments. See Fred Jameson 1978 (On Realism) and Schmitt 1973.

26 I take these terms 'apparatus' and 'dispositif' from the debates about the cinematic apparatus. See Heath and de Lauretis 1980 and T. Hak Kyung Cha 1980 (*The Apparatus*).

27 Apart from his remarks on 'Expressionism' already quoted, see also his writings, collected in Gehler and Kasten 1990a.

28 Cynicism is for him a phenomenology of polemical forms of consciousness, operative whenever two views of truth persist with equal force. 'Kygnicism' is a historically variable, adaptive form of resistance, allowing one to re-experience oneself as whole and

a sensuous, rational being, against the awareness of a constructed, artificial or arbitrary reality of power, logic or domination.

29 Cynicism is the enlightened false consciousness, the ability to live simultaneously two orders of rationality, the reasonable and the actual. It is the modernised unhappy consciousness on which enlightenment has worked at one and the same time successfully and in vain. It has learnt the lesson of enlightenment, but did not draw the consequences, and maybe could not. It cannot be reached by criticism, because it is already a highly self-reflexive consciousness.

(Sloterdijk 1988)

30 Sloterdijk attempts to do for Weimar Germany what Foucault did for the classical age of the seventeenth century: disengage the order of the reigning discourses: the military, the medical, the sexological, the political, etc. He calls them the cardinal cynicisms because in each case they constitute a defensive, self-validating 'closed' system. And rather than posit these discourses as objects of ideological critique, or denounce them as manifestations of false consciousness (with the implication of speaking from a position of true consciousness), Sloterdijk asks the Foucaultian question: 'How do they work?' 'What power-structures do they circumscribe, maintain and penetrate?'

31 There are three figures who, during the golden era of the silent German cinema, played a crucial prophetic role: the witchmaster Dr Caligari, the vampire Nosferatu and the gambler Mabuse. They are prototypes of a period of economic and social transformation, exemplars of a tyranny about to engulf the country.[...] These three demons of a hectic era are thus not only specific forms of expressionist film art. Cinema was writing the ethnographic and cultural history of a people, to whom the three figures hold up a mirror-image.

(Patalas 1962: 8)

32 Also, given the cliché sensationalist literary origins of the figure, Mabuse is a fantasy tailored to a contemporary film audience's expectations. He is 'behind' events that otherwise remain inexplicable coincidences in the life of the metropolis, but thanks to his many disguises, he makes himself 'invisible' in the crowd: dreams of omnipotence which are those of the cinema goer, projected onto the villain, made more powerful and attractive than the detective, through whom the spectator can, however, re-enter the helplessness and frustration that make dreams of ubiquity attractive in the first place. The detective and Mabuse are here two sides of the same desire, two sides of a properly cinematic desire – to be omnipotent and invisible, omnipotent because invisible.

33 Kreimeier 1987: 89–112.

34 Kreimeier, it should be said, uses a spatial metaphor of overlay or cover, rather than Kracauer's temporal one of foreboding and anticipation, yet the vanishing point for both is a historical reality they presume to know through the metaphorical meanings the present has attached to it.

35 In a similar vein, Peter H. Schröder argues that the exoticism of the early Lang is like a labyrinthine garden, planted in order to transplant another labyrinth, that of the metropolis, the luxuriating chaos of Berlin. See 'Orientalischer Irrgarten und Großberlin' in Schröder 1965: 670–5.

36 *Dr Mabuse der Spieler*, directed Fritz Lang, May–June 1922; script by Thea von Harbou, after the novel by Norbert Jacques, with Rudolf Klein-Rogge, Bernhardt Goetzke, Alfred Abel, Aud Egede Nissen and Gertrude Welcker. The novel was serialised by Ullstein, and the last instalments, featuring stills from Lang's production, were timed to coincide with the opening of the film. It was profusely reviewed and proved a huge success, turning a profit on its rather extravagant budget of 15 million marks. For details about authorship, tie-ins and marketing, see also the correspon-

dence between Norbert Jacques, Thea von Harbou and Fritz Lang, reprinted in Farin and Scholdt 1994: 217–55.

37 According to Lang, the film has lost its original introductory sequence: a brief, breathless montage of scenes of the Spartacus uprising, the murder of Rathenau, the Kapp Putsch and other violent moments of recent history. Lang maintains that when it first opened this sequence was intact; and it is unclear when the prologue was cut – whether in the twenties, when people did not want to be reminded of the troubles of the time, or later, by the East German archive, which owns the negative and may have preferred to excise the Spartacus material.

(Eisner 1976: 59)

38 See Eisner 1976: 57–8 for citations from Berlin newspaper reviews. Before *Dr Mabuse* was passed by the censors, 29 metres of film were cut from the street battles, it was X-rated, and in Sweden was banned altogether (see Töteberg 1985: 40).

39 The master-mind and manipulator Haghi in *Spione* is in this sense an elaboration of Dr Mabuse, though this time one of his disguises is clearly intended to resemble V.I. Lenin. See Brenez 1998: 120.

40 Fritz Lang 'A propos du Docteur Mabuse' (Eibel 1964).

41 'Ein brief von Fritz Lang', in *Caligari und Caligarismus* (Lang 1970). See also Lang: 'Fritz Lang remembers', *Focus on Film* no. 20 (Spring 1975) and 'Interview mit Fritz Lang', *Frankfurter Rundschau* (15 May 1971).

42 See E. Ann Kaplan, *Fritz Lang. A Guide to References and Resources* (Boston: G.K. Hall, 1981): 2.

43 D. Bordwell, J. Staiger and K. Thompson, *The Classical Hollywood Cinema* (London: Routledge, 1988): 82.

44 Paul Jensen *The Cinema of Fritz Lang*, 1969: 44–5.

45 Fritz Lang's polemical credo is 'Kitsch – Sensation – Kultur und Film', originally given as a lecture in Vienna, published in Beyfuss and Kossowsky 1924. But see also:

> The Decla took a double risk with the first film of its adventure cycle *Die Spinnen*: [...] an adventure film that consciously restricted itself to well-constructed, thrilling action without any literary ambitions. The action film had to come, like a force of nature, after the erotic film had lost its attractiveness and the detective film was on its death-bed. ... A return to Karl May.
>
> (Lang 1919: 43–4)

46 In this he is comparable to G.W. Pabst, whose *Die Freudlose Gasse* is based on a sensationalist novel by Hugo Bettauer.

47 Henry Fonda claimed that Lang remained a 'silent' director throughout his career and never got over the coming of sound. See Roberta Ostrov, 'Interview with Henry Fonda', *Take One* no. 10 (March/April 1972).

48 In several articles devoted mainly to *Dr Mabuse* and *M*, Noel Burch shows the degree to which individual shots in Lang can be temporally and spatially autonomous, which suggests that the system by which they combine is based on formal principles that implicitly break with both psychological realism and illusionist representational space (Burch, 'The Opening of Dr Mabuse', *Cinetracts*, 1981). Following Burch, Noel Carroll has compared the first sound films by Lang and Pabst.

49 See Tsivian (1995) 169–85.

50 See Burch's (1981) close analysis of the opening of *Dr Mabuse*.

51 See Pynchon (1972): 674.

52 He was also Thea von Harbou's first husband, whom she divorced to marry Lang.

53 Adorno 1951: 245–6.

54 A contemporary figure would be the boisterous, sordid – and in many ways none the less tragic – Muhamad Al Fayed, owner of Harrods and the Paris Ritz, self-advertised briber of Members of Parliament, father of the late Dodi of Princess Diana fame,

forever applying for British citizenship which successive governments continue to withhold from him.

55 In the scene at the Folies Bergères, for instance: not only do we see Hull being made the object of observation, when he thinks himself a subject, we have the tragicomedy of the elderly gentlemen throwing flowers frantically onto the stage, when the only flowers that Cara pays any attention to are those sent by Mabuse and containing the message to await instructions. The comedy is that the spectator is duped even when he thinks of himself most active, the tragedy is that we, too, are spectators, locked in the same mechanism as the diegetic spectator. By sharing Mabuse's perspective at this moment we have the image of the film director whose triumph it is to make the spectator believe that the spectacle is for him, that his pleasure is his own, when Lang indicates with lucidity and economy that the spectator of the cinema is caught in the imaginary of a *mise-en-scène* of vision, and this inescapably.

56 That a convinced Nazi like Pökler should be attracted to it says as much about Pynchon's apocalyptic pessimism regarding the United States, as it does about the German scientific and intellectual elite.

57 *M* is the most extreme example of a film about violence and aggression in which violence is presented not only by its absence but by the figuration of absence itself. In the opening scene, showing Frau Beckmann expecting Elsie's return from school, all the shots of the empty plate, the chair, the stair well, etc. relate to the violence of Beckert. What finds itself opposed is the waiting of the mother, via its metonymic representations, and the murder of the girl Elsie, also with metonymic representations, as if to define extreme aggression as the interaction of two kinds of absences symmetrically related.

58 This is the line taken by Lang's French critics, notably Jean Douchet and Gerard Legrand.

59 Lang's care for the specificity of his social world in *Dr Mabuse* is matched by his attention to detail, the carefully chosen decor in each of the settings. Close-ups highlight the planting/discovering/misplacing of clues: letters, notes, handkerchiefs, attaché cases, keys wrapped in balls of wool: a world of objects full of hidden significance, with close-ups making them even more mysterious.

60 D. Mellor (1978) *Germany – The New Photography 1927–33* (London: Arts Council) contains essays on Albert Renger-Patsch's *Die Welt ist schön* (1928) and Karl Blossfeldt, *Urformen der Kunst* (Berlin, 1928), including a review by Walter Benjamin.

61 Roland Barthes, 'The third meaning', in *Image, Music, Text* (New York: Hill and Wang, 1977) 52–68.

62 The discussions in film studies around metaphor and metonomy have surely not by accident focused also on Lang's work. But the analyses of Christian Metz and Thierry Kuntzel, while productive in clarifying the rhetorical code of classical cinema have perhaps not altogether come to terms with the transformational process involved, especially as far as their coexistence in a figural space is concerned, and the question of affectivity which is so clearly involved in the rhetorical operations of cinema, and may be said to be virtually absent in literature, except perhaps in the work of writers such as Bataille or the surrealists who consciously set out to explore the affectivity emanating from specific semiotic and rhetorical operations.

63 See Janet Bergstrom (1982).

64 The scene recalls that of *Metropolis*, with the slaves in their thousands building the Tower of Babel – an image of Asiatic or Egyptian despotism incarnate.

65 Borrowing from Jean François Lyotard, this other space could be called 'figural', as opposed to representational, and it might be here that the energies are generated that are rationalised by the viewer's memory as violence. See also Thierry Kuntzel, 'Le defilement', both as quoted by Maureen Turim (1989).

66 The intrigue ostensibly revolves around an investigation, but one never shares the investigator's point of view. A quest for power, it is also a power play, a contest between evenly matched antagonists, and finally, it concerns the possession of a desired object (Countess Told eventually replaces the desire for wealth, political and economic power). Mabuse is seen as having direct control through financial dependency (his footman George and the others of the Mabuse household), sexual dependency (Cara Carozza), substance dependency (Spoerri's cocaine addiction), and finally, psychic dependency through hypnosis.

67 Countess Told, it seems, is an object of desire for both Dr Mabuse and von Wenck, mainly because of her own lack of desire, which in turn makes her susceptible to Mabuse's scheme of 'playing with the lives of human beings and their fate'. She is the woman as enigma (the 'rich bitch') of many subsequent thriller films.

68 In a series of 'dissolves' the rapid rise of Schramm, as 'Kriegsgewinnler' and 'Inflationsschinder' is documented from street-corner black marketeer to owner of the poshest high-society hang-out in town.

69 See the review in *B.Z. am Mittag* (30 April, 1922), quoted in Eisner 1976: 58.

70 Mabuse's roving gaze picks out only two female spectators in the auditorium: one is occupied with her illicit lover, and the other punishes her husband's curiosity by snatching his pince-nez, as the showgirls come on stage.

71 See René Girard, *Mensonge Romantique, Verité Romanesque* (Paris: Grasset).

72 See Slavoj Zizek's discussion of Jacques Lacan's 'the signification of the phallus', in *The Metastases of Enjoyment*, (London: Verso): 201–2,1994.

73 Siegfried Kracauer, for instance, talks about 'dollar-dreadful rather than penny-dreadful, trash need not be untrue to life, on the contrary, life may culminate in heaps of trash such as no writer could ever amass'(Kracauer 1947: 82). Luc Moullet sees the film made up of 'societés secretes, vices cachés, hypnotisme ... ' L. Moullet *Fritz Lang* (Paris: Seghers): 26. Alfred Eibel: 'comme avant lui, Fantomas, Mabuse, dont les aventures sont aussi abracadabrantes, n'est autre qu'un criminel de génie devenu l'enemi public no.1' (Eibel 1964: 22).

74 See my chapter on Griffith's European legacy in Elsaesser (1990), *Early Cinema: Space, Frame, Narrative.*

75 In a crucial scene, a gradual alignment of body movement and looks eventually suggests that a character in one space (Nosferatu, in the Carpathian mountains) 'sees' a character in another space (Nina, sleepwalking in Bremen), across the body of the terror-stricken and supine Jonathan Harker, lover–victim of both Nosferatu and Nina. In Murnau, it is repetition, alternation and cross cutting between two spaces which gradually reveals their essential unity and 'correspondence'. See, for a more detailed analysis, the chapter on Murnau, in Part II, Chapter 3, this volume.

76 Gerard Legrand once called these forms of interactions 'les entrelacs de lang'. *Positif* 94 (April 1968): 1–7.

77 The narrative is constantly folded back and turned in upon itself, mainly by the way that blocks of narrative are edited into each other, in a process of montage, which, unlike Eisenstein's does not operate on the level of the shot, but the sequence: it is a semantic principle, not a syntactic one that is being applied (we may recall that it was Eisenstein, who while studying with Esfer Shub was put in charge of re-editing *Dr Mabuse* for the Soviet release version).

78 In this he is very similar to Haghi, the master-spy and international operator, in *Spione,* also played by Klein-Rogge.

79 *The Indian Tomb* which Joe May, the producer, 'took away' from Lang in 1921, was finally directed by Lang after his brief return to Germany in the 1950s as *Das Indische Grabmal* and *Der Tiger von Eschnapur.*

80 Burch 1981.

81 Edward Branigan argues in *Point of View in the Cinema* (The Hague: Mouton, 1982) that in classical cinema films do not narrate themselves but the act of narration creates the character who is thereby given the authority to narrate the story of which he is a character.

82 This is argued, for instance, by Lucy Fisher, 'Dr Mabuse and Mr. Lang', *Wide Angle* vol. 3, no. 3 (Winter 1979–80).

83 See 'La machine á hypnose: entretien avec Raymond Bellour', *CinémAction*, no. 47 (1988): 71.

84 Mabuse is also an image of the 'fixer' rather like Erich Pommer was a fixer. See Jacobson 1989.

85 I am here referring to the distinction made by Jacques Lacan between the imaginary and the symbolic look, which has been commented on for its significance in cinema studies by, among others, Slavoj Zizek, Kaja Silverman and Joan Copjec.

86 See Hal Foster, 'The "primitive" unconscious of modern art', *Recodings* (Seattle: Bay Press, 1985): 181–208.

87 On this distinction see Joan Copjec, *Read My Desire* (Cambridge, Mass: MIT Press, 1994) 15–38.

88 See also Jean Louis Comolli and Francois Géré, 'Two fictions concerning hate', in Stephen Jenkins (ed.) *Fritz Lang. The Image and the Look* (London: British Film Institute, 1981): 125–46.

89 The similarity of construction of *Hangmen Also Die* and of *Beyond A Reasonable Doubt* was noted by Jacques Rivette, 'La Main', in *Cahiers du Cinéma* 76 (November 1957).

90 As Ernst Jünger was to note in 1932: 'the more cynically, Spartan, Prussian and Bolshevik we lead our life, the better it will be'. *Der Arbeiter*, p. 201, quoted in Christian Graf von Krockow, *Von Deutschen Mythen* (Stuttgart: Deutsche Verlags Anstalt, 1995): 91.

91 About the sense of Weimar Germany as a 'topsy-turvy' world, see Joseph Roth: 'You're attending a masked ball and not reality – but you don't know how to get out of your costumes', and Robert Musil 'To read the daily paper takes more brain-power than possessed by Leibnitz, but no-one notices', quoted in Sloterdijk 1985, vol. 2: 872–97.

92 Both reprinted in Fred Gehler and Ulrich Kasten (eds.), *Fritz Lang. Die Stimme von Metropolis* (Berlin: Henschel, 1990a): 179–88, 202–6.

93 Jean François Lyotard, cited in K. Woodward (ed.) *Performance in Postmodern Culture* (New York: Coda Press): 90.

94 Cf. Raymond Bellour:

> In Siegfried, for instance: three warriors occupy almost the entire surface of the screen; they are so close that they cannot be seen in their entirety; between them are blank spaces, in the background a bare wall; the image is perfectly flat and the soldiers look like cardboard cut-outs; when Kriemhild's women pass behind them, following her, perspective suddenly returns so vividly that one feels it as being too deep, and it seems like another illusion.
>
> (Bellour cited in Jenkins 1981 (see note 11 above))

95 Pascal Bonitzer discusses Lang in his 'Partial vision: film and the labyrinth', *Wide Angle* vol. 4, no. 4 (1984).

96 Kristin Thompson, on the other hand, discusses Lang's *Die Nibelungen* as prototypical for Expressionist cinema in her *Eisenstein's Ivan The Terrible* (Princeton: Princeton University Press, 1984).

97 Even Lotte Eisner argues that Lang should be regarded as a director of *Jugendstil, Fritz Lang* (1976): 62.

98 Peter Sloterdijk (1985) *Kritik der zynischen Vernunft.*

2

THE OLD AND THE NEW REGIME OF THE GAZE

Ernst Lubitsch and *Madame Dubarry*

The historical imagination

A biographical detour may draw attention to the difference between two concepts that inform some of the thinking behind this book: 'historical imagination' and 'historical imaginary'. The historical imagination refers to nineteenth-century historiography, and in particular, romantic historiography, as in the works of the Scottish historian Thomas Carlyle and the French historian Jules Michelet. The historical imagination solves two related problems with regard to the writing of history generally and to the French Revolution in particular: to understand the kind of violence of social change that occurred during the Revolution, by embedding it in a metaphorical discourse. The French Revolution of 1789 seemed to the generation of 1848 a crisis of language – affecting the rational discourse of the eighteenth century no less than the 'organicist' discourse of Romanticism, which was itself a reaction to the rational discourse, though incapable of dealing with the emergent Industrial Revolution. Significantly enough, however, historians of the historical imagination, in confronting the French Revolution, had recourse to metaphors of material transformation, of productive relations, such as labour, travail, struggle – in other words, drawn precisely from the experience of industrialisation. They also relied on the vocabulary of the sublime and developed a new temporality of the instant, in order to focus on the historical process itself, but in terms at variance with an earlier historical consciousness, say that of Edward Gibbon, or even that of Edmund Burke. Second, historians of the historical imagination attempted to find a mode of representation appropriate to the new forms of agency emanating from the masses, and not sanctioned by divine power and authority. If the historical imagination takes account of the new history's different relation to violence, it often understands this violence as also part of a new performative mode (as expressed in the revolutionary journals of the time, with its theatrical aspects and its politicians–pamphleteers, such as Mirabeau, Danton, Robespierre, Camille Desmoulins and St Just). The Jacobins' own forms of self-presentation, for instance, had a marked preference for a second level of reference, dressing their performativity in the rhetoric and gesture of a Cicero, Marcus Aurelius or Julius Cesar. 'Playing at being Republicans', they distinguished themselves from courtiers, by using language more in keeping with descriptions of the ancient Greek city states or the Roman Empire. Yet for the truly novel insight – the violence of revolutionary spectacle as the spectacle of revolutionary violence – historians of the historical imagination adapted (mainly from Walter Scott) narrative forms and modes of narration able to dramatise such crowd scenes as spectacles of seeing/seen.[1] The intense theatricality of the Revolution's early years is also very conspicuous in Michelet's attempt to present it as the French People's self-celebration, described as the apotheosis of historical time and out of time altogether, in the realm of myth, or rather, in the temporality of revolutionary time as messianic time. Finally, historians used images of the body, their body – drawn from its pathology and symptomatology. Especially remarkable are the metaphoric discourses of the pathological body (in Carlyle's case drawing heavily on his intimate and painful knowledge of his own digestive system). They transform an older language of the 'sick' body politic and the need for drastic 'purges' into a new medical imaginary of the blood stream and hypertension, of nervous disorders and bodily discomfort, which stands in contrast to the rhetoric of youth and vigour of the Revolution itself.[2]

Philosophers of history have become only too aware of this legacy. How the writing of history will always construct itself as a metaphoric discourse about another history, or other histories, has been central to the work of Haydn White, who has extensively analysed the different modes and tropes that nineteenth-century historians deployed in their reconstruction of the past.[3] In the late 1960s – in 1968, to be precise, during the Paris street battles – I myself was reading the histories of the French Revolution of Thomas Carlyle and Jules Michelet in the green-shaded reading room of the Bibliothèque Nationale in Paris. As my fellow students in the streets were shouting 'l'imagination au pouvoir', I was wondering how much the all-devouring firestorms that Carlyle saw raging through the pages of history had to do with the all-too-literal fire raging through the pages of his first manuscript when the maid used them on one cold November morning to rekindle the kitchen stove! Or in Michelet's case, it seemed obvious that his constant invocation of 'le peuple' as the element in which the historian, no less than the Revolution itself, had to immerse itself in order to retain its momentum must have had something to do with his own predilection for mud baths in the South of France! But then again, what would Carlyle not have given if his own bowels had behaved with the same explosive force that he attributes to the Girondins of 1790?[4]

I adduce these reminders of the meaning-making power of a double level of reference at this stage in the hope of highlighting in Ernst Lubitsch's *Madame Dubarry* (1919) the inevitable charge of travesty that his account of the French Revolution immediately raises. Those who feel outraged are in good company: Lotte Eisner, in *The Haunted Screen* claimed that 'for Lubitsch, one-time shop-assistant, history was never to be more than a pretext for telling love stories in sumptuous period costume: silk, velvet and trimmings delighted his eye.'[5] And

Siegfried Kracauer, in *From Caligari to Hitler* lectured Lubitsch no less severely:

> the story's contempt for historic facts is matched only by its disregard for their meaning. [...] Instead of tracing all revolutionary events back to their economic causes and ideals, it persistently portrays them as the outcome of psychological conflicts. *Passion* (the American release title) does not exploit the passions inherent in the Revolution, but reduces the Revolution to a derivative of private passions.[6]

Considering that the film was shot in 1918/19, while running battles between Spartacists and the police were fought in the Berlin streets, and tens of thousands died of hunger during the first winter after Germany's defeat, it did take some chutzpah to portray the Revolution as an act of revenge by a jilted lover. To test how adequately Lubitsch portrayed the Revolution, Eisner and Kracauer read *Madame Dubarry* as if he were a historian of the 'historical imagination'. They treat the cinema as if it were itself a metaphorical discourse meant to render, reproduce and record another discourse, whose truth has already been constituted elsewhere. Yet, if one concedes that the cinema is not in the first instance a metaphorical discourse of the real but a particular kind of imaginary, whose own reality is neither to be conflated with its objects (the films), nor its referents (the stories it narrates about the real world), then *Madame Dubarry* may be making a significant contribution to the cinema's historical imaginary. This reveals an altogether different set of determinants.

There were first of all a number of economic reasons why the newly founded UFA was keen to make a historical epic with international appeal: since D.W. Griffith's film *Intolerance* had revived the fashion for opulent spectaculars in the Italian (pre-war) style, film companies in France, Austria and Germany tried to outdo one another by making films on epic subjects, with large sets and impressive casts. Although defeated in the war, Germany had the economic edge over France and Italy. Thanks to the rapid devaluation of its currency, it could produce these films at a fraction of the pre-war cost, even collecting tax relief by hiring demobbed soldiers and men and women from the vast army of the unemployed as extras for the crowd scenes. Paradoxically, therefore, it was the (potentially revolutionary) misery of the populace that provided a material basis for UFA and Lubitsch entering the world market with this type of film. *Madame Dubarry* proved to be an enormous success with the German public, and subsequently elsewhere, especially in the United States, where it helped to break the anti-German trade boycott.[7] As one of the very few German films ever to make a profit in the American market, it could be thought of as a film that by mocking history, actually made history – at least film history – for it also changed the lives of its four principals. Emil Jannings and Pola Negri (the stars), Hans Kräly (the scriptwriter) and Ernst Lubitsch himself, within two years of the opening of *Passion* at the Capitol Theatre in New York, found themselves on their way to Hollywood.[8]

How can the film's success be explained? Perhaps its secret lay in the fact of it being a travesty – understood as a particular double frame of reference that brought the events depicted to cinema audiences in both new and familiar ways. By doing so, it also redefined how cinema can relate to social reality other than by respecting historical facts. This double frame of reference in *Madame Dubarry* is, of course, not as with Michelet or Carlyle, to be found in the biography of Lubitsch or his collaborators. Rather, what was new and yet familiar were the many plot features and character situations that Lubitsch's historical epic shared with Parisian and Viennese operettas, a critically despised – but in the 1920s – still popular musical stage entertainment. Barry Salt was, to my knowledge, the first film historian to have dug up the relevant sources, not just for *Madame Dubarry*, but also for *Das Fidele Gefängnis* (*Die Fledermaus*, by Johann Strauss), *Die Austernprinzessin* (*Die Dollarprinzessin*, by Leo Fall), *Die Puppe* (*La Poupée*, by Edmond Audran) and *Die Bergkatze* (*Les Brigants*, by Jacques Offenbach).[9]

That Kracauer did not comment on this connection seems a pity, since his 1936 study *Jacques Offenbach and the Paris of his Age* is one of the most perspicacious social histories of the genre, thoroughly analysing the critical function – what he called the 'socio-biographical' element,[10] – inherent in the apparently irresponsible concoctions of mistaken identities, inverted class relations and sexual innuendos. Stressing the satirical and parodistic elements, he argued that the moment of truth of operetta as a form were precisely its light-footed improbabilities – so pointedly extreme that they exposed bourgeois rationality and class- and status-consciousness as no more than self-deceiving rationalisations: '[bourgeois Paris under Napoleon III] was living as if in a dream. Had they been awake, they would have recognised [in Offenbach's operettas] the implausible reality of their existence.'[11] In passing, Kracauer noted Offenbach's other unexpected frame of reference which gave his work an extra social 'truth-factor': the streets surrounding the theatres where operettas were staged, or more precisely, the Grand Boulevards, which not least thanks to Baron Hausmann's urbanist revolution had become a decisively modern social space, generating a new type of culture that not only embraced the so-called boulevard theatres, but also the grand-scale department stores, to which in the early years of the twentieth century would be added such movie palaces as the Gaumont and the Hippodrome.

Although many of Lubitsch's films thus borrow operetta subjects, the theatrical operetta as an institution had, after the war, entered into a state of terminal decline, in direct proportion to the cinema fulfilling its social function and taking over its forms. What arose on the back of this decline was therefore a popular cinema culture, or rather, a multi-media, sound-and-vision entertainment culture, in which the metropolis itself started to transform itself into an operetta-like ensemble, medial and mediated.[12] For instance, just as in operetta it is the women who have a lot to say and often the final word, so in the midst of this neon-lit world, the 'new woman' emerged as one of the key historical agents, inheriting the flair of Baudelaire's dandy roaming the streets of Paris, by becoming the *flaneuse*: going shopping, going out – which implied seeing and being seen, on the boulevards of Berlin no less than on the Grand Boulevards of Paris. She became prototypical for the so-called *Angestelltenkultur*: again, a phenomenon of Weimar modernity that Kracauer was the first to acutely analyse in its symptomatic importance, also for the cinema.[13] If this socio-economic context of cultural modernity can illuminate the success of Madame Dubarry, it also points to other features of popular cinema that remain puzzling if one does not add the diversity, technical proficiency and economic importance of popular music culture, which superseding operettas and variety theatre, manifested itself increasingly during the 1920s in Berlin's dance-bands, its amusement palaces, its hotel-lobby five o'clock teas, the spread of gramophones and the rise of radio broadcasts.[14]

Cinema and the historical imaginary: the metaphor of vision

To argue that 'operetta' in this wider sense is the intermediary medium and always already implicit, reference point of mainstream cinema in the Weimar Republic takes me further into the concept of the historical imaginary, in so far as it is relevant to how one might picture the relation of the cinema quite generally to social upheavals, including those associated with the French Revolution. It will bring me back to Ernst Lubitsch, precisely because *Madame Dubarry* takes up one facet of this relationship quite purposely, effecting the transfer of a historical experience – the inflation period after a lost war and a failed revolution – from one popular medium to another. A preliminary question once more concerns the metaphors and registers of discourse across which Weimar critics discuss modernity, social change and the emergent power of the mass-medium cinema in the early years of the Republic. Much of what contemporary commentators qualify in the films not only of Lubitsch as sentimental melodrama and fake operetta magic ('fauler Operettenzauber'), is dismissed on the grounds that it panders to mere surface appearance, betraying the expectation that the cinema should have an educational function and contribute to the enlightenment of the masses, in the form of unmasking social, i.e. capitalist evils. Yet this raises a paradox which could be summed up in the reflection that both the French Revolution and the cinema are the unruly and probably bastard children of *le siècle des lumières*: in one case, meaning the philosophers of the Enlightenment, in the other the Brothers Lumière of Lyon. What, beyond the feeble pun, is the connection?

It is striking how persistently the ideas of the French Revolution have been couched in terms of the metaphors of Light, of Sight and of Vision, and nowhere more so than in its civic ideals, its ideas of democracy, but also in its truth-claims. A reminder of just how strong this metaphoric link was can be found in Michel Foucault's *The Birth of the Clinic*:

> The ideological theme that guides all structural reforms from 1789 to Thermidor Year II is that of [the sovereign liberty of truth:] the majestic violence of light, which is in itself supreme, and brings to an end the bounded, dark kingdom of privileged knowledge and establishes the unimpeded empire of the gaze.
>
> (Foucault 1975: 39)

'The unimpeded empire of the gaze' – a major issue of the Revolution, according to Foucault – is the ideal of the all-seeing eye, the assertion of the primacy of vision in the expectation of dispelling the dark ages of feudal domination, secrecy. Hence the potent symbolism of the Bastille, whose storming was to have ushered in a society finally transparent to itself.[15] The fate of this double revolutionary heritage surrounding the metaphors of sight, spectacle and vision, and the epistemological discourses for which these metaphors are constitutive, is the historical link that joins the French Revolution and the cinema. As the quotation from Foucault hints at, there is to this legacy of the Revolution's investment in the discourse of sight another side, the verso of democracy: what we might call revolutionary despotism, which since the days of The Terror in 1792 has also claimed for itself the rage for transparency, for truth to be manifest to the eye (and as Foucault would add, to the ear:) the all-seeing eye of surveillance, the ubiquity of spying, of denunciations, of confessions, i.e. truth extracted from the individual, paid for with the price of life itself and practised by every autocratic regime since. George Orwell, with his 'Big Brother is watching you' has given a popular, but possibly inadequate metaphor for the political history of this violent gaze.

Yet it would be wrong to locate the origins of this double heritage of the gaze solely in the French Revolution. For instance, one aspect of violent revolutionary spectacle – the ritual of public execution – which is also related to vision and to justice being seen to be done, goes back to feudalism and the Church. Foucault opens his *Discipline and Punish* with a particularly spectacular account of regal punishment under the Ancien Regime: the putting to death of the purported regicide Damien in 1757, intending to draw a clear distinction between royal power writing itself onto the victim's body, and the people's justice embodied in the guillotine. One might say that the all-powerful gaze of the King is structurally opposed to the self-seeing, self-scrutinising, self-policing and self-purging gaze of the Revolution. It is Jean-Jacques Rousseau, for whom the eye is such a powerful organ that it makes the world not just visible, but transparent. His writings are the single most telling source for the ambivalence of the metaphor of the eye and sight, as Jean Starobinski has shown, for there the eye functions as a cognitive sense not in the way it does for Descartes, as that which enables knowledge by sustaining distance and separation between the subject and the object, but because the relation between sight and its object is reversible, allowing for a revelatory fusion, in which transparency is equated with knowledge, but a knowledge which is above all self-knowledge.[16] Yet Rousseau's existential metaphor of the eye is also dialectical, for its fervent exhibitionism is matched by an equally intense paranoia about being seen, being observed by an invisible ubiquitous and also punishing eye (not unlike that which accompanied the poet William Wordsworth as he rowed across Lake Windermere in *The Prelude*).

Rousseau's ideas, a few decades later, reappear in Hegel's *Phenomenology of Mind and Philosophy of History*, in which world history is recast in the image of the French Revolution. Hegel's subject–object division, the motor force of his system, whose dialectic can only be reconciled in the Absolute, has translated the revolutionary ideals of self-transparency into the philosophical concept of self-realisation, itself re-inscribed into history as the (objective and objectifying) movement of the world spirit. But the metaphor of vision has also had a profound impact on the everyday language of our Western, representational democracies. We demand, for instance, that justice not only be done, but be *seen* to be done; we expect 'open government' from our leaders, and we speak of a 'cover-up' when we suspect the democratic process is being perverted. If for the historical imagination the issue of the Revolution is on the one hand tied up with the question of metaphor, and on the other with the relation between the eye, vision and the subject, which is to say with distance and proximity and the geometry of representation, then the historical imaginary is concerned with the re-articulation of these issues across another reality, that of the (moving) image, and across a medium which presumes to the eye's transparency and all-seeingness, the cinema, but which is at once fundamentally technical and profoundly social. For with the advent of the cinema, the all-seeing eye is no longer a metaphor, but has become a practical reality, an apparatus, a complex ensemble of technologies and habits which installs the eye as supreme. Thomas Edison, for instance, waxed lyrical about the revolution his invention was to bring to mankind, though already in 1895 his ambition went towards what he called his 'kinetophonograph', a machine combining vision with voice, in the firm belief, as Noel Burch quotes him, that 'a total reproduction of life, presenting the human likeness and voice, the bodily envelope and its soul' constituted the true goal of human emancipation.[17]

The realisation that the cinema is not a *metaphor* of transparency, but its (deceptive) materialisation might explain why so much of film theory since André Bazin has been devoted to the question whether the cinema is a *means* of transparency – recording and reproducing the Rousseauist dream of self-transparent, self-evident truth – or whether it is an *apparatus* producing the *illusion* of transparency. Intriguingly enough, therefore, contemporary film theory is profoundly marked by the 'revolutionary' discourse of sight and the problem of its metaphoric status.[18] For instance, if one follows Jean-Louis Baudry, it introduced into the history of Western subjectivity a *dispositif*, a mental machine whose function it is, or rather whose efficacy lies in its ability not only to emulate the human psyche but to reverse the process whereby the biological human being enters into the order of the Symbolic, and becomes a subject, at the cost of radical and irreversible self-alienation.[19] Yet with this formulation, Baudry also acknowledges that the cinema is a philosophical machine, an infernal parody of Hegel's Absolute, so to speak, because in its complex negotiations of self and other, of perception, recognition and identification, this apparatus provides, in the strangely triangulated geometry of filmic representation (made up of a screen, a cone of light, whose source is hidden from view, and a seated spectator), an 'uncanny' reconciliation between subject and object. With this the cinema fulfils, both historically and ontologically, mankind's dream of self-realisation as a self-coherent, autonomous subject, but fatally, by depriving this self-realisation of its materiality, and also its 'history', if by history one understands the individual's unique existence as tied 'indexically' to place and linear temporality, as a succession of 'presences' made up of 'here and now'.

It is a thought also found in the critics of the Frankfurt School. For Adorno, for instance, film was the instrument of a not unpleasurable reconciliation of the spectator to his own reification, by the uncanny, comic or emotionally moving anthropomorphisms that the camera could lend to things. By humanising the world, giving it beauty and a 'soul', it endowed inanimate objects and mere shadows with feelings and life, the cinema seemed to have filled the gap between reality and its penetration by man's transforming labour: it anticipated the Revolution as the reconciliation of subject and object. Yet by taking it out of temporality, the cinema betrayed the hoped-for self-presence and self-awareness that made the Revolution necessary in the first place, voiding it of its promissory redemption. Georg Lukacs put it even more sharply, as early as 1913:

> The cinema is a life without measure or order, without being or value, a life without soul, mere surface ... the individual moments, whose temporal sequence brings about the filmed scenes, are only joined with each other insofar as they follow each other without transition and mediation. There is no causality which could link them, or more precisely, its causality is free from and unimpeded by any notion of content. 'Everything is possible': this is the credo of the cinema, and because its technique expresses at every moment the absolute (even if only empirical) reality of this moment, 'virtuality' no longer functions as a category opposed to 'reality': both categories become equivalent, identical. Everything is true and real, everything is equally true and real; this is what a sequence of images in the cinema teaches us.
>
> (Lukacs 1978 [1913]: 112–18)

Here Lukacs sketches a theory and critique of 'mediality', which already anticipates many of the positions of postmodernism, such as formulated by Baudrillard or Lyotard and encapsulated in the 'everything goes'. He also voices post-modernism's counter-positions, as in his warning against the hubris of instrumental reason in its technology-driven pragmatism ('everything is possible'), another legacy of the Enlightenment, though he does so from a philosophical perspective – that of a revolutionary transcendentalism and Marxist messianism

– to whose loss post-modernism thinks it may be the answer. In Lukacs' (or Hegel's) heroic view of human destiny the cinema appears like a pseudo-metaphysical short-cut, which signalled not only the end of bourgeois notions of the individual, as conceived by the French Revolution, but also of any critique in the name of the non-alienated self. For the obverse of the Hegelian vision, as Baudry also saw, was a world so penetrated by subjectivity that alienation becomes itself 'second nature', substituting without loss or regret for both the natural world and for human nature. This would be the world of consumption and specular seduction, the world of the audio-visual media, and the subject's narcissistic staging of itself. The reign of the (moving) image, in this view, has shifted the 'place' of the subject within the spatio-temporal universe, decentring it, and making both space and time a mere function of the motion picture, across which the subject is forever condemned to mirror and yet misrecognise him/herself. 'Appearance becomes Being': in it, the subject needs to learn to feel at home and at ease, across it the subject encounters the Other, even as it makes itself invisible to the Other.

Early German cinema and the gendered spectator

Thus, whether positivistically seen as the fulfilment of an 'age-old dream' (of Edison's self-transparency as technologically assisted self-presence) or more metaphysically as the betrayal of human life to 'true lies' (of primary narcissism and the imaginary of Jacques Lacan's mirror phase), the cinema emerges from these philosophical speculations as after all a legitimate, if rather problematic heir of the Revolution. While appearing – at first glance – to be the triumph of that all-seeing eye, it may, however, also come to be regarded as having put an end to the revolutionary conception of vision as the revelation of truth. For as the quotation from Foucault also hints: there is that other side to the Revolution and the two *siècles des lumières*: the tyrannical eye doubling the benevolent one. On the one hand, there is the spectre of the society of the spectacle (whose history starts with the Revolution and ends with Jean Baudrillard's 'simulacrum') and on the other, the 'panoptic' power which starts with the absent, all-knowing sadistic eye of Foucault's *Discipline and Punish* via Rousseau to Jeremy Bentham, and which ends with the omnipresent, but stupid eye of supermarket security cameras and spy satellites with their 'transparency without transcendence': the imposition of a new kind of discipline administered through the eye and its prosthetic extensions. Both 'archaeologies' point to the institution of vision in the sphere of public life as the very opposite of the political ideal that imagines transparency guaranteeing liberty and truth, which tempts one to regard the empire of the gaze as totalitarian, as that peculiarly modern form of power, which without an apparent apparatus of repression is none the less profoundly coercive.[20]

Yet taken by itself, this would leave out another history or archaeology – that of the cinema as a social practice, which finally points in a different direction, at least if my argument about Lubitsch and *Madame Dubarry* can be extended further. So far I have concentrated on a philosophical reading of a phenomenon, which needs also to be read historically and sociologically: that the advent of cinema during the first two decades of this century has brought about a transformation in the cultural significance of perception.[21] This complex process, admittedly, is not only due to the cinema. It may in fact be read the other way round, in so far as the cinema (or at any rate, its rapid spread and universal popularity) was, instead of cause, part of the symptomatic consequences of such a change in perception, which in Walter Benjamin, for instance, is tied to such diverse signs of modernity as assembly-line production methods and taylorisation, the rise of the metropolis, sensory overstimulation and the 'shock' experiences to which the individual is exposed in a mass society. In so far as the transformation also affected the relation of public sphere and private space, the cinema, as indicated above, also became implicated in the social transformation of gender, helping to redefine the roles of women and specify the meaning of their new visibility in this public sphere.[22] The history of the cinema is thus 'gendered', as it were, in that its emergence both reinforced but also upset traditional definitions of sexual difference along two axes: that of word/music and image (spoken–heard/seen) and that of the active and passive gaze (seeing/seen). Sociologically, this 'crisis' goes back to the very beginnings of the cinema, for viewed as a new public space, it opened up to women an area of presence, indeed of activity hitherto inaccessible to them, except at the cost of social status and 'respectability'. Women as cinema spectators had the right to a look that previously was denied to them, and films, knowing that they catered for women spectators, seemed ready to accommodate this different look. At the same time, public debates like the so-called reform movement, focused precisely on the cinema as a threat to morality. The 'reformers' talked about public health and safety, about fire regulations and work discipline, about moral dissolution and the danger: to the young, the impressionable and the unsuspecting. Yet what outraged them seemed to be the fact that the cinema allowed children and women an inquisitive, investigative, searching – in short, an active – look, which was immediately labelled immoral and dissolute. Male writers, from the bourgeois left or bohemian avant-garde circles were less public-minded. They revelled in the cinema as subversive, liberating and intoxicating (freely admitting to its archaic, erotic, narcotic, uninhibiting effects): quite candidly a writer like Jakob von Hoddis described going to the pictures as a kind of orgy, from which he emerged into daylight 'stirred and confused, tired and horny',[23] and Peter Altenberg confessed that he had not only taken a woman to the cinema who was probably too young for him, but that it gave him great satisfaction to yield without shame or embarrassment to the tears which a sentimental melodrama moved him to.[24]

The conservative bourgeoisie and the nationalist right tried to legislate against the cinema with a vehemence and intensity unparalleled since. When one comes across these often subtle, eloquent and even passionate testimonies today, one can read in them an interesting cultural phenomenon: they register by the very intensity of their concern the shock of this new gaze. The left polemicised just as much as the right:

> If one bears in mind that nowadays a film is seen by some million-and-a-half spectators […] of which at least half are from the world of women, then the magnitude of the danger the cinema represents cannot be overestimated. Furthermore, even a cursory glance into any of these cinemas will confirm that most of the girls and women present belong to the working class, our very own area of agitation. It is proven that the moving image with its vivid representations leaves an especially strong impression, even in men. Given their greater sensory receptivity and the predominance of the emotional life in women, the cinematic spectacle necessarily affects them even more strongly. […] Many look irresistibly drawn to what they see, even stirred to the innermost core of their souls.
>
> (Max Grempe, 'Against female idiocy in the cinema', quoted in Schweinitz 1992: 121)

On the other hand, there was the sophisticated, decadent culture of *Jugendstil*, of art nouveau, with its elaborate ornamentation, its vegetal traceries on cast-iron, bronze or domestic silver, its all-too knowing allusions and mythological references disguising promiscuous suggestions of sensuousness: for this world the cinema was also outrageous. First, for being so casual, so unceremonious and 'undressed', so paratactic and inconsequential in what it showed:

> Scenes from the Ganges were followed by shots of the pyramids, a domestic idyll of two young lovers seemed oddly foreboding when up came the tale of a maid abducting her mistress' child, and while we are still admiring the potato harvest, the Emperor's favourite regiment is parading outside Potsdam.[25]
>
> (Hans Heinz Ewers, 'Snake hunting on Java', quoted in L. Greve, M. Pehle and H. Westhoff (eds) *Hätte ich das Kino!* (Munich: Kösel, 1976): 18)

What was perhaps even more startling was that the cinema showed these sights, objects, and emotions with such insouciance and such impudence. Suddenly, nothing was safe and nothing was sacred before this inquisitive, curious, but also sentimental, prurient eye that was the camera. All the work of metaphor, of hint and allusion, of pleasing by teasing seemed to have become superfluous in the face of a 'democratic' eye which raided the world for the strange and the marvellous, for moving and bizarre sights. Viewed by the camera, everything seemed to become literally *ob*-scene, not only in the sense that things usually hidden became visible, but that looking itself became invested with a different kind of intensity which took away the cultural thresholds of the permitted look, letting it float between scientific, humouristic or pornographic coding.[26] Not yet inscribed in a stable social space, and no longer moralising, this new 'empire of the gaze' could develop revolutionary sedition that made the head spin of many a bourgeois intellectual. The novelist Alfred Döblin, for instance, seemed positively hypnotised in the cinemas of working-class Berlin: 'Pairs of lovers', he writes, are

> squeezed in the corner, but carried away by what they see, their unchaste fingers stop pawing each others' bodies. Consumptive children breathe flat gasps of air, and shiver quietly through every bout of fever. The men, exuding unpleasant smells, stare until their eyes are ready to pop out of their sockets. The women, in stale-smelling clothes; the painted street whores are bent forward on the edge of their seats, oblivious to the fact that their headscarves have loosened and are sliding down their necks.
>
> (Döblin 1908/1978: 37–8)

This subversiveness, some critics have rightly seen, affected most profoundly the commerce between the sexes, encased as these were, for the middle class, in rules of polite conduct and discourse. Before the camera, members of both sexes betray feelings, give away intentions, lend meaningful inflections to the most everyday gestures. But as important as this charging of the surface of things with significance and Eros, is the fact that early cinema admits for its female spectators the right to look on equal terms with men, and thus to appropriate the world in a mode not readily sanctioned socially.

One indication of how the new adventure of the probing eye translated itself into fictional stories and even genres can be found in the many Scandinavian but also French films from the 1910–19 era, featuring as their chief protagonists women – not as suffering wives, anxious mothers or lovers, but as detectives, master-criminals and adept helpers in the art of disguise or the hunting down of clues. Here it is noticeable that male characters when using disguise do so in order to change their class-affiliation and thus dramatise a desire for social mobility. Female disguise, on the contrary, is often the pretext for women to be present in places or to witness situations from which their sex is normally excluded, by virtue of a moral code or a social rule: for instance, when they enter a night club or a gambling casino. In these cases, the loss of social status is not valorised as such; what is at issue is the fact that the new role carries with it a different access to their own sexuality, even if this is mediated by male desire. A veritable compendium of this rich tradition in early cinema are, for instance, the first films of Fritz Lang, such as *Die Spinnen* (1919), or *Kämpfende Herzen* (*Four Men and A Woman*), (1920).[27]

The reverberations of this intense public debate, and its intuitively felt threat to male visual control can be followed throughout the war and into the early Weimar cinema: in its narratives (the inability of the males to inscribe themselves into the patriarchal order), the visual logic (the importance of the look, of off-screen space, the uncanny), and finally, the dimension of 'self-reflexivity', which makes so many of the films parables of cinematic spectatorship and allegorical figurations of film making itself. As a consequence, in the 'Expressionist' films of the early Weimar period, power relations and conflicts with authority figures less often lead to physical contact or direct interaction than they articulate themselves via the look, i.e. who is controlling the field of vision, who is looking at whom without being seen, who can immobilise whom by looking at whom. The most extreme example of this structure is obviously *Dr Mabuse* (1921), but it is equally in evidence in films like *Variety* (1925), or *The Last Laugh* (1924), the latter entirely structured around the (pleasurably perverse?) anxieties of being seen. Power relations are equated with a voyeuristic structure, via a hierarchy of gazes and views. But the gaze and power also encompass another pole, the pleasure of constituting oneself as the object of someone's look. As examined in a previous chapter, say that what characterises this 'Expressionist' cinema, pervaded by anxious males, is that power is equated with vision, and vision with knowledge, and knowledge with control, and control with anxiety in a power/anxiety/knowledge nexus almost entirely mapped on the axis seeing/being seen. The very dialectic of the on-screen and off-screen space in the German cinema lies at the heart of the problematic status of the image in these films, where one always has the impression that the image is doubly dematerialised: hyperreal because framed, enclosed, clearly marked as an image, and unreal because insufficiently articulated within a time space continuum of the cause- and-effect chain. The drama of vision and sight is at the core of the uncomfortable, anxious subject position that makes German silent films often difficult to follow in the logic of the actions not least because they speak a visual–narrational language that classical Hollywood narrative completely marginalised.[28] It is this notion of language, however, that is itself at issue, because it would seem that Hollywood already by the late 'teens had encoded its own style so rigorously and in such a rule-bound fashion, precisely in order to bring these floating moments, which modernity and the moving image introduced into culture under control, regardless of whether they related to morality or gender. The nexus power/anxiety/knowledge would therefore be one particular mode by which the Weimar cinema pays tribute to the pre-linguistic force of the moving image, though at the price of shifting the balance of the right to the look – not to men, but to the anxiety of men.[29]

Lubitsch and German cinema

My argument would be that the cinema of Ernst Lubitsch belongs to both traditions. Or rather, because it takes as its vantage point the 'operetta' world and derives from it a new visibility of gender and class, it can negotiate both the 'old' and the 'new' regime of the gaze. Not only is his a 'popular', mainstream cinema: it also provides a continuous, often caustic commentary on Weimar cinema's own neurotic relationship to vision and visuality. For instance, rather than about the anxieties of being seen, and the perverse power that derives from it, Lubitsch's films are about the pleasures of a good performance, and thus about that other side of exhibitionism. Furthermore, Lubitsch was a hugely popular director, appealing to every age, gender and social class, which already by the end of the 1910s had earned him the sobriquet of 'Berlin's American director'. He had joined the Max Reinhardt theatre in 1911 as an actor, and two years later had his first starring film part in a farce, *Meyer auf der Alm*. It established him as a household name and became the first in a series of Meyer films. A Jewish comedy character causing disaster wherever he goes, Meyer's ruthless if ragged charm always ends up winning him the boss's daughter. Lubitsch's first assignments as a director (*Der Stolz der Firma* (*The Pride of the Firm*) and *Schuhpalast Pinkus* (*Shoe-Palace Pinkus*) threatened to confine him to this milieu and its fantasies of social rise, but their success brought an association with Paul Davidson, a producer with international ambitions and the capital to build Germany's first purpose-built film studio: the Union Atelier in Berlin-Tempelhof. There, while continuing to make comedy shorts and parodies for the domestic market, Lubitsch began to embark on a series of costume dramas (*Die Augen der Mumie Ma* (*The Eyes of the Mummy Ma*), *Das Weib des Pharaoh, Sumurum* (*The Wife of the Pharaoh, Sumurum*)), historical films (besides *Madame Dubarry* the best known was *Anna Boleyn*) and full-length comedies (*The Oyster Princess*, *The Mountain Cat*, *The Doll*) which bought him a ticket to Hollywood. Particularly unusual were his staging of large-scale spectacles (such as the French Revolution), the *mise-en-scène* of crowds (e.g. the court of Henry VIII in *Anna Boleyn*), and the dramatic use of monumental architecture (as in his Egyptian and Oriental films, especially *Das Weib des Pharaoh*). The famed 'Lubitsch touch' of his American career was a reticent use of visual information, giving the spectator the pleasure of guessing the rest. The German films, too, worked with innuendo and inference, but they also exploited the chain reaction of a situation being taken *ad absurdum*.

One of the best examples of the 'German' Lubitsch touch is *The Oyster Princess* (1919), a satire on the Weimar Republic's newly discovered vogue for America, and on fantasies of affluence such as they could only have been nourished by years of extreme austerity suddenly confronted with raging inflation. Ossie, the temperamental daughter of Mr Quaker, America's Oyster King, wants 'at least a prince' for a husband, after reading in the papers of the Shoe-Polish King's daughter's wedding to a duke. A marriage broker locates Prince Nucki, handsome, penniless and wedlock-shy. He sends his servant to sound out the situation who, much taken by the splendour of the Quaker residence, announces himself as the prince. Impatient, Ossie takes him for a walk and is married to him on the spot, by the first priest who happens to be to hand. In her capacity as member of a teetotal club for daughters of American millionaires, Ossie has to deal with a particularly hard case: it is the real Nucki rescued from a drunken stupor on a park bench. The two fall in love, and Ossie cheats her husband – with her husband.

The film is a free adaptation of Leo Fall's operetta of 1907, *The Dollar Princess*, satirising the snobbery of American money about European titles and pedigree. Lubitsch and his scriptwriter Hans Kräly took this very premise as their target, for Nucki is ultimately more the charming windbag and *schlemihl* Meyer than an Austrian aristocrat fallen on hard times. Comic technique becomes social critique, when the Oyster King, in order to smoke a cigar after coffee, needs four servants: to take his cup, blow his nose, light the match and hold the ashtray. Henry Ford's taylorised assembly line is here applied to the Weimar Republic and its unemployed (film extras). Behind each guest at the wedding banquet, there stands for each course a waiter, five lines deep. The comedy derives from the image recalling but the mind repressing the waves of soldiers sacrificed in trench warfare: their tragic waste is suddenly made obvious in the opulence of a preposterous dinner. Another scene has the Oyster King relaxing over his morning paper: Ossie, enraged by his impassiveness, tears it away and shreds it. Impassively, her father reaches for another paper from his dressing gown … and another. Only first-hand knowledge of the mad logic of economic inflation could invest these gags of repetition and acceleration with such absurd probability as to give them the stamp of hilarious truth. What makes *The Oyster Princess* a comedy that endures – beyond the historical references, or its value as a document of the first audiences' starvation fantasies and anxieties – is the intelligence of its construction as an intricate comedy music-box. Mistaken identities and surprise twists are fitted together with such precision that the happy end is both inevitable, and when it comes, a satisfyingly elegant solution to the formal and moral problems the plot sets itself initially.

German Lubitsch thus stands at the dividing line between a cinema that emerged from variety theatre and operetta, and a cinema with bourgeois pretensions to literary and artistic status. His early films are performer-oriented, and they rely on the central character to establish a direct rapport with the audience. The actresses he uses, first Ossi Oswalda and then Pola Negri, have retained this ability, so absent from other Weimar films, to acknowledge and return the look, while the force of his satire derives from a certain blunt materialism which undercut pathos and lofty sentiments, operating as a kind of relativism, where sex and money subtend whatever motivations the characters appear to profess. In this fashion, Lubitsch, for instance, 'deconstructs' operas such as *Der Rosenkavalier* (1918) and *Carmen* (1918), Shakespeare's *Romeo and Juliet* (*Romeo und Julia im Schnee*) (1920) or *The Taming of the Shrew* (*Kohlhiesels Töchter*) (1920). For what is more susceptible to devaluation and revaluation, to semiotic trade and barter, but also to passion and deception than sex and money: especially in a period of raging inflation and precariously re-adjusting sexual mores after a world war, such as during the early years of the Weimar Republic?

This sort of blunt thinking is often associated with Brecht, and in a sense, Lubitsch anticipates the author of *The Threepenny Opera*, especially in the choice of a counter-point ('*Gegen-Entwurf*') from which to tell a fable and construct a vantage point 'outside'. Like Brecht a decade later, Lubitsch took classic drama subjects, in order to show that tragic inevitability or a tragic ending was often a matter of the author having repressed materialist motivations for the sake of aesthetic coherence or ideology. Typical of Lubitsch's materialism which is also a form of rough-justice egalitarianism, for instance, is the scene from *Romeo and Juliet in the Snow*, when the judge in order to decide the rights and wrongs of the rivalling families' case, puts the two sausages given to him as bribes on the scales of Justice to see which is heavier and finally bites into them to taste which is better – before pronouncing that both parties are at fault, and sentencing them to costs.[30] Again, these classics are 'deconstructed' in much the same way that Brecht, forty years later, in his *Practice Scenes for Actors* deconstructed *Hamlet*, *Macbeth*, *Romeo and Juliet*, or plays by Schiller, simply by inserting a scene which completely reversed the motivation of the characters, bringing out their self-interest or pointing to consequences that the original had strategically suppressed. Lubitsch practised his own alientation effects – precisely those of operetta – either by transposing the setting (from Verona to Bavaria), or by illegitimately mixing the genres (playing tragedy as farce), and thus involving his audience by undercutting their expectations while at the same time relying on their recognition.

But Lubitsch was not only a social satirist of turn-of-the-century Jewish behaviour and the debunker of theatrical and opera classics. His genius extended to becoming a radical parodist of the German *Autorenkino* or 'Expressionist' cinema (radical, in that he went to the root of the specular system that sustained it). If the Meyer films are a parodistic treatment of the theme of social rise which overtly and covertly occupies such an important place in the films about students, apprentices and clerks, especially as portrayed by Paul Wegener,[31] a film like *Die Puppe* parodies not only all the ETA Hoffmann-inspired stories about automatons and doubles, but also the Caligari–Cesare relations of German Gothic. *The Mountain Cat* makes fun of orientalism and Expressionist decor, when the absurdly ornamental scrolls on the walls are used as if they were particularly useless and uncomfortable pieces of furniture. Similarly, the scene in *The Oyster Princess* where the waiting suitor traces out the elaborate pattern on the Oyster King's entrance hall floor as if it were the ground plan for dance steps or a children's skipping game makes fun of a rhetoric of imposture that wants to pass itself off as imposing. In both cases an element of decor whose function it is to connote a 'style' and a class is suddenly foregrounded and materialises as an obstacle or a diversion. The comic effect is comparable to that achieved when one literalises a dead metaphor or acts out a clichéd figure of speech.

Critics have pointed to Lubitsch's background – the East-European Jewish 'rag-trade' in turn-of-the-century Berlin – as the reason for his preferred theme. They argue that 'clothes make the man' is his cynical tune, and that his preoccupation with disguise, appearance and deception are ultimately for their own sake.[32] Yet more to the point is that his films answer hypocrisy with cynicism, disinterested idealism with self-interested egoism. For what his early films show is that within authority structures based on a cult of appearances, indeed based on the systems of repression and displacement characteristic of the German art cinema, material motives such as money and sex, and surface values such as clothes, fashion and design actually allow for a reversal of power relations, for a different alignment of symbolic power. Faith in this reversibility makes Lubitsch see the tragic situations of 'expressionist' cinema such as those depicted in *Shattered* or *The Last Laugh* also as comic ones, giving them the 'operetta' twist. Maybe this is why the French Revolution proved such a promising subject, and the rise of a seamstress from a fashion boutique to the position of the most powerful woman in France seemed to him the more interesting revolution within the Revolution.[33]

Jeanne, the *flaneuse* of the roving eye?

The seamstress Jeanne, Lubitsch's heroine and the future Madame Dubarry, in this respect, inherits not French history, but the history of early (German) cinema already outlined. She is the character who takes on the audacity of a woman detective, the inquisitiveness of a cross-dresser and the boldness of the sexually

Figure 13 'May I take a look?' Emil Jannings (as Louis XIV) and Pola Negri (as Jeanne) in Ernst Lubitsch's *Madame Dubarry* (1919)

Source: BFI films: stills, posters and designs

active heroine. She combines the motifs of social mobility, but in doing so she redefines social power relations and phallic authority. With her character, 'the act of looking' enters a film no longer as the repressed element (in contrast, say, to the look of Jane in *The Cabinet of Dr Caligari*, which is immediately demonised),[34] but as a look that can actually change the relations of time and space. For instance, when in a later scene, as Madame Dubarry, Jeanne goes in search of Armand, she disguises herself as a young man in trousers and cape, looking even more attractive as she enters the tavern than she did in her 'sumptuous period costume of silks and velvets' derided by Lotte Eisner.

A closer analysis of the opening scene in *Madame Dubarry* may give some indication of the elaborate inscription of the look in Lubitsch's films, but also of his divergence from other Weimar directors. What is remarkable about this opening is that it immediately sets up a situation in which surveillance, control and the gaze are evident. Whereas her superior, Madame Labille is introduced with a double gaze, the subservient, smiling one to her customer, and the punishing one directed at Jeanne, Jeanne herself has a darting unfocused look, indicating a subversive, untamed personality in conflict with her superior, who, as so often in German cinema – though usually male – is both authoritarian and servile in turn. A 'false' match-cut between two point-of-view shots emphasises the contrast: there is a cut from Madame Labille smiling at the customer off-screen to Jeanne rolling her eyes and talking to her companions. We cut back to Madame Labille now looking off screen right, but with an angry expression. The three shots thus involve retrospective revision on the part of the audience, which turns out not to have developed a temporal sequence but a way of substituting for the point-of-view shot what one could call a 'point-of-ear-shot', because the connection is made through the laughter which, unheard by the spectator, alerts Madame Labille to Jeanne's unruliness. That is, the spectator has to put a visual cue together with an (unheard) aural cue to make sense of the scene. The sequence thus represents a structural conflict, and it sets the parameters for the rest of the film. Followed immediately by Madame Labille assigning Jeanne to leave with a commission, Jeanne responds by looking at herself in the mirror. After looking and being looked at she, so to speak, confirms her identity through her own mirror image (which is one of the most deceptive ways of fixing one's identity in an image, and already anticipating the look of the – male – other). Jeanne is stopped from doing this and leaves the shop under the disapproving gaze of Madame Labille. She walks in a straight line until she is off frame. The next shot shows her still walking straight on, but now diagonally across the shot, followed by the approving, interested gaze of a male passer-by who stops and then follows her. Intercut into this is a shot of Armand, her expectant lover, opening his window and scanning the street. We cut back to Jeanne, who drops her hatbox so that the passer-by can pick it up and thus she helps him motivate or rationalise his desire to follow her. We cut back to Armand, who has spotted her and waves. Jeanne enters the frame and she embraces Armand by the open window. The suitor is dropped, and the camera cuts to the interior of Armand's appartment, where he hides himself from Jeanne. She enters, but cannot find him and once more drops the hatbox, this time onto a chair. There follows a close-up of her feet, showing Armand's hiding place. After a general shot of Jeanne jumping up in panic, another one of Armand is seen from Jeanne's perspective. The next shot shows the lovers embracing, thus closing what is in a sense a complete mini-narrative, with conflict, development and resolution, very much along the lines of the early 'Meyer' films, such as *Meyer aus Berlin* (*Meyer from Berlin*), *Die Firma Heiratet* (*The Firm Gets Married*), *Schuhpalast Pinkus* and *Der Stolz der Firma*.

What is significant for my argument is that in *Madame Dubarry* each shot is motivated and determined by Jeanne. However, although at the level of the plot she takes the initiative and appears resolute, on the level of the dynamics of seeing and of who is telling this story, she is literally passed from look to look which is – as the film goes on – defined explicitly as being passed on from one man to the next. Unable to resolve the conflict of looking and being looked at, she is 'condemned' to manipulating other people into looking at her. Occasionally she becomes the look that others are already looking at, as in the scene at the Spanish Ambassador's house, where Count Dubarry sees her looking lasciviously at Don Diego, which initiates Dubarry's desire for her. Meanwhile standing outside, Armand is looking in but, as it were, blindly and ignorantly, the butt of the jilted Dubarry's laughter.

The narrative progresses by repeating this theme. Jeanne, in order to escape the punishing look, changes her situation by becoming the object of someone's desiring look: a passer-by, the Spanish Ambassador, and finally the King, by drawing attention to herself, exhibiting herself and turning herself into a spectacle to be looked at. At the same time, the unfocused look that she shares with Armand, turns more and more into the punishing or commanding look, as in the scene where after her fake wedding she looks out of the window and demands promotion for the first man she sees. Against her ascendant 'male' look is set the subversive, 'political' look that Armand has acquired as a result of astonished, envious, staring, hostile looks the masses conveyed upon him when he became their tribune. *Madame Dubarry* is thus coherent not at the level of the plot or the historical referent, which as all commentators have pointed out takes liberties with the facts of history, but at the level of enunciation and narration, where the film is tightly organised around the initial dilemma of looking and being looked at and the subject positions it entails in the different social situations which furthermore, are entirely defined as being related to those of authority and power. Lubitsch can take liberties with history precisely because his sequence of events is not strictly temporal, but is the permutation a given power-play, redefined by the film in terms of control of space and control of vision. Temporality is simply the by-product of a *mise-en-scène* organised around the articulation of spaces that are themselves constructed as 'views': images and compositions motivated by someone's gaze at someone else. This is especially noticeable when Jeanne looks out of the window into the park, towards the rabble angrily gathering outside the locked gates, or when she anxiously looks at Armand, as he enters the royal chambers, unsuspecting that he is about to meet his faithless former mistress.

The film is about the power of the look, both active and passive, or rather, the look as power and power as looking. One might even venture that what was scandalous about the film in the view of critics whose aesthetic sensitivities were based on narrative logic or verisimilitude, is that Lubitsch dares to make the opposition of looking and being looked at (which is the basic cinematic relation between spectator and screen) into the master difference that anchors other forms of difference. Power, politics, history, class and revolution are all defined along the divide of the viewing situation, itself triangulated between the looks circulating within the narrative, and the looks of the mass/audience at the screen. This in itself makes *Madame Dubarry* a typical Weimar film of its period. Where it is unique is that within this dialectic of seeing/seen, doubled by the metaphor of the viewing situation itself, its off-screen space does not automatically become the realm of power and authority, of the uncanny and the anxious male (as, for instance, in *Backstairs, Waxworks* or *Warning Shadows*). To put it another way, the figures of authority in Lubitsch do not, as they do in Lang, Murnau and others, seek to control off-screen space through invisible vision, or vision by intermediary, as happens in *The Cabinet of Dr Caligari*, *Dr Mabuse*, *Nosferatu.* Instead of 'who owns the other's look' becoming a struggle for power and dominance until the bitter end and thus a tragic conflict, a melodramatic show-down, or a depiction of the uncanny and the fantastic, Lubitsch's dialectic of point-of-view and off-screen space is essentially comic, by virtue of the reversibility of the inherent positions and the distribution of symbolic power they entail. Emblematic in this respect is the scene in which Jeanne, terrified that her former lover might be executed, substitutes the inkstand and the blotting sand on the King's bureau: a reversal that 'accidentally' commutes a death sentence into liberty. The one who looks can always be deceived by the 'show' put on by the one who is being looked at, which makes control elusive and power through perception inherently unstable. If voyeurism on-screen in Weimar cinema is always the sign of a duped and fallible vision, compared to the look emanating from off-screen, exhibitionism as performance (such as Jeanne's) is a form of control that holds the spectators' gaze both on-screen and off-screen.

Madame Dubarry, based as it is on an operetta, is for much of its action a comedy of disguise, mistaken identities and carnival-like fancy dress, which is why most spectators find the first part more entertaining than the second. In the first part not only is the look the chief instance that generates narrative progression and determines editing, it is a look that is unambiguously – and for the spectator most pleasingly – identified as a look of sexual jealousy and erotic desire. This, however, is very rarely the case in the 'Expressionist' film, where sexual difference is one of the most ambiguous and murkily articulated markers of division in the struggle for power and control – which, of course, can have its own bisexual and androgynous attraction, clearly manifest in the roles played

Figure 14 Types and stereotypes, costumes and cartoons: sketches by Hans Trier for *Madame Dubarry* (1919)

Source: Stiftung Deutsche Kinematek, Berlin

by Conrad Veidt, an actor for whom, not surprisingly, Lubitsch had no obvious use.

In the second half of *Madame Dubarry*, it is as if Lubitsch wants to become more seriously 'Weimar cinema', or rather, the logic of the story of the free-floating, reversible gaze he has to tell necessitates a staging of the breakdown of these sexualised power relations. With the death of the King, in whose person the convergence of the look of power and the look of pleasure are symbolically and literally manifest, the new regime of the gaze no longer holds, and power starts to crumble. The rupture is made explicit in the scene when the Sansculottes send a delegation to the King. As soon as they lay eyes on the King who is playing a game of blind man's bluff, he stumbles, collapses and is carried to his bed, never to appear again other than to die, covered in smallpox, as if each gaze of his subjects had left on his body a black, deadly mark. Lubitsch here works out what happens with the power of the look in a society more concerned with visibility and spectacle as the imposture of power and the irresponsibility of wilful blindness, rather than as a sign of fashion and disguise. As soon as politics is no longer conducted in terms of sexual or financial desire, which the play of voyeurism and exhibitionism can upturn and unmask, and instead, politics as power is directly eroticised as voyeurism and exhibitionism, one finds the emergence of repression, of violence and terror. The tragedy of Armand and Jeanne thus takes place against the background of a general devaluation of the look as an instrument of control, so that their respective promotion to positions of power via the look (she as mistress of the king, he as the people's tribune) have first to be undone before they can be united in love – which coincides with their death. Though in this case ending in melodramatic equivalence, it is possible to see in the action a potentially radical–democratic or at least anarchic–utopian principle, as if Lubitsch is suggesting that in the realm of the gaze and of disguise everyone might finally have an equal chance to participate in the enlightened rule of the lightly exchanged look. That Jeanne is sent to the guillotine is both the apotheosis of the law by which she lived – making a spectacle of herself – and a sign that she had herself ignored the look of another, that of the black slave. He is the one who betrays her to the mob, as if Lubitsch were here inscribing in the margins of his fiction yet another regime of the look, that of a 'third world' – merely exotic in the 1790s, but quite differently coded at the height of colonialism in the 1910s.

Surprise by surmise: *Madame Dubarry* as Lubitsch's first American film

If by 1919–20 Hollywood had established its hegemony on the European market, Lubitsch was the German director who responded to this challenge in the fullest sense, not just by rivalling the Americans on their own ground with sumptuous sets, production-values and epic subjects, but by rethinking the kinds of audiences written into his films. Whereas his early films had relied on shared cultural assumptions (the Mayer films) and a recognition of genres or dramatic situations (the parodies and pastiches), the history and costume dramas increasingly addressed themselves to an international audience where interest in purely national stories or knowledge of local issues could not be presupposed. Instead, each film, as it were, supplies in the opening scenes the set of references that allowed the audience to 'decode' the film.[35] To some extent already tried in *The Oyster Princess*, it is – as illustrated by my analysis of the opening scenes – fully worked out in *Madame Dubarry*, which is thus not so much Lubitsch's first historical drama as his first American film – in its narration and visual conception as much as in its subject and (successful) marketing.

What is 'American' about *Madame Dubarry* is mainly the first hour or so – paradoxically, the part that roughly coincides with the story taken from Leo Fall's operetta. But if the film seems divided into two parts, it is also because in the first part the division of the look and the division of the sexes overlap almost completely: men look, and the woman is being looked at.[36] In the second part, gender and the look are wrenched apart, and this – so my argument would claim – appears to be the real revolution, but also the line where American cinema and Weimar cinema part company. A woman, i.e. Jeanne, has appropriated the look, and opposite her she confronts not a woman, but a no longer feminisable mass – the people. Too poor to be able to play at disguise, they have with Armand acquired a male look, though as it turns out, one that is defective and unsteady. The power of the people is elsewhere: it consists of duplication, of seriality and manifests itself as repetition and replication – supported by the mass media. One scene that brilliantly illustrates this shift of register is the moment when Jeanne buys up the entire print-run of the satirical song lampooning her affair with the King. She has barely turned her back when the street-balladeer bends down to pick up another bundle from his supply, as if to suggest (like the Oyster-King and his morning newspaper) that there is always more where these have come from: the French Revolution was not for nothing also the revolution of journalists, newspapers, broadsheets and printing presses! In the Berlin of 1919, the Spartacists, too, built their street barricades out of the giant paper-rolls destined for the printing houses.

Lubitsch's German films thus in a sense complement what is missing in the Weimar art cinema, such as slapstick, comedy, filmic farce, in short, cinematic forms where aggression is represented directly on screen, rather than being repressed by such formal means as non-continuous editing or displaced into the dynamics of off-screen space. By making *Madame Dubarry* 'American', in a way that confidently mimics many of the rules of classical American narrative (which also privileges the point-of-view shot, and emphasises 'looking/being looked at' as a formal marker of sexual difference), Lubitsch counters German 'Expressionist' cinema before it had even established itself. On the other hand, Lubitsch is also a 'Weimar' director, in that he is able to critique the very regime of the gaze that came to be identified with Hollywood. American in outlook, Lubitsch is also very much a German director who finally shares the same preoccupations as Lang or Murnau, regarding the cinema as a new historical imaginary, rather than as a medium of the historical imagination. This is why *Madame Dubarry* needs its second part, needs to change register, and 'place' the regime of the gaze of *both* the German art cinema *and* of the classical American cinema.

To briefly summarise once more what is at stake. In the Weimar art cinema the spectator is, so to speak, caught in the cross-fire of protagonists seeking to control on-screen space by occupying off-screen space, and of point-of-view shots which are marked as subjective, i.e. identifying the viewer as the actual or potential victim of someone else's gaze. The effect is a position of knowledge, which when shared with the camera is inferior to that of the protagonist (we know less), but when superior to the protagonist, forces the spectator to identify with the point of view of the villain or the aggressor – a position of knowledge that produces the spectator as an unstable, threatened, split subject, as is familiar from the horror film (which is said to have learnt so much from 'Expressionist' cinema). In the American cinema, on the other hand, subject positions might be said to be too stable, because they install the spectator in the all-too-illusory wholeness of a socially and sexually fixed subject position. In both cases the positions of knowledge hold the spectator in the imaginary, in which off-screen space represents the symbolic field, whether explicitly identified with the Law and the Father or implicitly as the source of (narrative) Authority and Meaning, from which the spectator is excluded. It is in relation to both these 'regimes' that Lubitsch is different. In his films, the relation between point-of-view and off-screen space is one of implication rather than exclusion, and thus positions the spectator neither in the imaginary plenitude of narrative authority and voyeuristic spectacle, nor in the imaginary lack thematised in the permanent paranoia of off-screen narration and exhibitionist masochism. One might say that Lubitsch 'frees' the spectator by paradoxically drawing attention to that from which he/she is excluded – retrieving the off-screen neither through shot–countershot (Hollywood narrative) nor through the withholding of it ('Expressionist' cinema), but by implicating both character and audience in the very construction of this off-screen space, for instance, by introducing obstacles into the visual field, such as the famous doors, said to make up the Lubitsch touch. His off-screen space is thus different from that of most directors because unlike other German directors, he does not use editing to contrast or oppose two spaces, and instead, establishes a contiguous relationship between them, where one is a complex metonymic figuration of the other. And, unlike the American cinema where such contiguity usually connotes linear sequence in time, contiguity in Lubitsch opens space itself to cognitive play – the spectator is invited to hesitate between two possible alternative readings, for which temporal succession is all but irrelevant. Pictorial space – including off-screen space is thus clearly identified as always also a cognitive space – a metaphor of itself, as it were – which allows precisely for expectations to be deceived and disabused, for assumptions to be shown as erroneous, and anticipations constantly having to be revised retrospectively, in a game of wit and intellectual thought that puts characters within the film and spectators of the film onto the same footing, in a narrational mode that could be called 'surprise by surmise'.[37] Because it is based on the communication and sharing of roles, on setting up of constraints and then demonstrating their reversibility, Lubitsch's films escape the fixating of pleasure as power that make both Hollywood narrative and Expressionist films function so often as cinemas of domination, sexually as well as economically.

Once more, what the spectator learns are the 'rules of the game'. Visual pleasure in Lubitsch resides in acquiring not knowledge but competence – of playing or anticipating the next move, of being surprised that the next move plays yet another variation on the established paradigm. It is what makes the spectator–film relation ultimately so different in a Lubitsch film, for one is drawn into a game which is an eminently democratic one. The films make it appear as if everyone can play, that the values and stakes are not fixed from the start. In

Madame Dubarry both the opposition male/female and wealth/poverty appear, in the figure of Jeanne, as variables of each other, not because Lubitsch does not believe in either, or puts himself aristocratically above them, but because he believes in the revolution that would turn them from firm assets or predetermined constants into factors of mutability – they mark the beginning of a permanent reversibility of values. It makes his films both relativist, as befits someone who has seen a society collapse through inflation and revert to the anarchic economy of the black market, *and* optimistic, as befits someone who knew how to seize his chance in the symbolic world of seeing/seen – and being seen to see – which is the cinema.

History always returns twice, Marx said – once as tragedy, the second time as farce. Lubitsch would agree, but turn it round. For him, it is the ousting of comedy by tragedy that turns out to be the real drama of *Madame Dubarry*, which may after all be connected more directly to the revolutionary turmoil of the months during which it was shot than Kracauer gives it credit for. It shows, so to speak, the 'sunny' side of an inflationary world, the inherent possibility of a new beginning. Standing under the sign of chance, barter and the lucky break, *Madame Dubarry* may be said to speak to post-war Germany's revolutionary and utopian aspect, where the collapse of all values contains the hope for a new order and a new regime of the gaze. If Lubitsch appears to regret the (French) Revolution, it is because it tries to put an end to such a reversibility of values. The guillotine turns out to be what it is in Foucault – an extension of the castrating gaze of the Old Regime rather than emblem of the (film-) splicer of contiguity, token of a new regime of reversibility. *Madame Dubarry*, which seems to mock the Revolution, is in that very act of mockery and travesty the more faithful to it. For if, as Foucault implies, in the panoptic gaze, the tyrannical eye, the military and disciplinary monitoring and surveillance, it was the Revolution that betrayed its own libertarian belief in vision, democracy and self-transparency, then in Lubitsch's empire of the gaze, the Revolution – through the cinema of surprise and surmise, of inference rather than reference – returns to its own promise. The historical imagination may yet be able to acknowledge the historical imaginary, and even the invention of the Lumières may yet bring closer the kind of transparency once expected from *les lumières* – always provided it remembers its double registers of reference.

Notes

1 Carlyle probably in turn influenced a novelist such as Charles Dickens, who in his two novels of the revolutionary mob, *A Tale of Two Cities* and *Barnaby Rudge*, has – along with Edmund Burke – shaped the 'historical imagination' of late nineteenth-century England more profoundly than anyone else.

2 Foucault 1975, notably Chapters 2 and 5.

3 White 1973.

4 Elsaesser 1971.

5 Eisner 1969: 82.

6 Kracauer 1947: 48.
7 On the US reception of *Madame Dubarry* (*Passion*), see Pratt 1991: 34–70.
8 Only its producer, Paul Davidson, stayed on. Having made his name and fame with Asta Nielsen films in the 'teens and wanting to repeat the same with Pola Negri, he had hired Lubitsch to make Negri into a star. Davidson was also an important movie-palace entrepreneur, who by 1918 had built up the largest chain of luxury cinemas in Germany. In line with this logic, *Madame Dubarry* was the film chosen to premiere at the grand opening of Berlin's latest luxury cinema, the UFA-Palast am Zoo, on 18 September 1919.
9 The first hour [of *Madame Dubarry*] follows the narrative of Karl Millöcker's operetta *Gräfin Dubarry* quite closely – I am referring to the original 1897 version, and not the Theo Mackeben revision of 1931, which was called *Die Dubarry*.

(Salt 1992: 65–70)

10 Kracauer 1976: 9.
11 Kracauer 1976: 261.
12 For an excellent overview, see Paysan 1998: 44–66, 'aus dem Geist des Boulevards'.
13 Kracauer 1930.
14 German histories of the gramophone record stress how Berlin, from the early 1920s onwards, became the centre of technical developments, like improved microphones and amplifiers, but most important, it was the home of the radio broadcasts transmitting live from the many venues where new hit songs and their performers were launched as stars. See Günter Große, Von der Edisonwalze zur Stereoplatte (Berlin: Lied der Zeit, 1981), quoted in Paysan 1998: 52–3.
15 In *Madame Dubarry* Lubitsch several times condenses revolutionary action in the gestures of tearing down curtains and breaking into windows, and, of course, strategically deploying doors.
16 Starobinski 1988.
17 Burch 1979: 62.
18 Martin Jay has pointed out that in twentieth-century French thinking, the epistemology of vision is accompanied by another tradition, very hostile to the primacy of the visual, what he calls the anti-ocularist discourse. He traces this ambivalence from Bergson and Merleau-Ponty, from Sartre to Lacan, and from Foucault to Guy Debord. Although this is not the place to enter into Jay's argument in detail, it may be worth retaining that, given the major role played by French thought in the development of film theory, one finds reverberations of both the ocularist and anti-ocularist tradition within post-1968 film studies. Jean-Louis Baudry, for instance, could be said to belong to the anti-oculist tradition, and with the concept of the 'absent field' and 'suture', he and his colleagues took up the 'paranoid' but also 'expressionist' legacy of this particular discourse of vision (Jay 1993).
19 Jean Louis Baudry, 'Le cinéma – effets produit par l'appareil de base' (1970) and 'Le dispositif – approches métapsychologiques de l'impression de réalité' (1975). In English, Baudry's essays can be found in Rosen 1986.
20 The obligatory reference is to Paul Virilio (1988). However, in Virilio's genealogy of the visual technology of power, what is lost, Foucault would say, is history as resistance, as materiality, or what Marxists would call history as human labour.
21 In this context, one generally refers to the work of the German sociologist Georg Simmel, to Walter Benjamin's *Passagen-Werk* (1983), as well as Siegfried Kracauer's

early writings, such as *The Mass Ornament* (1995). Among the more recent cultural history studies one could name, apart from Martin Jay's, *Downcast Eyes* (1993) and Jonathan Crary, *Techniques of the Observer* (Cambridge, Mass: MIT Press, 1994).

22 See also Schlüpmann 1990 and Hansen 1993.

23 J. von Hoddis (1911)'Schluss: Kinematograph', quoted in Greve *et al.* 1976: 15.

24 Quoted in Jörg Schweinitz 1992: 170.

25 See also:

> Der Saal wird dunkel. Und wir sehn die Schnellen
> Der Ganga, Palmen, Tempel und auch Brahma,
> Ein lautlos tobendes Familiendrama
> Mit Lebemännern dann und Maskenbällen.
> Man zückt Revolver, Eifersucht wird rege,
> Herr Piefke duelliert sich ohne Kopf.
> Dann zeigt man uns mit Kiepe und mit Kropf
> Die Aelperin auf mächtig steilem Wege.
>
> (Greve *et al.* 1976: 15)

26 A good example of a writer's bafflement is the essay by Kurt Tucholsky ([1921] 1992): 214–18.

27 See the previous chapter on 'Fritz Lang's Traps for the Mind and Eye' (Part II, Chapter 1).

28 For further examples, see Part I, Chapter 3, this volume on 'Caligari's family'.

29 Weimar cinema seems more overtly beholden to the paranoid ontology of vision (the sense of being looked at, with a concomitant uncertainty of who it is that is doing the looking) than, for instance the American cinema of the same period. That it thus provides some very powerful subject effects (to do with the uncanny, for instance) seems undeniable. But instead of identifying this directly with state terrorism, as Kracauer does, it could with equal plausibility be attributed to the 'ocular terrorism' of modern Western epistemology. If the films of Ernst Lubitsch, as I argue in the following, invert this paradigm within Weimar cinema, his subject effects ought to be quite different, and so they are. His reliance on spectatorial complicity rather than on effects of the uncanny – on surmise and inference rather than surprise and shock – could be said to refocus viewer attention: from the traumatised eye to the tantalised mind.

30 The scene harks back to Heinrich von Kleist's village judge in *Der zerbrochene Krug* (*The Broken Jug*), but Lubitsch may in turn have inspired Brecht's figure of Azdak, the Judge of Misrule in *The Caucasian Chalk Circle.*

31 Elsaesser 1990: 171–89.

32 Lotte Eisner's dislike of Lubitsch seems to be partly motivated by his background in the 'Ostjuden' milieu of the Hausvogteiplatz, the traditional Berlin quarters of cloth merchants and rag-trade sweatshops. As indicated, she refers to him in *The Haunted Screen* as a 'one-time shop-assistant' (1969: 82), speaking truer than she imagined, if I am right in thinking that the association with the world of fashion and design gives not only early Lubitsch but Weimar cinema its (socio-stylistic) unity.

33 Lubitsch's cynicism is neither pessimist and misanthropic like Fritz Lang's nor male chauvinist like that of the young Brecht's, two (other) notable cynics of the Weimar Republic with whom Lubitsch has in common a belief in the instability of symbolic power. See also Chapter 1 on Lang in Part II of this volume and the discussion of the 'enlightened false consciousness' in the Introduction to this volume.

34 The reference is to the discussion of *The Cabinet of Dr Caligari* in Part I, Chapter 2, this volume.

35 In his American comedies of the mid-1920s, Lubitsch refined the narrative scheme I have been analysing to the point where the typical scenario (of, for instance, *Lady*

Windermere's Fan, *So This is Paris* and *The Marriage Circle*) goes like this: If A believes what B says but subsequently discovers that B has been lying, A is none the less still duped by B, if B knows something that A doesn't know. A on the other hand, can pretend not to have discovered that B has been lying. In other words, a lie is not cancelled by the truth but by making the person being lied to tell a lie himself. Only then, when both parties are in the Kingdom of Makebelieve, are they on an equal footing and the game can (re-)commence. Thus the 'American' Lubitsch develops narratives that are doubly symmetrical around an equation with at least two variables. Regardless of the location, but benefiting from their 'olde-worlde' social setting, they create just enough friction between claim and counter-claim, pose and imposture for the worlds depicted to detach themselves from any historical or social reference to become the pure artifice and pure structure which directors such as Alfred Hitchcock and François Truffaut so admired about Lubitsch.

36 See Mulvey 1975.

37 Such forms of indirection in Lubitsch led François Truffaut to speak of 'the Swiss Cheese called Lubitsch where it is the holes that count'. Lubitsch's style, however, makes ellipsis into a rhetorical figure, which strictly speaking, is neither temporal nor spatial, but narrational and cognitive. See Truffaut 1968: 12–14.

3

NOSFERATU, TARTUFFE AND FAUST

Secret affinities in Friedrich Wilhelm Murnau

'The Great Unknown'

Of the directors who have made Weimar Cinema famous, F.W. Murnau has always seemed the most enigmatic, though probably the one best loved by film makers and cinephiles.[1] When, in the 1960s, Lotte Eisner referred to Murnau as 'The Great Unknown', she did more than create a space for her pioneering study on the director.[2] The paradoxical blend of mystery and admiration she alludes to was at least in part due to the mutilation and destruction suffered by so many of his films, especially the ones made between 1919 and 1924.[3] Murnau's much-vaunted visual poetry was not helped by the fact that others of his key early films did not survive in the way he had planned or edited them. This includes *Nosferatu*: cut by distributors, incomplete or perishing prints of the film were later reassembled according to an idea of dramatic pace or continuity editing not always mindful of Murnau's own conception.[4] Looking back at this history of reception, it is evident that Murnau was appreciated by his contemporaries for his technical skills, then largely misappropriated or even forgotten during the sound period, and only 'rehabilitated' after the end of the Second World War, mainly by critics and archivists who had access to good prints. As with so many other directors of the silent era, chief honour must go to Henri Langlois, his assistant Lotte Eisner and the members of the *nouvelle vague*, whom Langlois's Paris Cinemathèque provided with their filmic education.[5] But it also suggests that there is something about Murnau's films which makes them peculiarly vulnerable to the physical degradation of the surface textures of the photographic image: in several senses, each frame is fringed with death, as Alexandre Astruc wrote, and meaning resides in Murnau's forms, as Rohmer argued.[6] More than Fritz Lang, Murnau is the director of a special kind of photographic indexicality, which again explains why among André Bazin's disciples his star should have risen so high.[7] It needs the original pin-sharp, luminous prints, in order to engage with Murnau's work at all, rather than the washed-out or smudged duplicate copies that for decades shaped one's view of the cinema of the 1920s, and the German classics in particular. As already argued in the Introduction to this volume, the study of Weimar cinema has benefited crucially from the technically exacting and historically informed standards of preservation become the rule since the 1970s, and few bodies of film have opened themselves up more startlingly than those of Murnau.[8]

One of the discoveries made in the course of re-viewing the films lies behind the argument in this chapter: that Murnau's painterly eye and pictorialist sensibility, the blend of dreamy haze and anguished longing emanate so strongly from his work not despite but because of the particularly advanced film technology and the ultra-modern, state-of-the-art studio techniques available to the director and promoted by Erich Pommer at UFA. The question this prompts me to return to are the affinities between the high romanticism of Murnau's visual style, his unparalleled poetry of the image, and the high-tech perfectionism, the proficient use of special effects in some of his major films. Struck by the sheer engineering skills required for films like *The Last Laugh* and *Faust*, one wonders what kind of mind of 'fire and ice', but also what kind of (self-)discipline was necessary to let poetic fervour and romantic delicacy translate themselves onto the screen with equal energy and brilliance?

Born into a family of well-to-do Bielefeld textile manufacturers in 1888, Friedrich Wilhelm Plumpe adopted the surname 'Murnau' in honour of an artists' colony in the Bavarian Alps. He was, according to his brother, a shy and sensitive child. Already as a boy, he 'overflowed with imagination. The dreams that seemed to weave themselves round his being at night surrounded him during the day as well.'[9] The person whom young Wilhelm was closest to was his elder half-sister, a painter who encouraged him to stage plays as a family entertainment (reminiscent of Goethe's hero *Wilhelm Meister*). After studying philology in Berlin, and then art history and literature at Heidelberg University,[10] Murnau became a pupil of Max Reinhardt, working as an actor and assistant director. In 1915 he was called up and served in the army.[11] In 1916 he transferred to the *Luftwaffe* where he flew combat missions, but after an emergency landing during fog, he came to spend the remainder of the war as an internee in neutral Switzerland. There, he won a national theatre competition and made propaganda films for the German Embassy.[12] The deepest wound the war inflicted on him seems to have been the death on the Eastern Front of his intimate friend Hans Ehrenbaum-Degele, poet and son of a Jewish banker and art-collector, whose mother Mary virtually adopted Murnau after his return from Zurich.[13] The Ehrenbaum-Degele villa in Berlin-Grunewald remained his home from 1918 until he left for America.

His earliest feature film, *Der Knabe in Blau* (1919) was produced and financed by the matinée idol Ernst Hoffmann, who also played the lead. The second, *Satanas* (1919) was an episode film modelled on Griffith's *Intolerance* (1916), with ancient Egypt, the Renaissance and the failed Spartacist revolution of 1918 as the locations for stories of evil and betrayal. Produced and written by Robert Wiene, *Satanas* featured Fritz Kortner as the pharaoh and Conrad Veidt in the roles of Satanas, the seducer. Preceding other famous episode films like Carl Dreyer's *Leaves from Satan's Book* (1920), Lang's *Destiny* (1921) and Paul Leni's

Waxworks (1924), its loss is especially regrettable for the historian. *Der Bucklige und die Tänzerin* (1920) and *Der Januskopf* (1920, a Jekyll and Hyde story with Conrad Veidt and Bela Lugosi) were exercises in the fantastic and macabre, and are also presumed lost. With *Der Bucklige und die Tänzerin* contemporary critics became aware of a distinctive directorial talent. For the first time one finds reviews that try to describe the special Murnau magic that has ever since been recognised and celebrated:

> I have never before experienced a film where camera and direction are able to surround the characters with the kind of atmosphere that breathes soul into them, that makes you believe you can actually smell the odour emanating from the hunchback's Javanese perfume.[14]

But Murnau achieved his first popular success with *Nosferatu – eine Symphonie des Grauens* (1922) and to this day this classic horror film has remained his best-known work. Subsequently, it was the big studio productions (*Großfilme*) made for UFA between 1924 and 1926 (*The Last Laugh*, *Tartuffe* and *Faust*: all three star vehicles for Emil Jannings) that gave Murnau box-office clout and a name in the film industry. As with so much else in Weimar Cinema, especially in its dealings with Hollywood, from Ernst Lubitsch's *Madame Dubarry* via E.A. Dupont's *Variety*, to *The Last Laugh* and Joseph von Sterberg's *The Blue Angel*, Jannings was also a driving force in Murnau's career.

Despite a meteoric rise to world renown (first in Germany, then in Hollywood), a number of myths both romantic and scurrilous attached themselves to Murnau's persona, not least because he jealously chose to protect his privacy.[15] A solitary person, he was evidently quite the opposite of an extrovert show business talent like Ernst Lubitsch or a society lion like Fritz Lang. In Weimar Germany, where the cinema had to fight hard to make itself socially respectable, Murnau – like his rival Lang[16] – allowed himself to be portrayed by the UFA publicity machine as a dandy, an aristocrat of the spirit, and a visionary of the new art.[17] A white lab coat became his trademark on the set, where he was addressed as *Herr Doktor*, because of his (uncompleted) university studies. Cultivating this aura helped him retain his aloofness: as far as one can judge, however, he thought of himself more as a footloose adventurer, restless, driven, and rootless – except in his art.[18]

After the international success of *The Last Laugh*, William Fox hired Murnau in January 1926 to work in Hollywood, much to the disappointment of Erich Pommer, who had counted on Murnau helping the German film industry to compete against the American companies, rather than becoming the prize trophy of yet another foreign talent-scouting shopping trip by a Hollywood mogul. Fox wanted Murnau because of his craftsmanship and reputation as a director who could reach international audiences. Besides, the studio was also keen to advertise its artistic ambitions by a name that connoted European style and sophistication.[19] In the Fox studio, too, 'Dr. Murnau' quickly acquired the reputation of being difficult and a recluse – not unlike Greta Garbo, one of his few close friends.[20] He was said to have consulted astrologers, occupied himself with Eastern philosophy and strongly believed in the occult. *Sunrise*, his first film in Hollywood was a box-office failure, but is now widely regarded as Murnau's aesthetic testament.[21] He made two more films for Fox (*Four Devils* and *City Girl/Our Daily Bread*), before breaking his contract and forming an independent production partnership with the documentarist Robert Flaherty to direct *Tabu*, set in Tahiti and intended as the first of a series of films on the South Sea Islands. But differences with Flaherty led Murnau to complete *Tabu* on his own, under considerable financial strain.[22]

'Where do you think you're going?' Doctor van Helsing calls out to Harker, in *Nosferatu*, 'you cannot escape your destiny by running away'. Murnau's last, ill-fated journey from Los Angeles to Monterey was a kind of 'Appointment in Samara'. It seems to have been undertaken in order to forestall the very destiny that was to lie in store for him. He died on 11 March 1931 in a freak automobile accident near Santa Barbara on his way to arrange his steamship passage to New York, after having been warned that he should avoid travelling on land. Only eleven mourners were present at his funeral. Whether part of the Murnau legend or authentic, the accounts of the circumstances of his death are a strangely apt tribute to his aura. It seals his life with a melancholy gesture of mysterious irony, not unlike that emanating from his films.

When *Tabu* opened on 18 March, 1931, only a week after Murnau's death, it brought the director more praise from the American press than he had had in the four preceding years. And yet, Murnau, in his last film, had swum against the current, both of Hollywood, still riding high on the phenomenal success of sound, and in Europe, where the films of Eisenstein and Pudovkin had in the meantime set the standards of art cinema taste. *Tabu* was in every respect their very antithesis: a film entirely devoted to creating the lighting effects and spatial compositions of his German studio films with natural sunlight and shade, filmed outdoors, on cliff-tops and in bamboo huts. Doom comes in the form of a ship, pushing its way gently into the perfectly framed, idyllic image of a peaceful port. In Murnau's cinema, it seems, few boats can hope to come home to a safe harbour – but they are expected, none the less.

Stimmung: Naturalism and Expressionism

The films at first sight only deepen the mystery of Murnau's true identity. Even among the extant films, after viewing *Schloß Vogelöd*, *Phantom*, *Die Finanzen des Großherzog* and *The Last Laugh* in succession, it is well-nigh impossible to distil from the diversity of the subjects a strongly personal *moral* statement of the kind attributed (wrongly or rightly) to Fritz Lang's pessimistic visions of fate, authority and power, or to G.W. Pabst's socially committed but coolly sardonic realist films.[23] If there is consistency, it lies, oddly enough, in the films' participation in the trends and fashions of Weimar cinema, and more tenuously, in certain preferences of the *mise-en-scène* for the fantastic: from the German *Der Gang in die Nacht*, *Nosferatu* and *Faust*, to the American *Sunrise*, *Our Daily Bread* and even *Tabu*, scenes of the supernatural, the other-worldly, of night-time, nightmare and transgression predominate in Murnau, rendered in a style that has the pictorial qualities so prized by Lotte Eisner: *Stimmung* – the play of light and shadow, the painterly compositions, the diaphanous transparency and yet tactile plasticity of the image. All these qualities are now generally associated with filmic Expressionism, not least thanks to Eisner's major book on the subject, *The Haunted Screen*. There, also with Murnau in mind, she suggests that German cinema of the 1920s is 'a development of German Romanticism, [...] modern technique merely lends visible form to Romantic fancies'.[24] To the extent that several other of the so-called Expressionist films more properly belong to the stylistic heritage of German Romantic painting (notably by an appropriation of Caspar David Friedrich, Carl Spitzweg and Georg Friedrich Kersting) rather than to the bold colours, the shifting perspectives and jagged lines of the artists associated with *Die Brücke* or *Der Blaue Reiter*, Eisner's formula of Romanticism plus cinema equals (filmed) Expressionism is apt, and also applies to Murnau.[25] On the other hand, directly transferring art-historical categories to a technical medium like the cinema renders a doubtful service to either, unless it also reflects the modernist and even constructivist break which the shift from a (craft) notion of technique to the (industrial) notion of technology implies for the idea of style. Perhaps 'lend' is the operative term in Eisner's phrase, because it leaves room for the possibility of mimicry and pastiche appropriation in this double transfer from (Romantic) painting to the UFA studio set, and from (Expressionist) avant-garde culture to the Weimar silver screens.

Looking at Murnau's work and keeping these historical provisos in mind, one gets a more hard-edged sense of the director's authorial signature, without losing sight of his acknowledged eminence as the silent cinema's outstanding lyrical genius. The newly restored prints, for instance, clarify Murnau's relation to Expressionist films to the extent that his work appears at some considerable distance from typically 'decorative' examples such as Robert Wiene's *The Cabinet of Dr Caligari* (1920), Karl Heinz Martin's *From morn to midnight* (1920) or Leni's *Waxworks* (1924). It is true, Murnau personally knew the poets Else Lasker-Schüler and Paul Zech, the sculptress Renée Sinténis and the painter Franz Marc, all of whom could be called Expressionists. But in so far as the notion of influence can be applied to Murnau's visual style, such early works as *Der Gang in die Nacht* and *Nosferatu* recall Post-impressionism rather than Expressionism. Mellowing the naturalism of the German cinema of the 1910s, Murnau renders it transparent towards symbolist nuance, but at times he also loads it with typically Wilhelmine ornament. The stills from his lost films, for instance, show mostly interiors, where draped furniture and heavily curtained salons pay tribute to the pre-war predilection for orientalism, colonial spoils and exotic bric-a-brac. Perhaps only the home of the hunchback in *Der Bucklige und die Tänzerin* shows 'expressionistically' jagged floor-patterns, to underscore the tortured body and the warped passions wracking his soul, which points to the correspondence between psychology and decor that is said to be the hallmark of Expressionist cinema, but also makes that fatally philistine association between avant-garde art and mental instability first insinuated by *Dr Caligari*.

Somewhat in passing, Lotte Eisner mentions an 'influence' on Murnau's films which seems more central as well as more evident than Expressionism, in visual values no less than in the deeper spiritual resonances: the Scandinavian cinema of the 1910s.[26] The work of directors like Viktor Sjöström and Mauritz Stiller, Urban Gad and Benjamin Christensen is marked by outdoor realism, a poetic treatment of landscape, and a very controlled, understated portrayal of psychological or even frankly melodramatic conflicts – no doubt indebted to the drama of Strindberg and Ibsen, as well as the novels of Knut Hamsun or Selma Lagerlöf, but realised in a visual style unique to Denmark and Sweden among European cinema nations during the formative period between 1909 and 1919.[27] Most of these 'Scandinavian' features are to be found in Murnau, and if one were to summarise his own contribution to the German cinema, it would be the evocative, because painterly depiction of the natural environment. From *Der Gang in die Nacht* and *Nosferatu* to *Sunrise* and *Tabu* Murnau was unsurpassed in blending an unfussily precise realism with exquisitely crafted artifice, whether on a large, studio-built set, as the street set and hotel in *The Last Laugh* and the cityscape in *Sunrise*, or for an intimate scene in *Faust* (the first meeting of Faust with Gretchen in Marthe's garden).

Murnau's debt to the Scandinavian masters consisted in his ability to adopt their naturalism and heighten it further in the direction of ordinary actions and simple gestures suffused with an atmosphere at once lyrical and uncanny, ethereal and mysterious, whose painterly precedents he did indeed often find in Friedrich for the outdoor and Kersting in the interiors. These were qualities which another Scandinavian director, Carl Dreyer, gratefully accepted from Murnau in return.[28] But Murnau also knew how to naturalise technological artifice, to take the elements of the UFA studio style and transform them into a language of homely/uncanny simplicity. For instance, despite the unforgettable make-up of the vampire in *Nosferatu* (1922) or the beetling antics of his acolyte Renfield, Murnau's direction is notable for its understatement and restraint, his spare, classical, often almost empty compositions. *Nosferatu* suggests the dawn atmosphere of sleepless nights, thanks to a meticulous attention to visual detail that sets off the more dramatically the appearance of the vampire himself, always framed in angled doorways and coffin-shaped apertures. The film was mostly shot on location in the Baltic ports of Rostock, Wismar and Lübeck, and for the Transylvanian parts, at the Castle Oravsky, in the High Tatras of Slovakia. In these latter locations, a rock, by the magic of framing and light, can look malicious and menacing, while during the sea voyage and the entry into the port of 'Wisborg', the mere lapping of water against a boat fills the image with foreboding. Murnau's lyricism was the result of applying in a distanced, almost clinical manner the technical mastery of German still photography and 'docu-

Figure 15 Waiting for the Master: Alexander Granach (Renfield) and Gustav von Wagenheim (Jonathan Harker) in F.W. Murnau's *Nosferatu-eine Symphonie des Grauens* (1922)

Source: Stiftung Deutsche Kinemathek, Berlin

mentary' camera-work to emotionally charged subjects associated with deep-seated fears and archaic feelings.

Undoubtedly, however, it was a film made prior to *Nosferatu*, *Der Gang in die Nacht* (1921) that showed Murnau at his most Scandinavian. It tells the story of the eye specialist Professor Boerne, who allows himself to be seduced by Lily, a young dancer. For her, he leaves his fiancée, Helen, and moves to a small fishing village. There he and Lily meet a blind painter (Conrad Veidt) whom the doctor is able to restore to sight. Lily falls in love with the painter and leaves Boerne, who returns to the city, embittered and vengeful. Knowing her lover is once more threatened by blindness, Lily pleads with the doctor, but he, still tormented by jealousy, tells her he will save the painter's sight only on condition that she kill herself. Lily takes poison, whereupon the painter refuses Boerne's help, saying that since all he wanted to be able to see was Lily, he had rather join her and 'go into the night'. Boerne, mortified, also commits suicide. As the second film on which Murnau worked with Carl Mayer (after *Der Bucklige und die Tänzerin*), the double love triangle in *Der Gang in die Nacht* has much in common with other of Mayer's so-called 'blind instinct films', including *Dr Caligari*. But its plot also follows in the footsteps of 'serious' film melodramas of the 1910's, such as Max

Mack's *Zweimal gelebt* (1912). Murnau, here, not for the first or last time (cf. *Der brennende Acker*, 1922 and *Sunrise*) juxtaposes country and city, across a story of fatal passion that can only end in death. However, unlike Wiene in *Dr Caligari*, Murnau in *Der Gang in die Nacht* (in this closer to Max Mack)[29] shows off fashionably modern interiors, while the sequences by the seaside are highly evocative of forlorn beaches in autumn. In the interiors, especially in the scenes featuring Lily or Helen, a subtlety of gesture and psychological nuance contrasts starkly with the histrionics of the men, not excepting Conrad Veidt.[30]

In so far as Murnau's films are 'Expressionist' at all, then, they qualify less by their visual style than by their stories. Focusing on tormented males with brooding minds and opaque psychological urges, they bear the trademark of Germany's most professional and prolific screenwriters of the 1920s: Carl Mayer and Thea von Harbou. Harbou wrote or co-wrote the scenarios of at least four, while Mayer was the writer responsible for no less than seven of Murnau's twenty-one films. Their collaboration was regarded as so important, and the personality of Murnau so baffling, that critics at the time assigned the creative authorship of a film like *The Last Laugh* to the scriptwriter Mayer, the cameraman Karl Freund, and the art directors Robert Herlth and Walter Röhrig![31] That critics expected Murnau to be an 'Expressionist' and then were disappointed that he did not behave like one (since he often included slapstick scenes and rather graphic humour) clues one also to some of the other distinguishing marks of his style: understatement, subtle nuance and allusiveness, i.e. the very opposite of Expressionist pathos.

Jo Leslie Collier has identified the recurrent plot-pattern underlying virtually all of Murnau's films, seeing in them archetypal tales of the Romantic legacy, even suggesting an affinity with the narratives of redemption that also inspired Wagner's operas:

> The story of a Murnau film most often begins with an already established pair, frequently husband and wife, leading what appears to be a happy, even idyllic life together. There is then some intrusion into the couple's life which creates a rupture between them. The first response to the intrusion is usually flight, by a single member of the pair or both together. There follows a reunion, but it proves only temporary: flight has served to postpone the crisis engendered by the intruder, but not avoid[ed] it. The intruder catches up with them [..], forcing them to confront [the crisis], sometimes successfully, sometimes not. There is one other element that must be added to this outline: at a point more or less midway through this sequence of events, there is presented a wish fulfilment dream, fantasy or subplot.[32]

Carl Mayer, Murnau and *The Last Laugh*

Given the consistency of this deep-structure and the debate about authorship, the Mayer–Murnau cooperation requires some further comment.[33] It was certainly widely discussed at the time. Willy Haas, for instance, could not imagine two people more different in appearance or manner – Mayer short, round and voluble, Murnau tall, reserved and formal:

> Carl Mayer, unusually effervescent, strongly moved and deeply sunk into every phase of a conversation, as if his body, like a small tree exposed to a violent storm, was being tossed helplessly hither and thither. Murnau, on the other hand, was just as unusually sober, every inch the Anglo-Saxon gentleman, *extra-dry*, with a very abstract grasp of the different aspects of a dialogical situation, and for the rest, exuding refined politeness and exquisite breeding.[34]

The strange mixture worked, for as Haas conceded, together they worked miracles, and *The Last Laugh* can rightly be seen as their most successful joint undertaking. It tells the story of the head doorman at the luxury hotel Atlantic, whose life revolves around his job, symbolised by a gold-braided uniform. One day, staggering under the weight of one of the trunks lifted from a carriage, he is observed by the manager who replaces him by a younger man. The doorman, pleading in vain for another chance, is made lavatory attendant. As he struggles out of his uniform, the proud giant of a man turns into a pitiful wreck. The uniform made him what he was also at home: head of the family, stern but benevolent patriarch in the tenement house where he lives with a niece and a housekeeper. At nightfall, he breaks into the manager's office. Secretly he puts on the uniform to go home, secretly he deposits it in the morning at the railway station left luggage. His life has become an anxious sham, and when his housekeeper catches sight of him at his humble job, even the uniform cannot prevent disgrace in front of the neighbours. Down below in his washrooms, the night watchman tries to console him, but the ex-doorman is ready to put an end to his life. Here, the authors take pity and let chance intervene: an American millionaire guest leaves him a fortune, and in a gesture to redeem a hundred humiliations, the 'last man' and his night watchman have dinner at the hotel, making every single waiter and maid attend to their whims. A carriage finally takes them off, not before they handsomely tip the entire staff, having 'the last laugh'.

The Last Laugh proved a key film of its decade, stylistically as well as thematically. Three tendencies of the German cinema converge to form a new synthesis: Expressionist acting, realism in detail and decor, and the *Kammerspiel* plot with its self-tormented characters. This braiding of closely observed detail with character psychology was Mayer's particular forte, developed also in *Scherben/Shattered* (1921), *Hintertreppe/Backstairs* (1921) and *Sylvester* (1923), each script giving precise directions for lighting, camera angles and close-ups. Mayer's ambition was to tell a story without inter-titles or explanatory comment, adding to the concentration on facial play, typical of German cinema, a pathos of inarticulacy and silent suffering thematised in the protagonists' plight. The anxious emotional muteness is offset in Murnau's film, however, by what *The Last Laugh* is perhaps most famous for: the 'entfesselte Kamera', i.e. the unchained or unfettered camera. Its fluid, mobile and (in the context of the film's pathos) eloquent command of the character's hidden feeling make the space it traverses so effortlessly into a wholly interiorised landscape of the doorman's psyche, while losing nothing of its biting social satire. It is especially memorably deployed in the opening scene, where the camera descends the hotel elevator and crosses the lobby, and in a drunken scene of compensatory fantasy, when the demoted doorman dreams that he himself is the triumphant victor over his younger rival. Emil Jannings incarnates the boastful joviality and self-centred complacency of the doorman with as much gusto as he undergoes the humiliations of stripped masculinity. Thanks to him, the real star becomes the uniform itself. The combination of almost sadistic repression and stylistic exuberance make *The Last Laugh* one of the most typically 'Expressionist' stories. But it is also a typical 'Depression' film from the first part of the 1920s, with its anxiety over downward social mobility and the stigma of age overpowering the satire of the Prussian penchant for uniforms. Mayer and Murnau show how someone makes a fetish out of status, not so much because losing one's job entails economic ruin, but because it is felt as the ultimate social disgrace, and it is a disgrace, because the society symbolised by the uniform, behind the mask of righteousness has already morally crumbled.[35] Yet the fairy-tale reversal at the end is also a kind of sadistic revenge on the doorman's own masochism. Murnau and Mayer have given a comic portrayal of the emotional chaos raging within the 'authoritarian personality', clinging to the trappings of office more desperately than to life itself. This doorman of the Atlantis hotel becomes an icon of the Weimar Republic, in his way even more fantastic than Caligari, more of an undead soul than Nosferatu, and yet more psychologically credible than the self-abasement of Jannings as the humiliated professor in *The Blue Angel*.

It almost suggests that Mayer was the (masochistic) Expressionist, and Murnau the cool, or even sadistic ironist. The two certainly seemed to complement each other in often unexpected ways. Yet Mayer also wrote scripts for Wiene, Arthur von Gerlach, Walter Ruttmann, and 'chamber plays' for Lupu Pick, Paul Leni and Paul Czinner, which resulted in very different films from Murnau's. *Nosferatu* (script: Henrik Galeen), *Phantom* (script: Harbou), *Sunrise* (script: Mayer) and *Tabu* (script: Robert Flaherty) have more in common with each other than any of them has with *Backstairs* (script: Mayer, director: Jessner) or *Berlin – Symphony of a Big City* (script: Mayer, director: Ruttmann). The same is true of Thea von Harbou (author of the screenplay of Murnau's *Die Austreibung*, *Der brennende Acker*, *Phantom*, *Die Finanzen des Großherzogs*).[36] She wrote the scripts for most of Fritz Lang's German work, as well as for films by Joe

May and Arthur von Gerlach, which, again, have little in common with Murnau's.[37]

Based on an immensely popular serialised novel, *Schloß Vogelöd* (script: Carl Mayer) for instance, is an amalgam of sensationalist high society hokum and a Hamlet-ish drama of passion, incest and revenge.[38] On one level, it is a picture of Weimar moral decadence, not unlike parts of Lang's *Dr Mabuse*, which, as indicated, also started life as a serialised thriller. On another level, the story has the logic of a recurring nightmare, trapping its characters in a hellish circle of frustration, desire and crime, each protagonist his own double and deadly rival. Murnau opted for evocative exterior shots of lakes and woods, rather than Expressionist stylisation. He sets off the improbably melodramatic plot against the spare decor of the interiors. The scene, where husband and wife suspect each other's mutual involvement in guilty designs shows both of them squeezed against the opposite walls of an immensely high-ceilinged hall heralds the more abstract, calculated *mise-en-scène* of *Tartuffe*, also about a theatrical performance, staged to unmask a villain.

Phantom (script: Thea von Harbou), on the other hand, affects the simplicity of a morality tale, but tries to heighten the drama of frustrated social rise with an existential *angst.* Lorenz, a humble clerk with a poet's ambitions falls in love with the rich ironmonger's daughter who once nearly ran him over in her horse and buggy. Rebuffed, he takes up with Melitta, a prostitute resembling her, in order to forget his phantom. To keep Melitta, he borrows from his aunt, and is drawn by a shady associate into robbing her. The aunt surprises them and is killed in the melee. Lorenz goes to prison, but Maria, his loyal fiancée is waiting for him upon his release.

The ordinary young man, drawn by a combination of naiveté and idealism into the most sordid of crimes was a fairly common subject in the popular literature and cinema of the time, and resembles motifs from *The Student of Prague*, *The Street* and *Berlin Alexanderplatz*. In the circumstances and the victim of the cold-blooded crime one finds echoes of Dostoevsky, with whose Raskolnikov the novel's hero was once compared. Murnau was commissioned to make the film in time for the sixtieth birthday of Gerhart Hauptmann, celebrated in 1922 as Germany's greatest writer since Goethe. Despite its celebrity status, *Phantom* was long thought lost, until a copy turned up in the Moscow Film Archive in the 1960s. It adds substantially to one's knowledge of early Murnau, not least because the nightmares of the protagonist on his slide into the criminal demi-monde are depicted with Pabstian relish. These sequences also show off the extraordinary sets designed by Hermann Warm, as in the scene where the houses of the little town seem to rear up and engulf the hero, an effect repeated in one of the dream sequences in *The Last Laugh.*

So versatile and adaptable were these two screenwriters that they could serve more than a single voice, and yet, Expressionist films did function, for the relatively brief period between 1920 and 1924, as a 'genre', in two senses: a *genus* with a strong family resemblance between its individual specimen, and a collectively worked (proto-)type, based not as much on a specific art historical style or even a unique or unified *Weltanschauung* as Eisner had argued.[39] The genre reflects the common denominators among a remarkably tightly knit community of professionals – no more than two dozen names – operating as teams and skills networks, many of them first brought together by Erich Pommer via his old firm Decla (and Decla-Bioskop), and subsequently dominating the creative input at UFA.

The notion of a collectively worked genre also suggests another hypothesis about Murnau and Mayer which somewhat depersonalises or recontextualises the 'odd couple' of (Jewish) expressionist and (Aryan) *extra-dry* ironist pictured by Haas. If the German cinema of the early 1920s owes its semblance of stylistic unity that has earned it the label 'Expressionist' mainly to the stable personnel in key positions, notably the writers, cameramen, (male) actors, art directors and set designers, then the squabbles over creative authorship already mentioned take on another meaning. Among the key professionals in the film industry, the set designers probably left the most lasting impression on the surface look: Hermann Warm, Robert Herlth, Walter Röhrig, Erich Kettelhut, Walter Reimann, Otto Hunte and Paul Leni are the ones that shaped the look, insouciantly adapting, appropriating, parodying or plagiarising art history as well as the avant-garde scene in whose (coffee-house, cabaret or club) fringe they participated.[40] For contemporary critics, they ranked second only to the cameramen: Guido Seeber, Karl Hoffmann, Karl Freund, Fritz Arno Wagner, Eugen Schüfftan, Theodor Sparkuhl, Günther Krampf were the names singled out,[41] followed by Emil Jannings, Conrad Veidt, Werner Krauss as the star actors. In this ensemble, the directors for the most part were treated as a vital ingredient, but not always as the controlling force: often in reviews, the *Spielleiter* (a term taken from the theatre) featured quite low on the list. That a small number of individual directors, notably Lang and Murnau (and the now perhaps unjustly neglected Ludwig Berger),[42] none the less imposed themselves as singular artists points to stylistic idiosyncrasies *within* shared preoccupations, rather than against them. Murnau would be a good example of a director whose work, as mentioned, participated in many of Weimar cinema's generic and thematic trends, but to whom UFA, after the success of *Nosferatu*, entrusted their most important star, Emil Jannings, and through him, some of their most market-oriented, 'international' projects. It is not surprising that Murnau's distinguishing role (like that of Lang) seems to have been to set himself and his team special kinds of technical problems, realised in ways that were to inspire European and American film makers,[43] but more practically, serving as prototype-projects for the German film industry, trying to consolidate a world-market position. The experimental character of the three Murnau/Jannings films would thus have been part of the Pommer–UFA policy, as it was with Lang's mid-1920s UFA ventures: both directors were asked to make films that could also function as large-scale research-and-development programmes, helping to establish the UFA brand-name and maintain the studio's edge in terms of its technical infrastructure and its reputation for innovation.

This would be Murnau's 'corporate identity'.[44] Within such a studio-defined premise, his own style, seemingly devoid of ostensibly 'personal' themes is arguably another matter. One might venture that a Murnau style and thematics was hiding inside the Weimar style. For him, UFA's penchant for Romantic, small-town settings, with Gothic decor (*Altdeutsch*) or rococo preciousness and Biedermeier personalities, did duty as a foil for his own artful camouflage, rather than as the expression of a personal idiom or an aesthetic–ideological credo. Murnau, by becoming a leading UFA director none the less kept the studio's commercial priorities at arm's length by distilling from them a peculiar obliqueness and distance, at the bottom of which would either be the irony and a quirky sense of humour observed by Willy Haas, or the melancholy banked-down passion, shot through with longing and *Weltschmerz* emphasised by Eisner. The mixture can already be seen in *Nosferatu* (made for Albin Grau's Prana Film, and not an UFA prestige project), which is justly famous for its sense of dread and heart-stopping anguish, but also displays unexpected moments of tongue-in-cheek humour and high-spiritedness. Especially in the figure of the naive Harker, never at a loss to play down the portents of evil and disaster, however palpable they might be breathing down his own neck, one thinks one can recognise an indulgently 'personal' touch, whether as a sardonic self-comment or as the empathetic portrait of a loved friend. However, to appreciate Murnau's importance not only for the German cinema of the 1920s, but as a pioneer in the history of visual form, one should guard against identifying the man too quickly and too anecdotally with his work. The temptation is to let the mysteries of his private life transform him into a character from his own films (in this instance, evenly divided between ghost-like Nosferatu and light-hearted Jonathan Harker). Similarly, elliptical story telling need not be the inevitable consequence of a reticent and introvert personality.

Narration and editing: *Nosferatu*

Yet Murnau's style of narration not only requires a special kind of attention from the viewer, it also asks for some kind of film-historical context. By narration I do not mean the story *per se*, as much as the manner of its telling (the ironic moments, the humour, the information that is left out, or only ambiguously hinted at). This obliqueness in turn affects not only the tone of a film, but the feeling one has of a structure which escapes the mere retelling of the plot. *Nosferatu*, *The Last Laugh*, *Faust* and *Sunrise*, for instance, are films that convey the sense of a narrative at once simple, because of a folk-legend, fairy-tale 'inevitability', and mysterious, because the overall meaning and shape remain inaccessible to linear cause-and-effect logic. By contrast, the structure of *Schloß Vogelöd*, *Phantom*, and *Tartuffe* immediately intimates complexity: in the power relations that obtain between the characters, how they interact, how they spy on or try to ensnare each other with disguises, one senses the presence of subterfuge, signalled by framed tales and nested narratives.[45] While these features of plot and the interplay of characters may have their Weimar template in Mayer's *Kammerspiel* dramas of instinct and repression, and Murnau's realistic daytime nightmare settings point to the Scandinavian cinema, the lacunary indirection of Murnau's editing, his narrative pace and scene dissection may lead one to a different source: the cinema of D.W. Griffith, and especially his *Intolerance*.[46] A short discussion of narration in *Nosferatu* may help to make the point. The plot, it will be remembered, revolves around a young estate agent, Jonathan Harker/Thomas Hutter,[47] who, hoping to better his professional prospects, visits a mysterious client far away, who expresses the wish to buy a property in Harker's home town by the Baltic Sea. The client, Count Orlok/Dracula, turns out to be a vampire, much taken by the picture of Harker's wife, Nina. Equipped with coffins and native soil, the Count makes his way across the sea to his new home, and installs himself opposite the couple, bringing with him the plague. The young woman, sensing the danger of his presence, one night retains her dreadful visitor until daybreak, saving her husband and the city. Adapted from Bram Stoker's novel by a specialist of the neo-gothic macabre, Henrik Galeen (*The Golem*, *Waxworks*, *The Student of Prague*), *Nosferatu* is none the less quite different from other Expressionist horror films, for Murnau's special skill lay in deriving such effects from the most realistic and even idyllic settings, using his actors to make the story seem natural and everyday, before the framing, the decor and a highly complex montage style imbued the images with supernatural life and an eerie poetry. Second, the narrative in *Nosferatu* is deflected from linearity by the different voices, successively or simultaneously called upon to tell the tale. Starting with Harker's boss who sends him to Nosferatu, via the Book of Vampires, the Paracelsian professor's commentary, the ship's log, the town's chronicler of the plague, all the way to the insert shots of contracts, documents, diaries, newspapers – so many agents of the narrative, relaying information, more or less reliable. Not unlike Nosferatu himself, mastermind but also enmeshed in the events, the majority of the characters are at once 'inside' the fiction and also standing apart from it.

Thus the lines of force, of attraction and repulsion that link Nosferatu and Harker and Nosferatu and Nina (but draw in everyone else, too) weave a subtle net of communication and dependency, of transfer and substitution. In short, they make contact. But what establishes itself is *soul contact* rather than *sight contact* (i.e. eye-line matches), charging the film with a kind of energy that gives the act of vampirism (as well as its complement, the plague) its extended metaphoric significance, reverberating throughout the film. This mutually sustaining symbiosis that mingles love and revulsion with petrified fascination and drifting abandonment, succeeds in taking over the Demeter, her unfortunate crew and the burgers of Wisborg, but also the natural history lesson of the professor, who seems to trace a malevolent genealogy from plant life to animal existence, from carnivorous orchids, polyps, spiders and flies, rats, hyenas and horses, all the way back to the playfulness of a small kitten. But a similarly fatal (food-) chain of eating or being eaten goes from Nina's anxious possessiveness as Harker sets off, to the servility of the peasants, the dangerous hospitality of Nosferatu, the craven dependence of Renfield, the sadistic exploitation of the ship's crew by its master, until it returns full circle with Nina's sacrifice, offering herself to Nosferatu's terrible visitation.

When one looks more closely at the editing, Murnau's style appears distinct and original, if only for the fact that, quite unusually for a German film of the period, *Nosferatu* has over 540 shots. To Alexandre Astruc it seemed as if, with every frame a Murnau film starts anew, suggesting that the director treats an individual scene, and sometimes the single shot itself as a self-sufficient unit: in its formal composition, how it determines figure movement, what gestures it elicits.[48] To classically trained spectators, this has the effect of slowing the film down, making them wonder not only about the connection between one shot and the next (a link that we are meant to 'fill in' for ourselves), but unsure about what is happening *in* the frame, since often enough, what is shown does not seem to advance the narrative, but depicts an action at the point preceding or following the climactic moment. Thus, when Harker first discovers Nosferatu's crypt full of coffins, the scene is edited in a way that makes us unsure of what it is exactly that Harker has seen, and how much of what he has seen he has in fact taken in. Murnau here relies on breaking the rules of continuity editing and above all (in a scene so crucially concerned with 'seeing') he almost completely avoids using point-of-view shots of Harker.[49] Instead, the impression is that it is Nosferatu who watches Harker, even though the vampire, his eyes closed and hands folded, lies dead in his coffin.[50] Disconcerting as this may be, it draws the spectators – those willing to see with their inner eye as well – into what Rohmer and others have called Murnau's imaginary space, one following a different logic of spatial disposition and temporal succession.[51] Although almost always taking its cue from the perceived sensible world, it finds its emotional focus in the urgency of a desire, an obsession, an anxiety or a wish, but one perhaps needs to distinguish this 'dream logic' from the unhinging subjectivity connoted by the painted sets, shadow play and distorted angles of *Dr Caligari*, *Warning Shadows* or *Waxworks*. Murnau instead eliminates, pares away and *under*plays what Expressionist *mise-en-scène* strains to display, overplay and double (with its shadows, for instance). A shadow in Murnau absorbs the figure casting it, registering, in the famous silhouetting shots of *Nosferatu* or *Tartuffe*, a trace, a physical absence and temporal deferral, rather than connoting the oppressive presence of the *Doppelgänger*.

Such hollow voids or spaced gaps come into existence (mostly outside and beyond what the images actually show) because narration keeps the action purposefully unspecific as to its time frame, equivocating about what happens when and in what sequence, and most importantly, by a skilful vacillation about who is active and who is passive, who agent and who patient. Hence, several causal chains seem to exist side by side, interlaced with each other by a complex, and at first sight disorienting alternation between different action spaces and locations. To take one of the most striking examples: as Harker makes his return on horseback, and Nosferatu smuggles himself into the ship's hold and into Wisborg, we see shots of Nina at the seaside, longing for the return of her beloved. This cross-cutting between Harker, Nosferatu and Nina is not for reasons of suspense, at least not in the way one normally understands it, when faced with an agonising will-he?/won't-he? situation, or when witnessing the proverbial race-to-the-rescue. It repeats the editing rhythm of a previous scene that is even more striking: Harker, terrified by the approaching vampire, presses himself against the side of his bed, and Murnau cuts to Nina, back in Wisborg, starting up from a nightmare. Is she dreaming what we are seeing? As if he had heard her silent scream, Nosferatu ceases to advance towards Harker and abruptly turns around, looking off-frame to the right. Cut back to Nina, now sleepwalking, advancing to the left and extending her arms in a gesture of welcome. To whom is it addressed? Is it to Harker or the vampire? The logic of the imaginary space constructed by the editing implies the latter, intimating a fatal attraction and anticipating the final embrace. What Murnau builds up in such scenes is a kind of architecture of secret affinities, too deep or too dreadful for the characters to be aware of, and even for us, happening only at the edge of perception, but none the less lodging in the spectator, too, that attraction swinging between horror and fascination that the vampire exerts on the protagonists.

This uneasy balance of incommensurability also applies to the hero's initial situation, the founding moment of the narrative and its lack, which has explicitly economic as well as sexual overtones: Harker undertakes his journey to Transylvania in order to make money and improve his prospects for advancement in his firm. His ambitions entail ignoring the entreaties of his bride, from whose sexuality and domesticity (flowers, the cat and kittens) he seems positively anxious to escape. The journey thereby has all the signs of a necessarily devious detour: if the economic motif, doubled by the sexual one, splits the couple, Nosferatu unites them, in the characteristic structure of the wish-fulfilling fairy-tale, where the constitutive lack is being overcompensated by the emergence of another force, another order of being, displaying a different degree of intensity. But underneath this compensatory function of Nosferatu giving the couple what they do not know they lack, all the characters are closely meshed and interwoven: Renfield, the estate agent, manipulates Jonathan, but he is himself the tool of Nosferatu, who in turn comes under the power and influence of Nina, who thereby closes the gap of her anxiety/frustration about not being able to exert influence on Harker. In the battle between the sexes, both partners call upon Nosferatu as their sorcerer's apprentice, and both get more than they bargained for. But in another sense, the protagonists are important to the narrative only in so far as they can enter into such substitute relationships. More explicitly than in almost any other film of the German fantastic, *Nosferatu* is the enactment of a deal, a bargain, an exchange, where there is a peculiar incon-

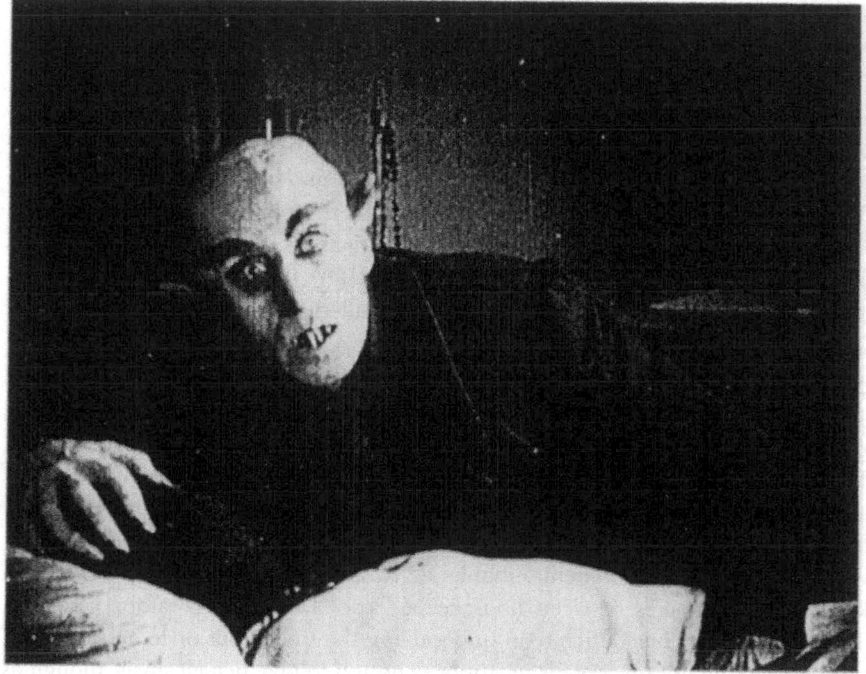

Figure 16 Surprised by the Light: Max Schreck as the demon lover in *Nosferatu* (1922)
Source: BFI films: stills, posters and designs

gruity about the entities being exchanged. One scene especially makes this explicit. As the Count is about to sign the papers, Harker accidentally (?) displays/exhibits the medallion that bears the image of Nina. Nosferatu grasps it, and it is this image, which is being exchanged between the men, that is substituted for money that would otherwise seal the deal. In a business based on real-estate, Nosferatu acquires a view of Nina (the house is nothing to him but an observation post) and Harker gains social status (for having a Count as his client). If Nosferatu is Harker's double, in so far as Nina acquires the lover that Harker seems so reluctant to be, the 'undeadness' of desire is shown to have social consequences: Nosferatu brings with him the plague, itself seen as the reverse side of trade, or at least, this particular kind of trade: for Nosferatu is both captain and cargo, producer and product. All three protagonists thus belong together and share a secret affinity because each is both active and passive, instigator and victim, caller and called upon: just as it befits the status of agency in such a drama of death, undeath and desire as enacted by *Nosferatu.*

Tartuffe: dissembling hypocrisy?

Nosferatu, produced by an independent firm, owes much to the exceptional artistic as well as financial commitment from Albin Grau, who was responsible for the scenery and the costumes, but seems to have been the driving force behind the production.[52] By contrast, *Tartuffe* appears to have been a reluctant commission for Murnau. Since UFA had Jannings under contract, Pommer, after the success of *The Last Laugh*, wanted to exploit the box-office potential of this winning team. Murnau, from his point of view, was keen to be given *Faust*, which had initially been promised to Ludwig Berger, UFA's third star director, and who is still credited with the original manuscript, called 'The Lost Paradise'. A deal was struck, and Murnau agreed to shoot *Tartuffe*. Once one makes allowances for what must have seemed an ingenious solution to the problem of filming the classic Molière play, namely the addition of a framing story, Murnau's film within the film is exquisitely crafted. In the tale, a young man, in order to persuade his uncle that he is being robbed by his housekeeper, disguises himself as a showman and screens in his travelling cinema the story of Tartuffe, a pious bigot, who tries to cheat his friend Orgon of his worldly goods. Although not without some comic moments, thanks to Rosa Valetti as the shrewish housekeeper, the analogies between housekeeper and Tartuffe are rather laboured. The nephew, too, has difficulty in undeceiving the uncle, but once he throws off his disguise, the housekeeper is incautious enough to give herself away, though as Willy Haas pointed out at the time, her deception is quite different from that of Tartuffe, further weakening the parallels.

Tartuffe's misogyny, especially regarding the older woman, resembles the unfavourable depiction of the various harridans in *The Last Laugh*. Perhaps the dowdy moral of the wrapping, so to speak, helps to give the diamond inside the extra sparkle, according to the stylistic principle of counterpoint Murnau was fond of elaborating in most of his films. The sluttish household of the uncle, which so upsets the nephew, is contrasted with the palatial residence of Orgon, and the down-to-earth peasant venality of the housekeeper is split between the highly strung and nervous anxiety of Elmira and Tartuffe's oily obsequiousness. To convey how pleased Tartuffe is with himself and his wily impersonation of piety, Murnau lets Jannings perform little intricate moments of servility and grave concern. Tartuffe's self-delight starkly contrasts with Elmira's self-disgust, who, as Orgon's faithful wife, makes herself the bait in order to expose Tartuffe's cupidity. Having to endure the sight of his gross appetites (culinary and sexual), she almost faints from nausea, but perseveres, in order to eventually unmask the lecherous hypocrite.

But this question of who is unmasking whom, in what order and to what purpose is indeed one of the most puzzling aspects of the film and irritating for a reviewer like Kracauer, but a possible source of interest in the present context, in which duality, duplicity and the relation between 'hypocrisy', self-reference and irony are examined. For Kracauer, the film is doubly symptomatic: it simulates content by an excess of technique and is thus typical of what he calls the 'paralysis' of the stabilising period of the Weimar Republic between 1924 and 1929. As with his account of *Dr Caligari*, he sees the fact that Mayer had written a 'framing' story as a 'fudge' and compromise, indicative of vacillation and indecision. But he also has a second objection, directed at Murnau: 'This *Tartuffe*, far from bringing home hypocrisy to the audience, was itself Tartuffish, for it flattered an audience anxious to leave things in the depths untouched' (Kracauer 1947: 147–8).

Willy Haas, on the other hand, loved the film, and once more appreciated a peculiar tension between Mayer's dramatic conception of Tartuffe as 'elemental', and Murnau's reticent *mise-en-scène* of the Orgon mansion as nobly baroque, counterbalancing, if not containing this irruptive force. Haas calls Jannings 'a single, healthy, indecent belch […] as if the earth itself was emitting gas', and contrasts him to the 'marble goddess' Elmire and the wishy-washy Orgon. The labyrinthine disposition of space made up of staircases, corridors and bedrooms is oppressive when dominated by Tartuffe, but undulating like curtains of lace when the saintly Elmire spins her own spider's web in which to trap Tartuffe. What strikes Haas is that Molière's comedy is now much closer to tragedy because of a strange duplicity: Murnau lets the spectator glimpse a more 'psychological' constellation, in which Tartuffe 'deep down' is a fanatically austere ascetic, who tragically cannot resist female beauty, the lure of Orgon's wealth, and his own dammed-up libido. Orgon is a gutless and impotent pedant, and Elmire the 'subconscious' seductress. Luckily, Haas, concludes, Murnau does not give in to this temptation of 'turning Molière on his head', but the cat is out of the bag, so to speak, because he adds, half-apologetically, that Molière is after all not Shakespeare, whose Shylock we now cannot imagine other than as a tragic figure.[53] This dual focus on hypocrisy seems to me intriguing and illuminating. It once more shows a Murnau ironically distancing himself from his primary source, at the same time as he seems willing to implicate himself in a play of reversals that is just a-symmetrical enough to be uncanny and unsettling – too unsettling for Kracauer, at any rate – yet it is able to sustain the formal *mise-en-abyme* also on the moral and psychological plane. Or as Haas put it: shaking one's head in disbelief is, after all, not the least plausible form of understanding.

Faust: portfolio film for Hollywood or travelogue for Germany?

As so often with big-budget productions in the 1920s, *Tartuffe* was the film with which UFA inaugurated one of its refurbished luxury cinema – in this case, the Gloria Palast in Berlin. Its film-within-a-film metaphor was therefore more than usually apt. The premiere of the film and the inauguration of the Gloria were themselves set in a frame by a prologue on the opening night, in which the star of the film, Lil Dagover performed 'live' with a group of dancers and a full-size orchestra.[54] The peculiarly performative character of these UFA *Großfilme* within metropolitan culture, and the multimedia strategies of their domestic or international exploitation are a good index of the German film industry's growing self-confidence. UFA increasingly adopted production concepts similar to those of its US rivals – or at least tried to: the background to Murnau's last German film *Faust* (1926) is a reminder that UFA could and did overreach itself, though as so often with apparent failures, they are, with hindsight, sometimes more instructive than successes. Murnau, as indicated, was a 'corporate' director, in the sense of being entrusted with prestige productions. Already with *Phantom* in 1922, made to celebrate the sixtieth birthday of Germany's then best-known novelist and playwright, Gerhart Hauptmann, Murnau had been assigned a high-profile 'national' film. But *Faust* was rather different in scale. Along with Lang's *Die Nibelungen* (1922–4) and *Metropolis* (1926–7), *Faust* was not only in subject matter a 'national' production, it also became the outstanding technical achievements of the Weimar cinema, with such a dazzling display of special effects that it remained unsurpassed until Stanley Kubrick's *2001 – A Space Odyssey*, almost fifty years later. Faust's aerial voyage, the miniaturisation of the sets, and a host of other, no less impressive optical and design marvels are an indication of UFA's unique roster of creative personnel and the studio's ambitious aim at surpassing international (i.e. Hollywood) standards, making *Faust* proof positive of the UFA company's determined effort to appear on the world market as equals of the US studios. The cast was to have been international on a grand scale, with Jannings (ahead of Conrad Veidt) the only German actor with a world-wide following and a reputation in the United States. He was also to have been the only German among the principals: Gösta Ekmann as Faust was imported from Sweden, Yvette Guilbert came from France, and as Gretchen, Pommer had signed Lilian Gish. Or so he thought: Gish insisted on a Hollywood cameraman, Charles Rosher, but both the unions and Pommer balked. At the last minute, Camilla Horn replaced Gish as Gretchen. She had first come to Murnau's notice as Lil Dagover's double on *Tartuffe*, and her Gretchen role, ironically enough, even secured her a (brief) contract with United Artists.

Besides the international cast, the other key ingredient of the film was to be its 'Germanness'. This was not necessarily that evoked by Goethe, and more by Gothic: the film attempted to reinvent a typically 'medieval' Germany, or rather, that of the Reformation, of half-timbered houses, steep cobbled streets in crooked townscapes, of mountain ranges and valleys, deep forests and waterfalls. In other words, a tourist Germany, but one sufficiently saturated with art-historical markers to make it plausible that the whole Northern Renaissance from Albrecht Dürer to Lukas Cranach, from Mattias Grünewald to Albrecht Altdorfer would be called upon to provide the authenticating iconography.

Despite the setback with the leading lady, the international marketing strategy was partially successful, and the film, while not the expected blockbuster, performed nowhere near as catastrophically as *Metropolis* the following year. Here, the new technology of special effects showed its efficacy in perfectly

Figure 17 Cutting a dashing Prince of Darkness: Emil Jannings in F.W. Murnau's *Faust* (1926)

Source: BFI films: stills, posters and designs

mimicking any desired style of painting, architecture or decor, not only Germanic or Gothic, because, improving on the manner of the early 1920s episode films, *Faust* was conceived as a time-travel travelogue, sending Faust on voyages through time and space. Well before the era of mass air travel, it took him on a plane trip and a space voyage, and introduced him to splendidly foreign settings, like the Renaissance Court of Parma. Journalist after journalist filed behind-the-scenes reports. Taken on an UFA studio tour in 1925, Siegfried Kracauer watched some of the special effects being tested:

> The[ir] evocative powers […] lend themselves particularly well to the domain of the supernatural. [*Faust*] uses them extensively. In a hall [i.e. a studio stage] previously employed by pirates for their life of thievery, the planet Earth now expands *en miniature*. Faust will fly through the air from one backdrop to another. A wooden roller coaster that curves down to the valley describes his aerial itinerary. The camera glides down the chute and, thanks to expert guidance, spews forth images of the journey. Fog made of water vapour produced by a steam engine

> envelops the range of appropriately sculpted mountain peaks from which Faust emerges. For the horrible crash of the foaming deluge, some water is sprayed through a side canyon. The wild urges subside when the wheat covering the fields and meadows beneath the jagged, pine-covered summits rustles in the wind of the propeller. Cloud upon cloud wafts eastward, masses of spun glass in dense succession. Upon Faust's landing, huts surrounded by greenery will most likely shimmer in the blazing, high-wattage glow of the evening sun.[55]

UFA's self-advertising effect was to present to the world a sort of 'portfolio' of the German film industry as state-of-the-art, and of Germany as ready to receive tourists: another secret affinity of modern technology and romantic longing. Not least for these very reasons – the calculatedly commercial nature of the enterprise, its blatantly 'painterly' style, and the barrage of special effects, the German critics were scathing. Predictably, they snorted with contempt at the kitsch travesty of German art, and the sacrilege of turning the complex drama of Goethe's two-part play of enlightenment faith in perfectibility coming up against fallible human nature, and still affirming the hope of salvation, into a middling 'opera' libretto. The script, written by Hans Kyser, an experienced screenwriter, cut back the drama to the scope of Gounod's opera, adding motifs from both Marlowe and the chapbook Faust, and confining Goethe's contribution mainly to expanding on the tragic love story of Gretchen. Dr Faust, unable to accept the fact that all his science cannot rescue his home town from the plague, signs a pact with the devil. But his miraculous powers of healing only make him more suspect to the crowd, and he is forced to flee. After many an adventure, he meets Gretchen, seduces her and leaves. Accused of murdering her child, Gretchen is condemned to die at the stake. There, Faust curses his thirst for youth, is changed back into an old man, and seeks out Gretchen through the fire and smoke. He promises to die by her side, and with this act of love, Faust saves both her soul and his own, leaving Mephisto, as in the prologue, to haggle once more with the Archangel.

Given that the critics seemed to be looking for content and denounced the form, while the film industry was interested in form, taking the content primarily as a way of showing off the form, the example of *Faust* would offer some parallels to the situation with *The Student of Prague*, discussed in an earlier chapter, where Paul Wegener and Guido Seeber tried to find the right story material to show off their special effects. If one therefore sees *Faust* as an anthology of stylistic features, studio high-tech and a celebration of cinema as magic around partly rather conventional and partly fashionably fanciful story material, it also confirms that among German film directors, no less than among the cameramen and designers, an almost scientific interest in experimentation existed, exploring visual effects and technical possibilities for their own sake, but also encouraged by Pommer because of sound economic reasons, as the medium- and long-term R&D investment of UFA. At first glance, Murnau is an unlikely candidate for such an attitude. According to one of his chief cameramen, Karl Freund, Murnau rarely looked through the view-finder himself.[56] He had little interest in the nuts-and-bolts of film technology and was awkward with his hands. Jim Shepard, in his *Nosferatu in Love* has a brief account of the subject:

> [Karl Freund's] working habits are as ordered as his equipment. During a break once, I [i.e. F.W. Murnau] watched him take a delicate shutter apart. This was of special interest to me because, as a young man, I too had taken a shutter apart, and knew what to expect. I had removed the screws from the front and lifted off the top, whereupon the entire internal economy of the shutter exploded in my face and scattered across the floor.[57]

Yet there can be little doubt that Murnau, besides his prodigious visual imagination and his preternaturally acute sense of framing and camera movement, possessed a lively interest and his own kind of mastery of the special effects so astonishingly on display in several of his films. In *Faust*, for instance, right from the opening moments, when during the prologue in heaven, the Archangel appears and light pierces the clouds as if we were witnessing creation itself (pipes were installed to blow jets of steam against a backdrop, lit by a battery of anti-aircraft searchlights), the spectacle is meant to enthral all the senses.[58]

How is it possible to account for this duality between the 'all-thumbs dreamer' and the 'all-out demon' of the special effects department? Klaus Kreimeier has pointed to Murnau's experience as a *Luftwaffe* pilot, suggesting that the tender soul had none the less shown a remarkable appetite for the 'storms of steel', thus conforming in his sensibility of high Romantic with a taste for modern technology to the type of aristocratic German dandy, most famously embodied during the Weimar years by Ernst Jünger.[59] In fact, the obsession with gliding camera movements and intricate spatial set-ups, confirming that the 'unfettered camera' is now associated as much with Murnau as with Karl Freund, does suggest some analogies with Murnau's perception of the curved space and unbounded vistas as experienced by a pilot. Jim Shepard, drawing cunningly on Paul Virilio, has his Murnau rhapsodise about flying almost in the manner of Saint-Exupery, the author of *The Little Prince*:

> He began to understand flight as a new manner of perception: whereas the old way had been to look from a stationary point at objects before you, here you moved *through* and swept *across* the image. The act of taking aim was itself a geometrification of seeing, by technically aligning ocular perception along an imaginary axis. The French called it *ligne de foi*, the faith line. What sort of image could the photographer record with such an advantage? What sort of image could the *motion picture* record?
>
> (Shepard 1998: 62)

The most ingenious approach to Murnau, the Faust with two souls stirring in his breast, however, is that chosen by Eric Rohmer, when in his study of *Faust*, he posits the existence of two films in one: that of the studio or the international film industry, and that of the modernist Murnau, tackling some very specific, apparently technical, but ultimately metaphysical problems of space and spatial organisation. In one of the most lucid and captivating studies of an individual film, Rohmer, as one film director about another, details the logic of spatial organisation in the film with almost delirious diagrams, showing the kind of movement in several dimensions underpinning especially the much-maligned Gretchen scenes. From another vantage point, of course, Rohmer splits the problem in two, 'rescuing' in classically *Cahiers du cinéma* fashion the true *auteur* from the exigencies of the industry, exploiting but ultimately failing to prostitute his profligate genius.

Murnau, masculinity and the homosocial subtext

What if one does not altogether follow Rohmer in this act of over-identification? How 'personal', for instance, was the stake that Murnau had in his films? Given that he lived for his films, was prepared to leave behind not only his native country, but also cancelled his contract with Fox in Hollywood, one can assume that there was a very powerful drive at work, and in light of his last film, *Tabu*, it is not altogether improbable to assume that part of this drive was erotic, if not directly sexual. Ever since Lotte Eisner, in *The Haunted Screen* remarked on the guilt feelings Murnau had about his homosexuality and the pressures he was under from very homophobe German legislation,[60] the issue of sexuality in Murnau's films has been on the agenda, notably his intense, but highly ambivalent representations of bodily presence and physical beauty. Some, for instance, have seen *Tabu* as Murnau's intimate film diary and the ultimate home movie: beautiful bodies diving into the deep for pearls, darting canoes, languid and yearning limbs stretched out or embracing.[61] But in its distillation of a sombre, ominous and uncanny mood out of daytime heat, empty landscapes and restrained framing, *Tabu* is a companion film to *Nosferatu*, with the old priest of *Tabu* impartially but implacably pursuing the young couple, thereby fulfilling a rather similar dramatic and visual function as the vampire. The French surrealists admired *Nosferatu* mainly for its eroticism, contrasting the anodyne puppy love of Nina and Harker with Nosferatu's necrophiliac lust, musty and potent at once, exuding the aroma of dank crypts and leathery flesh.[62] As with the example from *Tartuffe* discussed earlier, these moments have in common the sense that revulsion and fascination with bodily pleasures and bodily excesses are difficult to keep apart. When Tartuffe is finally alone with Elmira in her bedroom, the scene makes explicit a lewdness and gross indecency which, in the very similar constellation of Nosferatu visiting Nina, is symbolistically underplayed and estranged by the uncanny naturalism Murnau is able to extract from this most unnatural encounter.[63]

Comparing *Nosferatu* and *Sunrise*, Robin Wood has argued that sexuality itself is branded in Murnau's films as the source of evil.[64] Nosferatu, according to him, stands for carnal desire in general (in the tradition of vampires, he lusts after male and female victims), and so Nina, expressing that mixture of desire, curiosity and horror so typical of the film, must die along with Nosferatu. The vamp (!) in *Sunrise* is Nosferatu's soulmate: both are depicted as strong, active, unnatural, night-time creatures, in contrast to the domesticated females, but also when compared to the naive males, who can transgress or be tempted, but, like the youthful heroes of Germanic legend, always preserve their innocence. One could amplify Wood's reading by way of a gender-complement, the barely disguised misogyny in several of Murnau's films, where women exercise a kind of diabolical power and embody everything that takes from a male his dignity and self-esteem. For instance, the Baroness Safferstädt, demanding a 'crime' from her lover as proof of his devotion (*Schloß Vogelöd*), the monstrous housekeeper in the framing story of *Tartuffe*, to complement the vamp from the city in *Sunrise*. The tenement block in *The Last Laugh* is a nightmare of chattering, spying, deriding, castrating matrons, which makes the dualism in the doorman's soul, represented by his authoritarianism when in uniform and his abject submission when it is taken away (by a stiff matron, in charge of huge cupboards of starched linen) merely the internalised extension of the opposition between tenement house and hotel washroom, which – paradoxically, given its social status – turns out to be a haven of male friendship and solicitude. These now all-too-readable references to a prime site of homosexual desire all but subvert the film's 'humanitarian' or sociocritical message. As with the improbable plot premise (a doorman in a plush hotel would never do a porter's job, Fritz Lang is said to have derisively remarked, when he heard about the story his colleague was shooting on the adjacent lot) and the so-called 'tacked-on' happy ending, such perversely wish-fulfilling fantasies would seem to have their roots in a narcissistic childhood idea of omnipotence, culminating in a homoerotic scenario, in which the doorman and the night watchman ride off as the perfect couple, with the young beggar boy they have just picked up as their 'son' in tow.

In some ways, the love triangles in *Nosferatu* also could be read in a way that brings out their hesitating, reversible ambivalence. For instance, the relation Renfield–Jonathan–Nosferatu is similar to a number of other representations of homosexuality in German films from the immediate post-war period, of which the best known is probably Richard Oswald's *Anders als die Anderen*, in which a young Conradt Veidt is seduced by an older man, played by Reinhold Schünzel.[65] One way, therefore, of interpreting the initial situation in *Nosferatu* would be to see the film superimpose two kinds of scenarios, one developing around the explicitly homosexual relationship between Nosferatu and Renfield, and the other around the befriending of Harker by Renfield, whereupon the older man introduces a younger friend to a very 'experienced' queen. The same could be said of the protagonists in *Faust*: are Mephisto and Faust not also a couple, especially on their extravagant travel adventures, and could one not argue that the emphasis placed in the film on the tragedy of Gretchen merely highlights the homoerotic bonding it is meant to camouflage?[66] Is the 'excessiveness' of the Faust–Gretchen part, commented upon and heavily criticised, not, as so often in Weimar cinema, a sign that something else remains in hiding, and thus marks the textual body with the energy of disavowal?

But how 'autobiographical' were these (con)sensual or anxious ambivalences? For a novelist like Jim Shepard, they are crucial to his empathetic creation of a tale of sorrow and guilt, love, longing and self-abjection. In *Nosferatu in Love* Murnau's creativity seems to need grief as a protective armour behind which it feeds on lascivious thoughts furtively indulged. On the other hand, Siegfried Kracauer was not the first critic to suggest that Weimar narratives in the 1920s

Figure 18 More Goldwyn than Goethe? The Eternal Female in *Faust* (1926)

Source: BFI films: stills, posters and designs

were symptomatic of a predicament in male self-images and male sexuality: *From Caligari to Hitler* (1947) gives this theme of damaged masculinity its fullest iconographic and psychoanalytic reading, not least by tying it to a sociopolitical analysis of the authoritarian personality and the vanishing of paternal authority. As discussed in an earlier chapter, the stories preferred by 'Expressionist' cinema (whether scripted by Carl Mayer, Thea von Harbou, Henrik Galeen or Hans Kyser) focus on male crises of identity (signalled in the motif of the double) and toy with bi-sexuality (love triangles in which the two males are usually 'best friends' and show an obvious, sometimes fatal, but rarely verbalised attraction for each other). In this respect, Murnau's films are neither an exception nor are they unusually explicit. For instance, in its imperious demand for tragic sacrifice from everyone, *Der Gang in die Nacht* is typical for that strain of masochistic melodrama which Kracauer has identified as part of Weimar cinema's frequent gestures of male abjection. Doubles abound in Murnau as they do in other directors, whether by way of disguise (*Schloß Vogelöd*, *Tartuffe*) or across a split male character (*Faust* old and young, *The Last Laugh* at the hotel and at home, the hero of *Phantom* timid by day, a criminal at night). Likewise, there are several crucial films, where a pure, almost asexual love is threatened or destroyed by the intrusion of another male's predatory attentions – to the man (Nosferatu/Harker, Wigottschinski/Lubota in *Phantom*, Mephisto/Faust, Tartuffe/Orgon, Hitu/Matahi in *Tabu*). But these depictions could be ranged side by side with the troubled male–male relations to be found in, for instance, *Variety*, *Danton*, *Metropolis*, all the way to *The Threepenny Opera* and *Berlin Alexanderplatz*.

Thus, if there is displacement of (hetero-)sexuality in many Weimar films into anguished looks, sexually more potent doubles, and mirror images reflecting the repressed, darker sides of male desire in Weimar Cinema, this complex would then be more than the cultural background against which Murnau's representations of beauty and eroticism might have to be seen. If his films carry some special secret message (about Murnau the man) in the narratives, it is unlikely to be about a love that dare not speak its name, but rather of passions that find fulfilment in distance and contemplation, sometimes of an idealised self-image, as in *Faust*, whose hero is seduced chiefly by an image – that of himself as a beautiful young man.[67] This is indeed the moment of a very special *frisson*, an extreme point in Murnau's cinema, so much of which is about mediated desire, desire of an image, for an image: the open secret of film making itself, intensely eroticising the very act of looking, but also every object looked at by a camera.

Light and volume

That the world is beautiful when viewed through a lens is the devil's pact to which it seems, our century has as a whole succumbed, and which Murnau's *mise-en-scène* resists, framing the image once more and making the viewer share the very process of metamorphosis. Scenes such as the transformation of Faust from old man to Renaissance prince, or the many dramatic uses to which

Mephisto's cape is put,[68] draw attention to the way Murnau animates the space within the frame. Robert Herlth has given a telling account:

> I had always designed the sets first and drawn in the figures afterwards. But under the influence of Murnau I now began to sketch the people first. We thus came, by our third film, *Faust*, to adapt the space to the actor: for example, Gretchen's mother's room became merely a frame for the robust presence of Dieterle, who was playing Valentin. And Faust's study was not designed as a single room, but, in accordance with the shots, in four separate parts. The hall in *Tartuffe* consisted merely of a wall: its dimensions were suggested by the shape of Jannings walking up and down with his breviary in his hand – all that was needed was an effect of relief. Depth of field, which the specialists made such a fuss about at the time, was to us in this particular case, immaterial.
>
> (Herlth, 'Dreharbeit mit Murnau' in Eisner 1973: 86)

Murnau rarely adopted the habit of staging scenes in depth as practised by the French, nor did he take on the clipped realism of the Americans – with its reliance on shot–countershot, the variations of angle and constant reframing for the sake of keeping up pace and momentum. The German cinema during the 1920s often returned to frontal compositions reminiscent of the (melo-) dramatic tableau. Murnau, however, used the two systems (deep-focus sets, and flat, foreshortened spaces) as contrasting alternatives within the same film (*Phantom*, *The Last Laugh*, *Faust*), thereby extending the emotional space towards the screen: as suddenly as the depth of a frame opened up, it could, in the very next shot, become suffocatingly close and ominously encroach upon the spectator. It was one way that Murnau integrated outdoor photography and natural locations into his psychological interiors. By concentrating much of the emotion on the gaps or distances between the shots, he developed the drama in the implied space that surrounds the frame, always absent and yet always palpable.

Herlth also confirms how crucial Jannings was to the films not only from the commercial angle, but in terms of setting the reference point for the sets, the decor, the dimensionality and depth of space. In films like *The Last Laugh*, *Faust* or *Tartuffe*, Jannings' upright or slumping, sweepingly expansive or furtively lurking though none-the-less always massive bulk contributes the real drama. Yet, as so many critics before and after Rohmer have pointed out, the lighting techniques are crucial if not decisive, because it is the lighting that gives this shape of Jannings not only its volume but also its energy. A good example is the opening scene of *The Last Laugh*, often quoted because of the mobile camera, swooping down the open lift shaft, travelling across the vast lobby, and passing through the glass door into the open, all in (almost) one single shot.[69] However, it is as if this movement is orchestrated by the towering figure standing outside, flailing his arms and hailing taxis with his whistle. And what ties these motions together, animates them from within is the light, falling first on the steel cage of the lift, bouncing off the chandelier in the lobby, its reflections caught in the revolving glass panes, intensifying in the headlights of the approaching cars and finally, emitting the appropriately high note, becoming that sliver of silver which is Janning's whistle. In fact, the main reason why it is pouring with rain in this scene is for the light to catch itself once more in the wet, glistening folds of the doorman's capacious oilskin, before Jannings takes it off to reveal the shimmering gold braid and buttons of his livery.

'Art', Murnau is reported to have told Robert Herlth, 'consists in eliminating, but in the cinema it would be more correct to talk of "masking"'.[70] Murnau seemed to prefer light to come into the frame from a hidden, covered, or unknown source. Alternatively, he liked to exaggerate the effects of a visible light source, such as Mephisto swinging his lantern in *Faust* or the moonlight casting its pallor on the illicit lovers in *Sunrise*. This practice has direct implications about motivation and causality, leaving both ambiguous. It is one of the devices chiefly responsible for 'psychologising' the protagonists (the German speciality), in contrast to the American cinema's concern with motivational realism. Furthermore, it underscores a general tendency in Murnau's films to suspend linear time and turn it into space. In order to suggest the temporal and causal reversibility of the action, for instance, the characters' glances are often isolated, the eye-line matches are subtly de-phased, and figure motion is abstracted, or arrested in mid-thrust. As if the air had become solid, and light itself had turned to matter, its shafts, instead of bringing clarity, are in *Faust* the very force against which the hero has to fight, creating an oddly perverse balancing, in which 'white' connotes mass and aggression, while black is 'light', soft and yielding. 'Rembrandt lighting', when used by directors such as De Mille, in Hollywood practice usually also serves, besides dramatic emphasis, also atmospheric purposes. But in order to naturalise such overtly artificial lighting, it is often motivated in explicitly psychological terms and based on physical verisimilitude, rather than interiorising and spiritualising its effects, as it is in Murnau.

As discussed in an earlier chapter, the lighting developed by German cinematographers like Freund, Wagner and Carl Hoffmann is intent to simulate the tactile values of oil painting. It lends the image the ability to attract the spectator's desire for touch, a desire frustrated not only in the literal sense, but also metaphorically, thanks to the stylisations and the quality of the fetish-object, endowed with a value that exceeds its representational properties and is not connected to its realism. The special kind of luminosity that comes from objects being lit and at the same time radiating light, brings forth the illusion of a special kind of 'essence'. As indicated by Herlth, this not only applies to objects: characters, too, are in Murnau's films often treated no different from other forms for which light models volume and depth, two properties that suggest a special presence, mainly because the light source is so often indirect, shielded or placed off-frame altogether. Lighting thus enacts in the most efficacious manner, and on the plane of perception, the relations that obtain in Murnau's cinema between cause and effect, motivation and meaning, origin and presence: they become substitutable, available for metamorphosis. Herein perhaps lies the secret of Murnau's style, that fluidity of forms, those startling analogies and parallels through which the real world, brilliantly evoked by his cinematographers, becomes none the less a 'forest of symbols', and the chief reason for his reputation as *the* poet of the silent cinema. But at the same time, lighting also embodies the relations that obtain in capitalist society between process and product, labour and value: they, too, become exchangeable. A spectacle of an emanation, an unmotivated presence that trades on behalf of the object as artefact, lighting lends the world of the commodity its semblance of self-sufficiency and autonomy, deciding the 'romantic' issue of the mirror and the lamp in favour of the mirror *as* lamp, and the lamp as the spotlight: heightening the glamour of display.

Absorption and theatricality

Yet it also allows for another reading, perhaps more appropriate to the erotically so polymorphous sensibility of Murnau, and none the less not in conflict with the glamour of display. As Janet Bergstrom has suggested, a 'new erotics of looking' can be discerned in Murnau which transcends or bypasses altogether the male/female polarity implied in seeing/seen, in favour of the veiled gaze of contemplation.[71] This contemplative stance fits well with the slowing down of narrative in Weimar cinema discussed in an earlier chapter, and it contrasts with the harsher rhythm of American-style shot/countershot, point-of-view editing or the cut on action of Lubitsch, Lang and Pabst. Put in more historical terms, Murnau's meditative gaze might allow us to reconsider the cultural debates which Murnau confronted, at least in his German films. It, too, is an intervention in the *Kino-debatte*, taking positions around spectatorship, the cult of distraction, and the relative pressures of narrative and spectacle in Weimar cinema. Yet, while it allows one to come back to Lotte Eisner, and her claim of Murnau being 'influenced' by Caspar David Friedrich or Max Reinhardt, one does so by another route: Murnau stakes a claim in showing how the cinema is beholden neither to literature nor the theatre, working instead with papier-mâché, toy-sets and industrial equipment, in other words, in the idiom of kitsch, to create a world inhabitable by a very special gaze that can oscillate between the illusionist depth of old stereoscopic photographs, and the pictorial flatness of modernism at its most sophisticatedly 'primitive'. Perhaps Murnau remembered the art-historical theories of Wilhelm Worringer's 'abstraction and empathy', or perhaps not. To be against theatricality, or rather, to counteract theatricality by giving the cinema its own distinctive scenic space, was merely to remain within the candour of Weimar cinema's star directors, 'educating' their audience into ways of possessing the world (and being possessed by it) through looking. Which is also where even Murnau's visuality differs from the spectatorship of the fine arts, the contemplative gaze appropriate to a museum or a gallery: Murnau's films from the mid-decade – and the revived reconstructions on large screens make it palpable – deploy the high-tech of UFA to the fullest, where it is a matter of allowing the spectator to enter his space, to inhabit it, being absorbed by the image's several whirlpools of energy. Created by the always changing distribution of light and mass, they make the viewer vertiginously lose balance, disoriented by the depths modulating into pure surface, and surface undulating into unexpected depth.[72]

Because he often kept his story material at arms' length, approaching it with meticulous care, but also with a certain deadpan or wistful irony, Murnau can hardly be called a 'spontaneous' director, keen to capture the fleeting charm of the lived moment, or lingering with his camera on an everyday scene, in the way that French directors might: Feuillade, Epstein or later, Renoir. The will to form, and the drive for abstraction that Murnau shares with Lang make his work sometimes seem remote, as if his figures were indeed already touched by intimations of mortality that the Murnau myth in France projected into them. But as the discussion of his style has tried to show, much of his experimentation with space, volume, light and rhythm was designed to wrest the cinema from the hold that both art history and the stage had had, especially over German art cinema, and to do so, without handing the cinema over to the fascination with the matter-of-factual of *Neue Sachlichkeit* realism, or the constructivist ethos of montage cinema. In this respect, Murnau's films are also about the possibilities of cinema, trying to discover what forms emerge when inherent qualities of the medium – the discontinuity of shot from shot, spatial symmetries or gestural repetitions, alternations and visual echoes – are explored as design features of 'other worlds'. This might give another clue to the secret affinities between romanticism and technology, or rather, a different version of the seeming split, where the paradox could be regarded to have 'resolved' itself into the Faustian 'persona' of two souls in one body for Murnau the man, and the invention of the 'soul of cinematic glamour', for UFA, Fox and film history. If Murnau the man never felt he finally had to decide between the melancholy artist, the effete aristocrat and the military dandy, all of whom he at times styled himself after, it might have been because he trusted his 'masking', his '*extra-dry*', gentlemanly hypocrisy, 'hiding through light'. It allowed objects and people to acquire a glamour that could be read as radiance and spirituality, but which lent itself no less successfully to the seductions of the more canny, knowing glow of the commodity, what disenchanted detractors of *Tartuffe* and especially *Faust* were quick to label as kitsch, while it was also the very sign of a sensibility that secretes its sweetest cinematic poetry only when its aesthetic conscience is most keenly pricked by the fiercest onslaught of technology.

Notes

1 Speaking of Murnau as an enigma has a long history. In a famous essay by Willy Haas from 1925, Murnau emerges as 'unusually cool, every inch the Anglo-Saxon gentleman, *extra-dry*'. Haas ends on a note of slight exasperation: 'there is little that is

private, and what there is does not seem to matter. Shadows are hard to get hold of, even when they are as affable as this one', *Film-Kurier* 228 (28 September 1925).

2 Eisner 1964. This is still the most important study of Murnau's life and work, and the source I am drawing on for much of the biographical information. More recently, a fictionalised biography of Murnau has emphasised the homoerotic side of his personality, calling him *Nosferatu in Love.* See Shepard 1998.

3 Eight films of Murnau are missing presumed lost: *Der Knabe in Blau* (1919), *Satanas* (1919), *Sehnsucht* (1919/20), *Der Bucklige und die Tänzerin* (1920), *Der Januskopf* (1920), *Abend-Nacht-Morgen* (1920), *Gräfin Marizza* (1920/1) and *Die Austreibung* (1923).

4 In 1930, a re-edited sound version was distributed under the title *Die zwölfte Stunde*, and it was often this material that circulated in 16-mm copies in the 1950s and 1960s. In the 1980s, the composer Mauricio Kagel made his own *Nosferatu* on the basis of scenes from Murnau's film.

5 Maurice Scherer (i.e. Eric Rohmer), 'Vanité que la peinture', *Cahiers du cinéma* no. 3 (March 1951); Alexandre Astruc, 'Le feu et la glace', *Cahiers du cinéma* no. 18 (1952); Jean Domarchi, 'Presence de F.W. Murnau', *Cahiers du cinéma* no. 21 (March 1953); and Eric Rohmer, 'Le Celluloid et le marbre: de la métaphore', *Cahiers du cinéma* no. 51 (April 1965).

6 Eric Rohmer, *L'organisation de l'espace dans le Faust de Murnau*, 1980: 39.

7 The revival began with the essay by Maurice Scherer (i.e Eric Rohmer), 'Vanité que la peinture', *Cahiers du cinéma* no. 3 (March 1951), followed by Alexandre Astruc, 'Le feu et la glace', *Cahiers du cinéma* no. 18 (1952), Jean Domarchi, 'Présence de F.W. Murnau', *Cahiers du cinéma* no. (21, March 1953), to consolidate itself with Lotte Eisner's and Charles Jameaux' full-length studies in 1964 and 1965. Eric Rohmer returned to Murnau in 'Le Celluloid et le marbre: de la métaphore', *Cahiers du cinéma* no. 51 (April 1965) and in his book-length study of *Faust.* Jacques Aumont spoke of 'the emergence of a veritable Murnau-myth, in a specific context, shaped by the development of the "politique des auteurs"' (Jacques Aumont, 'Mehr Licht!', in M.Corvin (ed.) *Goethe et les arts du spectacle* (Bron: CERTC, 1985): 267–82, [271]).

8 One of the first to record this change was John Gillett. See his 'Munich's Cleaned Pictures', *Sight and Sound* vol. 47, no. 1 (Winter 1977–8): 37–9.

9 Robert Plumpe Murnau, 'Mon frère Wilhelm', in Eisner 1964: 12.

10 Angela Dalle Vacche has admirably researched Murnau's art-historical studies at the Universities of Berlin and Heidelberg in her *Cinema and Painting* (Austin: University of Texas Press, 1996): 163–6.

11 For biographical information about Murnau's war years, see also Eberhard Spiess (ed.): *Wenn ihr Affen nur öfter schreiben wolltet! Briefwechsel zwischen Friedrich Wilhelm Murnau und Lothar Müthel 1915–1917* (Bielefeld: AJZ-Verlag 1991).

12 This information is from Murnau's mother, cited in Eisner 1964. A slightly different version of events is given by Murnau himself in Hermann Treuner (ed.) *Filmkünstler. Wir über uns selbst* (Berlin, 1928).

13 Hans Ehrenbaum-Degele (1889–1915) was an Expressionist poet who with Else Lasker-Schüler, Robert Meidner and Paul Zech edited the magazine *Das neue Pathos.* See Bernhard Zeller (ed.) *Expressionismus. Literatur und Kunst 1910–1923* (Marbach a.N.: Schiller-Nationalmuseum 1960): 46 and 141–2.

14 *Film-Kurier* (9 July 1920), cited in Dietrich Kuhlbrodt, 'Fast ein Shakespeare: Murnau und seine Zeit', in K. Kreimeier (ed.), *Friedrich Wilhelm Murnau 1888–1988* (Bielefeld: Bielefelder Verlagsanstalt, 1988): 58.

15 The most scurrilous account can be found in Kenneth Anger's *Hollywood Babylon* (New York: Bantam Books, 1981): 245.

16 Lang paid an obituary tribute to Murnau at a ceremony in Berlin in April 1931.

17 See the entries on Murnau in 'Film und Filmleute von heute und morgen' in the fan-magazine *Mein Film* (1926), and in Hermann Treuner (ed.) *Filmkünstler: wir über uns selbst* (Berlin, 1928).

18 When I sit on the steps in front of my house (on Tahiti) and look over the ocean in the direction of Morero, when the sea thunders, wave upon wave, against the reef, [...] then I catch myself at the thought that I wish this was my home! But I'm not at home anywhere – I feel it the more, the older I get – not in any country, not in any house or home, not with any human being.

(Letter to his mother, quoted in Eisner 1964: 210)

19 Robert C. Allen, 'Fox, Murnau and *Sunrise*', *Quarterly Review of Film Studies* 3 (1977): 321–38.

20 They were introduced through Salka Viertel, Murnau's closest friend in Hollywood. 'Greta Garbo long kept Murnau's death mask, the man who had been as lonely as herself' (Eisner 1964): 222.

21 See the special issue on *Sunrise* of *Quarterly Review of Film Studies* 3 (1977), edited by J. Dudley Andrew.

22 For accounts of Murnau's partnership with Flaherty, see Salka Viertel, *Das unbelehrbare Herz* (Reinbek: Rowohlt, 1979): 147–56 and David Flaherty, 'A few reminiscences' *Film Culture* 20 (1959).

23 There are no persistent thematic or literary bonds to tie Murnau's straggling work together. Our notion of the film-director is of a grandiose self-publicist. [...] But Murnau never adhered to that pattern. Tentativeness was one of the keys to his life and work, and it cuts right across the grain of the world in which he worked.

(David Thomson, *A Biographical Dictionary of Film* (New York: Alfred A. Knopf, 1994): 532)

24 See Eisner 1969: 113.

25 Angela Dalle Vacche has argued that the rediscovery of Biedermeier art and especially Friedrich's paintings around 1906 have had an appreciable influence on German Expressionism (Dalle Vacche 1996: 180–2), see note 10 above.

26 When he made *Nosferatu*, he had already seen Sjöström's *The Phantom Carriage* of 1920. [...] But above all, he entertained a love–hate relationship with Maurits Stiller, whose *Sir Arne's Treasure* [1919] he could not but admire.

(Eisner 1964: 96; see also pp. 52–3)

27 See Paolo Cherchi Usai (ed.) *Schiave bianche allo specchio. Le origini del cinema in Scandinavia* (1916–1918) (Pordenone: Edizioni Studio Tesi, 1986).

28 Most notably in *Vampyr* (1930).

29 See Wedel 1996: 105–212.

30 Heide Schlüpmann has worked out the 'gendered' agenda of the film in '*Der Gang in die Nacht*: das Motiv des Blinden und der Diskurs des Sehens im Weimarer Nachkriegskino', in U. Jung, W. Schatzberg (eds) *Filmkultur zur Zeit der Weimarer Republik* (Munich, etc: K.G. Saur, 1992): 38–53.

31 Karl Freund, in particular, tended to downplay Murnau's role, at least in his correspondence with Lotte Eisner (Eisner 1964: 79–82). See also Eberhard Spiess, 'Carl Mayer: ein Filmautor zwischen Expressionismus und Idylle', *Filmblätter* (Frankfurt: Kommunales Kino, 1979): 11.

32 Collier argues that each major Murnau film corresponds to a Wagner opera: *Schloß Vogelöd* resembles *Parsifal*; *Nosferatu* is a take on *The Flying Dutchman*; *The Last Laugh* shows similarities with *Die Meistersinger*; *Sunrise* is Murnau's *Tannhäuser*; and finally, *Taboo* is his *Tristan and Isolde* (Collier 1988: 111–31).

33 See Collier 1988: 106–7.

34 For more biographical information on Mayer, see Bernhard Frankfurter (ed.) *Carl Mayer. Im Spiegelkabinett des Dr Caligari* (Vienna: Promedia, 1997).

35 'Wie ich Murnau kennenlernte', in W. Jacobsen, K. Prümm, and B. Wenz (eds) *Willy Haas, der Kritiker als Mitproduzent* (Berlin: Hentrich, 1991): 115.

36 The detumescence of the doorman in the supervisor's office is not that far from Nosferatu's at dawn in Ellen's bedroom.

37 With *Die Finanzen des Großherzogs*, Harbou wrote one of the least likely Murnau films, one which only recently has turned up again, and over which opinion is still divided: a somewhat improbable comedy that seems to belong more to Lubitsch, with its mistaken identities and cloud-cuckoo-land setting. From a plot summary: 'Hoping to rescue his miniature Mediterranean court from financial ruin, the Grand-duke of Minorca plans to marry the wealthy Grand-duchess Olga. After many intrigues and counterplots, he succeeds, only to discover that he is marrying for love.' One of the restored Murnau films, *Die Finanzen des Großherzogs* was first presented by the Munich Film Museum in 1977. John Gillett, reporting about 'Munich's Cleaned Up Pictures' describes the first viewing:

> The print has clearly been made up from several sources and is still missing some fairly fundamental scenes, but its sporadic progress, ... perhaps added to the fun of a story which seemed to involve, ... stolen letters, ladies in distress and the exploits of a rather thuggish gang with a midget among their numbers. In its use of real locations as a background to these mysterious goings-on, the film looked as though Murnau was paying homage to Feuillade. ... Some quirky characterisation also recalled the master, with a very good-natured performance by Mady Christians as the lady on the run, being made up by the hero to look ugly and so evade her pursuers. Equally fascinating was the early appearance of a genuine built-up Murnau city, all flashing lights, scurrying streetcars and busy hotel foyers, in this case looking ... forward towards *The Last Laugh*, which Murnau was to make immediately afterwards.
>
> (*Sight and Sound* (Winter 1977/78): 39)

Lotte Eisner is less enthusiastic, finding the film 'heavy going', and the acting 'stiff and false', but admits that her disappointment might be due in part to the bad print she had seen.

38 On Thea von Harbou, see Reinhold Kainer, *Thea von Harbou und der deutsche Film bis 1933* (Hildesheim: Olms, 1984).

39 Plot synopsis: The party assembled at the castle Vogelöd finds two uninvited guests in their midst: Graf Johann Oetsch, the brother of the Baroness Safferstädt's first husband, and Faramund, an itinerant monk. The sight of the former so unnerves the Baroness that she asks the latter to hear her confession about her first husband's murder by what she suspects was his own brother. Graf Johann, for his part, claims that Baron Safferstädt murdered his brother. The Baroness, in even greater turmoil, confesses to Father Faramund that, yes, the Baron had shot her first husband because half in jest and testing his devotion, she had wanted a crime, as proof of his love. Father Faramund, however, turns out to be Graf Johann in disguise, come to avenge his brother. The Baron commits suicide and the Baroness, too, drowns herself.

40 Eisner 1969: 12–15, 205–21.

41 Walter Kaul, *Schöpferische Filmarchitektur* (Berlin: Deutsche Kinemathek, 1971) for biographical sketches and background information. The Deutsche Filmmuseum Frankfurt has published studies of Otto Hunte, Walter Reimann and Hans Poelzig. *Kinematograph* 10, 11, 12 (1996–7).

42 For essays and biographical information on Weimar cameramen, see Michael Esser (ed.) *Gleissende Schatten* (Berlin: Hentrich, 1994).

43 Ludwig Berger (1892–1969) was the director, among others, of three of UFA's most commercially successful films of the early 1920s: *Ein Glas Wasser* (1922), *Der Verlorene Schuh* (1923) and *Ein Walzertraum* (1925). Berger went to Hollywood in 1926 on a contract with Paramount, possibly as part of the Parufament Agreement, for between 1927 and 1932 he directed films both in Los Angeles and Berlin. In the 1930s he made several very successful multi-language musical and operetta films, emigrated to the Netherlands in 1940, and returned to film making in West Germany in the 1950s, before becoming a leading director of plays on German television in the 1960s. There is no critical study of Berger, except for a useful collection of materials, with a filmography and bibliography. Hans-Michael Bock and Wolfgang Jacobsen (eds.), *Ludwig Berger* (Hamburg: CineGraph, 1992).

44 Apart from Hitchcock, for whom Murnau was an acknowledged source, directors such as Carl Dreyer, Edgar Ulmer and Frank Borzage have learnt from him. One of the most Murnauesque film dates from 1955, Charles Laughton's *Night of the Hunter.*

45 Most of Murnau's early films were produced by small companies not affiliated with UFA, with names such as Viktoria-Film, Lipow-Film, Helios-Film, Goron-Film, Prana-Film.

46 For a discussion of Murnau's *Phantom* in the context of 'frame tales', see Part I, Chapter 3, this volume, on 'Caligari's family'.

47 Griffith's German and European legacy is touched on above, in the chapter on Fritz Lang (Part II, Chapter 1).

48 Because the production company could not or would not pay royalties to the Bram Stoker estate, the names of the characters were changed, Dracula becoming Count Orlok, Mina Westenra becoming Nina, and Jonathan Harker becoming Thomas Hutter. In most current prints, one finds an inconsistent mix of Stoker's names and the Prana/Galeen cover-versions, often deliberately kept by archival reconstruction to indicate the composite sources of their print.

49 'In Murnau every image demands to be destroyed by that which follows it. Every shot announces its own demise' (Astruc, 'Le feu et la glace', *Cahiers du cinéma* no. 18 (1952): 10.

50 Janet Bergstrom, following Barry Salt, has argued that the Weimar cinema does not respect the basics of continuity editing, such as eye-line matches or 180-degree rules, and therefore cannot be said to 'break its rules'. This overlooks the fact that German audiences would have been perfectly aware of standard Hollywood practice, exposed as they were to American films, which in turn were copied by much of mainstream German cinema, so that, even by 1921, American scene dissection had become the norm. See also the discussion of Fritz Lang *Mabuse* in Part II, Chapter 1 and Pabst's *Pandora's Box* in Part II, Chapter 4.

51 This technique of creating the sense of the uncanny through a dead man's point of view is famously repeated in Carl Dreyer's *Vampyr* (1930), a film that, as indicated, renders homage to Murnau's *Nosferatu* in more than this one scene.

52 Eric Rohmer's remarks are echoed by Dudley Andrew: 'the essential meaning of the film is displaced – it is always elsewhere, and cannot be bound to specific spatial and temporal signifiers' ('The Gravity of *Sunrise*', *Quarterly Review of Film Studies*, 3 (1977): 366).

53 Bouvier and Leutrat, 1981. See also Enno Patalas, 'Arthur Robison – Albin Grau – Ernst Moritz Engert. Drei Schattenfiguren', *FilmGeschichte* 13 (June 1999): 49–53.

54 Jacobsen, Prümm, and Wenz 1991: 166–7 (see note 35 above).

55 Willy Haas, in *Film-Kurier* no. 22 (26 January 1926).

56 'Calico-World', Kracauer [1969] 1995: 284.

57 Eisner, 1964: 81–2.
58 Shepard, 1998: 137.
59 Murnau bent his huge torso down to the tiny, silent scene [the miniature sets] and smiled: 'If Goethe was alive, he would be interested in the movies. More than the writers are today. And he would be especially interested in this film. But everything, manuscript, acting, actors would not engross him half as much as these [special effects], because they are the only thing that would remind him of his own work.'

(Robert Herlth, 'Konturen von F.W. Murnau', *Filmtechnik -Filmkunst* (18 April 1931))

60 Klaus Kreimeier, 'Das Drama und die Formen: Versuch über einen Melancholiker', in Kreimeier 1988: 93. On Ernst Jünger and 'reactionary modernism', see Part IV, Chapter 2 on 'Modernity and modernisation'.
61 Eisner, 1969: 97.
62 A remarkable collection of stereoscopic photographic glass slides has come to light, taken by Murnau between 1921 and 1931. Besides historical buildings, landscapes, street scenes in New York and Chicago (which look like studies for his big city sets in *The Last Laugh* and *Sunrise*), there are male acts photographed in Berlin, Beverly Hills and Polynesia. See Heinrich Gräfenstein, 'Eine Hand aus dem Stereo-Off', *FilmGeschichte* 7/8 (June 1996): 21–3.
63 See Charles Jameux: *F.W. Murnau* (Paris: Editions Universitaires 1965): 26 (= Classiques du Cinéma 19).
64 [Elmira] is Nina once more, offering herself to a monster in order to save her beloved. And Tartuffe, like the vampire, is an image of rapacious, dehumanising lust, the inversion of Orgon's abstinence. Both positions are equally destructive of the true erotic.

(Collier, *From Wagner to Murnau* 1988: 120)

65 Robin Wood, 'Murnau Midnight and Sunrise', *Film Comment* 12/3 (1976): 4–9.
66 On *Anders als die anderen*, see Richard Dyer, *Now You see It. Studies on Lesbian and Gay Film* (London: Routledge, 1990): 7–46.
67 In this Faustian scenario, Hans Ehrenbaum-Degele would be the spurned Gretchen, and the model for Mephisto would be Walter Spies, a painter and musician, who left Murnau and Berlin in 1923 for a Gauguinesque life in the Dutch West Indies. The references in Spies letters from Djakarta to Murnau are comparatively rare, and it seems that the two did not in fact meet up while Murnau was filming *Tabu*. But that Murnau remained close to Spies is evident from the fact that he bought Spies' paintings and in his testament, left Spies a substantial sum. See Walter Spies, *Schoenheit und Reichtum des Lebens* [an autobiography in letters and memoirs ed. by Hans Rodius] (The Hague, 1994): 183, 296–7, 340.
68 Janet Bergstrom, 'Sexuality at a Loss. The Films of F.W. Murnau', *Poetics Today* 6/1-2 (1985): 185–203.
69 The capacious cape is, of course, like the Roman toga, a useful topic for speculation on masculinity, homoeroticism and the cinema, from Robin Hood and Dracula to Zorro and Batman.
70 For a detailed description of this scene, see Klaus Kreimeier, 'Wie in einem Taumel', in Esser 1994: 28–32.
71 Bergstrom 1985: 201.
72 In its ambivalences of pictorial dispaly, one might usefully discuss Murnau in the light of Michael Fried's distinction between 'absorption' and 'theatricality', as he relates it to nineteenth-century French painting, but extends it to formulate fundamental principles of art and spectatorship. Michael Fried, *Absorption and Theatricality, Painting and the Beholder in the Age of Diderot* (Los Angeles and Berkeley: University of California Press, 1980).

4

LULU AND THE METER MAN

Louise Brooks, G.W. Pabst and *Pandora's Box*

Itinerary of a Lost One

G.W. Pabst's *Die Büchse der Pandora* (*Pandora's Box,* 1928–9) has become one of the truly famous films of Weimar cinema, standing – along with *The Blue Angel* – in some sense paradigmatically for the period's twin identity around modernity and decadence, self-assured glamour and anxious descent into chaos. Yet for several decades after 1945, the film was practically unavailable, except as one of the very special treasures of Henri Langlois's Cinematheque in Paris. The star of the film, Louise Brooks, an actress from Wichita, Kansas was to have one of the most enigmatic careers in film history.[1] After the release of the two films she made with Pabst (the other one being *Tagebuch einer Verlorenen* (*Diary of a Lost One*), 1929) she became a Paris cult figure in 1930, but when she returned to Hollywood in the mid-1930s, she virtually ceased appearing in films, and literally became a 'lost one'. Langlois's infatuation with Louise Brooks caused him to feature a huge enlargement of her face – by then scarcely known to anyone – at the entrance to his 1955 exhibition, 'Sixty Years of Cinema':

> Those who have seen her can never forget her. She is the modern actress par excellence because, like the statues of antiquity she is outside of time. ... She is the intelligence of the cinematographic process, she is the most perfect incarnation of photogenie; she embodies in herself all that the cinema rediscovered in its last years of silence: complete naturalness and complete simplicity.
>
> (quoted in Card, 1958: 241)

Among those who could never forget Louise Brooks after Langlois's screening of her films was Jean-Luc Godard, paying homage to Lulu in *Vivre sa vie* (1962)[2] and James Card, curator of film at the George Eastman House, Rochester. He went in search of Louise Brooks in New York, found her in almost squalid circumstances and brought her to live in Rochester on a small Eastman House stipend.[3] While he encouraged her to write and take an interest in her own past, he also tracked down and restored *Pandora's Box*, so that we now, too, possess (in order to be possessed by) the 'image' of Lulu in this film as it had been seen by her first audience.

Pandora's Box was not a commercial success, and in the United States, for instance, only a cut and censored version was briefly in circulation,[4] at a time when the new phenomenon of the talkies eclipsed and consigned to oblivion many of the more outstandingly modern films of the last of the silent period. In Germany the film was widely known and discussed, but Pabst was attacked on several fronts. Even his most consistent supporter Harry M. Potamkin was disappointed and found the film 'atmosphere without content'.[5] A Berlin newspaper wrote about Louise Brooks's performance: 'Louise Brooks cannot act. She does not suffer, she does nothing'.[6] Alfred Kraszna-Krausz tried to prove Pabst's shortcomings as an adaptor of Wedekind's plays and complained about the film industry's general temerity of turning a literary classic into a silent film with nothing but laconic intertitles:

> Lulu is inconceivable without the words that Wedekind makes her speak. These eternally passion-laden, eruptive, undiscriminating, hard, unsentimental and unaffected words stand out clearly against her figure. […] The film is unable to reproduce the discrepancy between Lulu's outward appearance and her utterance.[7]

This assessment is in turn contradicted by Siegfried Kracauer who writes in *From Caligari to Hitler*:

> A failure it was, but not for the reason most critics advanced. […] The film's weakness resulted not so much from the impossibility of translating [the] dialogue into cinematic terms, as from the abstract nature of the whole Wedekind play. […] Pabst blundered in choosing a play that because of its expressive mood belonged to the fantastic post-war era rather than the stabilizing period.[8]

The almost unanimously unfavourable response to the film is interesting in several respects. Even if we can assume special pleading on the part of the literary establishment busy safeguarding its own territory,[9] the various complaints outline an ideologically and aesthetically coherent position: one that goes right to the heart of the film's special interest within Weimar attitudes to sexuality, class and the representation of women in literature and the visual arts. For the passages quoted are indicative of a resistance that, on the one hand, has to do with the difference between literary language and body language ('utterance/appearance'), reminiscent of discussions in feminist theory and psychoanalysis between speaking and being spoken to as a subject in discourse.[10] On the other hand, there is an evident irritation that Louise Brooks is neither active ('she does nothing') nor actively passive ('she does not suffer'), by which critics compare unfavourably one kind of body – that of cinematic representation – with another – the expressive body of the theatre performance. Contrast this with Langlois's 'Her art is so pure that it becomes invisible': praise that implies a diametrically opposite visual aesthetic. Furthermore, Pabst's choice of an American actress for the part caused consternation among German film stars. It gives the issue a further dimension if one considers his decision within the large-scale emigration of German film makers to Hollywood, the economic difficulties of the German film industry after the 1927 crash and especially the enterprising production company, Nero's bid to break, behind UFA's back, so to speak, into the American market.[11] But ideological attitudes towards America also played their part. Louise Brooks recalls a telling incident:

> As we left the theatre [after the opening of a UFA film, at the Gloria Palast] and Pabst hurried me through a crowd of hostile movie-goers, I heard a girl saying something loud and nasty. In the cab I began pounding his knee, insisting 'What did she say? What did she say?' Finally he translated 'That's the American girl who is playing our German Lulu!'
>
> (Brooks 1982: 95)

Kracauer's comments about the material belonging to the 'fantastic' period of Weimar cinema somewhat simplify this ideological–competitive move and countermove between 'Berlin' and 'Hollywood', reducing it to a juxtaposition of Expressionism and the *Neue Sachlichkeit* (New Objectivity).[12] But as so often, Kracauer did recognise a crucial tension in the film, even if, by calling Pabst's choice a 'blunder', he overlooks the extent to which the film actively re-interprets the inner relationship between Expressionism and *Neue Sachlichkeit.* For this 'American Lulu' gives Pabst a vantage point on *both* Expressionism *and* the *Neue Sachlichkeit*, as well as on the fundamental shift that the cinema (compared to the theatre) has brought to the representation of sex and class, libidinal and political economy.

In the following, it is the nexus of sexuality and class in *Pandora's Box* that will be the focus, but in relation to a certain 'zero degree' of mimicry and appearance. My argument will be that the cinema since the 1920s has mediated but also inflected the meaning ascribed to 'seeming' and 'being', changing their function as 'attributes' of identity – including those of 'national identity'. For perhaps the single most striking characteristic of Weimar culture was its 'cult of surface appearances', understood as a radical opening up of the boundaries of 'high' and 'low', and the values attached to surface and depth, with gender identity being a key marker of this shift. Explicitly sexual behaviour in public, open homosexuality both male and female, sexual ambiguity, androgyny, the play with sexual roles and the fascination attached to the shifting borders between male and female identity are what has fixed the period in the popular imagination: Isherwood's Berlin of *Cabaret* fame, but also Magnus Hirschfeld's research institute and his campaigns to decriminalise homosexuality. If there is some evidence for this obsession with sexuality in the 'serious' literature and the stage,[13] and even more evidence in the cinema, it is probably best documented in the club, bar and cabaret culture (on which Berlin still – or once more – trades as a tourist attraction),[14] while the fashion pages, the photos and drawings in quality magazines for a popular audience, like *Die Dame* or *Die Koralle* take the discussion about the 'new woman' and her sexuality into the middle-class home as shopping hints and life-style choices. Pabst's Lulu still teases the viewer today with uncertainty as to whether she is representative of a Weimar flapper, or anticipates the *femme fatale*, or neither, being a creature of another order altogether, that of a certain imaginary, at once typical of modern Germany's constant rewriting of its own social history and of the cinema as the discourse of the visible that gives this rewriting its repertory of apparently 'immortal' iconicity.

Wedekind's Lulu plays

The figure of Lulu that Frank Wedekind portrays in *Erdgeist* (1895) and *Die Büchse der Pandora* (1904) superficially belongs to the tradition of the *femme fatale*, the sexually alluring but remote woman, through whom men experience the irrational, obsessional and ultimately destructive force of female sexuality. The social and historical dimension of the figure is not my concern here, but many of the literary or visual embodiments, especially in the late nineteenth century have to do with projecting onto the desired woman an aggressiveness and destructiveness whose subjective correlation is guilt and self-punishment: for transgression, for violation, perhaps for desire itself.[15]

In the French literature of *décadence*, from Charles Baudelaire to Octave Mirbau, Huysmans and Villiers de L'Isle-Adam, as in the symbolist paintings of Gustave Moreau, this figure is a stylisation, often drawn from mythological characters (Salome, Judith, the feminised Sphinx) whose location in the orient and among the spoils of colonial wars gives a glimpse of a specifically political source of desire and guilt. In August Strindberg, Edvard Munch, Gustav Klimt and Egon Schiele, the *femme fatale* can also stand as a reminder of the violations of nature and instinctual life by the ascending bourgeois society and its consolidation in the patriarchal family. With Wedekind, a very specific social milieu, clearly marked by class division comes into view. More politically explicit, he locates the question of sexuality within an ideological field. The repression of female sexuality entails an intense eroticism suffusing everything that is asocial, primitive, instinctual, according to a topos that sees nature as devouring, whenever its nurturing function has been perverted. At the same time, Wedekind saw very precisely the hierarchical relation between social productivity and sexual reproductivity that the bourgeoisie had fought so hard to establish, and which lay at the heart of its 'sexual repression': it was the energy that had to be subjected to the labour process, regulated and accounted for. The bourgeois subject, for whom sexual passion is nothing but the inverse of the frustrations that make up his moral existence, is contrasted with the habitus of members of the lumpen-proletariat, located 'outside' – unassimilable or scornful – when it comes to the bourgeois dialectic of sexual renunciation and economic productivity.

By locating a deviant, instinctual and liberating social behaviour among circus people, artistes, petty criminals, and calling it true passion, Wedekind builds a fragile bridge with another class that also felt itself outside the social order: the declining aristocracy against whose notions of libertinage and of extravagant non-productive display the codes of the bourgeoisie had been developed. A non-repressive sexuality thus becomes the utopia where the lumpen class and the aristocracy meet in mutual tolerance and indulgence: the cliché situation of so many Viennese operettas and popular literature fantasies, the ones that served film directors from Lubitsch to Stroheim, from Max Ophuls to Willy Forst.[16] This kind of identification cannot maintain itself except as a projection that also invests the 'other' with the attributes that the self lacks. The attraction of the bourgeois for the lumpenproletariat arises, however, not from the similarity of position *vis à vis* a common antagonist, such as the working class, but out of a desire for a position 'outside' altogether. Wedekind's Lulu is without family ties, without social obligations, without education or culture; her psychological existence is free of guilt or conscience, her physical existence the very embodiment of beauty, youth and health, without any of the exertions one usually associates with their maintenance. Being outside the social order, she belongs to 'nature' – the only non-social realm that the plays can envisage. Sexuality therefore constructs itself primarily through negative categories, where non-family equals amorality and the non-social becomes the 'wild' on the animal level or the tropical plant in the vegetal realm. Several layers of self-projection are superimposed, yet it is the sympathy of the aristocrat for the lumpen that provides the basis for the glamorisation of these negative, somewhat demonic categories.

To leave it at this is to suggest a very schematic reading of the plays.[17] Wedekind's *Lulu* is in a sense not only a more radical critique of bourgeois notions of sexuality but also of the myth of the *femme fatale* itself. By critique I do not mean a denunciation of male double standards or a persuasively argued case for or against sexual freedom. For Wedekind, Lulu is a construct, not a sociological portrait: she represents in all her manipulative deviousness the only constant value, set against the relativity and dissolution of the so-called absolute and transcendental values. Through her provocation, she even serves as the projection screen for that epistemologically grounded, radical scepticism typical of turn-of-the-century Viennese philosophy and best known through the work of Ludwig Wittgenstein.[18] She can be the object of such male-projected, gendered doubt, one suspects, because Wedekind endows her with a kind of articulacy and energy that makes her the next of kin of another outcast altogether: the artist, traitor to his class whether aristocrat or bourgeois. She voices not only the artist's disgust with the members of all classes but with himself – which is why her predatory lust is allowed to vent itself against members of all constituted classes and convictions.[19] Wedekind's notion of female sexuality is thus even more abstract and conceptual than that of the French decadents. As the mask and (gendered) guise that the artist gives himself, she is distant and alluring, devouring and irresistible. As a woman she remains *terra incognita*, unknown even more than unknowable.[20]

Theatre and cinema: two kinds of spaces

For Wedekind, the conflict between class and productivity and between class and sexuality resolves itself only through the intermediary of art, and of an art that understands its own productivity as a form of elemental, natural expressivity. Yet in so far as Lulu is characterised by her *expressivity*, it is in response to the *repressivity* she experiences at the social level.[21] This means that she is less an artist than a performer, and the space where her expressivity can best articulate itself is the theatre. Voice and gesture, thought and body can be unified in the performance, and thus represent what one might call an image of non-alienated existence, the enactment of 'destiny as pure present'.[22] But such a 'pure present' does not escape social constraints, which is why Wedekind is careful to relativise the tragic pathos of his figure by such 'epic' devices as the prologue, the ringmaster and the animal imagery of the circus.[23] By stating in the preface that 'Geschwitz, not Lulu, is the tragic figure,' Wedekind seems to have a political agenda that enlists him in the sexual reform movements of his time.[24] The cinema, however, is still (or rather, once more) silent.[25] Its expressivity, the way it speaks to the mind and the senses, is distinct from that of the theatre, and therefore, other affective values attach themselves to gesture, performer or face.[26] With it, the relationship of expression to repression changes: conflict and contrast, antagonism and argument are perceived by an audience in forms specific to the new medium, though the antagonism to the theatre was far from absolute.[27] When Leopold Jessner staged *Die Büchse der Pandora* in 1911, he had written: 'Lulu is honest because she is woman, only woman, who however has succumbed to the pleasure of the senses, in an elementary form [Urwüchsigkeit] that cannot but bring disaster to us civilised beings, removed as we are from animal instincts'.[28] One recognises Wedekind's antinomies of nature and culture, as well as the decadents' welcoming gesture to the destructiveness of instinct. Yet, when in 1923 Jessner directed the film version of *Loulou*, with Asta Nielsen in the title role, it elicited a quite different response. Louise Brooks, who saw the film in Berlin, made short shrift of Jessner's adaptation:

> There was no lesbianism in it, no incest. Loulou the man-eater devoured her sex victims Dr Goll, Schwarz, Schön and then dropped dead in an acute attack of indigestion.
>
> (Brooks 1982: 94)

To Louise Brooks, *Loulou* was unintended camp, because Jessner and Asta Nielsen had ignored the fact that theatrical and cinematic body language are different not only in degree but kind; Jessner's idea of cinema is at fault, more than his conception of the central figure, since his 'Lulu is honest' was completely endorsed by Louise Brooks.[29] By 1927, the German cinema, not least thanks to familiarity with the American cinema, had drastically changed what was to be accepted as 'honest' in the visual representation of the erotic body and emotional affect. Fritz Rasp, also a favourite actor of Pabst's (*Diary of a Lost Girl*, *The Love of Jeanne Ney*, *The Threepenny Opera*) recognised this well:

> The first law of film acting has been for me right from the start to be very reticent with my gestures. When I came from theatre to the stage, I realized that acting for the moving image meant a complete break with the theatre and that the strongest visual effects [...] are achieved solely through the complete internalization of a role, for which one is the right type. That is why I prefer working for directors who have [...] recognized my physical appearance [...] so that acting in film, although this may seem paradoxical, is for me today not 'acting' at all but 'being'.
>
> (Rasp 1929)

Another difference between theatre and cinema is sociological, implying that in the late 1920s there were distinct class identities of audiences, which in turn affects the kinds of visual pleasure, curiosity and recognition-effects that bind spectators to the screen. Wedekind's plays engage his bourgeois audience's curiosity on a double level: the interest in the representation of the sexual 'other' of a predatory femininity, demonised and glorified in Lulu, and representation of a social 'other', symbolised by an aristocracy indulging its moral vices as if to complete its political ruin. In Berlin of the late 1920s, by contrast, as Louise Brooks remarks: 'the ruling classes publicly flaunted its pleasures as a symbol of wealth and power'.[30] Not only could the film not expect to shock with risky revelations, but the nature of the curiosity and fascination to which Pabst's *Pandora's Box* appealed had to be quite different:

> At the Eden Hotel, where I lived in Berlin, the cafe bar was lined with the higher-priced trollops. The economy girls walked the street outside. On the corner stood the girls in boots, advertising flagellation. Actors' agents pimped for the ladies in luxury apartments in the Bavarian Quarter. Race-track touts at the Hoppegarten arranged orgies for groups of sportsmen. The nightclub Eldorado displayed an enticing line of homosexuals dressed as women. At the Maly there was a choice of feminine or collar-and-tie lesbians. Collective lust roared unashamed at the theatre. In the revue *Chocolate Kiddies* [...] Josephine Baker appeared naked except for a girdle of bananas.
>
> (Brooks 1992: 97)

Louise Brooks's description of 'collective lust' highlights the sexually explicit, but also the sexually ambiguous aspect of Berlin high- and low-life. Perhaps more than is generally realised, the world of entertainment had already in the late 1920s become a central part of what defines sexuality and sexual difference for society as a whole, even if not in a direct, causally determining way. The cinema as the space of 'going to the movies' or 'going out' was as important as the films were, in providing specific role models via stars, fashion and decor.[31] What ultimately underlies the various 'Kino-debates' as the contest between theatre and cinema, between high culture and popular culture in Germany came to be known,[32] is a polemically conducted redefinition of the difference in status as well as a *de facto* convergence between various 'public spheres' in which the spaces connoted by the cinema, the theatre, operetta and popular entertainment vied with each other, not always fully aware of how they were all competing against the emergent power of 'shopping' and metropolitan consumption. From the perspective of the (classical) stage, the cinema represented an inauthentic sham world,[33] but considered on its own, or in the context of the modernity of popular (commodity) culture and consumption, the cinema turned into a socially coded realm that both filtered and substituted for public space.

Agency and ethics: beyond good and evil

Once sexuality is no longer circumscribed by biological categories, and gender roles no longer divide strictly along the binary lines of male and female, it is clear that sex is both more and less than a social construction: it functions within the broader symbolic field as one of the crucial markers of difference that exists in order to be transgressed. If one takes, among others, Louise Brooks's testimony about the profusion of sexualities and genders, roles and preferences, supply and demand in the Berlin of the late 1920s, then Pabst's film becomes a 'document of its time', as Fritz Lang claimed for his *Dr Mabuse, the Gambler* of 1921, which also features drugs, gambling and prostitution, though along rigidly heterosexual lines.[34] In *Pandora's Box* on the other hand, the perversity of sexual tastes and diversity of gender roles is entirely 'naturalised': perhaps one of the most startling and revolutionary aspects of the film, when compared with the so-called 'Aufklärungsfilme' from the early 1920s where 'deviancy' was clearly thematised as such.[35] Pabst places Lulu's sexual attraction to others invariably in the context of ambiguous gender attributes, though the film never comments on any of them, except by carefully differentiating the encounters. Throughout the relationship with Dr Schön, for instance, she is the androgynous Pierrot sporting a sylph-like body. With Alwa Schön an incestuous and homosexual element is always present. At her wedding to Dr Schön, Lulu reserves her most sensuous dance for the lesbian Countess Geschwitz, and on the gambling boat, she allows herself to be seduced by a young sailor, in order to exchange clothes with him.

Building on this reversibility of attributes, both the Wedekind plays and the Pabst film provide a principal ambiguity that also troubled the critics: namely, whether Lulu is a victim or an agent, whether she has a passive or an active role in the events of which she is the centre. Wedekind himself writes: 'Lulu is not a real character, but the personification of primitive sexuality who inspires evil unaware. She plays a purely passive role'.[36] The Lulu of *Erdgeist* is indeed the catalyst of the obsessions and neuroses, of the restless searching for meaning and value among the men she encounters. Yet this conception of her is rendered ambiguous precisely because she is a 'personification' of a fundamentally binary conflict between two definitions of femininity. As such, she has a positive presence, since for Wedekind, 'primitive sexuality' constitutes one side of the polarity which together with its opposite side make up an absolute value, the presumed 'essence' of woman. Artur Kutscher, one of the first serious commentators on Wedekind, saw this as a key ideological contradiction:

> The inner pivot of Lulu is also determined by Wedekind's attitude to the women's question. [...] The nineteenth century and its movements of emancipation 'masculinised' Woman, and literature from [...] Hebbel [...] to Strindberg gave more and more scope and significance to her struggle. Wedekind is an opponent of this movement, he wants to turn this 'culture' back to nature, and tries to emancipate, with a certain one-sided stridency, the female of the species ['das Weib'] from woman ['Frau'] by stressing animal instincts. It is, however, obvious from the whole conception of the character that he passionately endorses – influenced by Nietzsche in this – the values of reversibility and vitality.
>
> (Kutscher [1911] 1964: 121)

But critics did not always see Lulu as 'purely passive'. An English reviewer wrote: 'Wedekind reacted against German Naturalism and his plays are as full blown and direct as anything the Elizabethans could produce; indeed the nearest parallel to his Lulu cycle is *The Duchess of Malfi*, except that in the former case the woman is the active principle of evil.'[37] Agency is a crucial question because in our society moral evaluation of guilt or innocence, of evil or virtue attaches itself to intentionality and agency. Given the traditional gender division in terms of active and passive, Lulu's behaviour would find itself interpreted accordingly, and thus her function as a figure of projection for fantasies of power and control is also at stake. Pabst, it seems, resolves these questions, first, by using a script that reduces the number of protagonists and simplifies their narrative functions, and second by his choice of actress. With regard to the reduction of the action, *Pandora's Box* is a conflation of both *Lulu* plays, drastically cutting the first two acts of *Erdgeist*. By beginning with Dr Schön announcing to Lulu that he intends to marry the Minister's daughter, Pabst can precipitate the drama, without having to mention Schön's unlucky predecessors – Dr Goll or the painter Schwarz. Schigolch is the only reference to Lulu's past, the trapeze artist Rodrigo has a smaller, but still crucial part in the film, while the naive idealist, the student Hugenberg, is dropped altogether, his function of pleading in court and sacrificing himself being taken over by Geschwitz. Because Schön condenses in a single character the serial victims of Lulu in the plays, her ambivalent agency – half victim, half instigator is immediately established, finely balancing the various triangular relationships in which she finds herself. As to the choice of actress, the cameraman Paul Falkenberg reported:

> Preparation for *Pandora's Box* was quite a saga because Pabst couldn't find a Lulu. He wasn't satisfied with any actress at hand and for months everybody connected with the production went round looking for a Lulu. I talked to girls in the street, on the subway, in railway stations.
>
> (quoted in Brooks 1982: 97)

Louise Brooks had her own conception of the role. She, too, seemed inclined to see Lulu as a victim, although she also argued that at the end Lulu 'receive(s) the fate that has been her dream since childhood. Death by a sexual maniac'.[38] Ultimately, even for Louise Brooks, the transgressiveness of film had to do with agency, or lack of it:

> (B)esides daring to show the prostitute as victim, Mr Pabst went on to the final damning immorality of making his Lulu as 'sweetly innocent' as the flowers that adorned her costumes and filled the scenes of the play. […] How Pabst determined that I was his unaffected Lulu with the childish simpleness of vice, was part of the mysterious alliance that seemed to exist between us. […] When *Pandora's Box* was released in 1929 film critics objected because Lulu did not suffer after the manner of Sarah Bernhard in *Camille*. Publicity photographs before the filming of *Pandora's Box* show Pabst watching me with scientific intensity. […] (H)e let me play Lulu naturally […] and that was perhaps his most brilliant directorial achievement – getting a group of actors to play unsympathetic characters whose only motivation was sexual gratification. Fritz Kortner as Schön wanted to be the victim. Franz Lederer as the incestuous son wanted to be adorable. Carl Goetz wanted to get laughs playing the old pimp Schigolch. Alice Roberts, the Belgian actress who played the screen's first lesbian the Countess Geschwitz was prepared to go no further than repression in mannish suits.
>
> (Brooks 1982: 98–99)

In contrast to the 'driven' and desiring energy of the men, the female centre is all 'natural' stillness and simplicity. It is therefore quite possible to see the film in the terms that Louise Brooks suggests: Lulu as a child-like creature, whose attraction resides in her lack of guile and calculation, indulging in simple pleasures – among which are sex, but it might just as well be the bulging biceps of the trapeze artist Rodrigez, the sight of the old tramp Schigolch in the doorway, the fashion page in the illustrated journal *Die Dame*, or mistletoe at Christmas time in the dingy and draughty London tenement. But Pabst's Lulu is not one of those figures of the Victorians' obsessional psyche: the child bride, as in Edgar Allan Poe's stories, or the waif to be rescued and redeemed. Nor is she, despite appearances, a figure like Browning's 'My Last Duchess', who 'had a heart … too soon made glad, too easily impressed', who 'liked whate'er she looked at, and her looks went everywhere'[39]: Lulu's sexual ambiguity and indeterminacy has nothing to do with either puberty or virginity. And just as Pabst seems to want to redefine active and passive, he is at pains not to take up Wedekind's paradigm of the anti-social as identifiable with animal nature or tropical vegetation (by contrast, it is Dr Schön who keeps a particularly exotic and luxuriant plant in his office). Lulu is modern, in a manner that at the time would have been perceived as being typically American, even without the choice of a Hollywood actress for the part and the ballyhoo this created. But the film does not make 'Americanism' an issue as Pabst's *Joyless Street* had done a few years earlier. On the contrary, his Lulu, too, is without past or origin, and without any particular class attributes.[40]

Placed outside the spaces of family and personal history no doubt creates for Lulu a more immediately imaginary space, exploited by Pabst to underline that Lulu, in her relations with Schön – father and son – as well as with the sailor on the gambling boat, is merely the 'stake' in an all-male power play. When not stressing Lulu's sexual ambiguity, the camera shows all the male protagonists (with the possible exception of Schigolch) perpetually brooding, scheming and angry, as if to parody in their frustrated, restless state a very 'Germanic inwardness', in search of expression and self-realisation. Against this male world, obsessed with intentionality, goals and motives, Lulu appears to be exacerbating this, and is thus seductively sexual because she is a being of provocative externality, animated but without depth, attentive but without memory; persistent but without will-power or discipline: intelligent but without self-reflexivity; intense but without pathos. Her superiority resides in the fact that these 'effects-without-causes' are experienced by the men as both fascinating and threatening. This imaginary space is furthermore circumscribed by a double male fantasy: as the woman over whose possession father and son fight, she is also the phallic mother whom they wish to destroy – Dr Schön, the father demands that she kill herself (after 'humiliating' him at the wedding party) and Alwa Schön, the son, delegates to her his own parricidal desire, so that his guilt feelings become her crime. In this respect, the film elegantly condenses, as it were, one of the main theses of Kracauer's *From Caligari to Hitler* about male paranoia and its oedipal fixation. But the very elegance and sophistication of Pabst's narrative indicates that *Pandora's Box* is not primarily about the secrets of this (German) soul. It is more a knowing allusion to the many psychoanalytic and sexological theories circulating at the time, and the father–son rivalries so prevalent in the immediate post-war literature. A central complex of German Expressionism is depicted with serene indifference – an indifference to which Lulu gives a (provisionally) female form.

Spaces of desire: the pure image

Pabst's particular strategy is best illustrated in the opening scene. A man's back is turned to us. He seems to be writing something in a book. It is the meter man, reading the electricity meter in Lulu's apartment. We first see her, as she comes from the living room into the hall to give the man a small tip and to offer him a glass of liquor. Torn between looking at the bottle and looking at Lulu's revealing dress, the man drops some coins, but before he can pick them up the bell rings and rather grandly, he volunteers to answer the door. A shabby old man stands at the door, holding his bowler hat in a somewhat deferential manner. With another grand gesture, the meter man takes a few coins from his waistcoat pocket to give to the old man to be rid of him. But Lulu, peering over his shoulder, recognises the visitor, rushes out and flings her arms round the old man. She pulls him into the apartment, past the meter man and into the living room, shutting the door. The meter man, surprised and disappointed, stoops to gather up the lost coins, goes over to the chair and picks up his peaked cap and battered briefcase. With a final indignant glance at the closed door to the living room, he leaves by the front door. The scene shows a number of ambiguities. As I hope the description conveys, the meter man (whom the spectator only gradually perceives as such because without his official cap and with his back turned to the audience, he at first seems to be a kindly elderly gentleman) is caught both in a class and a sexual fantasy, which allows him, even if only for an instant, to be in the position of the owner of the apartment and desirable suitor. He becomes Schön the master, by the appearance on the doorstep of someone socially inferior to himself, someone whom he can patronise, by giving alms. Mirroring himself in the smile of a ravishing young woman, he becomes young and handsome himself, and the fact that his attention is further divided between sexual allure and alcohol allows him the illusory choice between two kinds of transgressions, of which the one he chooses, namely alcohol, may well be the consolation he seeks for the unattainability of the other.

In this brief episode, remarkable for giving us virtually no information about the plot, the normal social relations implied by master and servant (or mistress and servant), of favours rendered and money received, of alms, fees and gratuities – in short, an entire economy of exchange and value – is both shown in action and comically suspended. But it is not only the meter man's illusions that are shattered when the mistress of the house and the shabby tramp fall into each other's arms. The spectator, too, has no time to get his visual bearings, for the scene is staged and edited in a complex succession of camera movements, glance–glance shots and glance–object shots, whose function it is to give a fluid movement to the scene. It establishes hierarchies and relations between the characters, only to undo them again. There is, for instance, a noticeably 'false continuity' match: Lulu is looking off-screen right, when logically, according to the 180-degree rule, she should be looking off-screen left, which increases the sense of an imaginary space not quite obliterating but also not quite confirming the diegetic space of the hallway and entrance lobby.[41] The two doors – front door and apartment door – suggest a rather theatrical proscenium space, but it is the effect of editing and the dynamics of the rapid exchange of glances between characters in the many point-of-view shots of this scene that establish the illusion of a real space while at the same time undercutting it. Juxtaposed to this imaginary space, and counteracting the spectator's disorientation (which he shares with the meter man) is the image of Lulu, framed by the door and offering – via a close-up – to the spectator also, an almost impossibly radiant smile: the promise of pleasure and absolute plenitude. The disorientation increases the fascination, the dependence on the image, yet the very excess of the smile (excessive because not registering or responding to the meter man's lowly social status or Schigolch's shabby clothes) breaks the strictly narrative function of her presence within the frame, making her the figure of desire in and for the spectators' imaginary.

The scene is a kind of emblem of the film itself. First, in its view of social relations: Lulu, at the end of the film, when back in the world of Schigolch and past all sense of bourgeois decorum, will fling herself into the arms of yet another outcast – Jack the Ripper – with the same radiant smile. Second, the scene initiates a strangely displaced character identification, making the spectator enter the fiction via the meter man, whose lack of plot function turns the episode into a parable of movie watching as paid-for vicarious participation. With the exit of the meter man, sociologically speaking, the petit bourgeoisie – Kracauer's *Angestellten* and chief victims of inflation and downward mobility – disappear from the fictional space of the film. Yet they are the historical audience that the film addresses, the family men who besides going to the cinema also treat themselves to exotic drinks in the 'Riviera Room' of *Haus Vaterland*.[42] They may enjoy seeing themselves portrayed on the screen, but according to Kracauer, they take even more pleasure (and thus open themselves up to the interplay of pleasure and anxiety) in identifying with their betters. The meter man waiting in the hall of Lulu's apartment is also the office worker waiting in line at the entrance lobby of the Gloria-Palast for the star to appear or the show to begin. The prologue delicately points out how fragile his class identity is, and the interplay between the meter man's uniform and status recalls Murnau's *The Last Laugh* of which it is an oblique pastiche. Throughout Murnau's film about the hotel doorman who ends up being demoted to lavatory attendant at the same time hiding this from his housekeeper and niece, the pathos of his demise hides a deeper malaise concerning his male masochism.[43] In contrast, the erotic presence of Lulu in the opening scene of *Pandora's Box* ensures that male sexuality is not repressed by social disgrace, but openly stated. Lulu's total indifference to class and status depicts the predominant anxiety of the middle classes during the early Weimar cinema – loss of class status and proletarianisation – as a comic rather than a tragic motif, for as Lulu demonstrates, in a 'decadent' society of show and mimicking status, the 'sliding scale' of inversion and grades of identity is potentially limitless.

The opening scene also makes a statement about female sexuality and its power of attraction as well as of subversion in the field of (cinematic) representation: for Pabst, desire is depicted in the hesitation between two roles, between two glances. Lulu's 'essence' is in the realm of the sexual, but this realm exists nowhere except in these moments of choice and division, in the reversibility of the order of exchange. Lulu can be the object of desire for men and women, old and young, because her symbolic position is never fixed, because it criss-crosses class and gender, the law and moral authority. In fact, Lulu is most desirable when her appearance is caught in the crossfire of someone else desiring her as well, and her power constructs itself always in relation to someone else experiencing a crisis in their sexual identity. An example is the encounter between Dr Schön and his son Alwa, when the father, after having decided to give up Lulu in order to marry the daughter of the Minister, realises that his son is also sexually interested in Lulu. Suddenly his passion is once more inflamed by anger, hatred and jealousy. But the son, too, experiences his desire via someone else. He falls in love with Lulu only after having observed the jealous and passionate glances that Countess Geschwitz bestows on her in his studio.

Black holes and homosocial worlds

Such triadic structurations of desire also suggest a more directly 'oedipal' reading of the ending, for Lulu's murder by Jack the Ripper would complete a homosocial fantasy that is centred on Alwa. After the father has died in the son's arms, killed by the mother on whom the son has projected the guilt for his incestuous feelings, Alwa appears to have freed himself from his obsession. But Lulu's escape, thanks to Countess Geschwitz, and the appearance of Casti Piani on the train trap Alwa once more in a masochistic, self-punishing role. Powerless against the father figures that continue to surround him, he displaces his masochism onto Lulu, with whom he necessarily identifies, creating a curiously dyadic bond with her. In the London scenes, the regressive oral and anal aspects are heavily underscored: the three live in filth, and their abode is penetrated by wind, rain, fog and cold. The skylight window, pictured as a black hole, is constantly blown open. All three are exclusively preoccupied with oral gratification. Alwa readily devours the piece of mouldy bread that Lulu breaks off for him in disgust. Schigolch sucks his empty brandy bottle like a baby, before he finally settles down to a Guinness that he has scrounged and a big Christmas pudding – showing a return to the beginning of the film where both he and the meter man preferred oral pleasures to sex. Alwa's infantilism – he is in turn enraged and petulant – underscores the sadomasochistic stalemate of his unresolved oedipal dilemma. Emerging from this at once impenetrable and penetrating fog is Jack the Ripper. He functions as Alwa's double, the ambivalently psychotic side of his infantile dependence, and in the encounter between Jack and Lulu the two sides of Alwa's personality are fully played out – the tender yielding and seductive anima and the punishing, destructive animus. It is a scene portrayed without violence and struggle, hence disturbingly archaic, where the very tenderness indicates a fantasmatic and also regressive quality. As Jack leaves and meets Alwa at the front door, a sign of recognition seems to pass between the two men that sets Alwa free and allows him, too, to disappear into the fog, as if he had finally found in this complicity salvation from his tormenting sexual ambivalence.

Such a reading of the film centres it on Alwa, surely a contentious choice in terms of the plot, but suggestive of one aspect of how the film engages the male spectator. For a differently gendered reading it would be necessary to assume that Lulu, after challenging the oedipal and patriarchal law by placing herself outside it, had succumbed to this logic the very instant she herself manifests sexual desire, as she clearly does for Jack the Ripper. In this sense her death inscribes itself in a hysterical reassertion of patriarchy – the woman is sacrificed so that the homosocial order of men can continue, cemented by a perpetually displaced, repressed homosexuality and a de-sexualisation of women, represented by the female members of the Salvation Army whose maternal gestures accompany and frame the entire episode like a silent chorus of ministering angels. None the less, however poignant the tenderness that leads to murder, it is without pathos or the element of horror one associates with such a scene. The tenderness lingers, but a cool irony ensures that the end is anti-climactic, a dream that is already faint, and fading, as it occurs, into the darkness that envelops all.[44] The shock of the film not ending with a shot of Lulu is profound, because it prevents the (male and female?) viewer from constructing her as victim, thus recovering one's emotional investment in her. It is even more disturbing as an absence because Pabst provides neither fetish nor symbolisation, if it is compared with the famous 'absence' of Elsie in Fritz Lang's *M* metonymically present through her ball and the balloon.

Two-faced trade-offs: body-languages beyond pathos

What is Pabst up to in the scene? Could it be that he distances himself from the early Weimar socio-sexual imaginary that Kracauer implied in *From Caligari to Hitler*, that Klaus Theweleit castigates in *Male Fantasies* and that Maria Tartar has analysed in *Lustmord*? By showing these psychoanalytically over-determined constellations as if he were citing them, Pabst seems once more to distance himself from their sociopolitical reality, inspecting with almost clinical detachment the 'male body' of Weimar patriarchy in crisis, while speaking from a quite different position than the sexualised cultural critique at once ecstatic and apocalyptic that is so typical of Wedekind's plays, Vienna *Jugendstil* and Expressionist art, such as Egon Schiele's paintings, Oskar Kokoschka's *Murder Hope of Women*, Brecht's *Baal* and *In the Jungle of the Cities*, or the post-war drawings of Otto Dix and Georg Grosz. That Pabst's cool seems also different from our own merely enhances the fascination still emanating from this in many ways so politically incorrect film.

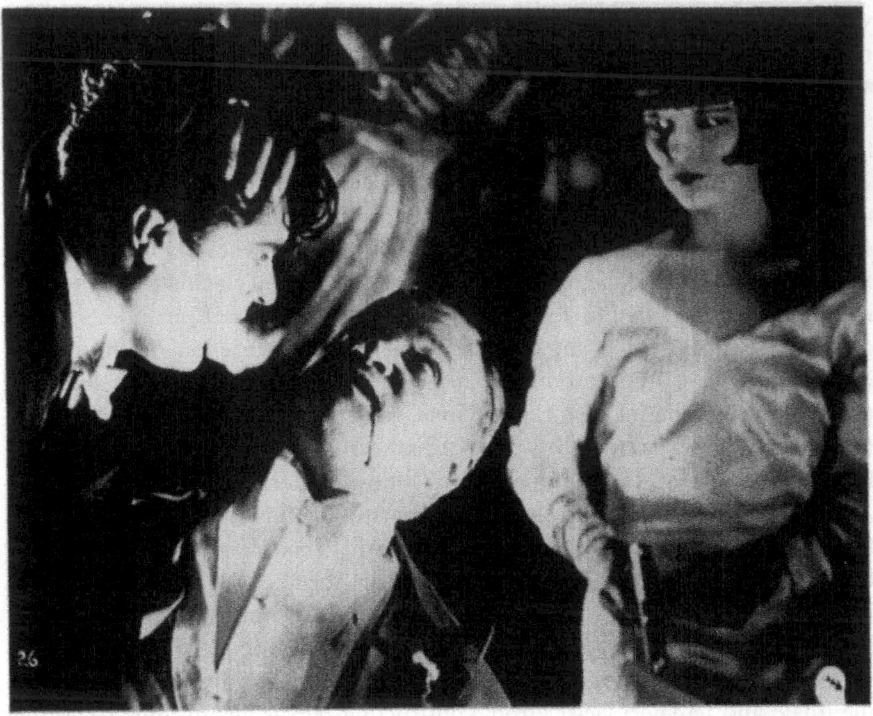

Figure 19 Mercurial menace to the Male: Lulu with gun on her wedding night in G.W. Pabst's *Pandora's Box* (1928)

Source: BFI films: stills, posters and designs

One source of its dynamics and its fundamentally perverse eroticism is the stark but always modulated and often subtly shaded contrast between Lulu's agility, the diaphanous and transparent quality of her body or body image, and the solidity, the heavy, black body mass of the men that so often block her pathway. Lulu's body is in motion even when she stands still, because motion might carry her away at any instant, unmotivated, mercurial and unpredictable. Just as Lulu smiles, and one hesitates to say why or at whom, and from what inner eye, so her body moves without this motion inflecting her gestures with intentionality. With the men, however, every move, every finger and eyebrow is heavy with significance. We mostly see the back of Fritz Kortner, who plays Dr Schön. His acting style and Pabst's use of his bulk to fill the frame, stresses the bull-necked, looming and cowering nature of his physiognomy. Such a body conveys to perfection (in that it translates into kinetic-gravitational force) the complex interplay of willpower and instinctual drive, of anger and repression, of frustration barely controlled, finally flaring into aggression and masochistic, self-tormenting, suicidal despair, which makes Dr Schön be the quintessential contrast to Lulu, and one that becomes paradigmatic for all the men in the film.

After Schön's death Alwa, Rodrigo, or Count Casti-Piani merely have to affect a scowl, a frown, bend a shoulder or raise an arm, and one immediately associates these gestures with the body of Dr Schön, or rather, what he stands for in terms of ruthless, brutal and inflexible will, against Lulu's fluidity and lightning changes of place. As the opening scene shows, Fritz Kortner's back is not even the first among a long line of backs in the film that finally, in the London scene, spread blackness everywhere. Dr Schön's back and its doubles are thus the very image of motive, design, intentionality, the world of cause-and-effect, of self-realisation as self-imposition, to which correspond self-abandonment and self-pity and finally violent death as their negative mirrors. By contrast, it is difficult to assign to Lulu – and Louise Brooks's acting – a similarly psychological–physiognomic 'consistency'. She is always 'in-between' – between the meter man and Schigolch, between Schigolch and Dr Schön, between Rodrigo and Schigolch, between Alwa and Countess Geschwitz, between Alwa and Dr Schön, between Rodrigo and Alwa, between the stage manager and Dr Schön, between the state prosecutor and Countess Geschwitz, between Casti-Piani and Alwa, between Casti-Piani and the Egyptian. What complicates matters is that the shifting positions are not all grounded in sexual desire, otherwise sexual desire would indeed emerge as the elemental, irrational asocial force that it is in Wedekind.

In *Pandora's Box* sexual desire has as its asymmetrical double almost always the political economy, with money accompanying the sexual link between the characters, but also crossing it in the opposite direction. This is a banal observation, if one sees Lulu as a prostitute who trades sex for money, but evidently sex and money stand in a more complex relationship to one another in the discursive registers of the film. Although Lulu is a kept woman, it is none the less she who is seen giving money: to the meter man and then to Schigolch, for instance. Then, there is Dr Schön who finances Alwa's theatre revue, as a way to prevent Lulu from getting involved with his son. Schigolch introduces Lulu to Rodrigo because 'men like Schön won't always pay the rent', but Rodrigo has no sexual interest in her. Countess Geschwitz supports Lulu financially because she is in love with her, but the favour is not returned. Casti-Piani blackmails Alwa on the train but he, too, is not interested in Lulu sexually. On the boat Rodrigo also tries to blackmail her, and it is only with a complicated sexual ploy that sacrifices Countess Geschwitz that she can get rid of him. By this time Alwa is no longer interested in Lulu sexually, yet constantly demands money from her. The police are offering a reward for her arrest and the Egyptian is quoting a price for her body: Casti-Piani, before deciding, simply calculates which is the better deal. In the London scenes where Lulu is most explicitly shown as a prostitute, we never see her with clients or in a financial transaction, and she eventually gives herself to Jack the Ripper precisely because he has no money and is thus – like herself – outside the cash-nexus. Sexual desire emerges as one particular manifestation of a generalised structure of exchange, and, in the case of the men, it seems wholly bound up, but not identical with money and finance. Unlike female subjectivity (about which the film may or may not have much to say), male desire has a precise exchange value for which either money or sex can serve as accepted currency: Lulu is that which allows both desire and money to circulate. Complicity reigns at all levels, and the reward offered by the courts opens up an unbroken chain between police, Alwa, Casti-Piani, the Egyptian slave trader, Rodrigo and Geschwitz: it is as if the law fixes Lulu's price, so that everyone else can enter into the exchange, in order to trade most favourably with the same stock.

The scene on the gambling ship makes the relations explicit. While at the tables, men and women play cards or bet on the roulette wheel, Casti-Piani and the slave trader bargain over Lulu, and a dangerous sexual gamble is started by Schigolch between Rodrigo and Countess Geschwitz. All three of these transactions finally decide Lulu's fate, but they do so negatively. It is a gender-bending role change that saves her life when she trades clothes with the sailor boy. What at the plot level appears to be the logic of suspense, or of melodramatic complication is at the symbolic level an instance of the relativity of values in a given society. It is also historically located, with the gaming tables and the mad rush for the stakes, when Alwa has been caught cheating, inevitably recalling the Wall Street Crash of 1927 and the gambling imagery of Lang's *Dr Mabuse der Spieler* (1921), itself linked to the 1921 lift-off of hyperinflation. In Pabst's film, however, a new kind of equivalence under the sign of interminable exchangeability is shown to exist between desire, sex and money, generating an endless chain, which seems both the motive force behind the men's anger and frustration and the reason why they are, despite the different oedipal and class configurations, mere substitutes of one another. The London episode is here doubly ironic. It takes us back to the world of the lumpen-proletariat, a world outside Weimar bourgeois society (of which the gaming tables are both parody and apotheosis) where the nexus bracketing capital and productivity and sex and money no longer apply, and the whole libidinal economy of exchange becomes meaningless. Jack the Ripper and Lulu are not endowed with the kind of supersexuality that the Lulu plays project onto the lumpen-proletariat. Instead, she is at her most maternal and child-like and he is clearly impotent. At the same time, they meet at Christmas, amidst the dispensations of the Salvation Army. In other words, Pabst sarcastically takes them outside all constituted forms of exchange into limited and utopian forms of exchange: those of the gift and of grace and salvation. Targeting Wedekind's social romanticism and the emergent capitalist logic of exchange, while gently mocking the institutionalised otherworldliness of religion and philanthropy, Pabst's ending is so anticlimactic because it is built on a series of mutually undercutting ironies around the trope of the 'end of symbolic exchange'.

Spectatorship: back-stage battle stations

The gambling ship, as indicated, is a the fictional metaphor for the economic chaos of the Weimar Republic, letting the mechanics of inflation, de- and revaluation inflect sexual difference and briefly challenge the symbolic position of women within this patriarchal society. But it is also literally and metaphorically a 'free zone', part of something 'outside' where the rigid divisions and differences can realign themselves. As such, economic chaos could be, as I suggested in the case of Lubitsch (see Part II, Chapter 2), a 'chance' for a more radical or permanent state of suspension and reversibility. But just as in Lubitsch, the 'Revolution' as the new bourgeois, patriarchal order catches up with Jeanne, so in Pabst, speculative capitalism is not the preferred site for the 'permanent revolution' one may have in mind. Instead, and in order to critique the economic (dis-)order as the 'ground' of gender and social agency, Pabst brings into view another emergent institution that is radically transforming social agency, because of re-figuring subjectivity and representation, sexuality and the image. This institution is the new order of the spectacle and it appears in *Pandora's Box* as a critique of theatre from the vantage point of the cinema, this time not focused on acting as agency, but on *mise-en-scène* as that which allocates the roles and rules of spectatorship.

At the centre of the first part of the film and as its climax, Pabst has put a scene that takes place in the theatre. In terms of narrative progress, it is the point where all the threads so far introduced are tied into the proverbial Gordian knot, which Lulu eventually undoes at a stroke. We are at the opening night of Alwa's revue. Lulu suddenly refuses to appear on stage because she has seen Dr Schön enter, accompanied by his official fiancée, the daughter of the Minister. Despite everyone's protestations and entreaties, Lulu remains adamant. The tension mounts, the stage-manager is frantic. Eventually, Schön agrees to see Lulu in her dressing room. But no amount of aggression, verbal or physical threats, appears to move Lulu to a change of mind. Dr Schön, eyes blazing with hatred, cannot resist the seductive force of her negativity. Sexually aroused, he embraces her at just the moment when a frantic Alwa, accompanied by Schön's fiancée, anxious about his absence, enters the dressing room. Profound consternation occurs all round, except for the theatre manager and Lulu, who, triumphant, sweeps past the shocked assembly and leaves the dressing room in the direction of the stage. The scene ends with a brief exchange between father and son (similar to the one where the two had struck a bargain over Lulu's appearance in the revue), to the effect that Schön will marry Lulu even though it will be his ruin. What gives the scene its force is primarily the editing as it cross-cuts between the building up of tension and mounting chaos both on stage and back stage, and the ever more single-minded determination of Lulu to provoke a showdown, once and for all. But determination is perhaps the wrong word, because it makes her appear to be too active, when in fact it is the strength of her refusal, her negativity, the control she keeps on her absence that cause the events to take shape and finally resolve in her favour. Pabst here recasts the central 'moral' issue of the Wedekind plays: is Lulu active or passive, evil or innocent? The answer that the film gives in the scene just described is that she is neither, that it is a false dichotomy. Instead, it has become a matter of presence or absence, of spectacle, image and *mise-en-scène*. Lulu puts on the show of her own disappearance and reappearance. The spectacle of her person, about which she controls nothing but the cadence and discontinuity of presence, is what gives rise to desire and fascination. Lotte Eisner, trying to describe the magic of Louise Brooks' acting after a visit to the set in 1929 homes in on the same phenomenon:

> And this Louise Brooks, whom I had scarcely heard speak, fascinated me constantly through a curious mixture of passivity and presence which projected through the shooting. ... [She] exists with an overwhelming insistence; she makes her way through these two films [i.e. *Pandora's Box* and *Diary of a Lost Girl*], always enigmatically impassive. (Is she a great artist or only a dazzling creature whose beauty traps the viewer into attributing complexities to her of which she is unaware?)
>
> (Lotte Eisner, 'A Witness Speaks', quoted in Brooks 1982: 107)

What Lotte Eisner does not discuss is the role of Pabst's editing technique in achieving the effect of an enigmatically impassive presence. Film historians usually credit him with a particular type of (classical continuity) editing style that makes the transitions from shot to shot especially smooth, dynamic and imperceptible, the so-called 'cut on movement':

> At the end of one cut somebody is moving, at the beginning of the adjoining one the movement is continued. The eye is thus so occupied in following these movements that it misses the cuts.
>
> (McPherson 1927: 26)

At the editing table, one can clearly follow how Pabst breaks down a scene into smaller and smaller units, in order to reassemble, intercut and build up the fragments into a complex crescendo of frantic motion. Like no other European director of the 1920s, Pabst combines speed of narrative with the simultaneity of action spaces, which places his style somewhere between the Russian montage school and classical Hollywood. The simultaneity effect in the theatre scene is derived from the logic of parallel editing and alternation, combining the glance–object shot of a Kuleshov with the glance–glance shot of Griffith, which is to say, the *mise-en-scène* of glances and the organisation of the look. It essentially reconstructs the action into the terms of seeing and being seen, of who looks at whom, across which intercut pieces of business, dramatic fragments or parts of the decor. Lulu disappears from the stage, because as the inter-title says, she 'will dance for the whole world, but not in front of that woman' meaning Schön's fiancée. But it is for Schön's fiancée and son that her tantrum in the dressing room is staged. Once they have seen her and Schön in each other's arms, the show is over. Not to appear in public means the chance to re-stage a private oedipal drama in a space carefully poised between public and private, thus exacerbating

Figure 20 Young love or puppy love? Lulu (Louise Brooks) and Alwa (Franz Lederer) in *Pandora's Box* (1928)

Source: BFI films: stills, posters and designs

the inherently voyeuristic exhibitionist relationship between audience and performer.

With it, the battle of the sexes, the question of possession, of who belongs to whom and who controls whom becomes a battle for the right of the look and the image, the position of the subject – as seeing or seen. Dr Schön's undoing, in the film's terms, is precisely that he, supreme possessor of the right to look, emphasised by his glittering monocle and his scowling, piercing eyes becomes himself the object of the gaze: in other words, an image that in terms of classical narrative is 'feminised'. The star, especially the female star, pushes the implications of this gaze to its limits.[45] Such a limit is Pabst's Lulu: she has no gaze, hence the fascination of her smile. It is so open as to appear empty, unfocused, mirror-like. The few times she frowns or looks puzzled, Pabst neutralises her gaze by inserting a cut that disperses or disorients its direction, as in the mismatch of the opening scene. The difficulties of finding the right actress discussed earlier in the chapter, as well as Louise Brooks's detailed account of the shooting, confirm the importance that Pabst attached to the look that poses no threat. At one stage he considered Marlene Dietrich for the part but is reported to have said: 'Dietrich was too old [!] and too obvious – one sexy look and the picture would have become a burlesque' (Brooks 1982: 96.)

In the scene at the theatre, the private oedipal family spectacle is set within the public exhibitionist revue. The one seems to be the reason for the other, each space subject to an asymmetrical exchange. Superficially, the contrast takes up a division evident in Wedekind: that between the various bourgeois family feuds where Lulu makes her destructive presence felt and the 'circus ring' in which she is exhibited among the wild and beautiful animals. Pabst's similarly double perspective is, however, neither sociological nor biological. Instead, we have two kinds of theatricalisation, two kinds of visualisation that effectively put both private and public worlds under the scrutiny of a gaze. One might say that the film contrasts the world on-stage with the world back stage, but Pabst's concept seems more complex and more reductive; the usually comic effects of such a division, say, in the Warner back-stage musical are actually undercut by the deadly seriousness of the power struggle enacted in what has become a single space – that of the theatre as an infernal machine that no longer knows an 'outside'. In the traditional theatre the area back stage is hidden from view, the 'repressed' part of the performance so that a (cinematic) representation of the disjuncture between back stage and on stage invariably draws its ironies from the disjuncture expression/repression, scene/'ob'scene, the hidden and the revealed. This disjuncture is precisely what Pabst critiques in Wedekind's contradictory and patriarchal conception of sexuality and social class. Against Wedekind/Jessner's Loulou the man-eater, he makes Lulu the bright-eyed American starlet, and sets a modernist/constructivist view of spectacle and visual pleasure against the classical theatre's view of stage, ramp, proscenium, curtain, and the illusion of a self-generated enactment of reality. Less than two years before Pabst made *Pandora's Box* the Weimar Bauhaus published in its house journal the text and picture of a 'kinetic object-box', Heinz Loew's 'Mechanical Stage-Model', intended as a manifesto 'about stage mechanics in general':

> guided by a mistaken feeling, today everyone anxiously tries to hide from view on stage any kind of technical process. Which is why for a modern audience back-stage is often the most interesting spectacle, since we live in the age of technology and the machine.[46]

This seems close to the spirit in which Pabst conceived the scenes at the revue as a deconstruction of theatre stagecraft by a constructivist cinema. If the theatre represses and displaces the split between the spectacle and that which produces it, *Pandora's Box*, although dedicated to the creation of illusions like all realist cinema, adds another dimension of unreality by showing the mechanics of presence and absence, across which an imaginary of 'realism' must necessarily take shape. The cinema needs theatrical illusion in order to both conceal and reveal its own devices. When thus observed by the cinema, this theatre review is a clockwork mechanism gone berserk: a ceaseless, syncopated succession of instances caught in motion, responding violently to the animation filling the frame, while incapable of containing the elements that traverse it. People and objects enter and exit from left to right, but also vertically: the stage manager is suddenly hoisted into the flies; scene shifters blot out the main protagonist; decorations and pieces of costume disappear off frame as if through an imagined trap door. A piece of moving scenery cuts in half a space that seemed a solid set. The very instability of the elements on view, and the constant changes of perspective and angle make it impossible to conceive as three-dimensionally solid the space extending beyond and outside the frame: the illusion sustains itself by constantly collapsing, and the recovery from this implosion produces a fascination with the 'not-there' that is deeply fetishistic.

At the same time, everyone in the frame is double: both actor and spectator, both participant and audience. The performers crowd around as gawpers when Lulu and Dr Schön have their argument, and from the moment Schön and his fiancée become visible they are performers in their own domestic – but also more and more public – drama. And Lulu triumphs by making theatre actors as well as society ladies her spectators, willy-nilly. The only spectators notable for their absence, because never shown, is the first-night audience in the theatre. Why? Their perceived presence would immediately 'anchor' the fictional space and take away that hovering effect of indeterminacy. By allowing the cinema spectators to decide and define their own position of spectator unambiguously, the diegetic audience would have been too convenient a stand-in, creating a *mise-en-abyme* on a direct axis of duplication between the act of viewing the film and that of the staged performance, both firmly located in narrative time and space. This position of knowledge the film withholds: refusing to provide the sequence with its master shot, Pabst indicates his own constructivist–relativist sympathies. The cinema here defines itself *through* the theatre *against* the theatre. Confronted with a need for distanciation not unlike that advocated by Brecht, Pabst did not choose expressionist psychodrama, comic opera or 'No-plays' for his *Verfremdungseffekt*, but chose American film acting and continuity editing – neutral, minimal, pure surface and exteriority. Bauhaus kinetics, *Neue Sachlichkeit* and dada metamechanics create the robot Lulu at the interface of sexuality and technology. Who else to play it better than Louise Brooks, former flapper, wind-up Hollywood doll and trained dancer from the Ziegfeld Follies?[47]

The image disavowed by a look

Lulu is forever image, framed in the doorway or by Rodrigo's biceps, dancing in front of Schigolch or in a Pierrot costume hanging from the wall. In the jealous encounter between Countess Geschwitz and Alwa Schön she is present as the costume sketches that Geschwitz has drawn, and a little later, Dr Schön points an empathetic finger at the same sketches when he tells Alwa that one does not marry women like Lulu. In court she is on display in the witness box, snapped by a press photographer. This very photo Count Casti-Piani recognises in the newspaper when her face appears from behind the compartment door on the train to ask him for a light. Finally, the Egyptian settles on a price after he has shuffled through a pack of photos which catch the spectator in a typical hesitation about how to read the image as that of the 'real' Lulu (within the fiction) when, in fact, it is 'merely' her photo (within the fiction). The nature and function of the look thus appears to be subject to the same divisions and ambiguities that structure the signifying materials of the narrative: class, gender, body – articulated across motion, spectacle, frame. A closer analysis of the relation of the tight head-on shots of her looking into the camera to other types of point-of-view shots, especially where we are not shown what she is looking at, or the relation of off-screen space to on-screen space would confirm Pabst's systematic use of these shots in order to keep our narrative comprehension in the register of hesitation and ambivalence. This is the more noticeable, given the pre-eminence of another, directly gendered look, of which Schön's stare is evidently the paradigm: the look of patriarchy – exacerbated and parodied in the look of and through the monocle, which witheringly, at one time or another hits Lulu, Schigolch, Alwa and Geschwitz. As the look of the father and the law, its force is never broken or subdued; after Schön's death, it is merely passed on to the state prosecutor's monocle, then to Alwa's scowl and Rodrigo's frown. Of all the sexualised men in the film, only Jack the Ripper's eyes are as unfocused as Lulu's.

The film establishes sexual fascination through the disavowed and hidden power of this look. For the spell to be broken, one simply has to imagine Lulu returning the look in defiance rather than acknowledging its force by constituting herself as picture and image. To imagine Lulu turn round and stick out her tongue at Dr Schön – the way, for instance, the heroine of Bunuel's *Un chien andalou* mocks a similarly castrating stare – would be to realise how it changes the film, breaking the atmosphere and tone, because it would upset the delicate and invisible balance that has displaced the opposition between active and passive: 'one sexy look and the picture would have been a burlesque'. The peculiar ambivalence that surrounds the encounter between Jack and Lulu feeds on the fact that here, both characters transgress the logic of the look specific to their symbolic role in the fiction. Once this logic is broken, so is the fascination on which the narrative relies for its paradigm of indeterminacy.[48] Again, only one conclusion seems possible: the moment Lulu manifests desire and appropriates the look defined by the film as 'male', she suffers death at the hands of the psychotic male, tormented by castration anxieties. But given the difficulty in *Pandora's Box* of defining the referential categories 'male' and 'female' according to who looks and who is being looked at, or aligning either with eye-line matching and point-of-view editing the classical narrative model as elaborated by feminist film theory seems to apply only up to a point. In so far as the ending is a kind of 'disenchantment', the breaking of a spell, it establishes as radiantly imperishable the image of Louise–Lulu while extinguishing her as the character Lulu in the fiction. This 'reality' of her image is the result of an excess of looks, all finally unable to seize her, rather than the product of these looks, to which it

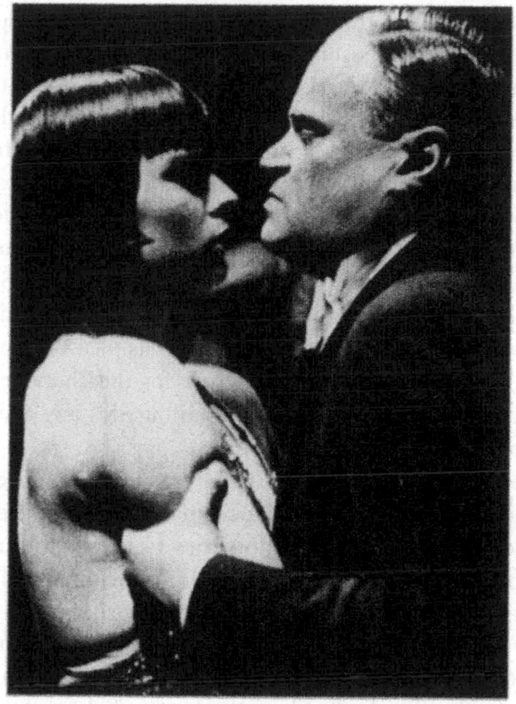

Figure 21 Apprehension against incomprehension? Louise Brooks (Lulu) in the grip of Fritz Kortner (Dr Schön) in *Pandora's Box* (1928)

Source: Stiftung Deutsche Kinemathek, Berlin

is confined: the image, one might say, is so radiant because of the ultimate powerlessness of the male looks. In this respect, Lulu would be the intermediary, the figure that allows for the communication and exchange of different 'looking' positions. For her response to the look of the Father is not to return the look with a suitably aggressive gesture, but to constitute herself as image and spectacle for the same or another subject's visual pleasure. An obvious example is the moment on the train when in response to Alwa's sullen frown, Lulu, as if by chance, attracts the interested and pleased eye of Count Casti-Piani. Similar reversals structure the entire courtroom scene, where Countess Geschwitz, in order to divert attention from Lulu, makes an admittedly angry rather than a pleasing spectacle of herself, which leads directly to the fake fire alarm and Lulu's successful escape. 'Hiding in the light' and 'overexposure' seem to work as a form of empowerment for Lulu, a sort of masquerade of excessive visibility.

This division of labour between looking and being looked at, however, does not work in the same fashion throughout. Pabst's use of the point-of-view shot and his editing establish a constant transfer or slippage between the various characters' point of view and that of the camera; since for the spectator, characters are stand-ins, markers of position in the field of signification, whose function it is to split – systematically and in constantly changing dramatic context – the attention of the viewer, Pabst's visual style here introduces subtle but significant variations on the norm of classic realism. A brief reminder of the role played by the meter man in the opening scene: the spectator participates in his point of view, 'moral' as well as optical. Yet although he is on the screen for no more than a minute or so, his gaze, his back and his preference for liquor are all 'preserved' for the fiction, as these semantic attributes are split between Schigolch, Schön and the mobile, hovering, alternating point of view, making hesitation and indecisiveness the very definition of spectatorship and its pleasure in this film. Pabst's insistence on Lulu as image, as framed picture for the characters in the film as well as for the spectator, renders even more ambiguous any distinction between the character's look and that of the spectator.

By far the most disturbing, because virtually unreadable (unreadable not in its narrative logic but in the logic of the glance–glance, facial expression, space and gesture) is the death of Dr Schön. Schön tries to persuade Lulu to kill herself after he has surprised her in the conjugal bedroom with Alwa's head cradled in her lap. Pabst stages the scene in a series of medium shots, with Lulu and Schön cut off at the waist. As Schön tries to force the gun into Lulu's hand, both of them are reflected in the bedroom mirror. From then on it is almost impossible for the spectator to decide whether he is looking at Schön or his mirror image, whether Schön is looking at Lulu, at the camera or at himself. The expressions on their faces subtly and continuously change as they struggle – they change from surprise, anger and anxiety until the emotive quality or intentionality of their expessions become indecipherable. Finally, a faint column of smoke rises between their faces, Schön looks pleased, Lulu surprised, but then Schön's features become rigid as his body begins to slide out of frame and blood trickles from his mouth. Lulu's expression glazes over, but also becomes intently curious as the camera pulls back to show her holding the smoking gun. As she turns from the mirror, her body is obscured until it is virtually smothered by Schön's slumped body. The scene ends with Alwa entering the room, looking fascinated and horrified at his father's dying face. The very discrepancy between the highly melodramatic, but none the less coherent narrative situation and the elaborate manner of its staging splits the spectator's perception and viewpoint in ways that subvert the action (who does what to whom?) and gender identification, in favour of a sliding scale of emotional expression, a puzzled scrutiny attempting to decipher face and gesture. Its effect is to make the scene hallucinatory, i.e. it allows one to locate several 'imaginaries' of the characters in the oedipal situation enacted in this primal scene. These imaginaries include that of Dr Schön, from whose point of view the scene could also be narrated, representing his struggle and ultimate failure to possess Lulu, to fix, limit and define her – if necessary by the act of marriage – in order to mould her to the negative identity of his obsessions (a bas-relief of a Pieta on the wall acts as a comment on this scene). Schön at the wedding is depicted as a man whose life is suddenly and dramatically out of control, so much so that only a pistol shot can put an end to the chaos. In so far as the wedding party turns into a repetition of the chaos at the theatre, the ways in which Schön put a stop to the first one (by proposing marriage to Lulu) and to the second one (by proposing that Lulu commit suicide) are structurally identical: a caustic comment on the bourgeois institution of marriage? Actions designed to terminate uncertainty reverse themselves and turn against the agent, for Schön also can be seen as a latter-day Student of Prague or Caligari, with whom his double has finally caught up.

But why should the narrational perspective and narrative point of view be mainly that of Dr Schön? What the ambiguity of bedroom scene suggests is also an allegory of cinematic perception and spectatorship. In the staging of Dr Schön's death the act of viewing itself becomes an activity situated in a different space, because it is presented as a series of views of identifiable objects or part-objects (hands, faces, backs, etc.), unenclosed by a master shot and therefore constantly implying what we do not see, and evoking a space where we are not. The cinema here is never what is shown: it is also what the shown implies or demands in the way of the not-shown and not-seen. The different kinds of repetition, elision and recognition create a hesitation on the threshold of perception that seems to serve a single aim: to make Lulu a phantom, a fetish reality in the register of the hyper-real, whose sexual presence is nothing other than the mirror-doubles the male characters are fated to carry about with them. Being an object of desire for everyone in the film, she preserves herself by being nothing and everything, a perpetual oscillation in the dramaturgy of conflict and aggression. The fact that Dr Schön cannot possess her and dies in the attempt to do so, gives an indication of Pabst's concept of the Lulu figure: to create a presence without an essence, heightened to the point of overexposed clarity solely by the play of difference and duplicity. The cinema, at the point in its history where it seemed poised to inherit the theatre, becomes for Pabst a mirror-image machine that turns the desire for possession into an obsession with the image, and the obsession with the image into a maze of divided, discontinuous, partial views whose identification and interpretation always entail a fine and final doubt – who is this me in the cinema that the beautiful stranger is smiling at up there on the screen?

The image in the cinema – how can it touch me if it cannot be touched? The androgynous, untouchable body of Louise Brooks would seem to be the ideal support for a project that sets out to transform the image of woman into an imaginary object, so that it can survive any kind of physical destruction, be it the ravages of age or sexual murder. If the first part of the film demonstrates that it is as impossible to possess Lulu as it is useless to try, and the second part exemplifies an equally useless attempt to fix her as an object of use or as an object of exchange in an economic–libidinal transaction, then the ending 'liberates' both these systems of constraint, beyond physical–sexual desire, beyond economic exchange, into the realm of the image. Jack the Ripper kills Lulu in the gentlest manner imaginable: extinguished by his back, she disappears from the field of vision, becoming the non-seen after the looked-at, asserting her indestructible intangibility against the alternation of presence/absence that traverses the film.

A fatal weakness: robots with maternal memories

Earlier I claimed that the meter man never returns. I must now revise this statement. We see him first reading/writing in a book, then turning round and seeing Lulu, as the spectator sees her and when he sees her. The meter man is thus the first spectator, turning from reading/writing to looking. In a different guise he returns as the last spectator. After Jack the Ripper kills Lulu, he steps out of a doorway, glances at Alwa, tightens his raincoat and walks off into the fog. After a brief hesitation, Alwa, too, begins to walk off disappearing into the night. They seem like men leaving the cinema: not the Gloria Palast, but the sort of cinema that caters mainly for men in raincoats or cloth caps. Both look disappointed and disenchanted as if the spectacle had finally revealed its emptiness. Its nothingness, had proved to be 'a masquerade that shows that there is nothing there'. Jack the Ripper, as long as he looks into Lulu's eyes is held by her image, the smile that fascinates with its radiant openness and indeterminacy. It is only when in the embrace he looks past Lulu that the knife appears as the object of his own obsessions, like the 'knife-phobia' of the protagonist in Pabst's *Secrets of a Soul.* Past the image, past the smile, he encounters once more only himself, his own anxieties. Jack the Ripper as a stand in for the spectator, wanting to grasp the presence that is Lulu, finds that he is distracted/attracted by the flickering candle and the glittering object: oscillating between the source of light and its reflection, his gaze traverses the woman, making her an image, a phantom, a fading sight in the *laterna magica* of his tormented psyche. This, once again, suggests an allegory of spectatorship and the cinematic apparatus: indeed, the pleasures of cinematic spectatorship are of a voyeuristic nature, and they enact a fetish fixation. And yet, Pabst's point-of-view structures, his *mise-en-scène* of mismatches and the manifold divisions of his film's textual system depend finally not on the woman's body, on what of it is hidden or revealed, nor on the aggressive male look directed at her: it is as if on all these (theoretical, moral, ideological) positions Pabst had anticipated a counter-argument or a re-statement. Sexuality in *Pandora's Box* is the infinitely deferred moment, the constantly renewed movement *away* from identity, and the film sustains this movement by the creation of a specifically cinematic imaginary that has no equivalence in either literature or the theatre. Pabst called his film not *Earth Spirit* but *Pandora's Box*: this Pandora's box is also the cinema-machine, the machinery of filmic *mise-en-abyme.* The achievement, in other words, is to have presented sexuality *in* the cinema as the sexuality *of* the cinema, and to have used as his starting point the crisis in the self-understanding of male and female sexuality that characterised his own period, the Weimar, of wounded male egos confronting the 'New Woman'.

At the same time, Pabst does not posit an essence of cinema as the 'ground' for a new society of the spectacle, any more than he believes in an essence of sexual identity. The extensive play on Büchse (box) at the level of the signifier – can of film, camera, Freudian 'symbol' of the female sex – disperses the fixity of the signified, be it woman or cinema. This is where in some important respect, the Louise Brooks of *Pandora's Box* can be compared with the Maria of Fritz Lang's *Metropolis*, the man-created robot woman. Significantly enough, the figure of Lulu cannot be conceived as a mother Her eroticism is constructed on the paradigmatic opposition to all the traditionally female roles, and yet, while the same is true of the *femme fatale*, with the latter it is a sociological and biological paradigm to which she is contrasted rather than the technological–constructivist one that seems to underlie Pabst's conception of Lulu.[49] In Pabst's other film with Louise Brooks, *Diary of a Lost Girl*, the heroine does have a child, illegitimate and eventually taken away from her. It is this fact that fundamentally changes her character, making her the classic female victim, and the film more like the classic social melodrama. It is as if with the introduction of the biological function of women, one cannot escape sociology and bourgeois morality, whereas in *Pandora's Box* it is precisely the absence of these motifs that makes the cinematic erotic shine out so brilliantly but also so coldly. Indeed, Lulu's hint of a maternal function for Jack the Ripper is precisely that which makes her fallible and vulnerable. The film thus becomes a parable of the new woman, created by man, whose fatal weakness are her maternal 'memories'. The eroticism in Lulu is paradoxically that of the creature that comes to life, the auto-eroticism of the creator and the narcissism of the creature: a relationship only too familiar from the Sternberg–Dietrich Pygmalion myth, which Pabst very nearly anticipated with Louise Brooks three years earlier, but also, in his purportedly disparaging remark, already questions. This eroticism is one that, however, plays on a concomitant anxiety: that of the creature that emancipates itself from the creator, the sorcerer's apprentice, a motif which with some justice might be called the key motif in German cinema ever since *The Cabinet of Dr Caligari*, itself in a tradition where the robot of *Metropolis* constitutes the decisive transformation from 'medium' of Golem to vamp and woman.[50] It is this genealogy that might give one a clue to the mysteriously truncated subsequent career of Louise Brooks. In her essay on Pabst she reports that at the end of her work with him he took her aside:

> 'Your life is exactly like Lulu's' he said, 'and you will end the same way.' At that time, knowing so little of what he meant by Lulu, I just sat sullenly glaring at him, trying not to listen. Fifteen years later in Hollywood with all his predictions closing in on me, I heard his words again hissing back to me.
>
> (Brooks 1982: 102–3)

What Pabst meant by 'Lulu' is perhaps precisely this: a woman, an American actress, made by the film industry into a star becomes an object among objects, alive only in front of the camera. Louise Brooks's struggle with Hollywood as documented in her autobiographical essays bore out exactly what it meant for an intelligent, articulate woman to be a 'thing among things'. It is as if, at the very threshold of becoming a star, Louise Brooks made a film which had as its subject the psycho-pathology of this very star system, against the background not of Hollywood nor its ideological critique, but in terms of a very specifically German 'settling of scores' around Expressionism, the theatrical performance as social and representational space, around avant-garde Modernism and the modernity of cinema. In this respect, the film is indeed the 'tissue of arguments' that it was disparagingly called by Kracauer, testifying to the degree of 'abstraction' that the German cinema, even in its commercial productions, was engaged in. The enigma of Louise Brooks is thus in part the enigma of film making *per se* and *par excellence*, and the very film that might have made her a star allowed her to see what being a star entailed, in the mirror of a film that dramatised and contrasted the liberating pure externality of the 'American' character (the hope of Modernism for most of the 1920s) with the contorted inwardness of the 'Weimar psyche'. Against its obsessiveness, but also its moral essentialism, her externality signals not objectivity (and certainly not New Objectivity), but the object status and objectification of a subjectivity and sexuality – that of women, but also, finally of men – which in the film has neither name nor place. It was as if in the debate between patriarchy on the one side, and technological modernism on the other, Louise Brooks had glimpsed, albeit at first unconsciously, in her defeat with Hollywood, but later with full lucidity, the blank that both left for woman as a site of representation and agency.

Pabst perceived this perhaps more acutely than most of his contemporaries.[51] His emphasis on the cinema creating its own time – that of the motion of the camera, whose signifiers the characters become and to which they lend their gestures, faces and expressivity – and its own space, that of editing and lighting, of the cut on movement or the cut according to the dynamics of the gaze (glance–glance, glance–object) – makes Louise Brooks embody the principle of the cinema itself, in its distinctiveness from literature, theatre and the other arts. But in this very principle lies an objectification of human beings and an anthropomorphism of technology, such as the cinema has introduced into the culture of Modernity – rendering a reality in its own right. It makes Langlois's praise of Louise Brooks that I quoted at the beginning: 'she is the intelligence of the cinematic process' so apt and so ambiguous. For this intelligence is the principle of divisibility and division itself, of exchange and substitution, as it constitutes the symbolic logic of Western culture and capitalism. By contrast, it is a sign of Louise Brooks's intelligence that she decided not to become the objectified commodity that the logic of this process demanded of her. What Pabst could not have prevented, if ever he had wanted to, was the shift, whereby the film industry, seizing on the woman's body, and focusing so much on spectator pleasure, turned the cinema into an obsessional, fetishistic instrument, seemingly betraying its modernist (Nietzschean) promise of 'reversibility and vitality', by making this Modernism instrumental and subservient to the logic of capital and the commodity. It might seem, finally, a poor bargain: Pabst's film tries to sustain a modernist project, *against* Expressionism and *for* the cinema, where the cinema is assigned the task of performing a 'holding operation', being the lesser evil, because, if it cannot bring about the permanent revolution, its indecidability, hesitancy, indeterminacy does at least keep things in suspended animation, corroding with its cynicism, its scepticism, its irony all the impostures of spectator power. But the price is high: it leaves the woman-as-image 'inside the system' to be commodified, or rather, as the necessary currency lubricating not only the system of male exchange, but also the exchange of goods, the capitalist system of consumption. Because what has kept it going? According to Kracauer, 'the little shopgirls', according to Pabst, *Die Dame*: the woman as commodity becoming consumer. This is where a new dialectic might open up, or rather, here would be the point of another reversal, where 'woman' does have a stake. What if Lulu the 'modern woman' had stepped out of the 'picture' into the street, to enter the space of consumption, but instead of street walking, she had gone window shopping? Might the mirror of consumption have 'freed' her differently than expiring in the male gaze, her 'purchase' allowing her to break the vicious circle between (bourgeois) production and (maternal) reproduction, by suspending both?

Notes

1 For biographical information on Louise Brooks, see Card 1958; Tynan 1979a: 45–78; Brooks 1979: 97–9; Paris 1989.

2 Godard's references for this film were Renoir's *Nana*, Dreyer's *La Passion de Jeanne d'Arc* and Pabst's *Pandora's Box*. Pabst himself was reportedly inspired by Dreyer's film. But see also Peter Wollen, 'Brooks and The Bob', *Sight and Sound* (February 1994): 24–5.

3 Card 1958: 242.

4 Apparently, all references to the possibly incestuous relation between Schigolch and Lulu, the fight of father and son over the same woman, and the lesbian attraction to Lulu of Countess Geschwitz were removed by appropriate cuts and changes in the intertitles (Clipping file, *Pandora's Box*, British Film Institute Library, London).

5 Potamkin 1933.

6 Quoted in Brooks 1982: 95.

7 Kraszna-Krausz 1929: 27.

8 Kracauer 1947: 178–9.

9 Fifty years later, Kenneth Tynan, man of the theatre, could afford to be more charitable: '*Pandora's Box* belongs among the few films that have succeeded in improving on a theatrical chef-d'oeuvre', 'Dream Woman of the Cinema', *Observer Magazine* (11 November 1979b): 38.

10 Kristeva 1980 and Rose 1984.

11 See the chapter on UFA and the importation of American stars such as Anna May Wong for Dupont and Eichberg, or Lilian Gish for Murnau's *Faust*.

12 Saunders 1992 and Horak 1992.
13 Tatar 1995.
14 On this 'boulevard culture' of the 1920s, see Szatmari 1928. For a more recent history, see Wolffram 1992. A good overview can also be found in Paysan 1998: 46–66.
15 For an examination of the *femme fatale* in film and feminist theory, see Doane 1991, which also contains a most illuminating discussion of *Pandora's Box* ('The Erotic Barter': 142–62).
16 See also the chapters 'It's the end of the song' and 'To be or not to be', (Part III, Chapter 3 and Part IV, Chapter 1, this volume).
17 A concise sociological analysis of Wedekind's Lulu can be found in Galassi 1975: 84–7. But see also Gail Finney, 'Woman as spectacle and commodity: Wedekind's Lulu Plays,' in Gail Finney: *Women in Modern Drama: Freud, Feminism, and European Theater at the Turn of the Century* (Ithaca: Cornell University Press, 1989): 79–101, and J.L. Hibberd, 'The spirit of the flesh: Wedekind's Lulu', *The Modern Language Review* 79 (April 1984): 336–55.
18 I have tried to elaborate on this in my 'Presentation of Stanley Cavell' (*ASCA Brief*, Amsterdam, 1998), a short commentary on this complex 'Vienna, skepticism, melodrama' as I see it present in Stanley Cavell, *Contesting Tears* (Chicago: University of Chicago Press, 1996).
19
> The curse on our literature today is that it is much too literary. We know of no other questions and problems than those that crop up among writers and intellectuals. We see no further in our art than the limits of our interests as a class. To find back to great and powerful art, we would have to move much more among people who have never read a book in their lives, and for whom the simplest animal instincts serve as a guide to their actions. I have tried to work along these lines in my play *Earth Spirit*'.
>
> (Frank Wedekind, *Die Büchse der Pandora*, Act I (1990) [my translation])

20 Wedekind's image of woman seems to stand in the tradition which goes from Freud's remark, 'What does woman want?' via Otto Weininger and Karl Kraus, not forgetting Fritz Lang's notion of the 'Weibsteufel/She-Devil'. For Weininger, see Slavoj Zizek: Otto Wininger or, 'Woman doesn't exist', *Metastases of Enjoyment. Six Essays on Woman and Causality* (London: Verso 1994): 137–64.
21 'When writing the part of Lulu, the main problem was to depict the body of a woman through the words that she speaks. With every line of hers I had to ask myself, does it make her young and beautiful? (Wedekind, quoted in Kutscher [1911] 1964: 128).
22 Lukacs [1913] 1981: 3–4.
23 It is here that one can see how crucial Wedekind was for both the drama theory and staging practice of the early Bertolt Brecht.
24 Wedekind confessed to Kutscher that he had declared Geschwitz the tragic figure in the preface, because he hoped to deflect the legal objections to his play, raised at three successive trials in Berlin, Leipzig and again Berlin. In the preface to the play, Geschwitz is characterised by Wedekind as 'non-nature', i.e. outside the binary oppositions of nature/society, and male/female:

> What the courts did not object to was that I had made the terrible fate of being outside nature ('Unnatürlichkeit') which this human being has to bear, the object of serious drama. Figures like [Geschwitz] belong to the race of Tantalus. [...] I was driven by the desire to snatch from public ridicule the enormous human tragedy of exceptionally intense and quite fruitless inner struggles.

(*Die Büchse der Pandora*, Preface (Kutscher [1911] 1964: 127) (my translation)

25 For an overview of the debate around 'how silent was silent cinema?', see among others, Altman 1997: 648–718.
26 Lukacs [1913] 1981: 3–4.
27 On the relation of theatrical to cinematic space, see Tsivian 1996: 264–76.
28 Jessner 1979: 213.
29 For the discourse of 'honesty' in relation to Louise Brooks, see Hastie 1997: 3–24.
30 Brooks 1982: 93.
31 On Kracauer's description of 'Haus Vaterland' see my 'Cinema – The irresponsible signifier', in *New German Critique*, no. 40 (Winter 1987): 71–5.
32 Kaes 1983.
33 See discussion of Lukacs' remarks in Part II, Chapter 2.
34 See Part II, Chapter 1, this volume, on Fritz Lang's *Dr Mabuse.*
35 On Richard Oswald's *Anders als die anderen*, see Richard Dyer, 'Weimar – less and more like the others', in R. Dyer, *Now You See It. Studies on Lesbian and Gay Film* (London: Routledge 1990): 7–46.
36 Quoted in Brooks 1982: 94.
37 Pandora's Box, microfiche file. BFI Library, London. Programme note, no date, no source given.
38 Brooks 1982: 98.
39 Browning 1920: 54.
40 The film strongly hints that Schigolch is her father, and possibly 'initiated' her sexually. But there is also the suggestion that both might be Jewish - he in his gestures and looks, she by having a candelabrum on her sideboard.
41 One might argue over how firmly this 'American' rule of continuity editing was adhered to in Weimar cinema and whether it was considered a rule at all, but the disorienting effect exists, in a film which, for the rest, is perfectly capable of creating the illusion of a coherent scenic space, especially when it needs to complicate it, as in the back-stage scene discussed below.
42 See *Die Angestellten* (1930) in Siegfried Kracauer, *Schriften* vol. 1 (Frankfurt: Suhrkamp, 1971): 91–101 and 286–7.
43 See Part II, Chapter 3 on Murnau, this volume.
44 This part of the chapter refers to an exchange with Mary Ann Doane, subsequent to a paper of hers, first given in my 'Weimar Cinema' graduate seminar at the University of Iowa, 1979. See also footnote 1 in Doane 1991: 284.
45 I am alluding here, of course, to Laura Mulvey's argument in 'Visual pleasure and narrative cinema' (1975).
46 The 'kinetic object box' and the text are reproduced in *Film als Film*, Catalogue Kölnischer Kunstverein (1977): 88.
47 Kenneth Tynan called Louise Brooks 'this unbroken, unbreakable porcellain filly' (Tynan 1979b: 45).
48 Today, one might call it the 'performative' aspect of Lulu's sexuality. See Andrea Weiss, who also talks about the 'mobility' of Louise Brooks's sexual identity in *Vampires and Violets* (New York: Penguin Books, 1992): 24. Amelie Hastie comments on this: 'recognizing Brooks' sexuality as "mobile" accents her movement not simply in the space between sexual identities, but within the space of the identities as well' (Hastie 1997: 9).
49 Pabst made several films starring Brigitte Helm, the 'Maria' of *Metropolis*. The most intriguing is *Die Herrin von Atlantis*, suggestively analysed in the terms I am here proposing by Karl Siereck, 'The primal scene of cinema: four fragments from *The Mistress of Atlantis*', in R. Rentschler (ed.) *The Films of G.W. Pabst* (New Brunswick: Rutgers, 1990): 135–42. See also Hermann Kappelhoff, 'Der weite Himmel', in *Der möblierte Mensch* (Berlin: Vorwerk 8, 1994): 195–224.

50 See the more extensive discussion of the motif of the sorcerers' apprentice in Part I, Chapter 3, this volume on Caligari's family'.

51 There have been a number of recent studies on Pabst (in German), all of them extensively discussing *Pandora's Box*: Hermann Kappelhoff, *Der möblierte Mensch: G.W. Pabst und die Utopie der Sachlichkeit* (Berlin: Vorwerk 8 Verlag, 1994): 157–79; Gerald Kroll, *Pandoras Schätze* (München: diskurs film, 1998): 265–329; Klaus Kreimeier, 'Die kalte Persona' in W. Jacobson (ed.) *G.W. Pabst* (Berlin: Argon 1998): 31–40.

Part III

TRANSPARENT DUPLICITIES

Comedy, opera, operetta

1

HALLO CAESAR!

Reinhold Schünzel, a German Chaplin?

> There are plenty of fine moments, but as comedy it falters, for lack of structure and a central dramatic idea. Schünzel who plays Caesar [...] is on a slippery slope. What he is famous for, his wicked flippancy, his cynicism, his tongue-in-cheek silliness is in danger of turning into a mannerism.
>
> (*Lichtbildbühne* no. 108, 1927)

> Maybe it is true that [...] the material would have been more suitable for a three-reeler than a full-length feature. Szakall, who is a very successful variety artist, has many a fine sketch to his credit. If he gives up writing film scripts, it won't be a great loss. Nobody needs to be good at everything. And Schünzel ought to be reminded that if he didn't just trust his acting skills but took more care over his story material, his successes would be even greater.
>
> (*Kinematograph* 8 May 1927)

Popular cinema?

Reading the reviews from 1927, it seems that critics at the time did not quite know what to make of *Hallo Caesar!* (1927, director: Reinhold Schünzel, script: Szöke Szakall, with Reinhold Schünzel).[1] They saw a ragbag of more or less successful routines, gags and visual jokes, poorly motivated by a flimsy plot; they criticised the sentimental interludes that detract from the underlying comic premise; and they thought that the acting was over the top. Yet they implicitly made the actor–director's own past performances the measure of their present dissatisfaction, thus confirming that in the mid-1920s, Reinhold Schünzel was a household name, considered by the critics to be a major film maker and a comic genius. With our knowledge of classic German (or Weimar) cinema still largely drawn from Lotte Eisner's *The Haunted Screen* (1969) and Siegfried Kracauer's *From Caligari to Hitler* (1947), this comes as quite a surprise. Here is a popular comedian–director–producer, in the tradition of Charlie Chaplin, Buster Keaton and Harold Lloyd, unknown internationally and barely remembered by German film historians. *Hallo Caesar!* in particular is something of an archaeological discovery. A small chink of light in the received opinion that perceives German cinema as the dark mirror of the nation's soul and authoritarian traits, this film might conceivably give a glimpse of some of the other layers that made up Weimar film culture and popular cinema.

Figures such as Schünzel raise important questions about European and national traditions of comedy in and out of the cinema, about the transitional period between 'early' and 'classical' cinema and the changes from performative to narrative modes, about national film style and the international film industry, and finally, about the discourses that constitute a popular star or performer as a brand-name. Schünzel's persona and work also redresses the traditional emphasis on expressionist versus realist film making as the dominant dualism of the period and reintegrates this part of Weimar cinema into an international production context. No national cinema has suffered more from the neglect of the popular in favour of the art cinema and *auteur* cinema. This is probably due to three factors: first, the scarcity of material that has survived.[2] Second, the bias of the Weimar cultural elite either for the art film, or for American popular cinema, notably slapstick comedy. Third, the general belief that the German cinema has never been capable of good comedy with the exception of Lubitsch – who went to Hollywood.

Reinhold Schünzel – a typical Weimar film career?

Born in Hamburg in 1888, Schünzel started acting as early as 1912 in a 'Volkstheater' and by appearing in comedy sketches for a travelling troupe. By 1916 he had begun working in films, but first profiled himself as an actor in the so-called 'Sittenfilme' (sex education films) of the post-war period, where he played diabolical figures – seducers, homosexual extortionists and swindlers whose smooth exterior disguised sadistic villainy and fiendish lusts. Of these essentially melodramatic roles probably the best-known is in *Anders als die Anderen* (*Different from Others*, Richard Oswald, 1918/19), where he blackmails Conrad Veidt over a homosexual affair. He is equally impressive as the double-dealing Duc de Choiseuil in Ernst Lubitsch's *Madame Dubarry* (1919) and the cold-blooded seducer in *Das Mädchen aus der Ackerstrasse* (*The Girl from Acker Street*, Reinhold Schünzel, 1920). From the mid-1920s onwards, Schünzel developed an alternative persona, essentially comic, the Berlin street-wise good-for-nothing, turning a notorious 'local' character into a nationally recognised type. Often he played characters of the lower orders (servants, waiters, out-of-work artisans) acting as go-between to facilitate fantasies about social mobility and careerism in a society where class was about to be superseded by appearance and raffish style. In this, he was very much a composite identification figure for his primary target audience, the upwardly mobile class of artisans-to-office workers, entering en masse the new service industries – Siegfried Kracauer's *Angestellten*.

Schünzel carefully nurtured a number of show-business myths centred on being a man of the people. Stories put out by his studio's press office described incidents in which he was 'mistaken' for Reinhold Schünzel in provincial towns or working-class districts. His favourite plot material in the comedies involves impersonation, mistaken identity, role reversal, con-tricks and deception, which hints at a deeper connection between his sinister and his comic roles:

> There is no second [actor in Germany today] whom one believes more readily capable of all imaginable evils as Schünzel, effortlessly gliding straight from the slippery slope of the big city onto the scene. We see him, thanks to his cruel realism, in the midst of a milieu which only with his presence fully comes to life. Violent and overpowering, he is sinfulness made flesh. His cynical brutality, his duplicitous eroticism and diabolical insidiousness are truly daunting.[3]

Internationally, Schünzel did not become famous until the sound era, when he directed some of the most sophisticated comedies of the 1930s, such as *Viktor und Viktoria* (1933; in English: *First a Girl*, director: Victor Saville, with Jesse Mathews), *Die Englische Heirat* (*The English Marriage*, 1934), *Amphytrion* (1935). Eight of his films were also made in French, usually co-directed by Roger Le Bon, or Henri Chomette.[4] He also acted in international hits like G.W. Pabst's *Die 3-Groschenoper* (*The Threepenny Opera*, 1931), where he played the servile-sentimental police chief, Tiger Brown, or in the German-language version of *Le Bal* (Wilhelm Thiele, France 1931). Although Jewish on his mother's side, his films were such big box office that Goebbels was anxious to keep him on after the Nazi takeover in 1933, and he continued to make popular comedies well into the mid-1930s. When he eventually left for Hollywood in 1937, after censorship difficulties over *Land der Liebe* (*Land of Love*, 1937) he arrived to a very hostile reception from the German émigré community. Under contract to MGM, directing four films for them between 1938 and 1941, he somehow managed to antagonise Louis B. Meyer, who apparently made sure that Schünzel would be out of work as a director. The rest of his career is made up of small parts in anti-Nazi films, such as an SS officer squeezing a pimple while torturing an old lady in Fritz Lang's *Hangmen Also Die!* (USA, 1942), *The Hitler Gang* (John Farrow, USA, 1944), and Alfred Hitchcock's *Notorious* (USA, 1946), where he plays the guest of honour at Claude Rains's rather strained dinner party and comes to a sticky end. Schünzel's filmography includes directing credits for 45 films between 1918 and 1941, and he acted altogether in 140 films between 1916 and 1953.

Author, actor, showman, type

Celebrating Schünzel as a rediscovery, it is tempting to think of him as an *auteur* (writing, directing, producing, acting all in one) but this is misleading. He comes from a tradition (in fact, rather similar to the milieu that gave Lubitsch his start) where the performer is perforce a *metteur en scène*, if only of his own persona. Contemporary reviews, however, did make a distinction between Schünzel the director and Schünzel the actor. As a director, he was first regarded as a realist with a feel for detail, for seedy settings and underworld types (*Das Mädchen aus der Ackerstrasse* is often quoted as the first realist feature film), while his comedies won praise for their understatement. As an actor, by contrast, he was accused of developing exaggerated mannerisms and hamming it up: a dualism the critics resolved by ritually admonishing Schünzel the director to restrain Schünzel the actor.[5]

The Schünzel persona relies heavily on the transvestism of operetta, with its preference for role reversal, and the definition of erotic desire around exchange and substitution. Often, social status and sexual status are conjugated against each other (the impostor who pretends to be the rich uncle from America, or the village simpleton who is suddenly sexually desirable when he becomes heir to a fortune). As the quotation above suggests, Schünzel uniquely combined sentimentality, ruthlessness and cynicism in his roles: opportunist but irreverent, the boy-next-door with a heart of gold but also the street lout without a conscience, and capable of unspeakable brutality. Perhaps most characteristically, the Schünzel persona is also marked by sexual ambivalence: a homosexual or bisexual subtext is the most conspicuous common denominator between his

Figure 22 City-snob, rake and dandy: Reinhold Schünzel publicity still (circa 1924)
Source: BFI films: stills, posters and designs

diabolical seducer of the late 1910s and early 1920s and his comic persona from the mid-1920s onwards. Aptly, Klaus Kreimeier calls Schünzel 'the unreliable type, par excellence':

> in his roles he translated all that was irridescent, cynical, duplicitous about the culture of Weimar into a sometimes shamelessly crude, at other times subtly nuanced and elegant language of gestures.[6]

Hallo Caesar! was filmed during June/July 1926, produced by Schünzel's own firm, with himself as co-writer, director, producer and leading actor. Executive producer was Fritz Großmann, whom Schünzel seemed to have relied on regularly during that period. 1926 was a good year, and Schünzel was at the height of his career.[7] After the enormous success of the Emil Jannings' film *Alles um Geld* (*Everything Turns Around Money*, 1923) Schünzel was also taken seriously as a director, and during the next six years he was involved in more than thirty films as director or in a leading role. With seven films, the 1925–6 season was one of the best. Those directed by Georg Jacoby (*Der Hahn im Korb* (*Cock of the Roost*, 1925); *Der Stolz der Kompanie* (*Pride of the Regiment*, 1926); *Der Dumme August des Zirkus Romanelli* (*The Clown from Circus Romanelli*, 1926) as well as *Fünfuhrtee in der Ackerstraße* (*Five O'clock Tea in Acker Street*, Paul Ludwig Stein, 1926) and *Der Juxbaron* (*The Baron of Fun*, Willi Wolf, 1926) crystallise and define Schünzel as a comic. In *Hallo Caesar!* his own comic qualities condense these into a multifaceted but none the less readily identifiable type. A poem by the title 'All Star Cast', clearly implies that Schünzel is, with Conrad Veidt a figure in the front row (of the cinema's publicity machinery).[8] But as one of the trade papers pointed out, this was also a function of his astonishing rate of output: 'Schünzel works without a break, and that is the publicity which serves him best'.[9]

Similarly, judging by the ads placed by UFA studios in the 1926 trade papers, Schünzel had also become a bankable director. In the context of the famous Parufamet Agreement, several Schünzel productions are specifically announced for the 1927 season, and in the UFA Annual Preview[10] much is made of the anticipated December 1927 premiere of *Üb'immer Treu und Redlichkeit* (*Be Loyal and Honest*, 1927) and for April 1928, next to 'a Portenfilm' appears 'a Schünzel-Film' (presumably, *Gustav Mond ... Du Gehst So Stille* (*Gustav Moon ... You Move So Silently*, 1927–8). Such PR work suggests a few questions: was Schünzel at that time valuable to UFA as a star director or as star actor? The comparison with Henny Porten points to the latter, but the fact that both 'Schünzel films' were actually directed by him does not exclude the former, especially since in the same 1927–8 season two more Schünzel films are released through UFA: *Herkules Maier* (1927) and *Adam und Eva* (1928), both with Schünzel in the lead, produced and supervised (as 'künstlerischer Oberleiter') by him, but with directorial credits going to Alexander Esway and Rudolf Bieberach. This raises a further issue: were the Schünzel films of the mid-1920s intended for export or for the domestic market? The press releases continue to sell Schünzel to a broad public in Germany, especially provincial audiences:

> In between his important productions he is always concerned to make more modest films, which are above all destined to ensure that a certain public – that of the small cinemas – does not forget him.
>
> (*Die Filmwoche* no. 9, 1924)

The Schünzel anecdotes published in the *Filmkurier* of January 1928 have one single point: to show how, whether among the revolutionaries on the barricades in 1919, among the Berliner street-wise adolescents, or among the working men and Viennese cab drivers, Schünzel is a familiar face: though apparently much better known in his roles as criminal, aristocrat or dandy, than as comedian. Schünzel's own biographical sketch on the other hand tries to prove that right from the start, behind the serious (theatrical) roles, the comedian in him was irrepressible:

> [I must have been] deeply benighted, when I honestly believed I would give the world a new Hamlet or Don Carlos. The Swiss knew better: their stifled laughter was an eye-opener, they discovered the comedian in me. It was a relief no longer having to be afraid of the audience laughing at me.
>
> (*Filmwelt* no. 4, February 1925: 12)

In the same article Schünzel boasts of his services to ordinary films for ordinary people:

> I don't want to appear immodest, but permit me to point out that I am proud to have been the first director in Germany who, in the age of the big budget films, dared to make a film on location in Berlin, about the fate of a little servant girl.
>
> (Ibid.: 15)

Was Schünzel, as a comic talent, a creator of comedian's comedy or merely an actor of comic parts? A comparison with the early Lubitsch is quite telling. In films where Lubitsch not only directed but also played the lead (*Meier aus Berlin* (*Meier from Berlin*, 1916), his persona 'Meier' was a character already familiar from variety theatre and newspaper cartoons, so that – parallel to developments in the USA – the persona could rely on a certain amount of audience foreknowledge, increasingly the basis for the fixed characters of comedian's comedy like Chaplin's Charlie, 'Stoneface' Keaton, 'Rubberface' Al St John, or 'Babyface' Langdon. Lubitsch soon abandoned comedian's comedy and concentrated on directing, perhaps precisely because the 'Meier' type he had helped to bring to the screen proved geographically and ethnically too limiting, cutting out potentially important audiences and becoming – as much popular European comedy seems to have been – inexportable.

Schünzel did not go down the Lubitsch road until the 1930s when he began to acquire an international reputation for directing erotically suave 'sophisticated comedies' (*Viktor und Viktoria, Amphitryon*) following, precisely, the (American) Lubitsch tradition. What the German film industry did not seem to be able to marshal in the 1920s, compared to the international competition, were slapstick comedians of wide appeal, who could measure up to Max Linder, Ben Turpin, Chaplin and a host of others. This is not to say that there were not many actors who excelled in comic parts, such as Siggi Arno, Curt Bois, Victor Janssen and Julius Falkenstein, but none of them managed the breakthrough to being a star whose (brand)name alone conjured up a one-man-genre and guaranteed box-office success.[11] Schünzel, it would seem, was a compromise figure between a comic character actor and a German star comedian to compete with the popularity of Chaplin.

One of the largest ads of the Reinhold Schünzel–Film GmbH in the *Lichtbildbühne* April 1928 reads in bold letters: 'Reinhold Schünzel promises a full house for every movie-theatre owner'. Underneath four new productions are previewed: *Der Harem des Mister Fox* (not completed), *Aus Dem Tagebuch eines Junggesellen* (*From A Bachelor's Diary*, 1928), *Don Juan in der Mädchenschule* (*Don Juan at the Girls' Gymnasium* (1928), and *Michel im Weltkrieg* (not completed), each title advertised with the phrase 'Schünzel as … ' following the manner of Charlie as tramp, as gold prospector, as widower. In the satirical poem 'Kino, Kino über alles', Hans Harbeck counts Schünzel among the greatest.[12] One can assume that part of this comparison ('Keaton, Chaplin, Schünzel, Pat and Lloyd') is wishful thinking, or all-too obvious publicity, for these comparisons had already prompted one critic to vent his doubts, when in a review of *Gustav Mond* he noted with some exasperation: 'the fact must just for once be stated that Schünzel is no Chaplin, Harold Lloyd or Buster Keaton',[13] against which must be set articles in *Das blaue Heft* or *Das Acht-Uhr-Abendblatt,* where Schünzel is emphatically described as on a par with Lloyd and Keaton.

Hallo Caesar!

There is much to suggest that Chaplin served as a role model for the character of Caesar, in the way that physically demanding comedy and slapstick routines are combined with a modest and ultimately sentimental plot. Chaplin's films (and thus his fame), came to Germany relatively late, but when they did, proved irresistible, especially to the critics. He became the yardstick, not so much of comedy, but of film as art. Especially the influential Berlin critics such as Willy Haas and Hans Siemsen idolised Chaplin. Siemsen went as far as to castigate his countrymen for continuing to worship war heroes such as the Kaiser or Hindenburg, when the rest of the world had found the true modern hero – the little-man-in-the-street, suspicious and undermining authority.[14] Schünzel may well have been suspicious of such reverse hero worship of Chaplin, but as his marketing proves, he knew that emulating Chaplin was good for the box office. Considering Schünzel's furious rate of productivity (seven films in 1926, three of them as director), *Hallo Caesar!* would seem to have been a routine film intended for the domestic market:

> Schünzel has his eye with this – by no means cheap – film firmly on an audience ready to laugh at the slightest occasion, without making too high a demand on its entertainment.
>
> (*Lichtbildbühne* no. 108, 1927)

Both the identity of the star and character he plays are announced in the title of the film – Schünzel *is* Caesar! The plot of the film contains the most popular theme in Weimar entertainment – mistaken identity satirising dreams about social climbing, which can be found in films, popular fiction and especially in operettas. Schünzel himself made a film of one of these operettas, namely *Der Juxbaron* (*The Baron of Fun*). There is also an American influence in Weimar cinema, where the chase after the Hollywood contract replaces the chase after the rich American uncle's inheritance. Other episodes (the taxi ride after he arrives in Karlsbad, for instance) are comic episodes reminiscent of the Mack Sennett school of American slapstick. Schünzel knows his audience: with *Hallo Caesar!* the director imitates certain popular Hollywood genres, while making the characters and plot recognisable to the Germany of that era. A review of *Gustav Mond ... Du Gehst So Stille* (*Gustav Moon*) identified very clearly this aspect of Schünzel's films:

> Despite the viewer being familiar from earlier films with this kind of character, Schünzel still enchants in much the same way as Harold Lloyd and Buster Keaton do. In particular, when the frame is as cleverly mounted as it is here, and a few sensations in the American manner are added for good measure.
>
> (*Kinematograph* 25 December 1927)

In other words, Schünzel, is perceived as a director who is not targeting the American market, but is providing the same kind of entertainment aimed at a German audience. In a sense, it shows much more clearly than do the art films and prestigious spectaculars of Weimar cinema, how popular taste and the German market had become Americanised (i.e. taken over by US firms) by the mid-1920s. The consciously populist streak in *Hallo Caesar!* is evinced by the title itself – the actor and the main character converge – and also because of the title – 'hailing' the hero – it is almost as if there were an imaginary public applause as the star comes onto the stage. This brings *Hallo Caesar!* into the realm of a narrative mode that is still very performance-oriented, and some of the faint praise that the film received from the critics reflects the preference for the totally narrativised full-length feature film. However, *Hallo Caesar!* was still conspicuously made with an eye to the 'numbers principle' of early cinema, perhaps an indication that the audience it was aimed at had not yet become familiar with the full-length feature film and was quite satisfied with an evening of two and three reels, provided there was a recognisable star character, in this case the Schünzel/Caesar persona. There was in fact a topical debate about the desirability of re-introducing two-reelers into the programme, especially for provincial theatres.[15] Several other factors indicate that *Hallo Caesar!* belongs to what Tom Gunning has called 'the cinema of attractions', as opposed to the 'cinema of narrative integration'.[16] The format of 'showing and telling' (as opposed to just 'telling a story') is very apparent, with Schünzel often taking the audience into his confidence with a wink, or an exaggerated gesture. From the beginning of the film (at the hairdresser's salon), to which he follows the pair of legs that first attract his attention, Caesar obviously revels in the role of love-struck beau, failing to seduce the lady with his conjuring tricks and talented miming, but at the same time seducing the audience, which, of course, is his real aim. Thus, we have a twofold spectator position: a narrative one, concerned with the progress of the love interest, and a performative one that justifies Caesar's claim to be the vaudeville artist he so desperately desires to be. This is even more apparent in the subsequent scene, when the lady departs and Caesar rushes after her. Her departure occurs after he has placed his 'bride' in a chair, asking the hairdresser to give her a fashionable hair cut. The 'bride' is one of the salon's dummies from the shop window and the hairdresser is already halfway through cutting the dummy's hair before he realises his mistake. In this scene, the camera has temporarily abandoned both Caesar and the real love-object of his attention. The gag, carefully prepared by Caesar, is wholly staged for the benefit of the audience. In fact, the lady of his dreams all but disappears from the film, and we are as surprised as she is – and as Caesar is – when she turns up again on the Karlsbad promenade.

A whole series of scenes, notably those in the Berlin coffee house, are built up as separate 'numbers', with the coffee house an ideal setting for creating performers and audiences, spectators and exhibitionists. It is as if a constantly gathered diegetic audience doubles and 'represents' the actual audience in the cinema – a clear indication that the film is very conscious of its own performative mode (which has nothing 'theatrical' about it), making *Hallo Caesar!* not so much a 'primitive' film, but one that 'knows its audience'. It is this aspect of Schünzel the actor–writer–director–producer that makes any attempt to rescue or rediscover Schünzel as *auteur maudit* implausible, at least for the 1920s. In performance-oriented films like *Hallo Caesar!* he belongs much more to the (by no means unimportant) category of 'film maker as showman', a category that can be followed from Méliès to Keaton, from Jacques Tati to Jerry Lewis, and from Federico Fellini to Woody Allen – directors, in other words, whose talent and film material has often been enriched by drawing on non-narrative traditions, such as the circus, variety acts, cabaret and stand-up comedy, but in the

German context, the intertext is also operetta, which already in 1913 had been denounced as being 'the worst enemy of German theatrical art' (mainly because it deflates dramatic pathos).[17]

Irony or nostalgia?

One could go further and argue that *Hallo Caesar!* is not only a satire on the film industry and show business, but is also quite a cunning and sophisticated evocation of an earlier cinema, partly alluding to it ironically, partly out of nostalgia, and thus inscribing possibly two kinds of audiences – one might refer to them as cosmopolitan populist and rural popular audiences. There is, for instance, little doubt that the film is full of allusions and in-jokes difficult to understand and pick up on today. The basic theme of the all-important contract to go to America for a variety artist is still discernible: it is a satirical swipe at the German film industry, which especially in the year of the Parufament agreement and with UFA on its knees, was basing too many hopes on American input. The search for American impresarios had a very topical flavour that was even more apparent from an item in the film industry trade journal *Lichtbildbühne* dated 7 July 1926 (the month *Hallo Caesar!* was filmed) about Carl Laemmle, studio head of Universal visiting Karlsbad on his annual European holiday. It reads:

> Laemmle is now the centre of a number of Berlin film people who have joined him in Karlsbad, to shake hands with him, partly as friends, partly for business reasons.

Schünzel's Caesar could not have put it better, and Laemmle, himself of Czech origins, is of course similar to the character of the American tycoon disguised as 'Herr Lehmann', in *Hallo Caesar!*.

A double irony produces the happy ending. Despite all his troubles, Caesar gets the contract and the woman. But in actual fact, the 'right girl' is really the wrong girl, for the daughter of his landlady is, as the film makes abundantly clear, the maternal type and home-loving, with her roots firmly planted in a small town. She is destined to wilt and wither, if transplanted to Berlin, in spite of the American vaudeville circuit. The owner of the elegant pair of legs, who turns out to be the daughter of his new boss, would of course be the perfect partner, personally as well as professionally, and she does not seem to be disinclined towards Caesar, except at the very end of the film, when she generously gives up the hero to the other girl. Thus, the plot – described by the critics as feeble when judged in terms of drama and suspense – is quite a witty take on substitution and exchange: Caesar chases the wrong 'American', while he already has the right one as his friend. He pursues the right woman (the boss's daughter) but she is the wrong choice, and he gets the right girl who really loves him, but who may well prove to be the wrong one for his professional ambitions. This criss-crossing of erotic and economic object choice would not have been out of place in a

Lubitsch comedy, such as *The Marriage Circle* (USA, 1924), *Lady Windermere's Fan* (USA, 1925), *So This Is Paris* (USA, 1926) and already anticipates the more explicit and vertiginous exchanges in *Viktor und Viktoria* or *Amphitryon*. What appears to be a happy ending in *Hallo Caesar!* is, in true comedy fashion, simply the beginning of tragedy in another register: say, *Sunrise* (F.W. Murnau, USA, 1927).

Equally remarkable, and as a kind of counter-current to the daring 'simple tale simply told' is the film's technical sophistication, mainly in terms of lighting, which – unusually for the period – has been influenced by the UFA *Großstyle* of film. It is very 'American' in this, using several light sources, for instance, in the evening and night scenes, lighting up the characters in outline for some of the dramatic scenes, and giving them unusual depth of field, as in the daytime shots of the environs of Karlsbad, where the landscape and the undulating line of the houses are offset against the horizon. At night, for example, at the fairground, the space is clearly divided into several planes of action, often with an extreme foreground, to emphasise depth, or direct attention to the glances exchanged between the characters. In the interior scenes, Schünzel has learnt from Griffith as well as Chaplin, as in the extended gag with the water jug and the wash-basin in the hall at the bottom of the stairs, where there is an asymmetrical and very powerfully dramatic space typical of early 1920s Griffith, organised to cut out depth, and to emphasise the lateral, since the whole point of the gag depends on entrances and exits, off-screen right and off-screen left, doors and corridors.

But even if the references to the Hollywood style are not self-conscious quotations, but merely the adoption of a convention, there is no doubt that entire scenes in *Hallo Caesar!* are very deliberate pastiches on the classics of film history. This is especially noticeable in parts of the film that do little in order to advance the plot, such as the hotel fire. A veritable anthology of screen gems are found. Apart from the Méliès-type 'féeries' that match Caesar's profession as a juggler and magician, there is Lumière's *L'arroseur Arrosé*, lovingly recreated precisely in the middle of what is obviously Edwin S. Porter's *Life of an American Fireman*, alluding to the fact that every film producer at the turn of the century re-staged the popular hits of his competitors. The hotel fire itself, with its Marx Brothers routines and Tati-esque mime sequences (the fire-chief endlessly and futilely giving morse hand-signals to his subordinates) could no doubt, with all its different gags and phases, be traced back to precise examples, whether from Max Linder or Fatty Arbuckle and Ben Turpin. The episode, although renewing his courtship of the boss's daughter, has little other dramatic significance except to show off Schünzel-the-actor's skills of mimicry and impersonation (for one kind of audience) and Schünzel-the-director's skills as parodist and pasticheur (for another, or for the same audience who are getting a whole repertoire of old favourites for the price of one admission).

Figure 23 Harold Lloyds' straw boater: Reinhold Schünzel in *Hallo Caesar!* (1927)

Source: Stiftung Deutsche Kinemathek, Berlin

The avant-garde, the popular and beyond ...

Obviously, there is a danger of making too much of this, and ending up claiming that *Hallo Caesar!* is a sort of deconstructive avant-garde masterpiece. This would be unfair to Schünzel, and the point is rather an opposite one. Even a quite ordinary, run-of-the-mill production, such as *Hallo Caesar!*, a mass-market product made for the general public, can be quite multilayered to the historically curious gaze. It also raises the question – as in the chapter on Lubitsch (Part II, Chapter 2, this volume) – of what is the relationship between the popular and art cinema in Weimar cinema. Are they 'twin brothers' or doubles, parasitic on each other, while each is also capable of pastiching the other? Without being definitive, there are certain indicators that give a clue, because they apply, not only to *Hallo Caesar!* but to much of Schünzel's other work: stereotypical plots, comic or dramatic set pieces; cross-generic intertextuality and allusionism; plagiarism and self-plagiarism; spectacle-attraction over narrative integration; the entertainer/showman as opposed to the director/artist; the star persona defined by his/her roles, but also existing outside in the world of show-business. Finally, a popular film will be made famous by the powerful attraction of the star rather than the genre or the director: a Henny Porten film, a Harry Piel film, an Emil Jannings film, which once more makes the dual status of Schünzel as director and star symptomatic for the possibility of crossovers (from star–actor to star–director and vice versa).[18]

In *Hallo Caesar!* there is, for instance, a perspective from which the different points of entry, such as the cosmopolitan–populist and the provincial–popular converge, making any hard-and-fast division between avant-garde and mass culture unnecessary. This would be the question of sexuality and sexual ambiguity already alluded to, and the significance that the Caesar persona takes on in this light. Schünzel had a screen presence that was very unsettling in terms of gender, an ambivalence that was due not to his sexual preference, but to his style, not to the representation of any specific 'vice', but to the social role of gender. At first glance, *Hallo Caesar!* is no exception. What could indicate a homoerotic counter-current to the plot's heterosexual romance is, for instance, the unsatisfactory, anti-climactic 'formation of the couple', and Caesar's relation to Herr Lehmann (he dances the tango for Herr Lehmann and dons a huge paper-mâché nose, then the two throw confetti at each other and behave like Laurel and Hardy: their childish pranks only cease when Caesar resumes, much to Lehmann's annoyance, the pursuit of his daughter). In addition, the lady's suitor is outrageously foppish and effete, and Caesar's own juggling tricks are anything but innocent (the billiard balls juggled on a walking stick and the bunch of flowers constantly sprouting from his trouser pockets. At the same time, there are mother-in-law jokes, and an obvious delight on the part of Caesar in fragmenting (the pair of legs, the revue-girl's bottoms), regimenting (the three girls in the coffee house) and fetishising (the dummy in the shop window) the female body, all of which – if not supporting the homosexual subtext – none the less seem to mark the film as being mildly hysterical with regard to female sexuality and phallic masculinity.

Such a reading, admittedly, does not delve very deeply into the social roots of the Schünzel persona, but it underlines its double register of appeal. Female dummies and straw boaters, pairs of legs and chorus lines, walking sticks and billiard balls, bouquets of flowers and missing pearls – sound like a list of props either for a Busby Berkeley musical or an experimental film like *Ballet Mécanique*. Perhaps the point where the avant-garde and the popular merge in the Schünzel persona requires a different definition of his sensibility as a performer. The figure that comes to mind is that of the dandy, a term that despite its complex cultural baggage seems to me to best capture the ambivalence and duality of many of Schünzel's characters – their subversiveness towards social norms, including sexual norms, but also the fact that this subversiveness is ultimately very conformist, since one of the main attributes of the dandy is his style and his narcissism that he wields aggressively, like a weapon. But Schünzel, especially in his comic parts, is perhaps too little of the aristocrat and too much the populist really to qualify as a dandy. Which is why, despite the anachronism, one might think of him as an early candidate for camp, in the limited sense that he lovingly devotes himself to popular and even bad taste, not necessarily out of an attachment to kitsch objects or sentimental situations *per se*, but out of an enjoyment of the spontaneity and eccentricity inherent in the act of choosing these objects and situations, in the face of educated or highbrow disapproval and distaste. If Schünzel and *Hallo Caesar!* are in some sense camp, it is thus only to the degree that the term valorises three distinct moments that I have tried to isolate in the film: the performative–exhibitionist stance, the sexual ambiguity of several of the characters and the evident love of cliché and pastiche in the plot, the gags and the comic turns.

Yet there is a final aspect to which one should draw attention. Many of the motifs and scenes highlighted can also be read as instances of doubling, of mirroring, and as exploiting the pleasure of seriality. This, too, is a feature where historically, avant-garde sensibility and the popular had a common cause, for right across the spectrum of the arts, seriality and symmetry became something of a key metaphor during the so-called 'second machine age' in which Weimar amply participated. We find it as a celebratory metaphor of energy and vitality in revue girls and bio-mechanics, in the New Photography and representations of Fordism, in the passion for 'time and motion studies' and the jazz idiom. In short, it became Weimar's code for 'Americamania'. In *Hallo Caesar!* doubling and the series appear not only in the plot, the coffee-house girls and the rehearsing Tiller troupe, the otherwise unmotivated introduction of the (male) Kretschmar twins and their act, but also in the structure, i.e. the double and triple comedy of errors, which elevated to a moral mirror-maze, fairly loses its ideological content: social rise. Schünzel's most loving attention in *Hallo Caesar!* ultimately belongs to the mechanical, the serial and the compulsion to repeat. This makes him almost our contemporary: he has, to use a cliché, faith in doubles and in fakes because they are some of the perennial passkeys to the popular.

Notes

1 The film tells the story of an unemployed variety artist who follows a famous American impresario from Berlin to Karlsbad in search of work. But Caesar, told that all it takes to be hired on the spot is to startle the tycoon with a surprise performance, mistakes several well-heeled tourists for the American, baffling them with juggling a plate and a billiard ball on his walking stick. In actual fact, the real impresario is a casual acquaintance of Caesar's who calls himself Herr Lehmann. In the end, Caesar gets the contract and, for good measure, a bride as well.

(Synopsis from *Lichbildbühne* no. 108, 1927)

2 The copy of *Hallo Caesar!* that I was able to study came from the Cinemathèque Municipale de Luxembourg, and was kindly made available to me by the late Fred Junck in 1989. The Hamburg CineGraph collective organised the first retrospective of Schünzel in 1988. The proceedings of the conference, which contain the first version of the present chapter, were published as Hans Michael Bock,

Wolfgang Jacobsen, Jörg Schöning (eds.) *Reinhold Schünzel, Schauspieler und Regisseur* (Munich: text + kritik, 1989).

3 C. Phoenix, 'Reinhold Schünzel', *Deutsche Filmwoche* 18 (30 April 1926).

4 *Le petit écart* (Reinhold Schünzel and Henri Chomette, Germany, 1931), the French version of *Ein kleiner Seitensprung*; *Ronny* (Reinhold Schünzel and Roger Le Bon, Germany, 1931), French version of *Ronny*; *La Belle Aventure* (Reinhold Schünzel and Roger Le Bon, Germany, 1932), French version of *Das schöne Abenteuer*; *Georges et Georgette* (Reinhold Schünzel and Roger Le Bon, Germany, 1933), French version of *Viktor und Viktoria*; *Idylle au Caire* (Reinhold Schünzel and Claude Heymann, Germany, 1933), French version of *Saison in Kairo*; *La jeune fille d'une nuit* (Reinhold Schünzel and Roger Le Bon, Germany, 1934), French version of *Die Töchter Ihrer Exzellenz*; *Les Dieux s'amusent* (Reinhold Schünzel and Albert Valentin, Germany, 1935), French version of *Amphitryon*; *Donogoo* (Reinhold Schünzel and Henri Chomette, Germany, 1936), French version of *Donogoo Tonka*.

5 There is evidence that Schünzel tried to keep the two sides of his life quite separate: most striking is the contrast between his publicity photographs as director/producer, with a monocle in the dandified manner of Fritz Lang, and some of the stills from his films, in which he appears more like one of Dr Mabuse's low-life disguises, or where he casts himself as a 'Berliner Pflanze', a proletarian rough diamond (see the group photograph in the Schünzel file at the British Film Institute).

6 Klaus Kreimeier, 'Der Großstadtgauner', in Thomas Koebner (ed.) *Idole des deutschen Films* (Munich: text + kritik, 1997): 79.

7 For a complete filmography with extensive credits, see Schöning 1989: 82–117.

8
Ich säh's so gerne: Conrad Veidt den blassen,
In einem Film mit Baby Peggy spielen [...]
Und Reinhold Schünzel mit den sanften Mienen –
Ich säh ihn gern als Mary Carr Entsprossnen [...]
Wo wär' solch Paar wohl schon vordem erschienen?

(*Filmland* no. 4, February 1925)

9 *Filmwoche* no. 9, 1924.

10 *Lichtbildbühne* no. 151, 1927.

11 It is true, Harry Liedtke und Harry Piel made enormously popular films, and their names were synonymous with the parts they played, but they embodied only one kind of hero, that of the adventurer and daredevil, and not that of the comic anti-hero. For an overview of German film comedy, see Thomas Brandlmeier, 'Early German film comedy' in Elsaesser 1996b: 103–13 and H.M. Bock and W. Jacobsen (eds), *Der komische Kintopp* (Hamburg: Cinegraph 1997).

12
Und dann Grotesken, die mit froher Wucht
den Geist der Schwere treiben in die Flucht
und an der Hand von Unsinn immer siegen
Die Keaton, Chaplin, Schünzel, Pat und Lloyd
Lachpillen in das Publikum gestreut
bringen das älteste Gebälk zum Biegen.

(Hans Harbeck, 'Kino, Kino über alles', in Herbert Gunther (ed.) *Hier schreibt Berlin* (Berlin: Internationale Bibliothek, 1929): 105)

13 *Lichtbildbühne* no. 305, 1927.

14 Hans Siemsen, *Charlie Chaplin* Leipzig: Feuer-Verlag, 1924. See also Tom Saunders' chapter on the reception of Chaplin in Germany, and who writes: 'Siemsen read Chaplin's iconoclasm as a much-needed corrosive to German prostration before social status and political authority' (Saunders 1994: 186).

15 See, for instance, an article in *Lichtbildbühne* no.151 (1927): 20.
16 Tom Gunning, 'The cinema of attractions: early film, its spectator and the avant-garde', in Elsaesser 1990: 56–62.
17 Erich Oesterheld, 'Wie die deutschen Dramatiker Barbaren wurden', reprinted in Kaes 1978: 96–100 [98].
18 Actors in the 'Publikumsfilm' (as popular films were known in the 1920s) would not come from legitimate theatre and highbrow acting traditions (such as Max Reinhardt's theatre where virtually all actors of the German 'art cinema' began), but from the Volkstheater, the variety theatre. Similarly, narrative material would not have been adaptations from literature, but drawn from theatrical melodrama, farce, vaudeville sketch, operetta, serialised newspaper fiction ('Groschenromane'), and romance fiction (generically known as 'Courts-Mahler', after the most popular woman author or 'Gartenlaube', after the magazine of that title).

2

TRANSPARENT DUPLICITIES

Pabst's *The Threepenny Opera*

Preliminaries

To write about Pabst's *The Threepenny Opera* is to venture into a minefield of received opinion. Even if one side-steps the booby-traps of literary adaptation and refrains from any debate about the faithfulness of filmed classics, one ends up caught up in the 'barbed wire' of Brecht's powerfully polemical defence of his intellectual property in the *Dreigroschenprozess*, his docu-report of the court case he and Kurt Weill brought against the production company. Add to this Pabst's ambivalent role within the Nazi film industry, and the arguments seem to be in favour of assuming that the film maker had 'betrayed' Brecht.[1] Any assessment of the film in its own right may come to look like special pleading, but since the film has most often been discussed in the context of Brecht,[2] a reversal of perspective promises its own alienation effect. I propose to dispense with the question of the law suit and the circumstances of the production as quickly as possible, and consider, in light of the film itself, whether Pabst's approach to the material has a coherence of its own. This should allow some conclusions about Pabst as Brecht's contemporary, and the basis on which the *The Threepenny Opera* deserves to be considered a major work of Weimar Cinema.

The law suit and its legacy

With regard to the merits of the *Dreigroschenprozess*, commentators usually study Brecht's version. This seems reasonable, especially since his purpose in writing up his experiences with the film industry are interesting for two reasons. First, it will be remembered that Brecht, from about 1928 onwards, practised a strategy of cultural intervention, wanting to make his presence felt in virtually every debate and through every existing medium of artistic production. Brecht, in Benjamin's words, sought 'never to supply the apparatus without trying to change it.'[3] Not only did he work in the theatre, he also wrote radio plays and participated in musical life via his collaborations with Weill, Hindemith and Eisler. He was active in proletarian associations such as the Rote Wedding and wrote learning plays for factories and workers' clubs. He involved himself in film making with Prometheus Film, and with Slatan Dudow and Hanns Eisler made *Kuhle Wampe*.[4] He wrote very different plays for the theatre – for such different publics or non-publics – for example, *The Mother* and *St Joan of the Stockyards*, making the years between 1928 and 1933 among the most productive of his life.[5] The *Dreigroschenprozess* must be seen in this context. Second, Brecht who lost his case (while Kurt Weill accepted an out-of-court settlement and did rather well financially) was able to take the legal debate onto the high ground of political theory and ideological critique. By focusing on the contradictions between bourgeois notions of artistic autonomy on the one hand and capitalist notions of property on the other, Brecht demonstrated that bourgeois law, though called upon to defend intellectual rights of ownership, cannot in practice legislate against a material concept of ownership, even if this leaves bourgeois ideology in tatters as a result.[6] Since Brecht believed neither in artistic autonomy nor in the capitalist mode of production, he could claim to have instigated the law suit in order for the system to reveal its own contradictions: hence the sub-title 'soziologisches Experiment', which became a prime example of Brecht's conceptual interventionism ('eingreifendes Denken').[7] The *Dreigroschenprozess* was a sociological experiment not only about individual authorship under capitalism, but a materialist account of the structure of the film industry itself determining the nature of the products.[8] In an interview to Kraszna-Krausz, not quoted as often as Brecht, and given on becoming the Head of 'Dacho' (Dachorganisation der Filmschaffenden Deutschlands e.V.), Pabst implicitly comments on the controversy and points to one of the historical reasons for the ambivalent position of the creative personnel in film making: 'A process [of production developed during stormy commercial prosperity means that] the originators of mental–creative work were (and are) not able to decide sufficiently for themselves. They are used as *material* nearly always.' Pabst is here astutely political, when he goes on to make the case not only on behalf of (relatively privileged) writers, but of 'film workers' generally, including technicians, stressing, for instance, the importance of unionisation. 'The social question of the film-worker remains unsolved as long as the film is the exclusive property, that is to say: "goods" in the hands of the manufacturers and his renters' (Kraszna-Krausz 1931:122). Brecht and Weill, when taking out proceedings against Nero, knew that they could count on maximum publicity. The whole affair attracted much press coverage, well beyond the trade journals of the film industry and the arts pages, because *Die Dreigroschenoper* was 'hot property'[9] at the time, in fact, the hottest there was! As a consequence, the law suit was personalised and publicised to an extraordinary degree, with every critic feeling he had to make a stand. When writing up the *Dreigroschenprozess* Brecht had a large file of clippings on which to draw.[10] There is some doubt whether he ever saw the film, either then, or subsequently.[11]

The circumstances of production

How did the situation seem from the point of view of Nero Film, and by extension, the German film industry? Kurt Weill had sold the film rights of *Die Dreigroschenoper* to the Berlin representative of Warner Brothers, who went into co-production with Tobis Klangfilm[12] and Seymour Nebenzahl as owner of Nero Film. On 21 May 1930, Brecht signed a contract with Nero Film-AG, giving him 'consultative rights' ('Mitbestimmung') on the script, but no powers of a veto.[13] There were to be three versions of the film – in German, French and English, a practice not uncommon for major productions in the brief period between the advent of sound and the invention of dubbing.[14] This already indicates that the companies involved were not only hoping for world-wide distribution. From the start the film was conceived to be an expensive production,[15] indeed, it was said to have had the 'biggest sets for a German movie ever.'[16] Nero, with its aggressive production policy (other major Nero films during these years included Pabst's *Kameradschaft* and Fritz Lang's *M*) wanted to break into the international market, and also to strengthen its hand against UFA, the distribution giant in the German and European market. For Warner Brothers, teaming up with a German independent producer was a way of keeping a foot in the door. Much, therefore, was riding on the success of the project and its smooth production. Pabst, in the interview already quoted, is aware of the wider historical implications, and also of his own dilemma as creative artist and representative of a professional body within the film industry:

> Once before, eight years ago, Germany was able to determine the development of the silent film. Then Germany, like the whole rest of the world, succumbed to the American film. Now for the second time the fate of the European film is lying in the hands of Germany. France, England have already succumbed afresh to American money. Russia has not yet succeeded in finding a productive attitude to the sound-film. America's production however has driven into a blind alley, out of which the way will scarcely be found alone [*sic*]. Germany is uncommonly enabled by its literary and musical past to determine the shape of the sound-film of tomorrow, if ...
>
> *A.K.K.:* ... if the German industry will not be Americanized in spite of all that. If the Russia of the silent film won't remain eternally the 'Mecca' of the German critics.
>
> *G.W.P.:* ... and if the German film-workers will at last determine their fate–and with it the fate of the German film – all by themselves.
>
> (Kraszna-Krausz 1931:125–6)

The Threepenny Lawsuit was, in this respect, a minor episode in the international struggle of the major companies to stitch up the European market, with mixed results. It may have been good box office publicity for the international release of the film, but there is evidence to suggest that the delays and the terms of the eventual settlement put paid to plans for the English-language version.[17] Weill sued Warner/Nero because of the music, rather than for any alterations in the text, nor for fearing that the social message of the play had been blunted.[18] In the contract he was guaranteed exclusive control over the music to be used. The grounds on which he was able to litigate successfully was that apparently, in the scene of the Beggar's final march on Trafalgar Square, a single trumpet call was inserted that Weill had not composed.[19] Weill's settlement is, so to speak, a counter-example of a Brechtian *Messingkauf*: Nero bought from Weill the trumpet call he had not composed.[20]

Brecht and Pabst: two different approaches to the cinema?

When considering how 'faithful' the film is to Brecht, one is looking at two sources, rather than simply at the 'original' Brecht–Weill opera: Brecht wrote a fairly detailed treatment for the film, as stipulated by his contract. Since this script was published,[21] several critics have tried to extrapolate from it Brecht's implicit conception of the film, comparing it to Pabst's interpretation.[22] Most take the view that the film is somehow 'fatal to Brecht'.[23] The exception is Chris Horak, who in a careful assessment of Brecht's script, the film script by Leo Lania, Bela Balasz and Laszlo Vajda,[24] and Pabst's actual interpretation of both, comes to the conclusion that 'Pabst's film is ideologically more correct, from a Marxist point of view'[25] than either the opera or Brecht's script or that of Lania, Balasz and Vajda.

The argument generally revolves around two basic issues: first, whether Pabst's concern for a more classical continuity style, integrating the songs into the narrative, and leaving out as many as he did (from the 'Ballade von der sexuellen Hörigkeit' and the 'Tango Ballade', to the 'Henkersballade' and Mack's prison song) constituted a betrayal of Brecht's epic form, and undermined the role of the street singer and various protagonists, who in the original step in and out of their fictional roles. Second, whether the changes made to Brecht's treatment by the scriptwriters somehow inverted, attenuated or otherwise falsified the political message Brecht wanted to convey. On the first issue, Horak maintains that Pabst's direction of the actors (many, such as Ernst Busch, Lotte Lenya and Carola Neher drawn from the first or second stage production) 'comes closest to the Brechtian conception of epic theatre',[26] in so far as dialogue is pared down and sparingly used (this, of course, also due to the technical difficulties of combining music, camera movement and spoken word in one take).[27] The characters, in the love scenes for instance, look straight out towards the camera, breaking the illusionist space of the diegesis.

Discussions about the second point – alterations to the storyline – have focused mainly on the ending, and the motivation for the rivalry between Peachum and Macheath. In the opera, Peachum puts pressure on Tiger Brown, the police chief, to avenge Macheath's seduction of and elopement with Peachum's daughter Polly. In Brecht's treatment, the sexual shenanigans are secondary, and the rivalry is between the bosses of two competing businesses, both leeching on the middle classes: Macheath's gang of professional thieves and fences (the 'Platte', numbering around 120 men), and Peachum's similarly sized Beggar syndicate. Lania, Vajda and Balasz's script once again personalises the antagonism between Peachum and Macheath, and sends Peachum to a dismal fate, after his beggars have turned upon him. The finished film represents a compromise, or rather, a skilful synchromeshing of the two narrative motors driving the conflicting interests, notably by making Polly, the female lead, a much stronger character. At first a typically 'romantic' figure, love-struck, vain and innocent, Polly turns herself into a hard-headed businesswoman: she is the one who, during Macheath's stint in jail, leads the gang into going legitimate, and sets the terms on which both Tiger Brown and old Peachum join the bank. The ironic twist is that she does it 'out of love', as if running a bank was no different from keeping the house tidy for her husband's return. Brecht, in his film treatment, is mainly interested in working out the logic of capitalist dog-eat-dog-or-join-the-pack, making the play more like *Arturo Ui* by introducing the logic of move and counter-move into the linear flow. The transition from opera to film gave Brecht a chance to maximise on the cinema's ability to suggest through editing, new connections and new chains of cause, effect and consequence.

Reading *Die Beule*, one cannot help feeling that Brecht was having fun being hard-boiled and cynical. He must have known the problems his ideas would encounter in production. Some scenes are more dada than epic theatre, with sketches of the dramatic situation and characterisation that are broad caricature.[28] Montage sequences underline the didactic Gestus of the whole. Brecht tried to use film as a medium that 'reduces' lines of dramatic development, intent to get from A to B in the shortest possible time. At worst, Brecht is trying to sabotage the project from the start, at best *Die Beule* is intended as a critique of the dominant modes of the 'stylised' author's film prevalent during the early 1920s.

Brecht creates causal relationships, Weimar cinema dissolves causal relationships. Brecht is elliptical, in order to force issues into contradictions, whereas Expressionist cinema uses ellipsis to suspend causality, to introduce ambiguity, and to open up parentheses. Where Brecht is interested in metonymy, Weimar cinema employs metaphor; Brecht goes for satire, pastiche, irony, Expressionism for pathos, self-tormented psychology, primary process imagery. Brecht's is a text of verbal aggression, the Weimar cinema revels in texts of mute represssion. Brecht' affectivity is all invested in punning and 'Witz' (i.e. the saving of psychic energy) whereas the Weimar cinema's psychic economy is more like dream-work: it, too, shifts the burden of representation onto figures of condensation and displacement, but without the corresponding semiotic or comic pay-offs. What is generally missing in Weimar films is not attention to detail or objects, but their concretisation within the image, and also within the intellectual movement of a scene. Expressionist abstraction is, as Brecht recognised, the very opposite of the kind of reduction or short-cuts ('Verkürzung') he was after. It is a form of symbolic generalisation that opens the event to its contamination by the categories of the imaginary: reversible, inward, existential, psychoanalytical. Historical specificity and the 'social gestus' are almost always absent.

Yet Pabst's work, too, operates a critique on Weimar cinema, while at the same time, exploiting to the full what had made the German cinema internationally famous in the 1920s. He parodies, for instance, the expressionist mania for charging objects with a life of their own. In one of the night scenes, as the gang steals the furnishings for Mackie's wedding, one sees an armchair scurrying through the streets, shot at and followed by a policeman. Here Surrealism is invoked to deflate Expressionism.[29] More importantly, though, Pabst has rethought in terms of his medium the issues that Brecht raises in the original and his film treatment.[30] *The Threepenny Opera* is not so much a film about the contradiction between moral codes and business practices (the theme of capitalism's own betrayal of the ideology that supports it, as indicated, also a major theme in the *Dreigroschenprozess*), instead, Pabst concentrates on the duplicity of representation itself, and of filmic representation in particular.

To phrase the contrast between Brecht and Pabst in these terms may seem paradoxical, given that Brecht, too, criticised bourgeois modes of representation, and above all, the canons of realism and verisimilitude. But Brecht's notion of representation was language based, and in his film work, he seems to show little interest in the crises of representation brought about by the new culture of the image, however perceptive, according to Benjamin, he was about photography.[31] For Brecht the primacy of language always remained: a writer's hope, coupled with an enlightenment belief in the demystifying powers of the word.[32] Before exploring this point further, it is worth mentioning that *The Threepenny Opera* is also 'Brechtian' in ways perhaps different to those mentioned above. To the extent that it engages with a recognisable fictional scenario, the narrative is a standard Weimar oedipal situation: a man steals a daughter from a father, who becomes violent and homicidal, but is essentially powerless to intervene, since in the process the daughter emancipates herself from both father and lover. This scenario, which is similar to, say, a Heimatfilm like *Die Geier-Wally* (E.A. Dupont, 1921), is deconstructed by Pabst, who lets the material interests ('business') triumph over blood ties and family interests – except that in the end, family interests and business interests are made to coincide perfectly. What in other Weimar films gives rise to melodrama (or comedy) here becomes a parody, for the purpose of a materialist critique of the bourgeois family. Rather than depicting a story of betrayal and jealousy (Macheath, unfaithful to Jenny is betrayed by her to Peachum, who betrays him to the police) which would amount to psychologising the Brechtian plot, the film is true to Brecht's consistent 'de-oedipalising' of family relationships, as can be seen in *Mother Courage*, *Galileo* and even *The Caucasian Chalk Circle*.

Pabst's concept of cinema

Pabst's cinema, especially where it deals with political or social issues, has always supported its dramatic conflicts by underpinning them with another structure altogether: that of visual fascination, the treachery and irony of appearances.[33] Revolution, as in *The Loves of Jeanne Ney*, or the turmoil of post-war inflation, as in *The Joyless Street* are grist to the same mill, where power is defined across its hold on the machinations of make-believe. In this, of course, he is not alone among the major Weimar directors: Fritz Lang and Lubitsch, too, worked with the very structures of the cinema, as the power play of appearances.[34] Pabst's obsession with the shifting configurations produced by the false ontology of the filmic image can, I think, be usefully compared to that of Lang: the logic of *The Threepenny Opera* as a film rests on its place within this wider, also typically Weimar preoccupation. Pabst's Mackie Messer (especially as portrayed by Rudolf Foster) is above all the hero of many disguises: the opening song, already in Brecht, emphasises both his ubiquity and invisibility. But the way that he is introduced in the film as he leaves the brothel in Drury Lane emphasises another point. One of the girls passes his cane to him through the window, he tugs at it, she playfully refuses to let it go and the cane unsheathes to reveal a lethal dagger, the 'teeth' in the famous song. There is no doubt that Mackie is associated with the realm of the look and yet both cane and dagger become metaphors for his personality. In this respect, he is a second cousin to Dr Mabuse, equally dandified, though more darkly intelligent and tormented than Macheath. But whereas Mabuse connotes the mesmerising power of capitalism itself with its breathtaking manipulation of the mass media and public institutions, Mackie Messer's power is founded on erotic power, the register of seduction, which in Mabuse is a mere by-product, a consequence of deploying the kind of intellect needed to wield social power. The Mackie of the film seems incapable of the deeds attributed to him in the Mack the Knife song, however much we see him actively encouraging the legend, and, indeed, be a slave to its claims.

Apart from retaining certain epic elements already mentioned (the songs, the street singer–presenter), Pabst has thus retained a typical ambivalence. In the guise of a critique of 'moonshine and romanticism', the opera had romanticised the proletarian *demi-monde* of the brothel, the pimp, sexual libertinage and anti-bourgeois moral sentiment. Brecht's film-treatment goes some way towards excising this lumpen-sentimentality. Pabst returns to the element that undoubtedly had made the opera such a hit, but adds a telling nuance, in that he uses the performative cabaret mode to redefine the main protagonist's social status as a celebrity. For instance, the first time we see Mackie Messer head-on is when he joins the crowd listening to Ernst Busch singing the Mack-the-Knife song. His gaze into the camera introduces a view of the crowd and motivates his search for Polly and her mother. Pabst then cuts to the crowds moving closer to Ernst Busch singing. Then the film cuts to Mackie, followed by a policeman. Mackie twirls his cane in response to the line about the teeth that no-one can see. A tracking shot from a high angle (at the level of Ernst Busch standing on a platform) follows the crowd milling about before it identifies with (and follows) the diagonal movement of Polly and Mrs Peachum.

Here the camera, at first moved by Macheath in pursuit of Polly turns out to be the narrative agent of the street-singer's story telling, weaving the character of Mackie and the setting into the song, and constructing a narrational *mise-en-abyme* effect rather than a distancing device, by its complex shift in 'focalization': singer, song and the one sung about are like a set of Chinese boxes.[35] Pabst shows how Macheath is distracted from his quest for Polly, because he gets caught up with listening to the song that celebrates his exploits, which introduces both the motif of vanity and self-display, and the extent that he, too, is implicated in the universe of the 'show' that so completely dominates the world of the brothel, but also that of Peachum's beggars. The young man through whom the audience is introduced to Peachum's business and whose real poverty lacks credibility until he is dressed in rags, looks at himself in the mirror, gazing at his image in wonderment and awe. The scene is similar to an earlier one at the wedding, where the pastor, anxious to get away, catches sight of himself in a mirror and is rooted to the spot by his reflection. Later, at a moment of great danger, with the police in hot pursuit Macheath looks at himself on a 'Wanted' poster, and encouraged by this boost to his ego, sets about seducing another female passer-by. In these instances of recognition/miscognition, the characters lose themselves in the phenomenon of fascination itself: but only Macheath captivated by his own image makes narcissism the chief resource of his power over others.

Eroticism as seduction has in Pabst's cinema much to do with the character's ability to control the image, which in turn is a control of one's own appearance and disappearance – witness Mackie's compulsive Thursday visits to the 'whores at Tunbridge', elaborate charades of regularity and surprise, geared not towards the sensuous extension of moments of pleasure, but the *mise-en-scène* of an ever more skilful vanishing artist. From this it would seem that the power of fascination is ambivalent in respect of gender. In *The Threepenny Opera* Mackie, phallic hero *par excellence*, is 'feminised' by his flaunted narcissism, assuming the function of a fetish, and becoming the love object of both males and females: of the masculinised Jenny, the ultra-feminine Polly and of Tiger Brown, his buddy from the Colonial wars. In his dependence on this circulation of desire and its frustration (and the social machinations that result from it), Mackie's position is similar to the role occupied by Lulu in *Pandora's Box*.[36] No doubt, his eroticism brings into Pabst's text a subversion quite different from that intended by Brecht, and makes Mackie an ambivalent narrative agent, halfway between possessor of the look that furthers the plot, and the look that acknowledges 'being-looked-at-ness': longingly, suspiciously, angrily, admiringly. Yet Pabst's re-working of the central figure is, as it were, only the localised instance, the evidence of a structure of perversity and narrational reversibility that allows the director to bracket it with another structure of fascination, also perhaps erotic, but in the first instance, directed towards the social world – the fascination emanating from the

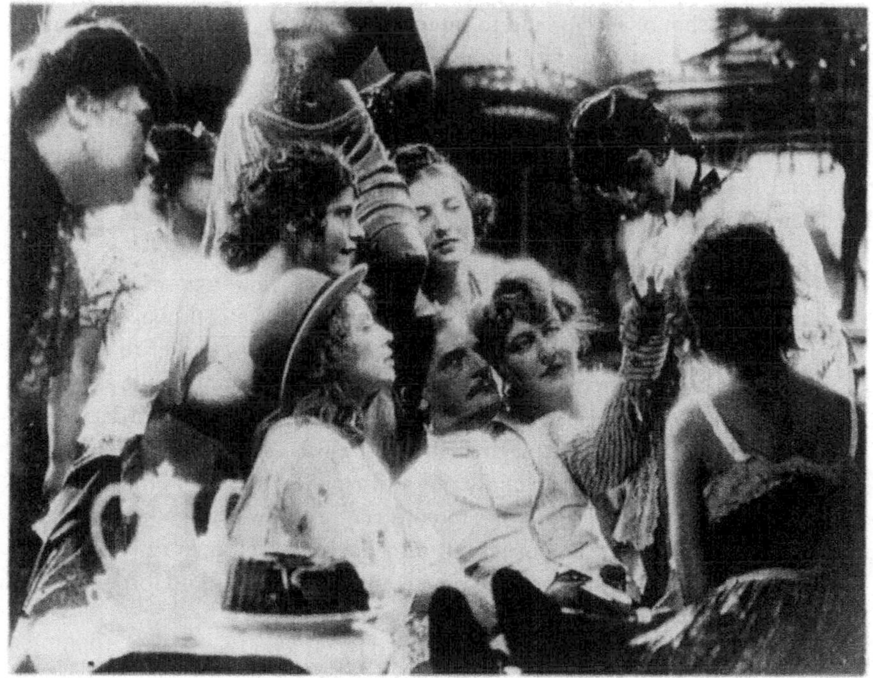

Figure 24 Mack the Knife (Rudolf Forster) having his fortune read by Jenny (Lotte Lenya) in G.W. Pabst's *The Threepenny Opera* (1931)

Source: BFI films: stills, posters and designs

different sham worlds that vie for the spectator's attention. There is the world of Peachum's beggars, that of Tiger Brown's forces of law and order, of capitalist business practices, of respectability and of Jenny's sexuality – all of them dominated by display and masquerade, which find their corollaries in the wedding feast and the brothel visits, and culminating in the crowd scenes and the sham-revolution of the beggars' procession.

Uniforms and dummies, windows and doors

One of the criticisms levelled against *The Threepenny Opera* was that Pabst allowed it to become a set designer's and an art director's film.[37] But the evident emphasis on textures and materials, decor and props rather underlines the inner logic of Pabst's conception, and the continuity that exists between 'classical' Weimar cinema of the 1920s and the sound films of the early 1930s. For a distinctive feature of German silent cinema, and part of its pioneering role in film history, is the 'designed' look of so many of the films, based as it was on the close collaboration between director, scriptwriter, cameraman, art director and editor. This labour-intensive and costly production method allowed directors to pre-design each shot or set-up, and to integrate characters, lighting, figure movement and editing in a way Hollywood had to acquire by importing the star talents from Germany in the 1920s: Lubitsch, Murnau and Pommer among others.[38] Here, then, was a further reason why the collaboration with Brecht was bound to be difficult, given Brecht's unwillingness to subject himself to this apparatus, and Pabst's habit of planning scenes very carefully, but improvising story details and dialogue to fit in with the visual conception:

> In framing a scene from the pictorial point of view and in understanding how to use the camera for pictorial effect, he is probably one of the greatest. [...] What makes it rather difficult for a writer to work with Pabst [is that] he has to supply the whole structure and at the same time he has to creep, as it were, into Pabst's personality in order to present a story to him, a story which Pabst always sees in pictures, not in scenes [...]. Pabst is certainly not a disciplined person, in the sense of being able to organise a story, to construct. And so if the other man, like Brecht, is just the opposite, but also unable to tell a story, darting from point to point, then you have no counterbalance and no force that supplies the structure, the skeleton for the story.
>
> (Leo Lanja, interviewed by Gideon Bachmann, 1955)

To the extent, therefore, that Pabst's *The Threepenny Opera* coheres around a principle of unity of style, it is still very much an example of a 'cinema of metaphor' in the tradition of the 1920s,[39] although it also follows the constructivist principle of 'coordination' and the fashion precept 'rhythm of design' through accessories. Pabst also shows his sense of humour in this respect: when Mackie is in prison, even his socks match the bars of his cell. Two metaphoric strands run through the film. One is centred on puppets and dummies, statues and objects d'art; the second on windows, partitions, doors and Mackie's prison cell. Scenes are not only frequently marked off by a fade-out or black leader (thereby minimising narrational contiguity), but are portayed under a different 'master image', for instance, the window of the brothel and the Milliner's shop window are 'condensed' in the scene where Jenny opens the window to signal to Mrs Peachum and the police; the mirrors in the dance hall anticipate those at the wedding and in Peachum's house; the stairs at the warehouse serve as an altar for the wedding ceremony, they allow Macheath to do his dictation and office work, and they visually 'rhyme' as well as time Tiger Brown's entrance with the gang's exit; at Peachum's the stairs dramatise the family quarrel, and in the brothel, they show Mackie make his escape. Both metaphoric series function either in tandem or as counterpoints, and both are integral to locating the film in a play of the human and the mechanical, of inside and outside, open and closed, of mirrors and walls, light and darkness, in short, a play of doubles and oppositional pairs entirely centred on sight, illusion and imaginary space, a combination that fairly defines that intensification of visual pleasure in Weimar cinema, which could be described as a peculiar fascination with the fake.

Puppets appear very early on in the film. Before it properly begins, and during the chorus from the Threepenny Song, doll-like representations of the leading characters are seen moving around in the manner of the Seven Deadly Sins or the Foolish Virgins on a medieval cathedral clock. Their use is first, an indication of the narrational effects to come (as described above), which place Mackie both inside and outside the double fiction of the song and the narrative. Second, the playfulness of these figures on the screen raises a question. Who controls the mechanism activating the power politics and who finally, pulls the strings and is thus in charge of the show?[40] The motif is taken up when we see the dummy bride in the shop window, stripped bare by Mackie's 'bachelors' a few scenes later on, with one of the thieves doffing his hat to her, very nearly the same as the hat doffed to Mackie in the dance hall, and then to Tiger Brown. He is the character most closely associated with the metaphoric chain of events that goes from dressed dummies to dress uniforms, from bowler hats and etiquette, to the imposture of office and authority – most graphically shown in the scene where one of Macheath's men allows himself to be caught 'red-handed' by the police in order to deliver the wedding invitation, hidden in his deferentially lowered hat, 'personally' to Tiger Brown.[41] Visually, the images of the bowler hats and their self-importance are echoed in the grotesquely inflated barrels dominating Macheath's warehouse.[42] Morally, the motif leads to Peachum, his dummies as beggars, and his beggars as the rent-a-mob dummies of the powers-that-be. Yet there is such an awareness in the film of the play on reversal and ironic inversion that Pabst not only introduces a slave motif in the brothel (full of statues of negresses), but also in contrast, there are white plaster statues of Greek goddesses in the warehouse. The latter appear most prominently in the film after Polly sings the ballad about the man with the dirty collar who doesn't know how to treat a lady, and when Mackie admonishes his men who find the song 'very nice' and exclaims: 'You call this nice, you fools – it's art!'

The metaphoric chain that links the many windows, trap-doors, partitions and skylights first of all draws attention to the sets themselves. In the warehouse, the camera pans slowly to reveal the entire brilliant display, but the scene is actually constructed as a series of rapidly changing passages to different fantasy worlds. The backdrop to the wedding, for instance, is the harbour and the moon, in keeping with Mackie and Polly's 'Moon over Soho' duet. But viewed solely as a stage set, it is now in keeping with the intensely felt phoney sentiments expressed. This is underscored by the fact that we first see it as a steel door, before it is hung with Chinese embroidery. After another song, announced by Polly and applauded by the guests as if it were a performance, a curtain is pulled, the marital bed revealed and a drawbridge is pulled up. The atmosphere of a country fair is combined with the sophisticated illusion of a backstage musical, and as in *Pandora's Box*, the stage and the mechanics of 'putting on a show', serve as a metaphor for the deceptiveness of representation, but also the pleasure of that very deceptiveness. The warehouse, an Aladdin's cave of capitalist production, here a surrealist accumulation of stolen goods and a hideous clash of styles, gives the wedding not only an air of unreality by celebrating the falseness of the world it depicts, it also turns the human players, but especially the figures of morality and law (the pastor and Tiger Brown) into mere props and objects – obsolete mementoes of a bygone age.

The structure of this scene contrasts with the scene in the brothel, but has a similar construction, built around the foregrounded architectural elements of the decor. Jenny's entrance is lit explicitly to recall the entry of Tiger Brown stepping through the skylight of the warehouse. But what is highlighted in the brothel are the different acts of transfer and exchange. Framed in the window, Jenny stuffs Mrs Peachum's bribe in her stocking, and, as if to underline her treachery, it is the same window that Mackie steps through immediately after. Jenny then opens the window making the fatal sign to Mrs Peachum and the policemen, before closing it again, while the other girls draw the curtains. The window makes this drama of entrapment and betrayal into a mini-stage, where the interplay and exchange of money, glances and bodies is performed, all of them having become

Figure 25 Matching Pair: Police Inspector Tiger Brown (Reinhold Schünzel) pleads with his best buddy Mack the Knife (Rudolf Forster) *The Threepenny Opera*

Source: Stiftung Deutsche Kinemathek, Berlin

interchangeable equivalences of transaction and transgression. Thus, even motifs that relate more directly to the political issues, such as the constant references to ledgers and accounts, bills, papers, lists, bail money and bank business are, as it were, introduced via references to visual exchanges. Conspicuous at the bank, for instance, is a sliding door with frosted glass, giving the opportunity for a kind of mock-Oriental shadow play, where each 'board member' takes a bow, without the spectator seeing the object of their deference. It is through this very door that Tiger Brown comes, as he slips from one high office to another, strutting into the room wearing his officer's uniform.

Charm and charisma: the power of Mackie Messer

One reason why the film contains so many sets with partitions, panes of clear or frosted glass, blinds and curtains, windows half lifted and suddenly dropped, is that they play a key role in defining Mackie Messer's method of authority, based as his 'authenticity' is on his impact on others as a show value. From the opening scene, when sash windows are raised, objects such as a glove and a cane are passed through – linking the inside with the outside. Extending the metaphor, entrances, exits and internal frames establish the paradigm of communicating 'vessels' that are so important for the dynamics of the film as a whole. In this respect, transparency and transport are the secrets of Mackie's success, and his power (of fascination, of attraction) resides in an ability to penetrate walls and summon people through windows. The scene where Mackie takes Polly to the dance hall, persuades her to marry him, and organises the wedding all at the same time, is Pabst's way of demonstrating a form of power in action, relying for its efficacy, it seems, entirely on glance and the gesture, on shadows spied through partitions, and messages passed as if by magic. Mackie looks at the camera (a point-of-view shot towards the two crooks, but without reverse angle follow-up), Polly looks at Mackie, while between them is a spherical wall-mounted light, that is a forerunner of the full moon seen later on. This set-up is repeated many times: the spectator is drawn into the imaginary space at the front of the screen, and witnesses the unexpected consequences of Mackie's look, thereby inferring the active power of that look. Thus Mackie does not have to do anything to win Polly. He is the man who makes things happen by simply being seen (to be).[43] In the dance hall full of mirrors that reflect other dancers, everything organises itself around Mackie – the source of a power that is economic, logistic and erotic – but in this scene he himself is framed as a spectator.

This play on vision establishes a double mode of control. At the level of the narrative, Macheath's power is defined as being active, but the mode in which this power is exercised and visualised is a passive one. At the level of the image, we observe a male character who is defined as 'phallic' but also as 'fetish', and the many scenes staged around windows, openings and partitions further dramatise a mode of interaction in which seeing and being seen are the two aggregate states of the same resource of power and control. Yet this very oscillation around active and passive once more focuses attention on Macheath's masculinity: is he is a man dressing himself in the traditional female mode, or is he, as object of desire, essentially a female, masquerading as a man? If Mackie is an ambiguous character in relation to gender, since he is not only erotic object, but also both producer and product of the narrative, a similar ambiguity surrounds the female characters – with one important proviso. While the film's image of masculinity is embodied in Mackie, that of femininity is split between Polly and Jenny. Pabst has always been recognised as an exceptional director of actresses and the creator of memorable women characters:

> Pabst has [in each of his films] displayed an interest in the mental and physical make up of his feminine players, with the result that he has often brought to the screen women who have been unusually attractive in a bizarre, neurotic manner, very different from the brilliantly turned out, sophisticated but stereotyped women of American pictures, or the dreary young ladies favoured by British directors.
>
> (Rotha, 'The Threepenny Opera' quoted in Manvell 1973: 297)

Rotha goes on to single out the chance meeting of Mackie and the young woman in the street immediately after his escape from the brothel, which, indeed has the sort of eroticism of the *flaneur* that Baudelaire first tried to capture in his Eros-and-the-city poem 'To a Passer-by'. More crucial to the narrative as a whole is, however, the metamorphosis of Polly, and of how she transforms the aggressive eroticism of Jenny into a specifically masculine power potential. Polly's mode of subjectivity is emblematically introduced in the scene in front of the milliner's shop. Mackie's desire in the opening scene is born out of division: the frame is split, as it were, between his catching a glimpse of Polly while trying to rid himself of Jenny. Polly's desire is depicted more classically – for a female character – through the narcissistic doubling of an image. As the song ends on 'Mackie, what was your price', we see Polly in front of the shop window with the wedding dress. The camera is inside the window for this shot, then reverses the angle, and Mackie enters the frame, but appears on the same side as the dummy in the window display.[44] Polly sees the reflection and smiles. Only then does she turn around, and, with an expression of shock, sees the 'real' Mackie Messer standing next to her. From being the imaginary dummy groom next to the dummy bride, he becomes the spy who has eavesdropped on her fantasy. These are the terms around which the seduction in the dance hall and the consent to marriage play themselves out across the screen of Polly's romantic double vision: glance/glance into camera by Polly/Mackie Messer, involving the spectator in their erotic space. But Polly's narrative trajectory is, of course, the total transformation of this feminine imaginary. It ends with her assuming phallic power over both father and husband, staged in that extraordinary scene already mentioned, where all the thieves-turned-bank managers bow before an invisible presence, which we infer before we know it – it is Polly! Her desire, over-inscribed in the register of vision during the first scene, has become that ultimate of male power in Weimar cinema (of both Lang and Pabst) – invisibility.

Duplicity: the fascination emanating from the fake

A 1970s review of *The Threepenny Opera* has rightly drawn attention to the fact that duplicity is one of the film's central preoccupations: Tony Rayns even speaks of the film's 'frank duplicity'.[45] In one sense, of course, this is in keeping with Brecht's original, and indeed his film treatment. Whereas the opera had insisted on the moral duplicity, the film treatment wanted to focus on the economic and political implications of such duplicity. What makes the film appear at one level a retrograde step is that Pabst seems to celebrate the same duplicity which (in Brecht's treatment) the moral of the fable, the verbal wit and the logic of the dramatic conflicts are called upon to expose. However, Pabst has recognised that the kind of duplicity that the opera highlighted is more difficult to seize critically, since its effects are multiple. First, duplicity energises. Contradictions create differentials and differentials are the very life-blood of capitalism, its source of profit and power. Second, duplicity eroticises. In the play Mackie is attractive to women because he plays hot and cold, because of his double standards, making explicit the duplicity of bourgeois morals by holding up a mirror to it. Finally, duplicity is the source of humour and wit. Pabst has, consistent with his project of translating all these issues into the terms appropriate to the cinema, made a film in which the fake is not criticised by the authentic, but by the fake, raised to its nth power, ending up being authentically ironic and honestly cynical. This Pabst achieves by contrasting two distinct forms of cinematic space, both of them imaginary. There is the use of off-screen space at the side of the frame, mostly deployed for comic effects, and in order to underscore the social hypocrisy, cynicism and double morality enacted by the dialogue. Then, there is the space at the front of the action, into the camera and thus towards the spectator, in a manner apparently 'estranging' (breaking the illusion), but also implicating the audience through its performative dimension. But the most typical space of the film, a kind of meta- or hyper-space of representation, is that constructed in the form of an infinite regress in which a show appears within a show, a frame framing a frame. It is these cinematic markings of spatial extensions that create that constant awareness of the differentials and degrees of make-believe operating on the reality status of the image. They structure the intrigue and its logic more decisively than other, more directly social issues, and they, like all visual mirroring effects, powerfully fuel the fascination emanating from moral or linguistic duplicity.

If one were to read *The Threepenny Opera* – analogous to so many German films of the early 1930s, and especially those of Lang – as a statement about the nature of power in the age of mediated images and the manipulation of appearances, then the elaborate *mise-en-scène* of Mackie Messer's charisma could be seen, by itself, as a mystification of the source of power. But what is the power with which the film is finally concerned? Not economic or political power directly, but the new category of spectacle power. Therefore, one might argue that what was at issue for Pabst was first and foremost to conserve the 'brass value' of the opera, namely its popularity, its recognition value as a mass-media product – the source of its commercial appeal, in short, what had made it a 'hot property'. For by emphasising Mackie's and Polly's 'narcissism' or (as Benjamin would say, their 'exhibition value') Pabst enacts and also deconstructs them as role models for a generation, while acknowledging the new narcissism of the cinema itself. It is not so much, as Hans Oser jokingly put it, that 'every girl wanted to be Polly, every fellow wanted to be Mackie. Apparently, the ideal man was the pimp',[46] but that every spectator, male and female, wants to be in love with his/her self-image, across the desire of the other. Mackie and Polly have, what to this day characterises the successful consumer of mass-entertainment: 'style'.

Pabst, in this respect, contributed to Weimar cinema not so much a film version of a masterpiece by Brecht, nor a poem of post-romantic inwardness, psychological depth and meta-cinematic self-reflexivity, but rather, a different mode of displacing the technology of filmic production into an intensification of the erotic aspect of filmic reality, which became the heightening of the commodity aspect, the glamour, seizing not only the men or the women characters, but also the objects and the decor. Herein lies the peculiar achievement of Pabst's *mise-en-scène* in *The Threepenny Opera*. Like other Weimar directors, he was able to imbue the filmic process with value in itself, as an added attraction to the commodity stimulus of Brecht's property become artefact, which was the opera and became the film. Pabst rendered a service to Becht, by 'deconstructing the work, while preserving its social function within a new technical apparatus'.[47] Adapting *The Threepenny Opera* into the new technical apparatus also meant inserting something into the new social apparatus – that is to say, making it as perfect as possible in the most authentic mode of social being of this apparatus – transparent duplicity.

Notes

1 Roger Manvell (1973), without offering much evidence, claims that 'most of Brecht's acid sarcasm was softened away and his social satire largely lost'. Even John Willett, who admits to liking the film, thinks that Pabst and Brecht were antagonistic in their outlook:

> Gersch, like other students of Brecht, on the whole takes Brecht's view and argues that Nero … had political objections to the new material. … Personally I doubt whether this was due to anyone but Pabst, whose divergences from Brecht's views … were surely predictable from the start.
>
> (Willett 1984: 115)

2 See, for instance, *Screen* vol. 16, no. 4 (Winter 1975); *Cinématographe* no. 125 (December 1986): 38–9, 42–4 and *Europe* Special Brecht issue (January–February 1957).

3 Benjamin 1973a.

4 Ben Brewster and Colin McCabe, 'Making *Kuhle Wampe*: an interview with George Hoellering', *Screen* vol. 15, no. 2 (Summer 1974: 71–9).

5 Willett 1984.

6

> Capitalism in its practice is cogent (konsequent), because it has to be. But if it is cogent in practice, it has to be ideologically contradictory (inkonsequent). [...] Reality has developed to a point where the only obstacle to the progress of capitalism is capitalism itself.
>
> (Bertolt Brecht 1978: 172)

7 Willett calls it 'a classic early media study to set alongside some of Benjamin's and subsequently Enzensberger's writings' (Willett, 1984: 116).

8

> The judges, bemused, finally seized on contract law to reach a verdict: Brecht lost his case on the grounds that he had voluntarily quit work on the screenplay; the cannier Weill, who had waited to be fired, won and was awarded damages.
>
> (Philip Kemp, 'Mud in your eye', *Sight and Sound*, October 1998: 26)

9 According to Jean Oser who worked on the film as sound man (supplied by Tobis): 'For five years, every girl wanted to be like Polly, talk like Polly, and every fellow like Mackie Messer. Apparently the ideal man was a pimp' (interview by Gideon Bachmann, reprinted in Manvell 1973: 299).

10 See Bertolt Brecht, *Dreigroschenbuch* (Frankfurt/M: Suhrkamp), 1973 for a selection of contemporary reviews and also Kracauer 1947.

11 John Willett seems to think he did (see Willett 1984: 117).

12

> Tobis had a monopoly on all sound film production in Germany because they had bought up all the Swiss, Danish and German patents. They were the only ones who could actually make sound films. You had to rent the sound crew and equipment from them. I was working for Tobis, and so when Pabst wanted to make a sound film ... I became editor for him.
>
> (Jean Oser, Interview by Gideon Bachmann, reprinted in Manvell 1973: 298)

13 See Gersch 1975: 48 and Willett 1984: 114.

14 See dates in Vincendeau 1988.

15 Oser says: 'You don't make a million dollar movie out of a story which should practically be shot in a backyard' (interview by Gideon Bachmann, reprinted in Manvell 1973: 299).

16 Ibid. This may be something of an exaggeration, considering the sets for *Großfilme* of the 1920s, such as *Metropolis* or *Faust*.

17 'Une version anglaise, *The Threepennies Opera* [*sic*], aurait également été tournée. Il semble qu'il s'agisse, pour l'essentiel, d'un doublage pur et simple de la version allemande' (Beylie 1976: 4). 'The film was released in France [...] and was a tremendous success. In Germany it was not a success and it was attacked quite often by the critics (Jean Oser in Manvell 1973: 299). *The Threepenny Opera* premiered in Berlin on 19 February 1931 and was banned by the *Filmprüfstelle* (the censor's office) on 10 August 1933. After a press show in Paris in March 1931, the French version was banned by the censors and only opened in November 1931, with some minor cuts, at the famous Studio des Ursulines. The cinema also showed the German version, uncut.

18

> Although the Theater am Schiffbauerdamm production was carried out strictly according to Brecht's directions, it would be a mistake to assume that critics or audiences were captivated by Brecht's bitter cynicism about the human condition. Rather, they were taken with Kurt Weill's jazz-influenced, easily singable score and songs.
>
> (Atwell 1977: 83)

19 This information is found in the interview with Jean Oser. Willett maintains that it was the music in the wedding scene that Weill objected to (Willett 1984: 115).

20 Literally: 'buying brass', in the sense of 'buying a trumpet for its brass value'. It indicated Brecht's approach to literary or artistic tradition, in relation to which he felt himself to be like a scrap-merchant, ruthless disregarding any other value than that of the 'material'. See also John Willet (ed.) *Brecht on Theatre* (London: Eyre Methuen 1964): 169–75.

21 Bertolt Brecht, 'Die Beule', first published in *Cahiers du Cinéma* no. 114 (December 1960), then in Bertolt Brecht's *Dreigroschenbuch*, vol. I, 1978: 102–16.

22 See Croce 1960; Stanbrook 1961; Gersch 1975; Willi 1984. These may usefully be compared to some of the original reviews of the film, e.g. those by Lotte Eisner (1969), Siegfried Kracauer (1947) and Paul Rotha (1933).

23 Croce 1960: 45.

24 Reprinted in full (with indications of cuts and alterations made during the shooting) in Manvell 1973.

25 *Jump Cut* no. 15 (July 1977): 20.

26 Ibid. Willett takes a similar view: 'At all events, the finished film is as distinctively a Brecht work as are his other collective works of the time, starting perhaps with the *Threepenny Opera* and not excluding *Happy End*, of which he chose to wash his hands; and so far as is now known, he was satisfied with it' (Willett 1984: 117).

27 Paul Rotha, in his very favourable review of the film, draws special attention to the prevalence of moving camera work in *The Threepenny Opera.* Since the introduction of the spoken word into film making, there has been a growing tendency to decrease the number of direct cuts in a picture, partly because of the desire to minimise the amount of different camera set-ups and partly on account of the difficulties attendant on cutting and joining the sound strip (reprinted in Manvell 1973: 296).

28 The central idea, namely that Peachum keeps in peak condition the bruise on one of his beggars' head, received from Macheath's men when they punished him for grassing on a robbery, may be good enough for a cabaret sketch, but is plainly silly as the dramatic premise for the multi-million movie.

29 'If the director has subverted the play's subversiveness, it is to the end of a poetic anarchy, irrational, beautiful and precise, where surrealism, expressionism and Marxism find a remarkable if fleeting common ground' (Rayns 1974: 162).

30 In this he is within Brechtian thinking, according to which an adaptation ought to constitute the 'deconstruction of the work from the point of view of keeping its social function intact while inserting it into a new apparatus' (Bertolt Brecht, *Schriften zur Literatur und Kunst* quoted in Gersch 1975: 51).

31 Bertolt Brecht's *Dreigroschenbuch* vol. I (Frankfurt: Suhrkamp, 1978): 135.

32 Josette Féral, 'Distanciation et multimedia, ou Brecht invers', in Pia Kleber and Colin Visser (eds) *Brecht Thirty Years After* (Cambridge: Cambridge University Press, 1986).

33 Barthelemy Amengual goes so far as to claim that the favourite Pabst shot is the low angle, and it functions as a kind of matrix or master shot, because it concretises the attitude of fascination (Amengual 1966).

34 See Part II (Chapter 1 on Lang, Chapter 2 on Lubitsch), this volume.

35 The narrational complexity of the scene is even more of a technical *tour de force* when one considers the difficulties of setting up such a scene with the sound equipment then available.

36 See Part II, Chapter 4 on 'Lulu and the meter man', this volume.

37 The set designer Andrei Andreev is often mentioned as responsible for its look, and a sumptuous volume dedicated to Hans Casparius makes a similar point.

38 See Salt 1979 for a useful discussion of set design in Weimar cinema. See also the chapter on F.W. Murnau, this volume. One of the most astute commentators on this feature of Pabst's style is still Paul Rotha, who talks of the film's dovetailed workmanship:

> Not solely on account of their individual merit as design do I draw attention to these sets, but because they are the envelope, as it were, of the film. Without the self-contained world that they create, a world of dark alleys, hanging rigging and twisting stairways, without their decorative yet realistic values, without the air of finality and completeness which they give, this film operetta would not have been credible. ... This is due not only to the settings in themselves, but the very close relationship maintained between the players and their surroundings, which has come about because the director and the architect have to all intents and purposes worked with one mind. Each corner and each doorway is conceived in direct relationship to the action played within its limits. This factor, together with the co-operation of the camerawork, builds the film into a solid, well-informed unity.
>
> (Manvell 1973: 295)

39 See Henry 1971, for the notion of a metaphoric space in relation to German films.

40 'It looks forward (in the integration of characters and setting) to [Jean Renoir's] *Le crime de M Lange* rather than backwards to *The Joyless Street*' (Rayns 1974: 162). Paul Rotha also commented on how Pabst emphasised the relationship of characters with their environment. Rotha (1933), also quoted in Manvell 1973: 295.

41 The motif of the bowler hat is reminiscent of Pudovkin and Eisenstein, and also of Hans Richter's dada-film *Ghosts Before Noon* (1928).

42 They were noted with amazement by Paul Rotha: 'On all sides of the set rise up great barrels, ridiculous barrels of absurd height and girth, yet how admirably original. Mackie's dressing room consists of smaller barrels placed slightly apart, behind each of which he vanishes in turn to complete his toilet' (Manvell 1973: 295).

43 Freddy Buache once commented that Rudolf Foster, when he kisses a women, keeps his hands in his pockets – in contrast to the actor in the French version, where Albert Préjean flings his arms around her (cited in Kemp, *Sight and Sound* October 1998: 28).

44 Very similar shots can be found in Lang's *M* and also at the beginning and end of *Fury*.

45 Rayns 1974: 162.

46 Gideon Bachmann, interview with Jean Oser (Manvell 1973).

47 Quoted in Gersch 1975: 51.

3

IT'S THE END OF THE SONG

Walter Reisch, operetta and the double negative

Operetta and the Lubitsch legacy

Already in 1982, at a conference on Early German Cinema,[1] Barry Salt drew attention to the fact that many of Ernst Lubitsch's German films were either directly based on or were inspired by operettas.[2] Implicit was the suggestion that this popular form of musical comedy had been a seriously underrated factor in the development of Lubitsch's style, carrying over into his American work. Since then, it has become almost self-evident that Weimar cinema as a whole cannot be understood without a knowledge of the forms of popular music drama and musical entertainment that were prevalent at the time. The re-evaluation of the role of sound in so-called silent cinema has furthermore provided a more historically informed account when discussing film music and its genres. For German cinema, for example, it is necessary to distinguish between filmed operettas and operetta films, between musical films and revue films and between musical comedies and films containing popular music.[3]

With regard to this, a number of points need to be made, by way of a cautionary reminder. For decades, German operetta films, musicals and revue films from the early 1930s to the mid-1940s seemed to be the most insidious vehicles for Nazi ideology to disguise itself as 'harmless' entertainment. In the 1970s, the Lubitsch scholar Karsten Witte (also present at the 1982 conference) had in fact analysed very precisely how they conveyed reactionary messages, in opposition to the parallel developments in the Busby Berkeley musicals in Hollywood. Witte cited musical comedy as the genre in which the regimentation of the body and the coercion of the look was most in evidence,[4] supporting his case with quotations from Kracauer's pre-war essays on 'The mass ornament' and 'Girls and crisis', which had already argued that dehumanising tendencies of (female) bodies in formation were prevalent in popular revue musicals.[5] Finally, commentators in the 1920s were all too aware of the operetta sub- and intertext of so many of the popular films of the time.[6] Apart from the word 'kitsch', there was probably no other word that expressed as much disapproval and derision among film critics as the word 'operetta'.[7]

I shared many of Witte's suspicions, until I met the Austrian scriptwriter, songwriter and director Walter Reisch, first at a conference in Venice, and subsequently, interviewing him in Beverly Hills in 1982.[8] As one of the key screenwriters at UFA in the early 1930s, he was, among others, also responsible for a number of 'Viennese' operetta films. Given that his collaboration with such dyed-in-the-wool Nazi directors as Geza von Bolvary, Gustav Ucicky, Carl Froelich and Karl Hartl did not exactly fit in with my image of the racially and politically persecuted Jewish émigré, I was forced to rethink my own position. For instance, Reisch's spirited defence of *Das Flötenkonzert von Sanssouci*, a film that even during its premiere had become notorious, because of the violence it provoked in left-wing militants, protesting against yet another Fredericus Rex propaganda film, sent me back to the director's bio-filmography.[9]

Walter Reisch and the myth of Vienna

The life and work of Walter Reisch (1903–83) is only sparsely documented in the specialised literature.[10] Most of what I was able to glean came from two Italian encyclopaedias that had evidently copied one another. An interview with Reisch by Joel Greenberg from the 1970s, significantly entitled 'The Tailor' was helpful.[11] The films, some of them very well-known, others – given the sheer number – more inaccessible, do not easily provide a key to his personality. A sad and painful memory is one at the Berlin Film Festival in February 1983, where Reisch, along with other exiles such as Franz Lederer, Wolfgang Zilzer, Hertha Thiele and Dolly Haas had been invited to attend a retrospective occasion dedicated to the actor Curt Bois.[12] Reisch was the only one among these illustrious UFA veterans who had not been honoured with a publication, which may have been the reason why, at the reception, he sat in his chair by himself, neither a name nor a face that the guests recognised. Reisch died, four weeks later, on 28 March 1983, two months before his 80th birthday – fifty years to the day when Joseph Goebbels had made his Kaiserhof speech to the German film industry, demanding that it should be 'Aryanised'. The sense of empathy and embarrassment I felt, and even more the caustic good humour with which he commented on his living death that evening in Berlin, was another reason why I wanted to look once more at the films he had been involved in during the 1930s.

Reisch belonged very much to the centre of the beguiling mythology and sardonic demystification associated with the Central European émigrés in Hollywood. His open house Sunday afternoons in the 1940s were an institution.[13] He either knew, or had worked with almost all the famous names: Fritz Lang and Ernst Lubitsch, Erich Pommer and Marlene Dietrich, Peter Lorre and Greta Garbo, Billy Wilder, Otto Preminger and Hedy Lamarr, the Siodmak brothers and Wilhelm Thiele, Charles Boyer and Ingrid Bergman. Perhaps it is because he was so much at the centre of the myth that he became invisible, or maybe he was – by his own admission – good at the same things that Lubitsch and Wilder were good at (story construction for light comedy, for instance), so that he was completely obscured by their larger-than life images. But Reisch may also be hard to track down, because he was chief architect of one particularly enduring myth, and like God in his creation, according to Flaubert and Joyce, such an artist is 'nowhere to be seen but everywhere to be felt'.

The myth is that of a Vienna, made up of waltzes and *lieder*, of exquisite emotional sacrifice and dashing but heartless young officers, of Franz-Joseph court intrigues, evenings with 'Heurigen' at the Prater amusement gardens, not forgetting the epitome of seductive naivety, the 'Wiener Mädl'. And Reisch was most certainly, if not the creator, then the adept translator into movies of some of this myth's most enduring figures. One only has to think of the stars he wrote for in the 1930s (noting only those who did not or did not need to emigrate in 1933): Lilian Harvey and Käthe von Nagy, Willi Forst and Paula Wessely, Brigitte Helm, Renate Müller, Sybille Schmitz and Hans Albers.[14] His screen credits tell their own story: *Die Pratermizzi* and *Ein Mädel aus dem Volk* (*A Girl of the People*), *Der Faschingsprinz* (*The Carnival Prince*), *Und dich hab ich geliebt* (*It Was You I Loved*), *Der Herr auf Bestellung* (*A Gentleman on Order*), *Zwei Herzen im Dreivierteltakt* (*Two Hearts Beating in Three-Quarter Time), Die lustigen Weiber von Wien* (*The Merry Wives of Vienna*), *Der Prinz von Arkadien*, *Ich und die Kaiserin* (*The Queen and I), Leise flehen meine Lieder* (*Softly My Songs Are Pleading), Maskerade*, *Episode*, *Silhouetten* and *The Great Waltz*. These titles seem to advertise their own irrelevance, but in the light of what self-existence does this myth of Austrian and Viennese life deconstructs itself: 'reality', 'politics', 'history'? The problem is twofold. First, there is the biography of Walter Reisch that demands reticence and precludes hasty judgement. As an Austrian Jew he probably did not have an easy life, either in Vienna or in Berlin, and as a screenwriter, not even in Hollywood was he spoiled for credit or attention. The second problem is the relationship of all Austrian film makers to their 'Big Brother' Germany. Austria had, almost since the beginnings of the cinema, nurtured an indigenous 'commercial' production sector, associated with names like Luise Kolm, Count Sascha Kolowrat, Willi Forst, Hans Moser and Paula Wessely. During the early period of sound films, Austria produced about 20 per year. Modest though it may seem, this number of films amounted to a distinct cinematic tradition, with a special kind of continuity in its themes and genres over a lengthy period. Hitler's rise to power in Germany in 1933 immediately affected film makers in Austria. Jewish directors such as Robert Wiene left Berlin for Vienna, but Austria could only serve as a temporary stopover. A clause in the Nuremberg race laws forbade the presentation of films with non-Aryan actors, which had an indirect effect on Austria's cinema, as access to the German market was a matter of survival, so that an early attempt was made to enforce the German race laws in Austria also, via the professional associations. In 1937, the combined financial and political pressure increased as a result of the extensive veto right in the affairs of Austria's Tobis-Sascha Filmindustrie AG enjoyed by the principal shareholder, the German Tobis. Furthermore, with the *Anschluß* in 1938 (i.e. Austria's annexation as 'Ostmark' into the German Reich), all existing organisations related to film making were dissolved and taken over by the German Reich Chamber of Film (the 'Reichsfilmkammer').[15]

Against this background, emigration becomes a blurred concept. The definition used, for instance, by Christian Cargnelli and Michael Omasta in *Aufbruch ins Ungewisse* includes artists who were forced to flee because of persecution by the Nazis as well as those who left the country in the 1910s and 1920s, mostly for economic and career reasons. But even in the case of those who left 'voluntarily', the dividing line between 'economic' and 'political' pressure is a thin one. As Fred Zinnemann wrote to Cargnelli and Omasta:

> As time went on I found that there was a second, deeper reason for my leaving, which became gradually clear. It was the enormous sense of not belonging, as expressed everywhere with typical Viennese charm: 'We have nothing against the Hebrew gentlemen; we would just prefer them going somewhere else.'[16]

The careers of emigrants such as Otto Preminger (born in Vienna, 1905) and Billy Wilder (born Samuel Wilder in Sucha, Galicia, 1906), whose films are by now synonymous with the Golden Age of Hollywood, are exceptions. The majority of the emigrating film makers (including technicians) had to struggle to make a success in the US film business. Some of them returned to Austria, but more often than not, to early retirement. A few, like Reisch, continued with their careers, both in the US and in German-speaking countries.[17]

With the transition to sound, 'Austria' had become a distinctive cinematic and aural idiom, not least because of the pleasingly lilting and attractively sensuous Viennese accent, cultivated by armies of highly trained stage actors from the Burgtheater and the Theater an der Josephstadt. The result was the so-called *Wienfilm*, a genre of erotic melodrama in operetta night-life settings, narrated in a tone of resigned irony, and most supremely embodied in the films of Willi Forst, whose decorative opulence as a director was perfectly matched by his world-weary elegance as actor (e.g. *Maskerade*, 1934; *Bel Ami*, 1938; *Operette*, 1940). Also excelling in the musicians' 'bio-pic' and cornering the market in other sub-genres of musical entertainment films (from operetta films to ice-skating revue films), Austrian productions in the 1930s and early 1940s were often quality investments, with stars like Paula Wessely earning huge salaries, and the brothers Hubert and Ernst Marischka breathing life and vitality into costume dramas and Heimat-films, which inaugurated prototypes that were to retain their popularity well into the early 1960s. While the Austro-Hungarian (or 'paprika') element was a crucial ingredient of the Nazi entertainment cinema, there existed no Austrian cinema strictly speaking between 1938 and 1945, since after the *Anschluß*, Austrian production companies became amalgamated in the Wien-Film company, at first majority-owned by Tobis, and in turn absorbed by the UFI holding company when Goebbels 'nationalized' the German film industry in 1941.

Felix Austria?

But there was another side to this story. It was not only in cinema that Austria's fate was tied to that of Germany in the twentieth century both literally and metaphorically. To use a few catch-words: the *Anschluß*, welcomed by the vast majority of Austrians with open (or rather, raised) arms in 1938, became in 1945 Austria's 'rape' by Nazi Germany, making extreme ambivalence towards Germany an important factor of Austrian identity.[18] On one hand there were complaints about colonisation, and on the other, there was the steady flow of tourist Deutschmarks. On one hand, there was cultural occupation, on the other, there were decades of a lucrative drain of talent from Austria to Germany. The 'feminised' image of 'felix Austria' often proved to be a convenient nickname, exculpating, for instance, Austrian anti-Semitism, while after the war, it helped to determine Allied attitudes when conferring 'occupied nation' status on Austria and guaranteeing its neutrality subsequently during the Cold War.[19] The 'colonisation' image, too, was double-edged, with film makers such as Lang, Reisch or Forst conducting themselves in Berlin in the 1920s and 1930s as Austria's cultural ambassadors but also as its 'double agents'. For if from the mid-1920s onwards, Austria was a lucrative 'market' for UFA films, there was also a 'reverse colonisation', in so far as much of what proved most popular in German cinema came from directors and stars 'made in Austria' and the Austro-Hungarian Empire. The list is well-known, and to the ones already mentioned, one could add: Joe May and Mia May, G.W. Pabst, Richard Oswald, Karl Grune, Carl Mayer, Robert Wiene, Ferenc Feher, Geza von Cziffra, Marika Rökk, Elisabeth Bergner, Rudolf Forster, Fritz Kortner, Jenny Jugo, Gitta Alpar and Richard Tauber. Some were Jewish, others were not. Some returned to Austria in 1933, others went further abroad immediately. The movement from Vienna to Berlin did not stop there: the much invoked and impressively versatile 'German invasion' of Hollywood in the 1930s was made up of many originating from Austria-Hungary, including the producers Arnold Pressburger and Sam Spiegel, the directors Otto Preminger, Billy Wilder, Fred Zinnemann, Berthold Viertel and Edgar Ulmer, the actors Oskar Homolka, Alexander von Granach and Paul Henreid, the musicians Max Steiner, Hugo Riesenfeld, Robert Stolz, Miklos Rosza and Hans Salter, as well as untold numbers of cameramen and art directors, screenwriters and editors.[20]

The distinctive voice of Austrian cinema has therefore always been extraterritorial, multiply refracted in the mirrors put up along the roads that lead from Budapest to Vienna, from Vienna to Berlin, from Berlin to Hollywood. Reisch, for instance, returned to Vienna in 1933 and, apart from writing screenplays for Willi Forst (*Maskerade*, 1934) also made several films, produced, directed and scripted by him, among them *Episode*, later remade in the US as *My Love Came Back* (1940), there directed by another émigré, Curtis Bernhardt.[21] Reisch, unlike Lubitsch, Lang, Preminger, Litvak or Sirk, was not involved either in writing films noir or in Hollywood's anti-Nazi films, although his wife, Liesl

Reisch, under the pseudonym of Poldy Dur, after the name of Paula Wessely's character in *Maskerade*, played in four anti-Nazi films (her only US screen credits), including *Margin for Error* (1943), *They Came to Blow Up America* (1943) and *The Hitler Gang* (1944). Nevertheless, Reisch, too participated in the additional paradox of Austrians representing the 'good' Germany in Hollywood, after having contributed his share to internationalising Central Europe in Berlin. There, as well as in Hollywood, Austro-Hungarian adventurers, exiles and émigrés may have added to a mythical Vienna, but it was both their revenge and a consolation.[22] For this myth, so often described and even more often denounced, mostly lives on as a result of being the object of its own irony and self-deprecation, and therefore does not dwell in a region where it can either be 'put right' or 'put aside'.[23] For instance, the bio-pic of Franz Schubert *Leise flehen meine Lieder* (1933, director: Willi Forst, script: Walter Reisch) opens with a shot of the Stephansdom, Vienna's famous landmark. As the camera pulls back, one realises that it is in fact a painting. No sooner does one register the *tromp l'oeil* then the picture begins to move, and one sees it being carried on someone's back to a shop, which turns out to be a pawnbroker's, where, of course, the painting – by now reduced from mythic landmark to tourist kitsch – is worth a mere pittance.

It's the end of the song: a late Weimar classic

At the time of my interviews, this film, along with *Maskerade*, *Ninotschka* and *FP1 Antwortet Nicht* was associated in my mind less with Reisch than with the directors Forst, Lubitsch and Hartl. Since then, I have also seen *Ein blonder Traum* (*A Blond Dream*), *Ich und die Kaiserin* (*The Queen and I*) and *Das Flötenkonzert von Sanssouci* (*The Flute Concert of Sanssouci*), which makes the Reisch-touch a more distinct signature, without necessarily allowing generalisations about his role in the development of the film operetta or the music film of the early 1930s. None the less, it suggests the possibility that among the outstanding works of Weimar cinema and early sound film, besides Fritz Lang's *M – Eine Stadt sucht ihren Mörder*, G.W. Pabst's *The Threepenny Opera* or Robert Siodmak's *Abschied*, there are a number of films scripted by Walter Reisch. These for me include *FP1 antwortet nicht*, *Das Lied ist aus* (*It's the End of the Song*), *Ich und die Kaiserin* and *Ein blonder Traum* and perhaps even the much-maligned *Flötenkonzert von Sanssouci*.[24] Reisch was co-author on two of these (*Ich und die Kaiserin*, *Ein blonder Traum*) and sole author on three (*FP1 Antwortet Nicht*, *Das Flötenkonzert* and *Das Lied ist aus*). The text of some of the most successful song hits are also by Reisch, including 'Flieger, grüß mir die Sonne' from *FP1 Antwortet Nicht*, which became, during the Second World War something like an alternative national anthem, because of its popularity among Field Marshall Goering's air force.

The list above should not be considered as a 'counter-tradition' to elevate the operetta film or the musical to the status of Weimar cinema's true contribution to film history, although there is more evidence for such an assumption than one might think, considering how internationally successful Erich Pommer's revue films were in the early 1930s, or how many of the émigré directors obtained their first contracts and assignments in France, England and Hollywood thanks to their collaboration on such films – Fritz Lang, Billy Wilder, Robert Siodmak, Curtis Bernhardt and Joe May, to mention only five film makers whose names would not immediately spring to mind in association with these genres. I am also not playing off mainstream popular cinema against the avant-garde, although this was indeed a trench dug especially deep with the coming of sound. Rather, my contention is that certain of these films testify to the same sensibility as the acknowledged masterpieces, but they also show the same fault lines of cynical make-believe, of an infinitely refracted and ironically broken relation to 'reality'. What makes some of them exceptional is the degree to which they sustain this in ironic self-awareness both in their forms of representation and their perception of truth: in other words, how far they are able to hold on to this 'transparent duplicity' which I have been locating in the vicinity of Peter Sloterdijk's 'enlightened false consciousness' of Weimar culture.[25]

This chapter focuses on probably the least known among the films for which Reisch wrote the script, *Das Lied ist aus* (1930, director: Geza von Bolvary, assistant director: Josef von Baky).[26] What made me curious was that Reisch, in the interview with Joel Greenberg, had described *Das Lied ist aus* as 'one of the most important pictures ever made in Germany', adding: 'Just like a Noel Coward play, very elegant, three or four characters, a few songs, no spectacle whatsoever, and practically no location work. It was Willi Forst's first serious part, the music was by Robert Stolz.'[27] That was all. He might have added that some of the songs became such hits that they survived the war and became popular evergreens: 'Adieu mein kleiner Garde-Offizier' ('Farewell, My Little Grenadier') and 'Frag nicht warum ... das Lied ist aus' ('Just don't ask why ... it's the end of the song').

As Reisch says, the story is very simple: Tilla Morland (Liane Haid), a successful (Viennese) operetta star, is being feted in the Carlton Bar by her admirers, who persuade the reluctant star to sing her latest hit, 'Adieu mein kleiner Garde-Offizier'. One of the bar's guests (played by Willi Forst) interrupts the song by calling loudly for the bill. She is incensed and demands that the troublemaker be found and punished. But the three admirers – the 'former', an impoverished count, the 'current one', a sheet music publisher, and the 'future one', a rich, but effete aristocrat[28] eventually gather at her home, their mission unaccomplished. She airily dismisses them and places an ad in the paper for a private secretary and bodyguard. Among the candidates, Tilla discovers that one of them is the troublemaker from the Carlton Bar and, on a whim, she hires him. He has a convincing explanation for his rude behaviour and turns out to be a veritable jack-of-all-trades – he can play the piano, sing, dance, make coffee, bake cakes, and his teatime sandwiches are the best Tilla's friends have ever tasted in their lives. Tilla falls in love with him, but he keeps his distance, despite her ever more sophisticated ruses to seduce him. Even her eventually quite sadistic attempts to break down his resistance leave him unruffled. Bored and frustrated, the jealous suitors have ganged up and started to spy on this new arrival. They let Tilla know that her private secretary visits a lady every night between 9 and 11 o'clock. On the evening of a big reception given in her honour by the music publisher, Tilla decides to slip out and find out where he goes, but discovers that he is visiting his grandmother, who mistakenly believes that she is the laundry girl. Learning by chance that her man is after all deeply in love with her, but too class-conscious to declare his love openly, Tilla rushes back to the reception. In the meantime, the publisher has used the opportunity to tell the unwelcome rival in no uncertain terms that a nobody like him cannot hope to make a woman of Tilla's tastes happy. Confronted with his secret by Tilla, dying to throw herself into his arms, he now disavows his feelings even more coolly, sending the love letter that Tilla had dictated to him in her desperation to the third suitor, the rich but ridiculous young fop. The latter can hardly believe his luck and marries Tilla on the spot, though not before taking advice from the secretary about how he can make her happy. The newly weds are off on their honeymoon, and those left behind once more gather at the Carlton Bar. The secretary joins the other two suitors, and once more the band plays 'Farewell, my little grenadier', and 'Don't ask why ... it's the end of the song.'

Das Lied ist aus is a comedy without a happy ending. Instead, it is full of world-weary resignation that was to become habitual in the *Wienfilm*, and the special trademark of *bel-ami*, *bon-vivant* Willi Forst. Strictly speaking, it is not an operetta film, except that the heroine is a singer, it is set in contemporary Vienna and the action takes place in the milieu of an operetta theatre. Apart from the opening song at the Carlton Bar, and a few musical numbers during the private soirée, there are no musical performances in front of an audience. As Reisch put it: 'no spectacle whatsoever'. He himself called it an 'intimate *Kammerspiel*', hinting at the Max Reinhardt theatrical tradition rather than referring to Carl Mayer's 'expressionist' *Kammerspiel* – or 'instinct' films of the early 1920s. What, then, is so unusual about this rather schematic plot that might make the film important in the way Reisch suggests? Perhaps it is this very schematism, the formally neat design and the classically simple structure. Striking a special note of self-reflexivity palpable throughout the narrative is an irony that constantly thematises the show-aspects of the action and comments on cinema itself. The film does not let the audience forget for an instant that they are – via the metaphoric stand-in worlds of theatre, cabaret and operetta – in the cinema: in one of the dance numbers, for instance, the song pointedly remarks: 'love ... is like a talkie', and – emphasising this with a sort of nonchalant double negative in another song 'you cannot go on singing all the time ... as if this was a talking picture'.

Several other songs confirm the kind of *mise-en-abyme* typical of Weimar films, the coming of sound both exacerbating and revitalising the customary dead-pan irony. For instance, the song with which Willi Forst first wins the heart of Liane Haid: 'wenn das Wörtchen "wenn" nicht wär' ('if only the word "if" did not exist') has its first verse end with: ' … then I'd tell lies like Baron Münchhausen', which is of course exactly what Forst is in the process of doing, when he tells Tilla she needs more happy songs in her repertoire like the ones he sings, rather than the nostalgic–melancholy 'Adieu, mein kleiner Garde-Offizier'. His song concludes with 'if only the word "if" did not exist', women would love me like they love Harry Liedke'. Given that Liedke was the biggest movie heart-throb of the 1920s, but somewhat in decline by the early 1930s, the reference could not be more explicit. It is, of course, himself that Willi Forst has in mind, so that the nameless, enigmatic private secretary here fantasises out loud about what it would be like to be Willi Forst! He slips neatly into his own (star-)identity from his fictional part. Similar semantic 'slippages' surround the homology of both the film title and theme song 'Das Lied ist aus', several times cited within the action, but each time alluding to something different, sometimes cynical–ironic, sometimes melancholy and resigned, depending on who is speaking and the kind of situation.

The sincerity of make-believe

It is worth studying in more detail how the sound films of the early 1930s consistently use anti-illusionist devices. Films like *The Threepenny Opera*, *M* or *The Testament of Dr Mabuse* spring to mind as prominent examples of montage experiments in sound–image counterpoint. Yet 'Brechtian' alienation effects also found their cinematic equivalents in the popular movie genres, mostly in musicals and comedies. Typical of a certain vein of self-referentiality in German films of the 1930s are comedies directed by Paul Martin, such as *Ein blonder Traum* and *Glückskinder*, sending themselves up via a double level of reference that uses 'America', Hollywood, Mickey Mouse and Coca Cola to suspend their own escapism.[29] Hanns Schwarz's comedies also have this dual register, notably *Einbrecher* (1930, starring Heinz Rühmann and based on a French boulevard play). It contains sophisticated effects exploiting the illusionist possibilities of the contrast between the human voice and its recorded equivalent, playing on the absence and presence of the sound source, and comically contrasting gramophone recordings and radio broadcasts with their 'live' embodiments. References to the cinema in *Das Lied ist aus* also have their parallels elsewhere. In *Ich bei Tag und du bei Nacht* (1932, director: Ludwig Berger) the heroine, visiting the residence of Frederick II at Potsdam's Schloss Sanssouci for the first time, is overwhelmed by the plush interior: 'what splendour – like the movies!' she bursts out. Finally, a star vehicle for the then very popular tenor Jan Kiepura (*Das Lied einer Nacht*, 1932, director: Anatol Litvak) cleverly uses a romantic comedy plot in order to distinguish 'Jan Kiepura', the actor–performer from 'Jan Kiepura', gramophone star. The conventionally pastoral story of mistaken identity with a fairy-tale prince/celebrity singer travelling incognito, who falls in love with a simple country girl, is here updated to include luxury trains, gas stations and open-top automobiles. The real modern twist, however, is that the singer's body is separated from his voice, the one impersonated by a confidence man on the run from the police, the other represented by gramophone recordings. The purpose of this is not so much to secure a happy fairy-tale ending, as to unite body and voice in the new (synthetic) identity of the performer and star at the end of the film, as Kiepura proves his 'real' identity in the court room by singing 'live' to the jury. The recording is once more synchronised with his own body, rather than lip-synched by the con-man. The film cleverly uses the sense of 'presence' produced by the recorded voice for its comedy of errors, in order to build up the reputation of Jan Kiepura the recording star for the new medium of the sound film. The *mise-en-abyme* of the two levels 'sound' and 'image' here have a precise objective, for they displace attention from the potentially deconstructive play of characters to the new star identity. In other words, perception shifts from person to product, and the rapt attention of the diegetic audiences participates in a blatant act of commodification. Anticipating some of the strategies of *Singin' in the Rain*, the brand-name 'Jan Kiepura' and the film *Das Lied einer Nacht* endorse one another by each becoming an advertisement for the other. The film literally features Kiepura's records, while the records promote the new genre of the sound film. The kind of duplicity in the representation of reality that, as the chapters in this volume have argued, is typical for Weimar as a period of major social turbulence, is here thematised around a major technological transition in a medium of representation – the change from silent cinema to sound film. Technologically mediated reflexivity, packaged as life-style modernity in both *Das Lied ist aus* and *Das Lied einer Nacht* proves to be a source of aesthetic fascination, which ends up boosting the commodity characteristic of the media experience, as it fetishises the technical effects in the figure of the human performer, making him a 'star'. Willi Forst and Jan Kiepura are not 'finally' themselves, they are identical with their media fictional characters, thanks to a doubled-up self-reflexivity.[30] However, the parallels between a film like *Das Lied einer Nacht* and *Das Lied ist aus* also help highlight the differences. Although it is not intended to claim for the latter an *auteurist*–modernist reflexivity and condemn the former for its crassly transparent commercialism, such self-reflexivity in the age of consumption none the less sustains in *Das Lied ist aus*, an egalitarian, if not democratising moment, by constantly undercutting and ironically relativising the signifiers of hierarchy and identity, while *Das Lied einer Nacht* eventually compacts these layers in the inevitable happy ending.

What also distinguishes *Das Lied ist aus* is the way the different elements of the action, the various situations and dramatic moments repeat themselves, or rather, find themselves mirrored across movements of addition and repetition. For instance, the fairy-tale and wish-fulfilling motif of the three suitors is played through several times, announced in the opening sequence with a minor detail, a visual gag that ranks the financial status of three according to the (descending) number of their respective dress-shirt studs, identified by the camera isolating them in three forward travelling shots. By staging a circularity into which the entire plot is folded, *Das Lied ist aus*, more elegantly than most Weimar films, is a variation on classical Hollywood practice, but with just enough of a modification of the initial constellation to give the impression of having 'worked through' the originating situation, in the cathartic mode of comedy and wit, rather than the more therapeutic mode of melodrama, as in the plays of Schnitzler, or the films of Ophuls.

The third 'schematic' and seemingly purely formal device that distinguishes *Das Lied ist aus* is complementary to the other two. It is the principle of alternation and inversion manifest in the editing style with a 'question and answer' pattern, which is a striking device also in Fritz Lang's *M*, where the viewer is drawn into the action not by the suspense of detection, but by having to infer the question to which a given sequence is the answer. A similar strategy can be found in *Das Lied ist aus*, with an additional layer of exchange provided by apparently identical repetitions. An example of the latter is the running gag of the instructions of how to alter Willi Forst's shirt collars. First, they are given by the grandmother to Tilla, when Tilla is mistaken for the laundry girl, and then Tilla passes them on with the bundle of clothes, to the real laundry girl whom she meets on the stairs on her way out. Tilla behaves as if she were the mistress of the house, so that the repetition not only contains a transfer from one person to the next, but also a functional reversal of the characters' respective social positions. The real irony of the transfer, however, resides in the fact that it was Tilla, as the mistress of her own house, who in the first place instructed her private secretary to change his, to her eyes, old-fashioned shirt collars. In other words, her request and command returns to her via the grandmother as a commission and a mandate: in a sense, it turns out that she has sent herself on the errand!

However, the request/command to have the shirts altered is itself a displacement and transfer: Tilla is not bothered by the style of the shirt as much as she is frustrated by the coldness of the man inside it. So, after getting hold of him by the collar in the hope of stealing a kiss, her disappointment turns the tender touch into a gesture of reproof. The motif of the 'piece of advice' that, as it is passed along, discloses its many-layered ironies, is itself once more doubled, because the exchange between the grandmother, Tilla and the laundry-girl takes place at the same time as the music publisher gives Willi Forst his piece of advice, namely to 'lay off' Tilla, in the guise of telling him about a stage play he has just read, in which a young man such as he, tragically does not know what to have and to do, in order to make a society woman happy. His advice, Forst will duly pass on to the bridegroom-to-be, in the course of a fox-trot lesson, where they have already reversed roles, because Forst plays the man to the groom, who takes the woman's (i.e. Tilla's) part. At the same time, this rhetoric of reversals has an ethical dimension, so to speak, because while the publisher is motivated by jealousy and prejudice, Forst's repetition of the advice is prompted by the melancholy resignation of someone who is prepared, for the sake of his love, to sacrifice himself.

The formal devices of *Das Lied ist aus*, therefore, are not an end in themselves. One way to sum up their message would be to say: only in 'fictional' modes can one discuss 'facts', and only in the form of a 'lie' can one speak truly about 'love', which is reminiscent of Umberto Eco's famous question: how is it still possible to say 'I love you', without immediately putting the sentence in inverted commas? This apparently 'post-modern' principle of mentally adding the gesture of quotation to any utterance that wants to pass for authentic is so central and so consistently applied in *Das Lied ist aus* that it may well be the best point from which to evaluate its place in Weimar cinema, and to understand why Reisch might have thought of it as one of the most important films made in Germany. The cardinal question of the film is that of the cinema itself, considered as the condition of 'reality in the age of its mechanical reproducibility': how can one be authentic in the medium of inauthenticity, how can

Figure 26 Romantic duplicity: Willi Forst and Liane Haid in Geza von Bolvary's *Das Lied ist Aus* (1930)

Source: Stiftung Deutsche Kinemathek, Berlin

the true disguise itself in all these masquerades of the false? The reply that *Das Lied ist aus* appears to give is: only across the double negative. Not merely because this acknowledges the treacherous nature of appearances, but also because such a negation of a negative has built into it the speaking position of an 'other', and therefore is at least potentially capable of dialogue, of give and take, of sharing and receiving.

Acknowledging the treacherous nature of appearances means to relativise and undercut even the most intimate of emotions, be it love or jealousy, sexual frustration or passion, by first letting the states of mind and heart manifest themselves in their 'false', 'put-on' form, where they immediately reveal themselves to be lies and impostures. A feeling changes its aim and turns into its opposite, or it changes its object and is transferred to another person. Because the song in the opening sequence touches Forst too deeply he disavows his feeling and derides it by interrupting Tilla's performance. She in turn calls him 'the most detestable, rude and ignorant man on earth', whereupon she proceeds to hire him as her secretary. He shows himself to be cold, correct and unapproachable, while she is burning up with passion, but perversely, this passion also gives her access to a sadistic fury of intensity that she converts into a power position that sets free her talent as a comedienne.[31] Much of this, no doubt, forms part of the normal erotic play between the sexes, for whom reversal of roles and the frustration of expectations is simply foreplay or the added spice of eventual conquest, and thus, so to speak, belongs to the standard equipment of the successful seduction, but is here performed to such perfection by both partners that it suggests, in its very negativity, their sexual equality. A utopian element becomes visible: extended to other areas of life, the 'erotetics' of question-and-answer could become the 'erotics' of dialogue, which in turn promises the 'ethics' of a democratic community, based on the negotiation of equality without being egalitarian. Taken only a step further, one can say that *Das Lied ist aus* sees itself as something of a swan-song to the ideals of 'Weimar', Germany's first attempt at a modern, democratic society, the more poignant because played out in the tragi-comedy of the 'new woman', faced, as we shall see, with yet another version of the Weimar 'damaged' masculinity.

Such a reading responds to the element of urgency and desperation in *Das Lied ist aus*, where the energies of change and renewal are constantly blocked, in everyone's full knowledge of their being blocked. The erotic passions are so intensely shown and displayed, while at the same time so thoroughly frustrated that display remains foreplay, and the circulation of libido remains stuck like the needle on the gramophone in the film's penultimate scene. Frustration being the ultimate pleasure principle of *Das Lied ist aus*, the movement of the narrative 'working through' its own blockages is transferred from depth-psychological exploration, to a kind of skimming along the hard surface of social inhibitions and class conventions, the sliding leaving its own traces in the punning linguistic slippages already referred to. However, because of the sheer effort put into keeping up appearances and deferring gratification, as well as because of the ingenuity invested in plotting them, one can assume that the deferrals are themselves pleasurable: to someone. This someone must be the spectator, since the hiding and disguising is in the service of another negotiation as well, namely the trade-off between modernist self-reflexivity and modernisation, both tied to the transfer of media technologies already discussed, in the process of which these technologies become fetishised as the glitz and glamour of the show. Early sound cinema's deployment of new media becomes an attraction in its own right, on its own behalf: the telephone and the gramophone take on a life of their own, as in the boudoir scenes, in which the bedroom with its furnishings are Tilla's stage, where she performs in order to melt her steadfast iceberg of a secretary. The bed, in fact, becomes her command-and-control centre, where the telephone on the side-table keeps Tilla in touch with the outside world and with her servants indoors. In one of the scenes, Tilla – after just having called him in – orders her secretary out again, because she is in the middle of an intimate telephone conversation, a show laid on especially to rouse his jealousy, since it was in fact a caller who had dialled the wrong number, and whom she now baffles with her outrageous love talk. No sooner has she completed this charade, she calls him in again, to make him witness to her bidding goodbye to a lover through the adjacent door. This tender and passionate farewell, too, is a mime act, in which she embraces herself, pretending to be pulled out of the door by her insatiable lover, the door-frame serving as the theatre wings or the movie screen, with the imaginary suitor placed in off-screen space.

The two scenes anticipate, in function as well as in their strategy of substitution, the device of the love letter she dictates to him. There, by a reversal that makes it also tragic, the intended addressee is no longer an imaginary lover, but the secretary, who – having learnt his lesson all too well in the bedroom charade – passes the letter on to the suitor, as if to punish Tilla with a real lover for her previous pretence of having an imaginary one. Yet, her action at this point is no longer dictated by the sadistic frustration of a woman spurned. Now it is the ruse of a woman in love, eager to make it easier for her shy partner to declare himself. Then, at a crucial moment during their non-exchange, a door opens and the song 'das Lied ist aus' can be heard played on the piano in the next room. Charged with new meaning by the way it intrudes into the scene, the hit record and evergreen-to-be, performed live, becomes a sadistic intruder, for it provides a caustic comment on the imminent end of the two partners' missed – as well as mixed – messages. Both are too late for their appointment with happiness, and it's the end of the song.

Self-reflexivity of a more traditional kind reaches its climax in a play-within-the-play scene. Placed at the centre of the film as its *mise-en-abyme* is a private puppet theatre performance given late at night to Tilla by Willi Forst. It is a fairy-tale love story for three voices with a happy ending, involving a prince, the postmaster and the postmaster's daughter. The prince falls in love, but how could he marry a commoner? Just as all hope seems lost, the postmaster confesses that the fair maiden is not his daughter after all, but the kidnapped child of a noble family, killed by robbers in an ambush. As the couple ride off in the wedding coach, the old man, finally freed of his burden of guilt, can die in peace. The puppet play reverses the genders, but mirrors the situation of the two protagonists, with the one difference that in the 'real' world of the film, no 'postmaster' intervenes to deliver the liberating message to its proper destination: only a pile of men's shirts continues to circulate. In other words, the media and means of communication are not only present, they mark the point at which mediated communication becomes meta-communication, as if to underline the 'felicity-conditions' of the face-to-face encounter between the central characters, which is to say, the impossibility of the face-to-face encounter in the modern love relationship, whose 'I love you' is always already placed, if not under erasure, then at the mercy of a medium instead of a mediator.

The episode of the puppet theatre is in this sense also an ironic, canny commentary on the characters' respective hopes and desires: 'she' wants 'him' to perform for her (repeating, mirror-fashion the opening scene, where it was the men who wanted Tilla to perform), but now her request is prompted by hearing the noise he makes sawing in the attic, where he is busy repairing the toy stage. Once more, he is the source of a disruptive noise, except that this one attracts her attention favourably, so much so that at the end of his performance she sidles up to him. But since he does not respond to her advances, she counters his indifference with an even colder rebuff that culminates in her capriciously complaining about his shirt collars. The over-compensation, or rather, the rejection of a rejection, is the most fundamental move of the film as a whole. While on one level it opens up a circuit of transfer and exchange that ends with 'him' able to confess his love for Tilla indirectly, via the 'medium' of the grandmother mistaking her for someone else,[32] on another, more abstract level, it confirms once more that only across the abyss of the double negative can an utterance affirm its authenticity, as well as its communicativeness.

In practice it means that each situation must enact a double act of deception, but under conditions where both parties at once know and do not know about the deception. If in the form of the double negative it becomes the 'minus times minus equals plus' principle recognised as one of the structural moves of the operetta plot,[33] it also points in the direction of both partners sharing a 'cynical–kynical' consciousness, in Peter Sloterdijk's sense. However, because both parties seem to be prepared to sustain these modes of negation right to the bitter end, such 'cynicism' becomes itself a heroic act of defiance, designed to keep in permanent suspension the level of reality as well as the level of reference, again suggesting a paradoxical kind of equality and mutual respect. For rather like the children's game of 'scissors, paper, stone', each element might change its place in the hierarchy of values, depending on the nature of its opponent: stone blunts the scissors, but can be 'wrapped' in paper, while paper is cut by the scissors, which in turn loses out to the stone. Thus, depending on the nature of the deception, either partner may retain the upper hand when countering deception with a dead-pan disavowal.

The flute concert of Sans Souci

That the game of dissimulation and disguise can have a 'political' as well as an erotic dimension is the lesson at the heart of *Das Flötenkonzert von Sanssouci* (*The Flute Concert at Sans Souci*), written by Reisch and directed by Gustav Ucicky in the same year as *Das Lied ist aus.* Under the motto 'all's fair in love and war' the combination becomes a concert in two musical keys, the cynical one of politics and diplomacy, and the melodramatic one of conjugal love and marital fidelity. The film is mainly remembered for the riots it caused at its premiere, when the communist left staged noisy protests against what they saw as pro-war propaganda, and *Das Flötenkonzert* has subsequently been cited time and again to illustrate the pro-Nazi tendencies in UFA productions after the takeover by Hugenberg and Ludwig Klitzsch.[34] Kracauer sums up the plot as follows:

> [Frederick] succeeds in thwarting conspiracies, outwitting slick diplomats, and winning battles where all the chances are against him. [He] secretly issues mobilization orders to his generals during a flute concert attended by the unsuspecting ambassadors of Austria, France and Russia, thus stealing a march on these three powers which, he knows, are all set to attack Prussia.[35]

With hindsight, the deceptive action taken by Frederick on the eve of what became the Seven Years War, whose necessity *Das Flötenkonzert* in 1930 seems to set out to prove, does indeed look like providing the perfect foil for justifying Hitler's 'preventive' war of 1938. But when reversing the historical telescope, another version seems just as plausible, especially since only the last ten minutes of the film deal with the marching orders to the troops. What leads up to it are a number of moves and counter-moves of deception and double-cross, in which the diplomatic intrigues are complicated by amorous intrigues, each intrigue at once inverting, undercutting and commenting on the other, in the mode of political and erotic cynicism made more familiar by *The Threepenny Opera* that premiered a mere two months later, with what in Part III, Chapter 2, this volume, I called its 'transparent duplicity'.

What would it mean to apply the same principle of transparent duplicity to *Das Flötenkonzert von Sanssouci*? It is in many ways a typical operetta story about court intrigue (double-) crossed with love intrigue, a virtual blueprint for what became the most successful example of the genre – *Der Kongress tanzt* (*Le congres s'amuse*, 1931, director: Eric Charell), which *Das Flötenkonzert* precedes by nine months. The plot involves the jealous and ambitious Count of Saxony, making common cause with Prussia's traditional enemies (Austria, Russia and France) in order to start a war against Frederick II. In the end, he can foil the plan by first having a spy at the Saxony Court, and second, anticipating the war by starting it himself. The film opens with a reception at the Court of Saxony, where every guest seems to be a spy or a double agent. Even the musician, the main protagonist, one quickly learns, is present on a reconnaissance mission for the King of Prussia. So many layers of game playing and imposture are peeling away in the first fifteen minutes of the action that it becomes difficult to keep up with who is spying on whom, who is in the service of whom and whether they are doing this in order to gain information or to disseminate disinformation. The spy motif associated with the Court of Saxony finds itself doubled by a love-and-jealousy motif at the Prussian Court of Potsdam, played already in a minor key at the Saxon Court, where the secret code word of mutual recognition among the conspirators turns out to be 'minuet galant'. At the Potsdam court, however, behind the suave politeness another conspiracy is in progress – between France, Russia and Austria against Prussia – of which the Saxony intrigue is, so to speak, its rococo miniature and *mise-en-abyme.* The motor that keeps these wheels-within-wheels turning is Frederick's musician spy, riding back and forth between Saxony and Potsdam, but whose own position is that of a framer framed, because of a flirtatious and sexually frustrated wife.

In a scene right at the beginning of *Das Flötenkonzert* one finds once more the double negative also typical of *Das Lied ist aus*, condensed into a formula that assumes programmatic status for several of Weimar early sound films: 'talking is often a better way to stay silent than silence', remarks the Count of Saxony, congratulating himself on a piece of successful deception, not realising – as the audience does – that he has in fact given away more than he wanted, because the supposed dupe realised what was happening but had his own reasons for

Figure 27 Viennese courtesy at the Court of Prussia: Otto Gebühr (as Frederic the Great) and Renate Müller in Gustav Ucicky's *Das Flötenkonzert von Sanssouci* (1931)

Source: Stiftung Deutsche Kinemathek, Berlin

'playing dumb'.[36] Such tactics of playing dumb, so as not to be caught out being too-clever-by-half resembles the strategy of the open lie as the best protection against being found out. These moves are not unfamiliar in a world of media-politics where straight-faced deception has become the secret of successful mass communication: 'I know that you know that I know' is the meta-level that retrieves such duplicity and mints it afresh as a form of validated authenticity, given that, in the words of Jacques Lacan's famous *double entendre* 'les non-dupes errent': those most proud of not being fooled are the real dupes.[37]

While Kracauer sees *Das Flötenkonzert* prospectively as an anticipation of the Blitzkrieg of 1938, the left-wing press at the time read it retrospectively: as yet another 'revanchist' story about the Versailles Treaty, which throughout the 1920s was widely resented as a humiliating national disgrace, much worse than losing the war itself. Walter Reisch evidently saw his film differently, and one can understand why: after all, the resentment against Versailles was a cliché, a standard trope of Weimar political discourse, and so were the stories of Frederick II's high and low cunning. The basic conceit of *Das Flötenkonzert* was to invent a story around a very well-known painting by the popular artist Adolf von Menzel, which shows Frederick surrounded by family, friends and dignitaries, playing his beloved flute. But instead of creating an anecdote that would give all these characters depicted by Menzel a pseudo-historical referentiality, Reisch typically inverted the proposition, so that the painting itself seems staged by Frederick in order to disguise something else – namely that in the presence of these dignitaries and ambassadors, Frederick has decided to give his generals orders to march on the enemy, during the interludes in the concert: the painting was itself a 'front', a facade and a ruse – a game for all to see, but with a false premise. We are back in the world of *Leise flehen meine Lieder* and the Stephansdom that turns out to be a painted 'front'.

It is the background to this background that Reisch's story tries to tell, crossing the political intrigue of who spies on whom at the Saxony Court, with an erotic intrigue involving Frederick's spy. While he successfully dupes the Count of Saxony in the political stakes, he is himself duped in love by his young wife, who – left alone once too often, on account of her husband's secret missions – is ready to deceive him with a smooth-talking courtier. The King, getting wind of the imminent affair, uses his own prerogative of regal duplicity to trick her into missing her amorous encounter by making sure that instead of her husband finding her at her secret date, she is dining with the King. The husband, having intercepted a love letter, sees his jealous anger wholly frustrated, because he now has to assume either that his suspicions where unfounded, or that His Royal Highness himself was courting his wife. In neither case can he act on impulse or drop his guard. For the sake of king, country and patriarchal morality, Frederick protects the wife from herself, the husband from his murderous rage, and the country from its enemies.[38] As in all the UFA films that Reisch was involved in, *Das Flötenkonzert*, too, works with the same sort of open duplicity, in which two lies almost make a truth, or at the very least deliver a cleverly devious set of ironies. In this reading, the ending in which Frederick double-crosses the double-crossers is therefore no more 'serious' than the rest of the film, and the accusation of having made propaganda for the Nazis must have seemed to Reisch as coming from those boorish Berliners who just could not appreciate a (Viennese? Jewish?) joke. But that, of course, was part of Reisch's own tragedy: neither could Hitler.

What is at stake is thus not so much this film or that, but a surprisingly supple yet consistently pursued strategy that could be called a 'culture': of irony and double reference, sustained by a rhetoric of indirection and double negation. Within this rhetoric a certain dynamic seems to unfold where energy and frustration, the permitted and the prohibited, showing and telling, telling and silence redefine each other and find a new adjustment as these originally private and dialogical values enter into the public arena of the new media world. The characters demonstrate the gain in libido that comes from not confronting obstacles head-on, but by a sort of mimetic reduplication, which at once confirms their recalcitrance by repetition and surreptitiously undermines it by comical exaggeration. The result is yet another mode of suspended referentiality typical of Weimar cinema as a whole, irrespective of genre and regardless whether it were made during the silent era or after the coming of sound, whether it were attached to the epic struggles of a Dr Mabuse or surrounding the somnambulant, nocturnal encounters between Cesare and Jane, or Nosferatu and Mina Harker. In this respect Weimar cinema knows two related narrational systems, which visually involves the use of off-screen space and cognitively implies the deliberate withholding of information. It is a structure that can have a tragic (melodramatic) component (as in *The Cabinet of Dr Caligari*, *Dr Mabuse* and *Nosferatu*) or it can be played in the register of comedy, as in these (operetta) examples from Walter Reisch's films and the films of Lubitsch, whose elliptical narration, it will be recalled, was aptly summarised by François Truffaut's phrase about the 'Swiss cheese called Lubitsch', because of the holes he leaves in the stories for spectatorial surmise.

The anti-Nazi film

Lubitsch, however, was also the master of the double inversion, in the mode of openly displayed duplicity, as demonstrated in his still underrated *To Be or Not to Be* (1943), which dares to make fun of Hitler, right in the middle of the war, by mimicking the regime's self-important theatricality with another layer of blustering imposture. To save their lives, a troupe of Polish actors impersonate their deadly enemies – an SS commandant and his henchmen – so perfectly that it confounds the Nazis themselves, catching them in the mirror-image of their own narcissism long enough for the actors to make their escape. Paradoxically, it is the Hollywood anti-Nazi film that here provides the genre in which Austrian and German émigrés can continue the Weimar mode with the greatest virtuosity. Because of the dominant legacy of Weimar style in exile purportedly leading to film noir, this proximity of the anti-Nazi film and operetta comedy has not always been appreciated, yet even more than film noir, its self-referentiality as well as its self-critical look at the parallels between political and show-business make-believe make the genre a serious contribution not only to the fight against Nazism and American isolationism, but also to a sort of self-examination, where an entire generation of Weimar film makers takes stock of its own historical imaginary.

One of the most prominent examples of the genre in this (self-) reflexive mode comes from Fritz Lang, whose anti-Nazi films *Man Hunt* (1941), *Ministry of Fear* (1944) and *Cloak and Dagger* (1946) use every opportunity to construct their scenarios around different kinds of falsehood, around the opportune lie as the manoeuvre to best counter the bigger lies of those who brutally put themselves in charge of truth. The battle for freedom, justice and morality in such films always takes place in the deceptive realm of images, because the moment of truth of an image is nothing but another image. Lang's stories are driven by no other principle as much as by their accumulation of trap-doors and false floors: a film as the elaborately set (mouse-) trap also for the spectator, as it catches mind and eye in the agonising prison labyrinths of a Piranesi universe. The most extraordinary example, as Jean-Louis Comolli and Gilles Deleuze have also noted, is Lang's collaboration with Bertolt Brecht on the anti-Nazi film, *Hangmen also Die* (1943):

> For Lang, there is no longer truth, but only appearances. The American Lang becomes the greatest film maker of appearances. Everything is appearance, and this new system transforms the ability to judge, though it doesn't suppress it. [...] Appearances are not deemed to be lies, because they give way to some deeper truth, but simply because they turn out themselves to be not-true: a character makes a slip, like giving away that he knows German when he is supposed to be a Czech nationalist. Under these conditions, it is possible to create new appearances in the light of which falsehood can be judged and is being judged: the resistance group fabricates false witnesses, so that the traitor who knows German is condemned by the Gestapo.
>
> Lang's relativism is Protagorean, where the judgement expresses the 'better' point of view and where appearances decide in favour of the better cause or individual (judgement as vengeance, or displacement of appearances). On this basis, one can appreciate the encounter between Brecht and Lang, and also their misunderstandings. For with Lang as well as Brecht, judgement and truth cannot exercise themselves directly in and through the image, but pass to the spectator, who is given the means to judge the image him/herself.[39]

In Lang's relativising universe, justice is not a matter of virtue or an abstract ideal, but, pragmatically, rather more a question of the 'better' lie at the right moment. This vantage point of the 'image' rather than of 'truth' also throws a different light on the encounter between Brecht and Lang, and also helps one understand their inevitable misunderstandings. What the two had in common was that truth cannot be apprehended directly in and through the image. Instead, judgement is passed to the spectator, who is merely given the means to perceive the image, the scene as constructed, as 'given to be seen'. Yet what in Brecht was a matter of sharpening a conflict to the point of producing a contradiction, became in Lang a determination to demonstrate the necessary fallibility of the opposition between truth and appearance. In one scene of *Hangmen also Die*, for instance, Brecht dramatises the dilemma of the young woman who urges the Heydrich assassin to give himself up in order to save the hostages, while she is quite prepared, a few moments later, to sacrifice another innocent, the woman greengrocer, in order to remain undetected herself. Brecht wants the spectator to see the potentially tragic contradiction between two value systems, the personal and the collective, and he does so by demonstrating the dependence of an emotional reaction on the social context. What fascinates him is the reversibility of the situation around this particular moral dilemma, but it is a scene that could equally well have been conceived for the stage.

Lang, on the other hand, is interested in how a man like the conspirator and the Heydrich assassin behaves, since he has nothing but disguises, and since his situation is a false one whichever way he plays it. The hero therefore deliberately and desperately engineers a play of falsehoods, not in the hope of staying alive, but in order to serve the cause as long as he possibly can. Sometimes, as in the scene where the lipstick marks are applied too perfectly to convince the police inspector Gruber of a passionate date, he loses, and sometimes he wins, as in the scene where the wounded man behind the curtain starts dripping blood, which the hero quickly disguises by 'accidentally' spilling the glass of wine he was about to offer the inspector. Good triumphs only because it has another layer of appearances up its sleeve. This 'truth' effect can only be achieved by filmic means and the specific resources of the cinema.

The example shows that between these two Weimar artist-intellectuals, a fundamentally different attitude to the cinema was at stake. For Brecht, from the point of view of the artist-as-producer, the cinema was at best a socially more convenient support for documenting the staging of theatrical performances, and at worst (seen from the point of view of its 'realist' potential) it was a technically very defective apparatus of distanciation because it permitted no division between play text and performance text. For Lang, on the other hand, images constitute their own reality, so that any critique of 'appearance' must situate itself at the reality of the image, and the search for truth can only be the play of the different *mises-en-scène* of falsehood. Good triumphs, when it does, mostly if it can bring more levels of 'falsehood' into play.

This may, in the universe of totalitarian politics, be too much of a utopian hope, but it locates fairly well the point where, as suggested, the anti-Nazi film meets the operetta comedy, both referring one back to the legacy of Weimar cinema in the New World, as a director like Billy Wilder practises equally astutely the duplicity of cynical comedy and the paranoia of film noir. Operetta is a genre whose musical form and subject matter is meant as an attack, whether in a mimetic–parasitic spirit, or by way of parody and pastiche, on high-culture self-importance. Given this aesthetic position on the margins, yet supported by a social class confident of its cultural claims and therefore both popular and profitable, operetta seems to have thrived, at least since Jacques Offenbach and Johann Strauss, from an ability to invert the relations of 'seeming' and 'being'. To simplify a little, one can venture that for the world of operetta, it is seeming that becomes the 'zero degree' of all values, rather than the forever unattainable or always already discredited world of 'being'. Extended to the realm of the intersubjective and the dialogical, it would indicate that the default value of any act of communication is its impossibility: only a tacit, sustained, and in each instance renewed special contract between the partners (in the world of the operetta, usually erotic), can give them the illusion of mutual understanding and meaningful exchange, as long as they abide by a set of (cultural, generic) rules.[40] Put differently, it is a matter of knowingly accepting deception and self-deception as the 'normal' state of existence, without expecting that the world of appearances might in the end be defeated by the revelation of reality's foundational ground.

If, therefore, operetta makes a virtue out of necessity, turning make-believe into a generically secured truth-standard, and thus the agreed basis of its own authenticity, then it stands to reason that early sound cinema should find in the operetta mode its own most 'honest' self-definition. For in view of the technical problems of synchronous sound, the 'all-talking film' was a special kind of achievement: it 'performed' synchronisation or the 'matching' of voice, music and sound-effects with an image. Radical scepticism was thus built into the very condition of the sound-film, so that the impression of reality was always already the simulation of an effect, rather than sound being a technological device to 'render' the impression of reality: the supplement, as always, exceeded its intended function as complement. Thanks to technology, a certain 'immediacy' presented itself as real, but based on such supplementarity, the impression of reality was but one of its possibilities. This in turn changed the relation of the spectator to his or her own sense perception, and thus altered the contract that the audience had with that which is represented.

When applied to *Das Lied ist aus*, it gives one another clue to its generic hybridity, neither an operetta nor a musical, neither a tragedy nor finally, a comedy. Rather, it is their 'theoretical' elaboration, making the structural features of all these genres productive for the emergent sound film and its ideology of self-confident but also self-cancelling illusionism. The basis for confidence would be that neither operetta nor the sound film refer to a world outside themselves, while none the less – in this respect quite different from any avant-garde–modernist 'immanence' ascribed to the autonomous work of art – claiming its right to a social space precisely because of the commercial priorities standing behind its 'fantasies'. As argued above, a film like *Das Lied einer Nacht*, is conceived as the extended self-advertisement of a singer-turned-star thanks to the mechanical reproduction of his voice. Second, even though only this 'inner' reference point exists, and even though this world is merely 'intransitive', such self-cancelling self-referentiality is not a given. As *das Lied ist aus* shows, it has to be negotiated progressively, painfully, across a series of comedies of errors, of misunderstandings, mistaken identities and well-intentioned deceptions. What the sarcastic and even at times sadistic display of cognitive traps, false bottoms and blind alleys prepares the spectator for is a peculiar kind of semantic surface density, enjoyable without anxiety or regret, precisely because of its lack of 'depth'. The historian Volker Klotz has pointed out how, in the world of the operetta, an apparent tautological self-reference is almost programmatically indispensable:

> [Operetta] can only blossom under the motto that Johann Strauss has given one of his sopranos: 'I love Love/I live Life'. This is how the operetta form is able to appropriate everything, and make its own whatever fills the senses. Not as external object, that might be graspable in this or that singular embodiment, but – to use a linguistic term – as its inner object, as deictic reflexivity. Once its basic structure has been recognized, such an inner object can only be mimetically staged: to love love, to live life. Whoever takes to heart this operetta motto, does so twice over, insofar as the opposition between desire and reality, between wanting and doing vanishes [...] but it does so by transforming both into a beautiful illusion. [...] The inner object must not be possessed or clung to, nor can it be a means to a utilitarian end or otherwise turned to individual advantage.[41]

The tautological, but in actual fact 'performative' nature of the inner object establishes another link between operetta and early Weimar sound film. It is as if sound, rather than adding a layer of 'reality', was turning action into 'speech acts', but in contrast to a speech act like 'I promise' binding the speaker to his utterance, the operetta – true to its 'inversive' relation to (bourgeois) norms – assigns a particular role to the spectator, namely that of an accomplice, with all the ambivalence inherent in such a notion of complicity. The many modes of mis-communication which *Das Lied ist aus* deploys as the supports of mediation, indirect speech and *double entendres* are not so much designed to deceive the protagonists, since all of them are at once too expert at the game, and too cynical in their expectations of anything else. Instead, the gaps create the spaces for the spectators to insert themselves as vicarious participants. Declarations of undying love are staged as if to illustrate the interchangeability of subjects in the transmission of the message: the love letter that Tilla dictates to her secretary, but which he thereby writes to himself is only the most tragic–comic instance of a whole line of declarations of love via third parties, opening a space between 'make-believe' and 'trust' whose playfulness is in fact its most serious guarantee of authenticity, while respecting the other's right to discreetly misconstrue the message. This, Willi Forst does with Tilla's declaration, passing on the letter to the suitor least likely to expect it. But in another scene, Forst, once more in his role as private secretary, answers Tilla's fan mail. Seated at the desk, autographing a pile of her photographs, he pauses, takes one of them and lovingly pockets it. Here, too, 'Tilla' dictates him a message, but this time he chooses to believe it as addressed to himself, even though, or maybe because, it is he who forges the 'sincerely yours' and the signature.

The curtain closed, but all the endings open?

Like the fictive stage play that is to scare him off starting a love-affair with Tilla, and the puppet show put on for her benefit, the agents of the drama are first made spectators of their fate before their status as addressees once more gives them the freedom to act on their own behalf. This reversal, too, is used to metaphorically point to sound cinema itself, with its retrospectively attributed agency across the synchronisation of body and voice, not least to valorise this new form of technological presence and sensory plenitude as the sole available mode of authenticity, in the full knowledge of its artifice. But it also drastically devalues film as an instrument of propaganda, since the demonstration of this artificial authenticity is one of which the spectator is an accomplice, having in each case to decide what value to allocate to his own scepticism, and whether to assign tragic, melodramatic or tragi-comic consequences to the state of affairs prevailing in the world of the protagonists. As Brecht put it in his play *The Good Woman of Sezhuan*: 'the curtain closed, but all the endings open'.

1930: *Das Lied ist aus*, 'it's the end of the song'. In retrospect, of course, the title carries its own allegorical burden. For by 1933 at the very latest, 'appearance' is arrested and reified into 'being', and deception passes itself off as the will to power supporting the new state. Weimar's kynical principle of the paradox sustained, as the best option among alternatives of which all are false, finds itself replaced by the Nazi's bare-faced cynicism, resolving contradiction by vigorously engaging their supporters in blunt or clever but in any case, straight-faced faking. Seen in this light, it was indeed a game not without risks, which the early sound film played with its public, when it put on the guise of the operetta, to conceal but also to reveal its many layers of duplicity. Judged positively, through the benevolent end of the historical telescope, one can argue that with its rhetoric of artificial authenticity, the Weimar sound comedy playfully set an impossibly high standard for cinematic truthfulness, almost that of an 'aristocratic' or elite mode of indirection for a mass audience. To put it less indirectly, this art of the inauthentic and the duplicitous is not a play with 'seeming' and 'being', and their reversibility, as an end in itself. It is an attempt at dialogue, forsaking the democratic ideal of absolute equality for the complicity of shared consent, extended over the abyss opening up in any act of communication. As a consequence, every representation claiming to be valid must bear the marks not only of its conventionality, but also of its negotiated conditions of possibility, which is to say, it invites active participation in its artfully staged duplicity. Such a form of exchange ultimately rests on respect for the other, because, courting the risk of (tragic) misunderstanding, it is prepared to tolerate the other also as radical 'other', even when she/he is unable or unwilling to bridge the abyss, or denies its existence altogether. Weimar duplicity practised the high art of tolerance, before it acted out the harder part of survival, as in *Hangmen also Die* and *To Be or Not to Be.* What separates the two, in time as well as ethics, is the moment at which one side decides to unilaterally cancel the 'rules of the game', declaring war on the undeclared, but mutually practised agreement to keep the duplicity visible.

Such moments, too, can be observed in the films Walter Reisch was involved in: for Georg Seesslen, *Episode* (1935, director:/script: Reisch) is a film that 'without wishing to, describes a chapter in the progressive fascistisation of the Austrian petit-bourgeoisie', adding, however, that it achieves its resolution 'without terrorizing one side or making the other pay with a total loss of self-perception'.[42] Reisch's dilemma is even more explicit in the final sequence of *Das Flötenkonzert von Sanssouci*, already quoted. What makes the seemingly endless parade of Prussian armies and Frederick's final address so awkward in its pathos, and so embarrassing in its calculated effect is the unexpected absence of any distancing irony. All of a sudden, no more false bottoms: the duplicity disappears from the fiction (the mutually sustaining and deflating military and marital intrigues), to arrogate a reality in 'history'. Frederick steps out of the film, as it were, to 'endorse' an assertion whose metaphoric reference aims at an extra-fictional present, where it becomes a cynical allusiveness directly addressing the audience: 'in Versailles our enemies conspired against us, we are surrounded and have to attack as our only means of defence'. Transparent duplicity turns into a skewed historical parallel, and operetta inversion is used as vehicle for a perversely prophetic time shift, which makes Frederick's duplicity not a memory from Prussia's past but a promise of Germany's future. Yet such a step out of the historical frame also leaves behind the 'frame tale' of the fiction, since it was precisely the embedding of politics in erotics and the embedding of both in the looking-glass game of masking, unmasking and re-masking that secured the fiction its authenticity, and thus its credibility, which in the end, it seeks to 'cash in' on behalf of a historic mission. To this extent, the film in its final scenes breaks its own code, distancing itself from its own mode of functioning, which is why it cannot ultimately prevent this mode from returning, and therefore turn against the ending itself. In so far as this makes the parades themselves seem merely another façcade, *Das Flötenkonzert* becomes readable as Frederick's own self-advertisement (the making of the statesman as wily fox, the human façade of modern power politics), rather like *Das Lied einer Nacht* advertises the making of Jan Kiepura, lending a human face to a technological invention. On the other hand, the end of *Das Flötenkonzert* is indeed also readable as the 'end' of duplicity, advertising the start of the parade of historical parallels, in the service of political legitimation and thus of state propaganda. As always in Weimar cinema, ambiguity is the better part of valour, and in its own way, *Das Flötenkonzert* starts with as many reversible frames as *The Cabinet of Dr Caligari*, except that the last one is torn away, making the story suddenly bleed into a more sinister necessity.

Das Lied ist aus, too, contains a reference to Versailles, and the question of responsibility for the war. In fact, it is the premise on which the film contributes a very special message, giving added meaning to Reisch's own evaluation of it as an important film. For it is Germany's (and Austria's) defeat that triggers the action, constituting the 'trauma' of which *Das Lied ist aus* is the peculiar 'working through', in the mode of recognition/repetition, identified by Freud to be equally essential phases of the mourning process. 'Adieu mein kleiner Garde-Offizier': the reason why the rude guest in the opening scene noisily provokes an éclat turns out to be his painful memories of having himself served in the Austrian army as a 'Garde-Offizier', and having been beaten and defeated. The film thus opens on the angry, resentful response to the lost war and the defeat in peace, but as an over-reaction, and a socialite's *faux-pas*. This gives it the opportunity to point to an alternative way of dealing with this damaged masculinity: via indirection and artifice, via subjunctive and optative: 'if only the word "if" did not exist', associated with that paragon of the Grand Lie, the Baron Münchhausen, who not only told the tallest tales and most improbable adventures, but who was also known for pulling himself up by his own boot-straps, which is to say, for making himself his own 'inner object'. Self-reference here takes on a fairly explicit political dimension, with the light-hearted song-text embedding a whole sub-text about shame and guilt, war wounds and psychic injuries. *Das Lied ist aus* brackets this 'serious' discourse and its political dynamite, by suspending its love story between the message of its songs, 'Frag nicht warum' ('Don't ask why'), 'Adieu, mein kleiner Garde-Offizier', and 'Wenn das Wörtchen wenn nicht wär' ('If only the word "if" did not exist'), which is to say, between the address of denial (don't ask), the temporality of regret (adieu), and the mode of hypothetics (if only).

As already suggested, these issues have a distinctly deconstructive ring about them. What in Peter Sloterdijk is the 'cynical reason' of the 'enlightened false consciousness' faced with the 'Weimar syndrome' of radical scepticism could also be called a post-Heideggerian anti-metaphysical metaphysics, part of postmodernism's 'anti-foundational deconstructivism', as propounded by, for instance, Richard Rorty in his dialogue with Derrida, *Contingency, Irony and Solidarity*.[43] Could it be that late Weimar cinema of the kind represented by Reisch, has passed on to us the playful glimpse of a none the less serious hypothesis, one that still awaits its realisation, namely that one does not need to be in the possession of 'the truth', to enter into dialogue with the 'other', and that one does not need absolute equality, in order to be committed to democracy? Such might be the message of *Das Lied ist aus* and it spikes it with an added irony, because it would de-negate its own modality and tense: since the word 'if' does exist, the resigned assertion proposed in the title *Das Lied ist aus* might both hide and reveal also a more hopeful question: *What if the song had only just begun?*

Notes

1 Barry Salt: 'The world inside Ernst Lubitsch', first presented during the 'Space Frame Narrative' conference at the University of East Anglia, September 1982. It is published in German as 'Die innere Welt von Ernst Lubitsch', in: Uli Jung and Walter Schatzberg (eds) *Filmkultur zur Zeit der Weimarer Republik* (Munich and New York: K.G. Saur 1992): 65–70.

2 See Part II, Chapter 2, this volume, on Lubitsch.

3 Michael Wedel, 'Schizophrene Technik, sinnliches Glück. Die Filmoperette und der synchrone Musikfilm 1914–1929', in Katja Uhlenbrok (ed.) *MusikSpektakelFilm. Musiktheater und Tanzkultur im deutschen Film 1922–1937* (Munich: edition text + kritik 1998): 85–104.

4 Karsten Witte, 'Visual pleasure inhibited: aspects of the German revue film', *New German Critique* 24–5 (Fall/Winter 1981–2): 238–63.

5 Siegfried Kracauer, *The Mass Ornament* (Cambridge, Mass: Harvard University Press, 1995): 75–88 and 'Girls und Krise', *Frankfurter Zeitung* (27 May 1931).

6 Herbert Jhering was known for his disgust with the flood of film operettas, but see also Rudolf Arnheim, 'Tauberton und Studio', *Die Weltbühne* 7 (11 February 1930): 246–8. By contrast, Willy Haas once remarked: 'I am highly suspicious about the enemies of [film] operettas. They are mostly educated snobs, dried-up exalted geniuses, expressionists, Pen-Club members, in a word, skeletons without flesh or juice', *Film-Kurier* no. 266 (12 November 1926). I am grateful to Michael Wedel for the Haas quotation (Wedel, personal communication).

7 Disapproving code words were 'Alt-Heidelberg-Schmalz' (reference to 'The Student Prince'), 'Donaukitsch' ('Blue Danube') and 'Zuckerbäcker' ('Viennese pastry').

8 Karsten Witte, 'Wien–Berlin–Hollywood', *Frankfurter Rundschau* (16 March 1978).

9 See my interview with Walter Reisch, 'Aviator, Greetings to the Sun: Vienna–Berlin–Hollywood', in *Pix* 3 (2000).

10 The most up-to-date information in German is the bio-filmographic entry by Frank Arnold in *CineGraph. Lexikon zum deutschsprachigen Film*, edited by Hans-Michael Bock (Munich: edition text + kritik 1984 ff., suppl. 4/D1).

11 'Walter Reisch: The Tailor', Interview by Joel Greenberg, in Patrick MacGilligan (ed.) *Backstory II. Interviews with Screenwriters of the 1940s and 1950s* (Berkeley, Los Angeles, Oxford: University of California Press 1991): 201–45.

12 Curt Bois is best known internationally, perhaps, as the old man 'Homer' in Wim Wenders' *Himmel über Berlin* (*Wings of Desire*), (1989), Bois's last film.

13 Christian Cargnelli and Michael Omasta (eds) *Aufbruch ins Ungewisse: Lexikon* (Vienna: Wespennest 1993): 172, 193.

14 Reisch wrote his first Hans Albers vehicle in 1929 – *Die Nacht gehört uns*, directed by Carl Froelich, which is also one of the pioneering German sound films. His best-known Albers film is *FP1 Antwortet Nicht.* On Albers's relations with the Nazi regime, see Michaela Krützen, *Hans Albers: eine deutsche Karriere* (Weinheim/Berlin, 1995).

15 See also my entry for 'Austria' in *Encyclopedia of European Cinema* (London: Cassell, 1995): 21–2.

16 Christian Cargnelli and Michael Omasta, *Aufbruch ins Ungewisse* (Vienna: Wespennest, 1993): 9.

17 Reisch made a film in Germany in 1956 (*Der Cornet*, based on a well-known story by Rainer Maria Rilke), which has recently been reinstated as a rare example of German Neo-realism: 'I did it without any studio-work. Real locations were chosen,

to depict the background to the story. No sets were built in Tempelhof or Geiselgasteig' (Walter Reisch, *Die Filmwoche* (3 September 1955), quoted by Fritz Göttler, in Jacobsen, Kaes and Prinzler 1993: 203–4.

18 See Robert H. Kayserlingk, *Austria in World War II* (Kingston, 1988).

19 Georg Tillner, 'Österreich, ein weiter Weg: Filmkultur zwischen Austrofaschismus und Wiederaufbau', in R. Beckermann and C. Blümlinger (eds) *Ohne Untertitel* (Vienna: Sonderzahl, 1996): 175–96.

20 Christian Cargnelli and Michael Omasta, *Aufbruch ins Ungewisse* (Vienna: Wespennest 1993) lists in its second 'lexicon' volume no fewer than 550 Austro-Hungarian film-related émigrés.

21

> Carneval: not a celebration of liberty but of decadence. 'Set in Vienna, 1922' is the laconic title appearing over the image of a female singer, who however, is not performing a typically Viennese song, but: 'Yes, we have no bananas'. We have no choice but to interpret this opening scene as a programme: every detail speaks of the 'problem' we are in the midst of. National and sexual alienation wherever we look; psychoanalytically speaking, the false gaiety of the singer's performance, surrounded by suspiciously pop-able balloons signal the absence of the phallus in the story we are about to witness. We are in a world of disempowered men, as becomes evident when the camera pans right, showing a pair of heavy-drinking women with their male companions fast asleep. A story-within-the story once more illustrates the point of male impotence and decadence: while the band plays a catchy Charleston, a woman deftly steals a man's wallet before stealing herself away. She immediately encounters another woman, narcissistically holding a hand-mirror and powdering her nose, with whom she exchanges a knowing glance, before the two of them grab each other and move onto the dance floor together. From left to right to left we witness the transformation of sexuality and gender, in a world where femininity 'falsely' impersonates itself.
>
> (Georg Seesslen, *Episode*, in Gottfried Schlemmer and Brigitte Mayr (eds) *Der Österreichische Film* (Vienna: Synema, 1999): 4.

22 Willi Forst later claimed that he had made his most typically 'Austrian' films when Austria had ceased to exist as an independent nation (Willi Forst, 'Der Wiener Film ist tot – es lebe der Wiener Film', *Film* 2 (May 1946).

23 The myth was serviced by Austrian stars and directors, but even more so – indicating its imaginary pull – by barely-natives such as Erich von Stroheim (whose parents emigrated in 1909) and Joseph von Sternberg (who left in 1914), and altogether non-natives such as Ernst Lubitsch, in whose films Vienna is present from Prince Nukki in *The Oyster Princess* to *Eternal Love* and *The Smiling Lieutenant*. Also deeply implicated in the myth were such importantly transnational, European directors as Max Ophuls (*Liebelei*, *Letter from an Unknown Woman*) and Ludwig Berger (*Ein Walzertraum*).

24 Other films prior to 1933 scripted by Reisch are *Hokuspokus* (after a play by Curt Goetz, Director: Ucicky), *Zwei Herzen im Dreivierteltakt* (Director: Bolvary), *Im Geheimdienst* (Director: Ucicky), *Saison in Kairo* (Director: Schünzel), *Leise flehen meine Lieder* (Director: Forst).

25 Peter Sloterdijk, *Kritik der zynischen Vernunft*, 2 vols (Frankfurt: Suhrkamp, 1985).

26 For instance, it is not listed among Reisch's credits in Ephraim Katz, *The International Film Encyclopedia* (London: MacMillan, 1980).

27 'Walter Reisch, the Tailor', 212 (see note 11 above).

28 Such, at least, is the pecking order of the suitors, according to (chorus-like) commentary of the two hostesses behind the bar.

29 *Glückskinder* is happy to plagiarise and at the same time pastiche the mid-1930s Hollywood screwball comedies, especially *It Happened One Night*.

30 Significantly enough, Tilla, the 'star' in the film itself, has second billing to Forst, who in the fiction does not have a name, possibly to shine more brightly as 'Willi Forst'.

31 The ironic–erotic play of reversal, with its sado-masochistic component is reminiscent of the 'Surabaya Johnny' song, performed by Polly in Brecht/Weill's *Threepenny Opera* and made famous by Lotte Lenya: 'Und als er kein Geld hatte/Und als er nicht nett war/Und sein Kragen war auch am Sonntag nicht rein/Und als er nicht wußte was sich bei einer Dame schickt/Zu ihm sagte ich nicht 'Nein'/Da behielt ich meinen Kopf nicht oben/Und ich blieb nicht allgemein.' The song applies to Willi Forst, except that as the modern, consumption-oriented version of the gutter-dandy Mackie Messer/Surabaya Johnny, Forst's collar stays white even when it is not Sunday. Although he knows how to treat a lady, he stays seductively 'cold and heartless'.

32 Is the kind old lady really his grandmother? Maybe the encounter is an elaborate staging, as it might be in a 'Third Man' spy-novel. We certainly do see Forst post a tell-tale letter after he walks out of the Carlton Bar.

33 'Minus mal Minus macht Plus' is the phrase used to describe Leo Fall's 'Madame Pompadour' in Volker Klotz, *Operette. Porträt und Handbuch einer unerhörten Kunst* (Munich: Piper, 1991): 73.

34 [Frederick II], a King who, if possible, surpassed all previous Fredericks in his resemblance to Hitler. Artistically on an average level, [*The Flute Concert of Sanssouci* and *The King's Dancer*] with their propagandistic implications found little understanding abroad. An American reviewer called *The King's Dancer* [another Fredericus film] a 'fine German costume piece' in an obvious attempt at indulgence. […] The whole series was a thorough attempt to familiarise the masses with the idea of a *Führer*.

(Kracauer 1947: 267)

35 Kracauer 1947: 268.

36 The court intrigues of *Das Flötenkonzert* seem to have inspired parts of Helmut Käutner's debut film *Kitty and the World Conference*, made just months before the outbreak of the war (1939). It uses a very similar sub-plot of mistaken identities, amorous imposture and spying, intertwined with world-diplomacy, but simplifies the programmatic phrase, making the female character remark: 'silence says more than words'.

37 Slavoj Zizek, *Looking Awry* (Cambridge, Mass: MIT Press, 1991): 69.

38 Several other scenes play on the trope of substitution: the foppish courtier, stood up by his dinner date, decides to eat the second pheasant himself, which inverts the logic of the husband forgetting altogether about the 'papers of state' once he has secured the incriminating letter from his wife's admirer as 'proof' of her infidelity.

39 Gilles Deleuze, *L'Image-Temps* (Paris: Les Editions de Minuit, 1985): 181.

40 See the chapter on 'inference' in Dan Sperber und Deirdre Wilson, *Relevance* (Oxford, 1995): 65–116.

41 Volker Klotz, *Bürgerliche Lachkultur* (Reinbek: Rowohlt, 1987): 190–1.

42 Georg Seesslen, *Episode*, in Gottfried Schlemmer and Brigitte Mayr (eds) *Der Österreichische Film* (Vienna: Synema, 1999): 15, 17.

43 Richard Rorty, *Contingency, Irony, and Solidarity* (Cambridge: Cambridge University Press, 1989).

Part IV

AFTER WEIMAR

Avant-garde and modernisation, emigration and film noir

1

TO BE OR NOT TO BE

Extra-territorial in Vienna–Berlin–Hollywood

'Strangers in Paradise'

Why was it that so many talented European film makers, actors, scriptwriters, composers, and set designers ended up in Hollywood? This question has attracted a considerable amount of attention from biographers and cultural historians, but mainly to flesh out with anecdote an answer already known in advance.[1] In particular, when writing about the exodus of people in the film industry from German-speaking countries, writers have their narrative emplotment more or less ready-made, for it is obvious that many were political refugees, first fleeing Europe because of fascism, then frustrated by uncouth and uncultured movie moguls and finally persecuted and witch-hunted by paranoid anti-communist senators in the USA. Prominently featured in this version of events are Fritz Lang and Bertolt Brecht, Expressionism and film noir, Thomas Mann and Arnold Schoenberg, Marlene Dietrich and William Dieterle. John Russell Taylor's *Strangers in Paradise* can be considered the definitive account and classic formulation of the liberal–intellectual political-émigré thesis, in which the story unravels within aptly titled chapters, such as 'The Gathering Storm', 'Hollywood Left and Right', 'The New Weimar', 'Hollywood at War', 'What We are Fighting For' and 'How to be Un-American'.[2] This canonical version does not lack either plausibility or testimony, yet nevertheless its self-evidence is deceptive.[3] In what follows, I intend to make the picture slightly more complicated, first, by extending it backward in time, and then, by coupling the political dimension with a second one: that of trade and competition, of contracts and markets. Finally, the anti-fascist war and the trade war have themselves a double in the cinema – the 'looking-glass war' of competing representations of identity and origin, where what it means to have a home and to have left it receives a further twist.

Immigrants or invasions, exiles or trading places?

While the cinema is undoubtedly *the* American art *par excellence*, it has long been recognised that migration, exile, and immigration are constitutive of what we mean by the American film industry. It is impossible to understand how Hollywood came into being without the knowledge that it originated when independent producers escaped the (Eastern) Motion Picture Trust to set themselves up on the West Coast – as a result of the interplay of ethnicity and family values as the tropes of economic–institutional bonding along with a disavowal of origins. If the latter reinforced the bonding, neither quite disappeared without trace. Even though the immigrants assiduously strove to be assimilated and integrated into the new society, sediments of habits and traces of defiance remained that when projected into an entrepreneurial future of dynastic ambitions and cultural aspirations defined the conformity of a self-made elite. Carl Laemmle was a German-born bookkeeper whose career began in a clothing store in Wisconsin; Samuel Goldwyn, born in Warsaw as Samuel Goldfisch, was a glove merchant from upstate New York before he married into the Lasky vaudeville family; Adolf Zukor was born in Hungary and made his first fortune as a furrier in Chicago before moving into penny arcades; William Fox was born Wilhelm Fried in Hungary and set himself up in New York's Lower East Side garment trade before buying up Blackton's bankrupt arcade business; Louis B. Mayer, born in Russia, moved from his father's scrap-metal business in Boston and bought cinemas in New England; Joseph and Nicholas Schenck also came from Russia, owning drugstores and amusement parks in New York while setting their sights upon the high-risk motion-picture business. Another Russian, Lewis Selznick, owned jewellery shops in Pittsburgh, gambled away a fortune made in movies, but fathered two famous sons who were to make the family name part of the Hollywood legend.

Yet ethnic memory or even the Jewish faith as such is perhaps not what was most remarkable about Hollywood's 'founding fathers.' The paradox of these first-generation Americans is that they played such a large part in transforming film production into the cartel known as the Hollywood studio system, precisely because they wielded a cultural influence over mass taste while claiming simply to be in a business. For even if they did not altogether 'invent Hollywood' as argued by Neal Gabler, by repressing and disavowing their own homeland and heritage,[4] they must have helped install at the heart of Hollywood an ambiguity regarding cultural identity that has typified the role of foreigners in Hollywood ever since – either assimilate and become 110 per cent American, or be European and exotic, but also 110 per cent! Such asymmetry and excess might in fact represent two hidden features that sum up this relationship to a 'centre' that is itself the projection of different kinds of otherness, hinting that the questions of émigrés and ethnicity, of homeland and Hollywood has to be located also in a broader context.

The contradiction is perhaps most noticeable among the German émigrés to Hollywood, arguably the largest group or, as indicated above, the one most written about. The story of Germans in Hollywood is complicated by two factors: They came from a country that, at least in the 1920s, could boast of a strong film industry, but they also came from a country that was politically a pariah – associated with war, aggression, and Prussian brutality after the First World War, which became in the 1930s the country that openly persecuted the Jews. As a consequence, two master-narratives compete for credibility. One is centred on the 1930s and 1940s and tells the story backward, with the émigré refugees fleeing Europe to escape a fascist dictatorship and the war, only to be humiliated in Hollywood by tyrannical, ill-read, and ill-bred movie moguls such as Louis B. Mayer, Darryl Zanuck, and Harry Cohn. This narrative gradually replaced an earlier one, also centred on a war. It described the Germans as invaders and as a flood, terms first used when *The Cabinet of Dr Caligari* (Robert Wiene, 1919) and *Madame Dubarry* (Ernst Lubitsch, 1919) made money for their (American) distributors, but the metaphors allude to militaristic national clichés in everyone's mind after 1918, when there was substantial resistance against the import of German films. The trade press of the time in particular was fond of using bellicose expressions and this reached a climax when Ernst Lubitsch came to stay and brought with him his whole retinue from UFA, the German studio conglomerate. David Robinson, in *Hollywood in the Twenties* echoes the mood when he writes: 'Ernst Lubitsch, the most successful and enduring of the foreign invaders'. John Baxter takes up the same theme:

> The arrival in New York on 24 December 1921 of Paul Davidson and Ernst Lubitsch – and the more flamboyant landing a few weeks later of Pola Negri [were the] harbingers of a flood that fundamentally changed the American film industry,
>
> (Baxter 1976, 36)

adding somewhat gleefully a few pages later, that the flood was eventually 'beaten back,' either because directors 'returned in disgrace' or because Hollywood 'ruined the brightest European talent' (Ibid.: 54, 65, 72).

One could argue that both Baxter's claim and his disclaimers are exaggerations, and indeed, I shall try to put forward a slightly different case. For instance, if the military vocabulary about 'invaders' has any justification, it applies more to Hollywood than to Germany: throughout the 1920s when there were talent-raiding campaigns masterminded and conducted by US studio executives coming to Europe for what Fritz Lang called 'trophy-hunting', the objective being to defeat a rival by buying out the best talent in order to exploit them internationally. On one of these shopping trips Harry Warner 'bought' Michael Kertesz in Berlin. Kertesz had taken refuge in Germany from Hungary, after the collapse of the Austro-Hungarian Empire, and in Hollywood he transformed himself into Michael Curtiz, the most dependable and inspired of Warner's contract directors, directing some fifty films for them in twenty years, among them a German-language version of Lloyd Bacon's *Moby Dick* (*Dämon des Meeres*, 1931) and (much later) everyone's favourite émigré film, *Casablanca* (1943). And Carl Laemmle's summer vacations during the 1920s in the (now Czech) spa towns of Marienbad and Carlsbad were notorious occasions when

Berlin film folk fell over themselves in the hope of getting a contract for work at Universal.[5]

Baxter, however, makes an important point. When discussing the émigrés of the film business, it can be misleading to focus solely on the directors, because Hollywood also wanted the popular stars (in the European market), whom the directors were believed to be able to deliver (apart from Pola Negri, Lubitsch also brought Emil Jannings, while Mauritz Stiller brought Greta Garbo). Hermann Weinberg, in *The Lubitsch Touch*, also recognised the nature of trade:

> The foreign 'invasion' had begun, though it was never a real invasion, for the European contingent had been invited one by one, nay, *lured* to come here. Thus on the heels of each other soon appeared Emil Jannings, Conrad Veidt, Erich Pommer, Alexander Korda, Paul Leni, Lothar Mendes, Lya di Putti, Karl Freund, Lajos Biro, Friedrich Murnau, E.A. Dupont, Ludwig Berger, Camilla Horn and many others – stars, directors, cameramen, and scene designers, leaving UFA all but bereft of many of its best talents.
>
> (Weinberg 1964: 47)

Even with the lesser talents, the aim was to make films destined for the foreign national markets at the expense of indigenous producers. Lubitsch's personal assistant, for instance, was a young man called Heinz Blanke, who later, behind the scenes, became one of the most important middlemen in the traffic between Berlin and Hollywood. From 1933 to 1962 he acted as a key producer for Warner Brothers under Hal Wallis.

The anti-Hollywood sentiment in Weinberg has been taken up by other writers, such as Siegfried Kracauer and Lotte Eisner, who speak of an exodus, a drain that left the German film industry deserted and depleted. Here the economic argument shades into the political argument, for it implies the notion of a steep decline of the German film industry in the latter years of the 1920s, leading inevitably to its artistic demise in 1933. But as George Huaco has pointed out, this narrative cannot be right, since films made in Germany in the late 1920s and early 1930s – *Menschen am Sonntag* (*People on Sunday*, Billy Wilder/Robert Siodmak, Fred Zinneman, 1929), *The Blue Angel* (Joseph von Sterberg, 1930), *Der Kongress Tanzt* (*The Congress Dances*, Eric Charell, 1931), *M* (Fritz Lang, 1931), *Die Dreigroschenoper* (*The Threepenny Opera*, G.W. Pabst, 1931), *Vampyr* (C. Th. Dreyer, 1932), and *Kuhle Wampe* (Hans Eisler/Slatan Dudow, 1932) to name but a few – are aesthetically as important, thematically as adventurous and stylistically as diverse as anything produced at the same time as Hollywood, quite apart from the fact that these films, among others, ensured that the German film industry was financially more stable and internationally more successful than at any other time in its history. The profits from a series of musicals produced by Erich Pommer and directed mostly by Hanns Schwarz, Karl Hartl, and Gustav Ucicky (all of whom stayed on in Germany) were enough to keep the UFA balance sheet positive, despite the studio's huge investments in the conversion to sound.[6] Considering how generally hostile avant-garde critics tended to be to the coming of sound, one wonders whether the political argument of the exodus after 1933 might not have found reinforcement in an aesthetic prejudice.

Wave after wave?

A more historically grounded assessment of the relationship between Germany and Hollywood, therefore, cannot be either solely economic or purely political. The two master-narratives of the 'German invasion' and the 'German refugees' at once contradict and complement each other, precisely because they are held together at another level, that of the ethnic imaginary, where the dilemma of the Germans of the 1920s as well as of the 1930s matches the situation of the 'founding fathers' of 1910–19. Hence, it is interesting to trace the peculiar cultural logic underpinning these interchanges. To start with the economic interchange: if the Germans did produce a flood, they certainly produced waves! But these waves need to be distinguished from one another. Lubitsch in 1921 could be called the crest of the first wave, and Murnau headed the second in 1925. After the success of *The Last Laugh* (1924) Murnau was imported with the more specific brief of bringing the values of 'cinema art' to Hollywood,[7] while behind him were those whom Hollywood regarded as specialists in particular styles or niche markets, such as E.A. Dupont and Paul Leni. Both, like Murnau, were known for exceptionally innovative, but also esoteric films in Europe (*Waxworks*, 1924, *Variety*, 1925). Dupont's and Leni's motives were primarily economic, or at the very least, professional: Hollywood made films with higher budgets, in better-equipped studios, for larger audiences.

Besides directors with some experience, such as Lothar Mendes and Ludwig Berger, this wave also brought adventurers with little previous experience to southern California, such as Fred Zinnemann, or with varied experience, such as Edgar Ulmer, who first visited as an assistant to Max Reinhardt in 1923, then came back as part of the Murnau troupe in 1925, returned to Germany in 1929, only to try his luck once more in Hollywood as an art director in 1931, until he came into his stride with *The Black Cat* (1933) and found a specialised niche as the most important director of Ukrainian and Yiddish films between 1935 and 1940. These film makers, then, were neither poor immigrants fleeing their country of origin to escape hunger in search of the American dream, nor were they political exiles and refugees. They were film artists and cinema professionals who were attracted because of the technology, resources and rewards that Hollywood could offer. This migration and 'talent transfer' is therefore first and foremost an expression of the extraordinary economic dynamism of the film industry generally during the mid- and late 1920s, and of the inescapably international character at every level of its operation, be it production, distribution, or exhibition. Nothing demonstrates this more clearly than another wave around

1930, which brought to Hollywood William Dieterle, Hans Heinz von Twardowski, Günther von Fritsch, and several other less permanent visitors. They were hired by Warner Brothers' Berlin subsidiary, Deutsche National, in order to make foreign-language versions of Warner films, with Dieterle being chosen because he could act as well as direct, and Fritsch because he had enough knowledge of Spanish to direct a Latin American version alongside a German one, saving Warner the costs of transport, board, and lodging on their imported labour. Germans thus made German films in Hollywood while still contributing to the American film industry, especially in the then-crucial overseas (European, Latin) markets. In a similar context, Dupont was able to revive his faltering international career by directing, between 1928 and 1931, a number of English-, French- and German-language versions for the London-based British International Pictures and its German subsidiary, Südfilm.[8]

Fighting fierce competition and forging strategic alliances was thus the *modus operandi* not only between Europe and Hollywood, but also between the different European national industries as well as among national producers. What moved people and personnel from country to country was often the sheer power of capital needing to stay in circulation within the various sectors of the (international) film industry. This is even the case with the wave that landed after 1933, and which with more justification can be called political refugees: Fritz Lang, Joe May and Billy Wilder, and later in the decade Robert Siodmak, Curtis Bernhardt, John Brahm, and William Thiele. One feature shared by these émigrés is that many arrived in Los Angeles not from Berlin or Vienna, but from Paris, where all of them had also directed films, while some came via London, where they had gone in the hope of being able to return to Germany once things improved politically (which proved a false hope). None had intended to seek his fortune in Hollywood, and all had to remake themselves culturally as well as professionally in order to prosper.

The Paris stopover most clearly indicates the mixture of economics and politics in the motives for emigration, because it points to the dominance of the German film industry over that of France from the late 1920s throughout the 1930s. Only the final wave of émigrés during the late 1930s and early 1940s, notably Max Ophuls, Jean Renoir, and René Clair (escaping from occupied France, or via Holland), and from Germany, Reinhold Schünzel, Frank Wisbar, and Douglas Sirk were to leave Europe for political reasons. The last three had a difficult time once they arrived in America, not least because the established émigré community regarded them with suspicion, since they were known for having made prominent and highly successful films for UFA after the Nazi takeover, such as *Victor und Viktoria* and *Amphitrion* (both Reinhold Schünzel, 1933, 1935), *Anna und Elizabeth* and *Fährmann Maria* (both Frank Wisbar, 1933, 1934), *Schlußakkord* and *Zu Neuen Ufern* (both Douglas Sirk, 1936, 1937). The most tragic case perhaps is that of G.W. Pabst, known in the late 1920s and early 1930s for his experimental (*Secrets of a Soul*, 1926), socially committed (*The Joyless Street*, 1925), new-realist (*Diary of a Lost Girl*, 1929), liberal (*The Loves of Jeanne Ney*, 1927), and critical-pacifist films (*Kameradschaft*, 1931). He too went to the USA in 1934, after making French and French-language version films between 1930 and 1933. When *A Modern Hero* (1934, made for Henry Blanke and Hal Wallis at Warner Brothers) was not a success, he resumed directing in France from 1936 to 1939. With a ticket on the *Normandie* to New York already booked, Pabst returned to his mansion in Austria, where he fell ill just as war was being declared, which postponed his departure indefinitely. Film historians have not forgiven him for 'missing the boat'.[9] Pabst's example underscores more dramatically than the meandering careers of Ulmer, Bernhardt, or Dupont that to speak even of 'waves' is misleading, since much of this was two-way traffic.[10] In the late 1920s and early 1930s in particular, individual trajectories were at once contingent and accident-prone before political events in Europe and Hitler's rise to power forced upon so many careers the fatal pattern of persecution, exodus, and blighted prospects. Although everyone who was in the public eye was affected by the changes in Germany after 1933, often it was actors, writers, composers, and singers who experienced fascism and anti-Semitism more directly as a threat to their lives as well as their livelihood. They made up the hard core of the political refugees. The directors, especially those with a reputation already established, had contacts abroad as a matter of course. They were familiar with the basic techniques and technology of picture making everywhere, and many knew the working practices in other studios, quite apart from the fact that language was less of a barrier to finding work than for writers or actors. Certainly during the 1920s, improved communication and sea travel meant continuous movement back-and-forth between Europe and America. John Baxter points to this when he writes:

> Many came to Hollywood – it is hard to find a single major European director of the period who did not make at least a token visit to Los Angeles – but only a fraction ... stayed there.
>
> (Baxter 1976: 54)

This, too, is not the whole picture. Behind the directors, there are the producers. Paul Davidson's role in getting Lubitsch to Hollywood has already been mentioned,[11] and Pabst was able to work in France because of his long-standing association with Seymour Nebenzal's Nero Film, which had connections with Warner Brothers and Pathé Nathan. But the close ties that the German film-making community had with Paris, London, and Los Angeles were in no small measure due to the vast network of contacts and incessant travel of a single individual: Erich Pommer, the head of production at UFA for much of the 1920s, who began as the German representative of Gaumont, worked for Eclair, had contracts with Paramount and MGM, in the 1930s produced films for Fox in France and the United States, worked with Korda in England, shuttled between London and Los Angeles for most of the 1940s, and returned to Germany as a US Army officer to reorganise the West German film industry in 1947. If at one end it is the impersonal, abstract logic of capital that provides the necessity as well as the energy for competition, collaboration, and exchange, at the other end, the engine that kept the revolving doors in motion was the charismatic personality of Pommer, either directly or indirectly.[12]

The dynamics of uneven exchanges

But what, one is obliged to ask, is finally being traded in this pattern of uneven and non-equivalent exchanges? What profit-and-loss ledger actually keeps score? Is it commodities, reputations, services, expertise, markets, know-how, patents? If one concentrates on the most tangible commodity, the films, it is obvious that very few German films from the so-called classical German cinema were commercial or even critical successes. After the flurry of excitement caused by *The Cabinet of Dr Caligari*, others apart from the press became more critical. As Baxter observes:

> By the time *Passion, Deception*, Buchowetzky's *Danton* and the remaining post-war epics had been released in the US, Hollywood's ardour for the German film was considerably diminished. Having bought every new production of any reputation in order to keep it from competitors, the studios viewed their accumulated holdings with alarm.
>
> (Baxter 1976: 55)

Baxter goes on to quote from an interview with a production head from Famous Players-Paramount who in 1922 was in charge of re-editing Joe May's eight-part series *Mistress of the World* (*Die Herrin der Welt*, 1921) for the American market. Dismissing German films for their 'shape that the most amateurish of American picture fans would laugh at', he finds that 'the German mind cannot condense. ... Editing seems a totally unknown art in the German film studio.' A similar, though more famous response was Randolph Bartlett's article 'German Film Revision Upheld as Needed Here' in the *New York Times*, 13 March 1927, a justification of the decision to re-edit Lang's *Metropolis* (1926). Bartlett argued that the cut and re-titled American version 'brings out the real thought' of the film, which Lang had somehow failed to put across in the original. As for the stars, not even Emil Jannings, winner of one of the first Oscars, was able to sustain a career in the United States into the 1930s, while Pola Negri, more famous for her romance with Rudolph Valentino and the feuds with Gloria Swanson than for her American films, criss-crossed between Hollywood and Germany throughout the 1930s and 1940s.

Yet what the focus on the films', stars' and the directors' fortunes in the United States loses sight of is that the battle was usually not about the American market, but about American influence on Western European, South American, or Eastern European audiences. As suggested by the investments initially made in multilanguage versions of films both in Hollywood and at Paramount's

Joinville studio near Paris, the US film industry was always vigilant about its dominant role in the field of exports, threatened, or so it seemed, with the advent of the talkies. Such profound technical and financial changes in the industry, such as the conversion to sound, make it doubly difficult to construct the narrative of film emigration to Hollywood around the prominent personalities of the times. Throughout the 1920s, film industry personnel came to Hollywood and their influence was in some ways more lasting and more profound than that of the directors or the films. Examples are cameramen such as Karl Freund, Theodor Sparkuhl or Eugen Schufftan, art directors such as Hans Dreier and Ali Huber, and composers such as Erich M. Korngold, Franz Waxmann, Max Steiner and Dimitri Tiomkin: each of them had very individual careers in Hollywood, and made inestimable contributions to their particular fields. Their expertise was recognised by the industry even if they were not always recognised by the general public. The work of Karl Freund, for instance, is worthy of major recognition. After being responsible for the camerawork in *The Last Laugh, Variety* and *Metropolis*, Freund not only became a key director of photography for Universal and MGM, and a director of eight feature films (among them such classics as *The Mummy*, 1932 and *Mad Love*, 1935). He was also an activist in the Society for Motion Picture and Television Engineers, and after the war worked in television as chief cameraman for Lucille Ball at the Desilu Company. He had also acquired – since the mid-1920s – important patents in the technology of sound, colour and optical instruments. These he exploited commercially through his own company, the Photo Research Corporation, which in turn had close ties with certain US defence industries working on guided weapons systems.

Freund thus had several 'visible' as well as 'invisible' identities as an émigré, moving seemingly with ease between his roles as film director, director of photography, inventor, patent holder, and businessman, a champion 'chameleon' in the survival stakes of southern California. The case of Henry Blanke, already mentioned, is also special, because of a career conducted almost entirely out of the public eye, and 'inside the whale', so to speak. His longevity as line producer at Warner Brothers throws a fascinating light on the forces that controlled, or at least shaped, the fate of many of the German émigrés. After working for Lubitsch until 1926, Blanke went to Berlin to be Lang's production manager on *Metropolis*, another sign that UFA conceived this film from the start with the American market in mind. He returned to Warner in 1927, only to be sent back to Berlin in 1928, when Warner opened their own production unit in Germany (Deutsche First National). There Blanke got to know William Dieterle, who made one of his biggest successes, *Der Heilige und ihr Narr* (*The Saint and Her Fool*, 1928) for First National. He also worked for the German subsidiary of another US firm – Deutsche Universal – headed by Joe Pasternak. With the introduction of sound in German first-run theatres in 1929, Blanke was recalled to Hollywood to oversee German-language productions, for which he hired Dieterle.

Dieterle, for his part, was only too eager to accept, having had to default on substantial debts incurred on a contract with the Silva Film company. In the files of the Bundesarchiv-Film Archiv, Berlin, there is a warrant issued for Dieterle's arrest, dated about the same time (July 1930) as an article in *Thüringer Allgemeine Zeitung* reporting Dieterle's 'sudden flight to America'. A month later, the Berlin trade journal *Film Kurier* ran a First National publicity still of Dieterle, his wife, and other German and French actors waving from a train that has just arrived at the Union Station in Los Angeles. In the Dieterle files of the Berlin Kinemathek there is also a copy of an out-of-court settlement dated January 1931, according to which Warner Brothers' New York office agreed to employ Dieterle for forty weeks, paying $400 per week to Silva Film in Berlin, while Dieterle received only $200 a week in salary. The incident neatly underlines the trade and barter between German and US firms, as well as Dieterle's status as a 'hired hand' when he first arrived in Hollywood. Ironically, the reason Silva Film could claim such high damages for breach of contract (2 million RM at first, though they seemed to have settled for 80,000 RM) was Dieterle's pull at the German box office, both as a leading actor and as a director. Blanke continued to work with Dieterle on many of the latter's more famous bio-pics (*The Story of Louis Pasteur*, 1936 and *The Life of Emile Zola*, 1937), but Dieterle had to pay off his debts to Warner by directing a number of remakes of films made by his former German colleagues such as Joe May's *Ihre Hoheit Liebe* (which became *Her Majesty, Love*, 1931), the Billy Wilder-scripted *Ihre Majestät Befiehlt* (which became *Adorable*, 1933), and Lubitsch's *Madame Dubarry* (which became *Madame Du Barry*, 1934). At the same time, Dieterle also directed some of the most fast-paced, action-packed and wisecracking pre-Hays Code Warner Brothers B-picture programmers, such as *The Last Flight* (1931), *Jewel Robbery* (1932), or *Lawyer Man* (1932). Only the arrival in Hollywood of his former teacher, Max Reinhardt, changed his image, when Reinhardt appointed him director of *A Midsummer Night's Dream* (1935). This became a prestigious success for Warner Brothers and upgraded the studio's image, at the same time rescuing Dieterle from remaining an unknown B-film director, after having already been a director of A-films in Germany. Could he be considered to be a refugee or was he an adventurer 'lured' to Hollywood or was he waiting desperately for that Hollywood phone call the Berlin press was always joking about? But although Dieterle and his wife were neither Jewish nor a prestigious European import, they provided a most welcoming Hollywood home for German political refugees, and used all their influence to obtain entry visas, affidavits, or contracts for Germans in need.

Dieterle's initial task – the remaking of German pictures for the American market – highlights a common feature in the careers of Germans and German-speaking émigrés. Understandably, many émigrés tried to sell adaptations of plays or films to the American studios that had already been successful in Europe. For example, the playwright and screenwriter Lajos Biro (originally from Hungary) sold Lubitsch the play on which *Forbidden Paradise* (1924, remade as *A Royal Scandal* by Otto Preminger in 1945) was based. He also wrote *Hotel Imperial*

(1927, Erich Pommer's first Hollywood production, and remade twice more, once by Billy Wilder as *Five Graves to Cairo*, 1943) and returned to London with Alexander Korda to write *The Private Life of Henry VIII* (1933, itself inspired by Lubitsch's 1920 *Anna Boleyn*). Such networks of ethnic bonding, trading on a common culture, and cashing in on kinship contacts became so notorious that Alexander Korda put a sign on his desk that read 'It's Not Enough to Be a Hungarian'. The obverse of the close-knit community that depended on one another but also 'vampyrised' one another were the often bitter personal feuds and rivalries that developed among the émigrés, especially prior to the late 1930s. The composer Kurt Weill, for instance, who became one of the most successful of the émigrés to be accepted in America, heartily detested his occasional encounters with fellow refugees, calling the evenings spent with them 'nights in the mummies' cellar' and complaining about the 'execrable German' spoken there – 'that awful mixture of Hungarian and Viennese', and bemoaning the fact that the subject of conversation was invariably gossip about other émigrés.[13]

Old World, New World

These stories are, of course, only too familiar among diaspora communities everywhere and in all eras. They illustrate the painful dependency, feelings associated with being uprooted from one's home, and the perverse need to reassert an individual identity in the face of a common fate. In artistic and intellectual circles such feelings were even more in evidence when the immigrants wanted to blend with the host culture. They tried to adopt a positive outlook about a decision forced upon them by external circumstances, but this was often tempered by feelings of resentment about loss of prestige and nostalgia for the status enjoyed back home. A deep distrust of American values in general and those of Hollywood in particular made integration unlikely. Personalities who held such opposing views, for example, Bert Brecht and Thomas Mann, Theodor W. Adorno and Lotte Lenya, Arnold Schoenberg and Hanns Eisler, were agreed on one issue: that Hollywood represented culture at its most corrupt, venal, and hypocritical.

How could such insistence on difference amid commonality and tacit consent amid divergence manifest itself in the work the émigrés were able to do? Did the split consciousness come up with its own imaginary coherence, or were the fault lines visible in the films the Germans produced, authored, directed, or otherwise creatively influenced? I have – in the context of the German 'contribution' to Hollywood *par excellence*, namely, film noir – argued for a more cautious and thus discursive rather than deterministic model of 'influence'.[14] Not only did the different cadres of foreign or exiled professionals affect the film industry in varying degrees and often unexpected ways – as in the case of Karl Freund or that of William Dieterle – but the logic of this impact is such that adequate terms have yet to be found. What can be said is that here the cultural forces transform and yet also instantiate the economic and political determinants. Hence my suggestion to call the resulting mind-set an 'imaginary', to indicate a relation between orders of being that cannot be thought of as either contiguous or complementary, while none the less exhibiting the binding force of a mutually sustaining fantasy. I have already signalled the ambivalence in the Berlin film world of the 1920s *vis-à-vis* Hollywood, reflecting the ambivalence of Weimar Germany *vis-à-vis* America in general.

Only against this historical backdrop of a complex cultural rivalry between the First and the Second World's most powerful industrialising nations can some of the contradictory attitudes of the various waves of émigrés be mapped, and it thus provides the ground on which, for instance, the films themselves can be read as the figures. The process is well illustrated by a director from the first wave such as Lubitsch, who epitomises the most salient features of the German–American film exchange. While the lure of America for Lubitsch was living in a society that had successfully entered an age of perpetual revolution and modernisation – in industry, lifestyle, and technical invention, from which emanated the glamour of speed, wit, and energy, what America wanted from Lubitsch was something quite different. Although he considered himself Germany's most 'American' director (having made satires of Germany's 'Americanitis', such as *The Oyster Princess*), Hollywood needed him to be an out-and-out European.

Once they had arrived in the United States, Lubitsch, along with other 'big-name' émigrés who came to Hollywood with an international reputation, realised that for the New World, they were representative of the Old World. They found Hollywood hungering for images of a Europe fashioned out of nostalgia, class difference, and romantic fantasy. Obliged to recreate and imitate a version of the world they had left behind, directors found their previous work in Germany little help in promoting their careers in America. In this context, Vienna became a key reference point – the master sign and key signifier of 'Europe' to America, comparable only to Paris in this regard. Lubitsch, a Berliner through and through, had to revive Vienna and the Balkans time and again, thus reversing the historical process whereby scores of directors, producers, writers – from the Korda brothers to Michael Kertesz, from Joe May and Fritz Lang to Billy Wilder, Walter Reisch, and Emeric Pressburger – had moved to Berlin to get away from the decadence of Vienna and the decrepit reality of the collapsing Austro-Hungarian Empire.

The secret affinity that existed between Hollywood on one side and Vienna or Paris on the other was that they were societies of the spectacle, cities of make believe and of the show. The decadence of the Hapsburg monarchy was in some ways the pervasive sense of impersonation, of pretending to be in possession of values and status that relied for credibility not on substance but on a convincing performance, on persuading others to mistake appearance for reality. There is a historical basis to this construction. One can envisage Vienna as a 'melting-pot' city, in which class conflicts and ethnic tensions are veiled by a kind of permeability between classes, a state of affairs dramatised in Frank Wedekind's *Lulu* plays, but most succinctly perhaps in operettas, where the lumpen-proletariat and the aristocracy can find themselves enjoying the same places, not least because they have a common enemy – the hard-working, production-oriented, upwardly mobile bourgeoisie. Similarly, the Paris that attracted Hollywood was the Paris of Jacques Offenbach, the operetta composer, during the years prior to 1848, the end of the Restoration period, and before the bourgeois revolution. The power of Vienna as a signifier haunted the émigrés well into the 1940s – Max Ophuls did not come from Vienna any more than Lubitsch did, but he, too, became a specialist in Viennese charm (admittedly a choice that predated his work in Hollywood, as his German and French films from the 1930s amply indicate).

Erich von Stroheim and Joseph von Sternberg are good illustrations of a more drastic reversal of signifiers. Fashioning for themselves identities as European aristocrats, they made their personalities into brand names, which, in the case of Sternberg was that of an 'Old World dandy'. Stroheim, with his boots, monocle and military 'pedigree', might be said to have demonstrated the Vienna principle to dizzying perfection. Although he was the son of a poor immigrant hat maker, he lived not only as an aristocrat, but an Austro-Hungarian aristocrat to boot, doubling the connotations of pretence, style, and play-acting and taking this persona from screen roles into his biography. In both his personal life and work, he chose a mode in which Prussian and Austrian impersonation did not seem to be at all contradictory (as they were in history). Indeed, they almost cancel out the falsehood in both, to make one totally convincing persona.

Sternberg made a film with Emil Jannings which, in the admittedly somewhat different context of the Russian Revolution, none the less is very poignantly intertwined with this subject. *The Last Command* (1928) was scripted by none other than Lajos Biro. The film is about a tsarist general who, fleeing from the Bolsheviks and now living as political refugee in the USA, is forced to make a living as a Hollywood extra in Los Angeles. As fate would have it, he is cast in an anti-Communist epic about the heroic last stand of a White Russian battalion. Obliged to watch a Hollywood actor play a tsarist general, his distress on observing the performance causes him to rush up to the director and explain to him who he 'really' is. The director eventually gives in, and – dressed once more in his full military splendour – the general-turned-pauper-turned-movie-extra is able to die the heroic death on the battlefield that life so ignominiously denied him, before the camera instead. Other directors of European origin also promoted themselves as more or less subtle versions of national stereotypes, for example, Chaplin and Hitchcock, and to a lesser degree, Dieterle, who affected the habit of wearing immaculate white gloves on the set during the shooting of his 1930s films. The Hollywood publicity machine ensured not only that the private self could be consumed as myth, but also that it was a highly coded and thus immediately recognisable myth.

Clichés in the air

The story of the German film émigrés thus presumes a twofold estrangement: from their own home, and from the view that their American hosts had of this homeland. The consequence of this was a kind of schizophrenia, which, in turn also gave them a double perspective on American society – one of admiration and the other a hyper-critical view, both perspectives vying with one another. The dilemma of the émigrés in this respect refigures the cultural attitude of the 'pioneers' who created Hollywood. Did they repress their ethnicity or did it give them a sharper insight into what it meant to be American? Many of the biofilmographies of the émigrés do in fact make little sense, if they are not read against the background of trade and barter (programmed by the economics of the film-industry) that I have tried to describe above. But they also need to be read within another context – that of 'mis-cognition' and recognition, across the gap that opens up between the two kinds of imaginary, represented by Europe's view of America and America's view of Europe. For however much a biographer might be tempted to construct the linearity of a lived life around the fates of the immigrants, émigrés, adventurers and exiles, it may be much more coherent to assume that many of them lived several lives, quite separate from each other, yet each responding with some degree of logic to the requirements of a particular film-historical or film-economic exigency.

Two striking cases in which mutual mis-cognition played a crucial part are the American debuts of Joe May and E.A. Dupont. May, an unwilling émigré, came to the US via Paris with Pommer, for whom the 1933 arrival was more critical than that of 1926, when he was wooed back to Berlin by the new UFA management. *Music in the Air* (1934), which Pommer and May undertook for Fox (continuing his Fox–Europe connection) was very much an émigré project, with Billy Wilder as co-scenarist and Franz Waxmann writing the score. Pommer had wanted an unknown actor to star, but the studio insisted on casting Gloria Swanson. May's films, including his 1928 success *Asphalt*, were quite unknown in the USA – perhaps a blessing in the light of the acid comments made about *Mistress of the World* – and he could only point to a recent work of his which had been remade by Warner Brothers, the already mentioned *Ihre Hoheit Liebe.* The film was not a success, though it must be said that its release coincided with the deep financial crisis of Fox, in the wake of the bid for Paramount, leading ultimately to the takeover of the company by Twentieth Century and Zanuck. *Music in the Air* was interesting as a project, not only because it was calculated to cash in on a number of Pommer/UFA films that did make waves in the USA, such as *Der Kongress Tanzt*, *Ein blonder Traum* (*A Blond Dream*, 1932), *Liebeswalzer* (*Love Waltz*, 1930) and some of the other early sound musicals, with which UFA, as indicated, was impressing the world and redressing its balance sheets. But *Music in the Air* had the added piquancy of being based on a Broadway hit by Jerome Kern and Oscar Hammerstein, that took an 'olde worlde' setting and a typical operetta plot as its subject. What was being exchanged in this film made by Europeans, and adapted from an American musical were national stereotypes in the form of mutual cultural complements, and maybe the film should have been called 'Cultural clichés in the Air'. May did not get a second chance until 1937, and apart from a few assignments in the 1940s, had no film career to speak of in Hollywood. Even his other venture, running a restaurant, called – how could it be otherwise? – *The Blue Danube* did not rescue him and his wife from the most desperate and humiliating penury.

Ewald André Dupont, too, saw his film-making career fizzle out in the Hollywood of the 1940s, but in order to understand the logic of his professional life, it needs to be reviewed as several, rather discrete 'slices', happening almost to different individuals. In contrast to May's enforced exile, Dupont was more of an adventurer. He signed a three-year contract with Carl Laemmle in 1925, came to Hollywood and directed *Love Me and the World is Mine* in 1926. His stay proved to be exceedingly brief, for by July 1926 he had severed his ties with Universal and was on his way again – not to Germany, but to London. The fact that by the end of 1932 Dupont was back in Los Angeles, and once again (briefly) under contract to Universal, before moving to Paramount and beginning

Figure 28 Paris, made in London, destined for America: Olga Tschechova (as Parysia) in E.A. Dupont's *Moulin Rouge* (1928)

Source: BFI films: stills, posters and designs

a tragi-comic roller-coaster ride to disgrace, oblivion, and a post-war comeback as a hack director, underlines the feeling that in his case, the term 'émigré director', with its political overtones, is peculiarly inappropriate. And yet, Dupont's diverse career moves do actually fit into some of the patterns outlined so far.

What made Dupont attractive to Laemmle was the major international success of *Variété*, a Pommer/UFA production that was neither Dupont's first film, nor his first foray into the milieu of artistes, circuses and wandering players (cf. *Alkohol*, 1919, *Der weiße Pfau* (*The White Peacock*, 1920), *Das Alte Gesetz* (*The Ancient Law*, 1923). What made *Variety* such a success was the blend of closely observed milieu, indeed sordid naturalism, with a particularly intense, brooding psychological study of male masochism, jealousy, and murderous rage. It was also a virtuoso display of film technique, with camerawork by Karl Freund, which could be fluid and unobtrusively mobile, or vertiginously drawing attention to itself in the scenes where it substituted itself for Emil Jannings' perception and feelings. Especially 'modern' were a number of set pieces (as in the famous scene filmed through a revolving fan) that were attributed to Freund but were used in earlier Dupont films, not shot by Freund (for instance, *Alkohol* and *Die grüne Manuela* (*Green Manuela*, 1923)). Yet, when Dupont arrived in Hollywood, what project was he offered? *Love Me and the World is Mine* (1928), after the novel *Hannerl and Her Lovers* and thus, as one critic commented, 'another piece of Viennese schmaltz'. It seems that, whatever directors had been famous for at home, all that American producers could think about was 'Old Vienna'. Furthermore, as with May, whose film was to give Gloria Swanson a comeback, and also reminiscent of Lubitsch who, it will be remembered, was called over by Mary Pickford to give her career a different turn (with *Rosita*, 1921), the Dupont project was intended by the studio as a vehicle for Mary Philbin, whose career had been in decline since *The Phantom of the Opera* (1925) and *The Man Who Laughs* (1926). The 12 April 1926 issue of the trade journal *Film Kurier* announced the completion of Dupont's first 'Super Jewel Film' *Hannerl and Her Lovers* (i.e. *Love Me and the World is Mine*), which was to be followed by *Romeo and Juliet*, also with Mary Philbin, and with sets designed by Paul Leni. On the same front page, the *Film Kurier* also carries the notice that *Variety* was being screened to the Paramount renters' convention in Atlantic City, on the first day in its Berlin version, and once more at the end of the week, in a version re-edited for the American market, 'to give the 400 representatives a chance to decide for themselves'. Clearly, in the world of a film-industry trade journal, the two items are not linked by the name of Dupont, indicating once more the subordinate status of the director.

Sound strategy?

Traditional wisdom has it that it was the coming of sound that most damaged the 'international' dimension of the cinema. In *The Shattered Silents*, a study of the

American cinema on the eve of the transition to sound, Alexander Walker recalls the films to be seen in New York during August 1926, when the Warner Theatre on Broadway showed its first Vitaphone sound programme:

> Next door or just down the street, were Rex Ingram's *Mare Nostrum*; Rudolph Valentino's *The Son of the Sheik*; King Vidor's *The Big Parade*; Sjöström's *The Scarlet Letter*, MGM's *Ben Hur*; E.A. Dupont's *Variety*; *The Waltz Dream*, another UFA film; and a whole repertory season of Emil Jannings' pictures. Sophisticated in their narrative-telling, international in understanding, without speech, yet intelligible in all languages, each one bearing the individual signature of a director, star or studio: such movies as these presented some of the silent cinema's finest flowering.
>
> (Walker 1979: 198)

Although it therefore makes sense to say that with the coming of sound, movies became not only more realistic but also more nationally specific, my argument would be that the introduction of sound was not a special barrier to, for instance, German directors moving between different countries in Europe, or between Europe and America. Neither did it displace the peculiar trade-offs just noted for Lubitsch or Sternberg, between an outsider's view of America and the American public's desire to see on their screens a particular view of Europe, which the émigrés were not averse to providing. On the contrary, the films of Lang, Preminger, Wilder, and Siodmak as far as urban America is concerned (*Woman in the Window* (Fritz Lang, 1944), *Laura* (Otto Preminger, 1944), *Double Indemnity* (Billy Wilder, 1944), *Phantom Lady* (Robert Siodmak, 1944)) and those of Ophuls (*The Reckless Moment*, 1949) and Sirk (*All that Heaven Allows*, 1956) with respect of suburban America shaped and fixed the (US) national mythology in very important respects. The 'Germanic' touch detected so often in the psychological thriller, in film noir and melodrama seems thus more convincingly argued once one takes into account these mutually sustaining 'national imaginaries' I have been outlining, rather than any direct, linear descent from Expressionism.

The complementary counter-example is Dupont. If *Variety*, or rather, its quasi-unanimous success with an international public as well as the critics was to haunt the director throughout his life, earning him the somewhat sadistic sobriquet of the 'one-time genius', Dupont figures by rights once more in the history of the cinema, with a film rarely recalled because of its aesthetic merits or its mythical resonance, and remembered rather for its technical novelty. In 1929, working by then for British International Pictures (BIP) in London, Dupont was responsible for the first European talking picture, an adaptation of a play about the sinking of the Titanic, which became *Atlantic* (1929) and was filmed in three versions, with Dupont directing the English and the German one, but not the French.[15] More multilanguage films followed: *Two Worlds* (a story reminiscent of the already mentioned *Hotel Imperial*, with Charles Rosher as cameraman) and *Cape Forlorn* (1931, the German version – *Menschen im Käfig* – had an all-star cast of Conrad Veidt, Fritz Kortner and Heinrich George) completed his deal with BIP, and Dupont returned to Germany.[16] What intrigues one is just what kind of link might exist between such distinctly disparate moments focused on the same name, beyond the pure accident of someone called Dupont having directed, among many other films, these two landmarks of film history. From Dupont's point of view, however, there is no mystery. In so far as European film makers have always, at least in principle, been recognised as artists, i.e. as independently creative individuals, Dupont can be seen to have tried, throughout his career, to produce work that resembles his 'persona' and is consistent with itself, rather like a writer or a painter. But since being an *auteur* in the cinema also implies having to survive, and remain close to the technological–economic means of production, this 'staying in the game' represents a director's true working capital, his currency within the industry and for the critics, who in the case of Dupont, never stopped playing off his previous success against his later flops. For work in Hollywood, *Variety* was both Dupont's launch pad and his meal ticket. But it also was the cage from which he tried to escape – though often enough by a sort of compulsion for repetition. His motto seems to have been 'repetition by variation', for every time Dupont found himself at the cross-roads in his career, he was tempted by yet another variation on the motifs of *Variety*: show business people entangled in the eternal triangle. After his arrival in Britain, his first films are *Moulin Rouge* (1928) and *Piccadilly* (1929, also set in the milieu of dancers, gigolos and show-biz people), and his first film after returning to Germany is called *Salto Mortale* (a triangular love story involving trapeze artists). The question that poses itself, however, is not what personal obsession or existential themes might Dupont the *auteur* have wanted to articulate across the themes of the circus, vaudeville or the world of the spectacle, but rather why, when arriving in Hollywood in 1926 at the height of his reputation, did he *not* make a film featuring a circus ring or a *ménage à trois* (that is, a remake of *Variety*), and instead adapt a popular Austrian novel (i.e. *Hannerl and Her Lovers*), the sentimental story (with a happy ending) of a young woman who has to choose between a paternal professorial type and a young lieutenant departing for a war from which he may not return? The second question concerns *Atlantic*, that is, how was it that Dupont found himself in the vanguard of sound film and the multilanguage versions when little in his previous work indicated this turn? The answer has to be sought in the dynamics of European production companies finding themselves with too small a national market to remain competitive. British International Pictures intended to break into the European and American market, and so it was looking for an 'international' director, with experience in its largest rival markets, namely, the United States and Germany. *Piccadilly* was the biggest production BIP had so far undertaken, the first of a series of 'prestige' films, which not only explains the presence of a German director, but also of American stars (Anna May Wong and Gilda Gray, inventor of the 'shimmy'). Dupont in effect found himself in a situation similar to that of Lubitsch when hired by Hollywood: the Trojan horse smuggled into enemy territory. The dynamics thus bear signs of a comedy of errors and mistaken identities, not without tragic potential, making history at times seem like a prankster. Comparable to Pabst's missed boat, some of Dupont's career moves are the result of awesome accidents, though in a direction opposite to Pabst's 'bad timing'. A Dupont project called *Der Läufer von Marathon* (*The Marathon Man*, 1932) involved location work in Los Angeles during the Summer Olympics of 1932. When the film opened in February 1933 in Berlin, Dupont had already seized the opportunity to stay on in America, for by May of 1933, he was back under contract with Universal, never to return to Germany, having suddenly become, after years as an international adventurer, a political refugee with the Nazis' seizure of power.

Cultural contraband

It is in fact around the anti-Nazi films in particular that the German émigrés once more became an important force, but also a source of controversy with the Production Code. While Fritz Lang was praised by the Motion Picture Association for the delicate handling of difficult domestic subjects such as lynching and blacks in *Fury*, when Pabst wanted to propose as his second Hollywood venture a film about a mad radio-operator (Peter Lorre) starting a proxy (European) war on board an ocean liner, the project was promptly vetoed by the Hays Office as unsuitable for overseas markets and thus as diplomatically tricky. Dieterle, on the other hand, did get himself involved in a number of politically sensitive films – there were endless squabbles with ambassadors from both Spain and Mexico over *Juarez* (1939); there was an issue regarding the Jewish origin of the hero over *Dr Ehrlich's Magic Bullet* (1940, about the inventor of a cure for syphilis); and *Blockade* (1938, about the Spanish Civil War) gave rise to trouble with the American Catholic Church.[17] The émigrés' brush with the Production Code over the anti-Nazi films highlights a number of additional ironies that only the exiles – the Jews, the refugees from Europe – could fully appreciate. In the anti-Nazi films, it was often the case that Jews who had fled from Hitler's Germany ended up playing SS men or high-ranking Nazis, these often being the only roles they could get because of their German accents (Reinhold Schünzel, Alexander Granach, Gustav von Wangenheim, Hans Heinz von Twardowski, Conrad Veidt, and Fritz Kortner in films such as Litvak's *Confessions of a Nazi Spy* (1939), Douglas Sirk's *Hitler's Madman* (1943), Fritz Lang's *Hangmen Also Die* (1943), or *The Hitler Gang*. Otto Preminger, blacklisted by Daryl Zanuck, was only allowed back to 20th Century Fox after his Broadway success as an actor playing the Nazi in *Margin for Error* (1943). But it is Lubitsch, underscoring the theatricality of the Hitler regime in his *To Be or Not to Be* (1942), who fully exploits the supreme irony of the émigrés' cultural camouflage. *To Be or Not To Be* brings back that imaginary dimension I briefly alluded to in the beginning, when I argued that in the traffic between Europe and America images are being traded, images of America, but also images of Europe: after the 'Viennese pastry' and 'schmaltz' of the 1920s and 1930s, it is a European political tragedy – a dictatorship practising genocide – that is caught in the mirror of a double reflection that seems to date back to the early 1920s. The extent and kind of involvement the émigrés had with the political realities of their time were thus refracted via the politics of make-believe, so that the stylisation of film noir, the double-entendres or sight gags of sophisticated comedy, and the 'imitations of life' of melodrama might turn out to be just as politically engaged as the anti-Nazi films.

By contrast, Dieterle's and Dupont's stories help to focus on the way in which some directors found it difficult to shape a coherent work out of several dozens of films. Their individual films do not seem to be more than the sum of the circumstances under which they were made, which may be the reason why they were made. Useful for the historian, because they become symptomatic of the forces at work in the film business, the films end up being more interesting for their incoherence, gaps and fissures, as I have tried to show in a case study of Dieterle's Warner Brothers bio-pics, notably *The Story of Louis Pasteur.*[18] Second, Dieterle's and Dupont's films, for all their qualities – and for all Dieterle's political intentions – never seem to engage with an awareness of this historical situation of the double reflection, as was the case of other directors who found

Figure 29 Two worlds, back to back, as émigré actors play Nazi occupation forces, and an American actor plays a Czech resistance hero: Brian Donlevy in Fritz Lang's *Hangmen Also Die* (1943)

Source: BFI films: stills, posters and designs

themselves caught up with the over-determined signifiers 'Austria', 'Viennese decadence', 'Germany' and 'America'. For what some émigrés achieved was to make a morality out of make-believe. Only by piling up the falsehoods could they get closer to a truth. Highly self-conscious and self-referential, their films are filled with the appearance and the many levels of irony involved in make-believe. This has always been recognised in the American films of Lubitsch and Lang, but it is equally the case for Wilder, Ophuls, and even Preminger. If the spectacle is false, it can none the less be judged only by another spectacle. And while it is the combination of economics and inter(natio)nal politics that must be seen as the driving force for the conversion to sound, the workings of the Production Code and for the cultural camouflage adopted by Europeans in Hollywood, there is a dimension to this counterfeit trade in images and imaginaries that is as politically delicate in its way as the issue of America's isolationism in the late 1930s, and as morally disturbing as the depiction of its gangsters in the early 1930s. When it comes to finally assessing the question of influence that the German émigrés among others had on Hollywood, it may not be so much this *auteur* or that film style, but rather something altogether politically more acute and yet intangible: is it not the immigrants, the 'invaders', émigrés and refugees that helped to make – for all of the world, including the United States – out of Hollywood a country of the mind: the supreme fiction of displacement, transport and virtual realities? If the dream-factory was thus partly 'Made in Europe', the worlds of make-believe, disavowal, deception and self-deception have their own share of historical reality, fashioned not least out of the contradictory triangulations of migration, national stereotyping and exile.

Notes

1 Among the extensive literature, one can best consult the following titles: Baxter 1976; Freyermuth 1990; Heilbut 1983; Hilchenbach 1982; Horak 1984a; Jay 1985; Kohner 1977; Koebner 1984; Palmier 1988.
2 Taylor 1983.
3 The outlines of this story are strangely congruent with another inter-American migration – that of the 1940s and 1950s, when East-Coast or Mid-West artists, show-business people and writers moved to Hollywood, often to leave again, disenchanted, or with careers blighted and lives destroyed. Heading the list are Orson Welles and Joseph Losey, but especially after the McCarthy witch hunts, it includes countless New York writers, Broadway actors, theatre producers and choreographers.
4 Gabler 1989.
5 Kohner 1977: 52.
6 The most comprehensive accounts can be found in Bock and Töteberg 1992 and Kreimeier 1992.
7 Gomery and Allen 1985: 91–108.
8 Higson 1992: 34–52.
9 Bock 1990: 228–30.
10 It is well-known that Louise Brooks became a star after being imported from Hollywood to work for Pabst on *Pandora's Box* and *Diary of a Lost Girl*. See Brooks 1982. What is perhaps less well-known is that it was Emil Jannings who, anxious to

restart his career in Germany, brought with him Josef von Sternberg to direct *The Blue Angel*.

11 Paul Davidson remained in Germany. After the formation of UFA, his once so brilliant career began to falter, and in the wake of a few false starts, he died in 1926, probably a suicide (see Bock 1984).

12 Hardt 1996: 141–62.

13 Quoted in Wolfgang Schivelbusch 1997: 34.

14 See Part IV, Chapter 3, this volume.

15 Jean Kemm directed the actors in the French version, but judging from the version I was able to see at the National Film Archive in London, he utilised almost all of the non-talking scenes shot by Dupont.

16 In Germany, Dupont once more became a big-name 'author', judging by his different studio affiliations. He took on the post of production head at Emelka (a Munich company) in February 1930, but his first film after returning to Germany was actually made for Harmonie Film Berlin (*Salto Mortale*, 1931), before directing a major hit for Emelka in 1932 (*Peter Voss der Millionendieb* (*Peter Voss, Gentleman Thief*).

17 Vasey 1996.

18 Elsaesser 1986: 15–32.

2

LIFESTYLE PROPAGANDA

Modernity and modernisation in early thirties films

The trouble with Nazi cinema

> Never has a country abused the cinema as thoroughly for propagandist ends as Germany under Hitler, never has a people been subjected to so many false images as the German people during the Nazi period.[1]

Wim Wenders' words – said as much in sorrow as in anger in a review essay from 1977 – point to one of the reasons why the films made between 1933 and 1945 weigh heavily on the idea of a national cinema: the movies are tainted goods.[2] Yet, from the vantage point of post-unification Germany since the 1990s, another reason Nazi cinema has remained a source of controversy is a fact whose implications are not always fully appreciated. In their day, these films were very popular indeed, with top productions reaching between 18 and 28 million spectators (up to 40 per cent of the adult population). For instance, more than 26 million Germans saw *Wunschkonzert/Radio Requests* in 1940, and 27 million went to hear Zarah Leander sing in *Die Große Liebe* (*Great Love*) (1942).[3] By then, of course, choice had shrunk to German films, and war-time conditions favoured cinema-going as the main entertainment venue.

Yet even allowing for special circumstances, or putting such popularity down to indoctrination – proof of the hold Nazism had on ordinary Germans – the puzzle remains, since many of the films made during those twelve years have retained their popularity to the present day. And this is still the case in spite of the ideological divides that separate the three generations who have grown up since the 1930s, not to mention the political divide that separated East and West Germans between 1948 and 1989. One of the few things that Nazi parents, sixties sons and daughters, and New Age grandchildren in Frankfurt/Main and Frankfurt/Oder have in common is that they all love Hans Albers in *Baron Münchhausen* (1942), and cannot imagine the Christmas holiday season without Heinz Rühmann taking sweet revenge on his teachers in *Die Feuerzangenbowle* (*The Punch Bowl*), first released in 1944. If anything, the desire to confirm a dozen or so comedies, adventure films and melodramas from the 1930s and 1940s as the nation's classics has grown since unification: UFA films occupy a prominent place in video stores, on TV and even on supermarket shelves. 'Die UFA 1917–1945', an anniversary exhibition in 1992, was an overwhelmingly – and to some, worryingly – popular success.

How then, to bridge the chasm that opens up between Wenders' remark and the persistent appeal of these films? This chapter cannot give an answer except to examine why the answer is so difficult. It is as if the cinema had become a second history of Germany in the 1930s, shadowing the first. The films are like a collective popular memory that (through generic artifice and photographic presence, but also via the now openly furtive pleasure) massively protests against what is felt to be a self-estranged, guilt-laden official history of inhumanity and atrocity. What at the time became an increasingly cynical version of normality, when the nation's entertainment media casually presented an everyday reality from which all signs – physical as well as political – of Nazi rule had been retouched, has since the 1950s (when the reality previously kept out of sight, was 'put back' into German minds, though not always their hearts) taken on a therapeutic function *in reverse*. The films now shield the mind from the terrible history, by giving people heart and something to hang on to. In the face of facts still too horrendous to be believed to be real and too oppressive to forget, it seems as if the need for a different kind of history, side by side with the official one, had found in the cinema of the 1930s and 1940s its screen memory also in the Freudian sense. It protects knowledge of itself thanks to the 'reality effect' attached to moving images, songs and the accents of yesterday's stars.[4] So used have viewers become to taking the fantasies of the past as an index, perhaps not of reality, but of 'the feel of it' that the permanent revival of Nazi-era entertainment films and music speaks to the unvoiced question of what it was like to have lived through those times, and 'not known', i.e. successfully disavowed reality and protected (rather than, as after 1945, protested) one's innocence. From this perspective, and in view of the dismal record of post-1945 German cinema, it is easy enough to feel that quite a few of the films from the coming of sound up to 1938 are more witty, more daringly erotic, more energetic and emotionally engaging than almost any mainstream German films since, so that the attraction of redemptive nostalgia becomes more difficult to resist, even among those 'born after', and thus not necessarily disavowing.[5]

One – admittedly extreme – strategy would be to accept the notion that all popular cinema is potentially fascist, if by this one thinks of it as being illusionist, rhetorical, using affect and emotion to overpower reason and give sensuous substance to fantasies, even where these are destructive to self and others. Such was the view of the Frankfurt School and their motto of 'mass-culture as mass-deception'. Inversely, one can hold the view that genre films, like popular music, the tabloid press and illustrated magazines, engage in obvious or subtle ways with their audience's needs and desires, which in turn relate meaningfully to the spectators', readers' or listeners' subjective perception of a given reality. Whatever the ideological intent and propagandist aims, mass audiences are not made up of zombies: they take what suits them from popular texts, being neither duped by authority, nor mistaking their own and other people's fantasies for reality. Either stance makes implicit assumptions about the economic but also the technological state of a society's popular culture, for instance that it is organised top-down and paid for by the state, or that it is market-driven and trades culture like other commodities. Thus, the validity of applying such models to German cinema of the 1930s depends at least in part on an analysis of the development and functioning of popular culture in Nazi Germany, keeping an eye on the wider picture, rather than focusing on the cinema alone. In the past, this analysis has seemed unnecessary. Nazi Germany was a totalitarian state: the evidence of cultural policy being rigidly controlled by the relevant state bureaucracies was so overwhelming that the idea of the films being open enough to allow for 'oppositional' or 'negotiated' readings would have seemed a preposterous form of revisionism. Recent work has now cast doubt on these certainties, whether one takes into account popular music, dance, fashion, travel or sexual mores, a more patchy picture is emerging about the culture of the everyday, and cracks are appearing in the monolith. In a well-known study from 1982, tellingly entitled *The Divided Consciousness: German Culture and the Reality of Life 1933–1945* (1981), the historian Dieter Schäfer describes four levels of ideological incoherence, where (according to him) gaps between ideology and practice made Nazi Germany a less top-down, 'closed' society than the Führer-principle would lead one to assume: First, market criteria were applied to many areas of production, including the entertainment sector. Second, the state safeguarded a number of apolitical spheres to strengthen its powers elsewhere. Third, 'personalised censorship' prevailed, meaning that prohibitions were implemented in an *ad-hoc* fashion, varying greatly according to region and local whim, not least because of divergent interests and rivalries among Nazi organisations and state bureaucracies. Last, where majority interests were at stake, state controls often failed.[6]

Schäfer's 'ethnographic' research shows (for instance, in the areas of recorded music, movie memorabilia, imported goods and sports items) how the tastes and indulgences of Weimar Germany persisted, with flourishing black markets and a semi-legitimate trade supplying not only party officials but also the grass roots. Although such 'holes' in the organisation of the film industry would be pointless to prove, some 'revisionism' has also taken hold in studies of UFA, regarding the film company's declared objectives, especially in the transitional period after the serious financial crisis of 1926–7, or when reconstructing 'spin doctor' Goebbels' film-policy aims and comparing them to actual practice.[7] To recapitulate briefly the direction of this revisionism: the Nazi cinema was a propaganda instrument in so far as it formed an integral element of what, more euphemistically, one could call a self-consciously modern communication and media society.[8] To this extent, the Nazi cinema formed part of a 'popular culture' as one understands it today, with show-business values, stars and glamour creating both a 'market' and the kinds of surplus value associated with cultural commodities. UFA, for instance, promoted diversification (into the music business, entertainment centres, real estate), as well as practising modern marketing strategies (publicity campaigns) and merchandising (product placement). Both these points – that Weimar tastes persisted and that Nazi cinema was part of a wider popular culture – cannot be fully understood unless one appreciates the extent to which Nazi Germany saw itself in competition with that other modern-media society underpinned by consumerism and a successful popular culture, namely the United States and Hollywood.[9] Even the popular arts and mass culture of Nazi Germany could not, it seems, escape the fact that technologically advanced media are investment-intensive, i.e. expensive. Except when financed by the state for military purposes (as they partly were towards the end of the decade), or when state-owned (like radio), the media in Nazi Germany were market-driven. In this respect, the cinema, not least because it was for the most part so strenuously 'apolitical', has proven a severe test for any attempt to sharply differentiate between modernism, modernisation and modernity.[10]

The coming of sound and the 'end' of Weimar cinema

The point is important, because German cinema on the eve of Hitler's rise to power usually conveys a very clear picture. The masterpieces of the classical period of Weimar cinema were due to the flourishing of exceptional talent in the creative ferment of the Weimar Republic, so that as the Republic disintegrated under the blows of the nationalist and fascist right, its cinema entered into decline: no more *Metropolis*, no more *Pandora's Box*;[11] a last flowering around 1930–2 with *M*, *Kameradschaft*, *The Threepenny Opera*, *Kuhle Wampe*, *The Blue Angel* – and after that, mediocrity and worse:[12] Leni Riefenstahl's *Triumph of the Will*, films about Prussian kings and other historical Führer figures.[13] Where the films are not open propaganda vehicles for the new rulers, they are the more insidious for camouflaging themselves as harmless entertainment.[14]

However, the film-historical evidence does not altogether bear out this story, since if decline there was, it was also due to success wooing talent away from Berlin to even richer pastures in America, well before forced emigration and Nazi anti-Semitism made Hollywood the Mecca of European film culture. The picture of steep decline around and after 1933 gets more complicated still if one factors in economic performance as an indicator of the German film industry's relative strength, for it was not until the political upheavals of the Republic's final years that UFA matured into a financially viable business and an international media conglomerate: the crucial restructuring dates from 1927, not 1933.[15] The most famous films of Weimar cinema had been the products of an author's cinema, an art cinema and even, briefly, an avant-garde cinema. But by the late 1920s elsewhere in Europe, too, the days of the filmic avant-garde were strictly numbered.[16] What was remarkable about the Weimar cinema into the early 1930s was how long such days of innovation and experimentation seemed to last, right at the heart of a wholly commercial enterprise, which by its very nature, should not have been able to afford them. After all, Hans Richter, Walter

Ruttmann, Lotte Reiniger – key figures of the German film avant-garde – were employed by UFA in the late 1920s and 1930s, and some of the notable 'independent' authors – among them Arnold Fanck and Leni Riefenstahl – had their films distributed via UFA. The reason for the decline of this art cinema was mainly technological: the coming of sound, which – notwithstanding what the strictures of modernists on behalf of the 'art of silent cinema' argued – was itself a kind of modernisation. Sound forced the film industry all over Europe to reorganise itself, squeezing out niche ecologies, and raising the financial stakes for independents wanting to get their films into the cinemas.

Sound film did indeed dispel much of the atmospheric romanticism of so-called Expressionism, just as it managed to integrate into the frivolous plots of its comedies and musicals some of the spare functionalism of the *Neue Sachlichkeit* ('New Objectivity', or 'New Sobriety') and the Bauhaus aesthetics. Optical sound, initially developed by German engineers ('Tri-Ergon') but not exploited until the Americans had shown the way, was introduced in German film making relatively quickly, thanks to the new UFA regime, controlled by newspaper tycoon Alfred Hugenberg, who had injected capital into the ailing giant in 1927–8. Under the direction of Ludwig Klitzsch, a seasoned businessman and a manager of talent, deals were struck with rivals both at home and abroad to prevent costly patent wars. While critical successes like *The Blue Angel*, *The Threepenny Opera* and *M* may in the history books be the outstanding examples of early German sound cinema, UFA's international hits and currency earners were musicals and comedies, usually shot in multi-language versions (mainly French and English, but also Czech and occasionally Spanish). *Der Kongress tanzt* (*Le Congrès s'amuse*), *Die drei von der Tankstelle* (*Three Good Friends*), *Viktor und Viktoria* (*First a Girl*), *Bomben auf Monte Carlo* (*Le capitaine Craddock* or *Monte Carlo Madness*), *Ich bei Tag und du bei Nacht* (*Early to Bed*) were fast-paced and witty films, and they carried a youthful, sporty and vital image of Germany into the world.

Sound also profoundly altered the production logic of picture making, so that even before the Nazi takeover in 1933, the German film industry was substantially transformed from a twin-track cinema of 'art film/prestige production for export' and 'genre films for home consumption', to a single-track national/international mainstream 'stars-and-genre' entertainment cinema, by dint of economic necessity and technological change even more than by political interference. In addition, sound cinema profiled new faces, with female stars such as Renate Müller, Lilian Harvey and Marika Rökk beginning to catch up in the popularity stakes with their male colleagues (Willy Fritsch, Heinz Rühmann and Hans Albers) and ensuring not only that the German film industry was by far the strongest in Europe (with over 500 sound films produced between 1930 and 1933), but was also able to lure talents from France and Italy to Berlin throughout the 1930s. Hence propaganda minister Goebbels' had an initially softly-softly approach to the film industry (for instance, in his famous Hotel Kaiserhof speech of March 1933). He had no interest in scaring away the foreign punters. Of course, UFA was in no doubt what Goebbels had in mind

Figure 30 'Sometimes a cigar': Sonnie Hale and Jessie Matthews in Victor Saville's *First a Girl* (1935), the English-language adaptation of *Viktor und Viktoria* (1933)

Source: BFI films: stills, posters and designs

domestically, since unprompted, it proceeded to rescind with immediate effect the contracts of its Jewish personnel, including Erich Pommer, the wonder-weapon of German export successes in the early 1920s, and called back from the US by Klitzsch in the late 1920s. It was the signal for an unprecedented exodus. Directors, producers, actors, writers and technicians left Germany by the hundreds. For some, France was their first stop. Others went to Austria, Britain, The Netherlands and Latin America. By the early forties, California was home to virtually all of them, often with the help of an earlier generation of film immigrants (among the most active in lending a helping hand: Ernst Lubitsch and William Dieterle), who secured contracts, visas, affidavits and letters of intent. The exception among the top directors was Pabst, who after a brief and unsuccessful time in Hollywood, returned first to France and then to Austria. The exodus seriously bled the ranks of UFA's human resources (as recognised by the UFA Board of Directors in their internal memos), but it did not cripple production for long. Enthusiasm for the cinema among German audiences continued unabated. Most of their favourite actors were still there on the screen

(Emil Jannings, Werner Krauss, Heinrich George, Hans Albers, Rudolf Forster, Willi Forst, Heinz Rühmann, Theo Lingen, Zarah Leander, Luise Ullrich, Magda Schneider, Käthe Gold, Marika Rökk and Adele Sandrock), and new ones were being 'discovered' (Kristina Söderbaum, Sybille Schmitz, Ilse Werner and Marianne Hoppe). The illusion that nothing had happened was rather easy to maintain, and for the public that wanted to, easy to believe in.

Export earnings suffered at first, because of a generally hostile trading climate to Hitler Germany, but this simply confirmed UFA's emphasis on commercial criteria and popular entertainment, and by 1936 the company had made up for the shortfall, partly by extending the East European and Latin American markets, partly by diversification. The best propaganda, according to Goebbels was entertainment, which could express the regime's populist ideology as an attainable ideal, while making no mention of its totalitarian reality. A new generation of often gifted directors lent themselves all too willingly to the task (for instance, Veit Harlan, Wolfgang Liebeneiner, Gustav Ucicky, Karl Ritter, Hans Steinhoff, Karl Hartl and Geza von Bolvary), while their erstwhile colleagues Billy Wilder, Robert Siodmak, Max Ophuls, Kurt Bernardt, Edgar Ulmer and many others had to try their luck elsewhere, assisted at least initially by the unusual acumen of producers Erich Pommer, Gregor Rabinowitsch and Seymour Nebenzal, or the Austro-Hungarians Alexander Korda and Arnold Pressburger. The forced exile, as already shown in earlier chapters, overlays itself with the 'brain-drain' from the previous decade, when American studio heads were successful in shopping for film talent in Berlin, before Nazi anti-Semitism made Hollywood definitively the capital of European film culture.[17]

The vast majority of the films made in Nazi Germany continued with the popular genres already established during the Weimar Republic: costume dramas, bio-pics, comedies, film operettas, history films, filmed literary classics and female melodrama. The genres more rarely seen were the Weimar street films and the detective films, which is to say, the social reality of the metropolis and city life, or the everyday life of working-class families. As in Hollywood films of the period, one misses the location work, which is why the notorious Nazi propaganda film *Hitlerjunge Quex* (*Hitler Youth Quex*) (1933) is such an exception, together with the two or three 'proletarian' films directed by Werner Hochbaum. The years 1930 to 1936 especially are one of the most interesting, if contradictory, periods not only of German but also European cinema. On the one hand, it was the time of the conversion to sound, of multi-language versions of films and the trade-off of stars across national boundaries, and on the other, the political changes had created a situation, where economic, technological and geo-political factors were so tightly meshed together that they generated the kind of ideological incoherence that could itself serve as one of the definitions of 'modernity'.

Broadly speaking, three kinds of modernism are involved in the transition period between Weimar and Nazi cinema: the 'modernism' of an artistic avant-garde; the 'modernisation' as it affects labour and work, with Fordist production-line techniques replacing the workshop and the craft practices when sound was introduced; and third, 'modernity' as a particular attitude to life, in Western societies usually associated with increased leisure time and new patterns of consumption. What makes these distinctions so tricky, but also crucial is that in the domain of cinema, it is not always obvious that one can play off 'modernism' (in the sense of an artistic avant-garde) against these different forms of 'modernisation' (in technology, industry and science) and 'modernity' (in lifestyles, fashion and sexual mores), seeing how parts of the filmic avant-garde accommodated itself to the forced modernisation undertaken by the new industrial power that was Nazi Germany in the mid-1930s, as it geared up to arm itself for another war of conquest. There were, as already indicated in previous chapters, several 'Weimar' cinemas, including, besides the art cinema, a wide spectrum of popular genre cinema, scientific film making, documentary and factual film making. If the author's cinema of Lang, Murnau and Pabst had, as Lotte Eisner among others argues, some of its closest, but also contested links with the theatre world of Max Reinhardt and Erwin Piscator (as well as with other Berlin boulevard impresarios),[18] the ties of the film world to the Berlin music scene (already evident in the days of 'silent cinema') both to its post-Wagnerian wing (Giuseppe Becce) and the 'new music' (via radio) are less well known. The different dance movements and aspects of avant-garde body-culture also played a significant role.[19] The most obvious links appear to be with the fine arts, given that the classic German cinema is so closely associated with German Expressionism, but as argued in an earlier chapter, one needs to see this 'influence' mediated via 'commercial art', fashion and design, rather than gallery art and avant-garde circles. The other literary and artistic 'modernisms' of the 1910–20 era, such as German Dada and French Surrealism found resonance in the 'experimental' work of Hans Richter, Viking Eggeling, Walter Ruttmann, Lotte Reiniger, Julius Pinchewer and Georg Pal, who were working at the interface between the avant-garde and industrial advertising, and were known mostly only to a small circle of the initiated.[20]

However, one area in which the cinema's avant-garde status had an international reputation was through the cameramen, cinematography, and still photography, where in any case, the Weimar Republic excelled, as new technologies in optics, lenses and fast ultra-sensitive film stock profiled the leading status of firms like Zeiss and Agfa. Thus, while little of the 'arts avant-garde' film activity survived into the 1930s, important impulses from the *Neue Sachlichkeit* found its echoes in the so-called 'New Photography' (now best remembered by books like Albert Renger-Patsch, *Die Welt ist schön* (1928); Karl Blossfeldt, *Urformen der Kunst* (1928); August Sander, *Antlitz der Zeit* (1929) (see Mellor, 1978)). The New Photography – not least because of the increasing popularity of amateur still photography and photojournalism – continued to flourish, even in the years of transition, and it is often difficult to separate out the 'political' affiliations and ideological choices of the leading photographers.[21] One only has to look at the Photography Annual *Das Deutsche Lichtbild* from 1930 to 1936 to realise how modernist abstraction and the Leica look gradually turned from pictures of machinery, close-ups of plants and urban street scenes shot from high-angle diagonals, to landscape, to 'ethnic' portraits, people in folk costumes or rural idylls to realise that there was never a simple cut-off point, nor a complete rejection of modernist photography. This had to do as much with the positive connotations of 'modernisation' also among the National Socialists and their fetishism of technology and engineering, as with the political affiliations or convictions of its chief practitioners.[22]

Modern photography in the cinema: Arnold Fanck and Willy Zielke

A good example of the continuing presence of the avant-garde, partly thanks to the Nazi's greater tolerance for modern photography, are the films of Arnold Fanck, in which nature becomes spectacle, and the celebration of the sublime. At least this is how it might appear at first sight in the many mountain films that have made Fanck's reputation. However, Fanck discovered the photogenic side of mountains and mountaineering almost as a by-product of his interest in photographic technique. Son of a wealthy factory owner, Fanck owed it to his asthmatic condition as a child that his parents sent him to the Swiss Alps for clean air and fortifying exercise. But Fanck also used his Alpine stays to indulge his early passion as an amateur photographer and dedicated engineer of cameras and lenses. Fascinated by rushing mountain streams and waterfalls, Fanck was intrigued by the problem of how to encompass a sense of movement and other typically kinetic experiences in photography. It is a tension that continues in his films. Fanck's films are trapped in the still photograph, attempting to freeze movement in the frame and to dynamise the image, often at the expense of narrative, suspense or timing. His plots, as dramatic as they may seem, would be equally at home in a pulp magazine. Very rarely is there any build-up of a drama. Instead, he uses a dramatic/melodramatic frame, which he develops only to put something else up front in the scene. As Thomas Brandlmeier has observed:

> Films like [*Das Wunder des Schneeschuhs* and *Fuchsjagd auf Skiern durchs Engadin*] are most closely related to the abstract film: diagonal division of the screen, traces, curves and signs in the snow, *Jugendstil* ornaments, circular cut-outs of images, little points emerging on the horizon, which rush up to the camera and then disappear out of the picture, in giant close-up.
>
> (Brandlmeier 1984: Lg 4, E1)

One can see in his work the continuation of a tension never quite resolved in the history of the cinema, between the desire to break down movement in order to scientifically analyse it (from Muybridge and Marey, to Messter and Ruttmann), and the desire to animate the inanimate, to use technology to create life and replace women (to be found in Edison, according to Villier de l'Isle Adam's *L'Eve future*, or driving Rotwang in Lang's *Metropolis* to make the robot Maria in the image of Hel.)[23] In Fanck's mountain films, which are therefore quite different from *Heimatfilme*, it is always the combination of technology (often represented by aviation) and nature, of two kinds of energy – man-made and elemental, through which the individual defines himself and in which the filmic image serves as an erotic–orgiastic cooling-off point in the wake of the initial conflict.[24] The challenge is whether the camera can confer on nature the aesthetics of the machine age, and use the mountains or icebergs in order to infuse the technological apparatus with the sublime and the elemental. Fanck represents the still photographer-turned-film maker, forever experimenting with lenses, exposure times and new developers. He introduced the tones and shadings of a good black-and-white photographic print into his films about mountains, ice and snow, using time-lapse devices, back-lighting, high contrast and dramatic separations of background and foreground. In this sense, Fanck's world was the opposite of that of UFA, if UFA stands for man-made environments, studio-reality, total control over exteriors and nature, recreating it in quasi-laboratory conditions. Even in a film as patently misfiring as *Der große Sprung* (*The Big Leap*) (1927) – an attempt at a German slapstick comedy in the style of Buster Keaton or Harold Lloyd – there is a sense of the unresolved contradiction between the spectacle of nature (the picture postcards of the change of seasons, of trees and valleys) and the grossly inflated body, with its toy-town propellers of Hans Schneeberger, the city-slicker and patsy, who thanks to tricks and technology, outwits the locals when it comes to winning the downhill race as well as the brewer's daughter.

> With Fanck's filming of nature it is easy to forget the meaning of technology in his films. It is precisely this solid, crafted aspect of his work and the thematisation of technology which is essential to his role of precursor of the *Neue Sachlichkeit*. Technical know-how is evident in every image. Fanck's experience as a photographer working with natural light sources, and as an officer in the newsreel service utilising slow-motion shots, converged in films like *Das Wunder des Schneeschuhs*. His ski books work with single image series, in the style of Muybridge. […] He was one of the first cameramen to employ the Ernemann slow-motion techniques, and he was the first to work with extremely long focal length. In 1938 he was among the first five purchasers of an Arriflex camera.
>
> (Brandlmeier 1984: Lg 4, E4)

The dialectic of the German film avant-garde is such that Fanck is in some sense closer to the *Neue Sachlichkeit* than the genre of the Bergfilm makes one think, while Walter Ruttmann, alternating between sentimentality and cynicism, is closer to the mountain film than his pedigree of the 'city symphony' suggests.[25] Luis Trenker's *Der verlorene Sohn* (*The Prodigal Son*, 1934), with its switch between Alpine peaks and Manhattan street canyons, can stand as an emblem for this ambivalence, but also openness that allowed elements of the admired *Russenfilme* to resurface in the 1930s. Traces can be found in many of the UFA *Kulturfilme* (educational documentaries) well into the late 1930s, after livening up such early sound films as *Nie wieder Liebe* (Anatol Litwak, 1931). The famous nightmare scene in *Ein blonder Traum* is a clever and very knowing pastiche of Soviet montage-style, proof of how the 'revolutionary techniques' of Eisenstein were domesticated in feature films.[26] The two chief representatives of the film avant-garde from the 1920s that seemed to make the move from Weimar to the Nazi regime without much of a break were, of course, Leni Riefenstahl and Walter Ruttmann, whose image and sound compositions sometimes boldly, sometimes vulgarly popularised the achievements of Vertov and Pudovkin, fitting their techniques of contrasting and alternating shot sequences into the sound film, often in strikingly innovative ways.[27]

Before looking at their work, another outstanding example of German *montage kino* illustrates the dilemmas that faced the remnants of the avant-garde: dating from 1936, *Das Stahltier* (*the Beast of Steel*), was made by one of Riefenstahl's cameramen, Willy Zielke. Commissioned by the Deutsche Reichsbahn to celebrate its centenary, Zielke's film was to document the history of the German railway, and the development from steam engine to diesel to electrification. According to Riefenstahl:

> Zielke had turned this difficult material into a thrilling picture. His locomotive looked like a living monster. The headlights were its eyes, the instruments its brain, the piston its joints, and the oil dripping from the moving pistons looked like blood. The impression was increased by the revolutionary use of sound-mixes. When the railway officials saw the movie, they were so horrified – according to Zielke – that they left the room speechless.
>
> (Riefenstahl 1987: 242)

The film was not only not shown, the Railway Board wanted all copies destroyed. Riefenstahl tried to intercede, and arranged for Goebbels to see a print. He thought Zielke showed talent, but found the film too abstract for the broad public: 'it could be a Bolshevist film' – 'but that's no reason to destroy the film', replied Riefenstahl. 'I'm sorry, but the decision is entirely up to the Reichsbahn, which has financed the film. I would not wish to interfere.'[28] More than the film's chances for a public screening were destroyed: Zielke's sanity suffered, and he was interned in a mental hospital, apparently blaming Riefenstahl for his committal. A reconstruction of the incident by Martin Loiperdinger, however, indicates that the issue of censorship was not about 'Bolshevism'. The Reichsbahn had envisioned a film that would publicise a hundred years of progress and the comfort of modern train travel. Instead, as Riefenstahl also noted, 'the carriages [in Zielke's film] crashed into one another with such force that the audience were thrown out of their seats'.[29] In the light of this, the failed intercession with Goebbels becomes anecdotal. The intriguing factor is that a *neusachlich* avant-garde photographer like Zielke, with an admiration for Eisenstein and Vertov came to make an hour-long industrial advertising film.[30] Loiperdinger gives a vivid picture of the shoot (reminiscent of the appearance of agitprop trains in the first Soviet years), as well as of the 'star of the film – a magnificent S 3/6 locomotive, the pride and joy of the German railways at the time'.[31] To appreciate why the preview was a disaster, one has to imagine Eurostar wanting to show off the London–Paris route, and being presented with a film that cut images of explosions, tunnel fires and twisted metal into the action. Hans Ertl, a cinematographer also present at the *Stahltier* preview, remarked dryly, that 'no person in his right mind would ever travel by train again after experiencing this crushing effect in the interplay of tracks, wheels, buffers and steam sirens on the big screen'.[32] The fact that such a misunderstanding, unimaginable today, was still possible at the time, is symptomatic for the theme of this chapter: here the two concepts of 'the modern' – the avant-gardist–modernist and the advertising–modernising – clash head-on, so to speak, without the incident necessarily shedding light upon the political antithesis of Bolshevik art on the one hand and Nazi aesthetics on the other. And yet it is clear that both Zielke and the Reichsbahn wanted to appeal to a new kind of *Lebensgefühl* (lifestyle, literally: 'life-feeling'): their differing understanding of its aesthetic expression and political implications is characteristic of the ambivalence of the time, as already noted by John Grierson about Ruttmann's work:

> What is more attractive (for a man of visual taste) than to let wheels and pistons whiz around to the rhythm of a machine, if he has little to say about the operator, and even less about the tin cans produced in the process? [...] This is why I consider the symphonics tradition of cinema a danger, and *Berlin Symphony* the most dangerous example of all.[33]

An avant-gardist on the margins? – Leni Riefenstahl

None of the lessons from Fanck and Ruttmann were lost on Leni Riefenstahl, either in her debut film *Das Blaue Licht* (1932) or when she started to shoot *Triumph of the Will* (1935). In 1934 – *The Blue Light* and *Victory of the Faith* notwithstanding – Riefenstahl was in many ways still a directorial novice, a fact that may have some bearing on the argument of how 'clumsy' or 'brilliant' *Triumph of the Will* is as a piece of film making.[34] In some ways it strikes one as the work of a gifted amateur, cine-literate and cinephile. In its relentless use of alternating montage, and the juxtaposition of individuals and crowds, its extreme use of point-of-view editing, it demonstrates that Riefenstahl had studied not only Lang

Figure 31 Leni Riefenstahl and her star actor on location for *Triumph of the Will* (1935)
Source: BFI films: stills, posters and designs

but also Eisenstein, Ruttmann and Gance, as well as the Americans, with utmost attention. It is the film of a camerawoman, who introduces a certain type of photographic aesthetic in vogue mainly for landscape and nature films into the hitherto tabooed areas of mass, power and politics. If *Triumph of the Will* is the triumph of form over substance, this is partly because it is a box of tricks, full of unexpected visual angles, eye-line matches and parallel edits, picked up from feature films, squirrelled away like a film-academy graduate, and then flamboyantly shown off in a commission from Hitler, an offer she could not refuse.[35] It is this 'experimental' dimension that to this day makes some documentary film makers her most ardent fans, professing to have 'learnt from her'. But these film makers also know that when helping themselves from *Triumph of the Will*, a little goes a long way, for part of the potency of this film is that, in its genre, it goes 'too far' – but on a road that live television broadcasts of media events have often travelled since. The salient feature, in a way, is not the extent to which *Triumph of the Will* has or has not influenced documentary film makers (there are tributes not only from John Grierson but also Paul Rotha), but rather what kind of causal link can be drawn from this film to the Nazi newsreel 'tradition', and the countless documentaries, industrial shorts and propaganda films made in the

1930s and 1940s. In this respect, the role of Ruttmann in *Triumph of the Will* is worth mentioning, because he was assigned to provide a historical prologue, presenting 'a mirror of the last twenty years' of the Nazi movement.[36] But, as is known, this material was never used, because, possibly on direct orders from Hitler, the project had shifted from 'a party film, dedicated to the struggle' to a film that was 'to give the impression of the most unmediated and veracious present'.[37] Rather than showing the Nazi movement emerging out of Germany's post-First World War social struggles, Riefenstahl's film was to 'authenticate itself as true and without precedents'.[38] In other words, it aimed at the transparency of the newsreel with the stylistic means of the illusionist feature film – two modes quite distinct from the constructivist credo of Ruttmann or indeed Zielke, and more in line with that of a Railway Board advertising film. The point on which Riefenstahl expends many pages of her *Memoirs*, namely refuting that there was re-staging and re-shooting on *Triumph of the Will*, as stated in Albert Speer's *Inside the Third Reich*,[39] is thus mainly revealing for the same reason as the Zielke fiasco: the constructivist–documentarist credo of the late 1920s fighting a last stand against the (industrial, political, commercial) advertising film.[40] Her montage of the 'documentary' material in *Triumph of the Will* is remarkable not least because of the contribution made during the editing stage by the sound mixes and Herbert Windt's score, sound being the obvious technology in which to be experimental at the time – a more crucial link between Ruttmann and Riefenstahl than their political views.

Triumph of the Will and *Berlin Olympia* have to this day remained, for an international public at least, the best-known films the Nazi cinema produced. The fact that Riefenstahl directed both of them weighs heavily against her when she protests her lack of interest in politics or propaganda. However, from a film-historical perspective, the films may not belong together as logically as is usually asserted. *Berlin Olympia* is stylistically quite different from *Triumph of the Will*, as some formal analyses have pointed out.[41] Yet even if one emphasises stylistic similarities (low-angle shots of erect bodies against an empty sky, and so on) there remain some substantial differences in terms of function. While *Triumph of the Will* was made mainly in order to bind the leaderless SA to the Party, after the Rhöm putsch and the 'Night of the long knives', and to celebrate the outcome of the plebicite that merged the position of President with that of Chancellor, thereby legalising the 'Führer' principle, *Berlin Olympia* was a compromise project, negotiated between the regime and the International Olympic Committee. Aimed to give the world an image of the games as supra-national, it was a celebration of youth in communal competition. That these symbolic representations are carefully 'constructed' is evident, and the kitsch prologue appropriately announces the 'poem set to movement' that follows, while none the less keeping to a strict formal–rhetorical schema. Here Riefenstahl's debt to the New Photography is also evident, making the film already in 1936 slightly nostalgic for the 1920s. And while avant-garde in the way it presented sports (in terms of abstract film, rhythm and dance), it was old-fashioned in another sense. It seems that the regime used the Games and Riefenstahl's film making also to 'front' an altogether different purpose, that of allowing the Ministry of Posts to test the new technology of television, putting out live transmission of the sports events in public places in Berlin and elsewhere.[42] Television and its potential preoccupied the various ministries involved rather more than the ideologically correct content of the Olympiad film.

Two issues come into play here. One is that the Nazis, while keeping a tight rein on film production, did not consider film to be their main propaganda medium. As far as the audio-visual media were concerned, it was radio that interested them, as a way of creating a 'technological presence', where its penetration into the home, its potential as a public-appeal address and alarm system was as significant as what was actually broadcast. During the war, simultaneous broadcasting and the emphasis on 'liveness' became a crucial part of the morale boosting, mass-mobilising function of the media – one of the reasons why *Wunschkonzert* proved such a huge success was that it took the radio request programmes between the home front and the war zone as its subject. Generally, though, for these mobilising objectives, the cinema, not being in real time, was only of limited use. One might even argue that the Nazi film industry was developed as an entertainment industry, in order for the films and the stars to act as inducements to rally spectators to the newsreels, rather like the function of feature films on television today, to get people to see the ads. None of these technological or media-political considerations seem to have occurred to Riefenstahl. The memoirs, for instance, make no mention of the presence of television cameras at the Games.[43] However, there is perhaps a more important reason why this did not occur to her. The way the cinema developed in Germany in the 1930s and 1940s was not at all in the direction of Riefenstahl's own idea of cinema. Not only was Riefenstahl an 'independent' producer/film maker in a film business increasingly centralised and industrialised, but – as already indicated – hers was in inspiration an 'art' and 'experimental' cinema, not a 'popular stars and genre' cinema. While her films, as well as Fanck's were released through UFA, UFA was not their production company. On the contrary, Fanck actually referred to himself as the 'Freiburg School', and had little but contempt for studio-bound film making as practised in Neu-Babelsberg or Munich. Riefenstahl was less radical about this than Fanck, but none the less, she, too, was committed to an outdoor faith in a cinema on location. By contrast, the dominant commercial cinema in Germany of the 1930s became, as already mentioned, more and more modelled on that of the United States studio-system.

In the 1930s and 1940s, UFA, Terra and Tobis – the three major production companies – were by and large run as studios turning out films designed to make money at the box office, and while they were broadly in line with the regime, they continued a production policy already well established in the 1920s. Its mainstay were genres whose formulas were often copied directly from Warner Brothers or MGM prototypes, such as the musicals or bio-pics. Where politics massively operated in the Nazi cinema, apart from the newsreels, was in the politics involving personnel (the compliance of UFA in Hitler's racial policy, and the personal patronage and grace-and-favours system encouraged by Goebbels). Riefenstahl's aversion to being identified with propaganda work and commissioned films has, it would seem, as much to do with her self-image as a 'film-artist' in the avant-garde tradition of the 1920s, as with retrospective political whitewash. There is no question, however, that both Riefenstahl's *Triumph of the Will* and her *Olympia*-film substantially contributed to the training of a great many cameramen and editors, who played a key role in the demagogical, but during the final years of the war, also shockingly realistic newsreels. The question this prompts, then, when viewed from the point of view of the film industry and film politics is how did Riefenstahl fit into the Nazi *cinema*, and the answer seems to be – not all that well. For one of the puzzling aspects of her career is why did she only make these two films if she was so important to the regime? The one other film she worked on throughout the 1930s and 1940s was *Tiefland*, and what she documents in her memoirs about this project is a tale of failures and endless disappointments, of lack of support and outright betrayal.

With the beginning of the war, and the gearing of the film industry into a more overt propaganda and morale-boosting machine, directors like Riefenstahl saw their opportunities for making films dwindle, and she became more and more marginalised compared to directors, who like top managers or the captains of industry, placed themselves in the service of the regime. These were directors like Veit Harlan and Carl Froelich, Gerhard Ritter, Gustav Ucicky and Geza von Bolvary who fitted completely into this industrial strategy, and who had the same cynical attitude to keeping production going at any price (cf. *Kolberg*) as Speer had in the armament industries, or Himmler with his calculus of 'destruction through work', which rented the able-bodied inmates of the camps, prisoners of war, or foreign nationals out to Daimler Benz, Krupp, IG Farben and the Peenemünde V2 rocket sites of Wernher von Braun. It may be Riefenstahl's resentment of this that made her so sensitive about the accusation of using gypsies from the concentration camp for *Tiefland*, because it adds insult to injury as far as her mostly aborted *Tiefland* project was concerned. On the other hand, it never seemed to have occurred to her that her cult of the body beautiful, however much in the 1920s it might have been a shock reaction to the torn and mutilated bodies returning from trenches, had become a blasphemy in a Germany, where bodies were mere labour power to be deliberately worked to death. Although it would thus be absurd to suggest that Riefenstahl was in any sense a victim of the Nazi regime, there is some truth in her assertion that she had little control over what became of her career, effectively already finished before the outbreak of the war.

Science fiction, reactionary modernism and the imagination of disaster

What is certain is that the national-socialist film industry neither supported nor tolerated an art cinema or authors' cinema, which made it rather similar to its arch-rival – Hollywood. On the other hand, it was in the 1930s that certain forms of state aid were introduced, e.g. the financially attractive film-prizes, or the so-called *Ausfallbürgschaften* (guarantees against loss), which were revived in the 1960s, in order to build up the famous 'authors' cinema' of the Federal Republic by means of a government-supported film-subsidy system. Alongside state aid, Nazi cinema invested a good deal of aesthetic prestige in genres that, while formally often surprisingly experimental, were none the less ideologically intended as propaganda – the feature-length documentary, the so-called *Kulturfilm* (instruction film) and the many industry advertising films, the latter a speciality of Walter Ruttmann, though as we saw, he was by no means the only director active in this genre.[44] Faint echoes of the European avant-garde remained few and far between in the Germany of the 1930s. As exceptions, they merely serve to underline the rule that 'modernism' and 'Third Reich' are fundamentally antithetical terms: the regime's official aesthetics was anti-modernist (as witnessed in the infamous 'degenerate art' exhibition of 1937), racist–populist (*völkisch*), and neo-classicist. But Nazi art practice, by contrast, represented a form of extremely eclectic historicism: the neo-classical bombast of Albert Speer's architectural follies was found side by side with the Hansel-and-Gretel cookie-cutter look of domestic architecture. Even on its own terms, in the frantic search for what was German, the Nazi 'invention of tradition' took the forms of a historicist 'return' of very different cult figures: the Bamberg Cathedral knight as icon of the Nordic spirit; Albrecht Dürer and Rembrandt as the epitome of 'German art'; Goethe and Schiller as the nation's Hellenic sages; and Wagner and Nietzsche anticipating their renewal. Argued the other way round, given the feebleness of Speer's and Hitler's showpiece art, with its insensitivity to any history of style, the period could also be described as one of pastiche, in which 'everything goes', as long as it has at some point been designated by art history or common association as 'German' and 'national' – a conglomeration of the Late Gothic, Northern European Renaissance, Classicism and Folk Art, Romanticism and even Decadence – the revenge, perhaps, of the 'half-educated' on the over-educated (of international modernism). In public life and for official commissions in architecture there was a similar pastiche using half-timbered designs reminiscent of the Middle Ages, the Gothic of the Hansa League, the Dürer Renassiance, Weimar Classicism, Biedermeier – with even the survival, albeit in modified versions, of the Bauhaus aesthetic and the international style: so-called 'Nazi-*Sachlichkeit*'. This conservatism in cultural politics and state-approved art, however, contrasted sharply with the modernising tendencies in the fields of science and technology, which Nazi Germany not only continued from Weimar, but also intensified and accelerated. The result was a society whose official culture was stridently anti-technical, anti-industrial, anti-urban on the one hand, but whose manufacturing practice was to force a frantic pace of industrialisation and engineering, because – in the absence of a colonial empire – it needed to develop the productive and industrial potential of its domestic territories. And this was not only in order to pursue its re-armament policies and expansionist ambitions towards Eastern Europe. Equally important was a domestic reason, namely to compensate the civilian population for working longer hours by raising their living standards, which is to say, by supplying them with consumer goods. As indicated, in *Das gespaltene Bewußtsein*, Schäfer (1981) examines some of the consequences of these very contradictory aims with regard to popular culture.[45] Transparent duplicity of the Weimar years, it would again seem, became the double standards of Nazi ideology and practice, while the enlightened false consciousness of Sloterdijk turned into the split consciousness of Schäfer.

If the contradictions at the heart of the Nazi regime have often been noted, they are usually analysed as a form of collective schizophrenia, or as a particularly cynical game of mass-deception by the ruling elite. But other historians besides Schäfer have rejected this approach, arguing that the paradox is in some sense more apparent than real, in that a number of intellectuals and writers (such as Oswald Spengler, Werner Sombart, Carl Schmitt, Hans Freyer and Martin Heidegger) had been elaborating such an ideological blend between archaic values with modern technology since the Weimar years. The dual focus might be called Germany's 'historical compromise', but Jeffrey Herf has dubbed it 'reactionary modernism'.[46] Put briefly, Herf's main thesis is as follows. Subsequent to the First World War, in an effort to rationalise the German defeat, many writers who were by inclination and temperament conservative, tried to come up with an explanation that incorporated the analysis of the left (especially of the communist left), while nevertheless retaining crucial elements of German nationalism and the feudal class structure in their vision of the nation's future, when trying to draw lessons from a traumatic history. Reactionary modernism's most interesting proponent from a media-historical perspective was the novelist and essay-writer Ernst Jünger. Despite his virulently anti-democratic and nationalist outlook, he realised that Germany had to modernise and industrialise, in order to achieve a sense of national identity within post-war Europe. Jünger was therefore anti-agrarian, anti-*völkisch* and anti-regionalist, praising the life of the metropolis, of industry, steel mills and shipbuilding in metaphoric language borrowed from volcanoes and fire, biology and meteorology. His project was to find an intellectually coherent but also emotionally satisfying synthesis between the belief in the German soul and a German destiny – advocating technology, industrialisation and investment in research and development as a way of realising this destiny. Similar strategies can be recognised in Ruttmann's *Metall des Himmels* (*Heaven-Sent Metal*) (1935) when ploughshares grow out of blast furnaces, and wheat grows out of ploughshares. But whereas Ruttmann's metaphoric transformations of objects is not without tongue-in-cheek playfulness, reminiscent of Hans Richter's dada films (*Vormittagsspuk* (*Ghosts Before Noon*), 1927–8; *Alles dreht sich, Alles bewegt sich, (Everything Turns),* 1929, there is little trace of humour in Jünger's writing. In Ruttmann's film, the irony is derived from a play upon scale: aircraft formations are made up of fountain pens passing over a flotilla of paper clips. In Jünger, switches of perspective are variations of detachment: the Olympian gaze from above alternates with the scientific curiosity of the entomologist close to the ground.

In effect, Jünger's modernism was concerned with a synthesis between nature and technology, or rather a reinterpretation of romanticism that combined the industrial exploitation of nature with a pagan faith in its beauty and grandeur. It saw no contradiction between an industry of heavy goods manufacture, of research into synthetic fibres or nuclear fission on the one hand, and a worship of nature as sacred, elemental and sublime. There was no sense of disjuncture because Jünger also found the grandiose and the sublime in man-made structures, especially when they were being destroyed. His famous baptisms of fire or his storms of steel were ways of intensifying and accelerating processes of violent rebirth and renewal. Jünger, in a sense, tried to be Caspar David Friedrich *and* F.T. Marinetti, but while his books and essays are full of the most dramatic descriptions of fighter planes going down in flames, or battleships sunk by a torpedo – typical boys' fiction material dignified with philosophical ruminations – the ideological impact of his work seems to have been little short of revelatory. Herf quotes passages from a 1934 book celebrating Jünger that underline the latter's significance for the Nazi movement:

> German youth owes a debt above all to Ernst Jünger for the fact that technology is no longer a problem for them. They have made his beautiful hymns to technology born from fire and blood their own. They live in harmony with it. They require no more ideologies to 'overcome' technology. Rather, they grasp it as the arm of the [movement's] idea. This was something new for us, this incorporation of matter into the meaning of events. Jünger has liberated us from a nightmare.[47]

If the passage refers mainly to Jünger's idea of the soldier–worker, a figure in whom the military ideals of discipline and subordination are merged with the communist ideal of the proletariat as the motive force of history, then the crucial move that made this amalgam both plausible and emotionally uplifting was that Jünger viewed both nature and technology from the perspective of the observer – the onlooker – that is from the gratifyingly safe and at the same time fascinatingly engrossed subject positions that large-scale visual events could give. Interesting in this respect is Jünger's use of the concept of 'total mobilisation'. For one of his retrospectively most pregnant thoughts was the role he assigned to spectacle and to the mass-media in this process of mobilisation. He was in many ways the leading media theorist the right produced in the 1930s, and he drew on much the same insights as had Walter Benjamin.[48] Jünger predicted a society of the spectacle,[49] in which he saw the political use of the audio-visual media not so much in their capacity to realistically represent a simulacrum of the world, but in the peculiar kind of appeal and presence the technology of radio and the cinema contributed to political life and the public sphere. As early as 1934 Jünger was referring to the 'Great War' as the first war that would enter history in the form of moving pictures, noting that events increasingly take place only to be captured in sound, word and image.[50]

As a theorist of the media, Jünger is perhaps more relevant in the age of television and camera-guided missiles than for understanding the cinema of the Third Reich. He followed closely the developments in photo-journalism and radio in the 1920s, drawing conclusions which could be quotations from Paul Virilio.[51] When one thinks of Nazi cinema, on the other hand, relatively few films of the 1930s are concerned with such spectacles of destruction or the 'new ice age' as Jünger describes them. At most, one could cite the science fiction films made in the 1930s, above all films like *FP1 Antwortet Nicht* (1932, Karl Hartl), *Der Tunnel* (1933, Kurt Bernhardt) and *Gold* (1934, Karl Hartl), which in many respects seem more like late additions to Lang's UFA special effects extravaganzas such as *Metropolis* (1927) and *Die Frau im Mond* (1929) than new developments. However, in one or two respects they do offer an interesting perspective on the ideological project that Herf calls reactionary modernism. This has less to do with creating an emotional acceptance of technology, although in *Gold* it seems that the main reason for the high-voltage generator to be situated in an underground shaft beneath the sea is to amplify the spectacle value of the final explosion, which not only blows up a mine, and engulfs it in water, but also churns up the sea like a torpedo hitting a battleship. More striking is the contradiction that opens up between the ideological solution the film offers and the real economy in which it is purportedly situated. This contradiction crystallises around the figure of the engineer, positioned ambiguously between both the workers and the boss, but also between the inventor and those that commercialise an invention. The reason the engineer seems so crucial is because he has to mediate between two sets of binary oppositions, that of the class discourse (already familiar from *Metropolis*, as the social utopia of mediator between head and hand), but also of the discourse of science and technology. In this latter respect, the films of the 1930s have as their ideological aim to radically separate science from technology. On the side of science is the figure of the professor or inventor – selfless, absent-minded, beneficial in his quest for pure knowledge. On the other side is the businessman: unscrupulous and megalomaniac, who stops at nothing in order to steal, sabotage or keep for himself the work that by rights belongs to others. The business man or financier is thus the one who applies science, who makes technological progress and productivity possible, but he is invariably seen as the villain. Here we have, in some sense, the romantic anti-capitalist, anti-technology vision intact, except that both sides need the engineer – the inventor in order to rescue him from his other-worldliness, and the businessman because only the engineer can make the invention 'work'.

The engineer's job is therefore to help materialise the immaterial (pure disembodied thought) and to moralise the material (pure inert matter). These oppositions and the mediating function of the engineer stand in glaring contrast to the actual relations affecting the processes of technology and invention.

Ever since Edison, invention has been 'industrialised', which means that application, diffusion and acceptance has to be closely tied to the process of invention itself. Where this is not the case, and products cannot be exploited through the market, private industry likes to pass the cost of invention (i.e. research and development) on to the state. Especially in the early 1930s, when German industry lived in fear of US takeovers, the question of who would bear the cost of industrial development was acute, and one can see behind the romantic figure of the engineer in *Gold* the massive absence that the film never names – the state, called upon to invest via government contracts, and then to manage overproduction either by building up a war economy or by helping industry conquer new markets. The engineer thus becomes a stand-in, the inadequate human figure asked to 'explain' the mysterious workings of capitalism and the market economy.[52] Failing to understand it himself, he can only become a saboteur, by blowing the whole thing up. *Gold* appeals not only to anti-capitalist anxieties; it also attempts to neutralise the social processes that make gold an economic value in the first place, namely scarcity. By destroying the machine that can make gold out of lead, the engineer reinstates the principle of scarcity over abundance, and thus safeguards not only the value of gold, but economic protectionism. In its search for the vanishing mediator, *Gold* gives a pre- or anti-Keynsian vision of capitalist crisis-management.[53]

Allo Berlin? Ici Paris!: Film Europa

In actual life, on the other hand, neither the conservative forces of the Weimar Republic nor the Nazi regime were altogether ignorant of the real economy, a fact that brings into view the third kind of modernism in the cinema of the 1930s. It is perhaps no accident that such science fiction films were rare, and that the cinema did not become the primary site of popularised versions of Herf's reactionary modernism. Instead, as detailed in Part 1, Chapter 4, this volume on the UFA, the film industry was familiar with its own kind of conservative revolution, which cannot be directly conflated either with the political calendar of Germany in the 1930s nor identified with the ideological project of reconciling technology with nature or modernising an agrarian society into an industrialised super-power – one additional reason, perhaps, why a reading of this cinema in terms of progressive/liberal vs reactionary/conservative does not always illuminate the inner dynamics of the German cinema of that time. UFA itself experienced a struggle over modernism that could be said to have split along the lines of inventor versus businessman. As we saw, thanks to Klitzsch, UFA had undertaken the kinds of modernisation in its internal structure that had rescued the company from going to the wall in the aftermath of the Depression. The transformation happened in two phases, one in 1927–8, and the other between 1929 and 1932. While the second one was the transition to sound, the first one was the incisive managerial modernisation programme.[54] Having travelled to Hollywood, Klitzsch not surprisingly adopted the US model, reorganising UFA practice from the director-unit system of production to the producer-unit system (the so-called 'Produktionsleiter-Gruppen', headed by names such as Günther Stapenhorst, Max Pfeiffer, Bruno Duday and Alfred Zeisler). It brought a greater division of labour within production and between production and distribution, with stricter budget management under each spending unit, and an intensified effort of promotion and advertising. Klitzsch's strategy made UFA financially sound within two years, and it was this management structure that stayed in place at least until 1937, ensuring that UFA remained market-driven and was run along profit oriented principles.[55]

It also meant that because UFA was an export earner and in many ways a multinational company, the films it made and distributed were not only intended for and determined by the domestic audiences. UFA knew that it supplied markets other than the German one – not the American one (a territory in which German films never gained more than a temporary foothold) but primarily those of other European countries and Latin America. Scandinavia, Central and Eastern Europe, Turkey and the Balkans formed the most lucrative international audience for German films, but it was the importance of Western European and especially French audiences that explains the direction that the second, 1929–32 UFA modernisation wave took. In principle a technological one (the conversion to sound), its consequences affected marketing, and through marketing the product itself, namely genres and film styles. It also goes some way towards explaining the choice of subjects, and above all, the kinds of (female) stars it promoted: Lilian Harvey (of English origin), Marika Röck and Käthe von Nagy (Hungarian), Zarah Leander and Kristina Söderbaum (Swedish) and Lida Baarova (Czech). A still underrated element in this process were the multi-language versions that today strike one as such anachronistic and unsatisfactory remnants of those early years of cross-licensing agreements and patent exchange. An example might be the film *Die Letzte Kompagnie* (1930), a rather strained effort when the use of sound and dialogue is considered in isolation from the film's political context. But given its generic identity between melodrama and 'Prussian film', one has to admire the thoroughly 'balanced' view it gives of the Napoleonic troops (a change from the anti-French caricatures of earlier propaganda films). Yet this balance may have less to do with the liberal – and Francophile – views of the film's director, Kurt Bernhardt. It could have been the result of strategic marketing, considering the international reputation of its star, Conrad Veidt, especially popular in France and Britain.

Paris was also the first destination of many of the émigrés after 1933, most of them hoping to be able to return to Germany in a matter of years, if not months. Thus, both artistically and politically, the Germans who first arrived in France experienced the early part of the decade as a much happier period than its turbulent ending, caught as they were by then in a threefold insecurity – they were enemy aliens, administrative embarrassments and refugees persecuted for their race or convictions. Many writers and politicians of the collapsed Weimar Republic have put on record how the unenviable choice between internment and deportation darkened life after 1940.[56] By then, the film makers had for the most part left for Britain or America, and in most histories of the cinema the German film emigration to France features at best as the waiting room, and the films produced there ways of passing the time until the contract from Warners, Universal or MGM came through. This somewhat casual estimation is, however, contradicted by first-hand accounts. Bernhardt, for instance, had no intention of going to America until he was forced to: 'Had you ever before [i.e. 1939] thought of going to the United States?' – 'Never. I had even rejected an offer from Columbia Pictures in 1936.'[57]

The stay in France affected members of the German refugee community in ways that differed from one profession to the next. For film directors, for instance, working in France was neither as new nor as traumatic and isolating a situation as it was for writers and other intellectuals. The film business was, after all, part of an international industry, where France, Germany and Hollywood competed for a share in the national and European markets – paradoxically by an altogether confusing mixture of collaboration and rivalry, where co-productions, mutual distribution deals and multi-language versions became the recognised currency.[58] German and French production companies leased and hired one anothers' assets, whether these were stars or production facilities, patents or distribution rights. At the same time, Hollywood companies, such as Paramount, had major studio facilities in Paris, while Babelsberg had French stars under contract, from Maurice Chevalier and Charles Boyer to Jean Gabin, and French directors, among them Jean Gremillion, Marcel L'Herbier and Julien Duvivier, made pictures in Munich and Berlin, some using the sand dunes behind Babelsberg for French-colonial or Foreign Legion settings.[59] Among the German directors working in France during the 1930s, besides Max Ophuls there was also G.W. Pabst, each of whom made six films there. Fritz Lang made only one, but Robert Siodmak made nine films, and Curtis Bernhardt four – not counting the French-language versions of their German films. The list of those who made one or two films includes Billy Wilder, Robert Wiene, Ludwig Berger, Wilhelm Thiele, Kurt Gerron, Max Nosseck, Richard Eichberg, Victor Trivas: in short, the 'cream' of German directorial talent of the early sound period.

Treating the Germans' exile in France as a mere episode might nevertheless be justified by the impression that few of their films were outstandingly successful with either the French public or elsewhere (though, as we shall see, some did better at the time than their critical neglect in subsequent decades would indicate). But looking at the films today (most of which have luckily survived), it is clear that a whole generation's work during almost a decade amounts to more than a thin slice sandwiched between the glories of a German career and its eventual Hollywood apotheosis.[60] Even granted a purely *auteur*ist emphasis, according to which Lang's, Ophuls' or Wilder's French films are judged to be 'inferior' to their Hollywood ones, it is important not to lose sight of several facts notably the complicated Franco-German cultural–industrial negotiations going back to the mid- and late 1920s known as 'Film Europa', and the producer power of four or five individuals, among whom were Seymour Nebenzahl and Erich Pommer, rival producers in Germany who now found themselves in Paris. Film Europe comprises Pommer's distribution agreement with Aubert in 1923, the Paris and Berlin Conferences of 1926 and 1928, as well as the sound-film patent agreements of 1930 with the US Majors.[61] The producer power has two variants. It is embodied in Nebenzahl who, as owner of Nero Film, the company responsible for almost a dozen of the émigré's films, had always been an 'independent' producer who moved easily – and controversially – in the world of film finance and distribution.[62] Pommer, formerly the all-powerful head of UFA's international production, on the other hand, worked in France for a Hollywood company, 20th Century Fox, in which capacity he was to provide work for many of his former UFA staff. Without Pommer and Nebenzahl's astute business sense and international connections, many of the directors, and especially scriptwriters, would not have been able to work in France at all. The producers for their part could mount projects in such apparently difficult conditions, despite the political turn of events in 1933, precisely because of the long-established and initially uninterrupted 'competition by co-operation' between the German and French industries. Having already set up, supervised and marketed French-language versions of most major German productions, Nebenzahl and Pommer (and on a lesser scale Rabinowitsch and Eugen Tuscherer),[63] moved into original French films as almost the 'natural' extension of their activities in the late 1920s. However, the French cinema was undergoing a major crisis with the coming of sound which accelerated its internal difficulties in restructuring its domestic production while holding on to its market share. Already in the early years of the new decade, it was clear that the German sound cinema would prove a formidable rival, with especially Pommer's UFA musicals becoming very popular with French audiences. They saw them in French-language versions, usually relying on established French stars to replace the German actors in the lead roles, and consequently, they often became major hits and helped the trade balance, even after 1933.[64]

German cinema's European hegemony created its own problems when, after the Nazi takeover, so many film makers crossed the Rhine in the direction of Paris. The perception of special job opportunities opening up for the refugees led to intense hostility among the French film personnel, aggravated by traditional chauvinism on both sides and the wounded pride of France's film industry no longer occupying its number one position. Tensions soon took on the more sinister hues of outright racism and anti-Semitism. The French trade unions in particular seemed susceptible to this kind of propaganda, which meant that the German émigrés could effectively find work only in either B-productions, undertaken by one of the many small companies that had sprung up in Paris or in 'international' productions, mounted by Pommer either for his new S.A.F. Fox-Europe company, or in the context of ACE (Alliance Cinematographique Européenne) agreements.[65] Under the circumstances it is not surprising that almost all the German directors had, as their first job in France, the task of providing the French language version of their last German hit. Ophuls did *Liebelei* as *Une histoire d'amour*, Nebenzahl persuaded (or some claim – forced) Lang to do French versions of *M-Le maudit* and *Das Testament des Dr Mabuse*, Ludwig Berger remade *Ein Walzerkrieg* as *La Guerre des valses*, and even Joe May turned *Ihre Majestät die Liebe* into *Tout pour l'amour*.

Lifestyle propaganda

If films like *Die Letzte Kompagnie* (*Chacun sa chance*) (1930, Hans Steinhoff, with Jean Gabin), *Die drei von der Tankstelle* (*Trois bons amis*) (1930, Wilhelm Thiele), *Ein blonder Traum* (*Le rève blond*) (1931, Paul Martin), *Allo Berlin? Ici Paris!* (Julien Divivier, 1932) *Der Tunnel* (*Le tunnel*) (1933, Kurt Bernhardt) forcefully underline the economic and personnel exchanges between France and Germany throughout the early 1930s, then the connections between the film industry and the record

Figure 32 Three is company: Lilian Harvey in Wilhelm Thiele's *Die Drei von der Tankstelle* (1930)

Source: BFI films: stills, posters and designs

industry, the newspaper and publishing world are even more far-reaching. For what the multi-language versions prepared for – among which musical comedies predominated – was the build-up of a very lucrative trade in sheet music and recorded music, where for the first time the kinds of tie-ins and merchandising deals were practised, on the back of which a star system developed that survived the multi-language versions. It is for instance noticeable that almost all the early sound musicals became classics since they were also those that contained hit songs that were sold in millions separately from the films: *Der Kongress tanzt* (*le Congrès s'amuse* (1931, Erik Charell), *Die 3-Groschen-Oper* (*L'opera de quatt'sous* (1930–1, G.W. Pabst) and *Die drei von der Tankstelle* or *Der Blaue Engel* (1930, Josef von Sternberg). These early sound comedies and musicals are also important for another reason: they were aimed at international audiences because so often they are about national stereotypes that comment on each other (e.g. the Lilian Harvey vehicles *Liebeswalzer*, 1930, Wilhelm Thiele; *Der Kongress tanzt* and *Ein blonder Traum*, 1932, Paul Martin). The films invariably dramatise two worlds (Europe/America in *Glückskinder*, Berlin/Hollywood in *Ein blonder Traum*, an automobile factory and a rural principality in *Liebeswalzer*) that comment on one another in a spirit that levels out the differences rather than reinforcing them.

In many respects, then, it is this ambiguously countervailing modernisation that took hold in the cinema: whether deliberately encouraged or merely tolerated, UFA continued to behave in its production policy and business practices like a modern multinational company even after 1933. In particular, its modernisation renewed the technological base and marketing infrastructure, in order to foster one of cinema's broader social functions – that of supporting a culture of consumption whose idea of a community defines itself via its leisure time. The films were thus propaganda – but first and foremost propaganda for the cinema itself, dramatising it as a world not only more real than the real world, but also the one that guarantees that the other worlds stay real and meaningful. For example, in *Ich bei Tag und du bei Nacht* (1932, Ludwig Berger), Käte von Nagy, when seeing Schloß Sanssouci for the first time, is dumbfounded, exclaiming admiringly 'wie im Kino' ('just like in the movies'). She is, of course, referring to the luxury of the movies, but also to a certain lifestyle that these films are advertising. This 'modern' lifestyle is composed of elements still very familiar today: tourism, consumer and luxury goods, the heritage industry and a redefinition of gender roles, at least as far as the empowerment of women as self-confident consumers is concerned.

The old question of art versus propaganda therefore has to be rephrased. If Nazi cinema is treated as part of Nazi art, and both are seen as propaganda for the regime's political or racial ideology, the initial contradiction remains. If one regards Nazi cinema as part of popular culture's propaganda for consumerism, and the films as above all commodities – fashioned, styled and marketed rather like refrigerators, skiing holidays in Norway, and entitlement vouchers for the Volkswagen – then their persistent popularity makes more sense. After all, we still share the same aspirations towards the good life embodied in lifestyles and consumption, and our sense of history, tradition, the nation and cultural identity is still shaped by the technological media (re-)constructing their human interest value and personal significance. Typically this can be seen in the ways the cinema of the early 1930s treated modern transport and tourism. There were, for example, the obligatory sports cars (*Liebeswalzer*, *Die Drei von der Tankstelle*); romantic adventures got an extra erotic charge from figuring out how twin-beds worked in modern sleeping car compartments (*Adieu Mascotte*, 1930); holiday destinations included the French Riviera (*Bomben auf Monte Carlo*, 1931), trips were made in luxury yachts in the Mediterranean (*Nie wieder Liebe)* or the North Sea (*Gold*), the films exemplified dreams of sailing boats and skiing vacations, or taking a plane to Rio and making tough business deals in Hollywood (*Glückskinder*, *Ein blonder Traum*). Such propaganda for the new lifestyle (which the Nazis promised to deliver to everyone, regardless of class) appeared to link the great outdoors with the latest fashion trends, to marry novelty travel and household gadgets with Germanic worship of Nature – for Nordic forests and Alpine waterfalls. Much of it involved electrical consumer goods and home appliances proudly displayed, and it was most intensely focused around the sea cruises of the *Kraft-durch-Freude* organisations for the working class. The luxury transatlantic voyages of the Hapag-Lloyd Hamburg-America line were famous for clever and witty advertising films made well into the mid-1930s, including one by Ruttmann.[66]

The Nazis were not only impressed by the Fordist assembly lines depicted in the cinema – the new lifestyle was concerned with motorcars and mobility, tourism and package holidays, imitating the Americans while pretending to outdo them, thanks to less decadent, but equally discriminating consumer demands.[67] The build-up of a modern entertainment industry, for instance, went hand in hand with promoting mass transport and pouring resources into constructing the motorways. Hitler's famous Autobahn might have been conceived as a job creation scheme and a preparation for war, but it was sold to the German people as a new lifestyle. For only when the motorway project entered into its alliance with the Volkswagen, the new people's car, did the vision take off and begin to take on a kind of reality. In his *Reichsautobahn* (1985) and *Der VW-Komplex* (1987) Hartmut Bitomsky has documented the secret alliance of fantasy and industry manifesting itself through this enduring symbol of pre-war and post-war Germany. Bitomsky has gathered contemporary material, such as newsreel footage, coffee-table picture books and extracts from feature films almost as if to make the case that these engineering feats and architects' commissions were forced through not even to transport real people in real cars, but to be shown before, during and after construction as an ongoing spectacle in which the great German public could participate.[68] In a sense, the motorways were built in order to be advertised, and advertised in order to be visually consumed, which is to say, in order to provide a sort of extension to the cinema, the promise of more kinetic pleasures, including nature as motion spectacle. On the screen and in photos, the concrete ribbons were photogenically caught snaking through the

Black Forest or along the Rhine Valley (they never really did open for the public prior to 1945), and one might be forgiven for thinking (barely anachronistically) of giant roller-coaster rides and theme-park leisure centres.

Many of the musicals and comedies also exploited what today one would call subliminal advertising and product placement. In *Nie wieder Liebe*, for example, Lilian Harvey has great difficulty in seducing Harry Liedtke – until she offers him the agonising choice: 'Hennessy or Martell?', while in *Glückskinder* (Paul Martin, 1936) which is set in New York, Coca Cola and Mickey Mouse are mentioned quite openly,[69] while in *Ich bei Tag und du bei Nacht* a giant bottle of Chanel No. 5, that timeless symbol of French sophistication, is integral to the plot. In fact, most films of the mid-thirties are an orgy of expensive watches and extravagant accessories. The characters lounge in interiors stuffed with the latest designer furniture. They walk up to Bauhaus curtains and squeeze elegant cushions into comfortable shapes, while sporting '*dernier cri*' ladies' hats or very fashionable double-breasted suits. Often enough, this visual opulence is accompanied by the strains of 'swing' music (the German version of jazz, and officially banned) on the record player, or perhaps one of the latest hit songs played casually on the piano. Cross-dressing, mistaken identities, and other erotic come-ons are frequent in what are sometimes shameless imitations of American screwball comedies (e.g. *Glückskinder*, a particularly blatant but none the less brilliant remake of *It Happened One Night*).[70] The leading lady of *Glückskinder*, Lilian Harvey is the perfect exponent of this make-believe sophistication. Born in England, and yet Nazi Germany's most popular female star, she was as to the manner born for the new lifestyle, quickly establishing her consumerist expertise in both modern and erotic matters. Nothing was too much trouble for this dashing and athletic woman when it came to getting a look-in on the man's world, with singing, dancing, driving cars and competitive swimming, modelling for painters, portraying real-life royalty, cracking safes and getting the better of international criminal organisations. No challenge was too daunting: 'la Harvey' could whip up a stunning evening gown even from a shower curtain, transforming herself from good pal to *femme fatale* in a matter of minutes (*Nie wieder Liebe*). What is more, she had to perform these metamorphoses with perfect timing, knowing exactly when to keep her superior knowledge of the 'real' situation to herself (sharing this knowledge with the audience) and when to play it out to best effect. As she puts it so well in *Nie wieder Liebe*, 'hier scheint *man* nicht, hier ist *Mann*' (literally: 'here things are not what they seem, they simply are', but wittily playing on the untranslatable pun of 'man' meaning 'one' and 'Mann' meaning 'male'). These moments pave the way for what, in the sense of Third Reich ideology, would count as modern, with films conveying the whiff of luxury and the habits of consumerism that seamlessly ties fashion trends to family values and sexual innuendo to stereotypical gender-roles.

Guilty by complicity? Between cultural pessimism and the optimism of consumption

'Just like in the movies', 'things aren't what they seem, they simply are': one is tempted to contrast this playful appeal to simulated reality with the quite different simulation machine celebrated by Ernst Jünger when he speaks of the society of total mobilisation needing the power of spectacle. The same aspect of the modern leads in one case to Jünger's extreme – and extremely aristocratic–ascetic – cultural pessimism, typical of high culture, and in the case of the films, to a rather more light-hearted – or is it merely irresponsible? – optimism–hedonism, so much more typical of popular mass culture. While from our own vantage point, neither feels entirely acceptable, it could be argued that the kinds of self-reference, of self-advertising and self-irony to be found in the films just mentioned are recognisable aspects of the modernising tendencies of the cinema as a whole, to which the German cinema of the 1930s is not only no exception, but which it helped to shape, making it in this respect, too, indicative of international tendencies, even as it became nationally specific and national–chauvinist. One would not expect this process to happen without internal strains, in so far as some of the component elements of this ideological marriage developed their own momentum among the consumers and recipients. This, too, is an aspect of the divided consciousness that Schäfer examines. Schäfer's four levels of ideological incoherence mentioned earlier on can now be looked at more closely. For instance, as to market-criteria prevailing in many areas of production, including in the entertainment sector, UFA is a good example, because complicated. To the extent that the company was the goose that laid golden eggs, and was (albeit a modest) foreign currency earner, it enjoyed a measure of autonomy.[71] As an important promotional tool for German goods and the German way of life, it was, however, closely monitored by Goebbels. But given that 'the new Germany' was trying hard to win sympathy and even international popularity (often succeeding, too: Mitford, Cunard, or the then Prince of Wales), UFA behaved with its films as if it were a trend-setter, a style guide and a brand-leader that had the *Zeitgeist* on its side. This confirms Schäfer's second point, namely that the state safeguarded a number of apolitical spheres to strengthen its powers elsewhere, and it may go some way to explain why even political liberals like Reinhold Schünzel or Detlev Sierck not only decided to stay, but managed to direct such typically German but at the same time topically European entertainment classics as *Amphitryon*, *Viktor Viktoria*, *Schlussakkord* (*Final Accord*) or *La Habanera*.[72] Schäfer's third point, that 'personalised censorship' prevailed, meaning that prohibitions were implemented in an *ad-hoc* fashion, is well-known from Goebbels' often capricious decision making, but it can also be illustrated from a related area, the German record industry, which supplied most of Europe with records, and had complicated cross-licensing agreements that meant that even records officially banned in Germany were none the less produced in Germany for sales abroad, and via a flourishing black market, re-imported into Germany.[73] This was evidently less true of the cinema, except in so far as the regime allowed older American films to be shown right into the late 1930s, and current American films – even those that never made it into the cinemas – were of course shown to both the Nazi elite and to UFA directors and personnel, with the consequence that Hollywood continued to exert a not inconsiderable influence on German entertainment films throughout the life of the regime.

Although it would be disingenuous to divide Nazi cinema simply into two separate periods, one from 1933–1938, the other from 1939–1945, there are none the less quite distinct shifts of gear and of direction. The film industry, in line with other industries, was switched openly to the exigencies of a war economy from 1938 onwards: the 'nationalisation' of UFA late in 1937 was followed by a buy-out of all other production companies in 1938, including those in Austria (after the *Anschluss*). Also in 1938, the import ban on US films was extended, and in July 1939, a bilateral agreement was signed with France. Later that year, the newsreels were doubled in length, and their programming made compulsory. Seen in this perspective, the 'modernisation' of lifestyles increasingly disappeared from the films with the build-up and the onset of war. The play with different worlds, the double reference or double negative so characteristic of Weimar cinema, including its popular cinema well into the 1930s (and a feature also of the German émigré contribution to Hollywood),[74] made way for a quite different *Lebensgefühl*, which also found its ideal form in film. Detlev Sierk (*Schlussakkord* (1936) and *Zu Neuen Ufern* (*To New Shores*) (1937)) was a master of maternal masochism which was to become one of the mainstays of the second period. Promoting the willingness to self-sacrifice, it idealised renunication, extreme self-exertion and even risk taking, making them subjectively 'consumable' in the form of or last-stand war films, culminating in Veit Harlan's *Opfergang* (*Sacrifice*) (1944) and *Kolberg* (1945). Can one therefore argue that with the gradual fade-out of the international 'market-orientation' of Nazi cinema, the interest in the modernism of lifestyles also vanished in civil society as a whole? Or did not, on the contrary, the German armies' apparently so effortless conquests in Europe between 1939 and 1941 reinforce illusions of worldliness, energy and drive? Some of the biggest box office successes of the early 1940s – the already mentioned *Wunschkonzert* (*Request programme*) (26 million spectators), *... reitet für Deutschland* (*... riding for Germany*) (22 million) and *Die große Liebe* (*The Great Love*) (the all-time record of 27.4 million) suggest not so much a greater concentration on a female audience, but a focus on this audience in a different role – as mother, wife, provider rather than the frivolous young thing of the previous decade – and thus as mature women embroiled in extra-marital affairs, late blooming passion or forced into situations where a mother sacrifices herself for the sake of her child. In this respect, the onset of the war does indeed become noticeable in those films, where it plays little or no part, such as the box office hits with Zarah Leander. It is striking, for instance, how many female melodramas from the 1940s thematise Madame Bovary's temptations, trials and tribulations, or those of her German literary equivalent, Effi Briest (*Der Schritt vom Wege* (*The Trespass*), 1939, Gustav Gründgens; *Romanze in Moll* (*Romance in a Minor Key*), 1943, Helmut Käutner).

Whether one takes the musicals and comedies, or the melodramas and stories of romantic sacrifice as typical for the Nazi cinema – either genre must be regarded as 'modern', if one is to understand them in their role as enduring parts of (technologically produced and mass-consumed) popular culture. For it would appear that the *Volksgemeinschaft* – the collective of Nazi ideology – only existed thanks to the technologies of spectacle (radio, parades, media events), for 'in reality', its representations were not ready-made, they made themselves and undid themselves throughout the years of Nazi rule. The 'elect' and the excluded, 'the people' was invoked and repressed, and it changed into different aggregate forms: undesirables, mob, citizens, by-standers, spectators, chorus – films of the 1930s and early 1940s 'work' on this notion incessantly but never manage to produce a stable representation. Siegfried Kracauer's late 1920s notion of the 'mass ornament' captures one side of the equation, intentionally conceived as ambivalent, with its implied polarity between 'taylorisation' and 'regimentation', and its shifting location of the centre of energy.[75] The other side

Figure 33 The summer hit of 1940: Ilse Werner and Carl Raddatz in Eduard von Borsody's *Wunschkonzert*

Source: BFI films: stills, posters and designs

of the dialectic would be the mass ornament of metropolitan life, of the movie houses and concert halls, race-tracks and dance halls – full to capacity, right up until 1945. Ideologically, the demand addressed to the individual to sacrifice him/herself for the collectivity stands in contradiction to the consumerist vision of individual domestic pleasures away from the mass. It is as if, once part of the collective, one is lost, already sacrificed, as if caught in a situation of war. No mediation seems possible, and yet at the level of the lived reality, around all the artefacts of popular culture, Schäfer found evidence of spontaneous collectivities such as the fan community or the youthful gang: would one dare to call them part of an anti-totalitarian 'resistance'? As Schäfer points out, where majority interests were at stake, the regime's controls often failed, but this failure is, as I have tried to show, built into the system, as itself a stabilising force.[76] Nazi Germany was not defeated because of its popular culture, but neither was its popular culture the secret of its ideological 'success': in this respect, its ideology was more like a ferocious rider, riding the proverbial tiger, wearing the consumerist smile. Today, it is democracy, still riding the tiger, still smiling.

To substantiate such observations, it is not enough to cite more film examples. One would, for instance, have to examine afresh what is 'modern' about the cinema in general. Perhaps one too often still thinks of film history moving closer and closer to realism, be this outer or inner reality. This is, however, a historical teleology partly owed to Neo-realism and its aesthetics – and ethics – whose aim after 1945 had to be, among others, to immunise film history against the 'propaganda' bacillus that Wenders so eloquently invokes in my opening quotation. Yet, the cinema's modernity, its historical function, might just as much be sought not in its (capacity for) realism, but in the very opposite – in the way the cinema 'de-realises' the dimensions of time and space, and 'de-materialises' physical objects: not only to make them appropriated by fantasy (of the better life, of personal 'empowerment'), but in order to make them available for a different order of value, whether one calls it 'glamour' and 'show value', or – more old-fashionedly – 'commodity fetishism'. Seeing how these 1930s films respond affirmatively to travel and sports, to technological gadgets and consumer goods, to modern means of communication and transport, to engineering feats and spectacular media events, we cannot disown them, just as we cannot merely embrace them. Perhaps it is because these films still have too much in common with the Americanism popular during the Weimar Republic, whilst also anticipating a consumerism that did not take hold until the 1950s that they stay with us, as traces of a troubled modernity, always already overshadowed by a playful but also 'played-out' post-modernity, haunted by the allure of Nazi aesthetics, what Susan Sontag termed 'fascinating fascism'.

So the ideological project that stands behind Nazi cinema – whether concerned with the relation between technology and Nature, or with a specifically modern sensibility expressed through mobility and transport – remains as ambivalent as it remains topical. If it proved ideologically incoherent, when judged according to the oppositional pair reactionary versus progressive, it did make sense within the kind of consensus around which popular modernism and technological modernisation converged. The common denominator would be consumption and 'lifestyle' aspirations, rather than totalitarian ideology: if this is the recognition-effect that today's German audiences respond to, when wanting to know what it meant to be alive in the period, it makes the protective screen doubly necessary, for how could it share a *Lebensgefühl* that also colluded with such unimaginable physical horrors and permitted itself unspeakable moral depravities, without thinking itself sharing also that lifestyle's hideous underside? What one can be grateful for, perhaps, is that present social realities and political values seem so different. Even television seems to 'protect' us from those 'others' who look upon our lifestyle cynicisms, self-ironies and post-modern media-events rather less charitably than we do ourselves.

Notes

1 Wim Wenders,'That's Entertainment – Hitler (1977)', reprinted in Eric Rentschler, *West German Filmmakers on Film* (New York/London: Holmes & Meier, 1988): 128.

2 For a list of recent publications, exhibitions and retrospectives, see Eric Rentschler *The Ministry of Illusion: Nazi Cinema and its Afterlife* (Cambridge, MA: Harvard University Press, 1996): 2–15.

3 Among the all-time hits, it should be said, was also *Jud Suess* (*Jew Suess*), seen by nearly 20 million in 1940, which since 1945 cannot be shown publicly, except in an educational context. Other once popular Veit Harlan films, such as *Die Goldene Stadt* (*The Golden City*) and *Opfergang (Sacrifice)*, however, do have devoted fans, as has the actress Kristine Söderbaum who stars in all three. On *Wunschkonzert*, see David Bathrick 'Radio und Film für ein modernes Deutschland' in Irmbert Schenk (ed.) *Dschungel Großstadt* (Marburg: Schüren, 1999): 112–31.

4 The writer Martin Walser caused a major public debate in 1998 when he claimed that Nazi crimes and the Holocaust had, in the last twenty years, been rehearsed in the German media in a way that diminished the possibilities of thinking their meaning into one's existence. Fearing the 'instrumentalisation of Auschwitz', he called the Holocaust 'the moral club to batter us with'.

5 *Einbrecher* (*Burglars*), *Glückskinder* (*Lucky Kids*), *Das Lied ist aus* (*It's the End of the Song*), *Amphitrion*, *Schlussakkord* (*Final Accord*), *Viktor und Viktoria*, *Nie Wieder Liebe (Never Fall in Love Again)*, *Ein blonder Traum* (*A Blond Dream*), *Ich bei Tag und Du bei Nacht* (*Early to Bed*) are titles that, I have to confess, I never tire of watching.

6 For an earlier investigation of the ambiguities of Nazi Germany between 'conservative' and 'progressive' tendencies, see David Schoenbaum's classic study *Hitler's Social Revolution* (New York: Doubleday, 1966).

7 Felix Moeller, *Der Filmminister – Goebbels und der Film im Dritten Reich* (Berlin: Henschel, 1998).

8 Erhard Schütz, 'Das Dritte Reich als Mediendiktatur: Medienpolitik und Modernisierung in Deutschland 1933 bis 1945', *Monatshefte* 87/2 (1995): 129–50.

9

> Hitler did not let himself be governed by backward visions of a medieval social order. In many ways, his model was the United States. Although he rejected capitalist economics and the democratic order of the USA, he nevertheless admired its technological–industrial development.
>
> (Rainer Zitelmann (1994), cited in G.A. Craig, 'A man of the people?' In *New York Review of Books* (20 November, 1997): 21)

10 Among the many recent books that have tried to grapple with this issue, two stand out, not least because of their very different approaches: Rick Rentschler, *The Ministry of Illusion – Nazi Cinema and its Afterlife* (Cambridge, Mass: Harvard University Press, 1996) and Linda Schulte-Sasse, *Entertaining the Third Reich – Illusions of Wholeness in Nazi Cinema* (Durham: Duke University Press, 1996).

11 As early as 1926 the future of the German cinema seemed compromised, all the more so since commercially successful American cinema had begun to make the box-office paramount. […] During the closing years of the silent era the image still managed to succeed, following as it did the traditional conventions of the chiaroscuro. But the sound film betrayed with words the mystery of gestures, and cruelly showed up the mediocrity of the current output. The veil of *Stimmung* would seem to be rent without hope of repair.

(Lotte Eisner 1969: 311)

12 Irretrievable sunk into retrogression, the bulk of the German people could not help submitting to Hitler. Since Germany carried out what had been anticipated by her cinema from its very beginning, conspicuous screen characters now came true in life itself.

(Siegfried Kracauer 1947: 272)

13 The great historical figures that were dramatised this way were: poets (*Friedrich Schiller*), sculptors (*Andreas Schlüter*), scientists (*Paracelsus*), explorers (*Carl Peters*), industrialists (*Der Herrscher*), statesmen (*Bismarck*), and kings (*Der grosse König*). All of them can be seen as a projection of Hitler, who was exalted in Nazi propaganda as an amalgam of such geniuses.

(Welch 1983: 147)

14 In the 1960s, the historian Gerd Albrecht introduced a sophisticated, but also somewhat sophist classification system which divides Nazi films into different categories of entertainment and political films. *Nationalsozialistische Filmpolitik* (Stuttgart: Ferdinand Enke 1969).

15 See Part I, Chapter 4, this volume, on Erich Pommer and UFA.

16 Cf. the famous 'Congres international du cinéma independant' of October 1929, held at La Sarraz, Switzerland, where Eisenstein, Ruttmann and Hans Richter made *Tempête sur La Sarraz*, a spoof of their own attempt to rescue the 'Virgin Independent Film' from the prison in which the 'Army of the Industrial Film' keeps her imprisoned. See Hans Richter, *Köpfe und Hinterkpöfe* (Zurich: die Arche, 1967): 122–3.

17 See the chapter on German influences on film noir (Part IV, Chapter 3, this volume).

18 Eisner 1964, Collier 1988, Salt 1990, Hake 1994.

19 This, too, could be divided between an avant-garde wing (the school of Mary Wigman and Laban) and a more commercial wing (Erik Charell's dance spectaculars).

20 Hans Richter, *Der avantgardistische Film in Deutschland* (Göttingen: Cineaste, 1953) and Birgit Hein and Wulf Herzogenradt (eds) *Film as Film* (Stuttgart: Hatje, 1979).

21 Ute Eskildsen and Jan-Christoph Horak (ed.) *Film und Foto der zwanziger Jahre* (Stuttgart: Hatje, 1979).

22 *Das Deutsche Lichtbild* (Berlin: Verlag Robert & Bruno Schultz 1927) ff.

23 Huyssen 1986: 65–81.

24 Gottfried Knapp describes the observatory telescope (in *Stürme über dem Montblanc*) as 'a sexual organ peering into the dark' (Brandlmeier 1984: Lg 4, E 4).

25 See Eric Rentschler, 'Mountains and modernity: relocating the *Bergfilm*', *New German Critique* 51 (Fall 1990): 137–61.

26 *Ein blonder Traum* (premiere: 23 September 1932) features a montage sequence of bicycle-wheels that pastiches the same montage sequence in *Kuhle Wampe* (14 May 1932).

27 Elsaesser 1994: 186–97.

28 Riefenstahl 1992: 243.
29 Ibid.: 242.
30 An intriguing question is how Zielke received the commission to make the film in the first place. It was probably because he had taught at the Munich photographic academy from 1927 to 1934 and had made a name for himself as a major representative of New Photography, as well as his good connections with Albert Gollwitzer, a Munich rail company executive, who recommended him to the Reichsbahn Board (Loiperdinger 1994: 50).
31 Ibid.: 52.
32 Hans Ertl, quoted in Loiperdinger 1994: 53.
33 John Grierson, 'Documentary: Symphonics', *Cinema Quarterly* (Spring 1933): 138.
34 Winston 1995.
35 In her memoirs, she dramatises herself pleading with 'the Führer' to release her from the project (Riefenstahl 1988: 480).
36 *Völkische Beobachter* (29 October 1934), quoted in Goergen 1989: 40.
37 *Film-Kurier* no. 287 (7 December 1934), quoted in Goergen 1989: 41.
38 Goergen 1989: 41.
39 Speer, who acknowledges the difficulties Riefenstahl had as an independent-minded woman with the party hierarchy, confesses, somewhat disingenuously, to being shocked when Streicher, Rosenberg and Frank agree to re-takes in the studio. Hess in particular, 'with his special brand of ardour, turned precisely to the spot where Hitler would have been sitting, snapped to attention and cried: "Mein Führer, I welcome you in the name of the Party Congress." He did it all so convincingly that from that point on I was no longer sure of the genuineness of his feelings' (Speer 1969: 75).
40 Riefenstahl 1992: 365–7. She does mention the many re-shoots necessary for the *Berlin Olympiad* film, mainly in connection with the stormy love affair she had with the American decathlon winner, Glenn Morris, which apparently made her miss some crucial heats.
41 Bordwell and Thompson, *Film Art* (1992): 47–55.
42 Brian Winston and William Uricchio, 'The anniversary stakes', *Sight and Sound* 1995.
43 As to the origins of television in Germany and the importance of the transmission of the Olympic Games of 1936, see also the essays in W. Uricchio (ed.) *Die Anfänge des deutschen Fernsehens. Kritische Annäherungen an die Entwicklung bis 1945* (Tübingen: Niemeyer, 1991).
44 Barry A. Fulks, 'Walter Ruttmann, the avant-garde film and Nazi Modernism', *Film & History* XIV/2 (1984), and William Uricchio, 'Ruttmann after 1933' in Goergen 1989: 59–65.
45 Schäfer 1981: 170–9.
46 Herf 1984.
47 Wolf Dieter Müller, *Ernst Jünger* (Berlin, 1934): 42, cited in Herf 1984: 80.
48 Bohrer 1978.
49 Guy Debord's *La société du spectacle* (Paris: Denoel, 1972).
50 Jünger 1934: 154–214.
51 Ernst Jünger, *Das abenteuerliche Herz* (Hamburg: Hanseatische Verlagsanstalt, 1930). See also special issue on Ernst Jünger, *New German Critique* 59 (Summer 1993).
52 This was also demonstrated in the figure of the engineer in *FP1 Antwortet Nicht* (1932). Recommended in this context is the chapter in Herf on the role of the German civil engineering associations as active, if often naive ideologues in Weimar and afterwards (Herf 1984: 152ff.).

53 A similarly overtaxed mediator, this time between medicine and metaphysics, is found in the figure of the doctor in various bio-pics from the 1930s, particularly *Robert Koch, Der Bekämpfer des Todes* (1939, Hans Steinhoff).

54 Kreimeier 1992: 258–67.

55 See also Saunders 1994 on the tensions within Ufa in the 1920s and the internal as well as external strategies the German studio system pursued in order to compete with Hollywood.

56 Hans-Albert Walter 'Die Asylpolitik Frankreichs von 1933 bis zur Annexion Österreichs', in: P.U. Hohendahl and E. Schwarz (eds): *Exil und Innere Emigration* (Frankfurt am Main: Fischer, 1973): S 47–63; see also Dieter Schiller, Karlheinz Pech, Regine Herrmann and Manfred Hahn *Exil in Frankreich* (Leipzig: Reclam 1981).

57 H. Belach (ed.) *Kurt Bernhardt. Aufruhr der Gefühle* (Berlin: Argon, 1982): 105.

58 For multi-language versions, see Ginette Vincendeau 'Hollywood Babel', *Screen*, vol. 29, no. 2 (Spring 1988): 24–39; Natasha Durovicova 'The Hollywood multilinguals 1929–1933', in Rick Altman (ed.) *Sound Theory, Sound Practice* (London/New York: Routledge 1992): 138–52; Joseph Garncarz 'Die bedrohte Internationalität des Films. Fremdsprachige Versionen deutscher Tonfilme', in Sibylle M. Sturm and Arthur Wohlgemuth (eds) *Hallo? Berlin? Ici Paris! Deutsch-französische Filmbeziehungen 1918–1939* (München: edition text + kritik 1996): 127–40.

59 See Charles Ford 'Paramount at Joinville', in *Films in Review* (November 1961): 541–44; Francis Courtade 'Die deutsch-französischen Koproduktionen', in Heiner Gassen and Heike Hurst (eds) *Kameradschaft – Querelle. Kino zwischen Deutschland und Frankreich* (München: CICIM 1991): 159–72.

60 'Intermède Français 1933–1939' is the relevant chapter heading in Dumont 1981: 91.

61 Andrew Higson 'Film Europa. Kulturpolitik und industrielle Praxis', in Sturm, Wohlgemuth (eds): *Hallo? Paris? Ici Berlin!*, 63–76 (see note 58 above).

62 On Nebenzahl see entry 'Heinrich and Seymour Nebenzahl', in H-M. Bock (ed.) *CineGraph. Lexikon zum deutschsprachigen Film* (München: edition text + kritik 1984) ff., Lg. 24, D 1–8. As for being 'controversial':

> this way Siodmak hoped to rid himself once and for all from the hypocritical paternalism of Seymour Nebenzal; all these years [1933–1936] Nero massively exploited the precarious situation of the emigrés, to blackmail them into taking on assignments. After *Le chemin de Rio* Siodmak breaks all contacts with his cousin Nebenzal and even in Hollywood, he refuses to speak to him again.
>
> (Dumont 1981: 111)

Similarly negative views also came from Fritz Lang, first in the 1930s and again in 1951, when Nebenzahl produced a remake of *M* (directed by Joseph Losey) against the express wishes of Lang.

63 Eugen Tuscherer, the brother-in-law of Curtis Bernhardt, was one of the producers of *Carrefour*. 'Six well known Weimar Republic film producers managed to found their own production companies in Paris [...] Max Glaß, Hermann Millakowsky, Seymour Nebenzahl, Arnold Pressburger, Gregor Rabinowitsch and Eugène Tuscherer', Jan-Christopher Horak: 'Exilfilm, 1933–1945' in Wolfgang Jacobsen, Anton Kaes, Hans and Helmut Prinzler (eds) *Geschichte des deutschen Films* (Stuttgart: Metzler 1996): 105.

64 On the 'matching stars' syndrome, a favourite topic of the press in the early 1930s, see Katja Uhlenbrok 'Verdoppelte Stars. Pendants in deutschen und französischen Versionen', in Sibylle M. Sturm and Arthur Wohlgemuth (eds) (1996): 155–68. See

also Part III, Chapters 1 and 2, this volume on Schünzel and Pabst's *Threepenny Opera*.

65 While Gremillon, L'Herbier, Lacombe, Valentin and others were busy making 100% French films in Berlin and Munich for ACE – *Geule d'amour*, *L'etrange M. Victor*, *Adrienne Lecouvreur*, *L'entraineuse* etc. – the Germans in France have to submit to all kinds of bureaucratic harassments by the French authorities, sometimes even disguising their names in the end-credits.

(Ginette Vincendeau, 'Des portes ouvertes seulement à contrecoeur – les cinéastes allemands en France', *Positif*, January 1988: 47)

As to the difficulties with the trade unions, see Leo Lania, in: *Das neue Tagebuch*, quoted in Dumont 1981: 94.

66 Walter Ruttmann's *Melodie der Welt* (1929/30) was sponsored and co-funded by the Hapag-Lloyd Shipping Line.

67 Adolf Hitler himself formulated the motto: 'Frugality is the enemy of progress. In this, we're like the Americans – we have high expectations' in *Monologe im Führerhauptquartier 1941–1944*, quoted in Erhard Schütz, 'Das Dritte Reich als Mediendiktatur', *Monatshefte* 87/2 (1995): 141.

68 See James D. Shand, 'The Reichsautobahnen: Symbol for the Third Reich', *Journal of Contemporary History* 19 (1984): 189–200 and Erhard Schütz, 'Jene blaßgrauen Bänder', *Internationales Archiv für Sozialgeschichte der Literatur* 18 (1993): 76–120.

69 Coca Cola had several bottling plants licensed in Hitler's Germany, and the slogan 'Coca Cola eiskalt' was widely used (Schäfer 1981): 118.

70 Eric Rentschler, *The Ministry of Illusion* 1996: 99–124.

71 In a confidential memo from March 1937, Klitzsch complained that the cost of producing a feature film had doubled over the previous five years, and that due to falling exports, UFA was running up an operating loss of 12 million marks. Two weeks later, the Deutsche Reich 'bought back' over 70 per cent of UFA stock, the first step in nationalising the entire film industry.

72 For the career of Reinhold Schünzel, see Part III, Chapter 1, this volume. For Detlev Sierck, see Jon Halliday, *Sirk on Sirk* (London: Faber and Faber, 1997 [originally 1972]). *La Habanera* is discussed in Rentschler 1996: 125–45.

73 Schäfer 1981: 176.

74 See Part IV, Chapter 1, this volume.

75 See Siegfried Kracauer, *The Mass Ornament* (Cambridge, Mass.: Harvard University Press, 1998).

76 Schäfer 1981: 171.

3

CALIGARI'S LEGACY?

Film noir as film history's German imaginary

The connection between German Expressionist cinema and American film noir has become one of the commonplaces of film history.[1] Examining it once more, recalling or explaining it might be regarded as a matter of simple historical scholarship: tracing the stylistic or iconographic echoes,[2] researching film maker's biographies,[3] and inserting both in European political history and – if a more sophisticated account is called for – in the context of national and international film economics.[4] I shall argue that before proceeding, there is an important question to ask. Does the connection itself rest on a sort of historical double bind that conflates two 'histories' (i.e. of German Expressionism and of Hollywood film noir), which are not only distinct, but to a large extent 'imaginary'? By placing them back to back, across a listing of German émigré directors, the histories are made to mirror each other in an infinite regress that has tended to produce a self-validating tautology, where mutually sustaining causalities pass off as film history what is in effect more like a time loop. However, precisely because this lineage from Weimar cinema to American film noir does not ultimately make sense as history if considered in terms of demonstrable cause and effect, agency and consequence, it is – and probably remains – of interest to film history. Both complexes describe aspects of the cinema that should be regarded as 'a veritable history of the false' in the cinema, rather than as examples of 'false history': another version of the German cinema's 'historical imaginary'.[5] This chapter, then, tries to sketch the affinity between the German cinema as a national cinema especially rich in such historical imaginaries, and film noir as a case pointing to the transnational nature of such historical imaginaries in the course of cinema's developments.[6]

Although 'film noir' is both a French term and concept, it is worth remembering that the term has been used not only to describe an American cinematic genre or style, but has also been part of several interventionist critical battles centred on the idea of 'European cinema'. European cinema – another imaginary entity whose meaning resides in a set of shifting signifiers – has several 'magnetic poles' that, at least since the end of the Second World War and the dismantling of UFA, are mainly in Paris and Hollywood.[7] In the 1920s, by contrast, the term 'Film Europe' could be envisaged thus: Paris–Berlin and

Berlin–Hollywood, as well as Paris–Hollywood – in each case it was never quite clear to what extent competition was not always also complementarity, a feature incidentally also true since 1945.[8]

The ambivalent nature of the relationship is succinctly exemplified by the 'invention' of film noir, which might be called the centrepiece of a 'politics of trading compliments'. Considering how film noir 'survived' the 1950s and gained ever-wider currency by efficiently subsuming several distinct discourses within French post-war literary and artistic life,[9] one is struck by the superbly back-handed compliment the term 'film noir' pays to the victorious United States, even in 1946![10] For in the years of its ascendancy to super-power status and political hegemony, paralleling its relentless colonisation of popular taste in everything from food to music, from clothes to movies, film noir credits the US – at the heart of its belief in progress and peaking in its national optimism – with a fiercely critical, authentically negative view of American society and its institutions, thus flattering precisely those (French) intellectuals whose (left-wing) political convictions and (surrealist) aesthetic predilections obliged them to pay this compliment in the first place.[11] One suspects that only in the Paris of the 1950s would such a self-critical, pessimistic world view as it is generally ascribed to film noir appear *per se* as a philosophical and political virtue.

Seen from the other shore, the compliment has been handsomely repaid by at least two generations of American directors who have come to recognise the virtues of their own cinema by looking at it through French eyes, a process that – at least with regard to film noir – culminated in Paul Schrader's celebrated 1972 essay 'Notes on film noir'.[12] Schrader was also the one who, explicitly and at length, associated film noir with German Expressionism and its cinematic legacy, pointing to its 'unifying' force:

> [W]hen, in the late forties, Hollywood decided to paint it black, there were no greater masters of chiaroscuro than the Germans. The influence of expressionist lighting has always been just beneath the surface of Hollywood films, and it is not surprising, in film noir, to find it bursting out into full bloom. […] On the surface the German expressionist influence, with its reliance on artificial studio lighting, seems incompatible with postwar realism, with its harsh unadorned exteriors; but it is the unique quality of film noir that it was able to weld seemingly contradictory elements into a uniform style.[13]

More recently, another American director has given a further twist to these back-handed compliments. Quentin Tarantino, in *Pulp Fiction* fully plays out and returns the homage of the surrealists, by drawing an explicit analogy between film noir and *humour noir*.[14] The transnational ironies of the situation were, if anything, underscored when Tarantino accepted the *Palme d'Or* at Cannes from a jury president who was none other than Clint Eastwood, a star whose own image originally owed much to the Spaghetti Western, yet another 'European' homage to Hollyood.[15] It is Schrader, though, who enables the point to be made that the German connection turns out, on closer inspection, also to be French. If German Expressionism functions in post-First World War European cinema rather similarly to the way film noir functions in post-Second World War cinema, it may well be because of the peculiarly French element embedded in the origins of the idea of German Expressionist cinema itself. It was, after all, Lotte Eisner's *L'Ecran démoniaque* (first published amidst great acclaim in Paris in 1952) that breathed a new kind of life into the slim and fading silhouette of Dr Caligari's Cesare and the murky shadows of *Schatten*, thus making the link with the most obvious and most often repeated stylistic hallmark of film noir – the lighting style and the highly contrasting shadows.[16]

But Eisner in her particular re-reading of German Expressionism does not only stress lighting – the famous *clair–obscur* – as the epitome of its stylistic definition. The book also elegantly situates itself within another cultural politics of the compliment, one that links the French reading of *The Cabinet of Dr Caligari* from the 1920s to the Franco-German history of the 1950s. As described and documented by Kristin Thompson among others, *Dr Caligari* achieved its international canonical status after the reviews it received in Paris rather than during its initial release in Berlin.[17] Garnering a reputation in Paris that allowed it to become one of the few world-wide export successes the German cinema has ever had, the film itself became almost regarded as a 'French' film.[18] As for the Franco-German history of the 1950s, it was Jacques Aumont who in passing pointed out just how crucially Eisner's essays and then her book influenced the 1950s French cinephile re-discovery of German cinema of the 1920s.[19] By contrast, while in the United States, it was Kracauer's book *From Caligari to Hitler* (1947) that shaped the image of Weimar cinema for the post-war period, in France Kracauer was completely ignored, and instead, Eisner's version of German cinema became the key reference point.[20] Historically, Eisner's *L'Ecran démoniaque* coincided with the invention of film noir by Nino Frank,[21]and especially its popularisation by Raymond Borde-Etienne Chaumeton's *Panorama du film noir américain*.[22]

A double political axis thus emerges from these multiple convergences. On the one hand, Eisner was determined to contribute her part to repairing the damage that Nazism had done to Franco-German artistic and intellectual relations, by harking back to German Expressionism as the 'good Germany', the Romantic Germany, the Germany that France – ever since Madame de Stael – understood and loved so well. Madame Eisner was uniquely qualified to fulfil this role, and for this, another generation of German film makers, notably Werner Herzog and Wim Wenders, were to be undyingly grateful. Herzog, for instance, dedicated *Kaspar Hauser* to Eisner and undertook a pilgrimage from Munich to Paris on foot to visit her in hospital.[23] For Wenders, making *The American Friend* (1977) with assorted French and American directors playing noirish gangsters in the colours of the tricolore, film noir proved a most satisfying synthesis of his own Franco-German, Germano-American cinephilia. On the other hand, the invention of film noir around *La Revue du cinéma* and later *Les Cahiers du cinéma* played its own role in precariously balancing Anglo-French relationships after the war, in a political climate where the still victorious left was anti-American politically, but pro-American intellectually,[24] before this political–cultural entente around the complex 'French intellectuals, America and Hollywood' received the next of its many twists with de Gaulle's exit from NATO in the 1960s:

> The French have a paradoxical image of the United States: on the one hand, it permitted victory in the struggle against Nazism and offers the image of a people whose standard of living is sharply superior to that of the French, who until at least 1955 were caught in an economy of scarcity inherited from the war and even the pre-war period. But, on the other hand, the United States is an imperialist menace that threatens to impose upon France values and a culture that are not its own: if the Americans are superior and even saviours in the military and economic domains, they are judged to be inferior and dangerous in the domain of culture.[25]

Thus, at film noir's hour of birth, two ideologically fraught discursive balancing acts came together in France around what one might call the compromise formation of appealing to 'Expressionism' (re-figuring the traumatic Franco-German relations) and the 'symptom formation' 'film noir' (re-figuring Hollywood–Paris power relations). A case, therefore, of a doubly over-determined historical fantasy, firmly located in the 1950s rather than the 1940s, and firmly located in Europe, rather than in America. A first conclusion, then, would be to contend that essentially, film noir has no essence, that its most stable characteristic is its 'absent-centredness', its displacements, its over-determinedness, whose ghostly existence as too many discourses, instead of cancelling each other out, merely seems to amplify the term's resonance and suggestiveness. Most noticeable is the term's historical imaginary as deferred action (*Nachträglichkeit*).[26] Film noir is thus in a sense a textbook example of how *not* to write film history, considering that never have so many causes explained so few effects, and never have so many heterogeneous determinants made so little difference in invalidating other, seemingly equally plausible lines of argument: all of them leading to that relatively limited corpus of films made between *The Maltese Falcon* (1941), *Kiss Me Deadly* (1955) and *Touch of Evil* (1958).[27]

Foremost among the self-evidently plausible arguments is the history of German directors in Hollywood (the so-called 'émigré' argument). Yet this story – itself quite contradictory[28] – connects only with difficulty to the *femme fatale* confronting the doomed male hero (i.e. the 'gender' argument), while the literary history of the hard-boiled novel – *pace* Paul Schrader – does not connect to the 'political' explanation of the war-weary veteran, Cold War paranoia and McCarthyism. Yet film noir, true to its nature as a 'symptom formation', is

Figure 34 Anxious moments: Marjorie Reynolds and Ray Milland in Fritz Lang's *Ministry of Fear* (1944)

Source: BFI films: stills, posters and designs

impervious to logic or evidence. No sooner has a mass of historical evidence disproved the expressionist lighting theory about film noir, then the thesis of film noir as the foreign director's preferred Hollywood version of the American dream returns, multi-headed – this time around another generation of exile émigrés – Roman Polanski (*Chinatown*), Alan Parker (*Angel Heart*), Ridley Scott (*Blade Runner*), Paul Verhoeven (*Basic Instinct*), Adrian Lyne (*Fatal Attraction*), Wolfgang Petersen (*In The Line of Fire*), Wim Wenders (*Hammett*) and Uli Edel (*Body of Evidence*) – with Michael Ballhaus or Nestor Almendros as cameramen to pick up where Eugen Schüfftan or Sol Polito had left off in the 1940s.[29]

Where, one wonders, does this energy come from which continues to be absorbed into that conceptual black hole that is film noir? If, some fifteen years ago, when a slim booklet called 'Women and film noir' was published in London,[30] much of the energy came from feminist theory and a materialist history of film noir as rooted in a doubly 'repressed return' (the traumatic return of men into civilian life and civic duties after the confidence-sapping horrors of war, mirrored by the women's return into the home and domestic duties after the confidence-boosting years in factories and fields), the 1990s conjuncture of film noir may be located at the opposite extreme, summed up fairly well in Dennis Hopper's phrase of film noir as 'every director's favourite genre'.[31] Here film noir functions as the very signifier of meta-cinema, of cinema made out of cinema, signalling perhaps its own kind of 'return of the repressed'.[32] More prosaically, given that there has been a massive return in mainstream cinema to modes, styles, motifs to which the label of 'noir' is readily being applied (not merely by film scholars, but by marketing men, fashion moguls and merchandisers), the existence of noir paranoia thrillers (Wolfgang Petersen's *In the Line of Fire*) and noir Westerns (Clint Eastwood's *The Unforgiven*), of noir horror (Alan Parker's *Angel Heart*) and noir sci-fi (John Cameron's *The Terminator*) not so much heralds the end of the term's historical, critical or even descriptive leverage as the end of the 'repression' model itself – depth giving way to surface, and signifying elements entering into a new circuit of meaning.[33]

It is at this point, where film history might itself be challenged for adhering too closely to models dominated by linear determinants and thus blocking these potentially different circuits of meaning, that the German input into film noir rightly returns. In order to grasp this turn, one needs to remind oneself of some of the signifiers in play. They are both impressive and incontrovertible, when treated as evidence for the supposed German 'influence':

- If one looks at the lighting codes of Expressionism (*claire–obscure*, the harsh, elongated shadows, extreme and unusual angles, the light playing on faces and creating their own psychologically saturated environment (*The Cabinet of Dr Caligari*), one recognises the expertise of a large number of German (UFA) cameramen, like Carl Freund, Carl Hoffmann, Eugen Schufftan, Fritz Arno Wagner, Theodor Sparkuhl, Rudolf Maté and Franz Planer who actually did go to Hollywood, or of the American Charles Rosher who trained at UFA, or the influence and expertise of set designers/art directors like Hans Dreier and Harry Horner who were prized studio specialists.
- The generic influence of the so-called 'Straßenfilme' is equally strong: from *Die Strasse* (*The Street*, Karl Grune, 1923) and *Dirnentragödie* (*Tragedy of the Whore*, Bruno Rahn, 1927) to *Die Freudlose Gasse* (*Joyless Street*, G.W. Pabst, 1925), *Asphalt* (Joe May, 1928) and *Mutter Krausens Fahrt ins Glück* (*Mother Krause's Trip to Happiness*, Piel Jutzi, 1928), a German obsession seems to be reproduced in the mean streets of Chicago, New York and Los Angeles.
- The German cinema also featured classic *femme fatales* before 1940s film noir: Louise Brooks (*Pandora's Box*, 1929) and Marlene Dietrich (*The Blue Angel*, 1930) immediately come to mind, but an even earlier figure would be Lya di Putti who with *Variety* had an appreciable success when it was first released in the United States in 1926.

Another parallel is the anxious, doom-laden male of film noir, whose antecedent is found in the 1920s only in German and Russian films. In Weimar cinema especially, the masochistic male has given rise to much comment: Emil Jannings with his broad back always bent and stooping (in *The Last Laugh*, 1923; *Variety*, 1925), or the panic-stricken adolescents of *Waxworks* and *Nosferatu*. Associated with these males is a certain personality: they seem to enjoy humiliation, but then lash out in irrational violence; they get entangled in love triangles in which an older man tries to assert his masculinity against a younger rival. Similar triangles are typically found in *Double Indemnity* or *The Postman Always Rings Twice*.[34]

- The psychopathic male, the compulsive sex murderer: from Jack the Ripper in G.W. Pabst's *Pandora's Box* to Peter Lorre's child molester in Fritz Lang's *M*, the German cinema seems to be the first home of the serial killer, from whence he turns up in Boris Ingster's *Stranger on the Third Floor* (1940, starring Peter Lorre) and Lang's *While the City Sleeps* (1956).
- Then, there are parallels in the story structures between German films from the 1920s and film noir: the tortured, convoluted narratives, the use of framing devices and *mise-en-abyme* (like *Dr Caligari*, *Waxworks*, *Shattered*, *Destiny* (*Der Müde Tod* and *Variety*) seem credible precedents for the flashback structures from the 1940s (*Stranger on the Third Floor*, *Detour*, *Criss-Cross*).
- Of all the possible influences, the most conclusive and prominent fact is that so many directors of films noirs are German, Austrian or European: apart from the most prominent such as Billy Wilder, Otto Preminger, Fritz Lang, Robert Siodmak, there is Curtis Bernhardt, Anatole Litvak, Jacques Tourneur, Rudolf Maté, Edgar Ulmer, Max Ophuls and Douglas Sirk.

From a historical perspective, what kind of credibility can one give to these lines of reasoning and pieces of evidence? Strictly speaking, very little. Now that historians of early cinema have begun viewing more extant films and have consulted more trade journals and professional publications, it would seem that in the tradition of David Belasco, directors like Ralph Ince, Cecil B. de Mille and countless other American cinematographers and directors, as early as 1915 used 'Expressionist lighting' in their films, though referring to it as 'Rembrandt lighting', 'fireside lighting' or 'Lasky lighting'.[35] Its re-emergence in the 1940s can therefore be accounted for entirely within the history of American cinematography and lighting practices. But why did it disappear between the late 1920s and the 1940s? The answer is that it did not. Marc Vernet has shown in an admirable study of the Warner Brothers and RKO films from the 1930s that countless films did indeed use these harsh lighting techniques. But the difference was that they were used in B-productions – films by little-known directors – which have rarely been looked at by *auteur*-theory influenced film scholars.[36] Furthermore, within the cinematic profession the Germans had a high reputation for skills that are rarely mentioned in the catalogue of 'influences', at least if the Austrian writer and director Walter Reisch is to be believed:

> Peter Lorre became a star here and he played in many Humphrey Bogart pictures. And Bogart was a man of enormous charity; whenever Lorre or somebody else came to him and said that there was a guy from Germany who had to run away, flee from Hitler, do something for him, give him some money, or an old suit, or a part, Bogart immediately, if Lauren Bacall wasn't looking, gave him money. One day Lorre came with a guy and Bogart asked 'who's he' and Lorre said 'he was a cutter at the Ufa, and believe me, if you were a cutter at the Ufa you had to be the top'. So it became a by-word with Bogart to say 'he's a cutter at the Ufa'.
>
> (Author's interview with Walter Reisch, Beverly Hills, 1982)

Reisch's story is also revealing in its focus on Peter Lorre, and thus on a certain conception of masculinity. With the exception of Marlene Dietrich (and possibly Conrad Veidt), Lorre was the only German actor who became a Hollywood star in the sound period, but in the 1930s he was firmly associated with the Mr Moto series, which had little to do with German Expressionism and nothing to do with film noir. Only in the 1940s, and starting with *The Stranger on the Third Floor*, did Lorre pick up the sort of parts that are reminiscent of *M*, thus modulating the Weimar-type of anxious male into an uncanny figure, mainly on account of his sexual ambiguities. When entering film noir territory with *The Maltese Falcon*, his characters' sexual deviancy becomes as crucial an issue as their foreignness: thus, the American cinema resolved the ambiguities of the anxious and psychopathic Weimar male by explicitly making him effeminate and a 'pervert', that is, taking over the homophobe stereotyping of homosexuals prevalent in American popular culture.

As far as generic influences goes, a better knowledge of American film history would also reveal an important American predecessor of 1940s film noir. For even if we discount the gangster films of the late 1920s and early 1930s, there is the genre of the newshound film of the 1930s in the manner of *The Front Page* and extending from *Satan Met a Lady* to *The Stranger on the Third Floor* that could provide 'missing links'. A more complex story of genre transformation has therefore to be invoked, but one that once again does not have to rely on precedents or influences from German cinema. The fact, for instance, that John Huston's *The Maltese Falcon* was already the third film based on Dashiell Hammett's novel of that title must give the historian pause for thought. And when one learns that the second *Maltese Falcon* was actually directed by none other than German émigré William Dieterle, the story gains an additional twist. For this film – *Satan Met a Lady* – is an intriguing and underrated film, not least for being an ideal candidate for film-noir status (the German émigré status of its director) without actually belonging to film noir. This suggests that the émigrés had in fact less influence on the emergence of the style we call film noir than other factors, a conclusion perfectly in keeping with what we know about the Hollywood film industry. For a more likely scenario 'explaining' the emergence of film noir in the early-to-mid-1940s would be based on the historical changes that the American cinema underwent in the late 1930s and 1940s as a consequence of decartelisation, the Justice Department's case against Paramount Studio and the changes in the Hays Production Code.[37]

To account for the *femme fatale* in American film noir, one would similarly do well to explore the censorship discourse of the 1930s[38] and study the generic intertext of the 'independent woman' from the early 1930s, especially as she developed in the newshound film and screwball comedy. On the other hand, remembering that Ernst Lubitsch owed his first Hollywood contract to his reputation as a director of *femmes fatales*, reintroduces the German cinema, but as *Rosita* showed, for him at least, this proved a dead-end.[39] The name of Lubitsch adds another sideways dimension to the presence of German directors in Hollywood, and the question of their 'influence'. For in order to write the history of the German exiles and émigrés, one would indeed have to abandon notions such as influence and causal agent, and invoke the historical imaginary I mentioned earlier. This historical imaginary not only contains the émigrés' cultural or emotional or artistic baggage, which has been so crucial in 'writing' the (good) German cinema 'back' into the history of world cinema. It also includes such 'what-if' histories as that in which William Dieterle directs *The Maltese Falcon* and not *Satan Met a Lady*, or *Dr Caligari* director Robert Wiene, screenwriter Carl Mayer and *Die Straße* director Karl Grune (all émigrés – to France and Britain – in the 1930s and 1940s) would be the most prominent Germans associated with film noir. Such a virtual film history would have E.A. Dupont, Joe May and G.W. Pabst – all of whom directed films in Hollywood – make films noirs, so that our theory of influence might have a satisfying degree of symmetry and closure. While Wiene and Dupont made films in Germany that were popular or at least released in the United States, Pabst and May developed stylistic features in their German films that one can recognise in film noir. None of them, alas, can be associated with film noir: the actual names are quite different, and – with the notable exception of Fritz Lang – it was the 'wrong' Germans that went on to make films noirs in America, meaning that few of their previous German films indicated a particular predilection for atmospheric gloom. One thinks of Siodmak, Wilder and Ulmer. Their first German film was *Menschen am Sonntag* – a more likely candidate for a theory of German influence on Neo-realism than on film noir! On the other hand, both Siodmak's and Wilder's films in France could be said to have prepared them for Hollywood crime and mystery stories.[40]

In short, in order to understand the presumed German ancestry of film noir, attention shifts to the German cinema in its transnational as well as international dimension, which involves a more differential account of 'film exile' than one usually finds in film histories.[41] A linear history of 'influence' would have to be combined with a lateral history of 'interference', which might best be figured by the double, if at first sight disrespectful metaphors of the circulation of cultural cliché and the backhanded compliment, which however, have a more serious

Figure 35 'We have ways...': George Sanders and Joan Bennett in Fritz Lang's *Man Hunt* (1941)

Source: BFI films: stills, posters and designs

function in that they both refer to mutually sustained imaginaries of 'otherness'. Here are some of what I consider the salient features of such a history of interference.

First, the logic of the system. Rather than subsume all the directors, stars and movie personnel in the general category of émigré, we would have to study, in each and every case, the precise reasons and circumstances that brought a German director to the United States. This is not only a condition of sound historical scholarship, but also a requirement for a fair consideration of every human fate that otherwise – even with the best of intentions – would remain hidden, blocked out and lost to history by such a blanket term. In each case, cogent reasons can be adduced, which give a very differentiated and historically highly instructive picture.[42] For instance, there were directors like Lubitsch or Dupont who were initially hired by Hollywood because they were deemed to be capable of making popular and profitable films, which meant that Hollywood had an interest in having them work for the American cinema rather than for a competitor like Germany. Others returned to Germany (for example, G.W. Pabst and Ludwig Berger), or shuffled backwards and forwards, with spells in Britain (for example, Dupont).

The top directors' self-interest, on the other hand, mirrored that of the studios. Coming from Europe's most technically accomplished film culture and film industry, they hoped to find in Hollywood not only fame, but the facilities and expertise that permitted them to remain 'state of the art' in their field. Other directors, also among the best in their country, were none the less swept to Hollywood on another wave, which reduced them initially to mere instruments of a different kind of logic. It was because of the profound changes that the film industry underwent internationally with the coming of sound at the end of the 1920s that William Dieterle came to Hollywood, and the (second) career of Dupont (after *Variety*, 1925) was in the era of sound, namely the dual-language versions by which Britain and Germany rivalled each other.[43] Reinhold Schünzel and Douglas Sirk, by contrast, had been hugely successful directors under Goebbels' UFA regime until 1937, and when they eventually came to the US in 1938–9, they both had at first a hostile reception and grave professional difficulties.[44] Even among the Jewish refugees and exiles, one can differentiate between those who wanted to settle in France (on the strength of their extensive professional contacts), and those who subsequently were forced to move further afield by either the anti-Semitism of the French film industry or by the German occupation after 1940, and those who merely waited there until their long-expected Hollywood contract and immigration papers arrived at the American consulate:

> I knew from the start where I wanted to go. At first, I lived in Paris for nearly a year, and it was there that I was able to direct my first film, *Mauvaise Graine* with Danielle Darrieux, who was only seventeen at the time. But Paris was never more than a stopover for me. The truth is, I would have come to Hollywood, Hitler or no Hitler, at least that was my ambition.[45]

The common element between all the émigré directors, on the other hand, is something else: a certain structural asymmetry between aim and consequence. One might even say that the discrepancy between intention and result, cause and effect not only obliges one to revise one's notions of this history, but that it is generically coded – to paraphrase the famous remark by Karl Marx concerning the repetition compulsion of history – as either tragedy or farce, or since we are dealing here with Hollywood, as either film noir or musical comedy, the two genres in which the émigrés did indeed initially excel. In which case, the task of the film historian would be to read history as a genre film, and to establish some kind of pertinent relation between the expectations that the German directors had of Hollywood, and what expectations Hollywood had of the Germans. I have indicated elsewhere the extent to which I think it can be conceptualised by a series of narratives and metaphors – that of repetition, for instance ('Play it again, Lajos' ...), or the trading of clichés between 'New World–Old Worlde'.[46] Prime examples of the latter trope might be Ernst Lubitsch, a 100 per cent Berliner and the most 'American' of German directors of the 1910s and early

1920s, who had to remake himself in the cultural image of 'Old Worlde' Hapsburg decadence (Vienna, Ruritania and the k.u.k. [*kaiserlich und königlich*] Austro-Hungarian monarchy) or the operetta Paris of Jacques Offenbach.[47] Joe May left Germany on the strength of his Berlin street film and film noir melodrama *Asphalt* (1929), but found himself immediately co-opted into the vogue for musical comedy revue films (*Music in the Air*, 1934), on which his former boss at UFA, Eric Pommer, had built a world-wide reputation. Upon arrival in Hollywood, Dupont was asked to do *Hannerl and Her Lovers*, based on a novel by the Viennese Rudolf Hans Bartsch, and thus a topic better suited to Max Ophuls or even Joe May, a Viennese by birth, than the director of *Varieté* and a native of Saxony. It was almost a repeat of the situation in Paris, around about the same time when Lang was shooting *Liliom* for Pommer while Ophuls was preparing *On a volé un homme*, also for Pommer. 'In my opinion' Ophuls later said 'this was a double mistake. Pommer should have done it the other way round. Lang would certainly have made a remarkable thriller, while I would probably have turned out a good romantic comedy'.[48] And so the comedy of errors seems to continue: apparently nothing but a series of spectacular mis-castings, nothing but mutual mis-cognition, at least if one insists on seeing it under the 'European' paradigm of the *auteur*, the artist and the coherence of a creative body of works.

The American perspective was quite different. The film industry took on the Germans because it was head-hunting the brightest talent everywhere, and keen to neutralise, for instance, the German competition, making sure that Hollywood had the personnel that could make for the studios' balance sheets the films European audiences wanted to see. This was the gamble they took, and often enough – one must add in all fairness – it did not pay off. More generally, what made the Germans a prominent force in Hollywood was their professionalism and their technical expertise. Thus, the most likely scenario is that their UFA training, their versatility and adaptability as skilled film personnel was and remained the basis of the émigré's economic and cultural capital in the eyes of Hollywood. The prosaic answer, then, to the question about the prominence of German directors in the film noir cycle is that the Germans were film professionals, that they came from a mature, developed film industry, which is why they could adapt themselves so well to Hollywood, and could leave their mark on so many different genres, cycles and modes, while none of this *per se* implicates their personal conviction, their desire for self-expression or, indeed, the question of what typically German traits they conveyed in their films.

More likely, my model of an interference history would oscillate between creative mis-matches and miscognitions on the one hand (with many a comedy of error and some lost illusions), and over-adaptation, assimilation and over-identification (this, too, often with a grain of comic or tragic irony). The latter is nowhere more evident than in the cruel irony that obliged German Jewish actors like Peter Lorre and Otto Preminger, Alexander Granach and Reinhold Schünzel, Felix Basch and Leo Reuss (Lionel Royce) to make their living in

Hollywood by playing – and even becoming in the public mind identified with – the Nazi villains from whom they had to flee:

> Robert Thoeren, a much sought-after screenwriter among the émigrés [once said]: 'In 200 years, a bright child in a class-room will raise her hand and ask: Sir, what did those Nazis actually look like? And then, they'll go to the archives and dig out all those films from the period, and they will discover that the Nazis were a purely semitic tribe, as demonstrated in the Hollywood films by Fritz Kortner, Sigi Arno, Curt Bois, Alexander Granach, Felix Basch, Kurt Katch and others.[49]

This story is, of course, at the core of Lubitsch's anti-Nazi satire *To Be or Not to Be*, which shows that the Jewish actors playing Nazi villains are themselves enacting a kind of *mise-en-abyme* or special case of the general 'Alice in Wonderland' logic that confronted the Europeans in Hollywood, where they were asked to 'be' what they had worked hard to leave behind – whether Austro-Hungarian Hapsburg decadence or the Berlin garment district, whether the Eastern European *stetl* and *ghetto*, or the Paris of picturesque poverty.[50] The effect of 'interference history' on the topic of film noir would be that its history (and the Austro-German involvement in its genesis) may well become part of the same spirit of 'to be or not to be', of make-believe impersonation: enacting 'German expressionism' or Teutonic gloom as the mimicry of survival – though more for the critics than the audiences. Film noir would then be one of the splinters in the sometimes sharp-edged and sometimes soft-focused but always ironically broken wall of mirrors the émigré cinema put before its American public, confirming Germany's central place in the cinema's historical imaginary as well as its marginal place in the cinema's economic history.

The career of one of the German émigrés – the one most closely identified with film noir, namely Robert Siodmak – certainly lends itself to an exploration of this historical imaginary, throwing into confusion not only the idea of authorial intentionality, but also unilinear causality and – as we shall see – even chronology! For when one looks at Siodmak's career, it displays all the accidents of a talented but not exceptional *metteur-en-scene*, working within a studio system and having the good fortune of a possibly even more talented brother, Curt Siodmak, who writes successful novels, commercial screenplays, and has excellent connections.[51] Many different genre films follow each other, and from *Menschen am Sonntag* (*People on Sunday*) (1928) and *Abschied* (*Farewell*) (1930) via *La Vie Parisienne* (*Life in Paris*) (1934) and *Pièges* (*The Trap*) (1938) not much seems to lead to *Phantom Lady* (1944) and *The Killers* (1946), even if one leaves aside *Son of Dracula* (1943), or *The Crimson Pirate* and *Dorothea Angermann*, two Siodmak titles from the 1950s. But if one takes *Phantom Lady*, arguably one of Siodmak's most successful films during his 'noir' period, and makes it central to his work, it is as if his whole previous film making rearranges itself, around a certain kind of coherence that, however, is less due to the benefit of hindsight, and rather follows the more involuted logic of a J.L. Borges story, doubling up on its own temporal and spatial causality. *Menschen am Sonntag* and *Abschied*, which have little trace of expressionist lighting, function according to a quite different – if not diametrically opposed – aesthetic to both Expressionism and the Kammerspielfilm (literally: chamber-play film) (often – wrongly – conflated with Expressionist cinema). At the other extreme, *Phantom Lady* could appear a textbook example of harsh contrasts, strong key lights, returning us to the street film and the claustrophobia of UFA-style studio-bound exterior scenes. It is as if, in exile, Siodmak 'remembered' the lighting style of Murnau, Pabst and Dupont:

> Upon my insisting, they gave me Woody Bredell as cinematographer. I told him about my friend Eugen Schüfftan, with whom I'd made *Menschen am Sonntag* and *Mollenard* and who was a great admirer of Rembrandt. The theory that the eye instinctively moves away from the brightest point and seeks out the darkest seemed to impress Bredell. He began to study Rembrandt's paintings.[52]

Phantom Lady, in which a young woman tries to find the 'other' woman who could provide her employer–friend, suspected of murder, with an alibi even suggests the title of a German Siodmak film, *Der Mann der seinen Mörder sucht* ('A Man is Looking for His Murderer'), except that this noir title *par excellence* is actually a comedy bordering on slapstick, in which a suicidal hero tries to cancel the contract he took out on his own life with an amateur killer.[53] In *Phantom Lady*, on the other hand, a scene where Kansas, the heroine, meets her boss in prison is lit like a scene out of *Variety*, while the scene with Kansas escaping from Cliff the drummer (played by Elisha Cook, Jr.) and running across the street to call the detective Burgess is wholly reminiscent of the German street film, such as Joe May's *Asphalt* – a concentration on the sound of footsteps and shadows, an atmosphere of oppression and metropolitan chaos, while simultaneously conveying the image of a city where everyone is alone, suggesting the threat to the anonymous individual in a crowd and the danger of the deserted street at night. The reason for her hurried escape from Cliff's dingy apartment is that Kansas, playing detective in order to track down the phantom lady who might provide her boss with an alibi, has herself become a phantom lady to the naive but none the less potentially vicious Cliff, impersonating a *femme fatale*, both metaphorically in her sexual allure and provocativeness, and literally, in that knowing her is going to prove fatal to both the barman and Cliff.

Phantom Lady is based on a novel by Cornell Woolrich, who meticulously describes not only many of the most noirish effects of Siodmak's *mise-en-scène*, including several pages on such lighting details as the difference between shadows cast by shafts of light from a strong steady source and a wavering flame's shadows on an uneven surface. He also depicts, down to the sound effects, the manner in which the secretary-turned-*femme fatale*'s Medusa stare becomes the discomfited barman's nemesis.[54] Should we therefore say that it is

Figure 36 Chilled and not stirred: Ella Raines in Robert Siodmak's *Phantom Lady* (1944)
Source: BFI films: stills, posters and designs

Woolrich who is the true author of *Phantom Lady*? Not at all, for we only have to go back a few years in Siodmak's career, albeit in another country – the France of 1938 – to find a clear precedent for the figure of 'Kansas' from *Phantom Lady* in *Pièges*. Here, too, a young woman, a so-called taxi girl is hired by the police as a decoy in order to track down who might be behind the disappearance of a number of young women, among them her taxi-girl partner. Like Kansas, the heroine of *Pièges* each time slips effortlessly into the role that is most seductive to the man she is trying to expose, whether it is an ageing *grand couturier* (Erich von Stroheim), a playboy industrialist (Maurice Chevalier) or a sadistic butler (who enjoys being humiliated by a 'tease'). Clearly, in the light of *Phantom Lady*, *Pièges* becomes the work of a cinematic *auteur*, deepening and further exploring a number of moral themes and stylistic effects.

The inverse, on the other hand, is not the case: *Pièges*, looked at in its own film-historical context, does not anticipate *Phantom Lady* half as much as *Phantom Lady* implies *Pièges*. For when we look at the latter without the benefit of the former (i.e. of hindsight), something altogether different becomes evident, namely an intertext that points in the other direction, to what I have called the 'looking-glass logic' of Austro-Germans in Hollywood. First of all, *Pièges* is a typical Landru story, and thus with an impeccably French pedigree, except that here Landru is split between the playboy industrialist and his friend and business associate – itself another parallel with *Phantom Lady*, where the true murderer turns out to be Henderson's best friend. But to confound the issue still further, this friend and business associate who turns out to be the serial killer of *Pièges* is played by Pierre Renoir, familiar to French audiences of the time as Maigret, the Simenon detective in Pierre's brother Jean Renoir's *La Nuit du Carrefour* (1936).

However, according to the logic of the time loop affecting the historical imaginary, *Pièges* should really have been made in Hollywood, and by Ernst Lubitsch (maybe as *Bluebeard's Eighth Wife*), because it illustrates to perfection the 'miscognition' factor of Austro-Germans as directors of Habsburg decadence or Parisian operetta, given the prominent presence in *Pièges* of both Erich von Stroheim *and* Maurice Chevalier. On the other hand, Chevalier's casting in *Pièges* makes once more perfect sense in the context of Siodmak's *La Crise est finie* (a Franco-German 'depression musical') and *La Vie Parisienne* (a Jacques Offenbach operetta), except that these two films should have been directed by Max Ophuls, who was already in 1936 inescapably associated with Vienna, musicals, operetta, duelling officers of the Habsburg monarchy or Parisian *fin de siècle*.[55] But just at this point when one seems to be able to account for a film like *Pièges* very satisfactorily as less an *auteur*ist work by Siodmak, and more the typical product of that generic intertextuality and star discourse so characteristic of popular French cinema in the 1930s, while also recognising in it the traces of that 'interference history' marking the relations between Germany, France and Hollywood, another intertextuality opens up, namely a literary one provided by none other than Cornell Woolrich, who in 1942 published a story called *The Dancing Detective*. In it, 'the investigator is a taxi-girl dancer being stalked by a serial murderer'.[56] So either Woolrich had seen *Pièges* (which is unlikely, since the film was not released in the US), or Woolrich is the true 'author' of *Pièges* (which is equally improbable, except in my film-historical fantasy, with its achronological, back-to-front circulation of signifiers), since *Pièges* was 'actually' written by a German screenwriter with a French pseudonym, basing it on the 'true story' from the Paris police records involving a Parisian serial killer of German nationality.[57]

To conclude I return to the initial notion of German Expressionism and film noir as two sides of a more pervasive, more generalisable strategy of cross-cultural compliments. I started by saying that film noir was originally part of the back-handed compliment that the generation of Nino Franck, Jean-Pierre Chartier, Raymond Borde, Etienne Chaumeton and others were paying to the United Sates by dignifying the land of unlimited opportunity with a tragic sense of life, because they recognised in B-movies, pulp fiction and low-rent angst the cultural mirror of philosophical Existentialism, cinematic *auteur*ism and high seriousness. I then argued in a similar vein, that the 'Expressionist' heritage in Hollywood could also be told as a story of such back-handed compliment-swapping, this time from Hollywood to Europe. But when we think of how

Hollywood movies from the 1930s, 1940s and 1950s have used European avant-garde movements from the 1910s and 1920s – German Expressionism, French Surrealism and Soviet Montage cinema – in order to represent situations of chaos and disorder, of pathology and madness, of Freudian dreams and homicidal manias in films as different as *Blues in the Night*, *San Francisco*, *Spellbound*, *Strangers on a Train* and *The Two Mrs Carrolls*, then the Americans, too, have never been quite without irony (and dare one say, *humour noir*) when dealing with Europe and showing their cultural deference. We are indeed back with *The Cabinet of Dr Caligari*: after all, as we saw, it presented Expressionism as the emanation of a sick mind.

Such, then, might be the 'real' history of the German origins of film noir. If in their deconstruction, the false histories have one advantage, it is that they let us glimpse so many different 'other' histories, like that of the B-feature, that of the emergence of the independents after the Paramount case, the valorisation of black-and-white after the introduction of colour, or the single irreducibly individual and unique fate of each and every German film maker, cameraman, cutter or sound technician who set out *Zu Neuen Ufern* ('to new shores') during those most turbulent years of the 1920s and 1930s. Yet one doubts that these histories will ever retain in quite the same way as does film noir's imaginary history, accompanied by, shadowed by, indeed overshadowed by its historical imaginary, which gives it such an aura and energy, such longevity and fascination, proving once more, how in the cinema little seems to separate a 'false' history from a history of the 'false', which in the case of German Cinema, is finally 'truer' than it probably knows.

Weimar cinema ... and after

Paradoxically, the constant metaphorical exchanges between German political history, European cinema history and the Hollywood film industry turn out to have been the necessary condition for giving 'Weimar cinema' its distinct film-historical space. Perhaps because all cinema trades in miscognitions, in projections of otherness, the different (imagined) looks of the other – whether imagined as benevolent, punishing or envious – have continued to affect the films made in Germany after 1945, and the image and idea West as well as East German film makers subsequently had of themselves.[58] The peculiarly complex relations extend not only to social and political history, but to the images circulating about this history, cast as these images are in horror and glamour, and attaching to themselves all manner of fantasies of power and pleasure, fascination and melancholy. Weimar cinema thus has remained ever since more than its industrial, stylistic or authorial histories, doubled by what I have here called its role as Germany's historical imaginary.

As a national cinema seen 'from inside' the Weimar intellectual establishment, the films of the 1920s were, in their majority, rejected as kitsch, that is, their 'performative' aspects received a predominantly negative valorisation. But

German national cinema looked at 'from the outside' was always recognised, judged and valorised along performative principles, i.e. as to how credible it put on a show as 'art' or quality entertainment. This is how UFA's rivals perceived the contest, not least because Hollywood itself set the precedent in mimicry and camouflage, 'stealing' talent, making remakes of successful films and generally 'impersonating' Europe when it suited its objectives.

In other words, running through Weimar cinema as an industrial practice are a number of divides which are only very inadequately described by the traditional distinctions of an 'art cinema' and a 'popular' or 'mainstream cinema'. What one finds instead are different gradations and versions of the same basic configuration of what I am calling 'impersoNation': a self-conscious self-reflexive one, where the films are, as it were, straight-faced imitations of romantic and gothic horrors, of medieval romance and national mythology. Conversely, the self-conscious operetta versions of those same interpersonal, social, sexual as well as national–historical traumas turn out to be proto-musicals in which history is the masked ball. In this sense, the cinema is always a kind of dance on the volcano, because it makes available the iconography of the nation or the fantasies of national history as counterfeit signs for a festival, a carnival.

The crucial arena of this historical imaginary are the subject effects and identifications associated with a national cinema, more particularly, how spectators 'appropriate' moving images and their representations, in order to deal with the various crises in which their life worlds are threatened, destroyed or reconstructed. The German cinema, in the 1920s, and possibly even more so in the 1930s and 1940s, provided social fantasies that stood in a particularly complex, inverted and 'disavowed' relationship to the lived situation of its audiences. This has long been assumed as applying only to Nazi cinema, apostrophied as a cinema of cynical lies and singular deception, of an abuse of the imagination for demagogic ends. But such a view is, ultimately, difficult to maintain for, in so far as it is true, it contains a truth that extends beyond Nazism, in both directions. It encompasses retroactively the Weimar cinema, and it prolongs Nazi cinema into post-war period. For how could it not, given that the aspects that I have highlighted are part of the processes of modernity and modernisation? In particular, I have argued that Weimar cinema is a function of a contested consumer culture and its 'commodity fetishism' and on the other hand, it fashions a national identity around the 'reification' of some of the stresses and strains evidenced by these processes.

The concept of a 'historical imaginary' therefore tried to name the way in which the perception of the German cinema's films, genres, stars and directors has been warped – but also valorised – by certain (a-)versions of Germany and the German character, reflecting and inflected by its political and social history, on which a twelve-year regime with its six-year reign of terror has exerted a quite overpowering pull – at once a vortex and an abyss from which the latter half of the twentieth century wanted at all costs to pull back from, but also a Medusa's mirror in which crucial aspects of this very same twentieth century are all too faithfully captured.

Can this Medusa's gaze on fascism as that which 'centres' the German cinema both retrospectively and prospectively on either side of the political divide that was 1933 ever be displaced? The present chapter has tried to refocus the extent to which the Weimar cinema has always been European, as well as centred also elsewhere, namely around Hollywood. This other centre (whether one calls it Weimar culture's fascination with 'Americanism', nascent consumer culture or the 'disenchanted' world of 'reification' and the commodity) which this study has tried to reinsert, may in the end be no less crucial, even if less fatal. It certainly suggests that the German cinema since 1945 has been the orbit of two epicentres – Nazism and Hollywood. It is a moot point, whether these two seemingly diametrically opposed poles held the cinema because of similar forces of 'modernity', or if they are of such uneven weight that to put them into a direct relation would be to travesty the histories they are part of.

What makes the German cinema perhaps unique are the peculiarly problematic and eventually tragic modes of intersubjectivity and subjectification that typified Weimar Germany, tied up with a particularly extreme and extremely dysfunctional relation between 'self' and 'other'. If one grants the cinema a prominent place in the manner in which a societal body or nation 'works on', but also 'performs' its modes of subjectification, then the new look at the cinema of 'Weimar and after' proposed in the preceding chapters may hopefully not only give a new understanding of the affective and discursive conditions of this particular national cinema, but also provide a perspective for how to understand contemporary modes of subjectification and their relation to the various imaginaries of identity and otherness that the sound and image media entice and solicit us with.

Ultimately, it seems to me, Weimar cinema invites reflection about how much 'history' there is in cinema and how much cinema there is in history. This is a task that current film studies is not particularly well equipped for. One can phrase it perhaps as follows – the lesson of the New film history in so many areas has been to de-idealise film history, by recalling its socio-economic base, by reminding one of the materialist conditions at once enabling and constraining the existence of films. In the case of the German cinema, this anti-idealist tendency has also had the effect of 'normalising' this cinema: to relieve the films, along with the idealist expectation of cinema giving us 'art', also of their 'demonic' and 'haunted' burden, mitigating the horrified stare at a cinema apparently so much in the grip of a symptomatology, so much fevering towards the politicial apocalypse, as it did appear to hindsight accounts, not only those by Kracauer and Eisner.[59] What this de-demonising and normalising makes possible for the first time is, precisely, to see other figurations appear, not necessarily only that of 'duplicity restored', which was the main theme of the preceding chapters, but also a dynamics of assimilation and exclusion marking the nation and its national imaginary, traversing also the culture of its commodities, once these have become the primary sites of subjectification and intersubjectivity.

Can this history of duplicity, in which so much of Weimar Cinema seems to be 'sublated' and suspended, tell us something about the cinema itself? As indicated above, the reversals and mirror relations that tie the German cinema to European history and the American film industry are necessarily the 'ground' against which Weimar cinema becomes visible at all. That such a ground is occupied by several imaginary histories, in turn nourished by projections and colonised by hindsight, only gives it an additional semblance of self-evidence. Even the melancholy fantasies of disappearance, decline, leave-taking and loss that have surrounded Weimar culture after 1945 have fed a peculiarly cinematic image of the epoch, as if the precious and perishable nature of the celluloid record, the losses sustained by the audio-visual heritage had fostered the impression of historical reality's slow fade to film. What, however, has also disappeared in the deconstruction of the tight alignment of German film history with Germany's political history is any illusion of a German film history sufficient unto itself and comprehensible within the chronological sequence of its names and titles, its -isms, movements, genres and periods. To the degree that moving images insinuate themselves as memories and promises, as parallel and alternative worlds into the lived lives of audiences, neither co-extensive nor entirely discrete, neither directly reflecting these lives nor mimetically doubling them, their historicity remains an open question. Hence my insistence, so often in the previous chapters, on non-synchronicity, retrospective rewriting and deferred action as crucial aspects of film history's temporality. It is not only Weimar cinema that will always have an 'after-life' that functions as its irrepressible supplement.

This after-life, therefore, calls itself for an after-word. I borrow it from the dedication in Theodor W. Adorno's *Minima Moralia*: 'Whoever wants to experience the truth about immediate, authentic life', he writes:

> has to seek out its estranged forms and shapes, tracing the objective powers that determine individual existence into its innermost recesses. If one tries to talk firsthand about spontaneous life, one behaves no differently than those novelists [...] who make their protagonists act [...] as if everything depended on their decisions. The Look at Life has become identical with the ideology, that cheats us of the knowledge that none is left.[60]

Although Adorno's grief could hardly have found comfort in any of the films here discussed or in the modern cinema as a space of authentic experience, there is a thought in his dedication that almost makes one take heart: 'If one day that semblance of life, which the world of consumption now still defends, however transparent its reasoning, has been vanquished altogether, then all that triumphs is the immorality of absolute production'. Among the many faces of the false in Weimar cinema, one might conclude, absolute production never quite triumphed, for the realm of transparent semblance was not only not vanquished – duplicity stood its ground as a modest, if persistent member of the resistance. Almost as if it had already anticipated the most famous sentence from this very *Minima Moralia*: 'there is no true life within the false', duplicity insists that since the existence of the cinema at least, there may be no true life *without* the false.

Notes

1 The present chapter was first published in a special issue of *Iris* 21 (Spring 1996) devoted to the 'Euopean precursors of film noir', edited by Janice Morgan and Dudley Andrew. A German translation appeared in Christian Cargnelli and Michael Omasta (ed.) *Schatten. Exil: Europäische Emigranten im Film Noir* (Vienna: PVS, 1997), whose editors kindly expanded my notes with additional research and quotations.

2 Barbara Steinbauer-Grötsch, *Die lange Nacht der Schatten. Film noir und Filmexil* (Berlin: Bertz 1997) gives an extensive list of iconographic echoes and repeated visual motifs.

3 See Jonathan Munby's essay on Robert Siodmak *Iris* 21 (Spring 1996): 74–88.

4 Thomas J. Saunders, *Hollywood in Berlin* (Berkeley: California University Press, 1994).

5 See the Introduction, Part I, Chapter 1, this volume and also my 'The New German cinema's historical imaginary' (1992a): 280–306.

6 What is meant by 'imaginary' in the Lacanian sense is the field of representations that a subject lives as his/her identity across self-images, alienated because structured by an (invisible) symbolic, and determined by the (inaccessible) presence of the significant other(s). The 'historical imaginary' transfers this dynamic of 'miscognition' to the notion of (a national, generic) identity, with a given history functioning as its symbolic, and the cinema as the mirroring field of representations. In the present example, it implies that the history of film noir derives its semblance of cogency from the mirror-confirmation (i.e. the imaginary relations) which its images and concepts entertain with the economic, linguistic and political (i.e. symbolic) factors structuring this history. The 'historical imaginary' of film noir thus has the function of simultaneously 'covering up' and 'preserving' the inconsistencies, multiple realities and incompatible entities named by German Expressionist style, political exile and the Hollywood film industry, constructing an effect of self-evidence by giving them a single name and a cause-and-effect 'history'.

7 For the German–French connections, see Heike Hurst and Heiner Gassen (eds) *Kameradschaft-Querelle* (Munich: CICIM, 1991) and Sybille M. Sturm (ed.) *Hallö? Berlin? Ici Paris!* (Munich: text + kritik, 1996).

8 See references in Part IV, Chapter 1, this volume, on 'Vienna–Berlin–Hollywood'. For German émigrés in Paris, see also Thomas Elsaesser and Ginette Vincendeau *Les cinéastes allemands en France* (Paris: Goethe Institute, 1983).

9 Among these discourses one could name three: one dignifying Hollywood B-movies with a high-culture cachet of romantic nihilism, a second giving the American cinema a literary pedigree by associating it with the authors of the *serie noire* (Dashiell Hammett, Raymond Chandler, Cornell Woolrich and David Goodis), as well as with Faulkner in America and André Gide in France. Third, there is the legacy of surrealism valorising the bizarre, violent and nihilistic as '*maudit*', '*insolite*' and '*sublime*' – terms that became the stock in trade of the critical vocabulary applied to films noir.

10 'The end of WW2 favoured in Paris the emergence of a noir sensibility […] expressing itself in many aspects that lay outside the cinema' (James Naremore, 'American film noir: the history of an idea', *Film Quarterly* 49/2 (Winter 1995–6).

11 'You have to ask yourself what impression people will get from life in the US when in twenty years' time you show them *The Postman Always Rings Twice* […] a people with

a hangover' (John Houseman, in *Vogue* (15 January 1947), quoted in Richard Maltby, 'The politics of the maladjusted text', in Ian Cameron (ed.) *The Movie Book of Film Noir* (London: Tayleur, 1992): 41.

12 Paul Schrader, 'Notes on film noir', *Film Comment* vol. 8, no. 1 (Spring 1972): 8–13. But see also the earlier essay by Paul Jensen, 'The return of Dr Çaligari – paranoia in Hollywood', *Film Comment* vol. 7, no. 4 (Winter 1971–2): 36–45.

13 Schrader 1972: 9–10.

14 Raymond Borde and Etienne Chaumeton refer to Frank Capra's *Arsenic and Old Lace* (1944) as *humour noir* (*Panorama du film noir américain*, 203).

15
> The vacuum of authority is a key moment of neo-noir. […] In *Pulp Fiction* Tarantino not so much quotes old films as he literalizes the previous roles of his actors, rewriting them, in order this time to reward or punish them for their earlier behaviour.
>
> B. Ruby Rich, 'Dumb lugs and femmes fatales', *Sight & Sound* (November 1995))

16 Lotte Eisner, *The Haunted Screen*, 1969: 17.

17 Thompson 1990.

18
> *The Cabinet of Dr Caligari* started in France a fundamental debate about the aesthetics of film which went well beyond the questions discussed in Germany in the 1920s. […] Basic principles of filmic creation and its effects are discussed by Louis Delluc, Emile Vuillermoz, Lionel Laundry and […] Ricciotto Canudo.
>
> (Jürgen Kasten, 'Boche Filme: Zur Rezeption deutscher Filme in Frankreich' in Sturm 1996)

19 Aumont 1989: 204–5.

20 On Lotte Eisner's influence, see also Bernard Eisenschitz, in Sturm 1996.

21 Nino Frank , 'Un nouveau genre "policier": l'aventure criminel', *L'écran français* 61 (28 August 1946): 8–9, 14. Calling the term an 'invention' shows the historical imaginary in *status nascendi*: the political condition of possibility, as it were, are the Franco-American trade negotiations of 1946 which in the area of film imports, once more opened the French market to American films. 'Film noir is a product of the Blum-Byrnes agreements, and to this extent […], it is also an American invasion', Marc Vernet, 'Film noir on the edge of doom', (quoted in Copjec 1993: 27).

22 First published in 1955 by *Les Editions de Minuit.*

23 'I dedicated the *Kaspar Hauser* film to Lotte Eisner', Werner Herzog interviewed by Kraft Wetzel, in W. Schütte and P.W. Jansen (eds) *Herzog-Kluge-Straub* (Munich: Hanser, 1978).

24 See, for instance, Jean Paul Sartre's enthusiastic reports from New York, reprinted in *Situations III* (Paris: Gallimard, 1949).

25 Marc Vernet, in Copjec 1993: 5.

26
> Speaking about film noir consists, from the beginning, in being installed in repetition, in taking up the unanalysed discourse of those predecessors, with pre-established definitions […] that are impossible to criticise. […] Film noir is, then, an affair of heirs disinclined to look too closely at their inheritance.
>
> (Vernet quoted in Copjec 1993: 2)

27 For such a definition of the classic film noir corpus, see Michael Walker, 'Film Noir: An Introduction', quoted in Cameron 1992: 8 (see note 11 above).

28 Even if one assumes (which one should not (see Part IV, Chapter 1)) that most of them came to the United States because of political reasons, the fact that many of them had to flee from racial persecution and Hitler's SS need not explain the

pessimistic, desperate tone of the films, except in a most superficial film-historical perspective, which psychologises the complex decision-making process of Hollywood picture making by focusing on an implausible degree of directorial self-expression.

29 Paul Kerr, reviewing Joan Copjec's *Shades of Noir*, details a long list of recent reprises, pastiches, parodies of film noir commonplaces and clichés. 'Murky waters', *Sight and Sound* 4/4 (April 1994).

30 See Kaplan 1978.

31 Hopper is quoted in the BBC documentary 'The Film Noir Story', 1994. Among the 'origins' of neo-noir, historians name *Point Blank* (1967), but also *Alphaville* (1965), and in the 1970s, *Chinatown*, *The Long Goodbye*, *Taxi Driver*, *Klute*; in the 1980s *Body Heat*, *Blade Runner* and *Fatal Attraction*, and in the 1990s *Pulp Fiction* and *LA Confidential*. See Ed Gallafent, 'Echo park: film noir in the seventies' and Leighton Grist, 'Moving targets and black widows', both in Cameron 1992 (see note 11, above). Also see Jerry C. Kutner, 'Beyond the golden age. Film noir since the 1950s', *Bright Lights* 12 (Spring 1994) and Paul Arthur, 'Los Angeles as scene of the crime', *Film Comment* 32/4 (July–August 1994).

32 At a point in (film-) history when television, the interactive media and other new technologies threaten to engulf that historic and aesthetic specificity which was the cinema, film noir seems to afford, thanks to its combined appeal to narcissism, nostalgia and negativity, a last look at the cinema itself, before it disappears, thus doubling the circle of mutual compliments alluded to earlier on, which united cinephile Europe with Hollywood, by adding film makers like Dennis Hopper saluting Hollywood in films by German cinephile directors (Wenders' *The American Friend*).

33 'Obviously, the concept [of film noir], developed post facto, has become all over the world part of collective memory'. As the dream image of past glamour it displaces history as much as it recalls it, usually in the service of cinephilia and commercialism' (J. Naremore, 'Film noir – the history of an idea', *Film Quarterly* 49/2 (1995).

34 See Debora Thomas, 'How Hollywood deals with the deviant male', in Cameron 1992: 59–70 (see note 11 above).

35 See B. Salt, 'The unknown Ince', *Sight and Sound* 57/4 (Autumn 1988): 271–2 and Jacobs 1991a: 250–8.

36 As to the question of 'influence', Marc Vernet has pointed out that in 1932, Warner Brothers made *Two Seconds*, a B-picture directed by Mervyn LeRoy and starring Edward G. Robinson in the role of the lone psychopath, pleading with his executioners in an uncanny reprise of the final scene of *M* (Vernet quoted in Copjec 1993: 28).

37 See, for instance, Maltby 1984.

38 Jacobs 1991b.

39 It was Mary Pickford who wanted to use Lubitsch's reputation for creating 'vamps' such as Pola Negri, in order to change her image from America's sweetheart to more adult roles.

40

> Along with *Abschied* (1930), *Stürme der Leidenschaft* (1932) and *Brennendes Geheimnis* (1933), it is *Mollenard* (1937) which is a key work of Siodmak's entire oeuvre, because like them, it announces several of the *noir* themes in the very distinctive hues that Siodmak gave them, opening up a window to his depth-psychological concerns. […] *Pièges* (1939), Siodmak's greatest success prior to the war […] has, as a Parisian film noir all the hallmarks of his American work: a rapid introduction, fast editing, sophisticated lighting effects, camera movements and gestures which only hint at the essentials.
>
> (Dumont 1981: 118)

41 For a sketch of such an account, see my 'European Cinema: Germany and Hollywood 1927–1934', in G. Muscio (ed.) *Before the Hays Code* (Venice: Marsilio, 1991).

42 The case of Lubitsch has already been mentioned. In the case of Murnau, it was the success of *The Last Laugh* that made him fit the agenda of Adolf Zukor and Fox. Lang, Siodmak, Bernhardt and Ophuls wanted to settle in France. G.W. Pabst wanted to go to Hollywood, but missed the boat. ... See also Part IV, Chapter 1, this volume, on émigrés.

43 E.A. Dupont, director of the Gaumont–British *Piccadilly* (1927) came to Berlin in 1929 to alert his colleagues to the challenge. His front-page article 'England follows America' ends with the appeal: 'you must create the international sound picture in Berlin, otherwise you will be excluded from the world market' *Filmkurier* (9 March 1929): 1.

44

> The Hollywood Actor's Gild has taken a decision against Reinhold Schünzel and accused him of what this column has been saying for several months: as a Jew tolerated by the Nazis, he allowed them to earn foreign currency [with his films] and abided by their anti-Jewish laws. I hope the protest succeeds [and gets Schünzel banned].
>
> (Paul E. Marcus, *Privat-Berichte* 15 (December) 1937, in Helmut Asper, 'Reinhold Schünzel im Exil', in Schöning 1989)

45 Billy Wilder, interviewed by Heinz-Gerd Rasner and Reinhard Wulf, in Neil Sinyard and Adrian Turner, *Billy Wilder* (London: British Film Institute, 1980).

46 See Part IV, Chapter 1, this volume, on émigrés.

47 Ruritania became the mythical place of high, typically comic-opera romance, made famous by Anthony Hope's novel and subsequent film, *The Prisoner of Zenda.*

48 Ophuls 1959: 177.

49 Walter Slezak, *Wann geht der nächste Schwan* (Munich, 1964).

50

> In Lubitsch's *Ninotschka* I played a Russian, in *So Ends our Night* a Pole, in Fritz Lang's *Hangmen also Die* a German, in *Halfway to Shanghai* a Greek and in *Voice in the Wind* an Italian. That's how international I became in Hollywood.
>
> (Alexander Granach, 'Wer bin ich? Ein kleines Selbstportrait' quoted in A. Klein and R. Kruk (eds) *Alexander Granach. Fast Verwehte Spuren*, Munich, 1994)

51

> When Robert arrived in Hollywood at the outbreak of the war in 1939 he was completely lost in this cruel town that only recognises people with a current hit to their name. I [...] practically forced my [B-picture] producer Jack Gross to entrust Robert with the direction of my screenplay *Son of Dracula* (1943).
>
> (Curt Siodmak, *Unter Wolfsmenschen* vol. 1: Europe (Bonn: Weidle Verlag, 1995)

52 Hans C. Blumenberg (ed.) *Robert Siodmak. Zwischen Berlin und Hollywood* (Munich: Hanser, 1980).

53 However, a similar idea 'inspired the independent producer Harry Popkin' to make *D.O.A.* (1950), a very effective noir thriller, directed by Rudolph Maté. See George Turner, 'I want to report a murder', *American Cinematographer* 69/8 (August 1988): 35.

54 See a detailed description in Reid and Walker 1992: 81–2.

55 As indicated above, Max Ophuls himself seems perfectly aware of the workings of the historical imaginary when he argued that *Liliom* (with Charles Boyer, directed in Paris by Fritz Lang) should have been directed by him, while he would gladly have given *On a Volé un Homme* to Fritz Lang (Ophuls 1959: 177).

56 See Reid and Walker 1992: 73–4.

57 Just as Eugen Schüfftan became Eugène Shuftan, the screenwriter Ernst Neubach took the pseudonym Ernest Neuville. For the story of the serial killer, whose name was Eugen Weidmann, see Dumont 1981: 123.

58 For discussion of some of these post-war self-representations, see my 'The New German Cinema's historical imaginary' in C. Wickam and B. Murray (eds) *Framing the Past: The Historiography of German Cinema and Television* (Carbondale: Southern Illinois University Press, 1992): 280–307; 'American friends: Hollywood in New German Cinema', in Geoffrey Nowell-Smith and Steve Ricci (eds) *Hollywood and Europe* (London: BFI Publishing, 1998): 142–55; and (with Michael Wedel), 'Defining DEFA's historical imaginary: the films of Konrad Wolf' (*New German Critique*, 2000).

59 See, for instance S.S. Prawer, *Caligari's Children: The Film as Tale of Terror* (Oxford: Oxford University Press, 1980) or Paul Coates, *The Gorgon's Gaze: German Cinema, Expressionism, and the Image of Horror* (Cambridge: Cambridge University Press, 1991).

60 Theodor W. Adorno, *Minima Moralia* (Frankfurt: Suhrkamp, 1970): 7.

BIBLIOGRAPHY

Adorno, T.W. ([1947] 1973) 'The culture industry'. In *Dialectic of Enlightenment*. London: Verso.

—— (1951) *Minima Moralia*. Frankfurt: Suhrkamp.

—— (1974) *Versuch über Wagner*. Frankfurt: Suhrkamp.

Albrecht, G. (1969) *Nationalsozialistische Filmpolitik*. Stuttgart: Ferdinand Enke.

Altman, R. (1997) 'The silence of the silents'. In *Musical Quarterly*, vol. 80, no. 4.

Amengual, B. (1966) *George Wilhelm Pabst*. Paris: Seghers.

Andrew, D. (1995) *Mists of Regret*. Princeton: Princeton University Press.

Angst-Nowik, D. and Sloan, J. (eds) (1987) *One-Way-Ticket to Hollywood. Film Artists of Austrian and German Origin in Los Angeles. Emigration: 1884–1945*. Los Angeles: Max Kade Institute.

Anon. (1979) 'Aspects of Expressionism (3) It Lives Again'. *Monthly Film Bulletin* (August).

Arnheim, R. (1979) *Kritiken und Aufsätze zum Film*. Frankfurt/M: Fischer.

Asendorf, C. (1997) *Super Constellation – Flugzeug und Raumrevolution*. Vienna: Springer.

Asper, H. (ed.) (1991) *Wenn wir von gestern reden*. Berlin: Edition Sigma.

Atwell, L. (1977) *G.W. Pabst*. Boston: Twayne.

Aumont, J. (1989) *L'Oeuil Interminable*. Paris: Seguier.

Bächlin, P. (1972 [1947]) *Der Film als Ware*. Königstein/Ts: Athenäum (Originally 'Der Film als Ware'. Doctoral dissertation, University of Basel, 1947).

Bachmann, G. (1955) 'Leo Lanja'. In *Cinemages 3: Six Talks on G.W. Pabst*. New York.

Balasz, B. (1924) *Der sichtbare Mensch*. Wien. Reprinted in B. Balasz, *Schriften*, vol. 1. Berlin: Henschelverlag 1982: 43–143.

Bandmann, C. and Hembus, J. (1980) *Klassiker des Deutschen Tonfilms 1930–1960*. Munich: Goldmann.

Barlow, J.D. (1982) *German Expressionist Film*. Boston: Twayne.

Barrington-Moore, J. (1991) *On the Origins of Democracy and Dictatorship*. Harmondsworth: Penguin.

Barsacq, L. (1976) *Caligari's Cabinet and other Grand Illusions*. Boston: New York Graphic Society.

Bartetzko, D. (1985) *Illusionen in Stein. Stimmungsarchitektur im deutschen Faschismus*. Reinbek: Rowohlt.

Barthes, R. (1975) *S/Z*. Trans. Richard Howard. London: Jonathan Cape.

Baudrillard, J. (1978) 'La mode retro'. In *Kool Killer oder der Aufstand der Zeichen*. Berlin: Merve.

Baudry, J-L. (1970) 'Le cinéma – l'effets produit par l'appareil de base.' In *Cinethique* 7–8.

—— (1975) 'Le dispositif – approches metapsychologiques de l'impression de réalité.' In *Communications* 23.

Baxter, J. (1976) *The Hollywood Exiles*. New York: Taplinger Publishing.

Behne, A. (1929) 'Kunstausstellung Berlin' *Das Neue Berlin* 9.

Belach, H. (ed.) (1979) *Wir tanzen um die Welt. Deutsche Revuefilme 1933–1945*. Munich/Vienna: Hanser.

Belach, H. *et al.* (eds) (1983) *Exil. Sechs Schauspieler aus Deutschland*. Berlin: Stiftung Deutsche Kinemathek.

Belach, H. and Jacobsen, W. (eds) (1992) *Richard Oswald*. Munich: edition text + kritik.

Bellour, R. (1979) 'Alternation, segmentation, hypnosis'. *Camera Obscura* 3–4: 71–103.

—— (1981) 'On Fritz Lang'. In S. Jenkins (ed.) *Fritz Lang: The Image and the Look*. London: BFI.

Benjamin, W. (1933) 'Rückblick auf Stefan George'. *Gesammelte Schriften*, vol. III. Frankfurt: Suhrkamp.

—— (1973a) 'The author as producer'. In *Understanding Brecht*. London: New Left Books.

—— (1973b) 'On some motifs in Baudelaire'. In *Paris, Capital of the XIX Century*. London: New Left Books.

—— (1979) 'A short history of photography'. In *One Way Street and Other Writings*. London: New Left Books.

—— (1983) *Das Passagenwerk*. Frankfurt: Suhrkamp.

Berger, J. *et al.* (eds) (1977) *Wem gehört die Welt*. Berlin: Neue Gesellschaft für Bildende Kunst.

Bergstrom, J. (1982) 'Violence and enunciation'. *Camera Obscura* 8–10 (Fall).

—— (1985) 'Sexuality at a loss: The films of F.W. Murnau', *Poetics Today* vol. 6, nos 1–2: 185–203.

Beylie, C. (1976) 'Quelques notes sur l'opéra de quat'sous'. *L'Avant-Scène Cinéma* 177 (December).

Bock, H.M. (ed.) (1982) *Paul Leni*. Frankfurt: Deutsches Filmmuseum.

—— (ed.) (1984ff.) *CineGraph. Lexikon zum deutschsprachigen Film*. Munich: text + kritik.

—— (1990) 'Documenting a life and a career'. In R. Rentschler (ed.) *The Films of G.W. Pabst*. New Brunswick: Rutgers University Press, 217–36.

Bock, H.M. and Töteberg, M. (eds) (1992) *Das Ufa Buch*. Frankfurt: Zweitausendeins.

Bohrer, K.H. (1978) *Die Aesthetik des Schreckens*. Frankfurt: Suhrkamp.

Bonitzer, P. (1985) *Décadrages; cinéma et peinture*. Paris: Edition de l'Etoile.

Bordwell, D. (1979) 'Our dream cinema: Western historiography, and the Japanese film'. *Film Reader* 4.

—— (1985) *Narration in the Fiction Film*. Madison: Wisconsin University Press.

Bordwell, D. and Thompson, K. (1992) *Film Art*. New York: McGraw-Hill.

Borwell, D., Staiger, J. and Thompson , K. (1988) *The Classical Hollywood Cinema*, London: Routledge.

Bottomore, S. (ed.) (1995) *I Want to See this Annie Mattygraph*. Gemona: La Cineteca del Friuli.

Bouvier, M. and Leutrat, J-L. (1981) *Nosferatu*. Paris: Cahiers du Cinéma/Seuil.

Brandlmeier, T. (1984) 'Arnold Fanck'. In H.M. Bock (ed.) *CineGraph. Lexikon zum deutschsprachigen Film*. Munich: edition text + kritik.

Brecht, B. (1978) *Das Dreigroschenbuch*, vol. I. Frankfurt: Suhrkamp.

Brenez, N. (1998) *L'invention figurative au cinéma*. Brussels: De Boek.

Brennicke, I. and Hembus, J. (eds) (1978) *Klassiker des deutschen Stummfilms 1910–1930*. Munich: Goldmann.

Bretschneider, J. (ed.) (1992) *Ewald André Dupont: Autor und Regisseur.* Munich: edition text + kritik.

Brooks, L. (1979) 'Why I will never write my memoirs'. *Film Culture* 69: 219–28.

—— (1982) *Lulu in Hollywood.* New York: Praeger.

Brownlow, K. (1968) *The Parade's Gone By.* London: Abacus.

Buache, F. (1984) *Le cinéma allemand 1918–1933.* Renens: 5 Continents.

Budd, M. (1990) 'Retrospective narration in *Dr Caligari*'. In M. Budd (ed.) *The Cabinet of Dr Caligari.* New Brunswick: Rutgers University Press.

Burch, N. (1979) *To the Distant Observer. Form and Meaning in the Japanese Cinema.* London: Scolar Press.

—— (1981) 'Notes on Fritz Lang's first Mabuse'. *Cine-tracts* vol. 4, no. 1 (Spring).

Burch, N. and Dana, J. (1974) 'Propositions'. In *Afterimage* 5 (Spring).

Card, J. (1958) 'The "intense isolation" of Louise Brooks'. *Sight and Sound* vol. 27, no. 5 (Summer).

Cargnelli, C. and Omasta, M. (1993) *Aufbruch ins Ungewisse.* Vienna: Wespennest.

—— (eds) (1997) *Schatten Exil.* Vienna: PVS.

Carroll, N. (1978) 'The cabinet of Dr Caligari'. *Millenium Film Journal* 2 (Spring–Summer).

Cavell, S. (1996) *Contesting Tears.* Chicago: University of Chicago Press.

Cherchi Usai, P. and Codelli, L. (1990) *Prima di Caligari: Cinema tedesco, 1895–1920/Before Caligari. German Cinema 1895–1920.* Pordenone: Edizioni Biblioteca dell'Immagine.

Ciment, M., Fofi, G., Seguin, L. and Tailleur, R. (1968) 'Fritz Lang à Venise'. *Positif,* no. 94 (April).

Coates, P. (1991) *The Gorgon's Gaze. German Cinema, Expressionism, and the Image of Horror.* Cambridge: Cambridge University Press.

Collier, J.L. (1988) *From Wagner to Murnau.* Ann Arbor: UMI Research Press.

Cook, D. (1981) *A History of Narrative Film.* New York: Norton.

Copjec, J. (ed.) (1993) *Shades of Noir.* London: Verso.

Courtade, F. (1984) *Cinema expressioniste.* Paris: Veyrier.

Courtade, F. and Cadars, P. (1972) *Histoire du Cinéma Nazi.* Paris: Eric Losfeld.

Crary, J. (1994) *Techniques of the Observer.* Cambridge, Mass: MIT Press.

Croce, A. (1960) 'The Threepenny Opera'. *Film Quarterly* vol. 6 no. 1 (Fall).

Dalle Vacche, A. (1996) *Cinema and Painting.* Austin: Texas University Press.

Debord, G. (1972) *La société du spectacle.* Paris: Denoel.

Diederichs, H.H. (1986) *Anfänge deutscher Filmkritik.* Stuttgart: R. Fischer, U. Wiedleroither.

Doane, M.A. (1992) *Femmes Fatales. Feminism, Film Theory, Psychoanalysis.* New York: Routledge.

Döblin, A. ([1908] 1978) 'Das Theater der kleinen Leute'. In A. Kaes (ed.) *Kino-Debatte.* Tübingen: Niemeyer.

Drewniak, B. (1987) *Der deutsche Film 1938–1945. Ein Gesamtüberblick.* Düsseldorf: Droste.

Dumont, H. (1981) *Robert Siodmak, le Maitre du film noir.* Lausanne: Edition L'homme.

Eibel, A. (1964) (ed.) *Fritz Lang.* Paris: Présence du cinéma.

Eisner, L. (1947) 'Notes sur le style de Fritz Lang'. In *La Revue de cinéma* 5 (February).

—— (1964) *Murnau.* Paris: Ramsay.

—— (1969) *The Haunted Screen.* London: Thames & Hudson.

—— (1973) *Murnau.* London: Secker & Warburg.

—— (1976) *Fritz Lang.* London: Secker & Warburg.

—— (1984) *Ich hatte einst ein schön Vaterland.* Heidelberg: Wunderhorn.

Elsaesser, T. (1982) 'Social mobility and the fantastic'. *Wide Angle* vol. 5, no. 2: 14–25.

—— (1983) 'Lulu and the Meter Man'. *Screen* vol. 24, nos 4–5 (June/July): 4–36.

—— (1984a) 'Film history and visual pleasure: Weimar cinema'. In P. Mellencamp and P. Rosen (eds) *Cinema Histories, Cinema Practices.* Frederick, MD: UPA: 47–84.

—— (1984b) 'Fritz Lang's *Metropolis*: innocence restored'. *Monthly Film Bulletin* (December): 363–6.

—— (1985) 'Weimar cinema and subject-construction'. Paper at SCS Conference, New York.

—— (1986) 'Film history as social history: the story of Louis Pasteur'. In *Wide Angle* vol. 8, no. 2: 15–31.

—— (1987a) 'Cinema, the irresponsible signifier, or the gamble with history'. *New German Critique* 40 (Winter): 65–89.

—— (1987b) 'Dada/Cinema?' In R. Kuenzli (ed.) *Dada and Surrealist Film.* New York: Willis, Locker & Owens: 13–27.

—— (1988–9) 'Secret affinities: F.W. Murnau'. *Sight and Sound* (Winter).

—— (ed.) (1990) *Early Cinema: Space, Frame, Narrative.* London: BFI Publishing.

—— (1991) 'European Cinema: Germany and Hollywood 1927–1934'. In G. Muscio (ed.) *Before the Hays Code.* Venice: Marsilio: 201–12.

—— (1992a) 'The new German cinema's historical imaginary'. In B. Murray and C. Wickham (eds) *Framing the Past.* Carbondale: Southern Illinois University Press: 208–307.

—— (1992b) 'Kunst und Krise. Die Ufa in den 20er Jahren'. In H.M. Bock and M. Töteberg (eds) *Das Ufa-Buch. Kunst und Krisen, Stars und Regisseure, Wirtschaft und Politik.* Frankfurt/M: Zweitausendeins: 96–106.

—— (1994) 'Leni Riefenstahl. The body beautiful, art cinema and fascist aesthetics'. In P. Cook and P. Dodd (eds) *Women and Film. A Sight and Sound Reader.* London: Scarlet Press: 186–97.

—— (1996a) 'A German ancestry to film noir?' In *Iris* 21 (Spring): 129–44.

—— (ed.) (1996b) *A Second Life: German Cinema's First Decades.* Amsterdam: Amsterdam University Press.

—— (1997) 'Berlin–Hollywood'. *Sight and Sound* (November).

—— (2000) 'Aviator, Greetings to the Sun': An interview with Walter Reisch'. *Pix* 3.

Esser, M. (ed.) (1994) *Gleissende Schatten.* Berlin: Henschel.

Falkenberg, P. (1978) 'Oedipal structures in French and German Cinema'. Unpublished paper, University of Iowa.

Farin, M. and Scholdt, G. (1994) *Dr Mabuse Medium des Bösen.* Hamburg: Rogner und Bernhardt.

Feldmann, G.D. (1985) *Die Nachwirkungen der Inflation auf die deutsche Geschichte, 1924–1933.* Munich: Oldenbourg.

Foucault, M. (1975) *The Birth of the Clinic: an Archaeology of Medical Perception.* New York: Vintage Books.

Freyermuth, G.S. (1990) *Reise in die Verlorengegangenheit.* Hamburg: Rasch und Röhring.

Gabler, N. (1989) *An Empire of their Own: How the Jews Invented Hollywood.* New York: Doubleday.

Galassi, F. (1975) 'The lumpen drama of Frank Wedekind'. *Praxis* (Spring).

Gandert, G. (ed.) (1993) *Der Film der Weimarer Republik.* Ein Handbuch der zeitgenssischen Kritik, 1929. Berlin: de Gruyter.

Gay, P. (1992) *Weimar Culture.* London: Penguin (1968, New York).

Gehler, F. and Kasten, U. (1990a) *Fritz Lang: Die Stimme von Metropolis.* Berlin: Henschel.

—— (1990) *Friedrich Wilhelm Murnau.* Berlin: Henschel.

Gersch, W. (1975) *Film bei Brecht.* Berlin/GDR: Henschel.

Ghezzi, E. *et al.* (eds) (1981) *Vienna–Berlin–Hollywood.* Venice: Berlinale.

Giese, F. (1925) *Girl-Kultur.* Munich: Delphin.

Goergen, J (ed.) (1989) *Walter Ruttmann. Eine Dokumentation.* Berlin: Freunde der Deutschen Kinemathek, 1989.

Gomery, D. and Allen, R. C. (1985) *Film History.* New York: Knopf.

Göttler, F. and Grafe, F. (eds) (1990) *Friedrich Wilhelm Murnau.* Munich/Vienna: Carl Hanser.

Grafe, F. (1976) 'Kein Monument'. In *Fritz Lang.* Munich: Hanser.

Greve, L., Pehle, M. and Westhoff, H. (1976) *Hätte ich das Kino! Die Schriftsteller und der Stummfilm.* Munich: Kösel.

Grossmann, S. (1926) 'Erich Pommers Sturz'. *Das Tagebuch* 5 (30 January).

Gunning, T. (1991) 'Weaving a narrative'. In T. Elsaesser (ed.) *Early Cinema: Space Frame Narrative.* London: BFI Publishing.

—— (1994) *D.W. Griffith and the Origins of American Narrative Film.* Urbana: University of Illinois Press.

Güttinger, F. (ed.) (1984) *Kein Tag ohne Kino: Schriftsteller über den Stummfilm.* Frankfurt/M: Deutsches Filmmuseum.

Hake, S. (1990) 'Architectural histories of *The Nibelungen*'. *Wide Angle*, vol. 12, no. 3 (July).

—— (1992) *Passions and Deceptions: The Early Films of Ernst Lubitsch.* Princeton: Princeton UP.

—— (1994) *The Cinema's Third Machine.* Lincoln: University of Nebraska Press.

Hanisch, M. (1991) *Auf den Spuren der Filmgeschichte. Berliner Schauplätze.* Berlin: Henschel.

Hansen, M. (1993) *Babel and Babylon.* Cambridge, Mass: Harvard University Press.

Harbeck, H. (1929) 'Kino, Kino über alles'. In H. Gunther (ed.) *Hier schreibt Berlin.* Berlin: Internationale Bibliothek.

Hardt, U. (1996) *From Caligari to California: Eric Pommer's Life in the international film wars.* Providence: Berghahn Books.

Hastie, A. (1997) 'Louise Brooks, star witness'. *Cinema Journal* vol. 36, no. 3.

Heath, S. and de Lauretis, T. (1980) *The Cinematic Apparatus.* London: Macmillan.

Heilbut, A. (1983) *Exiled in Paradise.* New York: Viking Press.

Heller, H.B. (1985) *Literarische Intelligenz und Film.* Tübingen: Niemeyer.

Henry, M. (1971) *Le cinéma expressioniste allemand.* Fribourg: Edition du Signe.

Herf, J. (1984) *Reactionary Modernism. Technology, Culture and Politics in Weimar and the Third Reich.* Cambridge: Cambridge University Press.

Herlth, R. (1976) 'Dreharbeit mit Murnau'. In L. Eisner (ed.) *Murnau.* London: Secker & Warburg.

Herzogenrath, W. (ed.) (1977) *Film als Film.* Catalogue Kölnischer Kunstverein.

Higson, A. (1996) 'Film Europe'. In S. Sturm (ed.) *Hallo? Berlin? Ici Paris!* Munich: text + kritik.

Hilchenbach, M. (1982) *Kino im Exil. Die Emigration deutscher Filmkünstler 1933–1945.* Munich: Saur.

Horak, J.-C. (1984a) *Fluchtpunkt Hollywood.* Münster: MAkS.
—— (1984b) *Anti-Nazifilme deutscher Emigranten.* Münster: MAkS.
—— (1992) 'Rin Tin Tin in Berlin'. In U. Jung and W. Schatzberg (eds) *Filmkultur zur Zeit der Weimarer Republik.* Munich/New York: Saur.
Huaco, G. (1965) *The Sociology of Film Art.* New York: Basic Books.
Hull, D.S. (1969) *Film in the Third Reich.* Berkeley/Los Angeles: University of California Press.
Hunt L. (1990) 'The Student of Prague'. In T. Elsaesser (ed.) *Early Cinema: Space Frame Narrative* London: BFI Publishing.
Hurst, H. and Gassen, H. (eds) (1991) *Kameradschaft/Querelle. Kino zwischen Deutschland und Frankreich.* Munich: Institut Français-CICIM.
Huyssen, A. (1986) 'The vamp and the machine: Fritz Lang's *Metropolis*'. In *After the Great Divide: Modernism, Mass Culture and Postmodernism.* London: Routledge.
Jacobs, L. (1991a) 'Lasky lighting'. In P. Cherchi Usai and L. Codelli (eds) *The DeMille Legacy.* Pordenone: Edizione Biblioteca dell'Imagine.
—— (1991b) *The Wages of Sin: Censorship and the Fallen Woman Film, 1928–1942.* Madison: University of Wisconsin Press.
Jacobsen, W. (1989) *Erich Pommer.* Berlin: Argon.
—— (ed.) (1992) *Babelsberg: Ein Filmstudio 1912–1992.* Berlin: Argon.
Jacobsen, W., Kaes, A. and Prinzler, H.H. (eds) (1993) *Geschichte des deutschen Films.* Stuttgart/Weimar: Metzler.
Jameson, F. (1974) *Marxism and Form.* Princeton: Princeton University Press.
Jarvie, I. (1970) *Toward a Sociology of the Cinema.* London: Routledge.
Jay, M. (1985) 'The extraterritorial life of Siegfried Kracauer'. In *Permanent Exiles. Essays on the Intellectual Migration from Germany to America.* New York: Columbia University Press.
—— (1993) *Downcast Eyes.* Berkeley: California University Press.
Jenkins, S. (1981) *Fritz Lang. The Image and the Look.* London: BFI Publishing.
Jensen, P. (1969) *The Cinema of Fritz Lang.* New York: Barnes.
—— (1971–2) 'The return of Dr Caligari – paranoia in Hollywood'. *Film Comment* vol. 7, no. 4 (Winter).
Jessner, L. (1979) *Schriften.* In H. Fetting (ed.) Berlin: Henschel.
Jossé, H. (1984) *Die Entstehung des Tonfilms.* Freiburg/Munich: Alber.
Jung, U. (ed.) (1993) *Der deutsche Film: Aspekte seiner Geschichte von den Anfängen bis zur Gegenwart.* Trier: Wissenschaftlicher Verlag.
Jung, U. and Schatzberg, W. (eds) (1992) *Filmkultur zur Zeit der Weimarer Republik.* Munich/London/New York: K.G. Saur.
—— (1996) *Robert Wiene, der Caligari–Regisseur.* Berlin: Henschel.
Jünger, E. (1934) 'Über den Schmerz'. In *Blätter und Steine.* Hamburg: Hanseatische Verlagsanstalt AG.
Kaes, A. (1978) *Kino-Debatte. Texte zum Verhältnis von Literatur und Film 1909–1929.* Tübingen: Niemeyer.
—— (1983) 'The debate about cinema: Charting a controversy (1909–1929)'. In *New German Critique* 40 (Winter): 7–34.
Kaes, A., Jay, M. and Dimendberg, E. (eds) (1994) *The Weimar Republic Sourcebook.* Berkeley: California University Press.
Kalbus, O. (1935) *Vom Werden deutscher Filmkunst, Teil I- Der Stummfilm, Teil II- Der Tonfilm.* Altona-Bahrenfeld: Cigaretten-Bilderdienst.
Kaplan, E.A. (1978) *Women in Film Noir.* London: British Film Institute.

—— (1981) *Fritz Lang, A Guide to References and Resources*. Boston: G.K. Hall.

Kappelhoff, H. (1994) *Der möblierte Mensch: Georg Wilhelm Pabst und die Utopie der Sachlichkeit*. Berlin: Vorwerk 8.

Kasten, J. (1990) *Der expressionistische Film*. Münster: MAkS.

—— (1994) *Carl Mayer: Filmpoet. Ein Drehbuchautor schreibt Filmgeschichte*. Berlin: Vistas.

Kaul, W. (ed.) (1970) *Caligari und der Caligarismus*. Berlin: Stifting Deutsche Kinemathek.

Koebner, T. (1984) *Exilforschung Band 2*. Munich: edition text + kritik.

Kohner, F. (1977) *The Magician of Sunset Boulevard*. Palos Verdes, CA: Morgan Press.

Korte, H. (ed.) (1978) *Film und Realität in der Weimarer Republik*. Munich: Hanser.

Kracauer, S. (1930) *Die Angestellten. Aus dem Neuesten Deutschland*. Frankfurt: Frankfurter Sozietäts-Druckerei.

—— (1947) *From Caligari to Hitler*. Princeton: Princeton University Press.

—— (1960) *Theory of Film. The Redemption of Physical Reality*. New York: Columbia University Press.

—— (1976) *Jacques Offenbach und das Paris seiner Zeit*. Frankfurt/M: Suhrkamp.

—— (1978) *Von Caligari zu Hitler*. Franfurt: Suhrkamp.

—— (1994) *History – The Last Things before the Last*. Princeton: Wiener.

—— ([1969] 1995) *The Mass Ornament*. Boston: Harvard University Press.

Kraszna-Krausz, A. (1929) 'G.W. Pabst's Lulu', *Close Up* (April).

—— (1931) 'G.W. Pabst before the microphone of German broadcasting,' *Close Up* (May).

Kreimeier, K. (1987) 'Fritz Lang 'Der Schlafwandler'''. In U. Berg-Ganschow and W. Jacobsen (eds) *Film ... Stadt ... Kino ... Berlin* ... Berlin: Argon.

—— (ed.) (1988) *Friedrich Wilhelm Murnau 1888–1988*. Bielefeld: Bielefelder Verlagsanstalt.

—— (1992) *Die Ufa Story*. Munich: Hanser.

—— (1998) 'Trennungen'. In W. Jacobsen (ed.) *Georg Wilhelm Pabst*. Berlin: Argon.

Kristeva, J. (1980) *Desire in Language*. Oxford: Blackwell.

Kurtz, R. (1926) *Expressionismus und Film*. Berlin: Lichtbildbühne. repr. Zurich: Rohr (1965).

Kutscher, A. (1911/1964) *Wedekind Leben und Werk*. Munich: Paul List.

Lang, F. (1924) 'Kitsch – Sensation – Kultur Und film'. In E. Beyfuss and A. Kossowsky (eds) *Das Kulturfilmbuch*. Berlin: Chryselius.

—— (1947) 'The freedom of the screen'. In *Theater Arts* 3 (December).

—— ([1953] 1964) 'A propos du Docteur Mabuse'. In A. Eibel (ed.) *Fritz Lang*. Paris: Présence du cinéma.

—— (1970) 'Ein Brief von Fritz Lang'. In Kaul, W. (ed.) *Caligari und der Caligarismus*. Berlin: Stifting Deutsche Kinemathek.

—— (1971) 'Interview mit Fritz Lang'. In *Frankfurter Rundschau* (15 May).

—— (1975) 'Fritz Lang remembers'. *Focus on Film* 20 (Spring).

Laqueur, W. (1980) *Weimar – A Cultural History*. New York: Putnam (1974).

Ledig, E. (ed.) (1988) *Der Stummfilm: Konstruktion und Rekonstruktion*. Munich: Schaudig.

Loewy, R. (ed.) (1987) *Von Babelsberg nach Hollywood*. Frankfurt/M: Deutsches Filmmuseum.

Loiperdinger, M. (1994) 'Die Geschichte vom *Stahltier*: Willy Zielke und die Reichsbahn'. *Filmwärts* 30 (June).

Lowry, S. (1991) *Pathos und Politik. Ideologie in Spielfilmen des Nationalsozialismus*. Tübingen: Niemeyer.

Lukacs, G. ([1913] 1978) 'Gedanken zu einer Aesthetik des Kinos'. In A. Kaes (ed.) *Kino-Debatte. Texte zum Verhältnis von Literatur und Film 1909–1929*. Tübingen: Niemeyer.

—— ([1913] 1981) 'Thoughts on an aesthetic for the cinema'. In *Framework* 14.

Lucas, G. (1997) *The Hitler of History*. New York: Knopf.

Lyon, J.K. (1980) *Bertolt Brecht in America*. Princeton: Princeton University Press.

Maltby, R. (1984) 'Film noir: the politics of the maladjusted text'. In *Journal of American Studies* 18.

Manvell, R. (1973) *Masterworks of the German Cinema*. London: Lorrimer.

Manvell, R. and Fraenkel, H. (1971) *The German Cinema*. London: J.M. Dent & Sons.

McGilligan, P. (1997) *Fritz Lang: The Nature of the Beast*. New York: St Martin's Press.

McPherson, J. (1927) 'Die Liebe der Jeanne Ney'. In *Close Up* (December).

Mellor, D. (ed.) (1978) *Germany – The New Photography 1927–1933*. London: Arts Council.

Mierendorff, M. (1993) *William Dieterle: Der Plutarch von Hollywood*. Berlin: Henschel.

Monaco, P. (1976) *Ribbons of Time: Cinema and Society. France and Germany during the Twenties*. New York: Elsevier.

Mulvey, L. (1975) 'Visual pleasure and narrative cinema'. In *Screen* vol. 16, no. 3 (Autumn).

Murray, B. A. and Wickham, C. (eds) (1992) *Framing the Past: The Historiography of German Cinema and Television*. Carbondale/Edwardsville: Southern Illinois University Press.

Musser, C. (1990) *The Emergence of Cinema*. Cambridge, Mass: Harvard University Press.

Naficy, H. (1998) *Home, Exile, Homeland*. London: Routledge.

Nowell-Smith, G. (1997) *The Oxford History of World Cinema*. Oxford: Oxford University Press.

Oesterheld, E. (1978) 'Wie die deutschen Dramatiker Barbaren wurden'. In A. Kaes (ed.) *Kino-Debatte. Texte zum Verhältnis von Literatur und Film 1909–1929*. Tübingen: Niemeyer.

Ophuls, M. (1959) *Spiel im Dasein*. Frankfurt: S. Fischer.

Ott, F.W. (1979) *The Films of Fritz Lang*. Secaucus, N.J.: Citadel Press.

—— (1986) *The Great German Films: From Before World War I to the Present*. Secaucus: Citadel.

Pabst, R. (ed.) (1926) *Das deutsche Lichtsspieltheater in Vergangenheit, Gegenwart und Zukunft*. Berlin: Prisma.

Païni, D. (1994) '*L'animal d'acier* et la nouvelle vision'. In *Cinémathèque* 5.

Palmier, J.M. (1988) *Weimar en Exil* (2 vols). Paris: L'Harmattan.

Panofsky, E. (1992) 'Style and medium in the motion pictures'. In G. Mast and M. Cohen (eds) *Film Theory and Criticism*. New York: Oxford University Press.

Paris, B. (1989) *Louise Brooks*. New York: Alfred A Knopf.

Patalas E. (1962) 'Das Phänomen Mabuse'. *Neue Züricher Zeitung*. 23 (March).

Paysan, M. (1998) ' … aus dem Geist des Boulevards'. In K. Uhlenbrock (ed.) *MusikSpektakel Film*. Munich: edition text + kritik.

Petley, J. (1979) *Capital and Culture*. London: British Film Institute.

Petrie, G. (1985) *Hollywood Destinies. European Directors in America 1922–1931*. London: Routledge & Kegan Paul.

Petro, P. (1989) *Joyless Streets. Women and Melodramatic Representation in Weimar Germany*. Princeton: Princeton University Press.

Petzet, W. (1931) *Verbotene Filme*, Frankfurt/M.

Plummer, T.G. *et al.* (eds) (1982) *Film and Politics in the Weimar Republic*. Minneapolis: University of Minnesota.

Pommer, E. (1920) 'Bedeutung der Konzerne in der Filmindustrie'. *Film-Kurier* 204 (13 September).

—— (1922) 'Geschäftsfilm und künstlerischer Film'. *Der Film* 50 (10 December).

Potamkin, H.M. (1933) 'Pabst and the social film'. In *Hound and Horn* (January–March).

Pratt, D.B. (1991): '"O, Lubitsch, Where Wert Thou?" Passion, the German invasion and the emergence of the name "Lubitsch"'. *Wide Angle* vol. 13, no. 1 (January).

Pynchon, T. (1972) *Gravity's Rainbow*. New York: Bantam Books.

Quaresima, L. (1985) *Leni Riefenstahl*. Firenze: La Nuova Italia.

—— (1990) '"Dichter heraus!": The Autorenfilm and German Cinema of the 1910's'. In *Griffithiana* vol. 13, nos 38–9 (October): 101–26.

Rabenalt, A.M. (1958) *Film im Zwielicht*. Munich: Copress.

Rasp, F. (1929) 'Sparsamkeit der Geste'. In *Film-Kurier* 130 (June 1): ii.

Rayns, T. (1974) 'The Threepenny Opera'. In *Monthly Film Bulletin* (July).

Reid, D. and Walker, J.L. (1992) 'Strange pursuit: Cornell Woolrich and the abandoned city of the forties'. In J. Copjek (ed.) *Shades of Noir*. London: Verso.

Rentschler, E. (1986) (ed.) *German Film and Literature: Adaptions and Transformations*. New York, London: Methuen.

—— (ed.) (1990) *The Films of G.W. Pabst: An Extraterritorial Cinema*. New Brunswick/London: Rutgers University Press.

—— (1996) *The Ministry of Illusion*. Cambridge, Mass: Harward University Press.

Rhode, E. (1966) *Tower of Babel*. London: Weidenfeld & Nicholson.

—— (1976) *A History of The Cinema*. London: Allen Lane.

Riefenstahl, L. (1987) *Memoiren 1945–1987*. Frankfurt/M: Ullstein.

—— (1992) *The Sieve of Time*. London: Quartet Books.

Riess, P. (1995) 'Popularize and/or be damned: Psychoanalysis and film at the crossroads in 1925'. In *The International Journal of Psycho-Analysis* vol. 76, part 4 (August).

—— (1996) 'Geheimnisse einer Seele: Wessen Film und wessen Psychoanalyse'. In *Jahrbuch der Psychoanalyse*. vol. 39.

Rohmer, E. (1977) *L'organisation de l'espace dans le Faust de Murnau*. Paris: Union Générale.

Rose, J. (1986) *Sexuality in the Field of Vision*. London: Verso.

Rosen, P. (1986) *Narrative, Apparatus, Ideology*. New York: Columbia University Press.

Rotha, P. (1930) *The Film Till Now*. London: Jonathan Cape.

—— (1933) *Celluloid*. London: Longmans Green.

Rother, R. (ed.) (1992) *Die Ufa 1917–1945 Das Deutsche Bilderimperium*. Berlin: Deutsches Historisches Museum.

Salt, B. (1979) 'From Caligari to who?' In *Sight and Sound* (Spring): 119–23.

—— ([1982] 1992) 'The world inside Ernst Lubitsch'. In U. Jung and W. Schatzberg (eds) *Filmkultur zur Zeit der Weimarer Republik*. Munich: K.G. Saur.

—— (1989) *Film Style and Technology: History and Analysis*. London: Star Word.

—— (1990) 'From German stage to German screen'. In P. Cherchi Usai and L. Codelli (eds) *Prima di Caligari: Cinema tedesco, 1895–1920/Before Caligari. German Cinema 1895–1920*. Pordenone: Edizioni Biblioteca dell'Immagine.

Sartre, J-P. (1949) *Situations III*. Paris: Gallimard.

Saunders, T.J. (1992) *Hollywood in Berlin. American Cinema and Weimar Germany*. Berkeley: University of Californa Press.

Schacht, R. (1925) 'Der Film und die Gebildeten'. *Der Kunstwart* 2 (November).

Schäfer, H.D. (1981) *Das gespaltene Bewußtsein. Deutsche Kultur und Lebenswirklichkeit 1933–45*. München: Hanser.

Schivelbusch, W. (1997) 'Turnip into asparagus'. *London Review of Books* (5 June).

Schlemmer, G. *et al.* (eds) (1990) *G.W. Pabst*. Münster: MAkS-Publikationen.

Schlüpmann, H. (1990) *Unheimlichkeit des Blicks*. Frankfurt: Stroemfeld.

Schmitt, H.J. (1973) *Die Expressionismusdebatte*. Frankfurt: Suhrkamp.

Schneider, R. (1990) *Histoire du cinéma allemand*. Paris: Cerf.

Schoenbaum, D. (1966) *Hitler's Social Revolution*. New York: Doubleday.

Schönemann, H. (1992) *Fritz Lang: Filmbilder Vorbilder*. Berlin: Edition Hentrich.

Schöning, J. (ed.) (1989) *Reinhold Schünzel. Schauspieler und Regisseur*. Munich: edition text + kritik.

—— (ed.) (1993) *London Calling*. Munich: edition text + kritik.

Schrader, P. (1972) 'Notes on film noir', *Film Comment* vol. 8, no. 1 (Spring).

Schröder, P.H. (1965) 'Orientalischer Irrgarten und Großberlin' In *Filmkritik* 12.

Schulte-Sasse, L. (1996) *Entertaining the Reich*. Durham: Duke University Press.

Schweinitz, J. (1992) *Prolog vor dem Film. Nachdenken über ein neues Medium, 1909–1914*. Leipzig: Reclam.

Schweins, A. (1985) 'Die Entwicklung der deutschen Filmwirtschaft'. Ph D dissertation, University of Nürnberg.

Shepard, J. (1998) *Nosferatu in Love*. London: Faber & Faber.

Silberman, M. (1982) 'Industry, text, and ideology in Expressionist film'. In S. Bronner and D. Kellner (eds) *Passion and Rebellion*. South Hadley, Mass: J.F. Bergin.

—— (1995) *German Cinema: Texts in Context*. Detroit: Wayne State University Press.

Simmel, G. (1997) 'Metropolis and mental life'. In N. Leach (ed.) *Rethinking Architecture*. London: Routledge.

Sloterdijk, P. (1985) *Kritik der zynischen Vernunft* (2 vols). Frankfurt/M.: Suhrkamp.

—— (1988) *Critique of Cynical Reason* (vol. 1). London: Verso.

Speer, A. (1969) *Erinnerungen*. Frankfurt/M: Ullstein.

Spiess, E. (1979) *Carl Mayer: Ein Autor zwischen Expressionismus und Idylle*. Frankfurt/M.: DiF.

Spiker, J. (1975) *Film und Kapital*. Berlin: Volker Spiess.

Spoto, D. (1984) *The Dark Side of Genius: The Life of Alfred Hitchcock*. New York: Ballantine.

Stacey, J. (1994) *Star Gazing*. London: Routledge.

Starobinski, J. (1988) *L'oeil vivant*. Paris: Skira.

Sternberg, J. von (1967) *Fun in a Chinese Laundry*. London: Secker & Warburg.

Studlar, G. (1985) 'Masochism and the perverse pleasures of cinema'. In B. Nichols (ed.) *Movies and Methods* (vol. 2). Berkeley: University of California Press.

Sturm, G. (1990) *Fritz Lang: films, textes, références*. Nancy: Presses universitaires de Nancy.

Sturm, S. (ed.) (1996) *Hallo? Berlin? Ici Paris!* Munich: text + kritik.

Szatmari, E. (1928) *Was nicht im Baedecker steht: Berlin*. Munich: Piper.

Szondi, P. (1986) *The Theory of Modern Drama*. Minneapolis: University of Minneapolis Press.

Tatar, M. (1995) *Lustmord: Sexual Murder in Weimar Germany*. Princeton: Princeton University Press.

Taylor, J.R. (1983) *Strangers in Paradise: The Hollywood Emigrés 1933–1950*. London: Faber and Faber.

Theweleit, K. (1989) *Male Fantasies*. Minneapolis: University of Minnesota Press.

Thompson, K. (1981) *Eisenstein's Ivan The Terrible*. Princeton: Princeton University Press.

—— (1985) *Exporting Entertainment*. London: BFI Publishing.

—— (1989) *Breaking the Glass Armor*. Princeton: Princeton University Press.

—— (1990) 'Dr Caligari at the Folies Bergeres'. In M. Budd (ed.) *The Cabinet of Dr Caligari: Text, Contexts*. New Brunswick: Rutgers University Press.

Töteberg, M. (1985) *Fritz Lang*. Reinbek: Rowohlt.

Traub, H. (1943) (ed.) *Die Ufa: Ein Beitrag zur Entwicklunsgeschichte des deutschen Filmschaffens*. Berlin: UFA-Buchverlag.

Truffaut, F. (1968) 'Lubitsch était un prince'. *Cahiers du cinéma* 198 (February).

Tsivian, Y. (1995) 'Caligari in Russland: Der deutsche Expressionismus und die sovietische Filmkultur'. In O. Bulgakowa (ed.) *Die ungewhönlichen Abenteuer des Dr. Mabuse im Lande der Bolschewiki*. Berlin: Freunde der Deutschen Kinemathek.

—— (1996) 'Two stylists of the teens'. In T. Elsaesser (ed.) *A Second Life: German Cinema's First Decade*. Amsterdam: Amsterdam University Press.

Tucholsky, K. ([1921] 1992) 'Verbotene filme'. In J. Schweinitz (ed.) (1992) *Prolog zu dem Film*.

Tudor, A. (1974) *Image and Influence*. London: Allen and Unwin.

Turim, M. (1989) *Flashbacks in Film. Memory and History*. London. Routledge

Tyler, P. (1962) *Classics of the Foreign Film*. New York: Bonanza.

Tynan, K. (1979a) 'The Girl in the Black Helmet', *New Yorker* (11 June).

—— (1979b) 'Dream Woman of the Cinema', *Observer Magazine* (11 November).

Uricchio, W. (1991) *Die Anfänge des deutschen Fernsehens. Kritische Annäherungen an die Entwicklung bis 1945*. Tübingen: Niemeyer.

Vasey, R. (1995) *Diplomatic Representations. The World According to Hollywood, 1918–1939*. Madison: University of Wisconsin Press.

Vernet, M. (1993) 'Film noir on the edge of doom'. In J. Copjec (ed.) *Shades of Noir*. London: Verso.

Vincendeau, G. (1988) 'Hollywood–Babel'. *Screen* vol. 29, no. 2: 24–39.

Virilio, P. (1988) *War and Cinema: The Logics of Perception*. New York: Verso.

Walker, A. (1979) *The Shattered Silents: How the Talkies Came to Stay*. New York: W. Morrow & Co.

Weber, S. (1973) 'The sideshow: or remarks on a canny moment'. In *Modern Language Notes* vol. 88, no. 6: 1131–5.

Wedekind, F. (1990) *Die Büchse der Pandora*. Darmstadt: Häusser.

Wedel, M. (1996) 'Max Mack, the invisible author'. In T. Elsaesser (ed.) *A Second Life: German Cinema's First Decades*. Amsterdam: Amsterdam University Press.

—— (1997) *Max Mack. Ein Showman im Glashaus*. Berlin: Freunde der Deutschen Kinemathek.

Wehling, W. (ed.) (1974) *Der Weg ins Dritte Reich. Deutscher Film und Weimars Ende*. Oberhausen: Laufen.

Weihsmann, H. (1988) *Gebaute Illusionen: Architektur im Film*. Wien: Promedia.

Weinberg, H. (1964) *The Lubitsch Touch*. New York: Doubleday.

Weiss, A. (1992) *Vampires and Violets*. New York: Penguin Books.

Welch, D. (1983) *Propaganda and the German Cinema 1933–1945*. Oxford: University Press.

Wetzel, K. and Hagemann, P.A. (1982) *Zensur. Verbotene deutsche Filme 1933–1945*. Berlin: Spiess.

White, H. (1973) *Metahistory. The Historical Imagination in Nineteenth-Century Europe*. Baltimore: The Johns Hopkins University Press.

Willemen, P. (1994) 'The question of the national'. In *Looks and Frictions*. London: BFI.

Willett, J. (1978) *The New Sobriety*. London: Thames & Hudson.

—— (1984) *Brecht in Context*. London: Methuen.

Williams, A. (1974) 'Structure of narrativity in Fritz Lang's *Metropolis*'. *Film Quarterly* vol. 27, no. 4 (Summer).
Winkler-Mayerhöfer, A. (1992) *Starkult als Propagandamittel*. Munich: Ölschläger.
Winston, B. (1995) *Claiming the Real*. London: BFI Publishing.
Witte, K. (1978) 'Preface.' In S. Kracauer *Von Caligari zu Hitler*. Frankfurt: Suhrkamp.
—— (1995) *Lachende Erben. Toller Tag*. Berlin: Vorwerk 8.
Wolfenstein, M. and Leites, N. (1971) 'The good–bad girl'. In *Movies: A Psychological Study*. New York: Hafner.
Wolffram, K. (1992) *Tanzdielen und Vergnügungspaläste*. Berlin: Edition Hentrich.
Wolffsohn, K. (1922–33) (ed.) *Jahrbuch der Filmin-dustrie* 5 vols. Berlin: Verlag der Lichtbildbühne.
Wollenberg, H.H. (1947) *Fifty Years of German Film*. London: Falcon Press.
Wood, R. (1976) 'Murnau. midnight and sunrise'. *Film Comment* 3: 4–9.
Zimmerschied, K. (1922) *Die deutsche Filmindustrie, ihre Entwicklung, Organisation und Stellung im deutschen Staats – und Wirtschaftsleben*. Stuttgart: Poeschel.
Zglinicki, F. von (1956) *Der Weg des Films*. Hildesheim/New York: Olms Presse.

INDEX OF FILMS

GENERAL INDEX

Lightning Source UK Ltd.
Milton Keynes UK
UKOW05f0826250517
301981UK00004B/21/P